PRODUCT TESTING
AND
SENSORY EVALUATION
OF FOODS

MARKETING AND R&D APPROACHES

F
N
P

JOURNALS AND BOOKS IN FOOD SCIENCE AND NUTRITION

Journals

JOURNAL OF NUTRITION, GROWTH AND CANCER, G. P. Tryfiates

JOURNAL OF FOODSERVICE SYSTEMS, O. P. Snyder, Jr.

JOURNAL OF FOOD BIOCHEMISTRY, H. O. Hultin, N. F. Haard and J. R. Whitaker

JOURNAL OF FOOD PROCESS ENGINEERING, D. R. Heldman

JOURNAL OF FOOD PROCESSING AND PRESERVATION, T. P. Labuza

JOURNAL OF FOOD QUALITY, M. P. DeFigueiredo

JOURNAL OF FOOD SAFETY, M. Solberg and J. D. Rosen

JOURNAL OF TEXTURE STUDIES, P. Sherman and M. C. Bourne

Books

ENVIRONMENTAL ASPECTS OF CANCER: THE ROLE OF MACRO AND MICRO COMPONENTS OF FOODS, E. L. Wynder, G. A. Leveille, J. H. Weisburger and G. E. Livingston

SHELF-LIFE DATING OF FOODS, T. P. Labuza

ANTINUTRIENTS AND NATURAL TOXICANTS IN FOOD, R. L. Ory

UTILIZATION OF PROTEIN RESOURCES, D. W. Stanley, E. D. Murray and D. H. Lees

FOOD INDUSTRY ENERGY ALTERNATIVES, R. P. Ouellette, N. W. Lord and P. E. Cheremisinoff

VITAMIN B$_6$: METABOLISM AND ROLE IN GROWTH, G. P. Tryfiates

HUMAN NUTRITION, 3RD ED., R. F. Mottram

DIETARY FIBER: CURRENT DEVELOPMENTS OF IMPORTANCE TO HEALTH, K. W. Heaton

RECENT ADVANCES IN OBESITY RESERCH II, G. A. Bray

FOOD POISONING AND FOOD HYGIENE, 4TH ED., B. C. Hobbs and R. J. Gilbert

POSTHARVEST BIOLOGY AND BIOTECHNOLOGY, H. O. Hultin and M. Milner

THE SCIENCE OF MEAT AND MEAT PRODUCTS, 2ND ED., J. F. Price and B. S. Schweigert

THE ROLE OF FOOD PRODUCT DEVELOPMENT IN IMPLEMENTING DIETARY GUIDELINES, G. E. Livingston, C. M. Chang and R. J. Moshy

PRODUCT TESTING
AND
SENSORY EVALUATION
OF FOODS

MARKETING AND R&D APPROACHES

by

Howard R. Moskowitz, Ph.D.

MOSKOWITZ/JACOBS, INC.
SCARSDALE, NEW YORK
and
TASC GROUP, INC.
EVANSTON, ILLINOIS

FOOD & NUTRITION PRESS, INC.
WESTPORT, CONNECTICUT 06880 USA

Library of Congress Catalog Card Number: 83-80575
ISBN: 0-917678-16-8

Printed in the United States of America

I dedicate this book to three mentors, who have guided me over the years, and encouraged me to write.

To my father, Moses Moskowitz, who showed me what the written word could do.

To the memory of my late professor and mentor, S. S. Stevens, who provided me with the foundations of this book over the years that I had the privilege to know him.

To Dr. Jerome Kosseff, who made me realize that people would read what I wrote, and use it in their own work.

To these three guides, I gratefully say "Thank You."

Finally, and most of all to my dearest wife, Mary, who stood by me all this time, and gave me the continued encouragement and strength to write this book.

PREFACE

I wrote this book to fill a gap in our knowledge of how to properly conduct product tests. The past two decades have seen rapidly growing interest in product testing by marketers and by R&D. The novice and the professional can go to different sources to learn about product testing, but it requires the practitioner to add the spice and essence of experience to that mix. Only through experience "in the trenches," slugging it out with problems, can the novice really learn how best to assess consumer reactions to foods. Armchair reading and research doesn't substitute.

This book fills part of the gap in our knowledge. It presents the spectrum of product testing, for both R&D and marketing. Moreover, it presents much of the material in "case-history" form, much as one might have material presented in a business course. The reader can see from these case histories the problem definition, the approach, and the outcome in clear register. The case-history approach to product testing does not set each fact down in black and white. Rather, it presents to the reader one approach to solving the problem. In that spirit, this book also presents one approach to product testing, gleaned from a decade and a half of the author's experience in a variety of contexts.

With this meager introduction, then, the author invites the reader to journey with him into the tortuous paths of business and science, where product testing becomes a tool both for knowledge and for profit.

CONTENTS

CHAPTER 1

INTRODUCTION — BACKGROUND TO PRODUCT AND SENSORY TESTING

INTRODUCTION

During the past fifty years the discipline of sensory analysis and product testing has matured from a quick and dirty method, used sparingly by food scientists, into a set of quantitative procedures which enhance the efficiency and accuracy of food product development, quality control, market research and marketing. This book treats the science of sensory analysis from both the practical and scientific viewpoints. For both the novice and the experienced sensory analyst, the food scientist and the marketer, this book illustrates the history, current procedures and possibilities of the science of sensory analysis.

To a great extent modern day sensory analysis and product testing owes its scientific underpinnings to the branch of psychology known as psychophysics. Psychophysics relates perceptions to antecedent physical stimuli. The science of psychophysics began a century ago in Germany. E. H. Weber and G. T. Fechner searched for quantitative laws of human perception, concentrating their attention on measuring man's ability to discriminate small differences, and relating those abilities to the physical stimulus intensities. As psychophysics advanced, its testing methods proliferated. Sensory analysts in the food, beverage and pharmaceutical industries soon realized that this science could provide for them the structure and quantitative methods needed to understand how people perceive and react to food.

In order, therefore, to fully utilize the procedures of psychophysics and sensory analysis, this volume dually orients itself to theory and to practice. On the theoretical side, the book illustrates what we know about scientific measurement of human perceptions and what scientists have learned about the perceptions of food-related stimuli. These data comprise the bank of information that the scientist and practitioner require in order to design adequate studies and avoid pitfalls. On the pragmatic, practical side, the book illustrates a practitioner's way of doing things, starting from problem definition, going on to study design and execution, and finally finishing with data analysis and interpretation. No product test analyst can hope to perform his or her job adequately unless the person implementing the study understands the purpose for the study, the background of the techniques, the limita-

1

tions of alternative techniques (as well as their strengths), and finally the optimal way to analyze the data and report them.

A SHORT HISTORY OF SENSORY ANALYSIS

A century ago, in Leipzig, Germany Wilhelm Wundt founded the first psychology laboratory. Wundt proposed to scientifically study the laws of human behavior, especially the laws of human perception. The studies continued almost uninterrupted for almost a half century, until World War II. Numerous studies appeared from German laboratories of psychology. The techniques developed there influenced psychologists and physiologists/biologists alike.

During the same time food science developed in parallel, albeit slowly. Emil Fischer had discovered glucose. Remsen and Fahlberg had discovered saccharin by accident in 1879, and the golden era of synthetic organic chemistry had just begun. Food processing came of age, with newly synthesized chemicals finding uses in foods for food processing and storage. The food world expanded its horizons outwards from the local supplier of farm-fresh food towards more regional, and ultimately national, distribution.

With increasing structure comes diversity of jobs and new requirements for technology. So too with sensory analysis. Observations on the taste potency of different acids made by Corin (1887) in France, for purely scientific reasons, became important later on in food processing. That one acid tasted more sour than another piqued scientific interest in the 1880s both as an observation and as a clue for the mechanism underlying the perception of taste sourness. Fifty years later, in the late 1920s and 1930s, these observations would acquire additional value. They would provide hints to the product developer how one could enhance the sweetness of beverages or the sourness of pickles, etc.

Studies of sugar sweetness and the sweetness of artificial sweeteners showed the same pattern of basic science leading to product development insights. In the late 1880s scientific interest focused on new sweeteners. In 1914 Cohn published a magnificent compendium on the taste properties of many thousands of organic compounds. *Die Organischen Geschmackstoffe*, summarizing extensive bibliographic searches through the literature of that time. These studies had appeared in chemistry journals, paralleling the leapfrogging advances in synthetic chemistry. Shortly after World War I food scientists joined the fray. Papers appeared on the enhanced sweetness of invert sugar which comprises a 50-50 mixture of glucose and fructose, made by subjecting sucrose solutions to acid or to the enzyme invertase. Other papers appearing at that time concerned the sweetness of such new chemicals as saccharin and dulcin, fostering as much interest in commercial application as interest in physiological mechanisms underlying the sense of taste.

The Growth of Methodology

Methodology, the science of method, emerged for food science in the 1920s. Alternative procedures for taste appeared in scattered places in the technical literature of the time. Although no systematic science of sensory analysis seemed to emerge from these disparate articles (which appeared just as often in chemistry journals and fragrance/flavor trade journals as in psychology journals), one could detect a slow and steady growth in the research concepts and techniques. Practitioners in the food and pharmaceutical industries continued to write about the need to improve the measurement of a product's sensory characteristics.

The developing science of sensory analysis borrowed test methods from psychology, on the one hand, and from trade practitioners on the other. The growth of agricultural industry generated better methods of commodity grading, sponsored by the U.S. Department of Agriculture. Expert graders for agricultural produce used point systems which allocated score points among the different characteristics of fruit, meats, and the like. Texture received scores up to a certain percent of the total, appearance received another percentage of the total score, etc. The expert panel method for quality grading achieved wide popularity, as scoring systems found use in grading for purposes of item classification.

Parallel to these developments in agriculture, psychologists in various universities reported studies on improving the measurement of perception by scaling. Traditional psychological research focuses on the processes of judgment and perception, not on products. It should come as no surprise, therefore, that the methodological studies pursued by psychologists more often than not concerned model systems, such as sugar-water, or simple odorant chemicals diluted in a liquid. Beebe-Center (1932) recounts in his critical book, *The Psychology of Pleasantness and Unpleasantness*, the history of these studies as they concern hedonics, or pleasure. As one reads through Beebe-Center's synopsis of the scientific work on the measurement of hedonics, one will come across numerous elegant studies on the measurement of sensory and hedonic reactions to model stimuli, similar to but not the same as actual foods. Researchers focused their interest upon simple stimuli which they could easily control and present. Little did they realize that the principles which governed liking/disliking of simple chemicals and pictorial or graphic stimuli would apply to the measurement of perception and acceptance of foods, pharmaceuticals and related consumer items.

Leon Louis Thurstone founded a psychometric laboratory at the University of North Carolina where he developed new methods for psychological scaling. Thurstone deserves special recognition for joining together psychological measurement principes with real-world stimuli (which contrasts with the previous disparateness of the two domains). Thurstone hypothesized that when people evaluate the acceptability of stimuli, whether foods, fragrances or model systems (e.g., simple chemical stimuli like sugar-water or imitation banana oil), they do so based upon an underlying or internal psychological scale of hedonics or liking. Observable behavior, such as direct preferences by paired comparison (wherein the individual chooses one stimulus over another), represents the outcome of the use of this underlying psychological scale. The closer the preference rating lies to 50/50 (no preference) the more likely that the stimuli lie near each other on the underlying psychological scale of liking. Thurstone's work represented a psychological approach to sensory analysis and hedonics. Through statistical analysis of paired comparison data Thurstone transformed these paired preferences into psychological scale values, and erected scales for the stimuli. Food scientists soon adopted the Thurstone procedure to scale preference of food stimuli, adopting virtually the entire mathematics intact, including the assumptions and the computational formulae. They applied the Thurstonian method to various problems (e.g., food preference ratings) in order to develop psychological scales for actual foods. The crowning achievement came with Thurstone's *Law of Comparative Judgement* (1927), which provided the rationale and technical foundation for analysis of paired comparison data.

During the mid 1930s psychology and food science grew rapidly and divergently. Psychologists discovered new avenues of interest in complex behavior, laws of thought and perception, and human motor skills. Food science prospered as it increased its technical background, coalescing the work of biochemists, rheologists (scientists who study the forces and flow of matter), food processing engineers, chemical engineers and a host of ancillary disciplines. The procedures and substantive data bases of these disciplines found ready acceptance by food scientists. Sensory analysis proceeded more slowly. Isolated from the stream of psychological research because of the ever-widening gap between disciplines, and hindered because of methodological difficulties, sensory analysis found itself a step-child to food science; a discipline one used but rarely respected. Equipment, hard facts and the glory of engineering conspired to steal the attention of serious workers interested in food research.

From time to time interesting tidbits on the sensory characteristics of foods appeared in one or another journal. In the United Kingdom Moir (1936) gave a dinner illustration of how color could affect the perception of food. At a dinner for the food group of the Society of Chemistry and Industry, Moir served foods absolutely acceptable in all ways, save that a number of foods possessed unusual colors. Some of the items appeared green when they should have appeared red, etc. Despite the acceptable flavor, many of the food scientists attending that dinner demonstration reported feeling sick and nauseated. The demonstration successfully illustrated the role of color in food acceptance, but stopped there. Moir did not investigate nor report the rules governing food acceptability versus the relative importance of color. One can read reports of similar anecdotal studies, published during the 1800s in *Science* and *Nature*, two leading research journals. The reports from *Science* and *Nature* occasionally presented anecdotal observations on scientific phenomena in sensory perception of foods and fragrances, with no rigorous experimentation.

World War II and the Emergence of Sensory Analysis

World War II and the problems involved in feeding armies proved a boon for sensory analysis. Preservation of military rations assumed paramount importance. The U.S. Army Quartermaster Corps, then in Chicago (currently in Natick, Mass.), expended considerable effect on studies to improve food storage and to augment food quality. Food quality, or the improvement of product acceptability, emerged as a key facet of food science. The bacteriological, physical and quality deterioration of foods under adverse storage conditions resulted in lowered product acceptance. Soldiers commented upon the poor quality of their rations, occasionally refusing rations outright because they felt the food tasted unpalatable.

During World War II the Quartermaster scientists seriously experimented with methods to assess and improve product acceptability. The war had unified science as never before. Applied scientists dug into he store of scientific information published up to that period for clues to beter assess food acceptance and product perceptions. Funds became available to test the different sensory evaluation methods, albeit on a small scale, in an attempt to improve the measurement of product acceptability. The refinements in measurement, the recognition of complexities in food product assessment and the methodological niceties would come later. Scientists directed their effort to measuring the overall impact of perception on acceptability, using whatever scales they had available.

During this period, in quite a different sphere of research, psychophysicists at Harvard University worked to discover physiological mechanisms of hearing, the measurement of loudness and the intelligibility of speech. Their interest focused on the use of these discoveries to jam the enemies' radar and detection devices. Led by S.S. (Smitty) Stevens, the Psychoacoustic Laboratory in the basement of Memorial Hall became the focus of intense research on the sense of hearing, but also became a leading center for measurement of sensory processes. Stevens had developed a lifelong interest in psychophysical measurement—the search for a unit of measurement and a measuring system for the private world of sensation. World War II interrupted this basic research goal at Harvard University, thrusting Stevens and his colleagues into applying their research techiques to real-world problems.

This war-time experience led to Stevens' development of a theory of scales of measurement (Stevens 1946), and an appreciation of the do's and don'ts for proper psychological measurement of sensation. These studies on psychophysical measurement led to new methods for measuring responses to stimuli, methods which later (in the 1970s) would add vitality and new vistas to sensory analysis of foods. But we have now overstepped the advances by two decades or more.

In 1953, after a decade of research on hearing and other sensory modalities, Stevens announced that he had discovered a simple procedure for assessing human reactions to simple stimuli, such as tones and lights of varying energy levels. The method of absolute judgment (later called magnitude estimation scaling) required only that the panelist assign numbers to reflect sensory intensity. No restrictions applied to these numbers except that the size of the numbers should reflect the intensity of the sensation. With this procedure, the time needed to develop a curve relating sensory intensity to physical stimulus level considerably decreased. Furthermore, the relation between the two domains, one sensory and the other physical, seemed lawful. A power function related the numbers of panelists used (so-called magnitude estimates) to physical intensities which the experimenter measured. The power function appears as Magnitude Estimate $= k$ (Physical Intensity)^n; n indexes the rate of growth of sensory intensity, and ranges from 0.2 to 2.0 or more, depending upon the sensory modality.

Unbeknownst to food scientists, who at the time worked with arbitrary scales in an effort to quantify panelist perceptions, Stevens' simple yet robust method of magnitude estimation promised a radically new and powerful approach to the sensory analysis of food. Stevens sought scales to parallel physical or instrumental measurement, and which possessed meaningful zero points and valid ratios. Kelvin scales of temperature, weight and distance measures typify the ideal ratio scales. Food scientists and, for that matter, most psychologists lacked these scales for the measurement of human perceptions. They relied instead upon makeshift, and other arbitrary scales comprising an arbitrary number of fixed points (1-5, 1-9, etc.) to represent graded degrees of perceptual intensity.

During the 1950s food science and psychophysics blossomed, albeit in separate corners of the scientific community. Psychophysics developed its methods, techniques, rationales and philosophies of measurement. Sensory analysis prospered, achieving increasing recognition in food science, and spawning numerous scientific papers in the food (and other scientific) literature. The two disciplines crossed occasionally, more often than not because one or another food scientist took the time to read the psychology journals and learn the methods which scientists reported. Roland Harper in the United Kingdom and Carl Pfaffmann in the United States deserve special recognition for their role in fostering an awareness of psychophysics in food science, and bringing the world of food problems to the attention of psychologists. Harper's work on the psychophysics of texture, with special regard to food products, had appeared in the 1940s just at the start of World War II (Harper 1947). In the 1950s he maintained close liaison with the food industry, introducing to the field new techniques such as factor analysis for evaluating sensory dimensions of food. Factor analysis reduces the many descriptive attributes to a few, uncorrelated primaries. Harper worked in food research laboratories and universities in the U.K. As a psychologist he continued to emphasize the importance of sensory measurement in his published works, thus increasing the awareness of psychology in general, and psychophysics in particular. Carl Pfaffmann, a physiologist by training and a biological psychologist and electrophysiologist by profession, influenced the food science community in yet another way. Pfaffmann's interest in the laws of hedonics (liking/disliking) concerned animal behavior, but later broadened to encompass human appetite and hedonics. Pfaffmann's research appealed to food scientists, and to scientific or R&D directors of large food corporations. Before long Pfaffmann became the de facto psychologist representative to the food and flavor industry, appearing before many a convention to present the techniques which behavioral scientists used to measure animal preference. Pfaffmann also performed

the valuable task of keeping alive the awareness of current and previous psychological work on hedonics and taste perceptions reported by
psychologists, much of which otherwise lay hidden in the all too often
unread psychology literature.

The middle and late 1950s saw a resurgence of interest in sensory
analysis by food scientists. Rose Marie Pangborn, who later trained a
generation of applied sensory analysts for industry positions (and thus
placed the practical side of sensory analysis on a firm, pragmatic
footing), began her career with research on wine tasting, and on the
reactions of overweight and normal weight fairgoers to desserts (Pangborn and Simone 1958). Pangborn inspired a new approach to sensory
analysis—a disciplined, scientifically rigorous research program using
impeccably purist procedures. Her analysis and reportage exemplified
the best in technically oriented scientific work. Pangborn investigated
numerous problems in sensory analysis, ranging from the taste
changes occurring in sweet-sour (or sweet-bitter) mixtures to the tastes
of sugars with different structures, and on to the more applied problems
of sensory analysis of different foods. We will return to her work a little
later. Suffice it to say for the present that much of current sensory
analysis owes its methodological foundation to Pangborn's carefully
controlled studies, and her rigorous analysis.

The late 1950s and early 1960s witnessed the start of the flood of
research in sensory evaluation of food. The general resurgence of
science, in the wake of Sputnik, stimulated advances in food science
and sensory evaluation. The U.S. Army Quartermaster Corps in Chicago, Illinois continued the tradition begun in the 1940s, during World
War II. Numerous scientific papers appeared bearing the name of one or
another government scientist from the U.S. Army Quartermaster group
in Chicago, Illinois. These papers covered a gamut of topics from surveys of food preference, to studies on the effect of monosodium glutamate, to basic studies on odor and taste perception. Dr. David Peryam,
Dr. Howard Schutz, Dr. Frank Pilgrim and a host of other scientists
passed through the Quartermaster Crops during this period. Food preference measurement using a 9 point hedonic scale became the standard
method to assess liking/disliking (Peryam and Pilgrim 1957). The 9
point hedonic still sees service today in many test locations, ranging
from taste-test laboratories in industry to malodor evaluation in health-
care laboratories.

For thirty years the Flavor Profile Method, developed by the Arthur
D. Little Company (Cambridge, Mass.), has remained a standard
procedure for quantifying the quality of flavor. Developed by A. D. Little,
Inc. in the late 1940s, the Flavor Profile Method represents yet another
stream of applied research readily adopted by a food industry searching

for quantifiation. We will discuss the Flavor Profle more in depth in Chapter 2 on descriptive analysis. The reader should bear in mind that the profiling method represents the first general technique for generating the sensory signature or fingerprint of a product. The Flavor Profile Method received many writeups and an extraordinary amount of publicity when it first appeared. Jean Caul, then of Arthur D. Little Inc. (and now of Kansas State University), published the background and general technical method in the *Advances in Food Research* in 1957, further adding to its scientific foundation and reputation. In time practitioners would copy the procedure, adding better scaling procedures, modifying the time required to develop a good group of profile panelists and streamlining the method in other ways. Yet even today, researchers can scarcely point to any other procedure that has so influenced the industry and our conception of the nature of flavor.

Psychologists became aware of the ferment in food science and sensory analysis during the early 1960s. Conferences comprising participants from the psychology disciplines, physiology and food science enhanced the cross fertilization of ideas. Morley R. Kare, who would subsequently become the director of the Monell Chemical Senses Center, chaired several of these conferences which encouraged interchange between basic science on the one hand, and sensory analysis on the other. These conferences on different aspects of taste/smell attracted food researchers interested in problems of taste and smell from both basic research and from the point of view of a single commodity. All too often researchers in food science, nominally interested in taste and smell in general, or in sensory evaluation in particular, actually approached the problem in terms of a specific commodity which concerned them, rather than approaching the chemical senses and sensory analysis as a topic unto itself. These conferences broadened the vision of those individuals.

During the 1960s psychophysics also blossomed. Stevens' original hypothesis that sensory intensity rated by magnitude estimation followed a power law attracted a sizeable research following in the U.S., Sweden, Japan and South America. Researchers began seriously considering magnitude estimation as the procedure to use when quantifying sensory responses. During the 1960s literally hundreds of scientific papers appeared on the relation between stimulus intensity and sensory magnitude. Among these papers appeared studies on odor intensity perception (Jones 1958) and taste intensity of sweets and salts (Ekman and Akesson 1964). Carl Pfaffmann's laboratory at Brown University (and later at the Rockefeller University) produced doctoral students specializing in taste psychophysics and electrophysiology. Donald McBurney and Linda Bartoshuk pioneered the use of magnitude estimation scaling to assess taste responses to simple and complex liquid stimuli. Stevens' laboratory produced one Ph.D. in taste research, the author, and Ekman's laboratory in Stockholm, Sweden produced yet another, the late C. Akesson. As the fertile areas of auditory and visual psychophysics became denuded of simple and interesting research problems, psychophysicists turned their interest to the chemical senses. At Brown University William Cain received his Ph.D. with Trygg Engen. Cain's thesis on odor intensity of simple aliphatic alcohols (propanol, butanol, etc.) represented an outgrowth of Engen's work on the application of magnitude estimation scaling to odor perception in general which, in turn, derived from Stevens' pioneering work.

The late 1960s saw the start of new approaches to sensory evaluation, fostered by the migration of psychophysicists into the food industry. Research at the U.S. Army Natick Development Center in Massachusetts concentrated simultaneously on improved methods of sensory analysis for food science, and basic studies on sensory mecahnisms. The behavioral scienes division of the Natick Laboratories, under the leadership of Dr. Harry Jacobs (himself a well organized physiological psychologist), carved out new paths in sensory analysis. Researchers at the Natick Laboratories represented the optimum mix of basic food scientists, traditional-minded sensory analysts, and psychophysicists imbued with the spirit of the New Psychophysics which S. S. Stevens had introduced the decade before. The Food Acceptance Laboratory of the Natick Laboratories carried out numerous taste tests for applied purposes, while simultaneously exploring alternative methods for sensory evaluation. Magnitude estimation received its first major test at the Natick Laboratories. A paper by Moskowitz and Sidel (1971) in the *Journal of Food Science* introduced magnitude estimation to the food industry as promising an improved technique for sensory measurement. This paper showed how the modern method of psychophysical scaling could improve sensitivity to product differences. Other studies appearing from the Natick Laboratories concerned more basic problems on taste and odor perception, the study of mixtures, and the use of newer methods (e.g., multidimensional scaling) for assessing the chemical senses and the perception of food. These approaches continued for more than a decade at Natick, as a new generation of research scientists received dual training in food science and in chemoreception (psychophysics/physiology of taste and smell).

THE 1970's-DECADE OF ADVANCES AND CONSOLIDATION

Psychophysics and food science suffered relatively little from the massive funding cuts authorized by the U.S. Government in the aftermath of the Vietnamese conflict. Researchers in the food industry used the new sensory evaluation techniques, coming to recognize and appreciate their value in guiding food product development. Such novel techniques as the Flavor Profile, the Texture Profile (Szczesniak, Brandt and Friedman 1963), and magnitude estimation scaling saw increasing use by researchers. As in other fields, first the intrepid individualist and then the hesitant explored new methods, finding that the methods yielded reliable results. In many instances the researcher adopted the procedures as a part of the regular product testing sequence.

During the symposium sponsored by the Sensory Evaluation Division of the Institute of Food Technologists in 1974, Herbert Stone and Joel Sidel (then of the Stanford Research Institute, Palo Alto) introduced an offshoot of the Flavor Profile Method, which they titled the Quantitative Descriptive Analysis method, or QDA (Stone et al. 1974). The QDA used linear scaling (a 6 inch scale line), rather than numbers. Panelists profiled their perceptions of a series of product characteristics by marking the line at the appropriate point to represent perceptual magnitude or intensity. Many practitioners in sensory analysis quickly adopted the QDA method because of its simplistic representation, and its ease of administration. Although the QDA did not provide the necessary information to guide product developers in modifying ingredient levels, nonetheless it did advance the science and broadcasted the technology of sensory analysis to yet a wider population. Novice researchers found in the QDA a method which concretized sensory analysis in general, and profile analysis in particular. An offshoot of the Flavor Profile, the QDA method achieved an early success and popularized the sensory analysis discipline.

MARKETING RESEARCH, PRODUCT OPTIMIZATION, AND THE PRESENT

Our final section concerns the present—the past four or five years. This half decade has witnessed innumerable advances in sensory evaluation, appearing in rapid fire succession. Traditionally, sensory analysts confined their discipline and practice to the R&D laboratory where they assisted in early-product evaluation, cost reduction and reformulation. In 1975 the author founded MPi Sensory Testing, Inc., a division of MPi Marketing Research, with the goal of introducing the techniques and philosophy of sensory analysis and the new psychophysics into marketing research and marketing. Marketing research deals with consumers. Product evaluation tests run by marketing research often use rudimentary, unsophisticated, and occasionally incorrect procedures for sensory analysis. Moskowitz's goal realized itself when the method of magnitude estimation achieved recognition in marketing research and marketing circles (Moskowitz *et al.* 1980). The techniques of multiple product evaluation (perfected at Harvard during the late 1960s, and at the Natick Laboratories during the 1970s), coupled with the needs of consumer research, provided the stepping-stone to the further refinement of product measurement. The hitherto esoteric science of psychophysics emerged full scale into industry, accepted at the basic science level at the bench, accepted by researchers and practitioners in sensory analysis, and finally accepted by manufacturers and marketers interested in consumer marketing research.

Coming shortly after the introduction of magnitude estimation, product optimization procedures emerged into the forefront of sensory analysis and marketing research. For twenty-five years statisticians (Box and Hunter 1957) have investigated one or another method whereby they could relate responses to physical stimuli. Statisticians developed the method of response-surface analysis, which allowed them to fit a mathematical equation to the dependent variable (e.g., levels of the reaction constituents, process variables, etc.). Moskowitz, Stanley and Chandler (1977) recognized the advantages of combining statistical model building together with magnitude estimation scaling and multiple-product testing to develop better response surface curves for product acceptance versus ingredients. Four years of experience in model development using the statistical approach, practical product development using experimental design methods, and rigorous test implementation using marketing research techniques for field execution made the method of product optimization for food products work. The introduction of model building methods to sensory evaluation paralleled, to some extent, the use and growth of econometric modeling in economics. Neither procedure guaranteed a perfect result, but the practitioner could feel secure that with the model building method the chances of error would diminish and the chances of success would improve. The feedback from and verdict on product optimization suggests that it does improve product acceptance. The interest and applications received by the method, and its commercial successes promise an excellent future, especially when the practitioner uses it to develop better products more rapidly, at lower research cost, and with lower cost of goods.

OF BOOKS AND JOURNALS AND CONFERENCES

No history of sensory analysis and product testing should fail to cite the milestones. Conferences, books and journals represent scientific and trade milestones. They signify the emergence of interest in the problem areas, the willingness of individuals to share their ideas and insights, and the desire of scientists and practitioners to publicize their findings.

Looking back at sensory evaluation over the past century we see a gradual trend towards the cohesion of the discipline. As mentioned above, the past hundred years saw the increasing number of articles published on sensory analysis. At first the publications appeared in trade related journals, with little attention paid to sensory analysis as an area of inquiry unto itself. The 1920s saw the emergence of sensory analysis, under the guide of odor and flavor science, in trade magazines. *The Perfumery and Essential Oil Record* and the *American Perfumer* magazines deserve special mention in this regard. Perfumers and flavorists earn their living by creating scents and flavors. It should come as no surprise that the renewed interest in sensory analysis should first reveal itself in these journals. Subsequent appearances in brewing journals, pharmaceutical journals and the like, as well as in psychology journals, further enhanced the visibility of sensory analysis.

The Institute of Food Technologists founded the journal called *Food Research* in 1937. From time to time short articles appeared in *Food Research* concerning one or another aspect of sensory analysis. Usually these short articles considered substantive topics; e.g., flavor or texture of a specific product, or an abbreviated treatment of the entire field of flavor research. Sensory analysis as a discipline submerged itself in the general topic of food processing or food ingredients, and when it emerged, it did so only in a cursory manner, or almost as an afterthought.

The post-World War II explosion of scientific knowledge led to increased frequency of publications in all disciplines. Sensory analysis shared in this growth. An increasing number of papers considered the sensory characteristics of food. Many papers discussed correlations between instrumental measurement and sensory perceptions. Again, however, the scientific literature relegated sensory analysis methods to a contributory science involved in, but not the focus of substantive food science and food technology research. Shortly after World War II the

U.S. Government sponsored a conference on flavor, in 1948, concerning the issue of flavor enhancement by monosodium glutamate (MSG). This conference appeared in book form in 1948 (Food and Container Institute 1948), providing one of the earliest conference proceedings on a topic specifically concerning flavor and flavor enhancement.

During the 1950s few books appeared on flavor, perhaps with the exception of a symposium sponsored by the Arthur D. Little Company and a vast compedium of information on the chemical senses (taste and smell) authored by R.W. Moncrieff in the United Kingdom (in several editions). Short resumes of conferences sponsored by the flavor societies of the U.S. and the U.K. appeared in trade journals. These small conferences, bringing together a group of experts from chemistry, psychology and food science, represented roundtable meetings, rather than extensive, large-attendance symposia. In 1953 the New York Academy of Sciences sponsored the first of its decennial conferences on odor, bringing together many researchers from basic and applied fields. Attendees at the conference, and at the subsequent 1963 and 1973 conferences, comprised representatives from food and non-food industries. These conferences exerted little effect on the field of sensory analysis other than providing background reading material to introduce the novice and the expert into other research on taste and smell.

Morley R. Kare, the Director of the Monell Chemical Senses Center, organized several conferences during the 1960s and 1970s. A conference in 1961 on physiological and behavioral aspects of the sense of taste, held at Cornell University, appeared in print a year later (Kare and Halpern 1961). A thin volume, the conference proceedings comprised contributions by various researchers, mostly in basic research in biology, physiology and chemistry, but one or two in applied food science. For the most part, this conference showed participants talking to each other and beginning to recognize each other's areas of interest and problems. The discussion session showed a growing appreciation of the need to understand the rules governing acceptance or rejection of taste materials.

A second conference, this time in 1965, sponsored by the Nutrition Foundation, appeared in print in 1967 under the title *The Chemical Senses and Nutrition*, edited by M. R. Kare and O. Maller. Significant contributions to sensory evaluation included a paper by Pangborn and an extensive bibliography on the chemical senses (including much food science literature) prepared by Pangborn and Trabue.

At the same time, in 1965, the first significant book on sensory analysis appeared, authored by M. A. Amerine (an enologist with a world famous reputation in wines), R. M. Pangborn (a sensory evaluation expert) and E. B. Roessler (a statistician). The volume entitled

Principles of Sensory Evaluation of Food, published by Academic Press as part of its Food Science Series, encompassed most of the literature on the chemical senses, methods of sensory testing, and statistical procedures used in taste testing. In lieu of any other textbook covering sensory evaluation, this text soon became the standard reference work in the field, read by graduate students and professionals alike. An encyclopedic work, the volume saw extensive service for reference purposes. As an introduction to the vast field of sensory analysis and allied disciplines, the volume introduced numerous individuals to the rich background of research.

The late 1960s saw increasing publications in sensory analysis. In Gothenburg, Sweden, the Swedish Institute for Food Preservation Research, SIK (now called the Swedish Food Institute), researchers under the direction of Professor Erik von Sydow and Dr. Birger Drake began to apply the principles of sensory analysis of food products to model systems and to food processing problems. They issued reports in mimeographed form describing these studies. The SIK report series contained individual items which would subsequently appear in the food science literature. The report series short-circuited the lengthy time needed between completion of research, manuscript preparation and submission, review process and final appearance in published form. (This process can last a year or two, and causes great dissatisfaction in the scientific community because it results in literature which loses currency when it finally appears).

Under the direction of Birger Drake and Birgit Johannsen (née Lundgren), SIK compiled an annotated bibliography on sensory evaluation which comprised entries from food science, psychophysics, pharmaceutical sciences, etc. This annotated bibliography, appearing in 1969, updated Pangborn's and Trabue's bibliography (1965) and provided short synopses of many articles. No serious student of sensory evaluation can afford to miss these two mimeographed volumes, as well as their companion updated volumes published by SIK in 1972. Later, O'Mahony and Thompson (1975) would compile the *Harvey's Bibliography of Taste*, which would augment the other reference lists.

Paralleling the spate of publications, working committees in professional organizations developed as well. The American Society of Testing and Materials (ASTM) in Philadelphia, an organization devoted to developing industrial testing standards, set up committee E-18 on sensory evaluation of materials in 1961. The founding members of that working committee comprised participants from the food, cosmetics and chemical industries. Twice yearly meetings soon attracted many participants from the food, cosmetics, and chemical industries, many from across the U.S., and from Canada and Europe. The ASTM E-18

committee divided itself into four working subcommittees, with different goals and orientations:
(1) Terminology
(2) Psychophysical theory and test method.
(3) Consumer testing procedures (and other applications of sensory analysis).
(4) Sensory—instrumental correlations.

During the course of the past twenty years, the E-18 committee presented symposia on visual appearance of materials and new methods for answering old problems in sensory analysis. Furthermore, these symposia appeared in print, along with specific volumes devoted to methods of sensory analysis. Those volumes have served countless numbers of novice sensory analysts as guidebooks for the proper testing procedures which one should follow in various test situations, and for different types of problems. ASTM E-18 has also pioneered a publication of key sensory evaluation information through the ASTM DS (Data Series) publications. E-18 published a compendium of thresholds for taste and smell, garnered by volunteer abstracters from the scientific literature of many different fields (DS-48). This volume appeared in a second edition as well, containing many new and updated entries.

THE 1970s AND LITERATURE AND MEETINGS — THE ERA OF GROWTH

Since 1970 sensory evaluation experienced unusual growth. Many more meetings, symposia and organizations appeared on the scene, accompanied by increased publication rate of manuscripts dealing with specific problems in sensory analysis.

The Institute of Food Technologists (IFT) began yearly symposia on topics concerning sensory evaluation, presented by the newly formed Sensory Evaluation Division. At last count, in late 1982, the division had over 800 members, drawn from diverse disciplines in industry and academia. Topics presented in the symposia ranged from overviews on uses and misuses of sensory evaluation, to new scaling methods (particularly Magnitude Estimation and the Quantitative Descriptive Analysis technique), sensory quality control, and the interface between marketing research and sensory analysis for the development and testing of new products.

During this period other symposia concentrated on specific topics pertinent to sensory analysis, either from a theoretical point of view concentrating on the chemical senses, or from a pragmatic point of view, concentrating on methodology. The European Chemoreception Research

Organization, founded in Holland during the summer of 1970, sponsored symposia on the processes of taste and smell. Some of the papers presented during these symposia pertain to methods for sensory analysis, albeit analysis of simple, non-food stimuli (e.g., model systems). The chemoreception meetings began to concern sensory scaling, oftentimes the scaling of specific products.

The American Society of Testing and Materials (ASTM), which we met before, sponsored still other symposia, specifically on the sensory analysis of appearance and on new methods for correlating sensory and instrumental measures. These two symposia reflected the growing interest in sensory analysis, and comprised contributions from food researchers as well as textile scientists and other researchers only tangentially related to the food industry.

Until 1973, sensory analysts lacked a journal concerning their scientific discipline, and published papers in other topic-related journals. During the Gordon Conference (summer 1972), D. Reidel Publishing Company in Holland announced the publication of a new journal devoted to taste, smell, and the sensory analysis of foods and other consumer items. This journal, *Chemical Senses and Flavour* (now called *Chemical Senses*), integrated research on topics as diverse as the molecular processes underlying taste and smell sensation and the statistical analysis of flavor scores obtained in discrimination tests. To date the journal has published six complete volumes, first under the Reidel name, and more recently under the sponsorship of the British abstracting company, Information Retrieval Ltd., in London.

A potpourri of other publications and symposia round out our historical overview. During the summer of 1974, the Swedish Institute of Food Preservation Research (SIK) in Gothenburg sponsored a symposium of sensory analysis of foods to mark the opening of a special wing of the institute that would house special sensory analysis facilities. During the same period, numerous conferences on different aspects of food each featured sections on sensory analysis, whether concerning texture (De-Man *et al.* 1976), chemical senses and nutrition (Kare and Maller 1977), or sweeteners (Shaw *et al.* 1978; Guggenheim 1979), etc. Many of these symposia subsequently appeared in published proceedings, comprising full-text versions of the presented papers. These collected volumes of manuscripts further enriched the literature of sensory analysis. For the first time the serious researcher interested in methods of analysis had at his or her disposal information from current and previous periodicals, collected papers dealing with unified topics in which sensory analysis played a small or often large role, and literature on test methods appearing in specific manuals on sensory evaluation procedures.

SHORT COURSES AND WORKSHOPS

Perhaps during the course of scientific development a certain point emerges in every scientific discipline, when critical mass occurs. One can point to short courses on newest trends, or workshops on specific procedures, as indications of that critical mass. Short courses, lasting 1-5 days, reflect forums for transmission of new or baseline information in a discipline. They have become increasingly popular as a method for allowing practitioners to keep abreast of new developments in the field, and as a teaching instrument to indoctrinate new workers in sensory analysis.

These short courses cover topics on sensory analysis ranging from basic introductory materials (e.g., how to run a triangle test or how to instruct panelists to scale liking/disliking by means of a hedonic scale) all the way to training practitioners in the field to do flavor or texture profiling.

Workshops provide another method for disseminating experience. In a sensory analysis workshop the participants go through different exercises which illustrate how one should implement a variety of different tests, including discrimination tests, descriptive tests and scaling/ranking tests. Some of these workshops have recently appeared in print, notably the exercises and results from one workshop on sensory analysis of foods, first sponsored in Switzerland by the Swiss Federal Institute of Food Technology (under the guidance of Professor Jurg Solms), and later held at the University of Manitoba, Winnipeg, Canada (under the guidance of Professor Mina McDaniel). The volume containing these exercises appeared in 1977, and provided a valuable compendium of practical information on how to run a sensory test, along with the empirical results from the 22 exercises (Vaisey-Genser *et al.* 1977).

AN OVERVIEW

Sensory analysis and product testing has come a long way in the past fifty years, developing from a catch-as-catch-can approach to an amalgamation of different disciplines. Today several food science departments in the U.S. and Europe and South America offer courses on sensory analysis. Two decades ago such courses barely existed. At the University of California, Davis, one can major in sensory analysis in preparation for a master's degree in food science. Such emphasis on curricula for sensory analysis cannot but help improve the quality of practitioners in the decades to come.

Linked with the growing academic respectability of sensory analysis as a separate discipline, we see also its growing utilization by the food industry. Fifty years ago, or even twenty years ago, sensory analysis provided rudimentary data, often in the form which marketers could not or would not use in making their decisions. Today, company after company has created and maintained a sensory evaluation function, more often than not closely linked with the R&D function. The sensory analyst serves the valuable role of keeping R&D abreast of consumer and panel reactions to test products. Marketing researchers conduct their own form of sensory analysis with consumers. They too recognize that the key to continued product success comes from both advertising and successful product delivery. Sensory factors, and an understanding of those factors in the marketplace, play an important role in the market researcher's job.

The future looks bright for sensory analysis and product testing as a discipline. We can look forward to the increasing maturity of practitioners in the field who, armed with the proper educational background, can synthesize information from other disciplines and apply it to their work. As sensory factors play increasingly important roles in differentiating one product from another, we may expect to see even greater emphasis on proper sensory analysis of foods. Furthermore, the growing nature of interdisciplinary work in food science cannot help but exert a beneficial influence on sensory analysis practitioners. Faced with queries from management and faced with inputs from psychologists, physiologists and statisticians, the sensory analyst has become, and will continue to remain, one of the key individuals responsible both for new product success and for the maintenance of current product quality and market share.

CHAPTER 2

DESCRIPTIVE ANALYSIS OF PERCEPTIONS

INTRODUCTION

A history of perception from the perspective of the past thousand years reveals that much interest focused on describing the characteristics of perceptions. Descriptive analysis becomes the necessary first step in a science of product measurement. It categorizes the different senses, and provides a language for communication of experience. Aristotle recognized five primary senses (vision, audition, taste, smell and touch). Each of these senses impacts on our appreciation of foods, albeit in different ways, and with different degrees of importance.

BACKGROUND OF PROFILING SYSTEMS

Fifty years ago few, if any, profiling systems existed. The nuances in flavor which we recognize today did not play an important role to food scientists then. Certainly food scientists recognized that flavor comprised many nuances, but the state of the art dictated the use of simple scales of overall flavor, whether rating flavor intensity, flavor acceptability, or in very rare instances, intensity of specific flavor notes.

E. C. Crocker, a food scientist with the Arthur D. Little Company (Cambridge, Mass.), proposed that the food scientist consider flavor as a complex of mixtures of varying sensations. This suggestion followed the trend of introspectionist psychologists, decades before, who attempted to describe sensory perception in terms of structural constituents discerned through introspection of one's sensory experience (Crocker and Henderson 1927).

A decade of research produced the Flavor Profile, a scientific method designed primarily to ascertain the components of flavor, and secondly, to scale their respective intensities. Appearing in 1947 in *Food Technology* (Caul 1957), the Flavor Profile method jolted many food researchers into the realization that flavor perception comprises many facets. Researchers seeking to amalgamate all flavor nuances into an overall flavor score often missed the critical factors which differentiated one flavor from another. Flavor did not mean only amount, but also type or quality.

The Flavor Profile procedure attracted interest and a loyal following in the food industry. Numerous spinoffs appeared in related disciplines, such as texture and cosmetics. Competitive systems emerged which used similar approaches with, perhaps, different scaling methods, such as the Quantitative Descriptive Analysis, or QDA system, developed at the Stanford Research Institute, Palo Alto, California (Stone *et al.* 1974).

In the early 1960s researchers at the General Foods Corporation led by Dr. Alina Szczesniak concentrated their efforts to develop a descriptive system to evaluate texture perceptions. Szczesniak cooperated with physical chemists and engineers to develop a system comprising a limited number of textural attributes, classified in the order of appearance and according to type of property (mechanical property, geometric property). These early research studies culminated in a classic paper on Texture Profile Analysis, appearing in the *Journal of Food Science* (Szczesniak, Brandt and Friedman 1963).

These early attempts to develop profiling systems recognized the empiricism involved in such undertakings. Food scientists realized that their system did not really represent how the nose/mouth or tongue really worked, nor did they conceive their set of descriptors as a finalized version whose combination of components would encompass the entire realm of flavor or texture perceptions.

THE SPECIAL CASE OF SMELL AND TASTE

The major advances in descriptive analysis started in Linnaeus' time, spurred on by increased interest in scientific classification. Like other researchers, Linnaeus tried to classify the attributes of taste and smell into primaries, or basic characteristics. We can smell thousands of different scents and taste hundreds of different tastes. Does this mean that thousands of primary smells and tastes actually exist? Or, can one uncover an underlying set of primary odor or taste sensations whose combinations, in varying proportions, reproduce the spectrum of sensory experience? Vision researchers, starting with Newton, faced the same problem in color perception when they searched for color primaries which, in concert, could reproduce the colors of the rainbow. Linnaeus searched for a general classification of odor sensations, paralleling the biological classification of animals and plants into phyla, genus and species, etc. His classification system appears in Table 2.1 along with other systems of odor quality classification.

Bear in mind that this pioneering approach, like others which would follow, bore the stamp of morphology, the science of structure and classification. Other approaches would bear the stamp of physiology,

TABLE 2.1
LISTS OF DESCRIPTORS FOR ODOR

Odor Classes: General

	Zwaarde-maker 1895 30 (sub) classes	Linnaeus 1756 7 classes	Henning 1915 6 classes	Crocker and Henderson 1927 4 classes	Amoore 1952 7 classes	Schutz 1964 9 classes	Wright and Michels 1964 8 classes	Harper et al. 1968 44 classes	Miscellaneous additional
1	fruity						hexyl-acetate	fruity	
2	waxy							soapy	
3	ethereal				ethereal	etherish		etherish-solvent	
4	camphor				camphor			camphor; mothballs	
5	clove	aromatic	spicy					aromatic	
6	cinnamon						spice	spicy	
7	aniseed						benzo-thiazole		
8	minty				minty			minty	
9	thyme		fruity						
10	rosy								
11	citrous						citral	citrous	
12	almond					spicy		almond	
13	jasmine	fragrant	flowery	fragrant	floral			floral	
14	orange-blossom					fragrant		fragrant	
15	lily								
16	violet								
17	vanilla					sweet		vanilla, sweet	
18	amber	ambrosial						animal	
19	musky				musky			musk	

	Zwaardemaker 1895 30 (sub) classes	Linnaeus 1756 7 classes	Henning 1915 6 classes	Crocker and Henderson 1927 4 classes	Amoore 1952 7 classes	Schutz 1964 9 classes	Wright and Michels 1964 8 classes	Harper et al. 1968 44 classes	Miscellaneous additional
20	leek	alliaceous						garlic	
21	fishy							ammonia;	
22	bromine							fishy	
23	burnt		burnt	burnt		burnt	affective	burnt	
24	phenolic							carbolic	
25	caproic	hircine		caprylic				sweaty	
26	cat-urine								
27	narcotic	repulsive							
28	bed-bug								
29	carrion	nauseous						sickly	
30	fecal							fecal	
31			resinous				resinous	resinous	
32			foul		putrid	sulfurous	unpleasant	putrid; sulfurous	
33				acid				acid	
34						oily		oily	
35						rancid		rancid	
36						metallic		metallic	
37								meaty	
38								moldy	
39								grassy	
40								bloody	
41								cooked-vegetable	
42									sandal
43									watery
44									urinous
(Non-olfactory)					(pungent)		(trigeminal)	(Pungent and 5 others)	

Source: Amoore (1969)

or behavioral mechanism, for defining odors as combinations of primaries (as vision scientists do in color primaries).

The biological stamp on descriptive analysis held scientific sway for more than a century, as different scientists proffered their own classification of tastes, smells, etc. Some of these researchers proposed classifications which seemed correct from armchair speculation. Others, with a more mechanistic viewpoint, offered systems which represented basic odor or taste primaries. These systems also appear in Table 2.1 for odor qualities.

During the middle of the nineteenth century, Fick (1864) proposed that the spectrum of taste sensations resulted from four different, non-overlapping groups: sweet, salty, sour and bitter, respectively. From time to time other tastes appeared, suggested by one or another investigator. The reader of German physiology literature of the late nineteenth century will notice qualities appearing such as insipid, alkaline, and metallic. The consensus soon became that four tastes, and no more, constituted the primary points of the taste spectrum. The entire range of different tastes derived from combinations of these four. Later work by von Skramlik (1921) on taste mixtures, suggested that the use of four taste primaries could only account for some, but not all, taste mixture sensations.

Odor classification presented considerably more complex problems compared to taste, as we saw above. Investigators suggested widely varying numbers of primaries. Occasionally, a system evolved specifically to deal with a certain set of stimuli. Some classification of odors dealt only with perfumes. Other systems covered the entire field of olfactory perception, attempting to account for the entire gamut of odor sensations. Issues became clouded as researchers offered numerous systems. One could not feel sure that a particular odor classification system pertained to ad hoc descriptions of existing odor sensations, or whether to the contrary, that the system proposed basic, physiologically meaningful primaries which underlay all olfactory sensations (Harper, Bate-Smith and Land 1968).

ODOR CLASSIFICATION SYSTEMS
—THE PAST TWENTY YEARS

Since 1950 or thereabouts, two widely divergent research streams have dominated the scientific scene. John Amoore (1952) hypothesized that there exist seven primary odors whose combinations should, in theory, suffice to reproduce all of the known odor qualities. Later work, on the phenomenon of specific anosmia (loss of sensitivity to a specific odor chemical, or class of chemicals such as musk odorants, or androsterone which smells urinous), led Amoore to increase the number of supposed primaries to more than 30. Amoore speculated that odor perception and odor quality behave according to a lock-and-key mechanism. Our olfactory receptor system, housed in the nasal mucosa, possesses a limited number of structurally different receptors sensitive to specific molecular shapes and sizes. These receptor sites show varying sensitivity to differently shaped molecules. By measuring sensitivity to many different odors from a wide variety of odor stimuli, and by testing a wide sample of individuals in the population, Amoore isolated specific chemicals, the so-called primary odorants. The loss of sensitivity to one specific chemical (e.g., iso-valeric acid, a sweaty-smelling chemical in the fatty acid category), unaccompanied by specific loss of sensitivity to other odorants, suggested that the chemical represented the basic or primary odor sensation (Iso-valeric acid thus exemplified the sweaty primary).

Amoore's approach illustrates the mechanism-based approach, biologically oriented. The descriptive analysis of perceptions becomes a tool whereby the investigator learns about the chemical itself, the configuration of the molecule and its relation to the receptor site. Product testers can use Amoore's system as a starting point for descriptive analysis of odor sensations if they keep one caveat in mind. Amoore's classification system possesses far too few odorants as references and an inadequate, sparse language to have much use in classifying odor perceptions in a pragmatic fashion. The system remains simply too sparse and lacks the necessary detail. One can obtain an idea of how the sensory system works, and an idea of what basic primaries exist for olfaction. One cannot describe the perceptual attributes of food aromas using the limited number of chemicals or a parallel but limited set of descriptor terms.

Roland Harper and his colleagues, working at the Food Research Laboratory at Norwich in England, took an entirely different approach. These researchers did not set out to discover biologically meaningful primaries. Rather, they confined their interest to developing a lexicon of descriptive terms which could find service as a language of food and drink. They concentrated their initial efforts first on a thorough survey of the extant literature, going back a thousand years. This survey appeared in book form *Odour Description and Classification: A Multidisciplinary Approach,* published in 1968 simultaneously in the United Kingdom and the United States (Harper, Bate-Smith and Land 1968). Their research culminated in a checklist of terms to describe odor perception. Harper and his colleagues recognized that: (1) the list lacked many terms and would always remain incomplete; (2) the list could describe the aroma of many food products, but not all; and (3) the list did not represent biological odor primaries, but rather provided the user with a lexicon of terms for pragmatically oriented description.

The authors selected 44 words, which they felt would cover the range of olfactory perception. The 44 words could not capture many of the nuances of odor. In fact, to capture these nuances one must use unique words pertaining to objects, rather than relying upon general quality words.

TABLE 2.2
ODOR PROFILING WORDS (HARPER SCALE)

Quality Scale													
Absent 0	Slightly 1		2			Moderately 3	4			Extremely 5			
Q						**S**							
Fragrant	0 1 2 3 4 5					Oily, fatty	0 1 2 3 4 5						
Sweaty	0 1 2 3 4 5					Like mothballs	0 1 2 3 4 5						
Almond-like	0 1 2 3 4 5					Like gasoline, Solvent	0 1 2 3 4 5						
Burnt, smoky	0 1 2 3 4 5					Cooked vegetables	0 1 2 3 4 5						
Herbal, green, cut grass, etc.	0 1 2 3 4 5					Sweet	0 1 2 3 4 5						
Etherish, anaesthetic	0 1 2 3 4 5					Fishy	0 1 2 3 4 5						
Sour, acid, vinegar, etc.	0 1 2 3 4 5					Spicy	0 1 2 3 4 5						
Like blood, raw meat	0 1 2 3 4 5					Paint-like	0 1 2 3 4 5						
Dry, powdery	0 1 2 3 4 5					Rancid	0 1 2 3 4 5						
Like ammonia	0 1 2 3 4 5					Minty, peppermint	0 1 2 3 4 5						
Disinfectant, Carbolic	0 1 2 3 4 5					Sulphidic	0 1 2 3 4 5						
P						**R**							
Aromatic	0 1 2 3 4 5					Fruit (citrus)	0 1 2 3 4 5						
Meaty (cooked)	0 1 2 3 4 5					Fruity (other)	0 1 2 3 4 5						
Sickening	0 1 2 3 4 5					Putrid, foul, decayed	0 1 2 3 4 5						
Musty, earthy, moldy	0 1 2 3 4 5					Woody, resinous	0 1 2 3 4 5						
Sharp, pungent, acid	0 1 2 3 4 5					Musk-like	0 1 2 3 4 5						
Camphor like	0 1 2 3 4 5					Soapy	0 1 2 3 4 5						
Light	0 1 2 3 4 5					Garlic, onion	0 1 2 3 4 5						
Heavy	0 1 2 3 4 5					Animal	0 1 2 3 4 5						
Cool, cooling	0 1 2 3 4 5					Vanilla-like	0 1 2 3 4 5						
Warm	0 1 2 3 4 5					Fecal (like manure)	0 1 2 3 4 5						
Metallic	0 1 2 3 4 5					Floral	0 1 2 3 4 5						

Source: Harper, Land, Bate-Smith and Griffiths (1968)

Table 2.2 presents the Harper list of 44 words and the scale. The words pertain primarily to odors encountered in food. Along with the list, Harper *et al.* proposed a 6 point category scale, ranging from 0 (not at all appropriate) to 5 (extremely appropriate). With the list of 44 words and with a scale to measure degree of appropriateness, the user could profile the sensory quality of complex foods as well as simple chemicals.

Table 2.3 presents some profiles which Harper *et al.* reported when panelists profiled the sensory attributes of simple chemicals (Table 2.3 shows profiles generated by unpracticed panelists, who had had little experience in product evaluation.)

TABLE 2.3
SOME REPRESENTATIVE PROFILES USING THE
HARPER 44 WORD SYSTEM[1]

Unpracticed Panelists Did the Ratings

Diethyl Sulfide		*Safrole*	
putrid	2.1	sweet	1.9
garlic onion	1.8	minty, peppermint	1.5
sickly	1.1	fragrant	1.4
sharp	1.0	aromatic	1.3
petrol	0.9	spicy	1.3
		fruity	1.0
Acetaldehyde		cool	0.8
herbal	1.4	etherish	0.7
fruity	1.3	floral	0.7
fragrant	1.2		
petrol	1.1	*Benzaldehyde*	
sharp	1.1	almond-like	3.9
etherish	0.8	sweet	1.7
light	0.9	fragrant	1.3
		vanilla	1.1
Ammonia		oily, fatty	0.7
like ammonia	4.6	heavy	0.9
sharp	2.2	aromatic	0.7
fishy	0.6		
Octanol			
soapy	2.3		

[1]Numbers reflect average ratings from an unpracticed panel.
Source: Harper, Land, Bate-Smith and Griffiths (1968)

Not all panelists agreed on their profiles in terms of attributes used and values assigned. A mean score of 3.5 on a 6 point scale could mean that some panelists felt the attribute appeared at degree 3 on the 6 point scale, whereas others felt that the attribute appeared at degree 4. On the other hand, the same score of 3.5 might mean that half the panelists felt that the attribute appeared at degree 5, whereas the other half of the panelists felt that the attribute did not seem at all appropriate to describe the smell.

DEVELOPING A PROFILE LANGUAGE
—HOW AND WHY

We have seen the wide variety of olfactory notes which researchers proposed to describe the nuances of odor sensations (Table 2.1). A similarly large number of descriptor terms (albeit not quite as extensive) applies to texture descriptions as well (Yoshikawa, Nishimaru, Tashiro and Yoshida 1970). If a descriptive system aims for wide use, it must balance inclusiveness with practicality. No descriptor system comprising as few as 7 terms can hope to achieve wide use, because the system fails to capture qualitative nuances. No system comprising 500 descriptor terms can succeed because the system contains far too many terms. The number makes the system unwieldy, complicated, and more troublesome to use and to analyze.

There may not exist an ideal number of attributes or characteristics for a specific profiling system. Our ability to process and transmit information regarding our perception probably increases with an increasing number of descriptive characteristics. In the region beyond 7, but certainly less than 100, any additional attributes probably will add little if any new information. People cannot process an unlimited amount of information using the large profiling system. As we shall see, this inherent limitation on man's ability to describe perceptions places a behavioral upper limit on the number of characteristics tapped by existing systems.

Armed with this insight, let us look at the methods currently used to develop descriptor systems and the methods used to reduce the wide number of descriptors to a manageable number.

Unprompted Description

Imagine, for a moment, sitting alone with a glass of wine and a piece of paper. You must describe your impressions. A typical person may look at the wine, taste it, swirl it about, smell it, and then proceed to jot down the descriptor terms. Generally the descriptor terms emerge in clusters, first rapidly, then slowly (contingent, of course, on the person's ability to write or perhaps to dictate into a machine). The cluster of descriptor terms appears as a mélange. They include terms relating to texture, appearance, taste and smell. Perhaps mixed among the descriptor terms referring to simple sensations lie other terms of an image nature (fresh, elegant) or terms dealing with acceptance (acceptable, liked, good flavor, etc.).

Unprompted description refers to just that. The reseacher leaves the panelist alone with the stimulus, allowing the panelist to search his or her memory for terms to describe perceptions. The investigator or interviewer provides no feedback, no encouragement and no indications whether the terms fall on target or off target in description.

Unprompted description procedures quickly generate an abundance of terms, quite a few of which possess idiosyncratic meanings appropriate only to the originator. On the other hand, the adept investigator working with a dozen panelists, each of whom participates in the same exercise separately, receives inputs that he or she can collate together in order to select the key terms, reject the redundant ones and identify the idiosyncratic and, perhaps, meaningless terms. Since the panelists do not interact with each other, the investigator knows that the list of descriptor systems represents each individual's own point of view, rather than a consensus.

Methods used to analyze lists of unprompted descriptions include counting the number of key words to estimate frequency of use; ascertaining the order of appearance of the terms to see whether any terms show prepotency, or tendency to emerge quickly as a top-of-mind descriptor; and higher order analyses to ascertain whether certain pairs of terms correlate with each other. Two terms might always appear together, in all instances, suggesting that the presence of one term predicts the presence of the other. In such instances one of the two terms may not provide additional information.

As a general rule of thumb, a good set of unprompted descriptors emerges from a panel of 5 or more individuals. Obviously, the more panelists, the greater the likelihood that the final list will properly represent all relevant characteristics; however, the optimum number of panelists remains a moot subject among practitioners.

Group Sessions (Focus Group Interviews)

During the past twenty-five years market researchers and product developers have relied upon group sessions comprising 8-10 individuals, led by a skilled moderator. These group discussions provide another means to generate the requisite list of descriptor terms. During a group session, the panelists (chosen from the target population) meet to discuss aspects of the product under consideration. The purpose of the group may hinge on evaluations of new packaging concepts, or types of packages, reactions to advertisements or a search of the participants' reactions to the specific product category (e.g., what do people think about children's cereals, or what do they think about the pasta products currently in market).

The discussions follow a pre-specified moderator's guide, which covers specific points. The structured discussion allows latitude for participants to express their feelings, and to use many different descriptions of the product. The moderator often tapes the discussions for further analysis.

During the course of the discussion group many terms emerge as participants talk about products. In contrast to the unprompted but focused task of describing a product, group sessions usually do not focus panelists on pure product description alone, although such a task could find its place as part of the moderator's guide. A moderator might bring the discussion around to a point where she or he encourages free descriptions of the products in the category, and use that portion of the focus group as input to develop the descriptor list. Also, group sessions encourage and become subject to interpanelist interactions. During a group discussion panelists interact with each other, influencing each other's reactions and statements in the group. This procedure simultaneously generates benefits and leads to problems. A very articulate, dominant panelist may overshadow other less verbal, but equally insightful, individuals. On the other hand, the synergistic effect of groups enhances the output. More ideas and more descriptors emerge in a conversation mode than in a person-by-person test mode, where each individual records the descriptors in isolation.

If the food scientist or market researcher limits the interviews only to consumers, he or she runs the risk of limiting the number of descriptive characteristics to buzz words often used in advertising, or to more general and non-specific, meaningless words, e.g., aromatic, flavorful and natural for flavors or beverages. To avoid this problem, the investigator should interview a broad spectrum of individuals, including consumers, marketers of the products and the technical scientists responsible for product development. Each group uses a different descriptive language. The scientist often uses specific, scientifically-defined terms which characterize a product in exact terms. The marketer knows terms from wide experience in marketing and promotion. The consumer knows the general buzz words and advertising copy language. Some attributes overlap from one group to another. Furthermore, each group session may produce similar words, but the meanings could differ depending upon the background of the participants. The sensory analyst must keep these factors in mind when developing the final compilation.

Prompted Description—The Kelly Repertory Grid

Beginning in the 1950s, considerable research interest focused on product description. Kelly (1955) suggested an excellent way to elicit a wide array of descriptive terms in a simple manner from consumers. To do so, he would present three items to the consumer (e.g., spaghetti, cheese, orange juice). These generate three pairs (spaghetti-cheese, spaghetti-orange, cheese-orange). For each pair, the panelist would state in what ways the items seem similar and in what ways they seem different. The interviewer records these reasons. The technique generates many different descriptor terms by forcing the individual to change frames of reference for each pair. The method turns into an enjoyable game, rather than a boring recitation.

TABLE 2.4
EXAMPLE OF OUTCOME OF REPERTORY GRID EXERCISE
WITH A TRIAD OF WORDS:
SPAGHETTI, CHEESE, ORANGE JUICE

		Quality Scale	
	Spaghetti—Cheese	*Spaghetti—Orange Juice*	*Cheese—Orange Juice*
Similarity	White Yellow Color	Food	Food
	Solid	Yellow/White	Flavor
		Soft	Yellow
		Caloric	Side dish
Difference	Starch	Hard	Hard
	Milk	Solid-liquid	Aroma
	Flavor	Sour	Caloric
	Bland	Chewable	Fatty
	Sharp Acid	Aroma	Sweet vs Pungent
	Cooked vs Raw		
	Main dish vs Snack		

Table 2.4 shows the results of a Kelly Repertory Grid analysis with a small group of panelists, presented with these three words in all pairs.

TABLE 2.5

ODOR AND TASTE QUALITIES AND THEIR AVERAGE SCORES FOR TWO REFERENCE JUICE (BLUEBERRY AND CRANBERRY) AND FOR GRAPE AND APPLE JUICES[1]

Attribute	Grape		Apple		Blueberry		Cranberry	
	nose N²=146	mouth N=142	nose N=153	mouth N=153	nose N=60	mouth N=69	nose N=108	mouth N=109
Total odor strength	5.99 (.16)³	5.40 (.17)	5.53 (.14)	4.75 (.14)	5.16 (.31)	4.15 (.25)	4.57 (.21)	4.12 (.22)
Apple-like	1.07 (.09)	1.36 (.11)	5.46 (.18)	5.11 (.19)	.77 (.16)	1.69 (.17)	1.43 (.15)	1.33 (.15)
Musty, moldy	1.81 (.13)	1.68 (.11)	2.10 (.11)	1.92 (.10)	1.68 (.21)	1.46 (.19)	1.32 (.13)	1.03 (.13)
Sweet odor	5.13 (.13)	4.83 (.13)	4.31 (.13)	4.02 (.13)	5.23 (.21)	3.90 (.24)	2.56 (.21)	2.46 (.19)
Spicy	1.80 (.11)	1.77 (.10)	1.84 (.10)	1.72 (.09)	2.19 (.22)	1.58 (.18)	1.69 (.14)	1.61 (.16)
Fermented, wine-like	2.68 (.14)	2.51 (.15)	1.99 (.12)	2.04 (.12)	2.20 (.22)	1.83 (.19)	1.60 (.13)	1.62 (.15)
Blueberry-like	1.67 (.18)	1.73 (.19)	.13 (.03)	.23 (.05)	6.30 (.25)	5.00 (.27)	.20 (.05)	.29 (.08)
Estery (hard candy)	2.37 (.16)	2.54 (.17)	2.11 (.13)	2.08 (.13)	2.23 (.27)	2.04 (.28)	1.61 (.18)	1.81 (.20)
Aromatic	4.23 (.17)	4.07 (.17)	3.81 (.15)	3.67 (.14)	4.15 (.34)	3.67 (.31)	3.12 (.21)	3.01 (.22)
Sharp, pungent	2.31 (.13)	2.11 (.13)	2.61 (.12)	2.39 (.12)	1.88 (.21)	2.01 (.20)	3.46 (.20)	3.42 (.24)
Cranberry-like	.33 (.06)	.42 (.06)	.33 (.05)	.54 (.08)	.39 (.09)	.73 (.14)	5.98 (.20)	5.28 (.26)
Woody, sawdust-like	.81 (.08)	.75 (.07)	1.15 (.10)	1.09 (.11)	.59 (.13)	.59 (.12)	.77 (.11)	.80 (.13)
Floral	3.21 (.16)	3.20 (.15)	3.18 (.14)	3.05 (.13)	3.45 (.29)	2.77 (.26)	1.93 (.20)	2.00 (.21)
Grape-like	6.33 (.15)	5.89 (.15)	.50 (.06)	.63 (.07)	1.55 (.20)	1.59 (.22)	.56 (.10)	.64 (.10)
Resinous	1.54 (.12)	1.43 (.11)	1.54 (.11)	1.49 (.12)	1.57 (.22)	1.33 (.20)	1.24 (.16)	1.30 (.17)
Fruity, berry-like	3.57 (.19)	3.75 (.19)	2.32 (.17)	2.33 (.16)	4.52 (.30)	3.86 (.30)	2.69 (.20)	2.49 (.22)
Green, cut grass	.57 (.07)	.56 (.07)	1.13 (.10)	1.04 (.10)	.44 (.11)	.57 (.15)	.74 (.14)	.77 (.14)
Fragrant	4.84 (.14)	4.61 (.14)	4.13 (.15)	3.85 (.12)	5.12 (.22)	3.90 (.26)	2.93 (.21)	2.86 (.21)
Earthy	.82 (.09)	.87 (.09)	1.19 (.12)	1.33 (.13)	.68 (.17)	.64 (.15)	.64 (.12)	.61 (.11)
Vinegar-like	1.50 (.12)	1.49 (.13)	2.16 (.11)	2.26 (.13)	1.22 (.08)	1.46 (.21)	1.90 (.20)	2.03 (.23)
Etherish, anaesthetic	.73 (.08)	.73 (.09)	1.31 (.12)	.94 (.11)	.48 (.12)	.61 (.13)	.69 (.11)	.66 (.10)
Pleasantness in odor	6.47 (.09)	6.38 (.09)	5.58 (.12)	5.59 (.10)	6.65 (.15)	5.43 (.22)	5.03 (.16)	4.82 (.15)

[1]Data on profiling from Von Sydow, Moskowitz, Jacobs and Meiselman (1974) using the checklist method and a 0-10 point category rating scale.

[2]N = Number of ratings from the panel.

[3]Numbers in parenthesis = standard error of the mean.

Note the change in reference that occurs when the pair changes. The panelist seeks new nuances of difference and similarity for each pair, which forces the emergence of a richer description.

Prompted Description—The Checklist Method

If the product tester possesses a large list of descriptor terms, it becomes possible to cull the large list and develop a smaller and more appropriate list of terms by eliminating extraneous terms. One can quickly pare down the large list of terms to a smaller list by asking panelists to categorize the terms as critical and non-critical. Only those terms selected as critical by a prespecified percentage of the test group remain in the final list. Von Sydow, Moskowitz, Jacobs and Meiselman (1974) used the checklist method to generate a final list of terms describing the perception of fruit juices, as Table 2.5 shows.

A checklist procedure does not add new terms. It represents the sorting of available descriptors into usable and non-usable ones. Nor does the checklist procedure by itself provide the rationale for the classification of descriptor terms into one or the other category.

A recent study on 800+ odor descriptors, conducted by Dr. A. Dravnieks and the author for the American Society of Testing and Materials (ASTM) Committee E-18 (Sensory Evaluation), concerned odor descriptors. Dravnieks had collected the large set of descriptors from numerous lists published in the scientific literature, as well as lists currently used by fragrance and flavor houses. In order to do further work on odor description, he had to reduce the list of terms to a manageable set. To do so, he instituted a round robin study, involving several laboratories, with the checklist method. Participants in the study classified each descriptor term as belonging to one of three classes: critical for odor description, important (but not critical), and irrelevant. Table 2.6 shows highlights of the initial part of the study, including those words classified as critical by more than 50% of the participants.

Finally, Table 2.7 shows the expanded checklist of attributes developed by Dravnieks, based upon the Harper list and his own studies of odor description.

DESCRIPTIVE SYSTEMS
—MEANING AND REDUNDANCY

All languages possess terms which vary in their degree of meaningfulness. Some terms may evoke such widely different connotations to

TABLE 2.6
FIRST 29 DESCRIPTOR WORDS FROM 800+ DESCRIPTORS

Panelists voted these as the critical descriptors for odor perception.

1. Rancid	9. Musty	16. Lemon	23. Anise
2. Burnt	10. Cinnamon	17. Mercaptan	24. Butter
3. Minty	11. Earthy	18. Peppermint	25. Smoky
4. Fruity	12. Onion	19. Putrid	26. Sulfidic
5. Almond	13. Vanilla	20. Cheese	27. Amine-like
6. Floral	14. Citrus	21. Aldehydic	28. Apple-like
7. Coffee	15. Garlic	22. Clove	29. Banana-like
8. Camphor			

Source: Dravnieks, personal communication (1977)

different individuals that they possess no consistent meaning at all. Other terms may home right in on a definition, so that many, if not most, people use these terms similarly. In addition, all languages comprise some words with synonymous or, at least, overlapping meanings. Descriptor terms for sensory perception do not and cannot exhibit total independence from each other. Overlapping meaning and redundant terms always exist. Sometimes people use two terms identically in some and, perhaps in all contexts. Other times people may use the descriptive terms similarly, but the terms may retain sufficient identity to warrant their joint use.

How can we define the meaning of terms? How can we detect and measure redundancy so that we can eliminate those terms which add no additional descriptive power?

Developing Meaning

In odor and taste description, meaning often shows up in *ostentive* definitions. An ostentive definition means a definition made by pointing to an object and saying that the object represents or possesses the characteristic in question. We often use ostentive definitions in odor description. Odor definitions, by and large, take on meaning by reference to a stimulus which possesses that odor. Goaty smell refers to the smell of goats. One can use a chemical to exemplify the goaty smell, but again the definition requires that we point to the object or to the chemical. We do not have fixed exemplars in our mind typifying goatiness. Similarly, anise smell receives meaning from its exemplar, anise, or anethole, the pure chemical reminiscent of anise.

TABLE 2.7
DRAVNIEKS' EXPANDED LIST OF ODOR DESCRIPTORS

	Quality Scale					
Absent 0	Slightly 1		2	Moderately 3	4	Extremely 5

Eucalyptus	0	1	2	3	4	5	Strawberry-like	0	1	2	3	4 5
Buttery	0	1	2	3	4	5	Stale	0	1	2	3	4 5
Like burnt paper	0	1	2	3	4	5	Cork-like	0	1	2	3	4 5
Cologne	0	1	2	3	4	5	Lavender	0	1	2	3	4 5
Caraway	0	1	2	3	4	5	Cat-urine-like	0	1	2	3	4 5
Orange (fruit)	0	1	2	3	4	5	Bark-like, birch bark	0	1	2	3	4 5
Household gas	0	1	2	3	4	5	Rose-like	0	1	2	3	4 5
Peanut butter	0	1	2	3	4	5	Celery	0	1	2	3	4 5
Violets	0	1	2	3	4	5	Burnt candle	0	1	2	3	4 5
Tea-leaves-like	0	1	2	3	4	5	Mushroom-like	0	1	2	3	4 5
Wet wool, wet dog	0	1	2	3	4	5	Pineapple (fruit)	0	1	2	3	4 5
Chalky	0	1	2	3	4	5	Fresh cigarette smoke	0	1	2	3	4 5

Leather-like	0	1	2	3	4	5	Nutty (walnut etc.)	0	1	2	3	4 5
Pear (fruit)	0	1	2	3	4	5	Fried fat	0	1	2	3	4 5
Stale tobacco smoke	0	1	2	3	4	5	Wet paper-like	0	1	2	3	4 5
Raw cucumber-like	0	1	2	3	4	5	Coffee-like	0	1	2	3	4 5
Raw potato-like	0	1	2	3	4	5	Peach (fruit)	0	1	2	3	4 5
Mouse-like	0	1	2	3	4	5	Laurel leaves	0	1	2	3	4 5
Pepper-like	0	1	2	3	4	5	Scorched milk	0	1	2	3	4 5
Bean-like	0	1	2	3	4	5	Sewer odor	0	1	2	3	4 5
Banana-like	0	1	2	3	4	5	Sooty	0	1	2	3	4 5
Burnt rubber-like	0	1	2	3	4	5	Crushed weeks	0	1	2	3	4 5
Geranium leaves	0	1	2	3	4	5	Rubbery (new rubber)	0	1	2	3	4 5
Urine	0	1	2	3	4	5	Bakery (fresh bread)	0	1	2	3	4 5

Beery (beer-like)	0	1	2	3	4	5	Oak wood, cognac -like	0	1	2	3	4 5
Cedarwood-like	0	1	2	3	4	5	Grapefruit	0	1	2	3	4 5
Coconut-like	0	1	2	3	4	5	Grape-juice-like	0	1	2	3	4 5
Rope-like	0	1	2	3	4	5	Eggy (fresh eggs)	0	1	2	3	4 5
Seminal, sperm-like	0	1	2	3	4	5	Bitter	0	1	2	3	4 5
Like cleaning fluid (carbona)	0	1	2	3	4	5	Cadaverous, like dead animal	0	1	2	3	4 5
Cardboard-like	0	1	2	3	4	5	Maple (as in syrup)	0	1	2	3	4 5
Lemon (fruit)	0	1	2	3	4	5	Seasoning (for meat)	0	1	2	3	4 5
Dirty linen-like	0	1	2	3	4	5	Apple (fruit)	0	1	2	3	4 5
Kippery (smoked fish)	0	1	2	3	4	5	Soup	0	1	2	3	4 5

TABLE 2.7 (Continued)

Quality Scale			
Absent 0	Slightly 1	2	Moderately 3	4	Extremely 5

Caramel	0 1 2 3 4 5	Grainy (as grain)	0 1 2 3 4 5
Sauerkraut-like	0 1 2 3 4 5	Clove-like	0 1 2 3 4 5
Crushed grass	0 1 2 3 4 5	Raisins	0 1 2 3 4 5
Chocolate	0 1 2 3 4 5	Hay	0 1 2 3 4 5
Molasses	0 1 2 3 4 5	Kerosene	0 1 2 3 4 5

Source: Dravnieks, personal communication (1977)

Terms having no ostentive meaning include such general terms as harsh, aromatic, and fragrant. These terms validly apply to thousands of chemicals. We can categorize chemicals which smell harsh, but when we point to 200 chemicals widely different in quality, each with a harsh note, what have we accomplished? We certainly have not succinctly defined the quality of harshness.

In food assessment, specific quality notes acquire meaning in the same way. A descriptive panel of individuals may generate a list of aroma, flavor and texture characteristics. To assign meaning to these terms, and to simultaneously ensure that all panel participants know what the terms mean, the panel should attempt to develop ostentive definitions. They must search for reference standards. In this way, the panel leader can ensure that each panel participant uses the terms identically and refers to the same stimulus, or means the same thing, when describing his or her perceptions.

Food scientists have recognized the importance of such ostentive definitions. They search for reference standards in taste, smell and texture perceptions. Vision researchers already possess such definitions in color. They can point to specific Munsell color chips which possess defined colors, or point to specific wavelengths of a single frequency in the spectrum as typifying a color. Tables 2.8 and 2.9 show some typical definitions, or reference standards, which typify specific sensory characteristics for odor in the Crocker-Henderson system. Later on we will see such standards for texture as well.

Measuring Meaning

For new descriptive terms having no specific physical exemplar to represent them, how can the researcher feel sure that the terms possess

TABLE 2.8

ODOR STANDARDS FOR THE CROCKER-HENDERSON SYSTEM[1]

Basic Quality	Chemical Reference Standard (score of 8 on the attribute)
Fragrant:	Methyl salicylate (8453)
Acid:	20% Acetic acid (3803)
Burnt:	Guaiacol (7584)
Caprylic:	2,7 Dimethyl octane (3518)

(first number = fragrant; second = acid; third = burnt; fourth = caprylic)
[1]9 point scale: 0 = none; 8 = extremely strong.
Source: Crocker and Henderson (1927)

TABLE 2.9

SOME REPRESENTATIVE PROFILES OF CHEMICALS
USING THE CROCKER-HENDERSON SYSTEM

6333	Sweet orange oil from California	8124	Heliotropin
5533	Lemon oil, Messina	5324	Hydroxycitronellal
6423	Cinnamyl acetate	7523	Alpha Ionone
7823	Allyl caproate	6343	Linalyl Acetate
7224	Benzoin Siam, Resin	7733	Citral
7473	Oil of Nutmeg	8423	Ylang Ylang

Source: Crocker and Henderson (1927)

meaning? Do panelists use these descriptive terms in similar ways? Do the terms signify the same things to different panelists, or does each panelist use the terms in such idiosyncratic ways that the same descriptor possesses no consensual meaning whatsoever. As simple a problem as this sounds, its solution poses considerable difficulties. During the past 50 years scientists have developed procedures to measure meaning, or at least to determine whether the term means the same thing to all individuals. Obviously one cannot easily dig into the panelist's mind and come up with an unambiguous answer to meaning. One can, however, employ various experimental designs and statistical analyses to ferret out meaning, or to determine whether or not individuals concur about meaning when they use the descriptive term.

The serious, experimentally-oriented query about the measurement of meaning did not emerge until the early 1950s. Prior to that, sensory analysts contented themselves either by working with well-practiced panels who shared a common vocabulary by virtue of common training, or else they worked with consumer panelists, and instructed panelists simply to measure overall global and often nebulous characteristics (e.g., overall flavor or overall texture). In the latter case, an adequate definition of specific attributes could not impact on the final answer, since panelists provided only an overall rating of their impressions.

Approaches to the problem of descriptive language perceptions changed in the early 1950s. C. E. Osgood and his colleagues, Suci and Tannenbaum, reported the results of their study to measure word meaning. Osgood, Suci and Tannenbaum hypothesized that one could measure meaning by having the panelist profile a word using a specific list of characteristics. This list and the method they used subsequently became known as the *semantic differential method*. Panelists presented with a test word would scale the word on the different bipolar scales. For example, the meaning (or at least Osgood's operational or definitional meaning) of flavor would appear as the profile of the word flavor on a series of bipolar scales such as hot-cold, strong-weak, new-old, etc.

Panelists find the semantic differential procedure and scale easy and fascinating to use. They scale the stimulus word, or an object (e.g., a flavor, a food, an aroma, a picture), using a limited number of attribute scales. The profile of rating operationally represents the meaning of the word. Similar profiles on a wide number of scales for two words represent similar meaning. In this system the nuances of meaning often disappear, since these nuances elude the net of terms set up by a limited number of gross, bipolar scales. Furthermore, the statistical analysis and interpretation of the semantic differential becomes straight-forward. The investigator can compare profiles of two descriptor terms to see how similar or how different they appear.

Osgood *et al.* went several steps further in their analysis, by using the statistical method of *factor analysis*. Factor analysis assumes that there exist a limited number of dimensions which underly meaning. In their empirical analysis of words, Osgood *et al.* identified three primary dimensions: potency, evaluation and activity. Factor analysis reduces the sets of scales on which panelists rate words to a few mutually perpendicular dimensions, or axes, and locates each scale, as well as each word, in this dimensional framework. The result allows the experimenter to pictorialize words as points in a semantic or meaning geometry. Words close to each other possess similar meaning; words far away from each other possess dissimilar meaning (See Fig. 2.1).

Some of the findings in descriptive analysis using factor analysis and its companion techniques will be discussed later on in this chapter.

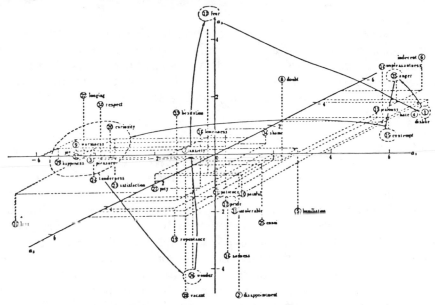

FIG. 2.1   SEMANTIC DIFFERENTIAL SCALING OF DESCRIPTOR
TERMS FOR EMOTION

(Source: Yoshida, Kinase, Kyrokawa & Y. Tashiro 1970)

For now we remain content with the observation that the investigator can represent meaning in terms of a set of underlying psychological dimensions, albeit statistically, by means of the statistical procedure of factor analysis.

Variability in Attribute Ratings

Another method for assessing meaning uses the variability around the average profile rating as a numerical index of consensus among panelists. When panelists scale a product using different descriptors, they generate a distribution of ratings. The average or mean rating represents the consensus value. Around that mean lies the distribution. Some terms generate means with large variation as indexed by the standard deviation of the ratings. Other attributes generate means with relatively small variation around them. Attributes which generate high variability may signal interpanelist disagreement and perhaps vagueness of definition. Some panelists may rate the same product low on these meaningless terms. The use of the attribute differs from one individual to another. Characteristics showing high variability represent the less meaningful characteristics. Each panelist may have his or her own idea of what the characteristic means, but the consensus shows wide divergence of opinion. Table 2.10 compares the averages and variabilities of several descriptor terms used in a study on fruit flavored beverages. Note that the simple sensory characteristics, sweet, tart and flavor intensity, exhibit lower variability around the average than other attributes, such as natural flavor or refreshing flavor.

DISTINGUISHING DIFFERENT TYPES OF ATTRIBUTES

A descriptive analysis panel can generate hundreds of attributes in a short period of time. Some of these attributes reflect sensory perceptions; others reflect hedonic responses such as "I like the product," "I dislike it;" whereas still others reflect image characteristics. The product tester must keep in mind that many hedonic or evaluative characteristics masquerade as sensory words. Natural flavor or refreshing may represent alternative ways of saying "I like the product" (Moskowitz, Jacobs and Fitch 1980).

TABLE 2.10
MEANING OF ATTRIBUTES DEFINED AS A MEASURE OF
RELATIVE VARIABILITY AROUND THE MEAN

Data from ratings of fruit flavored beverages.

	PRODUCT A			PRODUCT B		
	Mean	S.E.[1]	R.V.[2]	Mean	S.E.[1]	R.V.[2]
Sweetness	26	2.8	0.11	39	3.1	0.08
Tartness	40	2.9	0.07	23	2.2	0.10
Aroma Strength	24	2.3	0.10	41	3.9	0.10
Natural	48	6.9	0.14	53	7.4	0.14

[1]S.E. = Standard error of the ratings (base = 64 panelists who tried each product)
[2]R.V. = Relative variability = $\frac{S.E.}{Mean}$. Since the standard error grows in size with the size of the ratings, the R.V. or relative variability becomes a dimensionless number, independent of the size of the mean.
Source: Moskowitz, Jacobs and Fitch (1980)

DO WE LIVE IN THE SAME WORLDS OF TASTE AND ODOR QUALITY

Sensory Blindness and Descriptions

From time to time research reports in the scientific literature call our attention to the not-so-surprising fact that individuals differ in their perceptual worlds. We know from research on visual perception that some individuals cannot perceive red/green differences. These color-blind individuals perceive the two colors identically, and lack receptors to differentiate the two colors. John Amoore has spent 25 years investigating specific odor blindnesses, finding many individuals who show an unusually elevated threshold (or diminished sensitivity) to specific odorants. Through extensive testing of different chemicals with a wide number of otherwise normal panelists, Amoore identified chemicals which show widespread individual differences in sensitivity. A most dramatic case comes from the chemical androsterone. To unaffected, or non-anosmic individuals, androsterone possesses the unmistakable odor of sweaty urine. To anosmic individuals, lacking the particular receptor, androsterone smells haylike and sweet. Individual differences plague sensory descriptive analysis as well. Much as individuals try to be consistent, even with continued training, some specific off notes may elude those panelists exhibiting specific anosmia.

Similar individual differences affect the descriptive analysis of many commercial beverages sweetened with saccharin. Some individuals clearly detect and reject the bitter taste imparted by saccharin in artificially sweetened beverages. Other panelists report no bitter off-taste at all, or at least show no adverse reactions to any marginal bitterness which may emerge. Bartoshuk (1979) and her colleagues recently showed that saccharin bitterness insensitivity relates to one's inability to taste the class of bitter sulfur compounds known as the thio-carbamides. Anthropologists have used PTC or phenyl thio-carbamide as a test substance for years. Like saccharin, sensitivity to PTC classifies individuals into two groups of sensitive tasters, some who exhibit great sensitivity, others who exhibit little sensitivity. Consequently, we might expect that some of the variability in panel ratings derives from truly different perceptual capacities, rather than resulting from error or normal variability in assigning labels to perceptions. The product tester should take into account the combined roles of interpanelist variability in description and truly different perceptual environments as co-factors. These generate profile data comprising different opinions, even for the same food.

Cross-Cultural Differences in Sensory Descriptions

Benjamin Lee Whorf, the sociologist, conjectured that our environment influences our language and descriptive capacities. Eskimos, confronted daily with water and snow in different forms, and who rely upon snow as their ground and building material, possess many more

TABLE 2.11
DESCRIPTIONS OF TASTE STIMULI GIVEN BY ENGLISH AND SPANISH SPEAKERS[1]

		sweet (dulce)	combinations of sweet (dulce)	salty (salado)	combinations of salty (salado)	bitter (amargo)	combinations of bitter (amargo)	agrio	combinations of agrio	sour (acido)	combinations of sour (acido)	no taste (sin sabor)	combinations of no taste (sin sabor)	novel terms	TOTAL
														SELECTED RESPONSE	
Sucrose	mono-Eng.[2]	10	7											5	22
	mono-Sp.[3]	6												2	8
	bi-Eng.[4]	9	4											2	15
	bi-Sp.[5]	11												4	15
Sodium chloride	mono-Eng.			15	7										22
	mono-Sp.			8											8
	bi-Eng.			11	3									1	15
	bi-Sp.				15										15
Quinine sulphate	mono-Eng.					9	5			1				7	22
	mono-Sp.					6	1							1	8
	bi-Eng.					12	1				1			1	15
	bi-Sp.					11	2							1	15
Citric acid	mono-Eng.	1		1	1	1	1			3	6			8	22
	mono-Sp.			1						3	1			3	8
	bi-Eng.					3				2	1			9	15
	bi-Sp.					2	2	1		5	3			3	16
Water	mono-Eng.					1	1					2	2	16	22
	mono-Sp.											4		4	8
	bi-Eng.						1					5	1	8	15
	bi-Sp.											7		7	15

TABLE 2.11 (Continued)

		SELECTED RESPONSE													
		sweet (dulce)	combinations of sweet (dulce)	salty (salado)	combinations of salty (salado)	bitter (amargo)	combinations of bitter (amargo)	agrio	combinations of agrio	sour (acido)	combinations of sour (acido)	no taste (sin sabor)	combinations of no taste (sin sabor)	novel terms	TOTAL
Monosodium glutamate	mono-Eng.			8	7		1				2			6	24
	mono-Sp.			3	1		1	2			1			3	9
	bi-Eng.			6	2						1			7	16
	bi-Sp.		1	3	5		1				1			4	15
Sodium carbonate	mono-Eng.			4	1		3					1		12	23
	mono-Sp.			2	1		2			1		1	2	3	8
	bi-Eng.		1	1		4	1			1	1	1		7	16
	bi-Sp.	2	1			3	2			1			3	15	
Sodium benzoate	mono-Eng.	6	7		3	1	4			1	2			4	28
	mono-Sp.	2	2		1	1	2				1			2	10
	bi-Eng.	5	5	1	1	1					1			3	17
	bi-Sp.	4	4	2	1	2	1				1			1	16

[1] Numbers in boxes represent the number of times panelists used the term in free description

[2] mono-Eng. = monolingual English

[3] mono-Sp. = monolingual Spanish

[4] bi-Eng. = bilingual English

[5] bi-Sp. = bilingual Spanish

Source: O'Mahony and Alba (1980)

words than we do to describe the different nuances of snow and ice. A similar situation applies to perfumers and flavorists, who deal daily with many different notes of fragrances and flavors, and who must describe these nuances accurately.

Cultural differences, whether internationally or even occupationally, affect descriptions. Several studies on the taste names of primitive peoples (Chamberlain 1903; Myers 1904) suggest that these individuals often use more complicated, almost object-related descriptive terms to characterize the nuances of taste and flavor.

Recent studies on different taste names (O'Mahony and Alba 1980) have appeared in the psychological literature. English possesses similar, but not identical, words to Spanish. Certain flavor nuances in Spanish do not appear in English. Perhaps the Spanish descriptive terms reflect the different culinary environment and the preponderance of hot, chili-flavored foods. (See Table 2.11). Such cross-cultural investigations provide a unique research opportunity to determine how culture and cuisine affect sensory description.

THE DESCRIPTIVE ANALYSIS PANEL

How does one develop a descriptive analysis panel? How many members should the panel comprise? This section concerns the practical aspects of descriptive panel work from the point of view of the marketing researcher and the R&D analyst, who possess a minimum amount of time and money, and who cannot afford to expend substantial periods of time on training and perfecting a panel.

Defining The Problem—Descriptive Analysis For What?

Our first issue concerns the research goal. Why does the investigator want to develop the panel? Some panels owe their origin to attempts to answer a specific technical problem which develops during early product development, quality control or marketing. R&D may wish to develop a descriptive panel for a specific category in order to help narrow down alternatives in product development. A panel tailored for such a use comprises individuals who taste and evaluate recipes, describe the characteristics and, perhaps, indicate when the test product has the proper constituents to satisfy a target sensory profile. This analytic instrument, the panel itself, serves as a counterpart to laboratory instruments; it registers sensory reactions to products, classifies them and feeds back to the product developer that either he has achieved a specific desired flavor/texture profile, or that he has failed.

It indicates the gap between what the product tastes/smells/feels like, and what the product should taste/smell/feel like.

Another type of panel finds use in quality control, especially in factories. This descriptive panel comprises trained or experienced participants who evaluate these batches from plant runs, describe their perceptions and compare the descriptions against a predesignated target. When the production batch possesses an off-note, or fails to meet other quality specifications, the descriptive panel raises a red flag, signalling that something has occurred to modify the product. The descriptive panel reports only sensory reactions. Panelists should not report hedonic reactions (liking/disliking) since hedonic reactions from expert panelists may or may not represent consumer reactions and probably do not.

The product development panel should comprise individuals who can, and do show a desire to spend considerable amounts of time testing new formulations. Panels for new product development often test a variety of relatively unrelated products. The product tester may wish to tailor panels for specific product categories, rather than utilize the same panelists again and again to assess products from diverse categories. This decision depends upon the corporate resources, the time available for each panelist and the amount of work and diversity of product categories which one wishes to test. It makes no sense to develop specific panels for different categories if the range of products to be tested in a year's time exceeds a comfortable number. One should then develop a general descriptive panel. On the other hand, when the corporate sequence for product development involves only a few stable, recurring categories, then the product tester may wish to develop specific panels, tailored to each category, in order to assure data of the highest quality.

Who and How Many Participate In The Panel

From time to time the issues arise concerning panelist selection and optimal panel size. As product testing has grown over the past 30 years, practitioners have often used their good judgment to select panels of the right size and composition. No consensus exists among practitioners. Some practitioners prefer to use a small number of panelists (4-6), each of whom has received thorough training and indoctrination. The flavor profile panel uses the small group of closely knit, interacting panelists. The panelists receive extensive training, so that one need not worry that such a small number of individuals will generate meaningless ratings. Similarly, the QDA (Quantitative Descriptive Analysis) method and the Texture Profile method also employ a relatively small number of individuals who have each undergone extensive training.

Other practitioners prefer to use larger panels. In studies on the descriptive characteristics of odors and flavors, Von Sydow and colleagues at the Swedish Institute of Food Preservation Research have used many more panelists, sometimes 10-20 or more. These panelists receive less training than did those in the Flavor Profile group. Therefore, in order to assure a stable estimate of profile ratings, Von Sydow et al. needed a larger panel.

The author recommends a panel comprising 10 or more individuals, for two pragmatic reasons. (1) Individuals perceive and rate products differently, whether simple stimuli or complex foods. Thus, too small a panel can provide distorted ratings simply from lack of representation. (Ideally, one would like to use 30 or more panelists, but for descriptive work requiring in-depth analysis, such a large panel size becomes prohibitively expensive and unwieldly). (2) A small panel critically depends on the participation of each of its members. When one member cannot participate because of other corporate responsibilities, illness or vacation, his or her absence disrupts the panel. For a 5 member panel, one participant's absence diminishes the number of participants by 20%. For a 4 member panel, that same absence diminishes the panel size by 25%. Hence, pragmatically, panel efficacy in achieving its goal depends as much on each panelist's schedules as on panel ability.

Selecting and Training Panel Members—How

People do not come fully equipped to participate in descriptive panels. One need not have an extraordinarily sensitive palate or nose to participate in descriptive panel work. In fact, as Jones (1968) pointed out, perfumers do not possess any keener sensitivity than do ordinary working people. Panel members must show motivation. They should have the patience and ability to develop a vocabulary which they can apply to descriptive tasks.

Motivation. The desire to participate constitutes the first and most important prerequisite for a successful panel participant. Descriptive analysis requires a serious investment of time. The participant should realize the extensive time commitment demanded. Sometimes product profiling sesions conflict with other job requirements. The panel members should make every effort to leave sufficient free time for profiling work, rather than volunteer for participation but renege on his or her commitment when other requirements conflict.

Intelligence and Verbal Communications. Descriptive analysis requires an intelligent participant, albeit not a brilliant one. Intelligence allows the individual to verbalize his or her perceptions. The product tester should recruit articulate individuals, rather than shy participants, as members of the panel, in order to assure that the participants fully contribute their own ideas and perceptions to the group. The ability to communicate verbally enhances the participant's value to the panel.

Cooperative, Non-Domineering Personality. Personality styles affect panel performance. The domineering personality tends to force his or her opinion on the group, perhaps not overtly, but nonetheless effectively. A small panel comprising even one domineering panel member may report out the views of that panel member. Focus group moderators working extensively in marketing research studies with small panels of 10-12 participants, in single sessions, soon realize that the dominant member swings opinion in his or her direction, more by force of personality than by compelling argument about product description. Psychologists studying small group processes have found that a group personality emerges, representing the amalgam of inputs from the participants. The longer a panel remains in operation, regularly meeting and interacting, the more the group personality emerges, and the more influence the domineering member exerts. Domineering personalities can also result from corporate position. A panel comprising vice presidents of R&D, along with bench top product developers, secretaries and research assistants, may reflect the vice president's views more than it represents anyone else's. Furthermore, the other participants may not realize how subtly their views change as a consequence of non-verbal social pressure.

In-House Panelists versus Extramural Panelists For Descriptive Analysis

Quite often arguments for or against in-house panels revolve around the issue of objectivity in profile ratings. For a trained descriptive analysis panel, the optimal strategy dictates using individuals with high commitment and availability to participate. In most instances such requirements force the use of in-house panelists, generally from the corporate R&D facility. In a university setting, members of the food science department often participate. Extramural panelists recruited from the outside, become a valuable resource when the time pressures become so strong that these extramural individuals substitute for employees needed for other jobs. In both large and small companies, extramural panelists provide a convenient, tax-deductible business expense incurred during the course of product development. Furthermore, extramural panelists span a wide range of consumer types. The descriptive panel can comprise a group of individuals, tailored as to age, sex and brand usage.

DEVELOPING THE DESCRIPTIVE LANGUAGE
—THE GROUP PROCESS

How do a group of unpracticed panelists develop a language to describe product perceptions? Different methods for eliciting descriptor terms to characterize products proliferate. In the day-to-day panel work, pragmatics override completeness and technical accuracy. A small descriptive panel, comprising 4-8 individuals, may not possess the time nor breadth of experience to implement the necessary scientific steps to generate a large set of descriptors, cull out the unimportant ones, and then preserve and identify the key descriptors for further use.

Fortunately, in a small group, panelists develop a sense of group identity which allows them to converse freely with each other. Through give and take discussions, panelists will present different words for consideration. The feedback (more by vehemence of acceptance or rejection than by numerical counting) soon efficiently reduces the descriptor terms under consideration to just a few. Many panels work this way. They run the risk of selecting a narrow group of characteristics which lie top-of-mind. On the other hand, the group process strengthens panel cohesiveness, rapidly generates a set of terms and may require less work than does a full-fledged scientific analysis of descriptors accomplished in a more rigorous manner.

The product tester must keep in mind that whether panelists develop the language through rigorous screening procedures, or whether they develop the language through informal group dynamics, the descriptor list always remains incomplete. During the course of ensuing product assessment, whether the next profiling session or a session six months later, panelists will introduce new terms and eliminate some of the unimportant or redundant older terms. This process occurs because perception and reference frames fluctuate and sharpen rather than remain fixed. As individuals become increasingly familiar with the product, they will perceive additional characteristics in the products. Their descriptions change. Some characteristics emerge and others recede as panelists focus attention on the product. Hence, a fixed, nonchanging, permanent list becomes only an ideal, hoped-for goal. When achieved, the panel loses its dynamic aspect, and perhaps its value, becoming a rote descriptive instrument. Benjamin Whorf suggested quite similar processes for descriptive language in different cultures.

Perfumers and flavorists who work with many similar smelling or tasting compounds over months or years develop a rich language to describe that specific part of their daily experience. The Whorfian hypothesis applies to this process. The richness of a language directly correlates with the individual's experience with stimuli. Prolonged experience with specific types of stimuli lead to a richer descriptive language to differentiate those stimuli. Human beings use language to capture nuances, continually developing their terminology to keep pace with their perceptions. The focus becomes more precise as a result of experience.

How Feedback Affects Profile Ratings

The product tester can enhance results from descriptive analysis by providing feedback after individual profile evaluations. Feedback leads to specific improvements. It shows panelists where they agree with each other versus where they disagree with each other. It shows panelists what clues to look for when making their descriptive profile evaluations. This focusing of attention considerably enhances panel sensitivity to elusive hard-to-capture characteristics. It provides a reinforcing signal that the panelist has remained on target. It also improves learning by the psychological principle of reinforcement. Panelists like doing things correctly and learning that they have properly described the stimulus. This appreciation of reinforcement applies to all individuals, and motivates the panelist to try even harder.

A set of provocative experiments by McAuliffe and Meiselman (1974) in feedback in taste-naming demonstrates the power of correct feedback in improving one's ability to classify sensations. Other experiments (Harper *et al.* 1968; Moskowitz and Gerbers 1974) show how description changes even without direct feedback, but simply as the result of experience.

McAuliffe and Meiselman (1974) studied how feedback reduces the sour-bitter confusion (a confusion long known to behavioral scientists and food technologists). Panelists often mistake the sour and bitter tastes, labelling sour as bitter, and vice versa. To the expert product tester these stimuli taste quite different from each other. Yet, to at least 25% of the population sour and bitter taste so similar that they generate confusion. McAuliffe and Meiselman trained panelists to distinguish and label the two taste qualities. By presenting the panelists with taste stimuli comprising either bitter quinine or sour acid, and by giving the panelist the correct answer after each classification, they soon improved panelist performance. In contrast, the non-reinforced group showed much less improvement with the same number of practice trials.

Feedback can also occur without prompting from the outside. Sheer repeated experience, on a continuing basis, can increase one's ability to properly classify stimuli. For instance, Harper, Land, Bate-Smith and Griffiths (1968) reported that inexperienced panelists used many more descriptor terms than did experienced panelists to profile the same odor stimulus. One cannot infer from the study whether the experienced panelists perceived the stimuli differently or simply used a more parsimonious strategy to describe odors.

In another study on quality profiling of 15 odors, done for four consecutive sessions, panelists used more descriptor terms on day 1 than on days 2, 3 and 4 (Moskowitz and Gerbers 1974). This study, using 15 different odors, 16 different descriptors and repeated on four consecutive days (with four sets of profiles per day), suggests that with practice and repeated exposure the panelist changes his or her profiling strategy. At first, the unpracticed panelist uses many descriptor terms to cover all aspects of the odor stimulus. As the panelist begins to feel more comfortable with the task and becomes more familiar with the descriptor list, the profiling strategy changes. Effort expended in accurate description replaces effort to capture all attributes.

The continually changing strategy in profiling which panelists adopt as they become increasingly familiar with the profiling task requires that the product tester maintain vigilance on performance. The researcher cannot substitute novice panelists for experienced panelists during the course of a profiling session without changing the results, often substantially. For one, the two types of panelists have had different levels of experience, and will generate different profiles. For another, the experienced panelists will use fewer descriptor terms than the novice, just introduced. The mixture will produce a biased profile containing extraneous terms introduced by the novices.

Can We Enhance The Panelist's Ability To Describe Perception?

People can become expert perfumers, given a natural talent in chemistry and compounding, as well as a great deal of patience. Perfumers possess the same sensitivity as other individuals, but they possess a far greater trained ability to describe their perceptions in a meaningful way, using a standardized vocabulary. People have said that, to become a perfumer or a flavorist, one must possess an ability to recognize thousands of different odor notes. In actuality perfumers and flavorists simply describe their perceptions more accurately, with a more systematic language. Although no two flavorists or perfumers characterize a flavor or fragrance in exactly the same way, nonetheless, a perfumer or flavorist will point to specific notes in the fragrance or flavor which smell similar to standard reference chemicals. This descriptive capacity requires training and daily practice.

An interesting study on man's ability to recognize and describe many odorants and categorize them comes from the psychological literature (Lawless and Cain 1975). The studies investigated man's ability to unambiguously classify different odorants. With training one could substantially improve the panelist's classificatory abilities and thus descriptive capabilities. Furthermore, Lawless and Cain showed that mediating processes (making verbal or pictorial associations to odor sensations), improves the panelist's ability to classify an odorant.

Odor memory also plays a critical role. Unlike taste perceptions and texture perceptions, odor stimuli do not provide us with easy reference points for description. As we saw before, odor qualities derive from specific animals, plants or chemicals, rather than from general concepts for which a specific odor acts as an exemplar. This shows up in immediate and long term memory for smells. When psychologists test memory they find that memory for visual and auditory impressions far exceeds the memory for odor impressions, if testing occurs right away after exposure to the stimuli. When tested for ability to recognize the stimuli, panelists invariably score higher when presented with visual or auditory stimuli than when presented with odor stimuli. On the other hand, odor memory shows greater longevity. We do not lose our ability to recognize odors as rapidly as we forget auditory and visual stimuli. Odor memory possesses extraordinary stability or lasting power. The odor information which enters our memory system remains there, without noticeable decay, over a period of days, months and years. By that time, the visual or auditory memeory have long since decayed, and panelists show poor recognition memory when presented with visual or auditory stimuli a week or a month later (Engen *et al.* 1973).

What does odor memory have to do with a panelist's ability to describe perception? Very simply, effort involved in developing a trained profile panelist does pay off. The abilities developed in learning a descriptive system to characterize odors and flavors remain, and actual performance decreases very little over extended periods of time.

A panel trained for specific product evaluation (e.g., dairy products) should remain well-trained for a year or two, even though they meet infrequently. Odor recognition memory, and therefore panel ability to recognize and characterize flavor (and fragrance) notes, remains relatively constant. In terms of practical application, the product tester need only train the panelist once (albeit for an extended period of time). Panelists then need only short refresher exercises to bring them up to performance standards for subsequent panel work.

A POTPOURRI OF DESCRIPTIVE SYSTEMS AND STATISTICAL METHODS

The second part of this chapter concerns some of the more widely used descriptive systems (e.g., the Texture Profile Method), as well as a synopsis of empirical studies in the food field which have developed descriptor languages for taste, smell and texture. Each descriptive system considered here possesses a well-developed structure, including specified rating scales, reference standards, methods for training panelists, etc.

TEXTURE SYSTEMS

Szczesniak, Brandt and Friedman (1963) developed a comprehensive set of scales and reference standards to represent the multifaceted attributes of food texture. These authors, like their contemporaries in flavor science, realized that a snapshot of texture perception requires a panelist to assess a melange of different characteristics. Tables 2.12, 2.13 and 2.14 show the different scales, as well as the reference standards which Szczesniak *et al.* selected to exemplify graded levels of each texture characteristic.

Bare in mind the following key points with regard to the Texture Profile. (1) The system comprises an extensive list of characteristics which tap a full range of masticatory behaviors, as well as other secondary characteristics of texture. (2) The Texture Profiling system uses category or fixed point scales (e.g., 1-7, 1-9). A specific reference stimulus corresponds to each category on each scale. Reference standards play a particularly important role in anchoring the scale points to physically reliable stimuli. (3) The psychological intervals between adjacent scale points presumably reflect equal psychological intervals of perceived texture characteristics. In theory, the sensory distance between gumminess 1 and gumminess 2 equals the psychological

TABLE 2.12
STANDARDIZED RATING SCALES FOR MECHANICAL PROPERTIES WITH GENERALIZED STANDARDS

Intensity of parameter increases downward

Hardness
1. Cream cheese
2. Velveeta cheese
3. Frankfurters
4. Cheddar cheese
5. Giant stuffed olives
6. Cocktail peanuts
7. Shell almonds
8. Rock candy

Fracturability
1. Corn muffin
2. Egg Jumbos
3. Graham crackers
4. Melba toast
5. Bordeaux cookies
6. Ginger Snaps
7. Treacle Brittle

Chewiness
1. Rye bread
2. Frankfurter
3. Large gum drops
4. Well-done round steak
5. Nut chews
6. Tootsie Rolls

Adhesiveness
1. Hydrogenated shortening
2. Cheese Whiz
3. Cream cheese
4. Marshmallow topping
5. Peanut butter

Viscosity
1. Water
2. Light cream
3. Heavy cream
4. Evaporated milk
5. Maple syrup
6. Chocolate syrup
7. Cool 'n Creamy pudding
8. Condensed milk

Source: Szczesniak, Brandt and Friedman (1963)

TABLE 2.13
GEOMETRICAL PROPERTIES

Related to Particle Size and Shape		Related to Particle Shape and Orientation	
Property	*Example*	*Property*	*Example*
Powdery	Confectioners' sugar	Flaky	Flaky pastry
Chalky	Tooth powder	Fibrous	Breast of Chicken
Grainy	Cooked Cream of Wheat	Pulpy	Orange sections
Gritty	Pears	Cellular	Apples, cake
Coarse	Cooked oatmeal	Aerated	Whipped cream
Lumpy	Cottage cheese	Puffy	Rice pudding
Beady	Cooked tapicoa	Crystalline	Granulated sugar

Source: Szczesniak, Brandt and Friedman (1963)

TABLE 2.14
DETAILED TEXTURE PROFILE SCALE FOR GUMMINESS,
ADHESIVENESS AND VISCOSITY

		Standard Gumminess Scale			
Panel Rating	Product	Brand or Type	Manufacturer	Sample Size	Temp.
1	40% flour paste	Gold Medal	General Mills	1 tbs.	room
2	45% flour paste	Gold Medal	General Mills	1 tbs.	room
3	50% flour paste	Gold Medal	General Mills	1 tbs.	room
4	55% flour paste	Gold Medal	General Mills	1 tbs.	room
5	60% flour paste	Gold Medal	General Mills	1 tbs.	room

		Standard Adhesiveness Scale			
Panel Rating	Product	Brand or Type	Manufacturer	Sample Size	Temp.
1	Hydrogenated vegetable oil	Crisco	Procter & Gamble Co.	½ tsp.	45-55° F
2	Buttermilk biscuit dough	—	Pillsbury	¼ biscuit	45-55° F
3	Cream cheese	Philadelphia	Kraft Foods	½ tsp.	45-55° F
4	Marshmallow topping	Fluff	Durkee-Mower	½ tsp.	45-55° F
5	Peanut butter	Skippy, smooth	Best Foods	½ tsp.	45-55° F

		Standard Viscosity Scale			
Panel Rating	Product	Brand or Type	Manufacturer	Sample Size	Temp.
1	Water	spring	Crystal Spring Co.	½ tsp.	room
2	Light cream	Sealtest	Sealtest Foods	½ tsp.	45-55° F
3	Heavy cream	Sealtest	Sealtest Foods	½ tsp.	45-55° F
4	Evaporated milk	—	Carnation Co.	½ tsp.	45-55° F
5	Maple syrup	Premier 100%	Francis H. Leggett & Co.	½ tsp.	45-55° F
6	Chocolate syrup		Hershey Chocolate Corp.	½ tsp.	45-55° F
7	Mixture: ½ cup mayonnaise and	Hellman's	Best Foods	½ tsp.	
	2 tbs. heavy cream	Sealtest	Sealtest Foods	2 tbs.	45-55° F
8	Condensed milk	Magnolia	Borden Foods	½ tsp.	45-55° F

Source: Szczesniak, Brandt and Friedman (1963)

distance between gumminess 2 and gumminess 3. This assumption lacks empirical justification, however. (4) Different attributes use scales comprising different numbers of categories. Viscosity uses an 8 point scale, hardness an 8 point scale, but chewiness uses only a 6 point scale, and adhesiveness a 5 point scale.

The product tester quickly obtains a rather good idea as to the specific sensory characteristics of the different products. If the Texture Profile procedure served no other purpose, it would still add value because it simplifies communication by pointing to reference standards according to a prespecified scale.

When they developed the Texture Profile procedure, Szczesniak *et al.* positioned it for use with a trained panel who had undergone extensive orientation in scaling, and who had refined their descriptive ability so that all panelists shared the same, common meaning for each textural attribute. Szczesniak, Loew and Skinner (1975) presented a modified Texture Profile procedure for use with consumers, who had had little or no previous training. The approach remains the same—solicit scaled ratings on a variety of characteristics. The consumers do not undergo the extensive training, nor have they the experience and familiarity expected from an experienced, trained panelist. Nonetheless, the typical consumer can and does profile a complex textural perception into its components, perhaps with less interpanelist agreement, but still with no great, insurmountable difficulty. Figures 2.2 and 2.3 graphically display the consumer texture profile for two products, as well as for an ideal product, profiled with the same descriptor system and the same scale.

FLAVOR SYSTEMS

Caul (1957) extensively reviewed the background and methods used to develop the Flavor Profile for specific food items. In contrast to the Texture Profile, the Flavor Profile does not present specific reference standards intended for the novice. Many more flavor characteristics exist than texture characteristics. It becomes extravagantly expensive to develop general reference standards for flavor/aroma attributes when the number of basic characteristics looms so large as to become unmanageable. Hence, the Flavor Profilist uses a disciplined procedure to develop an ad hoc descriptive system which pertains to a specific product.

The system follows this sequence. The panel members, each of whom has already received training in descriptive techniques, discuss the product characteristics. This discussion focuses on the specific food

NOT AT ALL   VERY MUCH SO

CRISP	☐	☐	☐	☐	☐	☐
SOFT	☐	☐	☐	☐	☐	☐
AIRY	☐	☐	☐	☐	☐	☐
BRITTLE	☐	☐	☐	☐	☐	☐
CHUNKY	☐	☐	☐	☐	☐	☐
FLAKY	☐	☐	☐	☐	☐	☐
SOGGY	☐	☐	☐	☐	☐	☐
DRY	☐	☐	☐	☐	☐	☐
BAD	☐	☐	☐	☐	☐	☐
CHEWY	☐	☐	☐	☐	☐	☐
CRUNCHY	☐	☐	☐	☐	☐	☐
HARD	☐	☐	☐	☐	☐	☐
SLIPPERY	☐	☐	☐	☐	☐	☐
DOUGHY	☐	☐	☐	☐	☐	☐
GOOD	☐	☐	☐	☐	☐	☐
GRITTY	☐	☐	☐	☐	☐	☐

FIG. 2.2 TYPICAL CONSUMER TEXTURE PROFILE BALLOT FOR COLD CEREALS

Source: Szczesniak, Loew and Skinner (1975)

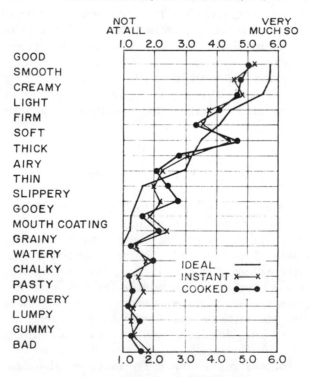

FIG. 2.3 CONSUMER TEXTURE PROFILES FOR PUDDINGS

Source: Szczesniak, Loew and Skinner (1975)

item and generates the key sensory characteristics which will later come under scrutiny through scaling. The group decides to accept or reject a limited number of terms for profiling. The group then evaluates specific products in order to develop reference standards which represent specific notes or sensory characteristics. This stage assures quality control (e.g., that the panelists in the group agree about the definition of each characteristic). The group generates a Flavor Profile by discussion and evaluation of specific products, using the fixed point scale shown in Table 2.15. The profile emerges from the interaction of a group of panelists who thoroughly discuss the sensory aspects of the product and develop a single, group consensus.

The flavor profile appears as a semicircle. The different rays extending from the center reflect specific characteristics. The overall circumference of the semicircle represents amplitude or balance of the specific note (see Fig. 2.4). By plotting two profiles side by side for the same product, before versus after treatment (or with/without specific additives), the marketer or product developer can visualize the net effect of the process or the changes which the additive causes to the specific notes. This visual representation lacks quantitative meaning. The flavor profile does not permit statistical analysis since the results evolve from group discussion in the form of a single profile, based upon a consensus judgement.

TABLE 2.15
FLAVOR PROFILE SCALE

0 = not present
)(= just recognizable threshold
1+ = slight
2++ = moderate
3+++ = strong

Source: Cairncross and Sjostrom (1950)

The Flavor Profile scale represents an unusual form of the fixed point category scale. The scale gradations represent verbal reactions to amount or intensity.

The Flavor Profile scale poses difficulties for statistical analysis of the ultimate Flavor Profile score. Although the Flavor Profile method lacks statistical analyzability (at least in its original form), the profile approach has proved extremely successful and utilitarian for diagnosing and visually representing problems to product developers and

Flavor by mouth

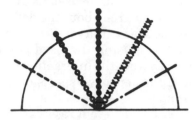

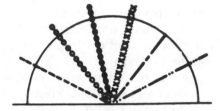

Boiled, seasoned

Boiled, seasoned, +0.5% glutamate

Legend:
------- Sweet
ooooooooo Salty
●●●●●●●● Peppery
xxxxxxxxxx Buttery
—·—·— Corn-like
—··— Mouthfulness

FIG. 2.4 PLOT OF THE "FLAVOR PROFILE" FOR A SPECIFIC PRODUCT; BOILED SEASONED SQUASH, WITH VERSUS WITHOUT ADDED MONOSODIUM GLUTAMATE

Flavor profile for boiled, seasoned squash, with and without monosodium glutamate. The lines emanating from the center reflect the flavor notes discerned by the panelists. The semicircle reflects the overall intensity of the flavor with the radius of the semicircule proportional to the overall intensity. (From Cairncross, S. E. and Sjostrom, L. B., *Food Technol.*, 4, 308, 1950).

marketers. The profile makes it possible and simple to visualize the change of flavor characteristics through the use of monosodium glutamate or the 5′ nucleotide flavor enhancers (e.g., inosine and guanydine monophosphate). Furthermore, recently The Arthur D. Little Company announced that it had taken steps to quantify the Flavor Profile ratings, making the ratings themselves and the profile amenable to statistical analysis. This statistical analysis represents an important step in the advance of flavor work, and brings the Flavor Profile into the era of current, scientific, quantitative approaches.

The Quantitative Descriptive Analysis System

Stone *et al.* (1974) reported the use of a modified profile procedure called the QDA, or Quantitative Descriptive Analysis system. Introduced to food scientists during a Sensory Evaluation Symposium in 1974, the QDA method quickly achieved popularity. Representing a modification of the flavor profile system, the QDA possesses both advantages and disadvantages as discussed in the following paragraphs.

Panelists undergo orientation at the inception of the study to train in evaluation. In searching for attributes, they cull out invalid descriptors and select key product descriptors.

To represent intensity, panelists scale using a six inch line having defined endpoints, as shown in Fig. 2.5 The six inch line typifies a semistructured continuous scale. The endpoints indicate the extremes of the sensory characteristics. The middle point occasionally possesses a mark as well. Panelists taste (or smell) a food sample, marking the six inch line where they feel the intensity of the specific characteristic lies.

Name _____ Date _____ Code _____

Please taste the water sample and answer each question in sequence, placing a vertical line across the horizontal line at the point that best describes that property in the sample. Take sufficient sample and time to evaluate each characteristic.

After you have answered all the questions, return this sheet, and the sample, and wait for the next sample.

If you have any questions, need more water, etc., ask the experimenter.

Thank you.

1. Aroma

| weak | moderate | strong |

2. Mouthfeel
   a) Effervescence

| flat | moderate | bubbly |

   b) Hardness

| soft | moderate | hard |

   c) Astringency

| weak | moderate | strong |

3. Flavor
   a) Sweet

| weak | moderate | strong |

   b) Sour

| weak | moderate | strong |

   c) Salty

| weak | moderate | strong |

   d) Bitter

| weak | moderate | strong |

   e) Chemical

| weak | moderate | strong |

4. Aftertaste

| weak | moderate | strong |

5. Overall

| dislike moderately | neither | like moderately |

Comments:

FIG. 2.5 INSTRUCTIONS AND RATING FORM (6 INCH LINE) FOR BEER

(McCredy *et al.* 1974)

Since the QDA (like the Flavor Profile) stresses assessment of multiple characteristics, the set of 6 inch lines generates responses which one must tediously convert to numbers by using a ruler to measure the relative position of the mark on the line. This labor entails additional effort better utilized by key-punching numerical ratings right onto computer cards for subsequent processing.

Although Stone *et al.* (1974) claim that the scaling method generates interval-scale data (like the centigrade scale: no fixed zero, but differences of scale values possess meaning), research has not substantiated that claim. Studies during the past twenty-five years, by psychophysicists interested in developing valid scales to use in sensory measurement, show that placing a fixed constraint at the end of the scale limits the panelist's freedom and generates biased data (Stevens 1975). Furthermore, in a study of auditory loudness, McGill (1960) found that with linear scales having fixed end points he could not replicate the findings of other sceintists who had allowed their panelists to use wide ranges of numbers, without predesignated endpoints.

The linear scale eventually provides numerical information for subsequent statistical anlysis. Stone *et al.* proposed the use of the analysis-of-variance technique which considers the data from two points of view: variance in ratings due to product differences, and variance due to panelists. The latter, or error variability, diminishes in a QDA panel after training the panelists. The reduction in variation due to a panelist's unique and idiosyncratic use of the linear scale occurs either by extensive retraining, or by eliminating that panelist's judgments from further consideration. In a sense, the QDA statistical analysis does what the Flavor Profile group consensus achieves. Both methods emerge with a consensus opinion reflecting the majority. The Flavor Profile system achieves this by means of group discussion; the QDA system achieves this by statistical averaging and analysis.

Graphic presentation of QDA data appear in Fig. 2.6 for a typical American beer. Like any multiple-attribute rating system, one best appreciates the QDA data graphically, as Fig. 2.6 shows. By comparing the profiles of current products versus the ideal, the product researcher can quickly ascertain how closely two profiles coincide with each other, as well as how closely they approximate the ideal, desired profile. The figure itself, as commonly drawn, possesses no additional significant information. If panelists rate products on 10 different characteristics, the issue of how to represent the data turns into the problem of developing a series of rays, projecting from a center point, with each ray separated from every other ray by the same angle. The profile values or intensities become distances from the center along that ray. A product with a weak overall impression and weak components appears as a compact circle or figure of irregular shape. A product with intense levels of specific characteristics, and weak levels of other characteristics, appears as a figure elongated on some axes and foreshortened on others.

Color and Appearance

Researchers have not developed specific systems for ad hoc product description of color and appearance. Perhaps taste, aroma and texture encourage profiling systems because they lack clearly defined and limited numbers of antecedent physical variables. Color specifications

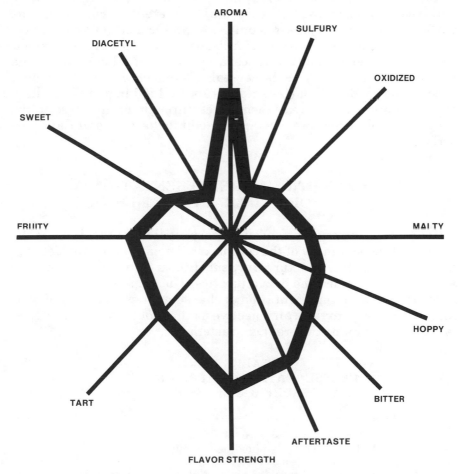

FIG. 2.6 QUANTITATIVE DESCRIPTIVE ANALYSIS OF A TYPICAL AMERICAN BEER
(McCredy, et al. 1974)

appear in various reference sources, with color samples of defined characteristics (either dye constituents or matching, simple mono-chromatic wave length values). Often the scientists or manufacturer can unambiguously specify the color of a product and find that color in a book of reference standards.

Forty-five years ago David Katz, then a refugee in Sweden from Nazi Germany, published his famous work on the characterization of sur-face appearance. In contrast to color science (which has become the domain of engineers and physicists), appearance research lacks a coherent organizing approach. Several researchers, including Katz, considered the various characteristics which comprise appearance. Table 2.16 presents the different modes of appearance which a color can assume, depending upon the way it presents itself. Note that surface appearance represents only one specific mode of appearance. The surface mode most aptly characterizes the appearance of food items. To further develop the appearance analog of a flavor profile, the investigator must measure the several different characteristics which specify the modes of surface appearance (Hutchings 1977). These characteristics best reveal themselves through profile descriptive groups as well, which we saw aptly facilitated aroma and flavor de-scription.

THE GEOMETRICAL REPRESENTATION OF SENSORY CHARACTERISTICS

Geometrical representations of sensory attributes provide a simple-to-understand summary of the complex interrelations among descrip-tive characteristics. A picture truly substitutes for a long explanation about the similarities and dissimilarities of descriptor terms. Further-more, the pictorial representation of characteristics, achieved by var-ious techniques, provides an objective method for illustrating interre-lations among many different characteristics.

TABLE 2.16
CLASSIFICATION OF APPEARANCE—
KATZ'S SURFACE CLASSIFICATION

---

(1) Surface touch—surface color
(2) Touching objects filling a space—filmy color
(3) Bulky touch—bulky color
(4) Touching through transparent film—transparent color

Source: Katz (1935)

Factor Analysis

The method of factor analysis (Harman 1966), which we met before in the measurement of word meaning (Osgood, Suci and Tannenbaum 1957), represents the most traditional method for pictorially representing interrelations among stimuli in a statistically valid manner. Factor analysis proceeds in a straightforward manner, summarized as follows.

The panelists scale each item in a set of stimuli on a variety of characteristics. For example, the stimuli might comprise different foods. The characteristics might represent a variety of different texture descriptors. The panelist would scale each food using up to several dozen texture descriptors. With two dozen descriptors and 20 foods, the panelist must assign $20 \times 24 = 480$ ratings to generate profiles of the 20 foods on the 24 sttribute scales.

The ratings for some characteristics or attributes often correlate with each other. Hardness and toughness may correlate with each other very strongly. Other pairs of attributes will correlate inversely with each other (e.g., hardness and softness). A product scoring high on hardness will score low on softness. Finally, some attributes do not correlate with each other at all.

Factor analysis places each descriptor in a geometrical space so that the descriptors which correlate highly with each other lie close together, whereas the descriptors which do not correlate with each other lie far apart. Furthermore, the number of orthogonal or perpendicular axes in the geometrical space may vary. One may wish to select a geometrical representation comprising only two axes. These two axes behave as mathematical primaries. Every texture attribute becomes a numerical expression which weights the contribution of primary A and the contribution of primary B. In effect, this numerical expression locates that texture descriptor in a unique point in the space on axes A and B. Similarly used texture descriptors possess similar weights of primary A and B, and thus lie close to each since they possess the same coordinate values on axes A and B. Sometimes a texture descriptor comprises only some amount of primary A, and none of primary B (see Fig. 2.7 and Table 2.17).

We have loosely talked about the dimensions of the geometry as primaries. The axes represent mathematical or hypothetical primaries, not behavioral ones. Factor analysis reduces the complete set of intercorrelations among factors into a set of mathematical primary axes, and locates the descriptors as points relative to those primaries. The researcher must name these primaries. He or she does so by ascertaining whether there exist texture descriptors possessing a lot of

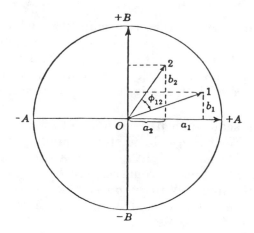

FIG. 2.7A

Geometric representation of two attributes in a two-factor space. The two vectors A and B represent orthogonal common factors, and the vectors 1 and 2 represent correlated attributes.

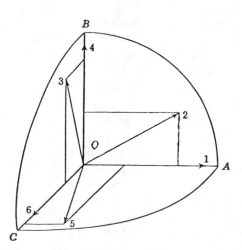

FIG. 2.7B

Geometrical illustration of the attribute configuration and the factor structure involved in Table 2.17.

FIG. 2.7A,B GEOMETRICAL REPRESENTATION OF ATTRIBUTES AND PRIMARIES FROM
FACTOR ANALYSIS

TABLE 2.17
AN ASSUMED FACTOR MATRIX F OF ATTRIBUTES 1-6
WITH THREE COMMON FACTORS

| | Factors | | |
	A	B	C
Attribute			
1	.9	.0	.0
2	.7	.4	.0
3	.0	.8	.3
4	.0	.9	.0
5	.3	.0	.9
6	.0	.0	.8

Source: Harman (1966)

primary A and no primary B. What characteristics do these descriptors share in common. The commonality defines the meaning of the mathematical primary. Table 2.18 shows a typical intercorrelation matrix and Fig. 2.8 the geometrical factor space (Hsü 1946) for odors.

Considerable literature on factor analysis in sensory evaluation has appeared, starting in the late 1940s. The studies published in the psychology literature and the food science literature concern primarily simple systems, such as odorants or foods rated along several dozen descriptor terms. A review of some of these results follows.

Odor Systems

Tables 2.19 and 2.20 present a short synopsis of work done on simple odors and complex odor mixtures to develop a geometrical space by factor analysis. Note that hedonics or liking often initially emerges as the first or second dimension from factor analysis. Experiment after experiment using multiple attribute ratings on different odorants continue to show hedonics as the initial primary dimension. Yoshida (1964) worked with perfumers to find a population supposedly immune to the hedonic properties of odorants, which represents the most critical property and the first characteristic to which panelists attend when judging odors. With such a panel of perfumers, different dimensions emerge first.

By and large the search for underlying odor primaries, by means of factor analysis, has not proved successful. For one, the primaries which emerge must accord with the range of different odors tested. A narrow range will produce a distorted view of the range of possible

TABLE 2.18

INTERCORRELATION MATRIX OF ODORS

(Each number multiplied by 100)

	1	2	3	4	5	6	7	8	9	10	11	12	13	14	15	16	17	18	19	20
1																				
2	05																			
3	-01	21																		
4	-10	05	-01																	
5	05	20	00	01																
6	-06	20	-17	20	44															
7	17	07	-22	-06	26	29														
8	25	16	10	13	11	10	21													
9	12	04	-09	13	18	41	10	21												
10	02	18	08	-02	13	08	12	-07	-01											
11	05	04	02	22	15	10	25	05	-15	17										
12	-01	14	04	-08	07	06	-10	37	08	-23	-03									
13	07	18	19	09	-10	08	16	04	-11	-01	05	31								
14	-12	18	-02	20	53	20	10	-21	05	38	13	-05	03							
15	10	10	12	11	29	38	-12	-05	74	04	05	03	-20	16						
16	27	13	17	10	-05	02	13	24	10	-05	26	27	45	-05	-13					
17	10	01	-03	38	10	29	-10	08	32	-03	34	12	10	23	37	25				
18	10	38	04	25	12	40	20	16	13	-16	17	08	10	20	16	20	20			
19	60	12	-05	-12	07	32	32	33	20	01	02	18	05	09	11	10	22	35		
20	14	08	-05	12	08	25	10	10	10	-12	30	30	-01	10	03	20	10	-07	20	
21	-14	16	16	34	27	-05	-38	-04	-12	27	14	-09	05	17	09	09	21	08	-24	09

1. o-Eugenol 2. Benzaldehyde 3. α-Ionone 4. Diethyl sulfide 5. Indol 6. Naphthalene 7. Eucalyptol 8. Anethol 9. Acetone 10. Trimethyl amine 11. α-Pinene 12. Geraniol 13. α-Terpineol 14. Skatol 15. O-Xylol 16. Linaloöl 17. Toluene 18. Amyl acetate 19. Methyl salicylate 20. Limonene 21. Pyridine
Source: Hsü (1946)

odor qualities. By testing a wide range of vastly different odors, the investigator runs the risk that the dimensions or primaries which emerge will possess such generality as to become totally unusable as definitions of specific odor qualities. Second, the researcher must make sure that he or she has properly named the primary. This becomes a difficult task, especially when one tests a dramatically wide range of odors as, for example, the study by Schutz (1964). What aspects do butryic acid, eugenol, and ethyl sulfide share in common? Research insights into the common factor of stimuli lying in a dimension become the basis for assigning a label to the dimension. Finally, factor analysis in the hands of a researcher parallels a scalpel in the hands of a surgeon. Some surgeons possess considerable talent for

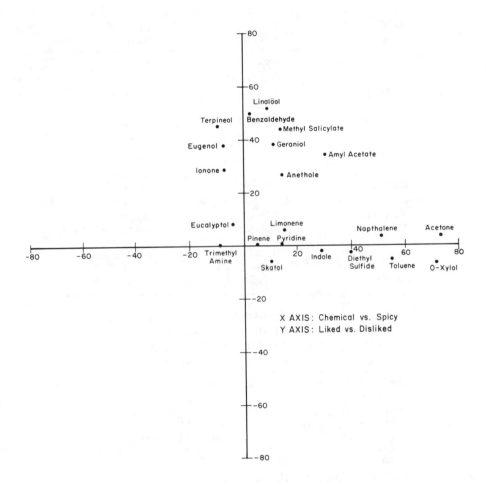

FIG. 2.8 FIRST TWO ORTHOGONAL FACTORS FROM HSÜ'S 1946 STUDY ON ODORS

Source: Hsü (1946)

TABLE 2.19
RESULTS OF FACTOR ANALYSIS ON SMELL;
EVALUATION OF ODORS (SCHUTZ 1964)

Ten chemicals evaluated on 29 word scales
(similarity of attribute to the chemical smell)

Factor A Fragrant	Factor B Ethanol	Factor C Sweet
Methyl-salicylate Benzyl acetate Isosafrole	I-Propanol Methyl ethyl ketone Ethanol	Methanol I-Butanol Vanillin
Factor D Burnt	Factor E Rancid	Factor F Oily
Guaiacol Eugenol Skatole	Butyric acid Skatole Octanol	Heptanol Octanol Pentanol
Factor G Metallic	Factor H Spicy	Factor L Sulfurous or Goaty
Hexanol Ethyl acetate Butanol	Benzaldehyde Amylacetate Pyridine	Butyric acid Eugenol Ethyl sulphide

TABLE 2.20
RESULTS OF FACTOR ANALYSIS ON SMELL;
EVALUATION OF ODORS (YOSHIDA 1964)
24 odorants evaluated on 25 bipolar scales

Factor 1 = pleasure. Scales with high loadings:

dull-sharp	vivid-lifeless
sultry-refreshing	oily-watery
pleasant-unpleasant	warm-cold
dirty-neat	vague-well defined
heavy-light	thick-thin
dark-bright	

Factor 2 = harshness. Scales with high loadings:

delicate-unrefined	pleasant-unpleasant
well defined-vague	warm-cold
soft-hard	sweet-sour
smooth-rough	permanent-temporary

Factor 3 = intensity or vividness. Scales with high loadings:

vague-well defined	small-large
weak-strong	dull-sharp

operating. So do some researchers who use factor analysis. The technical procedures and the implementation and analysis make sense, and generate insights. Other times, the scalpel becomes a dangerous weapon which does more damage than good. Factor analysis can create more heat than light when improperly used. The incorrect selection of attributes and stimuli, coupled with the extraction of too many dimensions (8+), or too few (2 or 1), obscures more than enlightens. When a researcher discovers eight basic factors one must question whether these factors apply to all odor perceptions, or whether these eight factors provide a provincial, limited solution applicable primarily to the particular odors in that particular study.

In odor description one should bear in mind that factor analysis and similar approaches based on correlations continue to provide valuable service. They point out redundancies in attributes where such redundancies exist. They point to similar characteristics by locating similarly used descriptor terms in the same geometrical region. Finally, factor analysis provides a method for data reduction. It simplifies a complex set of scales, reducing them to an easily conceptualized and visualized representation.

Figures 2.9 and 2.10 and Tables 2.19 and 2.20 show some of the published geometrical spaces (restricted, of course, to three dimensions). The reader should bear in mind that one can apply factor analysis procedures to actual chemicals, complex chemical mixtures (e.g., naturally occurring spices or perfume creations), and descriptor terms (where the technique turns itself around and the experimenter embeds these descriptor terms in the geometry).

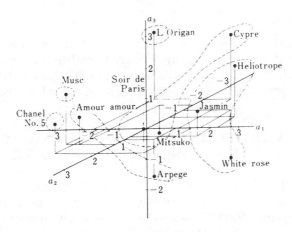

FIG. 2.9 PERFUMES
(Source: Yoshida, 1964)

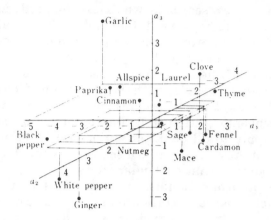

FIG. 2.10 SPICES
(Source: Yoshida, 1964)

Texture Systems

Experimenters have also used factor analysis to uncover the primaries for texture perception. The approach parallels the investigation of odors. Studies listed in Table 2.21 reflect the gamut of texture analyses, seeking to find basic dimensions on which people react to texture. Attributes which reappear from study to study include hardness-softness, viscosity (or thickness), brittleness, etc. Figures 2.11, 2.12 and 2.13 show geometrical representations of the texture space (Yoshida 1964).

Color Systems

Factor analysis applied to color perceptions reveals three basic primaries: red, yellow and blue. Rarely does the factor analysis data produce a startling new color space, except perhaps when the panelists involved suffer from one or another form of color blindness.

THE GEOMETRY OF DESCRIPTIONS —MULTIDIMENSIONAL SCALING

In the early 1960s psychologists focused interest on a panelist's ability to directly estimate the psychological distance between two stimuli (Shepard 1962). This method of directly judging sensory distance contrasts with the factor analysis approach (which correlates the stimuli based upon similar or dissimilar appearing attribute pro-

TABLE 2.21
TEXTURE PRIMARIES FROM VARIOUS STUDIES
USING FACTOR ANALYSIS

A. 7 Primaries (Yoshikawa *et al.* 1970) from naming attributes

> Hard-Soft
> Cold-Warm
> Oily-Juicy
> Elastic-Flaky
> Heavy
> Viscous
> Smooth

B. Evaluation of Texture (Moskowitz and Kapsalis 1974)

Evaluation of 39 food names on 11 texture attributes (unipolar scales and magnitude estimation scaling.)

Factor 1: Hard-Soft
(scales with high loading: crunchy, hard, brittle, crispy)

Factor 2: Tendency to remain cohesive after first bite
(scales with high loadings: crispy, tender, brittle, hard, mushy, chewy, crunchy)

Factor 3: Work expended in masticating
(scales with high loadings: chewy, then a cluster of crispy, crunchy, hard, brittle)

C. Evaluation of Texture (Moskowitz and Kapsalis 1976)

Evaluation of 71 food names on 15 texture attributes (unipolar scales and magnitude estimation scaling.)

Factor 1: Hard-Soft
(scales with high loadings: hardness, crunchiness, crispiness)

Factor 2: Cohesiveness in mouth vs Non-Cohesiveness
(scales with high loadings: cohesiveness, gumminess, adhesiveness)

Factor 3: Poorly defined external texture vs well defined external texture, when assessed visually
(scales with high loadings: creaminess, mushiness, spreadability)

files). When assigning distance judgments the panelist comes up with a rating which represents overall dissimilarity (or similarity) between pairs of stimuli. The panelist need not use specific attributes when making these judgments of overall dissimilarity.

A matrix of psychological distances emerges from this exercise. If a panelist rates the psychological distance or perceived dissimilarity between three stimuli, this results in $(3)(2)/2 = 3$ pair judgments (AB, AC, BC) The general rule dictates $N(N-1)/2$ pairwise judgments or

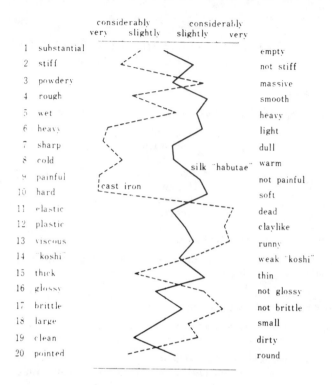

FIG. 2.11 SOME OF THE HAPTIC DIFFERENTIAL RATING PROFILES (ACTUAL TOUCH)
(Source: Yoshida, 1968)

dissimilarity for a set of N stimuli.

Given these ratings (whether numerical or points on a line, etc.), the analysis places the stimuli into a geometrical space of low dimensionality so that the distances between points in the geometrical space best correlate with the distances empirically judged by panelists when they assigned their ratings.

The 1960s and 1970s saw increasing use of the direct estimation procedure known generically as *multidimensional scaling*. Researchers used the method to uncover the primary dimensions of odor, texture and color perceptions. Multidimensional scaling has a major advantage over factor analysis because it eliminates descriptive terms as sources for dissimilarity ratings. When panelists scale the perceived dissimilarity between pairs of odors (or pairs of descriptor terms), they do not use adjectives to describe how they arrive at that rating. Researchers feel that these dissimilarity ratings, and the subsequent geometrical representation, do not depend upon any preconceived set of descriptor adjectives. Consequently, researchers feel that the dimensions which emerge more truly represent the basic, underly-

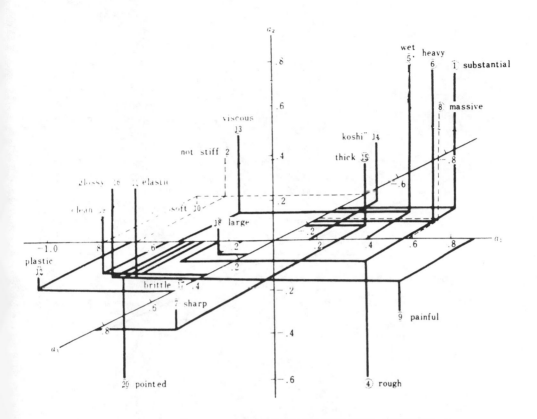

FIG. 2.12 FACTOR STRUCTURE OF RATING SCALES—TEXTURE
(Source: Yoshida, 1968)

ing psychological primaries, uncontaminated by predesignated descriptors.

As in all new developments, the initial papers on multidimensional scaling dealt with simple model systems and reanalyzed previous data. To validate the statistical and mathematical methods as procedures which truly provide an indication of underlying dimensions, the developers of multidimensional scaling used simplistic stimuli (e.g., geometrical figures of varying lengths, widths and shapes, etc.). These early studies validated the scaling method as one which uncovers underlying dimenions on which stimuli vary.

For descriptive analysis, consider the studies on odor, and texture reported by various experimenters, appearing in the following examples. In these studies the panelists scaled the overall dissimilarity

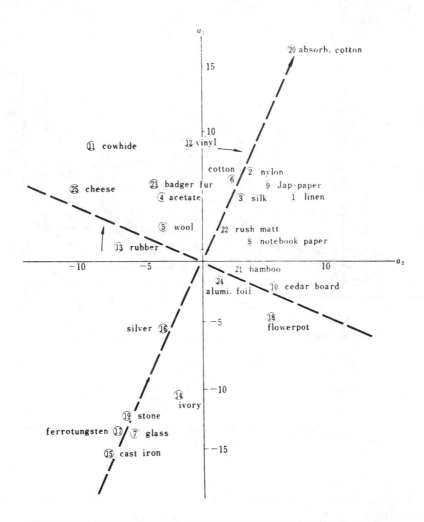

FIG. 2.13 MULTIDIMENSIONAL SCALING CONFIGURATION OF STIMULI
Obtained from the haptic differential rating (actual touch)
(Source: Yoshida, 1968)

(or similarity) between all pairs of stimuli. This excruciatingly
long task, sometimes demanding hours and days, generated geometrical maps similar to the maps emerging from factor analysis.
Again, for olfactory perception, hedonics or liking/disliking emerged
as the initial primary dimension, whereas for texture hardness-
softness emerged as the primary dimension. The most appropriate
description for remaining dimensions depended upon the specific
starting stimuli.

Results of Multidimensional Scaling of Odor by Direct Similarity or Dissimilarity of Ratings — Abstracts of Representative Studies

Yoshida (1964). *Odorants tested.* Odors and malodor including jasmine, skatole, heliotropin, vanillin, caproic acid, camphor, lemon, bergamot, trimethyl amine, cassia, acetic acid, menthol, coffee, isovaleric acid, musk ambrette, carbol, amyl alcohol, terpene, indol and anisaldehyde.

Subjects. One male and four females.

Method. Direct judgment of similarity among all pairs of odorants.

Results. Four dimensions extracted:
(1) Pleasant/unpleasant (terpene, camphor and menthol lying at the pleasant end, versus nitrogeneous odorants such as skatole, trimethylamine and indol lying at the other end).
(2) Sweet/pungent (sweet—vanillin; pungent—carbol and trimethylamine).
(3) Not interpretable.
(4) Not interpretable.

Yoshida (1964). Odorants tested. Representative perfume chemicals based upon Kainshow's classification scheme (skatole, olibanum, camphor and citral).

Subjects. Two specialist perfumers, one male, one female; and another group of 6 naive panelists.

Method. Direct judgment of similarity.

Results. Two meaningful dimensions extracted, although six factors statistically present.
(1) Resinous burnt versus sweet.
(2) High-pitched, vivid odors versus heavy, base notes.

Berglund, Berglund, Engen and Ekman (1973). *Odorants tested.* Twenty-one odorants spanning a range of pleasant to unpleasant, and high molecular weight to low molecular weight odors. All of the odorants matched to have equal subjective intensity (40% as strong, subjectively, as the odor of undiluted acetone). The chemicals: acetone, amyl acetate, anethole, benzaldehyde, benzyl acetate, butanol, butyric acid, ethyl acetate, ethyl methyl ketone, eugenol,

furfurole, geranial, guaiacol, heptane, heptanol, methol, methyl salicylate, nonane, octane, 2 phenylethanol and iso-valeric acid.

Subjects. Eleven subjects, practiced in the sensory analysis of
odors.

Method. Direct similarity estimates on a 0-100 point scale for all
pairs.

Results. They obtained large individual differences in the similarity judgments and concluded that we live in different olfactory worlds.
Hedonics represented the major factor. The remaining individual factors varied according to the specific panelist.

Engen (1964). *Odorants tested.* Various combinations of heptanol (oily) and amyl acetate (banana smell) mixed in varying
proportions.

Subjects. Thirteen individuals, each of whom compared the similarity of the mixtures to amyl acetate; and eleven other individuals
who rated the similarity of the mixtures to heptanol.

Results. A factor analysis of the matrix of similarity judgments
showed two factors. One factor appeared proportional to the percent of
amyl acetate in the mixture, and the other factor appeared proportional to the amount of heptanol in the mixture. In both factors, the
relation between loading on the factor and percent concentration
appeared as an S shaped curve.

Woskow (1968). *Odorants tested.* Twenty-five odorants: methyl
salicylate, eugenol, pyridine, safrole, benzaldehyde, guaiacol, citral,
n-butanol, toluene, anisole, *n*-propanol, acetic acid, *n*-pentanol, skatole, ethanol, *n*-butyric acid, *n*-nonanol, phenylethanol, vanillin, L-
menthol, D-camphor, *n*-hexanol, pinene, *n*-octanol and *n*-heptanol.

Subjects. Twenty unpracticed individuals.

Scaling. Instructed subjects to categorize the degree of similarity
between all pairs (1 = most dissimilar; 9 = most alike). All subjects
rated each pair.

Results. Three dimensions extracted:
(1) Hedonics liking/disliking (pyridine versus vanillin).
(2) Cool, woody (D-camphor versus *n*-octanol).
(3) No interpretation given.

PRAGMATIC CONSIDERATIONS AND
DESCRIPTIVE ANALYSIS

Descriptive analysis represents an exciting, growing area in product testing. It lies at the basis of all product testing, and provides insights into the multidimensional nature of man's perception.

For practical purposes, the product tester should keep in mind that descriptive analysis must effectively deal with the problem at hand. Cumbersome descriptive systems cannot do justice to pragmatic problems, because panelists just cannot cope with an unwieldly number of attributes. Panelists asked to scale a food product on a large number of attributes probably use only a selected number of characteristics, jettisoning the rest because of the pressure to finish the task. Researchers with experience in profiling often find that individuals do not use as many characteristics as they could, and use these in different ways. Some individuals use many different attributes to characterize a stimulus, whereas others use but a few. Recently, Dravnieks found the same results with a study of odor quality, using an expanded list of Harper-type descriptors, shown in Table 2.2. This means that the product tester must select a set of characteristics which panelists can understand and use; which do not drive away or discourage panelists from using the entire set; and which adequately describe the product and account for some, if not all, nuances differentiating one product from another.

A second point concerns the type of scale for the descriptor system. Scales comprise two major types: (1) a scale of amount whereby the panelist registers how much of an attribute the product contains; and (2) a scale of appropriateness whereby the panelist rates the degree to which a term fits a product. These two types of scales probe different aspects of description. For ratings of amount, we assume that the product comprises some defined level of each attribute, even if some levels achieve only a zero value (the product lacks that specific characteristic). When rating appropriateness, we conceive the panelist as locating the product in a geometry in which the separate axes comprise orthogonal or mutally perpendicular axes.

AN OVERVIEW

This chapter has illustrated the many facets of descriptive analysis which scientists, product testers and market researchers have available to them to describe the nuances of flavor, texture and visual appearance. The approaches which generate a descriptive profile vary from the very simple, virtually armchair scientific approach (by investigator fiat), to extensive statistical analysis of unprompted consumer descriptions of products. The methods for training consumer or expert panels in descriptive analysis also vary, from simple instructions to long-term, extensive training. Extended training generates a panel which acts as a highly precise measuring tool. Finally, the procedures for analyzing profile data also vary. The product tester can report group consensus data, or average profile ratings, from a number of panelists, measures of interpanelist variability, or even generate a geometrical picture of products and/or attributes in a geometrical space.

No descriptive method can provide the necessary data for all marketing and R&D requirements. The product tester or sensory analyst can use any or all of the foregoing procedures to secure a snapshot of the characteristics, or sensory attributes, which describe the product. On some occasions an expert panel may prove more useful than a consumer panel. On other occasions, large-scale statistical analyses of sensory profile data by factor analysis could answer key questions about how consumers perceive commonalities among several products, or point out key dimensions through which panelists differentiate two or more products. One need not limit the test to actual products, tested blind. One could also test branded products, and even concepts of products, to ascertain where they lie relative to each other.

As statisticians, product testers, psychologists and other parties involved in food learn more about how people react to foods and flavors, undoubtedly we shall see further developments in descriptive analysis in terms of better techniques for eliciting descriptors, improved methods for training and utilizing panels, and more powerful methods for analyzing descriptive panel data.

CHAPTER 3

PSYCHOPHYSICS—THE SCIENCE OF SENSORY PROCESSES AND ITS RELATION TO HOW WE PERCEIVE FOODS

INTRODUCTION

Psychophysics refers to a branch of psychology which relates sensory perceptions to physical stimuli. A century ago psychophysics, and the larger science of perception, comprised the vast majority of the then-current psychology. Today, psychophysics has undergone a renaissance. The scientific approaches which psychophysicists use to evaluate simple systems immediately translate into sensory analysis of complex foods. A look back into the history of psychophysics will reveal parallels with the history of sensory analysis at virtually every stage. Psychophysics has traditionally acted as a resource discipline for product testing, providing it with proven techniques to quantify human reactions to food

Like any other branch of science, psychophysics searches for regularity in nature. Relevant queries emerging from psychophysics include four major items. (1) What smallest stimulus level and change in a stimulus can we perceive? By what percentage does a stimulus have to increase in order for us to detect the increase? (2) How do sensory intensity and physical stimulus intensity correlate with each other? Can we accurately judge physical intensity, or do we distort the physical changes because of intrinsic distorting (or non-linear)factors in our sensory systems? (3) What basic facts emerge on the senses from research in pyschophysics? What information does psychophysics provide to help us better profile and scale different foods and thus better test products? (4) What procedures do psychophysicists use? Can we apply these procedures to sensory analysis? Can we improve some of the measuring techniques based upon psychophysical studies with simple stimuli, adapting these techniques to the evaluation of foods?

PART 1 — SCALING AND THRESHOLDS WHAT THEY MEAN AND HOW WE USE THEM

Scientists in any field of research and application look for hard data—a point, a measure or a fact which they feel remains invariant, or unchanged, and upon which they can base a law of behavior for a system. How does one find such invariants in perception? Do there exist constants in perception analogous to the constant of gravity?

Going back a century or two, let us put ourselves in the shoes of researchers seeking regularities of human behavior. We confront the empiricist tradition and the emerging scientific disciplines of physics, chemistry and biology with their observations of regularities and their constants.

Perception, too, seems to have a constant. The constant for perception becomes the physical intensity at which people make the simplest response: they either perceive or do not perceive. The physical level at which one just begins to perceive a stimulus we call the *perceptual threshold*. Thresholds indicate that level of physical stimulus which suffices to trigger perception. Presumably, according to these early researchers, the threshold value characterizes a sense modality. In a world lacking constants for perceptual processes, the threshold becomes acceptable and, more important, significant.

Researchers studied man's sensitivity to different stimuli to determine values for the threshold. By presenting stimuli at ever decreasing physical levels, investigators soon determined the lowest levels for a variety of different, easily manipulated physical continua.

Detection Versus Recognition Thresholds

There exist two types of thresholds: detection thresholds and recognition thresholds. To see the difference, let us consider the case of a panelist presented with increasing levels of quinine sulfate, a bitter tasting chemical. With no quinine sulfate in the taste stimulus (pure water), the panelist does not and cannot detect a stimulus. Therefore the panelist reports nothing there. Increase the quinine sulfate concentration just a little, and soon the panelist reports that he detects that the water seems different. The panelist cannot tell us why the water tastes different, but time after time he or she can reliably discriminate the adulterated, quinine sulfate solution from water. This lowest level we call *detection threshold*. The panelist detects that something has changed; the water tastes different. He or she detects, but does not recognize the stimulus.

Increase the concentration of quinine in water even more, and soon we reach a point where the panelist states that the water tastes bitter. The lowest concentration at which the panelist correctly categorizes the stimulus we label the *recognition threshold*. Most of the time the values differ for the detection and recognition thresholds. The recognition threshold values often lie several units of magnitude above the detection threshold. We require a higher intensity to categorize and recognize than to detect the presence of the stimulus.

As we might expect, sometimes a specific chemical exhibits several recognition thresholds, each of which lies above the detection threshold. As we increase the concentration of common table salt, sodium chloride, we reach a number of different recognition thresholds. First, at very low concentrations, table salt tastes sweet. Hence, table salt possesses a recognition threshold concentration for sweetness. As we further increase the concentration, the salt stimulus tastes bitter. Salt thus possesses a bitter recognition threshold. Finally, as we further increase the concentration, sodium chloride eventually provokes the typical salt taste.

Variability of Thresholds

Threshold values vary, often quite substantially, from laboratory to laboratory and from investigator to investigator. The supposedly invariant or unique point in sensory perception actually moves around, influenced by factors such as age, momentary states of attention and presentation procedures. A recent compilation of thresholds by ASTM (DS48 1973) shows disagreements about thresholds for virtually all odor and taste chemicals. Variation in reported threshold values occurs because: the threshold represents the lowest stimulus level that one can perceive; in the region around absolute detection level, stimulus concentration may vary by a factor of 3-4 provoking virtually identical sensory perceptions; and a large change in concentration around threshold exerts much less effect than we believe. In contrast, at supra-threshold level, a 3-4 fold increase in stimulus level produces a much more noticeable change in perception.

IN SEARCH OF PERCEPTUAL LAWS

One hundred and fifty years ago, the German physiologist E. H. Weber reported the results of studies on the ability to discern small differences between stimuli. Weber searched for a general rule to quantify our capacity for discrimination. Through tedious testing with pairs of weights, candles of different luminances, etc., Weber showed that discrimination behaves in a relative, not absolute, fashion. We discriminate percent changes in stimuli, not absolute changes. For example, suppose we lift a weight of 5 grams. How much heavier must we make a second weight so that we perceive the second weight as discriminably different? The answer, 5.1 grams. Now, let us consider a weight of 50 grams. Do we still require the same absolute increment in grams of 0.1g, or a second weight of 50.1 grams? Direct experimental observation reveals that the second weight must increase to 51 grams, rather than 50.1 grams, to feel discriminably heavier. Weber discovered that in order for a person to discriminate between two weights, the weights must lie in a constant ratio, rather than a constant difference.

This ratio increment remains fairly constant over a wide range of weights. The same percentage rule holds, albeit with a different ratio value governing each sensory dimension. This ratio increment we now call the Weber Fraction:

$$\Delta I/I = \text{Constant} \tag{1}$$

The change in physical intensity needed to produce a just noticeable difference (ΔI) varies in absolute size, but remains proportionally constant relative to the stimulus level from which it starts (I). Table 3.1 lists several representative Weber Fractions (also called JND's, or just noticeable differences). By and large $\Delta I/I$ remains fairly constant, except at the very low intensity levels where it dramatically increases. The German physicist-physiologist Helmholtz further studied how the Weber fraction varied with intensity, and expressed the ratio somewhat differently to account for the increase in the Weber Fraction at low intensity levels:

$$\Delta I/(I+C) = \text{Constant} \tag{2}$$

(C = additive constant)

TABLE 3.1

JUST NOTICEABLE DIFFERENCE (JND) FOR DIFFERENT SENSES

Sense Modality	Weber Fraction: ($\Delta I/I$)
Deep pressure, from skin and subcutaneous tissue	1/77
Visual brightness	1/60
Lifted weights	1/52
Loudness (1,000 Hz tone)	1/12
Smell (rubber)	1/11
Cutaneous pressure	1/7
Taste (salt solution)	1/5

Source: Boring, Langfeld and Weld (1935)

Weber's Law may not seem very important today, in light of our sophisticated tools for sensory measurement. A century ago Weber's Law of discrimination excited researchers, for it represented the realization of a science to measure the private world of perception. Such a numerical regularity of perception promised an ability to truly construct a science of perception, founded upon empirical laws that one could prove by scientific experiment and inductive reasoning.

G. T. Fechner and A Law of Sensory Intensity

A German philosopher-physicist, Gustav Theodor Fechner (1860) reported that he had discovered another general law of human perception. Fechner searched for a law governing perceived sensory intensity, as it relates to physical intensity. Could one develop a measurement system to truly quantify private sensory experience? Physicists have no trouble measuring length, width, mass and temperature. Human perception may yield to measurement, if one could only find the ruler for sensory measurement, and the appropriate unit of perceptual magnitude. Basing his approaches upon Weber's rule of discrimination, Fechner followed a train of reasoning which yielded an approach to measurement and a law for sensory intensity. The logic proved attractive, and subsequently led to substantial research. The logic follows the sequence below.

According to Weber, our ability to discriminate remains relatively constant, at least according to a percentage basis: $\Delta I / I = C$. We call this the JND, as discussed previously. If so, let us consider the unit of measurement as the JND, or the just noticeable difference. Starting from the lowest physical intensity which one can perceive (known as the threshold), let us experimentally determine that physical intensity I_1, just noticeable difference which appears stronger than the threshold level, I_0. I_1 will, of course, exceed I_0 since I_0 equals the threshold and I_1 lies just above the threshold. Furthermore, by definition, I_1 will lie 1 JND above I_0. I_1 obtains a score of 1 sensory unit.

Let us continue with this course of logic. Let us seek that level I_2, stronger of course than I_1 which lies 1 JND above I_1. To I_2 we assign 2 sensory units. By following this approach, either conceptually or in actual experimentation, one arrives at a sequence of physical intensities which possess 0,1,2,3,4...N sensory units. These physical intensities lie at 0,1,2,3,4...N JND units above threshold, by definition.

The sensory law of perceptual intensity becomes apparent by developing the mathematical expression relating sensory intensity (defined by the number of JND units) and physical intensity (defined by the actual physical measurement). By difference or differential equations this addition of JND's generates the so-called logarithmic law of perception, also known as Fechner's Law:

$$\text{Sensory Intensity} = k \, (\text{Log Physical Intensity}) + C \tag{3}$$

The coefficient k and the additive constant C vary as a function of the absolute threshold and the size of the JND, which remain unique for each sensory modality.

By this time, the reader should have an inkling of the tortuous experimentation one needs to follow in order to generate a logarithmic law governing perception. The lack of any other general rule led to the acceptance of Fechner's logarithmic law (or better, conjecture) as the rule of sensory intensity, at least up until the 1950s, when S. S. Stevens showed the way to a more direct, more valid measurement.

A review of the psychophysics literature between 1850 and 1950, in biology and psychology journals, as well as in chemistry and food science publications, shows many studies on one's ability to discriminate small differences in stimuli, motivated perhaps by a desire to lay the empirical foundations for different logarithmic equations as did Fechner. On the other hand, rarely did researchers spend the time or effort to actually generate specific logarithmic functions to describe sensory intensity. When researchers did carry out the research program, they discovered these two facts. (1) The tedium of the experiment often interferes with its results. One has a difficult time carrying out, to completion, a research program to determine the JND's for a sensory modality. (2) The resulting equation leads to contradiction. Consider the case of saccharin and sucrose, two sweeteners. Lemberger (1908) faithfully implemented the Fechner approach, determining concentrations corresponding to 1, 2, 3 ... 10 JND's for saccharin and sucrose separately. Presumably, these scales should produce equivalent perceived sweetness levels for equal JND levels above threshold. Saccharin at 5 JND's should taste as sweet as sucrose at 5 JND's. In actuality they differ in sweetness. Similar paradoxes apply to other sensory modalities. Stimuli at equal JND levels above threshold do not seem equally strong when directly compared to each other.

Fechner's logarithmic law gets quoted today, perhaps more often than really necessary. The middle of the twentieth century, starting in the 1930s with work at Harvard University, generally sounded the death knell for JND measurement as the unit for a general law of sensory intensity.

MEASUREMENT BY VARIABILITY
— L. L. THURSTONE

Principles of scientific research assume different forms. Structures of thought underlying scientific studies often submerge, only to emerge once again in different guise. Fechner thought he could build a sensory law by using discrimination capacity as a measure. About seventy-five years later, Leon Louis Thurstone (1927), the famous psychometrician, resurrected Fechner's measurement scheme in a different form, but with the same logic. Thurstone approached the general psychophysical law as a psychometrician, using the ratings of panelists and the variability around those ratings as external indications of the underlying psychophysical scale. According to Thurstone,we possess an underlying psychophysical scale which accounts for our behavior, whether the behavior reflects judgments of amount, or intensity, or judgments of preference. The scales differ for individuals, and differ, of course, for attributes and sensory modalities.

How does one go about discovering what underlying scales people use when they rate intensity? Fechner had measured JND's and cumulated them, but had not gone into any depth investigating the existence of such an underlying scale. Thurstone conceptualized the problem differently which led to a set of empirical methods for uncovering the scale.

His logic followed this pattern. Each person possesses an underlying scale which allows him or her to make judgments (e.g., that stimulus A tastes saltier than stimulus B, etc.) Each stimulus (e.g., sodium chloride of varying concentrations) lies somewhere along this underlying scale. If we instruct panelists to choose which of two stimuli seems stronger (e.g., which salt solution actually tastes saltier), panelists can readily do so.

This procedure, known as *paired comparison,* produces variable results. People do not show 100% consistency or accuracy. Give the panelist two stimuli of similar but not identical salt concentrations, and they may choose the saltier one only 55% of the time, choosing the less salty one (incorrectly) 45% of the time.The percent of time the panelist correctly selects the more intense stimulus in a pair varies directly with the distance between the two stimuli on the underlying scale. Thus, if one analyzes the variablity in paired comparison selections, e.g., saltiness or any other sensory or hedonic (liking) dimension, one can estimate the size of the pairwise distances between stimuli on the underlying scale. The panelist generally evaluates all pairs, choosing the more intense stimulus in each pair. This generates a matrix of choices, which provides a full matrix of data for subsequent processing. By processing a matrix of these paired comparisons, one can locate the different stimuli (e.g., salt concentrations) as points on the underlying scale. The scale has the property that the distance between stimuli on the scale relates to the number of times panelists choose the stronger one as seeming perceptually more intense. Closely spaced stimuli on the underlying scale reflect pairs of stimuli which panelists confuse. Pairs of stimuli located far apart on the underlying scale represent stimuli virtually never confused with each other when evaluated for relative intensity.

Thurstone had originally developed his psychometric approach for the measurement of value systems. Values possess no demonstratable physical continuum. On the other hand, by following Thurston's approach with well-defined physical stimuli, varying only along a single physical dimension, the researcher quickly develops the underlying J scale (or judgment scale) and the location of the different stimuli on that scale. This location of points reflects relative psychological magnitudes. One can correlate this judgment scale versus physical magnitudes. Table 3.2 shows paired comparison data for food, and Fig. 3.1 shows the scale which emerges from a Thurstonian analysis of the paired comparison data. In instances where one can generate such scale data and correlate it with physical measures, the curve approximates a logarithmic function similar to Fechner's logarithmic function.

Fechner and Thurstone each approached psychophysical measurement using scaling tools which seem today rather arcane and circuitous. Why, during a period of rapid scientific growth, could neither scientist instruct the panelist directly to scale relative sensory intensity and, thereby, avoid the complex series of assumptions and experimental tedium? We do not know. We do know, however, that both approaches stimulated considerable research effort, and antedated the extensive and more direct methods of scaling which we use today. Rarely do researchers use cumulated JND's or paired comparison scales as serious measures of sensory intensity. Rather, today's scientists use direct scaling methods, whether fixed point category scales or the increasingly popular method of magnitude estimation scaling.

FIXED POINT CATEGORY SCALES

In 1887 the Belgian investigator, Corin, reported studies on the measurement of taste of acids, using different acids at varying concentra-

TABLE 3.2
PAIRED COMPARISONS OF FOOD PREFERENCE AND
THEIR UNDERLYING SCALE UNCOVERED
BY THURSTONIAN SCALING

Proportion Matrix for Nine Vegetables Judged in Terms of Preferences as Foods*								
Vegetable	1	2	3	4	5	6	7	8	9
1. Turnips	.500	.818	.770	.811	.878	.892	.899	.892	.926
2. Cabbage	.182	.500	.601	.723	.743	.736	.811	.845	.858
3. Beets	.230	.300	.500	.561	.736	.676	.815	.797	.818
4. Asparagus	.189	.277	.439	.500	.561	.588	.676	.601	.730
5. Carrots	.122	.275	.264	.439	.500	.493	.574	.709	.764
6. Spinach	.108	.264	.324	.412	.507	.500	.628	.682	.628
7. String beans	.101	.189	.155	.324	.426	.372	.500	.527	.542
8. Peas	.108	.155	.203	.399	.291	.318	.473	.500	.628
9. Corn	.074	.142	.182	.270	.236	.372	.358	.372	.500
$\Sigma p_{i > k}$	1.614	3.001	3.438	4.439	4.878	4.947	5.764	5.925	6.494

*Food stimuli arranged in order of increasing $\Sigma p_{i > k}$ across the columns.

SCALE VALUES DERIVED FROM PREFERENCE JUDGMENTS

Vegetable								
1	2	3	4	5	6	7	8	9
−0.7	1.4	1.9	3.3	3.8	4.0	5.0	5.2	5.9

Source: Guilford (1954)

trations. Corin instructed the panelists to categorize their sourness responses in terms of a limited number of graded descriptor levels. The approach represents a fairly straightforward method to measure sensory reactions. In the intervening 90 years or so, many researchers have used fixed point scales to grade sensory intensity, and thus to generate curves relating physical intensity and sensory intensity.

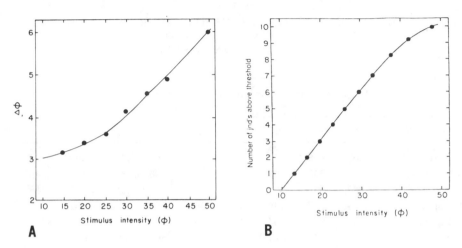

FIG. 3.1 RELATION BETWEEN PHYSICAL STIMULUS INTENSITY OF SCALED PAIRED
COMPARISON RATINGS (JND'S)

A. Discrimable physical difference ($\Delta \phi$) versus physical intensity (ϕ)
B. JND level versus physical intensity (ϕ)
(Source: Gescheider, 1976)

We can summarize the salient points of fixed point category scaling
as follows. (1) The investigator arbitrarily selects or develops a scale
comprising a limited number of categories. Some investigators prefer
to use 6 points, other 7 points, others 9 points and the like. The number
of categories, and whether one uses an odd or an even number of
categories, vary from study to study and from laboratory to laboratory, depending upon rather ill-defined rationales. (2) The panelist
uses the fixed point scale to grade different stimulus levels by selecting, for each stimulus, which one of the limited number of categories
best reflects magnitude. This requires discretion so that panelists do
not run out of numbers to use. (3) The category ratings generate a curve
when plotted versus the actual physical intensities (Fig. 3.2) (Schutz
and Pilgrim 1957).

Panelists find category scales easy to use, as long as they feel that
they have the opportunity to evaluate the entire range of stimulus
variations. By seeing the stimulus range at the start of the test session,
panelists can and do modify their use of the scale in order to accommodate the number of available scale points, and the wide or narrow
range of physical variation. The category typifies a direct, easy-to-use
procedure which has achieved considerable popularity in food science.
We shall discuss how to use the procedures, how to analyze the data

and how to avoid pitfalls in scaling in a separate chapter (Chapter 4) devoted entirely to intensity scaling.

MAGNITUDE ESTIMATION SCALING

In 1953 S. S. Stevens, a psychophysicist working in the Psychoacoustic Laboratory at Harvard University, reported the results from a series of simple, yet intriguing studies. Stevens instructed panelists to assign ratings to match the sensory intensies of lights of varying luminances, and sounds of varying energy levels. In one variation of the experimental design, Stevens deliberately omitted any fixed point scale, leaving the panelists free to assign numbers as high or as low as they wished to reflect relative sensory intensity. This omission did not affect panelist's ability to scale sensory reactions to stimuli, nor did it affect the reliability of ratings. The method, in fact, showed as much or greater reliability as fixed point scales.

Stevens initially named the method absolute judgment, but later termed the method magnitude estimation. The scaling procedure produced results which led to a stream of subsequent psychological research, which developed into a major technique for sensory measurement (Marks 1974).

The salient points of magnitude estimation (ratio scaling) follow. (1) Individuals differed in their selection of numbers to reflect sensory intensity. Some individuals used high numbers (10s, 100s), whereas other individuals preferred to use smaller numbers (fractions). (2) The ratings tracked or correlated with the physical variation, even though the panelists did not use a fixed point scale. One could quite easily correlate the panelists' numbers with the physical measurements. (3) The ratings appeared curvilinearly related to the physical levels, as shown in Fig. 3.3. In order to straighten the curve, Stevens suggested that one compute the logarithm of the rating, and correlate that logarithmic value against the logarithm of the stimulus intensity. Time after time, this transformation generated a straight line with a reproducible slope governing each sensory continuum. The logarithmic transformation appears at the right in Fig. 3.3. Figure 3.4 presents typical data for beverage sweetness.

We will return to magnitude estimation scaling in depth in Chapter 5.

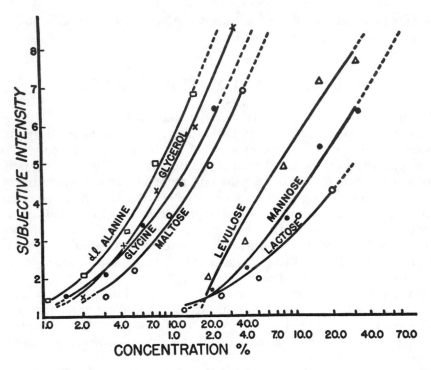

FIG. 3.2 TYPICAL CATEGORY SCALE RELATING SUGAR CONCENTRATION AND
PERCEIVED SWEETNESS
(Schutz and Pilgrim, 1957)

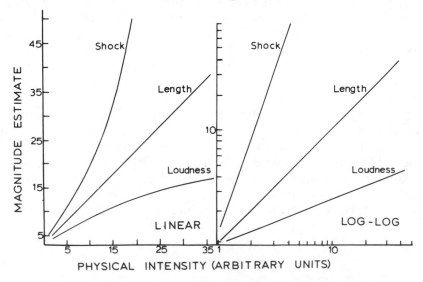

FIG. 3.3 SCHEMATIC MAGNITUDE ESTIMATION FUNCTION VERSUS
PHYSICAL INTENSITY

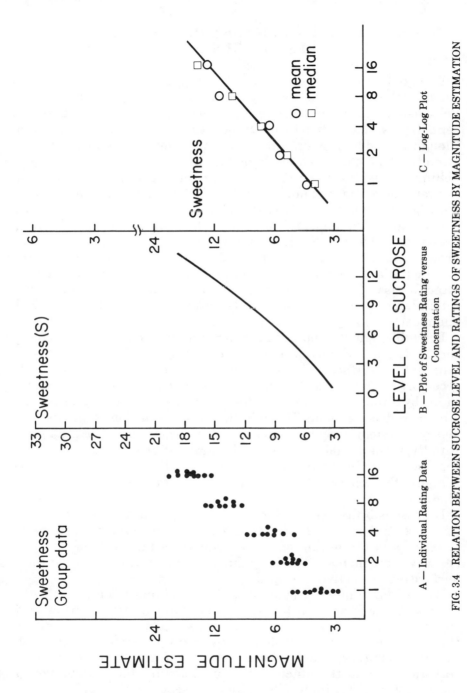

A — Individual Rating Data   C — Log-Log Plot

B — Plot of Sweetness Rating versus
Concentration

FIG. 3.4   RELATION BETWEEN SUCROSE LEVEL AND RATINGS OF SWEETNESS BY MAGNITUDE ESTIMATION

PART 2 — SENSORY PROCESSES
THE SENSES WHICH REGISTER FOOD

Each of our senses registers one or another aspect of food. Let us consider the apple. First we may see or smell the apple, bringing into play visual and/or olfactory inputs. These two sensory inputs represent the *distal senses*. The distal senses register information, even though they do not maintain an intimate, surface contact with the stimulus. The object, an apple or any other food item, can remain behind a glass partition (e.g., a jar in the supermarket) or remain entirely concealed, as under a napkin. Vision and olfaction nonetheless signal the presence of the stimulus.

Let us grasp the apple. We hold the apple, noting its weight. We bring into play the *kinesthetic* or *deep sense*, stimulating receptors which lie deeply embedded in the muscles and the joints. We sense heaviness and tactile volume that way. Simultaneously we stimulate vision and olfaction as well, as we perceive the apple with our eye, crush the skin a bit and, perhaps, release some of the esters and other flavor-critical chemicals.

Let us bite into the apple. We further stimulate the kinesthetic receptors located in the movable jaw and in the tongue. We touch the apple, stimulating surface contact receptors just as we stimulated touch receptors when we picked up the apple to put it into the mouth. Furthermore, by biting into it, we crush the apple's cells, distorting the apple, which produces a sound. The noise we generate further stimulates our sensory system, providing additional information about the apple. Finally, we taste and chew the apple, stimulating the gustatory receptors located on the surface of the tongue and in the roof of the mouth. We smell the apple while we chew it as well. We assess its texture while chewing.

Deep sensibility occurs when we ingest the apple. We sense the presence or absence of food in the stomach. Furthermore, food ingestion leads to the feeling of satiety which, in turn, comprises some sensory components, albeit deep, internal (interoceptive) rather than surface (exteroceptive) perceptions.

We could multiply this example a thousand times, considering specific foods one by one. The pattern of stimulation differs from one food to another. Some foods, such as celery, stimulate the tactile, kinesthetic and auditory sense systems significantly more than they stimulate the gustatory, olfactory and visual systems. Other stimuli, e.g., flavors, stimulate the olfactory system more than they stimulate any other system. They inform us of their presence by their effect on the overall flavor sensation. We would have a hard time differentiating a flavored versus a nonflavored item by touch, vision or audition. Yet, the difference seems immediate when we smell or taste the food.

Finally, the temporal order of stimulation varies as well. The distal senses first come into play. Vision may precede olfaction, or vice versa. The auditory impressions may precede taste if we crush the food item with our hands before tasting it (or otherwise deform the food as we prepare to eat it). We may entirely bypass olfaction by sipping the liquid food through a straw, and quickly swallowing it. In all instances our perception of foods remains fairly stable.

Modifying Perceptions By Eliminating Sensory Cues

As noted in Chapter 1, almost fifty years ago during a dinner for the British Society of Chemistry and Industry (Food Group), H. C. Moir put on a demonstration to show how colors affect one's perception of food. By changing the color of simple foods we normally eat, Moir reported that the dinner participants felt that the flavor had changed and that the food had become totally unacceptable, and sometimes sickening. Since Moir only varied the food color, the exercise showed that disturbing one of the sensory aspects involved in food perception could, and did, modify people's reactions to the food, whether these reactions concerned themselves strictly with sensory properties, or with hedonic, or affective, properties (e.g., liking/disliking).

Other researchers repeated this type of study with modifications. For example, in a study with candies colored atypically relative to their flavor, Kanig (1955) reported that most of the participating pharmacy students could not correctly identify the flavor when the color disagreed with the flavor (e.g., a green colored, but cherry flavored candy). Apparently, many people react more to the color of food than to the flavor when making their identification. Visual imputs seem to dominate gustatory and olfactory inputs as determining factors in flavor perception.

An unpublished study in the author's laboratory by Lennatta Glahn (1974) elaborated on the relative importance of vision and olfaction/taste as flavor determinants. Glahn speculated that the consumer population comprises two distinct groups of individuals: those who pay attention to their visual impressions, and those who pay more attention to their taste/smell impressions. The former constitute the *field-dependent* group. Their reactions and flavor identifications vary with the external, imposed visual framework. Miscolor a candy and these field-dependent individuals incorrectly identify the flavor. Correctly color the candy and these field-dependent individuals correctly identify the flavor. In contrast, the latter, *field-independent* group seemed impervious to the externally imposed visual modification. Members attend to their taste and smell perceptions when classifying flavor, rather than attending to the inconsistent visual stimulus.

We can take this study one step further by selectively eliminating some of the textural and olfactory cues. We know, for example, that panelists find it hard to identify an onion, or discriminate an onion from a potato, with the eyes blindfolded and the nose blocked (to prevent volatile chemicals from reaching the sensory receptors in the nose). In a study on the relative impact of different senses on food identification, panelists classified specific foods under three different conditions: no visual input, no olfactory input, and total input. Note that, in order to eliminate textural differences, the experimenter first shredded each food item to eliminate textural differentiation. Table 3.3 shows how difficult panelists found identification of foods when they operated with reduced input from their sensory systems.

TABLE 3.3
PROPORTION OF CORRECT IDENTIFICATIONS OF FOODS WITH
SUCCESSIVE RESTRICTIONS OF SENSORY INPUT
(Ground Potato, Carrot, Celery)

No Restrictions	Vision Reduced	Vision and Odor Reduced
75 of 75	66 of 75	56 of 75

Source: Vaisey-Genser *et al.* (1977)

VISUAL INPUTS TO FOOD PERCEPTION

We often fail to recognize how important a role vision plays in food perception and appreciation. Without vision we could not recognize the food at a distance. Anticipatory physiological responses might not occur as they do when we see a food without smelling, tasting or touching it. We derive some of the pleasure from a food by perceiving the food attractively presented to us. Indeed, to a great extent food service management concentrates on visual appearance as much as on taste/flavor acceptability. Without a visually acceptable appearance, the panelist may not extend his or her hand to bring the food close to the mouth in order to eat.

Physiology of the Eye

The eyes mediate visual perception. We react to a limited spectrum of light wavelengths, those between the range of 400 and 700 nanometers. We cannot detect light waves outside that limited range. Within that range, we associate each specific wavelength with a specific color, as Table 3.4 shows. The eye represents a complex, image focusing device, designed to provide information at a distance. A number of texts explain the physiological optics involved in visual perception, including a series devoted to the eye (Davson 1966).

TABLE 3.4
COLOR NAMES ASSIGNED TO SPECIFIC WAVELENGTHS

Color	Wavelength (Nanometers)
Violet	400-440
Blue	440-500
Green	500-570
Yellow	570-590
Orange	590-610
Red	610-700

Source: Davson (1966)

Physical Stimulus For Vision

Visual sensations result from reactions to electromagnetic radiation. We can detect light at extraordinary low energy levels, comprising just a few quanta of light. Table 3.5 shows how different energy levels appear visually to us.

When judging foods, we generally perceive the visual stimulus at room light level or dimmer. Rarely do food items glow, giving off highly intense light.

Color Vision—Receptors

The eye contains two types of receptors for visual perception: cones and rods. The *cones* subserve color perception and act as the important receptors for food perception. They process light information, and show sensitivity to light at moderate and high energy levels. Recent research suggests that three types of cones exist corresponding to three

TABLE 3.5
SENSORY INTENSITIES CORRESPONDING TO DIFFERENT
ENERGY LEVELS OF LIGHT

10^{10}	
10^{9}	Sun surface at noon
10^{8}	
10^{7}	
10^{6}	Tungsten filament
10^{5}	
10^{4}	White paper in sunlight
10^{3}	
10^{2}	
10^{1}	Comfortable reading
10^{0}	
10^{-1}	
10^{-2}	White paper in moonlight
10^{-3}	
10^{-4}	White paper in starlight
10^{-5}	
10^{-6}	Absolute threshold

Source: Graham (1965)

primary colors, although, from time to time, researchers suggest that color perception emerges from the reactions of two basic and opposing processes mediated by cells (opponent process theory). Rather than theorizing that the eye synthesizes color perceptions from specific combinations of the three primaries, the opponent process theory postulates two mechanisms. The particular balance of on/off of the two mechanisms generates the specific color.

Sensory Intensity of Visual Perceptions

Psychophysicists have investigated how various visual responses grow in perceived sensory intensity as a function of physical intensity. Perceived brightness conforms to a power function of luminance. For an extended source of light (e.g., the light emerging from a bulb, or an overhead fluorescent lamp, or even from a backlit bottle of juice in a supermarket), perceived brightness grows according to the 0.33 power of luminance. In practical terms, an individual with an illuminometer which registers a 1000-fold increase in actual physical luminance will probably perceive the brightness increment only as a 10-fold subjective increase. As researchers in visual perception continue to find, our visual system compresses the wide range of light to a narrower range of perceived brightness.

In very practical terms, the product developer can use this information when designing the level of illumination for lighting foods in stores. It requires a very large change in actual luminance to produce a smaller change in perceived brightness or luminance. If the light shines through the food, then the product analyst, interested in reactions to product illumination, can engineer a specific desired sensory perception using the power law relation: Brightness $=$ $k(\text{Luminance})^{0.33}$.

Saturation and Perceived Color Depth

Psychophysicists have investigated how people perceive increasing saturation of colors. Does saturation obey the same law of diminishing returns as visual brightness; i.e., does one require a large increment in saturation to produce a small increment in perceived color depth? Researchers working with well-controlled stimuli (including viewing systems which control the size of the target and the actual ratio of colored light to white light, thus, controlling saturation) have discovered that perceived saturation level of color grows more rapidly than actual physical saturation, measured with a color-imeter. To the product tester interested in correlating sensory and instrumental reactions, this finding means that small changes in the actual physical saturation of food color will generate larger changes in saturation as perceived by the consumer. The non-linearity of saturation differs from the non-linearity of visual brightness. Our visual system expands a small range of saturation to a larger range of perceived depth of color. Table 3.6 shows some empirical data on one's perception of the perceived magnitude of color saturation for a variety of colors, obtained via well-controlled viewing conditions, using precisely specified color stimuli (Indow and Stevens 1966).

Objects change in saturation when the scientist specifies the perception in terms of percent dye in the food. Most scientific work concentrates on the actual color, measured instrumentally. If, on the other hand, the product developer wishes to correlate the concentration of *dye* in a food versus the perceived color depth of the food, then he or she should take these precautions. (1) Do the actual experiment. Do not rely upon published saturation values when evaluating perceived saturation versus dye levels. The rules governing perceived saturation versus dye level vary according to the food, and according to the dye used. (2) Test the product in the same lighting conditions. Different lighting conditions comprise a different set of wavelengths. Some light

TABLE 3.6

RELATION BETWEEN PHYSICAL SATURATION OF COLORS AND
PERCEIVED SATURATION

Note that panelists viewed a lit field through an aperture. The numbers give
the exponent of the power function: Saturation = (Physical Saturation)^n.

	Low Brightness	Increasing Brightness $\longrightarrow$			High Brightness
	Exponent	Exponent	Exponent	Exponent	Exponent
Red	1.65	1.68	1.71	1.73	1.76
Yellow	1.58	2.60	3.45	4.29	5.04
Green	1.58	1.63	1.73	1.93	2.40
Blue	1.48	1.52	1.50	1.62	1.66

Note: For an exponent of 1, doubling the physical saturation doubles the perceived saturation. For
other exponents the table below shows what occurs perceptually.

Exponent	Doubling Stimulus Level Yields This Ratio of Perceived Saturation
1.0	2.00
1.33	2.51
1.66	3.10
2.00	4.00
2.33	5.03
2.66	6.32
3.00	8.00
3.33	10.00
3.66	12.64
4.00	16.00
4.33	20.11
4.66	25.28

Source: Indow and Stevens (1966)

sources, such as daylight, stimulate colors more equally than do other
sources, such as incandescent light (which brings out the reds and
yellows) or fluorescent light (which enhances the colder, blue colors).

A study of red dye level in wax versus perceived depth of red color
showed that the relation conformed to a power function, with exponent
around 0.55. This means that when the food scientist works with dye
levels commercially obtained, the behavior substantially differs from
that shown for physical stimulus specification using colorimetry. One

needs a large change in dye level to produce a smaller increase in perceived saturation (e.g., doubling the dye level yielded about a 1.67, not 2-fold, increase in redness).

Visual Perception of Areas and Volumes

Perception of geometrical figures has captured the interest of experimenters interested in whether we actually perceive areas veridically. When someone doubles the area of a square, does the square appear twice as large? In a study of area and volume, Teghtsoonian (1965) systematically varied the physical areas of squares, circles and triangles, allowing panelists to assign magnitude estimates to all. In one part of the study, Teghtsoonian instructed panelists to scale *perceived area*, but in another part of the study she instructed panelists to estimate the *actual area*. Only the instructions differed. Instructions modified how people scale areas and surfaces. When panelists scaled perceived area, without instructions about accuracy in measurement, their ratings grew much more slowly than actual physical area. The rules governing perceived area showed a power equation with an exponent of approximately 0.7. Doubling of the physical area produced only an increase of 1.62 in perceived area. Conversely, to double the perceived area required an increase of approximately 2.7 in physical area. When the panelists received instructions to scale the actual area, rather than the perceived area, the ratings approximated a linear function. Doubling the actual area doubled the magnitude estimate of perceived area.

A typical set of data on magnitude estimation of areas appears in Table 3.7. The same individuals scaled the perceived areas of circles, squares and triangles of varying area in random order. One stimulus appeared twice, as a reliability check to ensure that the panelists' ratings replicated themselves for the same stimulus. Importantly, the data shown in Table 3.7, gathered in 1978, show similar trends to data gathered with an entirely different group of individuals in a different part of the U.S. some thirteen years before.

Similar rules govern the perception of volume as govern the perception of area. When panelists scale the perceived volumes of shapes, their ratings fall along a decelerating curve. Large increments in volume always seem smaller than one might think, based upon the actual volumes.

Application to Product Measurement

An understanding of how color intensity and saturation area relate to their respective stimulus antecedents allows the product tester these

TABLE 3.7
RELATION BETWEEN ACTUAL AREA OF DIFFERENT SHAPES
AND RATED PERCEIVED AREA
(By Magnitude Estimation)

Circles		Triangles		Squares	
Area (cm^2)	Rating	Area (cm^2)	Rating	Area (cm^2)	Rating
7.1	7.8	2.0	4.7	10.1	13.2
19.7	10.0	7.4	10.7	17.9	18.8
43.0	31.1	24.8	22.5	72.4	47.6
91.6	52.2	64.9	49.7	123.0	68.5
145.3	69.5	104.0	65.4	123.0*	69.5
216.4	106.9	322.0	92.4	203.0	97.4
Power Law } Exponent n }	0.81		0.62		0.67

*Replicate
Power Law: Perceived Area = K (Physical Area)^n

specific benefits. (1) He or she can learn how panelists perceive products which the developer modifies, by increasing the dye level, or modifying color. One can correlate perceived depth of color with actual color saturation, instrumentally measured, to obtain calibration curves which tell the product developer the likely consumer perception of known colorimetric changes. (2) He or she can gain an appreciation of how people react to changes in area. Volume and area of foods influence some of our perceptions of food. The perceptual system contracts the larger volume or larger area of a food to a smaller perceived area or volume. In actuality, any mistakes in approportioning foods for product evaluation will appear less than what one measures.

AUDITION—THE SENSE OF HEARING

We rarely think of hearing as a key sensory input to food appreciation. Consider, for a moment, the perception of fresh celery, or our reaction to a limp, wet potato chip. We chew celery, and we crack, break and otherwise mutilate a potato chip while handling it and eating it. In these instances, auditory input plays a key role as an indicator of product sensory quality.

Psychophysical Measures of Hearing

From numerous studies comes the observation that, like visual impressions of area, auditory loudness versus sound pressure falls along a decelerating psychophysical curve. Large ranges of sound pressures transform to smaller sensory ranges of loudness. A power function with exponent 0.66 relates sound pressure (P) to perceived loudness (L): $L = k(P)^{0.66}$. The function appears roughly the same for noises (or irregular combinations of different tone frequencies) and for pure tones. At the extremes of tones, however, the exponent changes, increasing at the very high frequency levels.

The Auditory System. We hear through both ears. Like vision, hearing information travels along two channels. We thus use the information from both channels to tell about the intensity of the sound, its quality (or timbre) and the location of the object. Hearing sensations, especially as they involve food, may bypass the ear. When we chew a food we react to the sound energy conducted by bone directly to the middle ear. Our appreciation of the quality and texture of celery, and other chewable foods, derives from the modified sound quality which occurs when we break the cell walls, rupture them and create sounds. To an outsider listening, the noise made by our chewing sounds different, and less acceptable, than it does to us. We listen to a modified pattern of noises when we receive the auditory information by means of bone conduction.

Sound pressure differences provide the necessary stimuli for auditory perception. The sound pressure travels in waves, creating locally compacted and locally rarified masses of air (or liquid, if we swim underwater). These masses of compaction and rarifaction push against or relieve pressure on the outer ear drum. The pressure changes transmit themselves, through the ear drum, into the middle ear, by means of three bones which provide a sensitive mechanism for transforming sound pressure in air to mechanical motion against a membrane. These bones, the stapes, the hammer and the anvil, lie in the structure known as the middle ear.

Experiments On Hearing In Food Perceptions

Until recently, little or no work appeared of a systematic nature, exploring how differences in sound spectra (different wavelengths of sound) produced different perceptions. Vickers (1975) in her Ph.D. Thesis at Cornell University began a major study to isolate sounds which one produces while chewing a food, following earlier work by Birger Drake in Sweden (1963). As one might expect, the spectra for foods

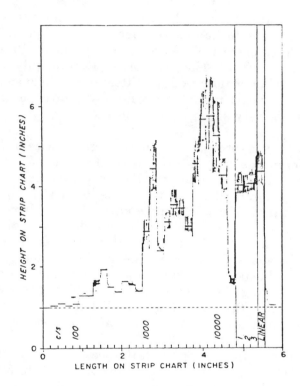

FIG. 3.5   SAMPLE OF SOUND SPECTRA GENERATED WHEN WE CRUSH FOODS
IN THE MOUTH
(C/S = Cycles per Second)

differ from each other. Figure 3.5 shows a typical set of spectra for different foods. The abscissa shows the sound frequency; the ordinate shows the amount of energy at that frequency in the noise. With experience, we should become capable of identifying foods by simply inspecting the spectra of sound energies one produces while chewing (Drake 1963).

Numerous areas of exploration remain for the food scientist interested in one of the last untouched areas of sensory perception of food. Auditory perceptions of the deaf, for example, differ from auditory perceptions of normal individuals. Partially deaf individuals may lack the ability to hear sound conducted through the air, but may detect and recognize the sounds conveyed by bone conduction. What differences exist between texture perceptions of normal and deaf people for those attributes of texture conveyed principally by hearing (e.g., crispiness, crunchiness)? Do deaf people rely on tactile perception more than do normal people when assessing these specific texture characteristics?

THE SKIN AND DEEP SENSES—
SOMESTHESIS AND KINAESTHESIS

Our skin and joints come equipped with a complex array of sensory receptors which provide us with multiple sources of information. The skin contains receptors for pressure (the Pacinian corpuscles), light and heavy touch, and pain, as well as temperature receptors. Figure 3.6 shows a schematic of the receptor systems in the skin.

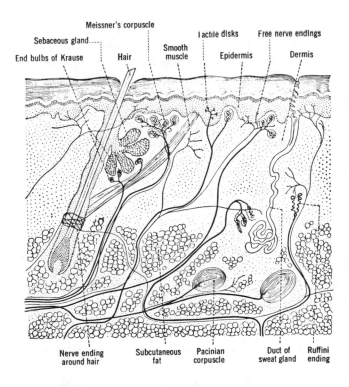

FIG. 3.6 SCHEMATIC OF THE SENSORY RECEPTORS IN THE SKIN AND JOINTS

Schematic representation of the nerve supply of the skin with sparse hair. Not all the endings shown exist in any one skin area. The heavy lines represent myelinated fibers, the light lines, nonmyelinated fibers.

Beginning a century ago, researchers attempted to determine the just noticeable differences for touch. How close on the skin can one stimulate two points with the panelist still able to discriminate the two points, rather than perceiving one point? This value represents the *two-point limen*, in classical psychophysical measurement. As expected, certain gross skin areas, such as on the back and the stomach, show higher two-point limens than the skin at the tips of the finger, or at the lips where we do much of our food sensing. We possess much greater ability to discriminate small spatial differences when evaluating stimuli on the lips or when touching the stimuli with the fingers.

Psychophysical Measures of Sensory Intensity

Researchers have generated substantial information on how sensory intensity of skin sensation varies as a function of stimulating conditions. Through magnitude estimation scaling, these results show two important facts. (1) Perception of thickness conforms to a power law with exponent 1.3. We expand small thickness differences to larger ones. We can test thickness perception by blindfolding the panelists, and instructing the panelist to rate the perceived thickness of blocks of wood held between the finger and the thumb. (2) Perception of temperature also conforms to a power law, but warmth and cold grow at different rates corresponding to different sensory mechanisms. In order to properly evaluate perceived temperature, we begin first by determining that temperature which seems neither hot nor cold. This temperature we call *physiological zero* (physiological zero lies around 35° C). We then present different temperatures to a specific portion of the body, either by shining a heat lamp on a part of the body, or by cooling a limited portion with a flow of water through a hollowed out brass block. When the experimenter follows this protocol and panelists assign magnitude estimates of hot or cold, respectively, the ratings produce a power function with one of two different exponents, depending upon whether the panelist scales perceived warmth (above physiological zero) or perceived cold (below physiological zero). We express these psychophysical functions as:

$$\text{Perceived Heat} = k(\text{Actual Temperature} - \text{Physiological Zero})^{0.7} \quad (4)$$
$$\text{Perceived Cold} = k(\text{Physiological Zero} - \text{Actual Temperature})^{1.7} \quad (5)$$

Although researchers seem not to have investigated the oral perception of temperature as they have skin temperature perceptions, the results probably would parallel each other. If so, we can conclude that people expand a small physical range of temperature gradation for cold into a much larger psychological range, but contract the range of heat perceptions. Furthermore, since the exponents for cold versus perceived warmth differ from each other, we might expect people to exhibit a larger psychological range of cold than of warmth.

The perception of pain has also intrigued investigators. Free nerve endings, distributed around the body, register the presence of the necessary stimuli for pain. In the mouth these free nerve endings respond to sharp pressure tactually applied, registering that as pain, as well as reacting to chemical irritants such as acid and chili spices which also register as pain. The perception of pain intensity grows more rapidly with physical intensity than any other sensory continuum studied to date. The psychophysical function for pain (determined via electric shock at varying amplitudes applied to the skin) shows a power function with exponent 2.0 or more. Behaviorally, a two-fold increase in physical amperage level produces a 2^2 or four-fold increase in perceived pain. The degree of acceleration of perceived pain versus physical stimulus level becomes more apparent as we increase the ratio increment to 10-fold, where the panelist feels a 100-fold more painful sensation.

THE CHEMICAL SENSES—TASTE AND SMELL

Chemical senses rank at the bottom in the hierarchy of sensory systems which the physiologist, psychologist and behavioral scientist study. In contrast, for food science they rank at the top. Forty years ago, one could summarize the published literature on taste and smell perceptions rather succinctly in a relatively short review paper or, at most, in a short book. Most of the current knowledge regarding taste and smell has appeared in the past twenty years in physiologically oriented journals, food and flavor journals, and psychology journals. Perhaps sensory analysis can count itself fortunate for the increased interest paid to the chemical sense, as scientists finding other fields well-explored turn their attention to chemoreception. Today, interest has expanded to the point where hundreds and, recently, thousands of articles appear yearly involving some aspect of taste or smell.

In the past, investigators often confused taste and smell perceptions, classifying them together or, occasionally, misclassifying smell sensations as taste sensations. Today, as a result of extensive psychological and biological investigations we know the anatomy and physiology, as well as the psychology, of both systems, and so we do not make such confusions. In popular parlance, however, people still confuse taste and smell when they talk about the flavor or taste of food. People usually consider flavor as the taste of the food, giving the taste or gustatory system the predominant role in registering food flavors. Quite the opposite; olfaction, perhaps the most neglected of the senses, plays the dominant role in registering flavor. Much of what we call flavor derives from olfactory input, some through the nose in the normal manner, and the rest through the nose in a reverse manner, beginning back at the bottom of the mouth and going upwards into the nasal cavity, through an opening and into the nose. The remainder of this chapter concerns the psychophysics and physiology of taste and smell.

THE SENSE OF TASTE

We possess two taste systems. Receptors of both systems inhabit organs in the mouth. The neural connections of the tongue reveal two distinct neural systems which innervate the tongue. The front two thirds of the tongue comprise units emanating from the chorda tympani, which itself emanates from one cranial nerve, the lingual nerve. In contrast, the back portion of the tongue comprises neural connections from the glossopharyngeal nerve, another cranial nerve. This division into two receptor systems has led some researchers in gustatory physiology to speculate that man really possesses two, not one, taste systems.

We receive taste information by responding to chemicals dissolved on the tongue, in the carrier liquid, and in saliva which we secrete from the salivary glands in the mouth (parotid gland). These taste stimuli must possess at least some marginal ability to dissolve in water, in order to reach the receptors located on the taste buds (see Fig. 3.7).

These buds contain various taste-sensitive cells. Some papillae contain taste buds which react to dissolved materials (e.g., fungiform, circumvallate), other papilla do not show sensitivity to any taste materials, whatsoever (filiform).

Mechanism of Taste

How does chemical information become sensory information? Physiologists have wondered about the "transduction" process for a century. Thousands of different chemicals excite the sense of taste. Yet, the concensus suggests that we perceive only *four* basic tastes. The other tastes really represent combinations of these four (recall Fick, as mentioned in Chapter 2 on descriptive analysis of sensations).

Two groups of researchers have offered opinions as to how the taste system recognizes quality. One group, led by Carl Pfaffmann (1974), assumes that there exists a set of four taste channels, or *labelled lines*,

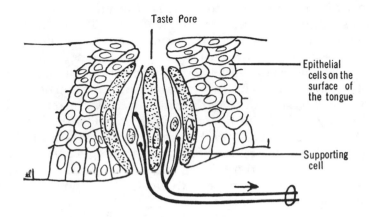

Taste Pore

Epithelial
cells on the
surface of
the tongue

Supporting
cell

FIG. 3.7 SCHEMATIC OF THE TONGUE SURFACE SHOWING THE TASTE BUD

which correspond to the four taste primaries. No matter what chemical configuration a molecule possesses, the molecule stimulates one, two, three or all four lines in varying proportions. The predominant or strongest stimulation determines the taste quality. All sensations in taste derive from that combination of primaries.

Some electrophysiological research on sensitivity to different taste materials supports the labelled line theory. Since the early 1960s, physiologists have measured the reaction of single strands or neural units in the chorda tympani by teasing out these strands, and laying them on electrodes. Application of taste solutions to the tongue of anesthetized animals, prepared in this way to dissect the specific units, showed tuning, or specific sensitivity. A neural unit sensitive to sucrose tends to fire, or react, to other sugars but not fire, or react, to salt. Statistical analysis of the sensitivities of single units shows groupings into four major categories: sweet, salty, sour and bitter, as typified by sugar, salt (sodium chloride), acid and quinine.

Erickson, at Duke University, and his colleagues in neurophysiology and psychology (Erickson, Doetsch and Marshall 1965) have hotly disputed the claim that taste possesses only four primaries, similar to the three primary colors in vision. Using methods wherein the investigor stimulates the entire tongue with a solution and records from dissected single units, Erickson reported that many so called single neural units exhibit multiple taste sensitivities. Some neural units fire or react to sugar and salt, others to bitter stimuli alone, and still other units react to stimuli of four basic tastes. According to Erickson, our brain receives a massive jumble of information from the neurons which transmit messages to it. This information fed to the brain contains within it signals about taste quality. The brain reorders the information, looking at the relative message rates of different neural units. This determines a pattern of stimulation across units. The *across-fiber* or across-unit pattern determines taste quality. We need not rely upon a labelled line which carries information pertaining only to sweet or salty, etc. Rather, the brain decodes the mass of information, looking at ratios of fiber reactions, etc. How the brain actually does this remains a mystery. Erickson developed a statistical model system which uses the relative firing rates of single units to a variety of chemicals. It converts those firing ratios to a message of taste quality. Erickson's model represents a statistical, rather than a deterministic treatment of taste perception.

Although we have limited our discussion to the neural foundations of taste perception, the reader should quickly grasp one fundamental difference in sensory analysis as implied from Pfaffmann's labelled line theory versus Erickson's across-fiber theory. According to Pfaffman, primaries in taste really do exist. Sweet, salty, sour and bitter typify basic processes of primaries which occur in the sensory coding of taste information. We perceive taste quality information which directly parallels the limited number of channels of information which the taste system possesses. According to Erickson, we may think we perceive basic taste qualities, but these qualities represent the results of statistical processing of a wider variety of input channels rather than the processing of information from four labelled lines.

Distribution of Taste Sensitivities on The Tongue

A century ago, researchers began to measure sensitivity to different taste materials as a function of position on the tongue. They found that the tongue showed a wide variety of sensitivities. Thresholds for different chemicals varied widely on the tongue. The anterior, front of the tongue, showed maximum sensitivity to sweet. The sides of the tongue showed greatest sensitivity to salty and sour materials, whereas the bitter tastes seemed to excite the posterior portion of the tongue, served by the glossopharyngeal nerve (see Fig. 3.8). Some investigators (e.g., Collings 1976) have challenged these original data and suggest that we possess different spectra of sensitivities, both in terms of (a) threshold, and (b) power function exponent. The different exponents mean that the same ratio increment in chemical concentration will produce different ratio increments of perceived taste at different parts of the tongue.

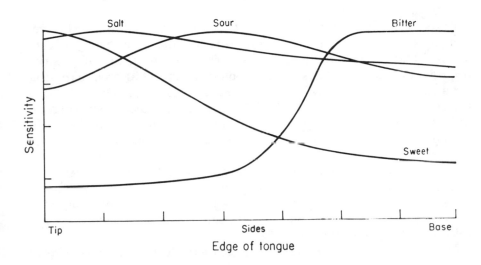

FIG. 3.8 TASTE SENSITIVITIES AT VARIOUS TONGUE REGIONS

Threshold Values

When considering the studies on thresholds and suprathreshold perceptions, we should keep in mind that many of the differences may result from stimulation of different portions of the tongue. Some investigators stimulated small, localized portions of the tongue. Whole-mouth stimulation, bringing into action many different receptors, will generally yield lower threshold values and more intense sensations than does punctate, discrete and localized stimulation. By stimulating the entire tongue, the experimenter stimulates many more available receptors, and thus increases the amount of information which reaches the brain about the taste material.

Thresholds for Taste

Taste thresholds span a very wide range of chemical concentrations. Some bitter substances possess taste thresholds as low as a thousandth or ten thousandth of a percent. Other chemicals, such as sweet sucrose or common cane sugar, reach threshold level only when they achieve a relatively high concentration of 0.5-1.0% in water.

Generally, bitter substances show the lowest thresholds, and the sweet sugars and carbohydrate chemicals show the highest threshold concentrations but not always. Table 3.8 presents absolute, or detection, thresholds as well as recognition thresholds for a variety of chemicals, arranged by groups.

For several decades now, scientists have wondered about the reasons for such wide differences in taste thresholds. Why do people seem so sensitive to bitter substances, in general, but show a lack of sensitivity to sweet and salt substances? Teleological explanations, searching for a cause in the survival value of taste sensations, suggest that the bitter materials (such as alkaloids) cause rapid death, even when an animal ingests a relatively small amount. Thus, in order to survive in the environment, the animal should detect poisonous bitter alkaloids at very low levels to avoid them.

The teleological explanation for sweetness leads to the converse hypothesis, namely, we should have become very sensitive to sweet materials. In nature sweet tasting materials contain nutritious sugars, a source of energy. We show much less sensitivity to sweets than this teleological explanation suggests.

More recent work on differences in taste in the thresholds concerns the chemical structures of taste materials, and how chemical structure affects thresholds. Researchers postulate that the differences in thresholds result from the physical configurations of the taste molecules. Some molecules more easily penetrate the receptor sites on the taste buds. Thus, they can stimulate the sense of taste at much lower concentrations. In contrast, the molecular configuration of sucrose and other sweeteners, which exhibit high thresholds, do not easily fit into the receptor. One needs a substantially higher concentration of sugar and sodium chloride molecules in order to ensure the same effective stimulation at the receptor site.

Taste Intensity Functions

For the past sixty years, researchers in various sciences have wrestled with the issue of measuring perceived taste intensity, often from the practical need to compare alternative acidulants or sweeteners, but more recently to learn how we perceive the strength of different taste materials versus changing concentration.

Often reports in the technical literature automatically, or at least implicitly, assume that perceived taste intensity relates to the ratio of threshold values. Thus, saccharin, with a threshold 1/200 that of sucrose, should taste 200 times as sweet. Many reports state that certain artificial sweeteners taste 2000-4000 times as sweet as sugar, especially the aniline derivatives discovered by the Dutch chemist,

TABLE 3.8
TASTE THRESHOLDS[1] OF A VARIETY OF CHEMICALS

Sweeteners		Acids		Salt		Bitters	
Sucrose[2]	0.01	Hydrochloric	.0009M	Lithium Chloride	.025	Quinine Sulfate	0.000008
Sucrose[2]	0.017	Nitric	.0011	Ammonium Chloride	.004	Quinine Hydrochloride	0.00003
Glucose	0.08	Sulfuric	.001	Sodium Chloride	.01	Strychnine Monohydro-	
Sodium Saccharin	0.000.23	Formic	.0018	Sodium Chloride	.03	chloride	0.0000016
		Butyric	.0020	Potassium Chloride	.015	Nicotine	.000019
		Oxalic	.0032	Magnesium Chloride	.015	Caffeine	0.0007
		Lactic	.0016	Calcium Chloride	.01	Urea	0.12
		Malic	.0016			Magnesium Sulfate	0.0046
		Tartaric	.0012				
		Citric	.0023				

[1]Concentration expressed in molar weight (molarity — gram molecular weight/liter).
[2]Detection threshold.
Source: Pfaffmann (1959)

Verkade, and the miracle fruit and monellin protein based sweeteners which exhibit a substantially lower threshold than sucrose. This direct translation of relative threshold values to relative sweetness values misleads. Just because we taste one sweetener at a much lower threshold than we do another does not mean that the former tastes much sweeter than the latter. Thresholds, by definition, represent the same point on the sensory intensity scale: the point at which the sensory intensity scale begins. Thresholds must equal each other perceptually, although the physical concentrations of different substances at threshold do not.

In order to truly measure taste intensity, the investigator requires a procedure which can quantify different levels of sensory magnitude. In lieu of an adequate sensory scale paralleling scales for physical measurements, early researchers turned to the tedious method of *equal-intensity matching*, previously used by psychologists. Let us reanalyze the match between sweetness of sugar and saccharin, reported by two groups of researchers in the 1920s, and shown in Fig. 3.9 (Moskowitz 1970).

In these studies the panelists tasted a number of different saccharin solutions. For each saccharin test solution, the panelists selected a sucrose solution which tasted equally sweet by direct comparison. Needless to say, such a procedure takes quite a while to implement. The panelist first tastes the saccharin stimulus, and then tastes the different sucrose solutions in order to find which sucrose solution matches. Panelists may, and often do disagree with each other. Thus, the average matching level of sucrose to a given saccharin level lies somewhere between the actual concentrations tested, and represents a consensus, intermediate value.

The results of this and similar studies generate equal-intensity matches. Some representative equal-intensity matches worthy of consideration appear in the next three paragraphs.

Magidson and Gorabachow (1923) and Taufel and Klemm (1925) reported matches between the sweetness of saccharin and sucrose as shown in Fig. 3.9. The matching function revealed that one needed a much smaller increment of sucrose to match a large increment in saccharin concentration. We deduce that, in terms of concentration, perceived sweetness of saccharin grows more slowly than perceived sweetness of sucrose. A large change in saccharin level equals (in sweetness) a smaller change in sucrose level. Furthermore, the two data sets shown in Fig. 3.9 lie atop each other. The matching function describes a nonlinear curve which straightens out when one plots the logarithm of saccharin solution versus the logarithm of sucrose solu-

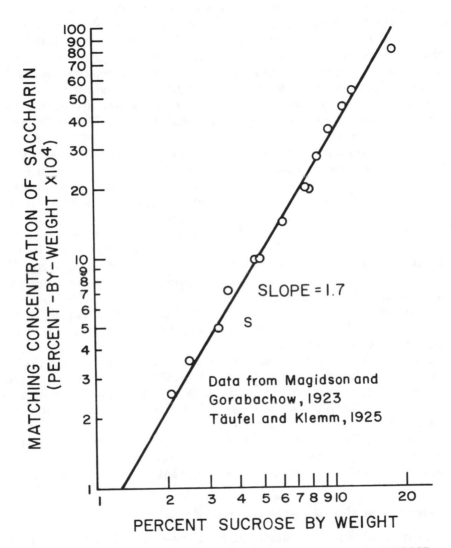

FIG. 3.9 EQUAL-SWEETNESS MATCHES BETWEEN SACCHARIN AND SUCROSE
Source: Moskowitz (1970)

tion. This leads to the important mathematical description of the matching function as:

log Saccharin = log k + 1.7 (log Sucrose) or   (6)
Saccharin = k (Sucrose)$^{1.7}$ (7)

A 10-fold increase in sucrose produces a necessary $10^{1.7}$, or fifty-fold increase in saccharin necessary to maintain the sweetness match.

Paul (1916) carried out a similar study on acids, matching a wide variety of acids against tartaric acid. Again, the matching functions showed curvature, but became straight lines in logarithmic coordinates. More importantly, Paul's study on acids showed that one could generate equal-intensity matches in another taste modality, sourness.

Pangborn (1963) also found panelists could reliably match the sweetness of different sugars when panelists matched levels of sucrose with glucose, fructose and lactose.

Equal taste-intensity matches, like equal loudness matches in audition, provide a method for measuring sensory intensity. The investigator need not worry about the panelist's idiosyncratic use of scales of sensory magnitude, nor about the validity of the sensory scale. On the other hand, other problems arise in equal intensity matching. (1) Equal taste intensity matches do not generate a true measure of sensory intensity, per se. Rather, the panelist acts as a balancing instrument, showing equivalence of two stimuli in terms of tasting equally sweet (or equally sour, etc.). (2) Taste matching takes a long time and fatigues the panelist. Fatigue introduces biases which affect the data, e.g., adaptation, or loss of sensitivity, because other, previously tasted materials still lie on the tongue, exerting their influence and interfering with the next stimulus.

Finally, a curious chapter in the history of equal-intensity matches comes from the reports on matches between sweet and salt. These *heteroqualitative* matches (to distinguish them from equal-sweetness or iso-qualitative matches) appear in Fig. 3.10. Panelists found a concentration of sucrose which tasted as *sweet* as a concentration of salt tasted *salty*. The matching data shows more variability than equal-sweet matches, but nonetheless panelists seemed to tap into a general measure of taste intensity to generate the equal intensity match.

Category Scales of Taste Intensity

With the growing popularity of category scaling in attitudinal and sensory measurement, it became only a matter of time before researchers in taste psychophysics would use fixed point category scales to quantify the perception of taste intensity. Category scales improved the science of measurement, because panelists could use a truly subjective unit of sensory intensity to represent taste strength, rather than limiting their ratings to equal sweetness matches.

With category scales one cannot say that a sweet stimulus rated 4 (e.g., on a 9 point scale) tastes half as sweet as a stimulus rated 9. On

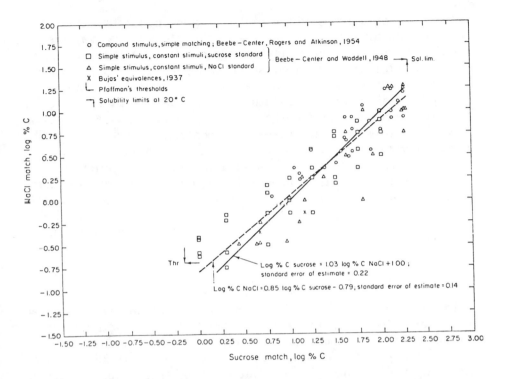

FIG. 3.10 EQUAL TASTE INTENSITY MATCHES BETWEEN SALT AND SUGAR
(From Beebe-Center, Atkinson and Rogers, 1955)

the other hand, the category scale illustrates how different in intensity two stimuli taste (whether they represent different concentrations of the same sugar or acid, or equal concentrations of different sugars or acids). Category scales ostensibly measure true psychological differences (although, in fact, they do not). Hence, the scientist can obtain a measure of relative difference between stimuli by using the scale. Keep in mind that one could not measure these psychological taste differences by relying on equal intensity matches (e.g., between sweeteners). By changing the unit of measurement from sucrose concentration to saccharin concentration, one also changes the size of the unit. The same two sweeteners, at different levels, would lie closer together on the sucrose-matching scale than on the saccharin-matching scale.

Recall Fig. 3.2 which shows a representative set of category scales for the perceived sweetness of various sweeteners, as reported by Schutz and Pilgrim (1957). The Schutz and Pilgrim data provide key improvements over previous, equal-sweetness measures, such as the capability to better measure differences of taste intensity on a common scale of perceptual magnitude; and a simpler, more efficient method for determining sensory sweetness levels with a measuring instrument, (the scale) that one can transport from location to location, and which maintains a degree of constancy independent of test conditions.

Category scales confirm that perceived sweetness does not grow equally rapidly with concentration for all sweet tasting chemicals. Some of the curves reported by Schutz and Pilgrim appear concave or bowed upwards. Small increases in concentration produce relatively larger increases in sweetness category rating. Other curves appear convex or bowed downwards. Small changes in concentration produce even smaller relative increases in the category rating for sweetness. Unfortunately, category scales with their unsupportable claims of equal-intervals between adjacent categories, their lack of a fixed zero and their arbitrary upper limit deprive the researcher of a better measure of relative sweetness.

Ratio Scaling of Taste Intensity

In the 1960s, Stevens (1969) reported the results of several studies which measured taste intensity using magnitude estimation scaling. Panelists used magnitude estimation scaling to rate sucrose sweetness and sodium chloride saltiness. The ratings generated scales of taste intensity similar to scales of loudness, brightness, etc. As he had discovered for so many other continua, Stevens reported that taste intensity also conformed to the general power law governing sensory intensity:

$$\text{Sensory Intensity} = k\,(\text{Physical Intensity})^n \tag{6}$$

In logarithmic coordinates this becomes a straight line:

$$\text{Log Sensory Intensity} = \log K + n\,(\text{Log Physical Intensity}) \tag{7}$$

For sugar and salt, sensory intensity equals the average magnitude estimate from a population of panelists. Physical intensity equals a measure of concentration, either molarity, molality or percent concentration. The parameters k and n vary with the particular use of numbers, and the slope of the function in logarithmic coordinates.

Recall the implications of the power function. It shows how rapidly sensory intensity grows with physical concentration. Since magnitude estimates possess ratio-scale properties, we can legitimately compare ratios of sensory taste perceptions to ratios of concentrations. For sucrose and sodium chloride the power function exponent exceeds 1.0.

This means that small ratios of concentrations produce larger ratios of taste intensities. On the other hand, for acid and bitter quinine, the exponents lie closer to 1.0, meaning that we transform physical ratios of concentration to equal, or even smaller, sensory ratios of taste.

Since the pioneering early work, many investigators have used magnitude estimation to measure the relative rate of growth of taste intensity for structurally different chemicals. These studies used one of two procedures to present the taste stimulus: (1) Sip-and-spit where the panelist sips the material from a cup from as little as 10 cc of material to 100 cc or more, depending upon the particular study—this method generates higher exponents for the power function of taste versus concentration (Meiselman 1971); (2) dorsal flow procedure where the panelist extends his or her tongue outside the mouth and a gravity fed system flows a continuous stream of taste material over the extended portion of the tongue to provide a steady stimulus, usually maintained at physiological zero tongue temperature (about 35-37° C)—the dorsal flow method generates smaller power function exponents (McBurney 1965).

Table 3.9 summarizes the exponents for different chemicals and tastes. Table 3.9 also indicates the ratio of concentrations needed to increase the taste perception by a factor of two.

TABLE 3.9
EXPONENTS FOR TASTE INTENSITY VERSUS CONCENTRATION

Taste		Exponent	Necessary Concentration Change to Double Taste Intensity
Sweetness of	Sucrose	1.3	1.69
	Saccharin	0.6	3.16
	Cyclamate	0.8	2.38
	Aspartame	1.0	2.00
Saltiness	Sodium Chloride	1.3 (sipping)	1.69
	Sodium Chloride	0.4 (dorsal flow)	5.66
Sourness	Citric Acid	0.7	2.66
Bitterness	Quinine Sulfate (depending on the study)	0.6-1.0	3.16-2.00

Some Observations on Ratio Scaling—Exponents for Taste

The early work on taste scaling concerned the exponent values for taste intensity. In the main these studies showed that taste perception generated different exponents. One general power function with a single exponent could simply not apply to the growth of different taste qualities versus concentration. For example, sweet sugars and salts generated an accelerating function versus concentration, whereas sourness of acid and bitterness of quinine generated a decelerating function versus concentration. These observations confirmed both Stevens' original work on simple taste scaling during the early 1960s, and observations by Beebe-Center (1949) with regard to the psychophysical GUST scale of taste intensity.

A further complication to mar the simplicity of taste intensity functions arose with respect to the different exponents for the same quality. Sugar sweetness grew as accelerating functions of concentration. Sucrose and fructose sweetness, in turn, behaved anomalously at high concentrations (Moskowitz 1971). The sweetness curves flattened out at concentrations above 1.0 M. This suggested unusual changes in the taste mechanism—perhaps an upper limit in the gustatory system for the appreciation of sweetness, or some unusual properties of the sweetener molecule. These same anomalies for sucrose and fructose sweetness appeared in equal-sweetness ratings which the Canadian investigator Cameron (1947) had reported some 24 years previously.

In contrast to sugar, saccharin and cyclamate sweetness generate very different sweetness functions. Saccharin and cyclamate sweetness ratings grow more slowly than concentration, not more quickly. This contrast with sweetness functions for carbohydrate sweeteners suggests either a different mechanism underlying the sweetness of artificial sweeteners, or the possibility that our perception of saccharin sweetness results from the simultaneous interaction of sweetness and bitterness, with each suppressing the other. Only sugar sweetness shows a true sweetness function, unadulterated by the continual presence of bitterness. When we measure saccharin or cyclamate sweetness, we really do not measure the underlying sweetness, but rather the dynamic equilibrium of a mixture, only part of which comprises sweetness (Moskowitz and Klarman 1975).

Finally, from time to time arguments arise regarding the true value of the psychophysical equation for sweetness and other taste qualities. What exponent does sweetness really possess? Academic as this query sounds, the answer carries with it profound consequences to the food industry. If perceived sweetness truly grows as an accelerating function of concentration, then we can conclude that small increases in sugar level entail larger increments in sweetness. Furthermore, quality control methods for sugar sweetened products, which aim at maintaining desired sweetness, must exert rigid controls on the sugar concentration. Small changes (e.g., downwards, for controlled reduction in concentration) should produce magnified reductions in perceived sweetness. They do, as shown in Table 3.10 which demonstrates the results of a beverage study in which panelists rated the sweetness of six different carbonated beverages, each with a different sugar concentration. Note the difference in perceived sweetness corresponding to the small change in concentration (Moskowitz, Jacobs and Firtle 1980). Similar considerations apply to products with other sweet substances as well.

TABLE 3.10
SWEETNESS RATINGS FOR SIX CARBONATED
SWEETENED BEVERAGES

Relative Sugar Level	Sweetness Rating (Magnitude Estimation)
100	83.0
95	77.1
90	69.3
85	54.0
80	46.5
75	43.5

Source: Moskowitz, Jacobs and Firtle (1980)

Some Observations on Ratio Scaling—
The Intercept of the Power Function

The early psychophysical work concerning magnitude estimation often overlooked the intercept, k, as an arbitrary factor in the psychophysical power function: $S = kI^n$. The intercept k varies with the size of numbers that panelists use. In the early studies, researchers focused their interest on the exponent without considering the additional information that the intercept could provide. The intercept would vary randomly, according to the idiosyncratic choice of numbers which the panelists exhibited.

With the study of different sweeteners, acidulants and the like, all scaled by the same panelists with the same number system, the intercept acquires importance as a measure of relative taste intensity for these reasons. (1) One uses the intercept, as well as the exponent, when calculating the expected taste intensity of a stimulus. (2) For any pair of stimuli, whether representing the same chemical at different concentrations, or different chemicals scaled under the same conditions with the same numerical scale, one can use the exponent and intercept to calculate the expected sensory intensity (by means of the power equation). The ratio of the magnitude estimates equals the sensory ratio. (3) If the exponent remains the same for two substances (e.g., two sweeteners, lactose and glucose), then the ratio of intercepts equals the sensory ratio of perceived intensities.

FACTORS WHICH AFFECT TASTE PERCEPTION

We can modify taste perception by changing various parameters of the stimulus, or in some cases by stimulating or anesthetizing the tongue itself. Researchers interested in changing taste perception usually do so by interfering either with the physical carrier of the stimulus, (i.e., by substituting a viscosified stimulus in place of a water solution), or by varying the area and location on the tongue which they stimulate.

Effect of Solvent on Taste

The solvent system delivering the taste material influences how strong the taste seems, as well as affecting our ability to detect the taste material. Observations going back more than 20 years on viscosifying the carrier solvent, revealed that the increased viscosity increased threshold, or lowered sensitivity, to taste (Mackey 1958; Mackey and Valassi 1956). In one study, Mackey measured detection thresholds for the different taste compounds presented in one of three different types of solvents: simple water solution, oil solution, or water thickened with a vegetable gum (sodium carboxy methylcellulose) so that the water viscosity equalled the viscosity of the oil solution. The results showed maximum sensitivity in simple water solution, where nothing interfered with the ability of the stimulus to get to the taste receptor site on the tongue. Detectability diminished and threshold increased maximally for the lipid, or oil solvent, suggesting the necessity of an aqueous solution. The thickened water solution (with vegetable gum) reduced sensitivity, but less than the oil solvent did. Panelists showed greater sensitivity to the chemical dissolved in a gum thickened solvent than to taste material dissolved in oil solvent. Viscosity plays a definite, but not the entire, role as a blocking agent to reduce taste. The type of solvent also plays a role.

In the other study on type of medium (gel, foam, liquid), Mackey tried to expand these results even further to determine whether the physical property of the solvent could modify sensitivity to taste. It did. By comparing detectability in liquids, gels and foams, Mackey found that sensitivity appeared greatest (threshold lowest) in water and lowest in gels. Again, we might expect these results by considering how well each system can block the access of taste molecules to the receptors in the tongue. A gel, with its almost-solid matrix, should block the entrance of taste-stimulating molecules to the receptor better than a liquid, wherein the molecules can move around quite a bit more.

Taste thresholds present only part of the picture. We must augment our knowledge by evaluating the effects of these solvents on suprathreshold taste intensity, where we obtain clear sensory impressions. Several studies have directly addressed these issues. An early study by Stone and Oliver (1966) on relative taste intensity in thickened solutions showed that panelists ranked the thicker solutions more sweet than thinner solutions. This unusual result contradicted their own threshold work, reported in the same study, where they found that panelists exhibited higher thresholds (lower sensitivity) for sweeteners in viscosified solutions. One difficulty with this study may derive from panelist confusion between thickness and sweetness. Since thick sugar solutions usually taste most sweet, panelists may have confused the added viscosity with added sweetener level.

Later studies by Arabie and Moskowitz (1971) and by Moskowitz and Arabie (1970) using magnitude estimation to rate sweetness, saltiness, sourness and bitterness of a variety of taste materials, with varying levels of the tasteless thickener, sodium carboxy methylcellulose, showed that taste intensity systematically diminished as solvent viscosity increased. Concentration played a far greater role in increasing taste intensity than did solvent viscosity in diminishing taste intensity. These investigators related viscosity, concentration and taste intensity by a power function comprising two factors:

$$\text{Taste Intensity} = k\,(\text{Concentration})^n\,(\text{Viscosity})^m$$

The exponent n for concentration far exceeded the exponent m for viscosity.

In general, viscosity seems to play a role in modifying taste intensity, albeit not an extremely important one. Other viscosifying agents besides sodium carboxy methylcellulose would probably produce similar results.

Effect of Temperature on Taste

People sometimes remark that food tastes different cold than warm. Complex foods, with volatiles, give off more volatiles when warm than when cold which, in turn, provides a more intense odor stimulus. Even in the case of pure taste stimulation, however, with no olfactory component at all, it appears that temperature differences may enhance or reduce perceived taste intensity. Which effect occurs, enhancement or suppression, seems not alltogether clear. Experimenters have reported conflicting results, adnmuch of the extant work appears in a summary table in Table 3.11.

TABLE 3.11
RELATION BETWEEN TEMPERATURE AND SWEETNESS:
A HISTORICAL PERSPECTIVE
(Moskowitz 1981A)

Reference	Conditions	Results
Luchtmans (1758)	Immerse tongue in water at 40-41° C or in ice-water.	Could not recognize sweetness of sugar.
Kiesow (1896)	Immerse tongue in water either 0° or 50° C. In other studies, Kiesow investigated intermediate temperature of solutions.	No taste sensation, even of concentrated stimuli. Solution temperature had little effect (e.g., at 5° solution sensitivity as great as at 30° C).
Schreiber (1893)	Measured thresholds of sucrose at 3 temperatures.	Threshold for sucrose: at 3° and 40° = 0.1M; at 0° C = 0.4M
Chinaglia (1915)	(a) Used a U-shaped tube on the subject's tongue to pass heated or cold water. Measured thresholds at 5°-50° C at 5° intervals.	Little temperature effect found.
	(b) Measured reaction time to taste stimuli at either 17° C, 37° C or 50° C.	For 10% sucrose, reaction time slower as the temperature diminished.
Komuro (1920)	Sprayed 200-500 cc of solution on tongue for 5 minutes. solutions at 10°, 20, 30°, 40°, respectively.	Thresholds for sucrose (grams of sucrose/litre) 10° = 12.30 G/L; 20° = 6.67 G/L; 30° = 5.66 G/L; 40° = 5.33 G/L.
Goudriann (1930)	Flowed taste solution of varying temperatures onto tongue. Stimuli at 10°, 15°-21°, 40° C.	For 10% sucrose, as the temperature rises, the sweetness rises.

TABLE 3.11 (Continued)

Reference	Conditions	Results
Hahn and Gunther (1932)	U tube used to flow solution over tongue. Limited temperature to 17°–47° to limit pain.	For sucrose, threshold drops down with temperature increase (from 17° to 32°) and then rises again.
Hahn (1936)	Evaluated adaptation curve by measuring threshold vs elapsed time since the continuing stimulation first applied.	Different adaptation curves appear depending upon temperature.
Shallenberger (1963)	Increase temperature and rate sweetness.	Sweetness increases with higher temperature.
Stone, Oliver and Kloehn (1969)	Magnitude estimates of sweetness of glucose and fructose + their mixtures at 5°, 22° and 50°.	No temperature effect.
Moskowitz (1973)	5 concentrations of glucose tested at 25°, 30°, 35°, 40, 45°, 50° by magnitude estimation.	Power functions fitted to sweetness unaffected by temperature. Maximum overall sweetness around 37°.

Although we do not know for sure the exact role of temperature on taste, because of the disparities in the scientific literature, we do know that as we warm or cool the tongue we modify the sensory information going to the brain. The tongue houses temperature receptors as well as taste receptors. Any modification of the stimulus or ambient tongue temperature will surely send additional, and perhaps interfering messages to the brain, to compete with the taste information.

Effect of Flow Rates and Flow Characteristics on Taste

Until recently, scientists failed to attend to the nature of oral stimulation as comprising a sequence of ebbs and flows of liquid on the tongue. With the advent of psychophysical scaling and the development of more precise methods for control, researchers recently investigated taste perception as a function of the type of flow over the tongue. In doing so, experimenters have utilized different types of flow (whole mouth sip-and-spit, whole mouth irrigation, dorsal flow over the extended tongue), different rates of flow, and different temporal characteristics of the flow. These present a fairly coherent picture.

Dorsal flow procedures, in which the panelist extends his or her tongue and a constant stream flows over the tongue, generate power functions with relatively low exponents. Whole mouth irrigation, via a forced flow under a pressurized system, generates higher exponents. Furthermore, the taste sensation seems stronger. Finally, the traditional sip-and-spit procedure, commonly used by researchers and representative of normal food and liquid ingestion, generates the highest power function exponents (Meiselman 1971).

Flow rates influence taste intensity, changing both the power function and the overall intensity of sensation. Meiselman (1971) reported some elegant work on varying the flow rate of liquid across the tongue. In order to achieve the necessary stimulus control, he developed a tongue chamber, fitting around the tongue, which permitted the stimulus liquid to flow over the surface of the tongue and escape by a second channel. Pressurized stimulus solution coursed over the tongue at varying rates. With higher pressure and thus faster flow, panelists perceived the stimulus as tasting more intense, even though the actual physical concentration of the taste stimulus remained unchanged. Panelists felt that the taste increased; not that the stimulus flowed faster. Furthermore, the effect of flow rate appeared dramatic, and even more potent than the effect of concentration. Changes in flow rate produced greater effect than the same ratio increments in concentration.

In recent years, investigators in various disciplines have studied the actual mechanical behavior in the mouth which occurs during eating and drinking (Halpern and Meiselman 1977). A panelist who drinks a liquid does not make that liquid flow steadily over the tongue and into the esophagus. Rather, people drink in a pulsatile fashion, ingesting small amounts at each pulse. The pulsatile drinking and ingestion modifies the sequence of oral stimulation. The tongue comes in contact with a pulse of taste material, not a steady flow. Furthermore, this pulsatile behavior reduces susceptibility to adaptation, as well as influences perceived taste intensity. Meiselman and Halpern (1973) investigated the relation between taste intensity and the pulsatile presentation of taste stimuli. As one might expect, pulsatile stimulation enhanced overall taste intensity.

Prior Adaptation To Taste

We live in a world which constantly stimulates our sensory receptors. Our tongue bathes in a pool of saliva secreted by the salivary glands. Saliva contains salts, mucopolysaccharides and proteins in various combinations. Each of these chemicals and most especially sodium chloride and other salts, continually stimulate the tongue. Yet, we do not sense the salt in our saliva, for we quickly adapt to the ambient salivary salt level. What occurs when we test individuals whose saliva no longer stimulates, because the saliva now contains only pure, distilled water, rather than the complex biologically emitted mixture? Can panelists with distilled water as their saliva taste salt at below salivary levels? If so, then prior adaptation to taste could strongly affect taste intensity. The distilled water replacement would regenerate sensitivity to salt at the low levels.

Eighteen years ago at Brown University, McBurney (1965) reported the results of adaptation on taste in his Ph.D. thesis. In one portion of the study, McBurney determined threshold values for sodium chloride, both with the presence of ambient saliva and after extensive rinsing with distilled water to eliminate the stimulating and adapting effects of saliva. The threshold values for salt in the presence of normal, ambient saliva appeared much higher than the corresponding threshold values for salt obtained after the extensive rinse with distilled water. As a general finding, the threshold value for salt achieved a value slightly higher than the ambient salt level in the mouth, 0.01 M. McBurney could thus modify the salt threshold by systematically varying the prior level of sodium chloride on the tongue (by pre-rinsing with different salt levels in the pre-rinse water solution).

In a parallel series of experiments, this time using suprathreshold test levels and magnitude estimation scaling, McBurney found that he could modify the psychophysical saltiness function (versus salt concentration) by systematically varying the level of salt. The function appears in Fig. 3.11. The reader should keep in mind that the saltiness function changes its shape at levels around and below the ambient salt content of the rinse solution (or in saliva), but remains unaffected at levels above the ambient salt concentration. For sensory analysis, we conclude that the ambient level of taste material in the mouth (especially salt, but perhaps bitter materials as well) primarily affects values lower than itself, rather than exerting any noticeable influence on higher concentrations. In practical terms, we generally detect and scale sensory intensities above the ambient level in a manner unaffected by the actual ambient level.

Implications of Adaptation for Product Testing

During the course of a product testing session, the panelist may taste a variety of different stimuli. Sensory analysts worry about adaptation, because it reduces sensory acuity and prevents panelists from detecting differences among stimuli.

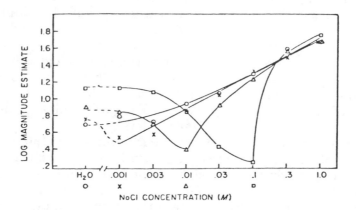

FIG. 3.11 RELATION BETWEEN TASTE INTENSITY AND CONCENTRATION OF SALT AS
ADAPTATION AFFECTS IT

Effect of adaptation on the sensation magnitude of NaCl. Each curve represents the response to NaCl
after adaptation to the concentration indicated by the respective symbols. The increase in sensation
magnitude as concentration decreases below the adapting level indicates the water taste.
Source: McBurney, 1965

Can and do adaptation and cross adaptation really exert such
strong effects? To answer this question, let us first consider what
occurs in normal drinking and eating. Recall that we eat and drink in
discrete steps, rather than in a continuous, adapting fashion which
would lead to rapid adaptation. We do not seem to lose any taste
sensitivity by continually eating when we follow this regimen of stimu-
lation-interruption-stimulation. We adapt only when we stimulate the
tongue in a continual fashion over an extended period of time, longer
than for normal ingestion. Furthermore, as we saw, adaptation occurs
primarily at concentrations lower than the concentration of the adapting stimulus. These findings imply the following considerations (1) In
product testing, we should worry about adaptation only when the
stimulus sequence comprises weak stimuli following shortly after very
strong stimuli. The opposite order (first weak, then strong) should not
affect taste sensitivity. (2) With short waits between samples (3 min or
so), most effects of adaptation should dissipate. Perhaps the primary
effect will involve a loss of some, but not all, sensitivity to threshold
level stimuli. Suprathreshold stimuli, which we clearly detect and
scale, should show virtually complete independence of previous stimuli, given this regimen of waiting between samples for a short period.
(3) When two stimuli have different taste qualities, adaptation
becomes rarer, and we need worry even less (McBurney and Lucas
1966).

Area of Taste Stimulation and Taste Intensity

Although we usually ingest food with our entire mouth, the sensory input comes primarily through receptors on the tongue, as well as receptors on the hard and soft palates, etc. We can severely restrict our sensory input by blocking the hard and soft palates with dentures, or by modifying the course of liquids over the tongue so that they flow only onto a restricted area. Each restriction modifies taste perception.

Anecdotal reports in the scientific literature suggest that patients with dentures have difficulty perceiving and appreciating the flavors of foods. Difficulties may arise from the unnaturalness of dentures. Furthermore, dentures hinder access of taste materials to the roof of the mouth, blocking both taste receptors and tactile/pain receptors. Finally, dentures may interfere with the normal breakup of foods in the mouth, which releases the volatile materials into the mouth and, therefore, into the nose by a pathway in the back of the mouth which leads to the nose.

One can also restrict the area of the tongue to a limited, pie-shaped portion of predefined area and shape. This restriction alters taste intensity. Smith (1971) instructed panelists to scale taste sweetness of saccharin solutions which varied both in molar concentration, and in the amount of tongue area that they stimulated. Smith had to construct a chamber to house the tongue and which allowed him to control the stimulus access. This chamber restricted access of the taste solution to specific tongue locations. By obtaining magnitude estimates of taste intensity, simultaneously varying area and concentration, Smith developed an equation which revealed the trade-off between area and concentration as co-determinants of overall sensory intensity:

$$\text{Taste Intensity} = K(\text{Area})^{0.15}(\text{Concentration})^{0.41}$$

Note that area plays a lesser role than concentration. The exponent for area, 0.15, means that to double sourness, with acid concentration held constant, one needs a 102-fold increase in the surface area stimulated. In contrast, the exponent for concentration, 0.41, means that to double taste intensity, with area held constant, requires a 4.50 increase in concentration.

TASTE MIXTURES, ADDITIVITY AND SUPPRESSION

Rarely do we taste stimuli comprising one of the four qualities alone. Most taste impressions comprise a combination of tastes, with 2, 3 or even 4 tastes present to varying degrees. Thirty-one years ago, Beebe-Center (1949) mapped out taste quality profiles for a variety of different foods. Even such predominantly sweet foods as honey stimulate tastes besides the predominant sweetness. Table 3.12 shows the taste profiles of some common foods, with the numbers reflecting the amount of GUSTS which each food comprises.

TABLE 3.12

TASTE QUALITY PROFILES OF DIFFERENT FOODS ACCORDING TO BEEBE-CENTER'S GUST SCALE OF TASTE INTENSITY

Food	Sweet	Bitter	Acid	Salty	Total
Consomme	1.4	1.3	4.5	7.9	15.1
Alsatian Wine	1.0	7.5	6.7	1.3	16.5
Cola	11.2	2.2	5.0	1.3	19.7
Pickles	1.0	1.8	18.0	3.2	24.0
Beer (Ale)	2.5	28.2	10.0	1.3	42.0
Grapefruit Drink	3.2	2.0	35.5	2.0	42.7
Coffee (No Sugar)	1.0	42.3	3.2	1.0	47.5
Coffee (5% Sucrose)	3.2	23.8	3.2	1.3	31.5
Honey	56.4	2.4	1.8	1.3	61.9

Note: 1 GUST = sweetness (or taste intensity) of 1 gram of sucrose dissolved in 100 ml of water.
Source: Beebe-Center (1949)

Scientists have extensively investigated taste mixtures in their effort to determine how we sense mixtures (the physiological/psychological approach), and to engineer specific taste impressions in actual foods (the technological approach). In order to do so, they have mixed together varying taste stimuli in water solutions (among other solvents), obtained ratings for the components tasted separately (e.g., sugar alone, acid alone, each dissolved in aqueous solvent) and then obtained ratings for the mixtures with both stimuli acting in concert. In some studies, the mixtures comprised components having the same taste quality. In other studies, researchers investigated heteroqualitative mixtures comprising components of different taste qualities.

Mixtures Comprising Components of The Same Taste

Practical application of taste research often concerns the taste of mixtures of pairs of sweeteners or acidulants. A food product developers may wish to enhance the sweetening power of a mixture of sweeteners by mixing together sucrose and glucose. Until cyclamate came under FDA ban, consumers could purchase commercially available mixtures of saccharin and cyclamate, premixed in a 1:10 ratio. These mixtures provided a more acceptable sweet taste than did saccharin or cyclamate alone, owing to the additivity of sweetness and to the suppressing effect that cyclamate and saccharin exerted on each other's bitter component. In many beverages today, we see mixtures of acidulants which provide added sourness, and perk up, or enhance, the flavor of the beverage. Fruit flavored beverages often taste far better with a mixture of acids than they taste when formulated with a single acid alone.

Researchers do studies to determine whether the mixture of like-tasting compounds generate an enhanced taste impression, over and above the taste impression which would emerge from the simple addition of the two components. We call this enhanced impression of taste intensity *synergism*. Until the advent of direct psychophysical scaling in the 1950s, investigators used cumbersome matching procedures to determine the presence and nature of synergism, and often ran into problems. A synopsis of Cameron's elegant work, appearing from 1944-1947, illustrates the approach and the problems which ensue.

Cameron investigated the sweet taste of mixtures of pairs of sugars, and mixtures of sugar with amino acids, in an effort to determine the underlying laws governing sweetness additivity. In order to carry out the experiment, but at the same time lacking a valid ratio scale to measure taste perception, Cameron used the method of equal-sweetness matches, as Taufel and Klemm and others had done some twenty years before. To measure the mixture sweetness (mixtures of A + B respectively), Cameron instructed panelists to follow this testing sequence. (1) Find the equally sweet concentration of glucose which matched the sweetness of mixture component A tested alone. A could represent glucose itself, fructose, maltose, etc., at a fixed concentration. Call this matching glucose concentration level A'. (2) Find the equally sweet concentration of glucose which matched the sweetness of mixture component B alone. B might represent an amino acid, or another sugar. Call this level B'. (3) Determine the concentration of glucose which tasted as sweet as the mixture of A and B. Call this C'.

This exercise generates a set of three glucose concentrations A', B' and C', the first two corresponding to the components, and the third to the mixture. Additivity occurs when $A' + B'$ equals C'. This calculation reveals whether or not sweetness obeys simple additive rules. Note that this procedure implies that the unit of sensory sweetness equals a unit of sugar concentration. Cameron chose glucose as the reference sugar. Therefore, glucose concentration became the de facto unit of sweetness: Had Cameron chosen sucrose as the unit of sweetness, panelists would have matched A to an equally sweet sucrose concentration, as well as matching B and C to equally sweet sucrose concentrations.

Table 3.13 shows some of Cameron's matches. In general, mixtures of sweeteners exhibit simple additivity when glucose serves as the reference sweetener, but not when sucrose or fructose serve as the reference sweetener. Mixtures of amino acids with sugars do not show additivity. The mixture tastes less sweet than one would expect on the basis of simple arithmetic additivity of the reference sweetener level.

TABLE 3.13
SOME REPRESENTATIVE EQUAL-SWEETNESS MATCHES

Matching Level (Mixture)	As Sweet As
1. 10% sucrose + 5.5% glucose	15% sucrose
2. 5% sucrose + 11.8% glucose	15% sucrose
3. 10% sucrose + 10.15% glucose	20% sucrose
4. 5% sucrose + 10.8% lactose	10% sucrose
5. 5% glucose + 9% lactose	10% glucose
6. 2% sucrose + 5% glucose + 10% lactose	10.1% sucrose
7. 6% glycine* + 3.9% sucrose	12% glycine*
8. 5% glycine* + 5.3% glucose	10% glycine*
9. 1% sucrose + 2% fructose	4.8% sucrose

*Amino Acid
Source: Cameron (1947)

Problems With The Approach. According to Cameron (and to other later investigators such as Yamaguchi (1970) and her colleagues in Japan who used equal-sweetness matches), the unit of sweetness measurement becomes the concentration of sweetener. We know, furthermore, that we can describe the relation between concentration and sweetness by a power function with exponent greater than 1.0 for most sugars. The exponent approximates 1.3 for sucrose and glucose sweetness. Hence, the addition of the same concentration to itself, each component of which shows a non-linear relation with numbers, should generate an overestimation. Specifically, adding glucose to itself should produce 2.46 units of matching sweetness. The approach appears below:

Addition in light of the power law of glucose sweetness

Arithmetic Addition
Glucose + Glucose = 2 Glucose = 2 Units of concentration
  Power Law Addition
1 Glucose + 1 Glucose = $(2 \text{ Glucose})^{1.3}$ = 2.46 Units of sweetness, not 2 units

Let us follow the same logic, this time with a sweetener such as saccharin which follows the law of diminishing returns. The power function of saccharin exhibits an exponent less than 1.0. Assume now that panelists match the sweetness of components and the mixture to equivalent concentrations of saccharin. Specifically, adding saccharin to itself should produce:

Saccharin + Saccharin = 2 Saccharin = 2 Units of Concentration = $(2 \text{ Saccharin})^{0.6}$ = 1.52 Units of sweetness, not 2 units

Unless the sensory system processes the sweet stimulus (or sour stimulus for acids) according to simple linear functions with unit exponents, the choice of the reference chemical will seem to suggest synergism or suppression, not additivity, even when the taste system adds together concentrations in a linear manner.

Moskowitz (1973) appears to have noticed this paradox first. It occurs in equal-sweetness (or equal-sourness) mixtures, and results from the definition of the laws of additivity. Once the researcher selects the method for calculating additivity for the experimental data, then any deviations of data from these calculations properly reflect synergism (excessive taste intensity relative to the expected sum) or suppression (the mixture tastes less intense relative to what we might expect, based on the expected sum, using the additive model).

Direct Ratings of Mixtures With The Same Taste

Recent work with taste mixtures by both Bartoshuk and Moskowitz highlight the advances in our understanding which emerge from direct psychophysical scaling. Both researchers used magnitude estimation to measure the sweetness of the taste components and taste mixtures. Moskowitz's work (1973 and 1974) concentrated primarily on ascertaining the degree of additivity for mixtures of sugars with each other and with artificial sweeteners. From a variety of experiments, he postulated two mechanisms which could underlie taste additivity, but the data did not strongly favor either one.

Addition of Concentrations. The taste system reacts to the concentrations of the components, adding the components together (after converting both sweetener concentrations to a common concentration unit), and then exponentiating that increased concentration by the proper exponent. This model agrees with the implicit model of additivity that Cameron used in his sweetness mixture studies.

Addition of Taste Percepts. The taste system adds together the taste perceptions as if they emerged from entirely separate channels. Only after the taste system transforms each component to sweetness does it add together the impressions to generate the mixture taste.

Since most taste materials exhibit power function for intensity with exponents between 0.8 and 1.3, the experimenter has a difficult time distinguishing between these two plausible models of taste additivity. In some instances the first model seemed to govern sweetness additivity, whereas in other instances the second model seemed more appropriate. Only if the exponent for taste intensity lies sufficiently far away from 1.0 can one determine which model of the two better describes the data (Moskowitz 1973).

Building on these results, Bartoshuk and her colleagues performed an elegant experiment to distinguish between the two models of additivity. Meiselman had previously demonstrated differences in the power function exponent for saltiness and sweetness using different methods of stimulation. When we test sugar or salt stimuli through normal sip-and-spit procedures, panelists' ratings generate a power function of exponent 1.3-1.5. When panelists taste the same sugar or salt stimuli by means of the artificial dorsal tongue flow, panelists generate power functions with much lower exponents, lying near 0.4-0.5. By presenting the same taste mixtures and components to panelists both by sip-and-spit and by dorsal flow, Bartoshuk artificially increased and decreased the power function exponents respectively, simply by virtue of the method of stimulus presentation. When she did this, she found clear evidence that the addition of concentrations, not the addition of sensory intensities, described the mixture taste intensity (Bartoshuk 1975).

Mixtures of Different Taste Qualities

Psychophysics shows us quite different results when we deal with mixtures comprising different tastes. Again and again, researchers find that the mixture components supress each other or, at most, they do not affect each other at all. They do not add as do components having similar taste qualities. Furthermore, one cannot usually predict the amount of suppression or whether the components will suppress each other to the same degree.

Studies on mixture suppression go back at least a century to anecdotal observations reported in scientific magazines, and to literature in the pharmaceutical industry. Reports stated that sugar suppressed the bitter taste of coffee, and the coffee itself diminshed the sweet sugar taste. Pharmaceutical journals discussed the problem of unpalatable medicines, and methods by which the pharmacist could disguise the unpalatable bitter taste of many medicinal elixirs. Quite often the pharmacist would add sugar syrup or glycerin, both of which provoke intense sweetness, in order to suppress the noxious bitter taste.

Systematic work on the suppressing effect in taste mixtures began a century later. Perhaps the earlier well-publicized systematic study appeared from the psychological laboratories at Harvard University, published in the *Journal of Psychology* by John G. Beebe-Center and colleagues (Beebe-Center, Rogers, Atkinson and O'Connell 1959). Beebe-Center had previously made a name for himself in the scientific study of hedonics, or pleasantness/unpleasantness. Together with his colleagues, Beebe-Center set out to quantify the effects which occur in mixtures. He used equal-intensity matching for his study on sweet/salt mixtures, although he had available to him his own GUST scale, published in 1949, ten years before his 1959 study on sweet/salt mixtures.

To investigate taste mixture suppression, Beebe-Center systematically varied the concentrations of salt and sugar in binary mixtures. A test mixture would contain a fixed concentration of sodium chloride, and a fixed concentration of sucrose. Panelists selected that concentration of unmixed sodium chloride which tasted as salty as the salt-sugar mixture. In other test sessions the panelists selected the concentration of unmixed sucrose which tasted as sweet as the mixture. From the panel, Beebe-Center determined a set of concentrations which tasted as sweet as specific sugar/salt mixtures. When panelists followed this testing regimen, evaluating several levels of sucrose (with salt held fixed), they generated equal-sweetness and equal-saltiness contours. According to Beebe-Center *et al*, one can mathematically express the concentration of sodium chloride needed to match a mixture comprising a fixed amount of sodium chloride and a fixed amount of added sucrose. The mathematics suggested that a constant percent or multiplicative reduction in perceived saltiness occurred for a fixed level of sucrose.

Beebe-Center's early data, and much of the subsequent results, show suppression in mixtures with differing taste qualities. One taste suppresses the other. More recent work by Pangborn (1960, 1961 and 1962), as well as by Moskowitz (1972) confirmed suppression in mixtures. Pangborn instructed panelists to scale taste intensity using category scales to express the taste intensity of sugar/salt and sugar/acid mixtures. In contrast, Moskowitz and Bartoshuk used magnitude estimation. With magnitude estimation they could express the total suppression as a percentage of the starting taste intensity. Moskowitz (1972) suggested that the total taste intensity of a mixture (e.g., sweetness + saltiness, for a mixture of sugar and salt) tasted approximately 40%–60% as strong as the arithmetic sum of the unmixed sweetness and unmixed saltiness. One could never make this claim or discover the percent reduction using the category scale method as Pangborn had done.

Practical Application Of These Findings

Often consumers reject products because these products possess off-tastes. Saccharin possesses a noticeable bitter off-taste together with sweetness. Commercially manufactured saccharin for the marketplace often comes in tablet form mixed with other chemical components, e.g., citrates, or salts of heavy acids. These heavier components produce a competitive taste perception which masks the bitter off-taste, thus suppressing some of the negative characteristics.

As noted above, pharmacy, health and beauty aids manufacturers often use taste-masking in order to reduce some of the noxious bitter tastes provoked by medicines. The addition of low levels of saccharin or moderate levels of sugar reduces the unpleasant bitter taste, and modifies the flavor characteristics in a more positive, acceptable direction.

TASTE MODIFIERS AND TASTE PERCEPTIONS

For the past century, researchers have studied the action of the so-called taste modifiers as clues to understanding how our taste system works. Two hundred years ago botanists reported that the leaves of the plant *Gymnema sylvestre* eliminated the sense of sweetness, at least temporarily (about 4-6 hr). At that time, and subsequently, the leaves of this shrub, which grows in India, found use as an anti-diabetic drug. Apparently, users of the leaves thought that by chewing the leaves they would make the sensation of sweetness disappear. They followed this illogically with the belief that the sugar in the urine of diabetics would also disappear.

Subsequent research showed that *Gymnema sylvestre* truly behaved as a general blocking agent for sweetness. Bartoshuk and her colleagues (1969) showed that a decoction of *Gymnema sylvestre*, placed on the tongue for a few seconds, interfered with a person's ability to detect the sweet taste; ratings for the sweetness of pure sugar solutions dropped down rather dramatically (Fig. 3.12). Sucrose, as well as virtually every other sweetener behaved in this manner. *Gymnema* reduced or eliminated the sweetness of each solution. Such observations led to the recognition of sweetness as a single sensory modality, provoked by a variety of sweeteners but based upon one physiological mechanism.

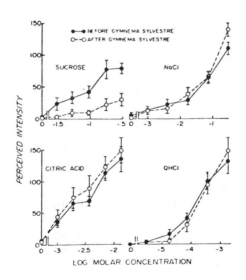

FIG. 3.12 RELATION BETWEEN SWEETENER CONCENTRATION AND RATED SWEETNESS BEFORE AND AFTER APPLICATION OF *GYMNEMA SYLVESTRE*, A SWEET BLOCKING AGENT

Source: Bartoshuk *et al.* (1969)

Gymnema's effect becomes even more apparent in sweet foods. A cola beverage or a chocolate pudding loses many of its flavor characteristics after a gymnema application. The cola beverage taste bitter, primarily because the sweetness no longer suppresses the bitterness introduced by the flavoring agents. The beverage tastes unacceptable, provoking bitterness and pain. Chocolate pudding tastes bitter and chalky. We still perceive the textural modifications caused by the sugar in pudding, but we no longer sense the flavor enhancing powers which sugar sweetness introduces.

Scientists have searched for other such general taste modifiers. One promising avenue has led to the Jujuba plant (Kennedy and Halpern, 1980) which seems to mimic the sweet effects of *Gymnema sylvestre* but on a smaller, less potent scale.

Miracle Fruit

A small plant grown in Ghana, *Richardella dulcifica* (or *Synsepsalum dulcifica*), possesses the unusual ability to make sour materials taste deliciously sweet. The so-called "miracle fruit" berry from Ghana contains a sweetening agent which comprises a large proteinaceous body (approximate molecular weight = 44,000), with the 5-carbon sugar molecules, arabinose and xylose, attached to it at one end. The molecule lies atop the tongue, attached to the rough tongue surface. In the presence of acid, the molecule splits at the sugar end. The arabinose and xylose sugar molecules enter the sweetness receptor site where they stimulate the sweet taste.

Miracle fruit provides a non-tasted reservoir of sugar on the tongue, which comes alive and exerts its effect in the presence of the acid molecule. Previously researchers thought that miracle fruit actually converted the sour taste to a sweet taste. It does not. The acid breaks the molecules and turns the effective stimulus into a mixture of acid (producing sourness) and arabinose/xylose sugars (producing sweetness). Studies with actual mixtures of arabinose and xylose in acid show sensory effects similar to the taste mixture effect exerted by miracle fruit in the presence of an acid (Bartoshuk *et al.* 1974).

In the 1970s the Miralin Corporation in Sudbury, Massachusetts tried to commercialize this taste modifer substance as a sweetener to replace cyclamate and saccharin. Miralin set up nurseries and developed a pilot plant extracting operation to process the berries. Furthermore, it developed a method to administer the protein in a chewable tablet form. Finally, Miralin developed recipes for foods which one could sweeten using the miracle fruit tablet. The problem with the product became Food and Drug Administration (FDA) clearance, and the limitations on product use. Effective use of the sweetener required the presence of acid in order to stimulate sweetness. In many instances, one could readily accomplish this by changing the product recipe. In other instances, such as beer, the inevitable sweetness in the presence of small acid levels proved unacceptable. Since the miracle fruit effect lasted for 3-4 hours after surface coating on the tongue, the problem of residual sweetness, unwanted in some foods, also plagued the developer. The Miralin Corporation eventually declared bankruptcy and the unique sweetener disappeared from the commercial realm.

MSG and the 5' Nucleotides

In 1912 in Japan, Ikeda reported the discovery in seaweed of monosodium glutamate (MSG), a naturally occurring salt of heavy glutamic acid. MSG provoked an unusual taste by itself which the Japanese named mouthfullness, and the Germans later named fullmouthedness or vollmundigkeit. When mixed with foods, MSG seemed to broaden or to enhance flavor, especially the flavor of foods containing nitrogenous flavor compounds (e.g., vegetables and meats).

Researchers in taste studied the effects of MSG by simple experiments in which they evaluated the ability of MSG to modify taste thresholds. They reasoned that if MSG truly acts as a taste modifier which changes the sensory system on the tongue, this effect should reveal itself as a decreased taste threshold. Sufficient anecdotal evidence accrued to suggest definite perceptual changes in the taste of food. However, a well controlled study by Lockhart and Gainer (1950) showed inconclusive results. MSG showed no dramatic ability to reduce threshold, nor did it elevate sensitivity to simple taste chemicals. To some researchers this suggested that MSG's principal role parallels the behavior of sodium chloride in taste mixtures: MSG adds its own flavor to the blend, and thus enhances overall acceptability just as sodium chloride (table salt) enhances the flavor acceptability of meat and vegetables by adding its unique flavor. Recent work on MSG in taste mixtures does suggest, however, that MSG may modify reactions in the neural system, possibly at the receptor site (Rifkin 1979, unpublished) by modifying some of the signals going up the chorda tympani. This could produce a change in overall quality, rather than produce a simple change in sensitivity to the stimuli. Howver, such a change in quality still does not rule out the possibility that MSG parallels the effects of salt, which changes the taste of a mixture by adding in the previously nonexistent quality of salt.

More recently, researchers have investigated the 5' nucleotides (e.g., inosinine and guanidine monophosphate). The chemicals exert effects similar to the flavor enhancing effects of MSG, but do so at substantially lower levels. Furthermore, according to published reports by Woskow, the 5' nucleotides truly sensitize the taste system, reducing its threshold. The Takeda Company of Japan has commercially marketed the mixture of 5' nucleotides (inosinine and guanidine monophosphates) under the trade name Ribotide, and uses these to replace MSG and to enhance flavor.

THE TIME COURSE OF TASTE SENSATIONS— BUILDUP AND DECLINE

Quite often researchers describe the taste sensations of new chemicals in terms of intensity, quality and time. One reads, for example, that the taste of citric acid begins with a burst of flavor which rises quickly. In contrast, malic or apple acid, a similar organic acid with slightly different taste properties, builds up to its peak more slowly and gradually. Both acids may taste equally sour at the end, but they show substantially different time courses. Differences in time course occur with saccharin versus sucrose sweeteners. Sucrose sweetness builds up more rapidly than does saccharin sweetness. When the sucrose solution no longer remains on the tongue the taste sensation rapidly diminishes. In contrast, saccharin sweetness builds up more slowly, and a bitter taste emerges shortly after the sweet taste begins its increase in taste intensity. When we remove the saccharin solution from the tongue, the sweet taste sensation slowly subsides. Panelists report a lingering sweet taste and an even more lingering bitter taste which only gradually dissipates. Two new sweeteners, the neohesperidin and neonaringin dihydrochalcones, which taste intensely and cloyingly sweet (Horowitz and Gentili 1974), provoke residual sweetness minutes after one rinses one's tongue to remove them. One can develop similar comparisons across qualities. Sweetness builds up more rapidly and decays more rapidly than bitterness, which we often sense even after rinsing the tongue to remove the stimulus (e.g., quinine).

In order to measure the time course of sensory intensity for taste perception, researchers use procedures which empirically chart the change of taste intensity over time. Several methods accomplish that goal. The panelist can assign numerical ratings over a period of time, writing these down on the answer sheet at prespecified, signalled intervals. More sophisticated methods require that the panelist draw a line on a chart recorder to reflect taste intensity. The chart paper moves continuously, at a specified rate, so that the panelist effectively draws a time curve to reflect perceived taste intensity. Larson-Powers and Pangborn (1978) published time-courses of perception with the chart recorder methods, in order to ascertain how the taste of the dipeptide artificial sweetener, aspartame, changes over time. In contrast, the continuous recording of numbers, albeit more cumbersome also provides an opportunity to record taste intensity, but in a discontinuous manner (since one does not record the intensities in between). McNulty and Moskowitz (1974) used the time-writing method to measure the bitter taste of anethole during continued exposure, in order to test McNulty's predictive model regarding flavor agent release from emulsion systems. Lawless and Skinner (1979) further used the discrete number-recording method to map the time-course of the perception of sucrose sweetness, as shown in Fig. 3.13.

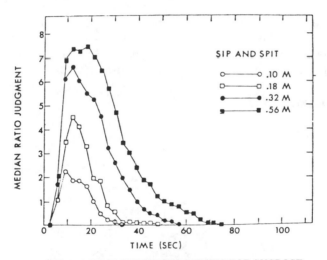

FIG. 3.13 TIME INTENSITY CURVES FOR SUCROSE
Source: Lawless and Skinner (1979)

We learn quite a lot from time-intensity curves which we would ordinarily overlook when focusing on single estimates of taste intensity. (1) Taste intensity changes dynamically over time, first increasing, then maximizing and then diminishing. (2) Different taste materials generate different curves. Some curves appear peaked with a sharp rise and decline, e.g., acids, sugars and salts. Other materials show flatter, more ragged time curves, e.g., artificial sweeteners and bitter agents. (3) In order to produce the most acceptable tasting food product, the product developer must fabricate a food which generates an acceptable time-course function for taste perception. For instance, when formulating a beverage comprising artificial sweeteners, acidulants and flavoring agents, the product developer should make every attempt to balance the flavor/taste impression so that the consumer tastes a mixture of sweet/flavor/acid at the same time, rather than first tasting the bitter flavor and the sour acid, and only later tasting the slowly rising sweetness produced by the artificial sweetener. The importance of such time-curve data reveals itself in the increasing interest of chemists in synthesizing an artificial sweetener having both potent sweetness (so consumers can use it at low concentrations) and a time-course of sweetness which parallels the time-course of sucrose sweetness as closely as possible.

OLFACTORY PERCEPTION

We often treat olfaction, or the sense of smell, as the lowest of the lower senses. In contrast to taste, touch, vision and audition, the nerves subserving the olfactory system go directly into the brain, rather than travelling to the thalamus, and then traveling onward from the thalamic relays to the brain (see Fig. 3.14 which shows the smell neural pathways).

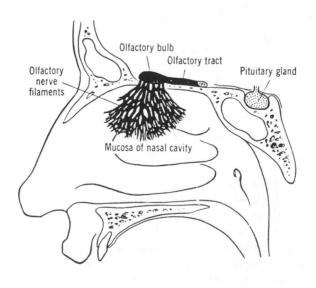

FIG. 3.14 SCHEMATIC OF THE OLFACTORY SYSTEM
Source: Gardner (1963)

Olfaction, like taste, generates hedonic reactions almost as often as it stimulates reactions of quality and intensity. Investigators often report that panelists first state that they like or dislike an odor, and only afterwards do they describe the quality and intensity.

Until recently, most researchers shied away from olfaction, finding research difficult because of poor definition of the stimulus, and difficult stimulus control. They considered olfaction a poor step-child to vision and audition, and a poor sister to taste and kinaesthesis, the two other lower senses. With the advent of direct psychophysics, however, researchers have shown renewed interest in the study of olfactory processes.

Physiology of Olfaction

The olfactory receptors lie on a broad sheet located in the olfactory mucosa in the nose. The mucosa lie out of the direct stream of air which we inspire when we breathe. Only about 2% of the air which goes through our nose ever reaches the mucosa. An even lower proportion of odor molecules reaches the mucosa when we suffer from a cold or some other blockage of the passageways. Nonetheless, the olfactory receptors exhibit sufficient affinity for odorant molecules so that, even with this low stimulus volume and the even lower concentration in air, we show unusual sensitivity. Some researchers, e.g., Stuiver (1958), have suggested that the receptors at the olfactory mucosa require only about forty molecules to trigger off the neural message to signal an olfactory stimulus.

These olfactory mucosa appear as a broad, flat sheet of brown colored cells. Scientists have estimated that we possess approximately 50 million single cells in our olfactory mucosa. Other animals possess even more. Moulton and Tucker (1964) estimated that dogs may possess about 200 million cells. Man belongs to the microsomatic group, possessing relatively few cells in comparison to the dog. The olfactory receptors connect to a smaller number of glomeruli. There, in the glomeruli, substantial spatial summation occurs. Investigators find it difficult to determine from which single receptor a signal arose, since many single receptors converge onto the far fewer glomeruli. Each glomerulus further feeds to the olfactory brain. One very important property of the olfactory system concerns the absence of a single neural path or strand going to the brain. Olfaction does not possess simple labelled lines. Rather, it comprises a multiple, interconnecting and complex set of converging neural inputs to the olfactory brain. For this reason, researchers have found it difficult to trace the course of a message from the receptor site to the brain. The extensive interconnections, and the difficulties encountered in teasing out specific receptors from the tightly packed olfactory muscosa make such anatomical tracings difficult if not impossible.

Anatomy of the Nose and Access to Receptors

Although of seemingly little importance to sensory evaluation and product testing, an adequate understanding of nasal mechanics provides the researcher with some useful insights into the perception of flavor. We inspire air through the nose, and the air passes over the olfactory mucosa. The air heats up and moistens while in the nose. Although we may smell hot or cold foods, the final air temperature appears to end up fairly constant. The nasal mucosa occasionally swell up blocking the nasal passage. When this occurs, we call the result a loss of *nasal patency*. Less air courses over the olfactory mucosa, resulting in a lower total stimulus concentration and, therefore, in less effective olfactory stimulation. Nasal patency diminishes during a cold, but appears greater just before a cold. These changes evidence themselves as diminished or heightened sensitivity, respectively. When we have a cold we lose most, if not all, of our ability to smell. This results from the blockage of the olfactory mucosa. The flavor of foods seems different.

Substances adsorb onto the surface of the mucosa. Our nose selectively absorbs vapor chemicals, releasing them at different rates. Our olfactory system acts as a separatory device. In theory, we could bias sensory analysis of food by smelling specific foods which adsorb quickly onto the mucosa, and then release slowly. Whereas the original stimulus (e.g., a musk chemical) may disappear, the residual molecules adsorbed onto the mucosa often release slowly and repeatedly stimulate the receptor. Compare this to the residual sweetness of the dihydrochalcones. Such a delayed stimulation could very well reduce sensitivity to new stimuli. Much of the time honored fear about testing several olfactory, or flavor-intense, stimuli too closely spaced in time could result from such an adsorption-release mechanism, which would effectively diminish sensitivity.

Flavor stimuli may reach the nose in the unusual, retrograde fashion, from the back of the mouth upward. This mode of stimulation produces olfactory perceptions which we misclassify as taste perceptions. In such instances, the flavor/odor molecules completely bypass the normal route to the mucosa.

THE OLFACTORY STIMULUS

During the past century, with the advent of modern organic chemistry, researchers have explored the olfactory properties of thousands of materials. As a consequence, researchers have sought to discover the structure/function requirements for an odorant to evoke an odor, and have come up with these general rules. (1) The odorant chemical must evaporate. We cannot smell a chemical which does not evaporate, even if only to a modest degree. The odorant must enter the olfactory mucosa, and therefore it must evaporate into air. (2) The molecular weight must lie approximately between 34 and 300. (3) Heavier molecules tend not to have an odor, although studies reported by Laffort (1968) with forced evaporation of metal (ordinarily non-odorous) show that panelists do perceive the stimulus to have an odor.

THE PERCEPTION OF OLFACTORY INTENSITY

Only in the last few decades have scientists seriously approached the issue of olfactory intensity measurement. A century ago, Hendrik Zwaardemaker (1895) attempted to measure olfactory thresholds by a tedious method. He developed the olfactometer, comprising a long tube mounted inside another tube. The inner tube contained the test odorant. The experimenter, usually Zwaardemaker himself, extended the outer tube to expose known lengths of the inner tube to the air. He then inspired the stimulus in the inner tube. The length that the tube extended represented a measure of olfactory stimulus concentration. With such a cumbersome device, Zwaardemaker managed to obtain quantitative estimates of threshold, measured in units he called olfacties (the length of the tube).

Zwaardemaker and his colleagues found their greatest measurement difficulties in the specification and control of stimulus concentration. At that time researchers did not possess accurate methods to measure concentration of molecules in air. They relied on the principles of chemistry, specifically Raoult's law which predicted the vapor concentration from liquid concentration. More often than not the odor stimulus levels did not agree with these calculations.

Olfactometry

No discussion of olfactory intensity can begin without a short discussion of olfactometry, for the simple reason that the type of stimulus presentation often determines the sensory threshold and the perceived stimulus intensity. Olfactometers of various types appear in Fig. 3.15, as presented and summarized by Andrew Dravnieks. These methods include the very simplest procedures, from presenting the stimulus from a liquid solution, all the way to complicated air-dilution mechanisms which deliver specific volumes of air with well-defined molecular concentration.

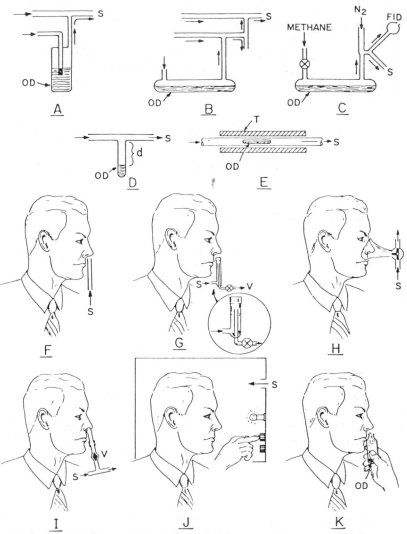

FIG. 3.15   VARIOUS METHODS FOR PRESENTING AND SMELLING STIMULI
Source: A. Dravnieks

Many scientific researchers today prefer to use air-dilution olfacto-meters wherever possible, rather than using liquid presentation. Air dilution olfactometry provides these specific research benefits. (1) It permits the accurate specification of stimulus concentration in air, rather than forcing the researcher to rely upon calculated concentra-tions, based upon a theory which may not apply to the actual stimulus. (2) It avoids aberrant or irregular concentration levels. A continual flow of odorized air does not depend upon a momentary build-up of odor volume which one removes by inhaling the same (see A in Fig. 3.15). Current olfactometers provide at least 100 ml/min to several liters/min of continuous, steady concentration of air. Breathing the stimulus in no way affects concentrations: In comparison, imagine breathing the stimulus from a bottle or a perfumer's blotter. With the first inspiration, the concentration of odorant changes above the liq-uid or blotter. Afterwards, several minutes must elapse, until the equil-ibrium above the liquid reestablishes itself. (3) It permits the researcher to substantially dilute the concentration to any level desired. In contrast, with bottles one runs into the problem that the liquid odorant in dilution can eventually become minute, but the odor level above the liquid remains constant as molecules escape from the solvent. The intrinsic odor of the solvent presents another problem. At very low odorant levels, the solvent itself contributes a relatively overwhelming odor.

We show great olfactory sensitivity. In very carefully controlled measurements with well-defined physical stimuli, scientists report that we can detect odorous stimuli at extremely low concentrations in air. Table 3.14 shows some threshold values for different chemicals. Olfactory thresholds vary from chemical to chemical. Generally, very low-weight molecules (e.g., ethyl alcohol) show much higher threshold levels than do heavier odorant molecules (e.g., octyl alcohol). Like taste perception, olfactory threshold studies must take into account detection and recognition thresholds. We can smell a chemical at low concentrations before we recognize its quality. In olfaction, the smell quality may change with concentration, so that a chemical could possess a detection threshold and a recognition threshold for one odor quality, as well as a higher recognition threshold where it stimulates another quality. However, sharp differences between different percep-tions of quality at various odorant levels seem less pronounced than the change in taste quality for a chemical such as sodium chloride. Researchers have not investigated the range of different thresholds for qualities of odor as extensively as they have for taste. Researchers have remarked that as a chemical increases in concentration, one begins to detect a harsh smell along with its characteristic quality.

TABLE 3.14
SOME REPRESENTATIVE OLFACTORY THRESHOLDS

Substance	Thresholds Mg/liter of Air
Ethyl ether	5.833
Carbon tetrachloride	4.533
Chloroform	3.300
Ethyl acetate	.686
Methyl salicylate	.100
Ethyl mercaptan	.046
Amyl acetate	.038
Valeric acid	.029
Butyric acid	.009
Propyl mercaptan	.006
Artificial musk	.00004

Source: Allison and Katz (1919)

This would suggest a detection threshold for another quality, or the entry of pain into the overall olfactory perception.

Distribution of Olfactory Threshold Values in the Population

Every biological process distributes itself statistically in the population. Olfactory thresholds do so as well. A single, average threshold value reflects the contribution of extremely sensitive individuals, and extremely insensitive individuals. Amoore, Venstrom and Davis (1968) have investigated the statistical distribution of thresholds in an effort to discover specific odor receptors. The thresholds of many, but by no means all chemicals, distribute statistically according to the normal or bell-shaped curve. On the other hand, quite a number of chemicals show two, non-overlapping distributions for olfactory thresholds. Some individuals show average sensitivity to the chemical. Other individuals show unusually low sensitivity and need a much higher concentration to detect or to recognize the odor. These insensitive individuals exhibit an olfactory deficit which Amoore believes reflects the loss of a specific receptor. Such partial, or specific, anosmia affects many individuals in the population for one or another chemical (see Chapter 2, classification; and Chapter 9, panel selection). Specific ageusia, or taste blindness, appears much more rarely in taste perception than anosmia in smell perception.

Category Scales of Odor Perception

Scientists began to use suprathreshold scales of odor perception for applied purposes in the food industry, and for air pollution measurement, where they needed to specify human reactions to known (or estimated) concentrations of odorant in the environment. Applied researchers often use fixed point category scales to rate different odorants for strength. Katz and Talbot (1930) measured noxious odors seeking a standard rating scale to express intensity of perception, and to correlate with odorant concentration. The scale comprised five points, compressing a wide range of perceptions into the small category range. The scale falls prey to the same biases which characterize all fixed point scales.

Ratio Scales of Odor Intensity

Psychophysical measurement of odor stength began in earnest with the revival of psychophysics in the late 1950s and 1960s, as scientists found themselves able to rapidly estimate sensory intensity using ratio scale methods, and to develop psychophysical intensity curves. Some early reports by Jones (1958) showed that odor intensity grew less rapidly than physical concentration. Odor intensity conformed to Stevens' power equation: $S = kI^n$, where S = sensory intensity, reflected by the magnitude estimates, I = physical concentration; and n = less than 1.0. The exponent for odor intensity lay around 0.5, meaning that an approximate square root law governs odor intensity. Continued research with dozens of chemicals, as well as with complex odor mixtures (e.g., perfumes, flavors, etc.), bore out Jones' initial finding that odor intensity grows more slowly than concentration, as a decelerating function. Table 3.15 lists some of the published exponents for odor intensity reported during the past 24 years.

Some of the important conclusions about odor intensity, as obtained by magnitude scaling, appear below.

(1) Odor intensity virtually always grows as a decelerating function of concentration, no matter what the chemical. In contrast, taste intensity functions often exhibit exponents both greater than 1.0 and less than 1.0, depending upon the chemical. (2) Intensity functions depend upon the olfactometric method of stimulus presentation. When the investigator uses air dilution olfactometers, the intensity functions show higher exponents compared to those obtained with the liquid dilution method where the stimulus concentration equals the relative odorant concentration in the liquid solvent. (3) With liquid olfactometry (odors presented in liquids) one can modify the exponent by changing the solvent. This modification represents a lack of parallel-

TABLE 3.15
EXPONENTS (N) FOR THE POWER FUNCTION RELATING
PERCEIVED ODOR INTENSITY (S) TO PHYSICAL
ODORANT CONCENTRATION (C)

Odorant	Exponent	Diluent
Amyl acetate	0.13	Liquid
Anethole	0.16	Liquid
Butanol	0.31	Liquid
Butanol	0.64	Air
Butanol	0.66	Air
Butyl acetate	0.58	Air
Butyric acid	0.22	Liquid
Coumarin	0.33	Air
Citral	0.17	Liquid
Ethyl acetate	0.21	Liquid
Eugenol	0.27	Liquid
Eugenol	0.64	Air
Geraniol	0.20	Air
Guaiacol	0.20	Liquid
Heptanol	0.16	Liquid
Hexanol	0.15	Air
D-Menthol	0.24	Liquid
Methyl salicylate	0.20	Liquid
Octanol	0.24	Liquid
Pentanol	0.21	Liquid
Phenylethanol	0.19	Liquid
Phenyl acetic acid	0.12	Liquid
Propanol	0.52	Air
Iso-valeric acid	0.21	Liquid

Source: Moskowitz (1976)

ism between the concentration in the liquid and the concentration in the air above called the headspace. Different liquid solvents possess varying abilities to retard or enhance the evaporation of the odorant. Hence, concentration in liquid may not show any simple relation to the vapor concentration above. (4) If we consider similarly structured molecules related to each other in a homologous series (e.g., butyl alcohol, pentyl alcohol, etc.), we find that the lower molecular weight members of the series show higher exponents and higher thresholds than do the higher molecular weight members. Cain (1969) found this relation in a study on the odor intensity of the *n*-aliphatic alcohols (propanol, butanol . . . octanol) using air dilution olfactometers to carefully control concentration. Each odorant followed a power function equation for growth of perceived intensity versus concentration. The exponent systematically decreased as the molecular weight of the odorant increased. (5) Power functions can describe complex mixtures with exponents lying in the range of simple chemicals presented in the same way. That means a perfume or a flavor, presented at various concentrations in liquid diluent, e.g., diethyl phthalate, shows a similar power function to many pure chemicals presented in the same way.

Equal Intensity Matches

Ordinarily researchers frown on equal-intensity matches in a study of olfactory intensity, due to the many difficulties which ensue from working with airspace above liquid dilutions of chemicals. With the increasing popularity of air dilution olfactometry, and the construction of simple and rugged olfactometers which deliver a constantly flowing odor stream at a variety of different concentrations, equal-intensity matches have begun to appear in the published literature. Dravnieks' 8-port air dilution olfactometer, described extensively by Moskowitz, Dravnieks and Gerbers (1974) and shown in Fig. 3.16, represents a popular device which allows equal-intensity matches.

Dravnieks has advocated the use of equal-intensity matches to n-butyl alcohol (butanol) as a method for standardizing odor intensity measurement. The panelist has in front of him or her the 8-port, continuous air dilution olfactometer delivering graded concentrations of butanol in air. These concentrations produce a wide range of perceived odor intensities. The panelist first smells the test odorant, and then tries to find a concentration of butanol from the set of eight controls which smell as strong as the test odorant. Dravnieks and associates have reported the results of numerous such matches (Moskowitz, Dravnieks and Klarman 1976). In a recent paper, four psychophysicists have suggested that the butanol scale, as developed by Dravnieks, merge with equivalent magnitude estimates assigned to the eight concentrations of butanol, in order to generate a general scale for odor intensity. A transformation equation relating butanol concentration to equivalent magnitude estimations (obtained by direct scaling of the eight butanol levels) follows the power equation:

$$\text{Magnitude Estimate Value} = 260 \, (\text{Concentration})^{0.66}$$

On this general odor scale, a value of 10 represents a moderate odor intensity, lying around 250 parts per million (Moskowitz, Dravnieks, Cain and Turk 1974).

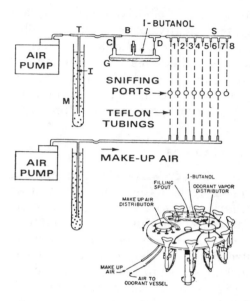

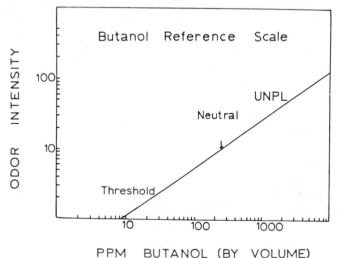

FIG. 3.16 AIR DILUTION OLFACTOMETER USED FOR EQUAL-INTENSITY ODOR MATCHES
  Schematic diagram of the air dilution olfactometer, showing the arrangement of the sources for saturated air and make-up air (top panel), and the arrangement of the eight ports around a circle (bottom panel).
  Source: Moskowitz, Dravnieks and Gerbers (1974)

FIG. 3.17 BUTANOL REFERENCE SCALE
  The butanol reference scale, plotted in log-log coordinates. The equation of the line equals: $S = 0.261(C)^{0.66}$ (or $\log S = 0.66(\log C) - 0.583$). The regions pertaining to threshold (2-5 ppm), neutrality (about 250 ppm), and unpleasantness (above 250 ppm) appear on the figure.
  Source: Moskowitz, Dravnieks, Cain and Turk (1974)

Whether or not the scientific community adopts the butanol scale or uses another reference odorant, it appears that equal-intensity matching has caught the fancy of experimenters in both industrial and academic laboratories. The equal-intensity match provides the same type of security of measurement as provided by equal-sweetness and equal-sourness matches in taste. With equal-intensity matches, a researcher inexperienced in sensory analysis need not worry that the panelists' idiosyncratic use of numbers will influence the data. Furthermore, the tightness of equal-intensity matches, producing less variability in the data compared to panel ratings, allows for a smaller panel size.

The deficits of equal-intensity matching remain the same as with taste intensity matches. One does not obtain a true measure of sensory intensity, but rather measures odor intensity expressed by a common reference chemical. Does the concentration of that chemical span the potentially wide range of odor intensity? Does the matching method permit discovery of laws of odor perception beyond simple equal-intensity matches? We cannot answer these questions directly, but if the olfactory system resembles the other sensory systems, then equal-intensity matching will come up against severe limits when researchers try to develop general perceptual laws while basing their data on a reference stimulus chemical. Such limitations plague auditory and visual researchers who cannot develop general laws by equal loudness or equal brightness matches. They must, as olfactory researchers must, use units of sensory magnitude independent of a single common physical stimulus.

Running An Evaluation of Odor Intensity:
Setup and Experimental Design

Psychophysicists have developed straightforward procedures to implement studies on odor intensity. Sensory analysts should know about these procedures, both for general background on psychophysics and as methods to rate the perceived flavor or aroma intensity of foodstuffs.

The basic steps follow. (1) Select the appropriate stimulus concentrations. Psychophysicists usually select a sufficiently wide range of concentrations, because they wish to learn how odorant intensity varies with concentration. The food scientist may wish to use a smaller range, because aroma intensities lie within a smaller range. Rarely does an aroma intensity really become as strong as the high concentrations of acetone and butanol to which psychophysicists have become accustomed during studies. If possible, the sensory analyst should explore aroma stimulus levels beyond those ordinarily encountered. This wider range reduces some of the risk that the ever-present variability around the average will disguise the basic pattern or trend in the ratings. (2) Present the stimulus concentrations to the panelists in random or irregular order, but not in ascending or descending order. Random order prevents the panelist from adopting a simple strategy of assigning increasingly higher or decreasingly lower numbers to the stimuli versus intensities. It forces the panelist to scale perceptions as he or she senses intensity. (3) Make sure that a reference stimulus lies within the set of stimuli tested. Since panelists use their own numbers, and since these numbers vary according to the individual panelist, one should use a common stimulus (or set of stimuli) to link together different studies. For example, when obtaining intensity functions for six different odorants, the researchers may wish to have each panelist evaluate five levels of each of two of the six odorants (total = 10 samples). In addition, the panelist should evaluate anywhere from one to five or more levels of a common odorant. Moskowitz, Dravnieks, Cain and Turk (1974) suggested that this odorant represent different concentrations of butanol, to allow comparison with the standard butanol scale. With this experimental design, the researcher can quickly compare ratings from one panelist who tsted odorants A and B to ratings from another panelist (who tested odorants C and D) even though A and B did not appear together with C and D.

FACTORS WHICH MODIFY ODOR PERCEPTION

Various factors change the perceived intensity of an odor. Researchers have just begun the investigation of odor intensity in the same systematic fashion as they have studied taste intensity. Hence, we possess less information for odor than for taste. Only recently have researchers used precise methods for stimulus control coupled with straightforward, easy-to-implement test procedures.

Flow Rate

More rapidly flowing stimuli, directed into the nose, smell stronger if the panelist receives the odorants in a blast. Unpublished observations by the author on the odor of butanol suggest that one can dramatically increase perceived odor intensity by forcing the same odorant into the nose at a high flow rate. The increased rate forces more odorant per unit time to course over the olfactory mucosa, and produces a stronger smelling stimulus.

Dirhinic Stimulation

We smell with both nostrils. By simultaneously smelling with both nostrils, we increase the perceived odor intensity slightly as compared to smelling with only one nostril at a time. Smell perceptions add from the two nostrils (Cain 1975).

Heating The Stimulus

Hot stimuli emit more odorant molecules because the molecules evaporate more quickly. Hence, a hot stimulus generates an increased odor concentration which, in turn, provokes an increased odor intensity. Conversely, a cold stimulus generates less vapor and, therefore, lower stimulus concentration.

ODOR MIXTURES

The science of odor mixture underlies the arts of the flavorist and perfumer. The flavorist and the perfumer must know how to mix chemicals and natural essences/extracts in order to achieve a desirable perception. Traditionally, much of what the perfumer and flavorist do relies upon historical, recorded experience that the individual learns while studying, as well as upon his or her individual experiences and creative bent. One often hears that perfumery and flavor creation represent arts, and that the secrets of odor mixtures do not readily lend themselves to scientific explication.

Scientists have studied the perception of odor mixtures since the last century. Zwaardemaker (1895) sought mixtures of odorants which would cancel each other out, and reported that a number of such mixtures actually did exist. For example, mixtures of beeswax and tolu balsam produced a noticeable loss of odor. However, it would appear that Zwaardemaker really observed the phenomenon of masking and reduction in intensity, and not true odor cancellation per se. Not until the advent of modern day psychophysics, however, did the science of odor mixture really receive its full due. Researchers working with direct magnitude estimation scaling of odor perceptions applied the rules of psychophysical scaling to odor mixtures, just as they had applied the rules (and techniques) to color and tone, as well as to taste mixtures. By scaling unmixed odorants and mixtures, the psychophysicist can determine how the mixture odor intensity fares versus the odor intensities of the components. Fig. 3.18 represents a summary of possible results (Cain and Drexler 1974).

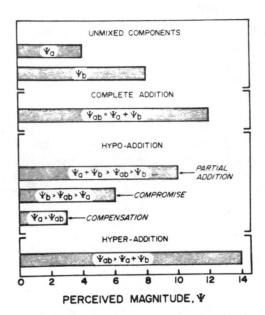

FIG. 3.18   MIXTURES OF ODORS

The perceived magnitude (ψ_{ab}) of a two-component mixture may differ from the perceived magnitudes (ψ_a, ψ_b) of its components. Various possibilities appear here. In this illustration the perceived magnitude of component a smelled alone = 4, and the perceived magnitude of component b smelled alone = 8.

Source: Cain (1974).

The Vector Law

Among the general rules governing odor mixtures, the vector rule of additivity seems to have stood the test of time, at least for binary mixtures. Developed in the psychological laboratories of the University of Stockholm by the Berglunds (Berglund, Berglund and Lindvall 1973), the vector law suggested that a fairly simple rule relates odor component intensities to odor mixture intensities. In a binary mixture of odorants, each component (e.g., amyl butyrate or pyridine) acts as a vector. The experimenter first determines the angle separating the two components. The experimenters can determine the value of the angle in a straightforward way. The odor mixture results from the vector-like addition of the component odor intensities, expressed by the simplest vector addition model:

$$(\text{Mixture Intensity})^2 = (\text{Component A})^2 + (\text{Component B})^2 + 2(\text{Component A})(\text{Component B})[\text{Cos } \alpha_{AB}]$$

Since the researcher can create the mixtures by selectively mixing A and B together, and measuring component odor intensities separately, as well as the mixture intensity, it becomes a straightforward matter to empirically estimate the coefficient of the angle separating the two vectors. Berglund *et al.* (1973) did so in a study of mixtures of malodors generated by dimethyl sulfide, diethyl disulfide (both of which smell like rotten cabbage) and hydrogen sulfide (odor of rotten eggs). For binary mixtures, they found that the value of α lay around 107°. Figure 3.19 shows how odor intensities add in this manner, and the results suggested by Berglund's initial studies.

The vector model looks promising as a simplistic model for describing binary odor mixtures. Other researchers have confirmed that the vector model applies to binary odors. Cain (1975) investigated the mixtures of pyridine (a harsh, unpleasant odor) and the odors of lavandin and amyl butyrate (fruity and apricot), respectively. In all instances, the vector model described the data with a similar angular separation (around 105°) between the odor vectors. Mixtures of pleasant smelling odorants (e.g., the pear-lily like smell of heptyl acetate

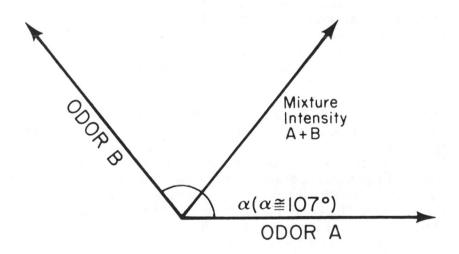

FIG. 3.19 SCHEMATIC OF THE VECTOR LAW OF ODOR SUMMATION FOR
TWO ODORANTS, A AND B

and the wintergreen smell of ethyl salicylate) also obey the vector law, but with an angular separation greater than 90° (Moskowitz, Dubose and Reuben 1977).

These studies suggest that a mixture of two odors smells intermediate to the intensities of the components, generally neither stronger than the sum nor weaker than the weakest component. Rarely does one find total suppression when using psychophysical scaling, in contrast to Zwaardemaker's contention that odor cancellation exists. One often finds changes in quality and a reduction in intensity, but one odor seems incapable of totally counteracting another unless the stronger odor smells substantially more intense. When the stronger odorant exceeds the weaker odor intensity by an extreme amount, we have total masking; not because of counteraction, but simply due to the overwhelming disparity in the odor intensities of components. A similar result would occur in mixtures of tastes, e.g., sweet and sour, if the acid component tasted overwhelmingly stronger than the sweet component prior to mixing. Then, the sour taste would overwhelm the sweet taste, and panelists would not detect any sweetness at all in the mixture.

Dirhinic versus Dichorhinic Mixtures

We possess two nostrils and, therefore, two channels of olfactory communication to the brain. Again and again we find that odor mixtures obey systematic laws for intensity. Do these laws hold when we present one odorant on one channel (the left nostril), and the other odorant on the second channel (the right nostril). The odorants do not physically mix. This question really concerns the nature of odor mixtures. Does the reduction of overall odor intensity occur because molecules in the mixture compete for the same receptors at the olfactory mucosa? If so, then we expect dichorhinic mixtures, mixtures with each odorant in a separate nostril, to show no suppression, since the two odorants stimulate different receptors. If we find evidence for interaction, then mixture suppression of overall intensity must occur at the brain which mixes together the information from each nostril. Cain (1975) showed that mixture suppression occurred in dichrohinic presentation. The vector law addition occurs at the brain, not at the receptor area on the mucosa. Dichorhinic stimulation, with separate odorants presented to separate nostrils, showed virtually identical changes in mixture intensity as did the control condition of presentation of the mixture to each nostril.

OLFACTORY ADAPTATION

Perhaps no sense seems more plagued by adaptation problems than does olfaction. Perfumers and flavorists working intensely with an odor stimulus, evaluating it in detail, restore their sensory acuity by leaving their workplace entirely for a few minutes to smell fresh air. Open a bottle of lavender oil in a room and one will perceive the same effect. With constant stimulation, the room first reeks of lavender. Then, the lavender smell disappears until one cannot detect it anymore. Leave the room, even for a few seconds, reenter it, and the lavender smell reappears in almost full force.

Note the relatively long time (60 seconds) needed for the odorant to disappear. Our olfactory sense possesses a robustness that we often overlook when we talk about the fragility of the sense of smell. We do not adapt to smell stimuli as readily as one might think. We need a substantial period of exposure in order to reduce our olfactory perception, so that we fail to detect the odorant stimulus (Woodrow and Karpman, 1919).

The Woodrow and Karpman (1919) study primarily concerned time to reach 100% adaptation. During that period, however, odor intensity diminishes before it drops to 0. Does the odor intensity diminish rapidly, or does it diminish gradually? In order to answer this question, the researcher must measure the time-intensity curve for olfactory perception in a manner similar to plots of time-intensity relations for taste perception. Several researchers have done this by presenting the stimulus to the panelist under constant conditions, and measuring either threshold after specific times, or having the panelist continually rate perceived odor intensity.

Threshold measures show a continuing decrease in sensitivity (a rise in threshold) with increasing time of adaptation. After the adapting stimulus disappears, recovery occurs. During recovery thresholds decrease, again systematically decreasing with increasing elapsed time since the removal of the adapting stimulus. Stuiver (1958), working with air dilution presentations of a constant odor stream, found that the sequence of olfactory recovery comprised two portions. The initial recovery occurred quickly. Panelists quickly regained their sensitivity to strong stimuli. Yet, a residual effect of adaptation remained which prevented sensitivity from returning entirely to normal afterwards. Panelists had difficulty detecting the lowest stimulus. This suggests that, in sensory analysis, continued or repetitive presentation of an odorant exerts its primary effect upon our ability to detect and recognize the very low stimulus levels lying around the threshold, but does not affect the easily recognizable suprathreshold levels. For those instances where the panelist must evaluate easily recognizable stimuli, one should not worry about the effects of adaptation as long as sufficient recovery time has elapsed.

One can trace the time course of adaptation. Ideally, the experimenter should use a procedure which does not require speech, because speech patterns set up currents of air in the nose which interfere with the steady stream. Berglund (1974) solved the problem by instructing the panelist to match finger span to perceived odor intensity. This matching operation generated a function relating finger span match to time since adaptation began. The function represented an equal-intensity matching function, commonly obtained by psychophysicists. In order to assign numbers to finger span and, thus, to assign numbers to odor intensity as panelists perceived it, panelists then calibrated their finger span scale by assigning numbers to reflect the perceived magnitude of finger span. The combination of odor intensity versus finger span and finger span versus numbers generated a match between odor intensity and numbers. Figure 3.20 shows the results, which depict how odor intensity decreased with time since the adaptation stimulus started. The equation describing the curve represents an *exponential decay function*.

Avoiding Olfactory Desensitization During Product Testing

Psychophysical measurement of sensitivity teaches the product tester how to avoid sensory losses during repeated product evaluation, especially in aroma/flavor profiling. To minimize the potential for olfactory desensitization, the product tester should: present the stimuli for short, not long, periods of time to avoid the buildup of adaptation; space the stimuli by at least 2–3 minutes, so that they do not fall into the recovery period from the previous sample; instruct each panelist to clear the nose by smelling something else, or at least by inhaling and exhaling rapidly in a non-odorized area; extend these precautions when working with stimuli whose odor levels lie near threshold, where adaptation exerts its greatest effect, and look for quality changes in an odorous mixture. The quality change indicates that some chemicals in the mixture have already undergone adaptation.

In all of these cases, the product tester should keep in mind that much of the material written about olfactory adaptation may not apply to the typical product testing study where panelists evaluate suprathreshold stimuli. As soon as a panelist evaluates moderate to

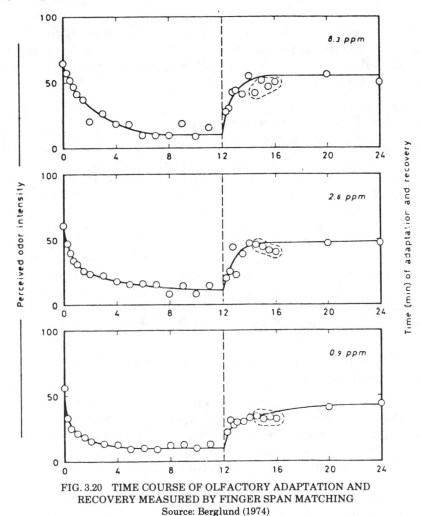

FIG. 3.20   TIME COURSE OF OLFACTORY ADAPTATION AND
RECOVERY MEASURED BY FINGER SPAN MATCHING
Source: Berglund (1974)

strong stimuli, the effects of adaptation will more than likely disappear, especially if the panelist takes the necessary break time between
samples to reestablish olfactory sensitivity.

Aroma Enhancement

From time to time flavor enhancers appear on the market which
claim to enhance aromas. Like their counterparts in taste (monosodium glutamate and the 5' nucleotides), these aroma enhancers
probably add their own nuances to the aroma, rather than changing
the physiological mechanism of olfaction at the mucosa. Chemicals

such as ethyl maltol and maltol add lift and brightness to aromas, especially to fruit-like aromas. One has a hard time showing that these chemicals do any more physiologically to change olfaction than would an ordinary stimulus mixture.

Aroma or Malodor Counteraction

Recent publications on malodors by Schleppnik (1981) concern the Veilex[R] system, a malodor counteractant. Through extensive research, Schleppnik isolated a number of chemicals which exhibit an unusual ability to mask malodors, especially the odors of fatty acids. These chemicals probably possess common masking ability shown by many odor mixtures, but have an enhanced capacity to mask specific malodor side-notes. The counteractants themselves do not destroy the chemicals in the malodor, but rather interfere with the perception of the malodor by adding specific sensory notes to the mixtures. Furthermore, they achieve their unique capabilities by exerting more masking or disguising effects than one might expect, based upon the intrinsic odor intensity of these chemicals evaluated alone.

Different sense Modalities Confused With Smell—
The Trigeminal Nerve

The trigeminal nerve, which responds to common chemical and pain stimulation, innervates the nose in parallel with the olfactory nerve. Thus, many of our olfactory impressions result from the conjoining of two different sensory inputs. One input comes from true olfactory information, the other input comes from the common chemical sense or irritation.

When we smell ozone or carbon dioxide, we sense irritation rather than a true smell perception. Ozone and carbon dioxide stimulate the trigeminal nerve, leading to irritation without necessarily stimulating the olfactory nerve. A key question thus becomes how to separate out the olfactory and the trigeminal inputs. One experimental method studies patients with trigeminal nerve loss which occurs with a section, or cutting, of the trigeminal nerve. These patients lose trigeminal input, and respond only to pure olfactory input. They show different sensory responses to odorants than do normal panelists with intact trigeminal nerves (Cain 1980).

The trigeminal input can also block, mask or inhibit olfactory sensation. By stimulating an individual simultaneously with an odorant and with odorless (but still irritating) carbon dioxide, the experimenter can reduce smell intensity without the panelist detecting the presence of the irritation. The trigeminal and the olfactory inputs interact with each other at the level of the cerebral cortex in the brain, where each modifies the input of the other (Cain 1980). For foods such as carbonated beverages, trigeminal inputs probably modify the olfactorily derived flavor perceptions in this manner. Carbonated beverages change flavor when they lose carbonation, in part due to the loss of the modifying influences of carbon dioxide, the trigeminal stimulus, modifying olfactory perception.

OVERVIEW

Psychophysics and sensory perception form a foundation for and an integral part of product testing. An understanding of how our sensory systems operate, whether in terms of physiology or perception, allows the product tester insights into the meaning of his or her data. Product evaluation studies partly depend on an understanding of how sensory systems work. Only by knowing the properties of the sensory receptors involved, the possibilities of sensory adaptation, the rules relating sensory magnitude and physical intensity, and kindred facts, can the sensory analyst, product tester, and marketer understand sensory reactions to products, and develop proper tests for assessing products.

CHAPTER 4

THRESHOLD DISCRIMINATION AND
DIFFERENCE TESTS

This chapter concerns the theory and method of threshold and discrimination testing. With these methods the product tester measures, respectively, (a) the lowest physical level of a stimulus which a panelist can detect or recognize, or (b) the panelist's capacity to discriminate between two similar, but not identical stimuli. Threshold measurement and discrimination testing occupy venerable places in the history of psychology, sensory analysis and product testing. They represent the historically first concrete methods for measuring sensory reactions. As discussed in the previous chapter, the threshold represents that lowest physical stimulus value to which the behavioral psychologist can attach a meaning—detection or no detection. To the scientist and product tester struggling with measurement of reactions in the complex world of food stimuli, the threshold concept represents a simple-to-define aspect of sensory perception. A similar attitude exists for measurement of discrimination, a capacity which Weber found fairly constant over a wide range, and which Fechner and Thurstone used as bases on which to erect psychological scales.

Threshold and discrimination testing find many practical applications. Quite often a manufacturer wishes to modify a product by adding a preservative to it. What maximal concentration of preservative can the manufacturer add before the panelist or consumer reports that the food tastes different, or that a noticeably new taste has emerged? For other applications, sensory analysts have used threshold measurements to screen individuals in the population as sensitive versus insensitive to specific attributes of products. Quality control procedures often dictate the selection of a panel of individuals with demonstrated sensitivity to a particular off flavor. The selection of sensitive panelists ensures that the public at large will not detect that off flavor in the food. Threshold measurement can screen the population and reveal groups of individuals with recognized sensory acuity.

Discrimination testing provides other practical advantages to the sensory analyst interested more in using the results of the test for product measurement and testing, than in understanding human sensory processes. When manufacturers modify a recipe or formula to achieve cost objectives (e.g., by replacing one flavor with a similar but less expensive one), they want to make sure that the consumer will not detect the substitution; or if the consumer does detect the change, that the new product tastes as acceptable, or more acceptable than the standard or control product. In a changing economy, ingredient shortages and price increases continually occur. Manufacturers try to reduce costs and increase profit margins by modifying the flavor, the sweetener, the color, etc. Witness the advent of artificial flavors with sensory quality profiles similar to those of existing flavors, and the widespread introduction of the sweeter high-fructose corn syrup in place of sucrose for many beverage formulations. Each modification of the product formula necessitates discrimination tests, with the goal of maintaining product identity after ingredient substitution.

Discrimination and threshold testing thus provide key tools for the sensory analyst and product tester. Proper execution of these tests provides important, practical benefits to the manufacturer. A well-designed study to measure thresholds or discrimination capacities can also elucidate some of the properties of our taste and smell sensory systems.

We will treat threshold and discrimination testing as methodological topics, presenting the various approaches, benefits and pitfalls by the case method. The case approach allows a clearer understanding of how the practitioner conceptualizes the problem and executes the studies using real-world data as examples.

THRESHOLD MEASUREMENT: CAN THE PANELIST DETECT THE ODOR IN LIQUID?

Our first case concerns the straightforward application of threshold measurements to determine the lowest concentration of an odorous compound which the panelists can detect in a liquid. Quite often manufacturers wish to add flavoring notes, preservatives, or chemicals to a product for functional, rather than for esthetic reasons. Or, from time to time, a batch becomes tainted with an off-odor, due to the residue from the previous batch or run which possessed a different flavoring. In each of these instances, the product tester can run a threshold test in order to determine the lowest concentration of a stimulus which the panelist can detect or recognize. In our particular case, the Chan Salad Oil Company (CSOC), a manufacturer of cooking oils, had an opportunity to purchase a new oil for use in salad dressings. On further inspection, a trained panel noticed an off-odor at very low concentrations. At those very low levels one could not smell the typical oil smell, but one could detect a smoky, harsh aroma. CSOC's technical director wanted to measure the threshold of this smoky

note. A very low threshold would mean that panelists, and thus consumers, could smell the note, and might reject the oil because of the
impurity in the oil. A high threshold implied that panelists and consumers would probably miss the smoky odor, and would accept the oil
for salad dressings.

The Stimulus

The first issue concerns stimulus. In what form should the product
tester present the stimulus for proper threshold measurement? Quite
often in odor work, panelists receive the stimuli in liquid dilution,
presented out of a cup. Sensory analysts select as solvents oil, water, or
the actual food product. Each of these three solvents modifies the
threshold for odor. The odor molecules selectively dissolve in the solvent and release into the air at different rates, depending upon the
type of solvent and its affinity to the odorant. In this instance, the
sensory analyst decided to dissolve the odorous oil in pure, odorless
cooking oil.

The next issue concerns the effective or real stimulus concentrations. Ideally, we would like to work with stimuli which span a wide
range of different concentrations, as well as know the exact concentration of the odorant in air above the liquid (the vapor phase concentration in the headspace above the liquid). For practical purposes in
product testing, one must use the dilutions of the odorant in the actual
liquid itself as the concentration measure. Rarely in applied product
testing can one expend the necessary effort to accurately measure
concentrations in the vapor phase. For the oil project, the sensory
analyst chose to express concentration as percent odorized oil in odorless oil solvent.

Choice of concentrations to test remains a perennial problem.
Should one choose a small range of concentrations within which to
work, with these concentrations bracketing the threshold level tightly
if previous reports have indicated an expected threshold value? Probably not. Threshold measurement requires the panelist to test a wide
range of different concentrations, ranging from 0 (nothing present) to
levels that the analyst knows clearly lie above threshold, and which
panelists can easily detect and recognize. Only by such bracketing can
we feel secure that we have accurately determined the threshold.

Ideally, the number and levels of concentrations should reflect: (1)
equal stimulus spacing in logarithmic terms (explained below), spanning the wide concentration range; and (2) a sufficiently narrow spacing between adjacent stimulus concentrations to ensure at least a
reasonable chance of ascertaining the threshold.

Spacing of Stimulus Levels

From Weber's early work (see Chap. 3), we know that the JND or just noticeable difference between adjacent stimuli equals a relatively constant percentage. For instance, if the JND value for taste lies around 0.4 ($\Delta I/I = 40\%$), then adjacent concentrations, starting at a point slightly above 0 concentration, should lie in a ratio slightly below 0.4 (e.g., 0.3). When the stimuli in the test increase by a constant percentage increment rather than by a constant additive increment, we call that *logarithmic spacing*. Table 4.1 compares logarithmic versus linear spacing for two stimulus sequences. We will generally obtain a better estimate of the threshold by using logarithmic (or constant percentage) spacing, rather than linear (or constant increment) spacing for these reasons. (1) The logarithmic spacing will array the adjacent stimuli at levels lying less than a JND apart above and below the absolute threshold. By doing so, one avoids the risk of having no one sense the stimuli slightly below threshold, and virtually all panelists detect the stimuli at the next level up, just above threshold. (2) The spacing will more adequately reflect the panelist's ability to discriminate stimuli from each other. Stimuli spaced logarithmically and lying above threshold will appear to grow in an even linear fashion with increasing concentration.

TABLE 4.1
COMPARISON OF LOGARITHMIC SPACING
VERSUS LINEAR SPACING

	Set 1		Set 2	
	Linear	Logarithmic	Linear	Logarithmic
	1.0	1	1.0	1.0
	3.0	2	1.5	1.5
	5.0	4	2.0	2.25
	7.0	8	2.5	3.375
Rule:	(Add 2)	(Double)	(Add 0.5)	(Multiply by 1.5)

Number of Stimuli

The best or optimum number of stimuli to test raises an age-old question in product and sensory measurement. Given a limited physical range of the stimuli, a large number of different concentrations will ensure a better estimate of the threshold value. One does not have to interpolate quite so much with the narrower stimulus spacing. On the other hand, having to test too many stimuli fatigues the panelist who searches for the sensory signal. Too many blanks or no-detection response decreases panelist morale, and may reduce the validity of any added information. Generally 4-8 stimuli should suffice if the researcher has a reasonably good idea of the threshold concentration. The spacing of the stimuli within a limit of 4-8 stimuli should take these factors into consideration: (1) the reasonable lower limit from which to start (0% or a definitely non-detectable lower value); (2) the reasonable upper limit at which to top off the stimulus range (stimulus levels that seem 100% detectable by all panelists); and (3) the JND or just noticeable difference. High JND values mean that the large percent changes in concentration will not enhance the ability to detect the difference, and require a wide ratio between adjacent stimulus concentrations for best results. In contrast, a low JND value suggests high sensory acuity in discerning differences, at least above threshold. A low JND value requires a smaller ratio between adjacent concentrations. Although the study concerns the threshold, nonetheless one should take into account panelists' ability to discriminate between adjacent concentrations when selecting the stimulus spacing.

Panelist Instructions

Threshold studies instruct the panelist to indicate whether one can detect (or recognize) the stimulus. The instructions may simply require the panelist to raise his or her hand in order to signal detection. On the other hand, the panelist may also rate his or her confidence level that he or she has correctly detected the stimulus. *Confidence ratings* allow the analyst an idea of the panelist's own criterion for stating that he or she detects the stimulus. Some individuals may always assign low confidence ratings, even when testing stimuli far above threshold. Others do the opposite, always assigning high confidence ratings, even when wrongly guessing.

The specific form which instructions assume can bias the panelists, forcing them to adopt a stringent or a lenient criterion in reporting detection. The panelist adopts an unstated criterion which governs whether or not he or she will report the presence of the stimulus in the threshold test. A *lenient criterion* dictates a detection response for a minimal number of sensory cues. Lenient criteria promote much guessing, and lead to many false alarms or false positives (the panelist states that he or she detects without the stimulus present). A *stringent criterion* promotes conservative behavior. Panelists refuse to state that they detect the stimulus until the stimulus becomes so intense that one cannot but admit to its presence. By wording the instructions to discourage false alarms, sensory analysts and product testers can shift the threshold upwards. Panelists will shy away from stating that they detect the stimulus until absolutely certain. In contrast, by wording the instructions to encourage guessing the sensory analyst will increase the number of false alarms, and lower the apparent stimulus thresholds. More likely than not, most panelists presented with the encouraging set of instructions will state that they detect the stimuli at a lower level, even if they must guess.

Stimulus Presentation

How does the sensory analyst or product tester present the test stimuli? Areas of concern in this regard include: (1) order of evaluating the stimuli—random or fixed; (2) number of stimuli at each concentration—one or several; (3) time period between stimulus evaluations—short or long; and (4) blanks (no stimulus present) or all actual stimulus concentrations, albeit below threshold.

Order of Evaluation. When panelists can evaluate the stimuli without carry-over effects from previous evaluations, the sensory analyst can then present the stimuli in random order. Intense samples can both precede and follow the weaker samples. The panelist evaluates each sample and indicates whether or not he or she detects the stimulus in that sample. This randomized approach particularly applies to acoustic testing, where ongoing adaptation rarely occurs and thus poses little or no problem to the panelists. People do not adapt to any great degree in hearing studies so that a loud stimulus presented first has little or no effect on a weak stimulus presented shortly thereafter.

In the measurement of aroma/odor or taste, threshold sequence can promote ongoing adaptation at the threshold level. As we saw previously (Chapter 3), Stuiver's (1958) work on olfactory threshold measurement showed that prior, strong and adapting stimuli do diminish sensitivity to subsequent test stimuli. When measuring aroma and taste thresholds, therefore, the sensory analyst should ensure long waiting times between samples. He or she must balance and control the stimulus order to ensure that the very weakest stimuli never immediately follow strong stimuli, or else present the stimuli in strict ascending order. The first two precautions eliminate some of the tightness of the study by prolonging time, or by introducing minor sequence effects. It then becomes impossible to truly randomize the order of stimuli.

Sequence of Stimulus Presentation. The panel leader can follow one of several courses in sequencing the stimulus to ensure the best results.

(1) He or she can present stimuli in ascending order until the panelist reports that he or she detects the stimulus; then stop the presentation and record the final stimulus level. The concentration at which the panelist states that he or she detects the stimulus becomes the estimate of the stimulus level. With this approach, the threshold depends upon the panelist's criterion. A panelist who adopts a lenient criterion will report detection at low levels, basing the report on flimsy sensory evidence. The panelist who adopts a stringent criterion will report no detection until absolutely sure. The researcher cannot differentiate between the threshold level and the panelist's criterion unless the panelist participates in the same study twice—once using a stringent criterion, and another time using the lenient criterion (Researchers have done this using the method of signal detection theory, explicated later in this chapter). Furthermore, the panelist may continue to state that he or she does not detect the stimulus when, in fact, he or she does actually detect the stimulus. The continued statements of not present set up a *response set*, or tendency to continue to state "not present," or "do not detect," simply by force of habit.

(2) Stop when the panelist has successfully detected stimuli, but not falsely detected blanks in several successive samples (e.g., the panelist correctly states that blanks contain no stimuli in four sequential trials comprising both stimuli and blanks).

(3) The panel leader can tell the panelist that the stimuli will appear in random order (sometimes present, sometimes absent) when, in fact, the stimuli appear in sequential ascending order. Perhaps the panel leader will intersperse 2 or 3 actual blanks, with no stimulus level between adjacent increasing concentrations, to confuse the panelist and disrupt his or her strategy. The presentation strategies to accomplish these goals appear as follows.

Straight Sequential—0, 1, 2, 3, 4, 5, 6, 7, 8, . . . 0 = nothing present = blank. 1, 2, 3, . . . represent systematic increases in physical concentration, whether logarithmic (preferable), linear (less preferable), or random change (least preferable).

Modified Sequential—e.g., 0, 1, 0, 2, 0, 0, 2, 3, 0, 5, 0 . . . With a modified sequential (or even with a straight sequential) design similar, but not necessarily identical, to the one shown above, the experimenter can prevent perseveration.

The modified sequential procedure lessens the bias, but depends upon fairly arbitrary rules to set up the stimulus sequence. The panel leader has the discretion to modify the sequential arrangement of the test stimuli by inserting blanks wherever he or she wishes. During the past forty years, however, a specified sequential procedure has proved popular which optimizes the selection and arrangement of the stimuli. The *choose 1 of n procedure* uses 2 or 3 (or even more) samples at each level. For two stimuli at each level, one sample contains the stimulus at a fixed level, the other(s) a blank. For instance, the experimenter might present these pairs, with 0 = blank: 0 0,1 0,2 0,3 0,4 0,5 0,6 0,7 . . . The panelist evaluates each pair of samples in fairly rapid sucession, indicating which sample in each pair contains the stimulus. At each stage, the probability of guessing equals 50%. This multiple choice method reduces the bias to perseverate by saying no detection or no stimulus. It also reduces the bias to adopt a lenient criterion and guess. The panelist must choose one of the stimuli. Psychologists often use this procedure, or a modified procedure comprising three stimuli (*ascending triangle procedure*), in order to obtain threshold values. In the triangle test, one of three contains the stimulus. The other two do not.

Measuring The Threshold For Odorous Oil—Specifics

Table 4.2 shows the results of the odor threshold test using the triangle method. The odorant stimuli (odorized oil) in oil solvent increased in concentration by a constant factor—the constant, or logarithmic, spacing of the stimulus on the concentration axis. A panel of 25 consumers evaluated each triangle of stimuli (2 blanks and 1 sample with odor stimulus present). Panelists tested the samples in ascending order, and in each triangle the panelists selected the stimulus containing the odorant.

We can plot the data in graphical form to visualize the threshold data. Figure 4.1 shows how percent correct choice varies with physical odorant concentration. The abscissa plots concentration of odorized oil in logarithmic values, and the ordinate shows the percent of the panel who correctly detected the stimulus at each concentration. Note the spacing along the ordinate (y-axis). The probability spacing compresses the middle and expands the extremes. This spacing exemplifies *probability spacing*.The ordinate follows the distribution of probabilities on the normal curve. When probabilities space according to a normal or bell shaped curve, the distance on the graph between 50% and 84% equals the distance between 84% and 98%.

Correcting For Guessing

The dashed line in Fig. 4.1 represents another way of computing the threshold value by correcting for guesses. Recall that in this threshold

TABLE 4.2
RESULTS FROM PANEL EVALUATION OF OIL ODOR

Concentration of Odorous Oil (%)	Percent Correct Detection (T)	Percent Above Chance (P)*
20	92	88
10	68	52
5	56	34
2.5	24	0
1.25	44	16

*To calculate percentage P, use formula: $P = 1.5\,(T - .33)$

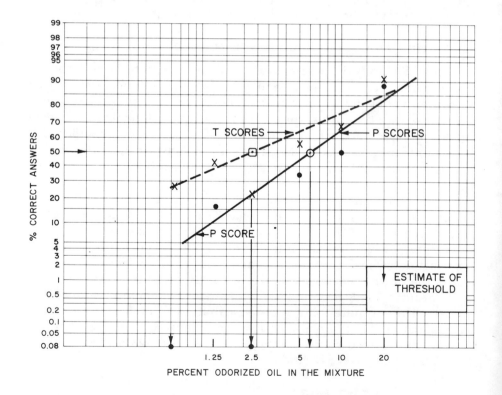

FIG. 4.1 RELATION BETWEEN ODOROUS OIL CONCENTRATION AND PERCENT OF PANELISTS CORRECTLY DETECTING THE ODOR

study on odor perception, the panelist selected which of the three stimuli in the triangle contained the odorized oil. By chance alone, a panelist can select one out of the three, or show a 33% probability of guessing (For 2 products, the probability of correct answers by guessing alone jumps to 1/2 or 50%. For four test samples, only one of which contains the odor stimulus, the probability of correct choice by guessing drops down to 1/4 or 25%, etc.). Guessing lowers the threshold value. Some practitioners advocate recomputing the probability of a correct guess by subtracting out the probability of guessing, according to a simple formula. For the 3 sample (triangle) case wherein the probability of correctly guessing equals 33%:

True Probability of Detection (corrected for guessing) =

$$\frac{P_{Correct} - P_{Guessing}}{1 - P_{Guessing}} = \frac{P_{Correct} - 0.33}{0.66} = 1.5 \, (P_{Correct} - .33)$$

For the 2 sample case, with guessing probability = 50%:

$$\text{True Probability of Detection} = \frac{P_{Correct} - 1/2}{(1/2)} = 2(P_{Correct} - 0.5)$$

Figure 4.1 compares the observed and the true probabilities of correctly detecting the actual odorized oil.

Calculation of the Threshold Value

Each of the foregoing procedures allows the researcher to estimate the probability at which a prespecified number of panelists in the population will correctly guess which sample from the set contains the stimulus odorant. We define threshold at that concentration at which 50% of the panelists correctly detect the stimuli. From time to time, researchers use more stringent or less stringent criteria to define threshold (e.g., the concentration at which 25% or 75% of the panelists detect the stimulus, etc.).

More often than not we must interpolate, usually graphically but also by equations, to estimate the concentration at which the probability equals 50% (see Fig. 4.1). The higher odorant (or stimulus) concentrations generate more than 50% correct detection, whereas the lower concentrations generate less than 50% correct detection. Through graphical estimation, however, one can best estimate that concentration which generates 50% correct detection, either with or without correction for guessing. In order to do so properly, the researcher should fit a straight data line to the detection probability versus concentration.

Straight lines usually (but not always) emerge when the analyst plots percent detection (in probability coordinates on the ordinate) versus the logarithm of concentration (on the abscissa). With such straight lines one can directly estimate the point at which the line intersects the 50% value on the ordinate.

Outcome of the CSOC Case Study

Based upon these data of detectability of odorized oil, management at the Chan Salad Oil Company opted to reject the odorized oil shipment. They felt that even by blending the odorized oil into their regular stock of odorless oil, consumers would detect the odor down to at least 10% or lower.

Other Refinements

Product testers can develop more rigorous procedures to measure thresholds by requiring the panelist to sort a large collection of test samples into two classes—those which contain the stimulus, and those which do not (Gridgeman 1959). Rather than presenting the stimulus in one of two or three samples (in a pair or in a triangle), the product tester presents the panelist with a set of 4-7 stimuli. Some of these contain the stimulus, and the rest do not (blanks). The panelist must sort the stimuli into two groups to reflect which contain and which lack the stimuli.

Methods requiring sorting allow more freedom from criteria in determining threshold than do the strict ascending or descending threshold methods. For one, panelists do not need to adapt a lenient or strict criterion. They know that one (or perhaps several) of the test samples contains the stimulus. They must correctly select (or sort), rather than simply say detect or do not detect. In effect, the sorting method represents a further refinement over the triangle test method. Table 4.3 presents some various sorting procedures and the chance probability of success, as reported by the Israeli scientist, D. Basker (1980).

ISSUES IN THRESHOLD MEASUREMENT

Simple as threshold measurement seems, it has generated strong controversies, and has given birth to a body of conflicting data in the chemical senses. We now consider some of the specific issues which have arisen.

TABLE 4.3
RECIPROCAL OF RISK OF CORRECT IDENTIFICATION
BY CHANCE IN SORTING TASKS OF VARIOUS DESIGNS

Total Number of Samples	Number of Samples Having the Stimulus Present						
	1	2	3	4	5	6	7
3	3						
4	4	3					
5	5	10					
6	6	15	10				
7	7	21	35				
8	8	28	56	35			
9	9	36	84	126			
10	10	45	120	210	126		
11	11	55	165	330	462		
12	12	66	220	495	792	462	
13	13	78	286	715	1287	1716	
14	14	91	364	1001	2002	3003	1716
15	15	105	455	1365	3003	5005	6435

For example: If 1 sample in a total of 3 samples has the odorized oil, then the probability of correctly guessing = 1/3 = .33 = 33%. If 3 samples in a total of 10 samples have the odorized oil then the probability of correctly guessing = 1/120 = 0.0083 = 0.83%.
    Source: Basker (1980)

Definition of Threshold—Point or Region

Chemists, physicists and other scientists accustomed to working with hard physical constants like to consider the threshold as a fixed point. From our data on odors and from extensive research in the literature, we know that threshold detection represents a probabilistic process, not a fixed invariant point on the concentration scale. Thresholds vary across individuals. Some of the variation results from inherently different sensitivity to stimuli. Other variations result from different criteria which panelists use when the test method allows such criteria to partly determine the threshold. Hence, we consider threshold to represent a region of uncertainty in which some panelists detect the stimulus, and others do not. The 50% value simply represents an arbitrary point in that region at which we find half the population falling into the class of detectors, and half into the class of non-detectors.

The size of the threshold region also varies. Some chemicals exhibit narrower regions of threshold variation than do others. In order to measure the size of the threshold region (with the 50% point representing the mean or average of the region), we look again at the threshold detection curve or the straight line when plotted in probability curves coordinates (Fig. 4.1). The slope of this line shows how the percentage of panelists correctly detecting the stimulus increases with increasing concentration. A steep curve or line implies a stimulus with a narrow threshold region. Most of the population exhibit detection thresholds within a narrow range. Increase the stimulus level slightly, and many more people will detect the stimulus. A flatter curve represents a stimulus with a broad threshold region.

Does The Threshold Really Exist

When first researched intensively by the Germans in the last century, the threshold appeared to promise a concentration on the stimulus scale (or a measure of physical energy) which possessed inherent reality and validity. Scientists hypothesized that the threshold value, whether fixed or varying across the population, reflected that minimal stimulus energy level which sufficed to activate the receptor. Researchers (e.g., Stuiver 1958) used the threshold value to calculate the number of molecules needed to excite a stimulation.

S. S. Stevens *et al.* (1941) hypothesized that the continuous curve relating concentration of stimulus to threshold really represents an artifact. In actuality, according to Stevens, the threshold represents a single point. Below that stimulus point an individual will not detect the stimulus. Above that point the individual will always detect the stimulus, all other factors held constant. We see the curve, not the step, because we average the thresholds from many different people. The average smooths out the all-or-none quantum step into a seemingly smooth curve.

SIGNAL DETECTION THEORY AND THRESHOLDS

In the 1950s a new view of threshold work and human detection processes arose in psychology known as Signal Detection Theory (TSD). Based upon work in radar detection (with signals in a noise background) done in the late 1940s (Tanner and Swets 1954), the theory of signal detection hypothesizes that the threshold value we observe in studies combines two processes: (1) inherent detectability of the stimulus (called d'); and (2) panelist criteria which bias the panelist's likelihood of stating that he or she detects the stimulus, given specific payoffs for correctly or incorrectly guessing.

According to TSD, the human sensory system continually operates in a background of noise, or low level sensory signals, created by random neural effects. We do not hear this noise. Rather, we assume its existence. The background noise varies. Sometimes the hypothetical neural noise seems loud, but rarely. Sometimes the neural noise seems soft, but also rarely. The bell shaped Gaussian, or normal, curve averages out to a specific neural noise level. Contrast this with Stevens' Neural Quantum Theory, NQT (Steven *et al.* 1941), which assumes absolute quiet without external stimulation.

When the experimenter presents the panelist with a stimulus, the bell shaped curve shifts upward by a constant amount equal to the stimulus value, as shown in Fig. 4.2. Again, signal + noise varies in a normally distributed way, just as noise alone did.

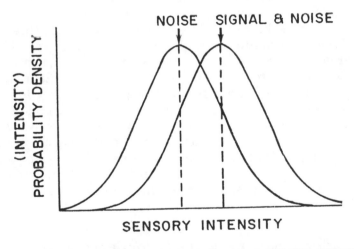

FIG. 4.2 SCHEMATIC DIAGRAM OF AN ONGOING NEURAL NOISE AND NEURAL NOISE + A STIMULUS, WHICH SHIFTS THE NEURAL LEVEL UPWARD

Threshold measurement studies determine the probability of stating that the panelist detects the stimulus correctly against the noise background. The panelist must respond basing his or her judgment on the belief that what he or she senses comes from: (a) the noise distribution, or (b) the signal + noise distribution.

Depending upon the reward for the outcome, the panelist may choose to always say signal present, to sometimes say it, or never say it. In fact, the probability of correctly detecting the stimulus and the probability of a false positive, saying present if the stimulus does not actually appear, link together closely, and vary with the payoffs for correct versus incorrect responses.

According to TSD, one can represent stimulus detection data seen in the laboratory as a combination of inherent detectability and effect of bias, resulting from the criteria which panelists adopt. Experimenter instructions, payoffs for correct versus incorrect responses, etc., influence these criteria.

TSD suggests that the threshold reflects as much response style and cognitive or behavioral criteria as it reflects true sensory functioning. By modifying payoffs or rewards and punishments for correct versus incorrect detection, one can modify the threshold value, in contrast to the Neural Quantum Theory (NQT) approach. According to NQT, the experimenter really taps into an underlying aspect of sensory process when panelists generate threshold measures. According to TSD, all threshold-related behavior follows a continuous, not a discrete, or all-or-none curve. The parameters of that curve result from both external criteria and payoffs, as well as innate sensory factors.

For a decade and a half, TSD posed severe threats to threshold concepts. S.S. Stevens pointed out, however, that in the typical TSD study one cannot possibly show the existence of a neural quantum, or an all-or-none sensory process. In TSD, the experimenter determines the panelist's ability to detect a stimulus (e.g., an auditory tone) by presenting the stimulus tone against the background of a noise under the experimenter's direct control. In order to avoid the vagaries of any so-called internal noise, the experimenter muddies the sensory input in an excessive and standardized manner. Any neural quantum which truly exists would disappear under such intense, extraneous noise stimulation. We should not feel surprised, therefore, that TSD research fails to find no evidence of a neural quantum.

Signal Detection Experiment: The Tabor Jam Company

Let us consider the case of a signal detection experiment applied to the evaluation of food. The Tabor Jam company, manufacturer of fine jams, receives shipments of strawberries from around the world. In its processing facilities, the Tabor Jam Company mixes the different lots of strawberries, adjusting the mixture until the flavor from the mixture tastes virtually identical to the quality control standard.

Management at Tabor wanted to run a project to ascertain whether, in fact, two jams taste different from each other. One jam contains more California strawberry than the usual source. Consequently, that lot may have a different flavor, perhaps more or less acceptable to the panelist. Let us follow the procedure according to the signal detection approach, rather than the traditional method.

Recall that in signal detection theory the experimenter hypothesizes that we do not possess an absolute threshold. According to TSD, people respond to constant sensory noise, and try to detect the signal (presence of California Strawberry flavor) in the presence of noise (flavors other than the specific California strawberry). Can the panelist distinguish the signal (or desired flavor) from the noise (other flavors)?

The experimenter would like to generate a curve similar to that appearing in Fig. 4.3. We call this the ROC or *receiver operating characteristic*. It plots the probability of a correct guess (detection of

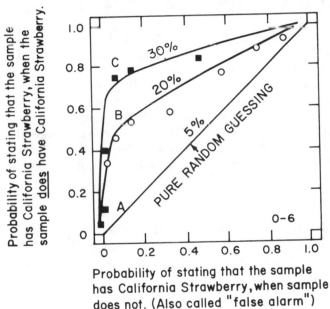

Probability of stating that the sample
has California Strawberry, when sample
does not. (Also called "false alarm")

FIG. 4.3   ISO-SENSITIVITY ROC
(RECEIVER OPERATING CURVE)

A—5% California strawberry added to jam sample
B—20% California strawberry added to jam sample
C—30% California strawberry added to jam sample

target, California strawberry sample) on the ordinate versus the total probability of guessing that the sample contains the California strawberry (whether correct or incorrect). As the panelist continues to guess that every sample contains the California Strawberry, we increase both the total number of guesses (abscissa) and the correct number of hits (ordinate).

Figure 4.3 shows three of these curves. The curves will differ as a function of the amount of added California jam, and sometimes one will appear as a straight line when panelists guess by random chance alone (see curve A in Fig. 4.3).

As the probability of correct guessing exceeds the probability of false alarms (guessing present without a stimulus), we find an increasingly concave curve (curves B and C). This occurs when panelists clearly detect the added California strawberry. If we increase the amount of added California strawberry in the blend, the curve will become even more concave.

Signal detection theory looks at two aspects of this curve: (1) the degree of curvature, and (2) the point on the curve.

The Degree of Curvature. Increasingly curved functions (A versus B versus C) reflect that the panelist can discriminate the stimulus (added California strawberry) from the noise. From guessing, we expect the straight line curve A. Here, the probability of correct guessing equals the probability of false alarms since the panelist really guesses at random. The degree of curvature relates to the ability to truly detect the test or target. A flat line means no detectability (curve A). An increasingly curved line (B and C) means increased detectability. Theoreticians call the detection capability d'. Sensitive panelists exhibit high values for d'. The d' value reflects the true sensitivity of the sensory system.

The Point on the Curve. Just where does the panelist place his or her probability of guessing correctly versus probability of guessing incorrectly. The panelist possesses constant detection ability indexed by d', a constant underlying sensitivity to the stimulus. Yet the panelist can behave conservatively, rarely saying present. This conservatism will produce low proportions of both correctly detecting the stimulus and guessing which yields a false alarm. On the other hand, the panelist can guess wildly. This strategy will generate a higher proportion both of correct responses and false alarms. Signal detection researchers claim that the payoff matrix, or reward structure, strongly influences where on that curve the individual probabilities lie. Should the experimenter make a guessing strategy pay off (reward correct guesses but not punish incorrect guesses), panelists will tend to guess present more often. After all, with only rewards and no punishment for errors, it pays to continue to guess present as often as possible. In such instances, we expect the proportions of correct guessing and false alarms to lie at the top right hand side of the curve. On the other hand, the experimenter may discourage guessing. The panelist may lose money for incorrect guessing (if the experimenter sets up a win-lose payoff matrix). False alarms may become so costly that the panelist waits until he or she definitely senses the stimulus before guessing "present." In this instance, and for the same intrinsic detectability of the stimulus, the probability of guessing diminishes radically. The probabilities will lie near the bottom left, but on the same ROC curve. Both the probability of correct guessing and the probability of a false alarm will drop down. In contrast, if the panelist has received rewards for guessing and punishments for incorrectly guessing, we expect the point to lie somewhere on the middle of the curve.

Through varying the rewards and penalties in the payoff matrix, the experimenter can move the panelist's proportions of correct guessing and incorrect guessing (false alarms) along the ROC curve. On the other hand, the shape of the ROC curve itself remains fixed, because it depends upon the innate detectability (d') of the stimulus.

In net, the experiment on signal detection of the flavor of strawberry jam, using California strawberry as the signal, shows these results. (1) With 5% California strawberry added to the jam, the panelists behave randomly in detecting the added flavor notes (see Fig. 4.3, curve A). This means that a 5% addition lies below the panelist's threshold. (2) 20% and 30% additions of the California strawberry product produce clear-cut detection of the changed flavor. The panelists may not know what has changed, but they can certainly detect the addition of the flavor. (3) By altering the payoff matrix (rewards for correct guessing, punishments for incorrect guessing), one can change the apparent proportion of correct and incorrect guesses.

This information helps management in the following ways. (1) If the presence of California strawberry adds acceptance, one needs to go above 5% to make a sensory impact. (2) If California strawberry reduces acceptance, one should definitely stay below 20% increase in the level of California strawberry.

Other Aspects of Signal Detection Theory

In traditional laboratory research psychophysics, TSD has received a lot of attention because it integrates motivation factors and sensory performance. The research procedures used to obtain the curves require the panelist to participate in long, tedious sessions trying to detect hundreds of stimuli. For auditory work, where fatigue plays a minor role, extended sessions pose no problem. It should come as no surprise that TSD data, for the most part, has attracted researchers studying auditory and visual perception. For taste perception, such extended or at least numerous sessions would become infeasible.

In recent years, however, experimenters have found other ways of estimating the probability of correctly guessing and the probability of false alarms. Estimates of panelists' confidence in detection correlate with these values. As a result, O'Mahony (1972) has developed methods to relate panelists' direct rating of confidence to the probabilities. Through a rating procedure, one can translate the panelist's rating of confidence in his or her statement of present or absent to the probability of correct hits versus false alarms.

Specifics of A Taste Experiment Using TSD

Let us consider the use of TSD in psychophysical (laboratory) evaluation. The study of O'Mahony (1972) on detecting the taste of salt provides an excellent illustration of how one can use the Theory of Signal Detection to determine the difference between a stimulus and the background noise. The study also shows how one can modify the apparent ability to detect a stimulus (from the supposed background noise of ambient saliva stimuli) by means of the approach. It will also augment our understanding of results from the Tabor Jam Project.

In the actual study, O'Mahony presented the panelists with salt stimuli, varying the concentration and the payoff matrix. In doing so, he obtained the ratings of panelists' confidence that they had detected the stimulus (when in fact he had actually presented the salt stimulus), and also estimated the false alarms.

In doing this experiment, he generated results shown in Table 4.4. Recall that a response to single stimulus concentration describes one of the ROC curves which appear in Fig. 4.3. The position on the curve derives from the matrix of payoffs for correctly detecting a stimulus versus incorrectly stating that one has sensed the stimulus, when in fact no stimulus has appeared (false alarms). Furthermore, recall that each individual concentration of a salt stimulus generates its own unique curve. The perpendicular distance of the curve from the top left equals the detectability of the stimulus, d'.

Signal detection generates two output indices in this salt detection experiment. The index value d' reflects the separation between the signal strength, or perceived strength, and the noise distribution. In terms of threshold value, d' acts as a measure of threshold. Of course, since we use data from the normal distribution, we have a difficult time converting d' to a concentration of salt or any other taste stimulus. On the other hand, we can measure the value of d' for different stimuli (e.g., sodium chloride, potassium chloride), or we can correlate the change in d' versus the salt levels we test (see Table 4.4). As the test level increases beyond the adapting salt level, the d' value increases as well.

TABLE 4.4

HOW THE ADAPTING SALT CONCENTRATION AND THE TEST SALT CONCENTRATION AFFECT d' (DETECTABILITY) AND P(Y/S) (PROPORTION OF CORRECT GUESSES) VIA SIGNAL DETECTION THEORY

Salt Level Adapting	Test	d'	P(Y/S)
10	11	0.41	0.606
	12	0.66	0.692
	13	1.03	0.771
30	31	0.48	0.618
	32	0.87	0.719
	33	1.19	0.801
	35	2.46	0.959

Source: O'Mahony (1972)

Can Signal Detection Provide A Useful Approach In Product Testing

In evaluating new procedures, the practitioner has to address the question of relevance. Specifically for TSD, does the procedure yield additional insights into the mechanism of sensory action per se, to aid the product tester? If so, does TSD provide a useful procedure to assess discrimination or threshold capabilities?

Currently, TSD methods seem attractive as a research approach in basic laboratory research. TSD allows the researcher to measure the separate components of (a) bias, which changes guessing behavior, and (b) innate discriminability, d'. TSD reveals that the apparent sensory threshold can change as a function of the instructions provided to the panelist.

In terms of method, as one might use in practical product evaluation, TSD has a role, but it seems too early to tell exactly how important the role will become. TSD does not generate immediately actionable data in terms of the measurements of threshold. One cannot specify a point on the continuum of stimulus concentration using TSD. One can specify a concentration by using actual threshold measurements done in the conventional manner.

In forecasting the future role of TSD, it looks like TSD will probably find itself playing two distinct roles. (1) TSD will enter into scientific research in the mechanisms of taste and smell, as it provides an alternative set of methods for measuring thresholds. (2) Panelist selection will have a basis in TSD. The experimenter can determine which panelists in a group seem most influenced by payoff matrices, and which panelists seem uninfluenced, or at least less influenced, by the payoff matrix. Those panelists who show little bias and behave almost independently of the payoffs represent the *field-independent* panelists, attending more to their sensory perceptions than to the externally manipulated rewards. These panelists may form the optimal nucleus of a test panel, either for discrimination testing or for other descriptive, or rating tasks.

OTHER ISSUES IN THRESHOLD MEASUREMENT

Variabilities In Threshold Measurement

In the measurement of threshold, the extensive presentation of various stimuli affects threshold. Thresholds for stimuli can vary over a wide range, often by a factor of 10 or 100, especially in tests of olfactory thresholds. Stimulus variation and momentary changes in sensitivity can play havoc with the supposedly single threshold value. We should expect, therefore, large variations in threshold values which appear in the literature. These high changes, in turn, correspond to rather small psychological ranges of odor intensity.

Uses of Threshold Values

Sensory analysts and others use threshold values for many different end uses. Specifically, the threshold provides three types of information. (1) Thresholds provide a measure of the potency of stimuli to evoke sensations. As we saw earlier, scientists during the past century and a half used threshold values as a measure of relative intensity. A stimulus with a threshold 10% that of another supposedly possesses 10 times the potency. Even today, scientists still use the threshold value as a rough index of the relative stimulating power of a stimulus. They often correlate the threshold value with chemical structure, to see what characteristics of structure produce high or low threshold values. (2) Thresholds measure the lowest level of stimulus (e.g., chemical) which a product can contain before the consumer senses an off-taste or off-flavor. (3) Thresholds have use as a measure of genetic relations among populations. Anthropologists study thresholds of populations using specific chemicals such as phenylthiocarbamide, or PTC (see Chapter 9).

MEASURING DIFFERENTIAL SENSITIVITY (JND'S)

How can the product tester determine whether or not two stimuli seem identical or different. Recall that psychophysics received its earliest impetus from E. H. Weber's pioneering studies on people's ability to discriminate between simple stimuli. Further studies elaborated on the human ability to discern small differences between stimuli.

Practical issues arise in the discernment of small differences between food or flavor stimuli. Let us explore the techniques of *difference testing* to answer some of the practical problems which arise time after time.

(1) The Flavola Company purchases lemon oil from sources around the world which it incorporates into its lemon flavored, dry-mix beverage. From time to time prices vary in the marketplace. The alternate sources of lemon oil seem acceptable, but will they generate a flavor which seems identical to the current lemon flavor? Or, does the current flavor seem so different from the lemon flavor obtained when using oil from South America, which Flavola has used for the past two years as its main component?

(2) A manufacturer wishes to reduce the concentration of sucrose in a carbonated beverage. Can the manufacturer reduce the concentration by 3% and ensure that panelists cannot discern the difference?

(3) We know that some individuals possess the unusual ability to discern small differences between otherwise similar tasting products. Does their rejection of a food with changed ingredients correspond to any acute differential sensitivity which they possess? Do they reject it because they discriminate?

(4) We wish to develop a flavor description and evaluation panel, but before determining the final panel composition we want to make sure that our panelists accurately detect small, but real stimulus differences. We want to know the range of abilities to discriminate in order to select only the best or most discriminating individuals for our panel. We will use the panel to assess the flavor quality of batches of product coming from the production line.

The Flavor Oil Supplier and Discrimination Testing

Any product tester working in foods comprising or incorporating natural flavors or other natural components obtained from several primary suppliers, at one time or another will need sensory quality control. Natural flavors and ingredients vary in quality. They comprise a multitude of chemicals, all in delicate balance with each other. Each flavor variation comprises many of the same chemicals, but at different relative levels. Figure 4.4 shows tracings of the chemical composition of two pear flavors derived from gros michel and valery. They have similar compositions, but components appear at different ratios. Can the panelist sense the difference between the two pear flavors by aroma alone or by taste in the final product?

In the case history reported here, it became necessary to determine whether panelists at the Flavola Company (and thus, ultimately consumers) could discriminate among three types of lemon oil: 100% current lemon oil purchased from South America; a 50/50 mixture of

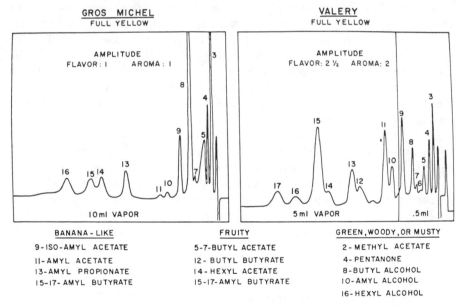

FIG. 4.4   GAS CHROMATOGRAMS (TRACINGS OF THE CHEMICAL COMPOSITION) OF
TWO PEARS: GROS MICHEL AND VALERY. EACH PEAK CORRESPONDS TO
A DIFFERENT CHEMICAL IN THE FLAVOR

lemon oil, half current and half purchased from Spain; and a 100% lemon oil purchased from the secondary supplier in Spain.

In any discrimination study, the sensory analyst should keep certain questions in mind. (1) Can panelists discriminate between samples in the product's final form? (2) If so, should the sensory analyst also determine whether or not the difference produces a less acceptable product? Or, should the sensory analyst simply implement the discrimination test without including other diagnostic questions? (3)

How can one best test the ability to discriminate? Does discrimination ability for this particular product emerge instantaneously after a short product evaluation? Perhaps, but perhaps not. Sometimes a panelist may require more extensive and longer exposure to the product, in order to learn about the stimulus in detail through repeated exposure to the lemon-flavored drink. We often overlook the fact that repeated experience may sharpen one's ability to discern differences, as the user detects other characteristics not immediately apparent on the first evaluation.

Stimulus Development. In order to test the stimulus in the most sensitive manner, the sensory analyst at the Flavola Company decided to use a bias-free method, the triangle test. In the triangle test, panelists tested three samples in random order. Two samples in the triangle comprised the same flavor (100% current), whereas the third sample comprised a different flavor (50%/50% mixture or 100% new product). In order to remove any bias in stimulus selection, half the panel evaluated this specific triangle: 100% current, 100% current, 100% new (items in random order). The other half of the panel evaluated the specific triangle: 100% current, 100% new, 100% new (items in random order). The panelist had to indicate which one of the three samples of the lemon flavor tasted different from the other two. The panelist tasted the flavor in a lemonade.

Although it appeared from informal testing that one could detect differences between the oils at 100% current level, the actual product (a beverage) contained the flavor at only a low level around 1/2%. By adopting a stringent criterion that panelists should not discriminate between the current flavor and the flavor with the Spanish lemon oil, the beverage manufacturer (Flavola's customer) would lose an opportunity to capitalize on a substantial cost saving. The second source, Spanish lemon oil, cost 80% of the current lemon oil and promised to become increasingly available, based on current weather forecasts. Hence, Flavola decided that it would test the current and substituted oils in the actual product, where a difference would play a much more valid role in influencing consumer reactions. It would then present the results to its beverage customer and suggest that it consider the cheaper, more available lemon oil from Spain as a component in the beverage.

Panel Selection. The Flavola company decided that for this initial test of current versus partially and fully substituted lemon oil, it would use an in-house panel of practiced employee panelists. These panelists do not fall into the class of true experts per se, but each panelist did have considerable experience in sensory analysis.

From time to time the sensory analyst faces the problem of which panelists to use. Should the panelists come from one's own internal staff, or should they come from an external source (consumers)? Chapter 9 deals in depth with the business and technical aspects of this issue. Here, the sensory analyst could have used internal or external panelists. The sensory analyst further recognized that even if the in-house panelists could detect a difference between the lemon-flavored beverage samples, that difference may or may not appear in the data generated by consumer panelists who regularly purchase and/or consume the lemon flavored beverage.

Panel Size. As with most in-house panel studies, panel size becomes a problem. The product tester often has a difficult time recruiting more than a handful of participants. Here, for the sake of expediency, the analyst selected twelve panelists.

Panel Composition. The panelists comprised individuals who regularly worked in the secretarial pool. They showed no special or enhanced sensitivity to product differences. On other occasions, the product tester may specifically tailor the panel composition so that the members demonstrate that they can discriminate differences between different samples. The sensory analyst could have selected lemon beverage users, or even users of the customer's brand.

The Study Itself. The study proceeded in a straightforward manner. The R&D group at Flavola prepared the test samples according to the customer's R&D specifications. The only potential negative point lay in the fact that, for such a small test, one relies upon small-scale bench-top sample preparation manufactured under nonrepresentative circumstances. Ideally, one would like to test discrimination capacity with samples that reflect actual pilot plant or production plant runs. Sometimes pilot plant and bench top results differ, because the bench scientist can rarely reproduce in toto the physical samples identical to those from actual plant runs. Some of the ingredients change during pilot plant processing. These ingredients might remain unaffected during bench-top preparation of prototypes.

The panelists reported to the test site. The test moderator (the product tester) oriented the panelists about the test. The instructions required the panelists to indicate which of the three samples seemed different from the other two. The product tester further instructed panelists how to test the samples: Accurate and adequate instructions play a vital part in difference tests, as they do in all product evaluation tests. The product tester should make every effort to clarify what the panelists should do in the evaluation, rather than leave the actual product testing up to the panelist's own discretion. The specific instructions concerned and stressed these points. (1) Evaluate the products singly. (2) Take a short sniff of the head space above the beverage for aroma information about the product. (3) Take short sips sufficient to fill the mouth as one normally does when drinking. (4) Swallow the product. (5) Do a short rinse between samples with water provided for that purpose served at room temperature. (6) Evaluate the second sample in a prearranged order. Each panelist followed a separate order of evaluation. With 3 samples, the panelist can evaluate the samples in any of 3! = 3 × 2 × 1 = 6 different orders. (7) Do a short rinse with provided water. (8) Evaluate the third sample. (9) Make a decision regarding which sample seemed different overall from the other two. (10) Set a specific time in which to do the evaluations with 30 seconds between samples as the minimum wait to clear the palate. (11) Make sure that the panelist rinses to remove the traces of the previous sample. Without such intermittent rinsing one cannot maintain panelist sensitivity. A residual taste in the mouth will begin to build up with subsequent stimulus tastings.

Results of the Study. Table 4.5 shows the result of discrimination testing between three sets of lemon beverage pairs: 100% current versus 100% current (control condition, which should yield random, or chance, discrimination); 100% current versus 50/50 blend; and 100% current versus 100% new, Spanish oil product.

TABLE 4.5
DISCRIMINATION TEST RESULTS—3 LEMON SAMPLES

	Pair	Pair	Pair
	100% Current vs 100% Current	100% Current vs 50/50 Blend	100% Current vs 100% Spanish Oil
Correctly discriminating	.41	.66	.83
Corrected probability (taking guessing into account)	.12	.50	.75

Furthermore, Table 4.5 shows the discrimination data in terms of the two measures of correctness in discrimination: percent correct and percent correct after correction for guessing (probability = 33% by chance).

The test results suggest these conclusions, which the sensory analyst submitted to the Flavola Account Manager to report to the customer, the beverage manufacturer. (1) As expected, the control condition (100% current) showed virtual chance, or random discrimination, as it should. (2) 8 of the 12 panelists detected that the 50/50 blend differed from the current blend. This ratio would occur only 1.3 times in 100 by chance (probability = 0.013), and thus we conclude that their discrimination of the 50/50 blend scored substantially higher than the 33% (or 4 of 12) needed for correctness by guessing alone (see Table 4.6 for the calculation of percentage corresponding to the statistically significant difference values). (3) 10 of the 12 panelists detected that the 100% new lemon flavor seemed different from the current blend. The probability that such a score will occur, if panelists truly cannot discern the difference, equals 0.00044 or 4 times in 10,000 trials.

The sensory analyst concluded that panelists could readily discriminate between the lemon oil mixture and the current lemon oil in the beverage. Panelists discriminated even more between the current beverage and the beverage containing the 100% replacement lemon flavor.

Some Implications of the Lemon Flavor Study: Decisions in an Economic Environment. Should the sensory analyst recommend rejecting the new lemon oil flavor at 50/50 substitution or 100% substitution? We now know that panelists detect the difference between the Spanish versus the current and partially substituted flavors. Some questions remain unanswered, which will prove important if the Spanish lemon flavor, in fact, promises a decided high economic advantage in terms of price and availability. Specifically, we know that panelists discern differences between current and the 50/50 substitution flavors. Should the beverage manufacturer consider a mixture of 25% new/75% current? If this mixture provides an economic, supply or marketing advantage, then the 25/75 mixture might prove a viable recommendation for further consideration. One would have to test that mixture as well.

We also now know that panelists can detect the differences in product flavor between the current and substituted lemon oils. Does this difference between the oils affect any other sensory or hedonic characteristics (e.g., flavor intensity, liking, purchase intent, etc.). Do panelists detecting the difference feel that the product's quality has diminished? Do panelists notice a change in beverage flavor or a change in beverage sweetness? Can they home in on which product characteristics seem different? Do panelists recognize that all other characteristics, with the exception of flavoring oil, have remained the same?

Obviously, the simplistic discrimination test above leads to many

TABLE 4.6
PERCENTAGE DISCRIMINATION AND PROBABILITY OF ACHIEVING
THAT CORRECT DISCRIMINATION BY CHANCE ALONE
(Triangle Test)

Problem   Example: 12 triangles, 8 correct, 4 incorrect triangles

Solution: Number of Combinations of 8 items in 12 $\times$
(Probability Correct)$^{Number\ Correct}$ (Probability Wrong)$^{Number\ Wrong}$

$$8C12 = \frac{12!}{8!(12-8)!} = \frac{12!}{8!4!} \times (.33)^8 (.66)^4$$

$$= 495 \times (1.406 \times 10^{-4})(.189)$$

$$= .013$$

more queries. Deeper evaluation of the results will ensue when the substituted lemon oil impacts on profit margins, on the marketer's ability to sell a product of consistent quality, etc. When faced with the issue of discrimination testing, the product tester should endeavor to learn more about the ramifications of noticeable differences in terms of changes in perception and hedonics. Different may not always mean worse. It may mean an improved product.

One common strategy combines discrimination testing with scaling perceptual characteristics. When the panelist selects the odd sample, he or she first makes a classification judgment reflecting an all-or-none rating; one product among the three falls into the class of different. In order to explicate the reasons underlying that difference, and to assess the magnitude of the difference, the panelist might fill out a rating sheet which probes attributes of the product, as shown in Table 4.7. The questionnaire can take one of several forms.

The product tester then follows these steps. (1) He or she instructs the panelist to provide a sensory profile of characteristics for the two products which seem identical, and a parallel profile on the same characteristics for the odd product. By comparing the two profiles, the sensory analyst can obtain a good indication as to what characteristics led to the selection of the different or odd product. More often than not, the simple flavor change generates changes in the other, seemingly non-related characteristics, such as beverage sweetness. (2) The product tester instructs the panelist to indicate the degree of difference between the two products (identical pair, odd product), rather than scaling each product monadically, or singly and separately. For

TABLE 4.7
EXAMPLE OF IN DEPTH PROBE OF PRODUCT DIFFERENCES

Which Product Seems Different From the Other Two?

A ——
B ——
C ——

Does the odd or different product:

Look same —— Look Different ——
Taste Sweeter —— Less Sweet —— Same Sweetness ——
Taste More Lemony —— Less Lemony —— Same Lemony Flavor ——
Taste Tarter —— Less Tart —— Same Tartness ——
Have More Lemon Aroma —— Less Lemon Aroma —— Same Lemon Aroma ——
Richer Flavor —— Less Rich Flavor —— Same Richness ——

example, the questionnaire might ask questions of this sort. Which product tastes sweeter, and how different do the two products seem? Which product tastes stronger in flavor, and how different in flavor? Which product do you like more?

Another strategy to further explicate the simple discrimination tests requires that the panelist freely describe the differences between the samples. Rather than forcing panelists to use a pre-set scale and set of descriptors, the sensory analyst allows the panelist to freely explain the reasons for difference in his or her own terms. While less amenable to quantification, free description can, nonetheless, reveal sensory characteristics impacted by the lemon oil substitute to which the sensory analyst or product specialist did not initially attend.

In net, based upon the data, the manufacturer decided to use a 50/50 blend of current lemon oil and Spanish lemon oil in order to take advantage of the cost savings, despite the ability of panelists to discriminate.

COST REDUCTION IN BEVERAGES—CHANGING SWEETENER LEVEL

As one might expect in an era of stationary growth and fairly rapid price rises, manufacturers try to increase their margins, but still maintain acceptability by reducing ingredient levels in products. This strategy reduces costs of goods but runs the risk of changing product characteristics, which may or may not lead to rejection by loyal consumers who represent the marketer's franchise.

In our second case in discrimination testing, we consider the soft drink manufacturer who wishes to modify the sugar level in a beverage, a root beer product. Generally, marketers decide during their product evaluation and strategy phase that they must reapportion funds among product costs, distribution costs, advertising and promotion. Quite often the first question that manufacturers ask concerns whether or not they can lower cost of goods in a meaningful manner by reducing the most expensive ingredient levels ever so slightly, while maintaining the same consumer acceptance.

We return, in this instance, to the historical use of the discrimination test to assess human sensory capabilities. We know from the scientific reports that panelists can and do detect small sweetness differences (around 10% change in the concentration of sugar). At the same time, we know from other published studies (Berg *et al*. 1955) that the JND for sweetness increases less between 5% and 10% in the presence of acid and other taste substances. The product tester who becomes involved with the cost reduction project can initially, but not necessarily accurately, estimate how much change in sweetener one needs for the panelist to detect the difference.

Published data in the scientific literature pertain to model systems, e.g., sugar in water. Rarely, if ever, do published data directly address the specific product with which the sensory analyst must deal. For the root beer, the fact that panelists probably cannot detect differences in pure water between an 11% and an 11.5% sugar + acid solution does not answer the specific question concerning root beer.

Case History—Root Beer

The Warren Beverage Company, which manufactures root beer, wants to reduce the amount of sugar in its root beer by as much as possible to save money. Every 10% decrease in sugar increases profits by 0.5%. The sensory analyst can tackle the cost reduction problem in at least two different ways. (1) Take a stab at the problem by trying one possible cost reduced formula to see whether consumers detect a difference in the formulation taste. Consumers can then try again, perhaps with a slightly less drastic cost reduction, with a smaller change in sugar level. (2) Evaluate several cost reduction alternatives in one project in order to evaluate a range of alternative cost reductions, and their impacts on the consumer response.

The first, or *sequential approach*, requires that the product formulator and sensory analyst guess about the single most appropriate sugar concentration in the cost reduced formulation. Perhaps historical data in corporate files will provide clues. In most instances, however, product flavors will have changed. Usually during a product's life cycle, formulations will have changed dramatically. Historical data often bears no meaningful connection with the current formula.

The second, or *systematic approach*, allows the sensory analyst to maintain a more detached, clinical attitude. One need not determine the single best opportunity for cost reduction. The cost-reduction project allows for an evaluation of different options, much as a psychophysicist evaluates a range of intensities for a single sensory continuum (e.g., sucrose sweetness). Furthermore, the method allows for interpolation to ascertain responses to levels of cost-reduced formulas not directly tested. We select the systmatic approach for illustrative purposes.

Stimulus Selection. By means of informal benchtop screening with some alternative formulations, the product formulator and the product tester may realize that they, and probably consumers, can detect differences between the current formulation and the cost-reduced formulations when one reduces sugar content from 11% (11° Brix) to 8.5%. One learns this quickly, and can roughly guess the feasible range of reformulation by informal testing with one's associates in the laboratory. From time to time formulators may use expert or trained panelists who have had considerable flavor experience. The ratings from these panelists do not, however, reflect a typical consumer reaction.

The root beer product, and especially the sugar in it, costs money. Therefore, the manufacturer wishes to reduce the cost of goods as much as possible. Furthermore, the root beer represents one of Warren's products, but not the major product. Thus, if the product developers make a mistake and reduce sugar too dramatically, the resulting loss of product acceptability will probably not damage the corporate image, or the acceptability of its major flagship brand. These facts lead the product developer and sensory analyst into a riskier, less conservative position when they select alternative cost reduction levels. Since one incurs little risk in modifying the brand greatly except perhaps for some disaffection by current consumers who show little or no brand loyalty, the product formulator and sensory analyst decided to test a wide range of sugar levels, ranging from 8.5% all the way up to 11%. In contrast, the manufacturer would tread much more gingerly and conservatively when cost-reducing the company's flagship brand, which generates most of its profits.

Sugar levels in the product varied in a systematic way in order to generate six alternative formulas with varying sugar concentrations: 11%, 10.5% 10%, 9.5%, 9% and 8.5%. The panelists comprised 30 untrained consumers who worked at the plant and in the product technical center, but who had received no special training in methods of sensory analysis. The panelists did consume root beer at home, and so represented the consumer population to some extent. The project proceeded in a manner similar to the foregoing lemon oil project conducted by the Flavola Company. Panelists received instruction in the method of triangle testing, and evaluated the root beer beverages in random order of triangles, so that from time to time one panelist might evaluate this triangle first: 11%, 11%, 10.5%, etc. Altogether they tested six triangles, and the results appear in Table 4.8.

TABLE 4.8
RESULTS OF THE TRIANGLE TEST FOR COST
REDUCTIONS OF ROOT BEER

Current Sugar Level	Percent of Panel Detecting the Cost Reduced Sample	Percent Corrected For Guessing
Versus	Percent	
11.0% (Current)	40	10.5
10.5%	50	25.5
10.0%	56	34.5
9.5%	66	49.5
9.0%	80	70.5
8.5%	93	90.0

By selecting the conservative product reformulation strategy of small cost reduction and small change in sugar, the Warren Company may miss an opportunity to gain additional revenues for the advertising and promotion budgets. Such conservatism would maintain brand quality at the expense of lowering potential profitability.

At this decision point the recommendation made by the product tester becomes important. Additional information regarding changes in product acceptability due to changes in sugar level (changes in flavor characteristics) might dictate selecting the more conservative strategy or the less conservative one. Although we did not obtain data on perceptual differences here, the product tester might wish to do so. The next case contains that information for further discussion.

Discriminators in the Population. Table 4.8 tells us that the number of panelists we can class as discriminators increases as the difference between test samples increases. We define discriminators in this instance as those panelists who correctly chose the lower or different Brix product in the triangle test. Quite often a manufacturer or laboratory group leader wishes to work only with those panelists who fall into the category of discriminators, feeling that these individuals may reflect more sensitive instruments for the measurement of product quality.

Our data for root beer tell us that discrimination behaves as a probabilistic process. Discrimination depends in great part upon the stimulus studied. A panelist who discriminates when the products lie far apart (8.5% versus 11%) may become a non-discriminator when the products lie closer together (10.5% versus 11%). Discrimination panels who perform well for an attribute of overall quality (overall difference) may perform poorly when asked to discriminate among products on a single specified characteristic. Had we modified the questionnaire and instructed panelists to select which product tastes the least sweet, we might find that many panelists feel that the products taste equally sweet (and guess randomly), but that these products differ primarily on root beer flavor. In contrast, other panelists participating in this project might feel that the products differ both in their sweetness and in flavor. By looking at the data from these latter individuals the sensory analyst might conclude that some individuals seem better able to discriminate flavor differences, whereas other individuals seem better able to discriminate sweetness differences. However, the same physical change produces both sets of discriminations. We conclude that discrimination behaves probabilistically, as a function of the differences between the products, and as a function of the characteristics to which the panelists attend. Furthermore, individuals pay differential attention to attributes. The same individual may show heightened ability to discriminate differences in sweetness evaluations, but no ability to discriminate in flavor evaluations (Moskowitz, Jacobs, and Firtle, 1980).

SELECTING TRAINING AND EVALUATING PANEL FOR DISCRIMINATION TESTING

In spite of its importance in product work, no standardized tests exist for selecting, training and evaluating panelists on discrimination for these reasons. (1) Products qualitatively differ from each other. Panelists who discriminate variations well in one product may not discriminate differences in another product. Since products differ so much in comparison to colors and auditory stimuli, the product tester must design specific discrimination tests for each product category. (2) No adequate criteria exist to define a discriminator. How does one differentiate a discriminating panelist from a non-discriminating panelist? All too often sensory analysts must develop their own criteria in lieu of recognized standards.

Two Approaches For Measuring Discrimination and Selecting Discriminators

Various methods can test discrimination in a scientific manner. We presently compare two radically different approaches here: the triangle, or sorting, method versus the rating, or scaling method.

Triangle (or Other Sorting) Procedure. A panelist can participate in various triangle tests which test discriminative ability on a variety of products and stimuli. The sensory analyst first selects the test stimuli. For food flavors, the test stimuli may represent different bitter or sweet materials. The panelists must show their ability to discriminate between stimuli of similar, but not identical concentration. A single triangle test allows a panelist a 33% chance to guess which product seems odd or different from the other two. A sequential triangle test cuts down the panelist's ability to guess. For example, back-to-back triangle tests (so-called double triangle) reduce the guessing chance by 2/3. As a consequence, the probability of correctly guessing the odd sample in both triangles equals $1/3 \times 1/3 = 1/9$. Only 11% of the population would turn up as discriminators by random guessing alone. One can further reduce the chances of including non-discriminators by making the requirements more strict. Discriminators would have to show correct judgement on three successive triangles (probability of doing so by chance $= 1/27$, or less than 4%). Moskowitz, Jacobs and Firtle (1980) used the double triangle method to select discriminators in the test population for beverage analysis. Qualifying panelists had to successfully pass a double triangle screening test. They received two identical and one odd beverage. As the concentration difference between the odd and the same samples increased, an increasing number of panelists fell into the class of discriminators. The number of discriminators grew as a direct function of the difference between the test and standard beverages.

The triangle procedure, or indeed any all-or-none procedure which demands that panelists show 100% discrimination behavior, falls prey to certain problems. For instance, one generally limits the triangle test to the specific product tested. How does the product tester know that a panelist who performs well on a double triangle test with that particular product set will also behave as a discriminator in another test with other product modifications? Furthermore, once a panelist fails in a triangle test for whatever reason, he or she disqualifies for inclusion in the category of discriminators. Suppose the panelist would have performed much better had one tested a slightly larger stimulus difference? Then the panelist would fall into the discriminator category. The all-or-none aspect of triangle testing can generate a biased estimate of the number of panelists in the population who truly qualify as discriminators.

Scaling Approach. Moskowitz, Jacobs and Firtle (1980) suggested an alternative, perhaps more sensitive and more reasonable method for discovering panelists in the population who seem able to discriminate. They recommended that panelists scale the intensity of a series of stimuli containing graded concentrations of a single component, such as sugar or quinine in water (model system) or in the actual product. Panelists' scaled data for intensity may or may not correlate with the actual ingredient level. Those panelists showing relatively high correlations between sensory ratings of intensity and stimulus concentration behaviorally discriminate between stimulus levels. In contrast, panelists whose intensity ratings show little or no correlation with objectively measured stimulus levels do not discriminate.

With such an approach (successfully carried out with a beverage), the results suggested that approximately 34% of the panelists fell into the class of discriminators when their task required scaling of six levels of sugar in a beverage. The advantage of this method lies in its ability to assess discriminative capacity across a wide range of intensities, with an objective reference standard (the physical stimuli) acting as a measure of discrimination. One need not worry that the discrimination capacity stays tied to the particular product formulations. However, like all other discriminative tests, this scaling procedure represents discriminating capacity for one product only; not for all products, or even for all similar products.

How Many People Should Participate
in A Discrimination Panel?

Product testers often have to address the issue of base size in product testing, whether for descriptive analysis, hedonics (liking/disliking) or discrimination. Good reasons underlie the query regarding appropriate base size. (1) A small base of panelists may show discrimination results similar to results from a larger panel. The small group average will show higher variability and less stability. Large groups of panelists generate more stable data than do small groups. Hence, the product tester who tests with a group of panelists, and finds that 6 or 10 show discrimination, would feel more confident in the ratings of 60% from 60 of 100 panelists than from 6 of 10. The variability or range in which one might expect the average to fall shrinks as the base size of panelists becomes larger. In actuality, the variability diminishes in proportion to the square root of the number of panelists. The variability around the average of 6 people of 10 will exceed the variability around the average of 60 out of 100 by a factor exceeding 3. (2) With a sufficiently large base size of panelists evaluating differences, virtually any small deviation from pure chance (50/50 for pairs, 33/67 for triangles) will ensure that the percent discrimination exceeds the chance probability. As one increases the base size ad infinitum, the average number of panelists who display discrimination should remain unchanged. On the other hand, the variability or scatter, around that average decreases. (3) Generally, the optimum size of the test panel should take into account the point to which the product has progressed in the formulation-production-marketing sequence. Early benchtop work may require as few as 6-10 individuals for a discrimination test. This small panel provides guidance. The sensory analyst or product tester should use the small base more as a guidance tool, rather than as a descriptive tool, to predict the population responses. Once the product has passed initial bench top screening, and the final changes made, consumer research with 50-100 panelists should suffice for better and more stable estimates of consumer discrimination ability. Finally, with confirmatory market testing, the sensory analyst or market researcher should aim for a much wider sample.

Discrimination Tests and Accidental Differences

Usually sensory analysts and market researchers use discrimination tests to detect differences between products. Sometimes such discriminations result from accidental variations in products. Take, for example, coffees. Two lots of coffee can taste significantly different and discriminable from each other for a number of reasons. Differences may result from the type of bean, or the location where the bean grew. These are biological differences which modify the chemistry of the same beans, and produce different flavors. Differences may originate in the preparation of coffee from the same lot, even though the starting material remains the same. A coffee perked at a higher temperature may taste different from a coffee perked at a lower temperature. The bean remains the same, but the preparation process modifies the stimulus composition. Differences may also arise from the serving procedure. A test coffee served slightly cooler than the reference coffee will taste different. In a discrimination test, the panelist may not realize which sensory signals generate the discrimination, but in many instances the products will just seem different. In test situations, panelists often strive to show how well they can perform on disrimination tests, by responding to small differences if those small differences constitute the only means to differentiate products from each other. The product tester always runs the risk that a discrimination study will highlight differences which ordinarily in real life the panelist might disregard. Faced with the absence of any other cues by which to differentiate two stimuli, the panelist will base a decision on those cues readily at hand. A similar focusing of panelist's attention occurs when rating the dissimilarity between sugars of equal sweetness. In a study where the panelist scales dissimilarities of products with widely different taste qualities (e.g., salt versus sugar versus quinine), different sugars would score identical or close. When the panelists evaluate the differences between sugars which all taste sweet, they look for other criteria such as texture and side-tastes on which to make the distinctions, even though such discrimination would never emerge in ordinary practice (Moskowitz 1972).

CAN WE IMPROVE DISCRIMINATION BY TRAINING?

Human abilities change with training though innate sensory capabilities themselves do not. One job of the product tester involves the selection and training of a discriminator panel for quality control work. We know that perfumers and flavorists appear to possess unusually acute discriminatory capabilities. Yet, presumably their noses and tongues fall within the range of physiological normality. These experts must perform their jobs using standard sensory apparatus, but they probably do so more efficiently.

One can train discrimination panels by feedback about discrimination. Engen (1960) reported that one could improve panelists' ability to detect and to discriminate by repeatedly exposing panelists to the stimulus, and by giving feedback. Although Engen studied the olfactory perception of simple chemical stimuli, his methods apply to food products and flavorings as well. However, we do not know the upper limit to which one can improve discrimination performance. Nor do we know the degree to which improvement can reach in discrimination performance. Nor do we know the degree to which improvement in discrimination through training and feedback given for one product category generalizes to performance with another category. Do wine tasters perform better in soup evaluations as well?

In a demonstration on feedback by Vaisey-Genser *et al.* (1977), panelists received feedback on their ratings of bitterness intensity. Each panelist scaled various concentrations of quinine for perceived bitter taste. As panelists received feedback, their performance improved. They more clearly differentiated the taste of different concentrations of material. The data became tighter as the panelists received additional feedback. Each individual showed a different pattern of ratings, and thus intensity rankings, as well as differential susceptibility to feedback. Some individuals learned quickly; others learned slowly. The correlation between ranking of the bitter solution and actual concentration provided an objective measure of the level of discrimination.

What occurs during this feedback process? Psychologists tell us that feedback acts as a reinforcer to increase the probability that the correct behavior will repeat itself. For product testing, therefore, feedback regarding correctness of discrimination (or scaling) reinforces the use of the specific cues which panelists use to aid in discrimination. Perhaps the panelist used rise time or build-up time of taste intensity on the tongue to discriminate between two bitter samples. If the panelist received a reinforcement for correctly discriminating two stimuli on the basis of time-course of taste sensation, the odds increase that the panelist will use the same criteria in the next discrimination test. Other panelists may use different characteristics. In fact, some of the differences in population responses to differences in products result from feedback. Perhaps certain panelists use differences of flavor, whereas others use differences in texture as aids to discrimination. We saw above that panelists in the population may qualify as discriminators for one set of sensory characteristics, but not for another. Perhaps this results from differential attention paid to the attributes. Differential attention, in turn, results from differential reinforcement during previous evaluations.

Auto-shaping, or self-reinforcement, also occurs, independently of external feedback from the product tester. A panelist who repeatedly tests different levels of a stimulus (e.g., sugar in a beverage, color in canned peas, etc.) or who repeatedly experiences different variations in a single flavor category (e.g., vanilla-like notes) soon learns to discriminate among the various samples. The typical panelist without such exposure, shows no such discriminative ability. Yet, our discriminating flavorist or quality control specialist may not have had a conscious awareness of reinforcement for making these discriminations. Reinforcement can occur in one's daily behavior. As an individual tastes or smells similar products, notes their differences in an informal manner, and then sees the product coding or source, that individual reinforces himself or herself in virtually an unconscious manner. Repeated experience and low-level attention to the discrimination task may work as well as finalized training in discrimination.

Auto-shaping or self-reinforcing behavior contributes to the perfumer's and flavorist's extensive discriminative powers. Through dint of experience and by the ubiquitous phenomenon of auto-shaping, the practitioner and artist fine tune their discriminating capacity, by paying attention to salient cues which differentiate one stimulus from the other. The unpracticed consumer also senses these cues, but disregards them. For this reason market researchers who study consumer reactions to products often insist on long-term users of products as participants in product discrimination studies. Such so-called heavy users represent individuals with extensive experience and who, presumably, have experienced auto-shaping, self-reinforcing behavior for the product category. The discriminative capabilities of such heavy users sensitize and attune them to differences in products resulting from reformulations. Light users, or individuals who rarely (if ever) use the product, possess the same sensory apparatus, but do not attend to the salient cues which differentiate the old and the reformulated products.

A DISCRIMINATION TESTING SEQUENCE IN PRODUCT DEVELOPMENT: FROM EXPERT TO CONSUMER PANELS

We finish this chapter with a program for intelligent use of discrimination testing by following the testing sequence from initial planning to consumer testing. As background for the discrimination studies, let us consider the case of the sweet and sour sauce, Polynesia, manufactured by the Mantell Manufacturing Company in New York. Polynesia leads the sauce market in the ethnic, non-tomato sauce category. The Polynesia formula contains sugar, flavorings, acid and other components in fixed proportions. Consumers in the U.S. and Canada have used Polynesia for approximately eleven years since the manufacturer introduced it, first in its limited test markets (New York and Milwaukee), and then nationally for 9 years. Polynesia owns 43% of the sweet and sour sauce market. Two other brands, A and B, share an additional 37%; and three other brands, X, Y and Z, plus some very small, local brands, share the remaining 20% of the market. Mr. E. Mantell, president of the company that manufactures Polynesia, has relied on the combination of excellent product quality, competitive pricing, extensive advertising and promotion to push the good taste of Polynesia to new consumers, as well as to reinforce current consumers. The manufacturer wishes to modify the product by reducing the sugar level to 88% of its current level (12% reduction). The 12% reduction will save money on the cost of the sugar.

This cost reduction issue represents a typical problem which marketers need to answer, and for which they use the services of a product testing group. The problem concerns the change in consumer perceptions, and ultimately change in acceptance, which the marketer risks by modifying the product for economic considerations. Let us begin with the sequence of product development and product testing to see where and how discrimination testing fits in.

Stage One: Initial Benchtop Reformulation

At this initial stage, the product development specialist fabricates potential cost-reduced formulations of Polynesia. These variations contain reduced levels of sugar. Sometimes they change in sugar and other ingredients to remedy the flavor and texture changes. Quite often tactics for divergent formulation suggest themselves, such as simultaneously reducing sugar but also reducing other ingredients (e.g., acid), to maintain an overall flavor balance. Perhaps the product developer feels that a 7% reduction in sucrose, rather than a 12% reduction, coupled with a reduction in the binding thickener would produce an acceptable product, whereas a full 12% reduction in current sucrose level alone would severely diminish acceptability.

At this point, the product development specialist probably does some informal taste testing at the bench, after formulating products and testing these reformulated products side by side versus current Polynesia. Some modified products will taste quite different than the current product, whereas others, with only marginal cost reduction, will taste virtually identical. Keep in mind that Mr. Mantell's executive vice president of marketing does not want to change the sensory characteristics of Polynesia when reformulating for cost reduction. Polynesia represents the Mantell's flagship brand, bringing in much of the corporate income.

Once the product developer has satisfied the basic requirement of developing some alternatives which show promise, the sensory analyst can implement discrimination tests. Let us consider the results of an initial discrimination test for three alternatives versus current Polynesia (see Table 4.9). The panelists comprised in-house, but non-expert, employees who generally participate in sensory analysis studies as surrogates for extramural consumer panelists. With these in-house panelists, the sensory analyst can make a first cut in solving the discrimination and cost reduction problems. The discrimination panel comprised 50 consumers. Quite often sensory analysts use base sizes of 30 or more in their studies, primarily because with a sample size of 30 one can begin using the normal or Gaussian, bell-shaped distribution in statistics as an appropriate distribution to describe the data.

TABLE 4.9
RESULTS OF THE DISCRIMINATION TESTING FOR POLYNESIA

	Stage 1: Informal Testing With 50 In-House Employees		
	Cost Reduction		
	A	B	C
	Product A has 12% sugar reduction	8% reduction	6% reduction
Percent showing discrimination in a single triangle test (Chance = 33%)	56%	42%	38%
Probability corrected for 33% chance	35%	14%	7.5%

Table 4.9 tells us the following. (1) Panelists can and do detect differences for product A (cost reduction by 12% reduction in sugar), because 56% of the panelists detected the correct or odd sample in a single triangle test. (2) Panelists have more difficulty in detecting differences in product B (8% reduction), and experience much difficulty (in fact perform at a statistical chance level near 33%) for product C (6% reduction in sucrose).

Stage Two: Consumer Discimination Test

Let us now go to the second stage of the research and testing. Soon after the results have come in showing discrimination at 12% cost reduction, the marketing manager along with R&D personnel may make various decisions. They may try another cost reduction (perhaps 6% reduction in sucrose + change in other key ingredients); or they may stop there, and do broad scale testing of one of the three reduced cost versions (e.g., B) with consumers. This second strategy assumes that the marketer wishes to maintain the current level of acceptability, and will sacrifice some of the additional profit accrued by using a higher than projected sugar level (8% reduction, not 12%) in order to maintain the consumer acceptance.

In stage two, the marketing researcher and the product tester meet in order to plan a full-scale consumer evaluation of the cost reduced products. In order to do so, the marketing researcher must: (1) select the product reformulations to test (B or C); (2) select the target population (here, current consumers of Polynesia); (3) select the test site and type of test (central location, quick taste tests or extended, home-use tests, etc.); (4) develop the appropriate questionnaire (one that probes only for a difference, or one that probes for reasons underlying that difference in order to ascertain what key sensory characteristics generate the discrimination); and (5) implement the study.

The marketing researcher who works with discrimination tests usually runs larger scale studies with many more consumer panelists, in order to represent the target consumer group. The marketing research manager for Polynesia selected a central location discrimination test. Furthermore, in consultation with the marketing group, the market researcher selected three markets for the Polynesia discrimination test: the central U.S. near Chicago (moderate awareness and use of Polynesia; 35% of the market); the Northeast area around Boston (moderate use of Polynesia; 36% of the market); and the West Coast San Francisco area (high use of Polynesia; 53% of the market).

The marketing researcher must tap the reactions of the consumer population. He or she uses the input from the small, 50-member panel; but in order to make sure that the data reflect the resulting market of consumers, the market researcher must work with the consumer. Furthermore, the use of Polynesia sauce differs by market. Polynesia shows a high share of the market in the West Coast (primarily among Californians), as well as a moderate share of the market in the Midwest. To the marketer, these represent key areas to test. To the product tester who implements the discrimination test, these differences in share of market reflect different experience levels with the product. We might expect the Midwesterners and Northeasteners to show lower or lighter use of Polynesia, and the West Coast consumers to show heavier use. Thus, carrying the logic one step further, a noticeable shift in the product which the consumer discriminates might adversely affect reactions in the West Coast markets, because in those regions consumers have obtained a deeper and longer impression of the product quality.

Such thinking characterizes the marketing research approach to product testing in general, and to difference testing in particular. The ability to discern differences may or may not track with acceptance.

However, the product tester must keep in mind that markets showing different usages may comprise consumers with different discrimination abilities for the products based upon experience and expectations about product identity.

In the Polynesia test, the market research group decided to use 150 consumers, 50 in each of the three markets. Furthermore, they decided to test with the 8% reformulation, which represented a substantial, but not overwhelmingly desired, cost savings over and above the 12% reduction previously requested by marketing. It appeared that the 12% reduction offered no real promise of maintaining product quality.

Note that at this stage the aim of the study remained the same: to introduce a cost-reduced, but perceptually identical product to Polynesia. The consumer market researcher contracted with an external field service to select a site, and to set up and implement the actual product evaluation test. The test comprised a double triangle discrimination in which one would expect only 11% of the population to successfully pick out the odd sample in a pair of triangle presentations.

The Questionnaire

In the second consumer phase study, the approach used a double triangle test and questionnaire which probed the following. (1) Which of the three products seems different from the other two? Note that the first project did not ask why or by how much, nor did it ask for preference. In fact, it simply asked for an all-or-none judgment of same versus different for the reformulated versus the current product.

(2) For specific characteristics, does the odd product have more, equal or less of each of these characteristics: sweetness, tartness, bite, flavor intensity, aroma strength, mouthfulness and acceptability (liking of the product overall)?

Note the depth to which this questionnaire probes the reasons underlying discrimination. If the panelist truly shows the ability to discriminate between products, then the additional information highlights the dimensions of perception which correlate with that discrimination. Quite often the product tester wants to know what to do with situations where the panelist seems not to show discrimination. In these instances, the analyst should exclude panelists' attribute data as invalid.

Results

The results of this consumer study appear in Table 4.10 which provides key information pertaining to: the number of discriminators in the first triangle versus the second triangle versus both triangles together; the number of discriminators by market, as well as the number of discriminators by individuals who describe themselves as heavy versus light users of Polynesia; and, for those panelists who evidence discrimination, their reactions as to how the cost-reduced Polynesia differs from the current Polynesia.

As we might expect, fewer individuals show discriminating ability in two successive triangles than in either one triangle or the other. This fact should become obvious when we consider that the probability of guessing remains at 33% for each triangle. As the panelists test two triangles, the probability of correctly guessing drops to 11%.

Also, approximately the same number of panelists showed discrimination in the first triangle as in the second triangle. This makes the sensory analyst feel more comfortable with the data. Had we found that more panelists show discrimination in the first triangle and fewer in the second triangle (or vice versa), we might conclude that the testing itself biased the discrimination scores by inducing fatigue or hypersensitization to differences, respectively. Little information on sequence effects has appeared in triangle testing (Frijters 1979), but such information would provide a wealth of important guidelines in product testing and discrimination. We do not know how many triangle tests a person can participate in without losing sensitivity. We find that by region, the West Coast panel shows slightly more discrimination (9 out of 50) than does the East Coast (6 out of 50), or the Midwest (7 out of 50).

Data Utilization For A Decision

By itself, the discrimination testing sequence just described provides additional pieces of information regarding consumer reaction to product variations. The manager responsible for product marketing will look at these results differently from the way the R&D sensory analyst will. Specifically, the marketer will ask these questions, and make a marketing decision which affects market share and profitability. (1) Can I change the Polynesia formula, and if so, can I change it sufficiently to impact on profitability? The product tester has provided information which shows that, for the 8% reduction, it may make sense to opt for a cost reduction. That small reduction maintains quality. By and large the marketer faced with this decision will select the 8% cost reduction, and act conservatively on the basis of the sensory information.

(2) What downside risks occur when reduction in sugar level reaches 12%? The risks divide into perceptual differences (panelist consumers can and do detect the difference rather readily) and potential loss in

TABLE 4.10
RESULTS OF THE DISCRIMINATION TESTING FOR POLYNESIA

Stage 2: Consumer Discrimination Test (N = 150 Panelists or Product Users, 50 From Each of 3 Markets: Northeast, Midwest and West Coast)

| | | By Market | | | By Usage | |
	Total	East Coast	Midwest	West Coast	Heavy User	Light User
Number of panelists showing discrimination						
1st triangle	65	20	21	24	23	28
2nd triangle	55	15	15	25	19	20
Both triangles	22	6	7	9	10	12

(Chance = 16/50 for 1 triangle,
(4-5)/50 for double triangle)

Among double triangle discriminators (in toto)

55% felt that B had less sweetness   B = cost reduced sample
43% felt that B had less flavor
17% felt that B had more tartness
81% felt that B had more bite
29% felt that B had more aroma
26% felt that B had less mouthfulness
24% felt that B had more acceptability
32% felt that current Polynesia had more acceptability

acceptability. Table 4.10 shows how discriminators perceived the sensory changes in the product. Note that as the sugar level diminished, those who correctly discriminated the change felt that the lower sugar product (8% reduction) had less flavor and more tartness, but tasted almost as acceptable as the current product. Consequently, the marketing manager decided upon the cost reduction.

In the subsequent chapter on optimization, we will deal with the issue of formulating a sauce, such as Polynesia, to optimize acceptability subject to maintenance of specific cost margins.

OVERVIEW

Discrimination testing represents the most traditional forms of product testing. It has grown during the past fifty years from the simple question of difference between two products, to questions about panelist criteria in making difference judgments and the mechanisms underlying discrimination testing. Threshold measurement, traditionally separated from difference testing, has itself become a complex scientific arena with its own theories and approaches.

Discrimination testing finds many uses. Properly applied, it can help the product tester and marketer classify stimuli into same versus different. Product quality control, product changes and marketing, in an era of inflation, all use discrimination or difference testing in order to measure and maintain current consumer perceptions of a product. In a sense, discrimination testing puts the consumer to the ultimate test of ability to differentiate products. Virtually always, however, the underlying aim remains one of maintaining the status quo, not changing it.

CHAPTER 5

INTENSITY SCALING FOR PRODUCT TESTING

INTRODUCTION

Sensory scaling lets panelists assign numbers to reflect perceptions, much as a testing machine generates numbers to represent the intensity of a stimulus on a specific characteristic. Without scaling, the sensory analyst must limit his or her inquiry either to descriptive testing which classifies the stimuli, or to threshold (discriminative) testing to find out the lowest level one can discern, or what small differences between magnitudes one can discern on a reliable basis. Sensory scaling, in contrast, requires the panelist to act as a true measuring instrument.

The product tester secures many advantages from a valid, reproducible sensory scale. (1) He or she can measure the magnitude of perceptions. (2) He or she can determine whether one perception seems significantly stronger or weaker than another, and by how much. Traditional discrimination testing can only indicate whether or not a significant number of panelists in the population can discriminate between two samples. It does not tell how perceptually different these samples seem. Most of the interesting differences among products lie in the supra-threshold realm where we perceive differences easily. We need a ruler or a sensory measuring stick to gauge the size of the difference. (3) Sensory scaling also allows the product tester to correlate the perceptual magnitude with physical stimulus intensity to develop a psychophysical equation. In Chapter 10 we discuss sensory-instrumental correlations.

TYPES OF SCALES

In 1946, S. S. Stevens suggested that sensory measurements, and in fact all forms of measurement, fall into one of four classes: *nominal, ordinal, interval* and *ratio* scales.

Nominal scales put objects into classes or classifications by naming, etc. By and large we do not usually consider nominal classification as a form of numerical measurement. Generally, one rarely considers nominal classification in a section on scaling, and we will not consider nominal measurement further.

Ordinal scales put stimuli into rank order, or choosing between two stimuli, by ascertaining which stimulus possesses more of a specific or criterion characteristic. We rank order sugars into those which taste sweetest versus those which taste less sweet, and those which possess a more insipid taste.

Interval scales put objects or stimuli on a scale. The interval scale has no meaningful zero level. However, the intervals between adjacent scale points do possess a meaningful zero and ratios of intervals have meaning. Our best analogy for an interval scale comes from the centigrade scale for temperature. Zero degrees centigrade does not represent a truly meaningful 0 (absence of heat) in the same way that 0 mass (absence of mass) represents the true starting point of the scale for mass. The scale developer arbitrarily chooses to place the origin of the temperature scale at 0° C, but goes downwards into negative numbers to measure colder temperatures. Traditional product testing often uses interval scales in the form of fixed point category scales (e.g., 1-5). As we shall see, such so-called category scales probably do not truly possess interval scale properties.

Ratio scales put objects or stimuli on a scale which possesses a meaningful zero, allowing for the computation of meaningful ratios. In the case of temperature, the Kelvin scale represents a scale having an absolute zero point which truly lies at the bottom of the scale. A temperature of 600° K implies twice as much temperature as a temperature of 300° K. We could not make that statement for centigrade scales as 600° C does not equal twice as much heat as 300° C. We measure mass, length, money, etc. in ratio scales with meaningful zeros. Ideally, the sensory analyst and product tester should strive to measure perceptions on a psychological ratio scale, just as scientists always strive, when possible, to express scientific measurements using a ratio scale. The existence of an absolute zero and the ability to conclude that two stimuli lie in a specific ratio permit the product scientist, the sensory analyst, and other users of scale data to develop mathematical models with potential scientific validity. Table 5.1 shows the properties of these scales (Stevens 1946).

RANK ORDER PROCEDURES

Sensory analysts often use ranking methods (pick the best product— e.g., the best 3 of 10 samples) to place stimuli into an order of merit. Although ranking methods allow only weak statistical analyses, both sensory analysts and panelists seem comfortable with ranking. Ranking has face validity. People can tell the stimulus A, a solution of sugar

TABLE 5.1
SCALE TYPES AND ADMISSIBLE SCALE TRANSFORMATIONS

Scale	Necessary Operation for Creating Scale	Permissible Transformations	Permissible Statistics
Nominal	Determination of equality	$X' = f(X)$, where $f(X) =$ any one-to-one substitution	Number of cases, mode, contingency correlation
Ordinal	Determination of greater or less	$X' = f(X)$, where $f(X) =$ any increasing monotonic function	Median, percentiles, rank order, correlation
Interval	Determination of equality of intervals or differences	$X' = aX + b$ $(a \neq 0)$	Mean, standard, deviation, Product-moment correlation
Ratio	Determination of equality of ratios	$X' = aX$ $(a \neq 0)$	Geometric means, coefficient of variation, decibel transformations

in water, seems sweeter than stimulus B, another solution of lower concentration. One can never underestimate the power of comfortable feeling in data collection. This feeling of comfort pervades all aspects of sensory analysis. It substitutes for rigor and motivates the adoption of face-valid procedures such as rank ordering.

Some Historical Results From Ranking

Much of the scientific evidence on sensory perceptions gathered during the first half of the twentieth century derives from ranking data. Let us consider the ranking of sugars of equal molarity in terms of relative order of sweetness (Chappell 1953). The panelists tasted the samples and placed the sugars into ranks. Panelists ranked sucrose as the sweetest taste, followed by fructose, glucose and lactose. Maltose tasted the least sweet. Considering the Chappell data for a minute, we experience satisfaction and psychological closure. The researcher has generated key information about which sugars taste sweetest, and which taste least sweet. On the other hand, delving a little deeper into the problem we can ask more penetrating questions. Specifically, how much sweeter does sucrose taste compared to fructose or glucose? Does the difference in sweetness seem large, or does fructose taste just slightly less sweet than sucrose? Rank order data can never tell the researcher the size of the sweetness gap between adjacent sugars.

Thus, the difference in sweetness might seem large for sucrose versus fructose (ranks 1 and 2, respectively), but seem quite small at the bottom end of sweetness (glucose versus maltose). One can never conclude that the ranks 1, 2, 3, 4, ... n (for n products) truly represent equal psychological distances or ratios. Chappell's sweetness ranks, and the values assigned to different sweeteners in the ranking system, reflect the particular selection of sugars.

Some Insights on Ranking

Ranking forces the panelists to implicitly compare all pairs of stimuli in order to ensure that the stimuli lie in the proper order. For two stimuli, the panelist makes one comparison. For three stimuli the panelist makes three paired comparisons, and for four stimuli six implicit paired comparisons. In general, for n stimuli the conscientious panelist makes $n(n1)/2$ comparisons. The number of such implicit paired comparisons appears in Table 5.2.

TABLE 5.2
NUMBER OF IMPLICIT PAIRED COMPARISONS IN RANKING

Number of Stimuli	Number of Implicit Paired Comparisons
2	1
3	3
4	6
5	10
6	15
7	21
8	28
9	36
10	45
11	55
12	66

We can conclude from these computations that, with a sufficiently large number of samples, rank ordering methods simply become too tedious and unwieldy. Ranking loses it attraction as a simplistic, utilitarian method. Furthermore, although scientists continually caution practitioners not to treat the rank orders as actual numerical equivalents of sensory magnitude, people, as they will, forget to heed these cautions. Practitioners often report the rank orders as if the ranks reflect numerical scores of intensity.

A Case History and Its Statistical Treatment

Let us consider the problem of ranking different levels of candidate peach flavor in a new product. The Becklum Food Company plans to introduce a peach ice cream. Management and R&D wish to rank order six different peach flavors in terms of perceived flavor intensity, to see which flavor produces the strongest sense impression. These peach flavors comprise different physical combinations of chemicals. The Becklum Food Company (BFC) wants its in-house sensory panel to report out which peach flavor submission tastes strongest in ice cream (at the recommended use level), and then to rank the various submissions in terms of flavor strength. BFC will select the most intense flavor at a moderate concentration of use if consumers later find the flavor acceptable in peach ice cream. For now, BFC wishes to find out whether or not the new flavor submissions seem to provide a strong peach flavor at a low or moderate concentration.

The study proceeded in a fairly straightforward manner. The product developer prepared samples of the base product incorporating the recommended flavor levels. The sensory analyst presented them to the panelists. In outward visual appearances, the six different samples seemed identical. They differed principally in the strength of flavor, although to a trained nose the peach aromas differed in terms of quality as well. The strongest peach flavor submission may have possessed a harsh note, whereas another submission may have had a slightly bitter taste which panelists might confuse with flavor, or which might detract from the flavor intensity of the key peach note. Panelists tasted each sample, expectorated, rinsed with water and proceeded to taste the next sample.

Often panelists adopt the test strategy of putting the strongest stimulus to the side until they evaluate another stimulus which tastes even stronger. After six tastings, the panelists select the strongest tasting product. They return to the five products which remain, and select the strongest of those, continuing in this manner until they have rank ordered the six samples. This takes time. Some panelists return to the final ranking and taste the products in order, to assure themselves that the products really lie in relative order of peach flavor intensity.

In terms of actual panelist time expended, this exercise varies according to the panelist's response style. Some panelists rush through the ranking in an effort to quickly finish the task. Other panelists adopt a more obsessive strategy, evaluating the final ranking in as much excruciating detail as they did initially. As a result, panelists differ in the time it takes them to complete the task, as well as in their own confidence of how well they have done.

Treatment of the Ranking Data

For a single panelist, the product tester reports the single rank order. If the individual panelists all agree, then the group data reflects data from a single panelist. However, by and large panelists disagree with each other. For measures of intensity we usually find the inter-panelist disagreement less pronounced than in measures of hedonics. Hedonics tap individual opinion over and above sensory reactions. In ranking the intensity of stimuli, panelists often agree quite well with each other, especially when the samples lie widely apart in the intensity scale. Sometimes panelists disagree with each other—primarily, but not always, about ranks of stimuli in the middle range where they confuse the rank orders. The most intense and the least intense samples generally show the most inter-panelist agreement. Panelists can err in ranking middle intensity stimuli by inverting ranks in the upward direction or the downward direction.

Table 5.3 presents the rank data from a panel of 10 individuals on the peach flavor ice cream. Note that the initial analysis presented the average ranking. A rank of 1 represents the strongest, or the most intense, and 6 reflects the weakest. Since individuals differ in their rank order, the theoretical range of 1 to 6 rarely emerges. Rather, the errors which panelists commit (defined as disagreements with each other) force the rankings to regress to a common middle range.

Do Panelists Agree With Each Other—A Measure of Dispersion

We can measure the dispersion of the rankings to get an idea of how well panelists agree or disagree with each other. Table 5.3 shows the standard deviation (a dispersion measure), and allows the analyst to report out the average ranking of the products (either in final terms, 1 to 6, or in terms of average ranks).

The analyst can also measure how well the group, in general, agrees with the final ranking by means of Kendall's W statistic. This statistic ranges between 1 = disagreement and 0 = agreement. The computations appear in Table 5.4.

Conclusions from the Peach Study

The analyst ultimately will report the ranking of the six peach flavors in terms of flavor strength, as well as reporting how closely the

TABLE 5.3
RANK ORDER OF FLAVOR INTENSITY BY PANELISTS
FOR 6 PEACH FLAVOR SUBMISSIONS BY FLAVOR
HOUSES FOR ICE CREAM

Panelist	Product (Submission)					
	A	B	C	D	E	F
1	6	1	4	2	5	3
2	5	2	4	1	6	3
3	5	1	4	2	6	3
4	4	3	2	1	6	5
5	2	1	3	2	5	4
6	6	1	4	2	5	3
7	6	2	4	3	5	1
8	6	3	2	1	4	5
9	5	4	3	2	1	6
10	6	1	4	2	3	5
Average Rank	5.5	1.9	3.4	1.8	4.6	3.8
Standard Deviation	0.70	1.10	0.84	0.63	1.58	1.48
Final Rank	6	2	3	1	5	4

1 = Highest (Strongest)
2 = Lowest (Weakest)

TABLE 5.4
ILLUSTRATION OF CONCORDANCE TESTING TO DETERMINE
THE CONCORDANCE OF RANK ORDERS BETWEEN PANELISTS
(Kendall's W Statistic)

$$W = \frac{12\,S}{k^2(N^3 - N)}$$

S = Sum of squares of the observed deviations from the mean of the ranked totals

K = Number of sets of ranking

N = Number of samples ranked

W = 0 = consistency

W = 1 = Inconsistency

S = 67.4   K = 10   N = 6

$$W = \frac{(12)(67.4)}{(100)(216-6)} = 0.0385 = \text{high consistency}$$

panelists agree or disagree with the final, average rank order. For example, from Table 5.3 we see that submission D ranks highest in strength, whereas submissions C, E, and F cluster close together; and finally sample A seems weakest. The analyst could, in addition, report some of the statistical analyses to further support these findings. By and large, however, the BFC analyst will probably present only the final results, reporting these in a simple, qualitative fashion. The analyst will leave the extensive, quantitative results for backup information only.

Some Caveats in Rank Order Evaluations

The product tester must cope with two major problems which pervade rank order studies: incorrect interpretation of the information by the ultimate users, and response styles of specific panelists which may reduce the validity of the findings.

Incorrect Interpretation. Rank order data appears attractive because it provides seemingly straightforward numerical measures of intensity (or of hedonics, as we shall see in Chap. 6). Despite the caveats in terms of scale interpretation, end-users of rank order information tend to use these scores as reflecting actual numerical ratings of the product. For our peach flavors in ice cream, it may come as no surprise that one will use the rank order of flavor intensity as a numerical measure of flavor strength with a slight inversion. A 1 versus a 2 may generate the incorrect impression that the stronger flavor submission tastes two times stronger than the weaker flavor submission by a simple inversion of the rank order values. Try as the product tester will, the end-users of rank order data continue to err by incorrectly interpreting the scale data.

Response Styles. To rank order a series of food samples requires intense panelist concentration to generate proper data. Some panelists feel that they must generate a perfectly correct set of ranks. These compulsive panelists labor meticulously over the stimulus set until they feel sure that they have put the samples into correct order. When evaluating visual impressions (e.g., brightness), taste impressions, or smell impressions, this meticulous behavior encourages ongoing adaptation and reduces sensitivity. A person cannot rapidly assess six peach flavored ice creams in continuing, round robin comparisons without losing some sensitivity. One must make at least $(6 \times 5)/2 = 15$ pair comparisons. Those panelists who feel so obliged may go through an additional 6 or more evaluations to check their rankings, for a

total of 21 evaluations. When done during a short test, these evaluations decrease sensitivity and, more critically yet more subtly, lower
panelist motivation. Quite often panelists complain that while rank
ordering a set of stimuli they lose track of their task and become
discouraged. The sensory analyst must guard against this loss of
motivation and sensitivity by reducing the task demands, e.g., telling
the panelist that his or her first impression of overall rank order
suffices.

VARIATIONS ON RANKING

Full ranking requires a considerable amount of time for large
numbers of products. The product tester can trim the task requirements considerably by strategies such as paired comparisons among
limited, specific subsets of samples, and choice or selection strategies
(find the strongest, and second strongest).

Paired Comparisons: Choosing The More Intense Sample

Let us reconsider the peach flavor problem executed in a different
way. The manufacturer has six different peach flavors, but also real-
izes that so many peach ice cream samples may discourage the panelists. Furthermore, the ice cream must remain cold during the entire
time, which may present technical problems. Additionally, while the
room heats up the ice cream, the panelist may grow tired of tasting so
many different samples which eventually seem to taste all the same.

To remedy these problems, let us consider a round robin exercise
quite similar to round robin exercises used in marketing research to
select the best product. With six products, we form three product pairs:
AB, CD and EF. With seven products we form the same 3 pairs plus the
seventh product, G. The panelist tastes ice creams A and B in a pair,
choosing that product which possess the stronger peach flavor. For a
panel of 10 individuals, 6 out of 10 may feel that A has a stronger flavor
than sample B, whereas the remaining 4 feel that B has a stronger
flavor. The same panel then subsequently tests the pair CD, again
selecting the sample with the stronger peach flavor. Table 5.5 shows
the results. The panel selects D as having more peach flavor than C, by
a margin of 8 to 2. Finally, we repeat the exercise for E and F, and find
that F possesses more peach flavor.

During the second go-around in the round robin, we now reduce the
sets of pairs to a triple of three products: A, D, and F. These comprise
one pair, AD, and F. Panelists feel that A possesses the stronger peach

flavor. Finally we pair A, the winner, and F; and find that A possesses more peach flavor than does F. We select A as our final choice for the strongest peach flavor. Table 5.5 shows the sequence and the decisions.

TABLE 5.5
ROUND-ROBIN PAIRED COMPARISON TO GENERATE A RANK
ORDER OF THE FLAVOR INTENSITY OF PEACH ICE CREAM

Round 1	
A versus B	7 chose A as stronger, 3 chose B
C versus D	8 chose D as stronger, 2 chose C
E versus F	6 chose F as stronger, 4 chose E
Round 2	
A versus D	7 chose A as stronger, 3 chose D
Round 3	
A versus F	6 chose A as stronger, 4 chose F

The paired comparison method for incomplete ranking provides these advantages over standard rank order evaluation. (1) It requires fewer stimulus comparisons to discover the most intense sample. (2) Panelists need not evaluate too many pairs of samples in the same session. (3) We can separate the testing sessions or, in fact, use different panelists to test any or every pair. Market researchers follow this latter strategy when searching for a winning product among a set of 6 or more alternatives. A panelist evaluates only one pair of samples from the set. Different groups of panelists, at different times, evaluate the various pairs.

The incomplete paired comparison method possesses these disadvantages. (1) Panelists do not rank the full set of samples. The strategy selects only the most intense sample. (2) Panelists may shift criteria when evaluating different pairs. The specific context of the test situation, the varying cues and the criteria by which panelists make their rank order choices each influence the criteria used. On one occasion panelists may choose A over B as more intense, because peach flavor A tastes truly stronger than flavor B. When confronted with A versus D, panelists may hesitate. A and D seem about equally intense, but D has a stronger or faster rise time in flavor intensity, whereas the peach flavor of sample A increases more slowly as the panelist tastes the ice cream. So, D seems more intense, not because of true flavor intensity, but because when confronted with a difficult comparison situation the panelist uses another (and ordinarily ignored) criterion on which to base a choice. (3) The sequential paired comparison may generate inconsistencies, or intransitivities, because different panelists participate and use different criteria. In theory, one might rank A more intense than B, and rank B as more intense than C, both by paired comparisons. Yet, as market researchers and sensory analysts will vouch, a direct paired comparison of A and C shows that panelists feel C to have a stronger flavor intensity than A. Different criteria for choice, different panelists, etc. all contribute to this. In contrast, when the same panelist rank orders the entire set of stimuli at the same time, he or she usually uses the same criteria. A shift in criteria cannot dramatically alter the results, since the panelist presents the final rank order for consideration, rather than presenting sequential paired comparison data.

Choose The Strongest Or the Two Strongest

Panelists report having fewer problems when confronted with taste instructions to pick 1 of n, as compared to ranking n of n in order of intensity. Picking 1 of n parallels the method of paired comparisons used to select the strongest ice cream flavor (Table 5.5). However, the panelist goes through the paired comparisons internally, rather than explicitly. The strategy of picking 1 of n reduces the time required for rank ordering to choose the winner, or the top two products. It cannot generate an entire ranking of the product set. Consequently, the product tester will not know how the weaker products fare.

An Overview on Rank Order Measurements

Rank order techniques remain popular for scaling perceptual intensities, both in laboratories and in consumer tests. The attraction of a simple task for panelists to perform encourages the frequent use of ranking for product testing. Rarely do practitioners, or even theoreticians, realize the difficulties into which panelists get themselves when panelists must rank a large number of different samples. The critic of sensory analysis, in particular, or of human sensory measurement, in general, finds psychological solace and comfort in that the panelist simply compares two products every time. That the panelist need not use numbers also overjoys those critics who believe panelists incapable of virtually anything beyond simple selection or ranking.

Relaxation of the panelist's task through ranking, rather than scaling, brings with it negative consequences, however. Specifically, ranking data defy analysis with standard statistics. Rather, they require so-called non-parametric or distribution-free statistics. Non-

parametric statistics make no inference about averages or variabilities of numbers from underlying statistical distributions. Assuming
nothing about the distribution of data (assuming nothing regarding
normality or the Gaussian, bell-shaped distributions), non-parametric
statistics proceed in a conservative and relatively less sensitive, or
even insensitive, manner. Where parametric statistics might show
differences among samples, non-parametric statistics on the same
data might not. Additionally, one cannot develop meaningful curves
relating rank order data to physical intensity. Recall that a major goal
of psychophysics focuses on equations or curves which reveal how
perceptions change as a result of specific changes in physical intensity. We cannot develop these equations with ranking data. What can
one say regarding changes in physical intensity? Do the ranks
change? If so, how does the ranking relate to different levels of sugar?
When the panelist rank orders a set of sugars of different concentrations, we can only correlate the rank order of sweetness with the rank
order of concentration to see how well they agree. We cannot, however,
predict the change in rank from actual changes in concentration.

FIXED POINT CATEGORY SCALES

We next consider the fixed point category scales which product
testers, many psychologists and social researchers often use to quantify subjective impressions. In its most typical form, the fixed point
scale comprises a limited set of categories (e.g., 2, 3, ... 100), representing graded, discrete levels of intensity. These fixed points presumably
represent equally spaced gradations of magnitude, with the psychological or perceptual difference between adjacent intervals equal along
the entire scale. On a 9 point scale, for instance, the 9 points presumably span the range between virtually non-perceivable (1 on the scale) to
the strongest possible perception (9 on the scale). Furthermore, the
eight intervals, 1-2, 2-3, ... 8-9, should represent equal psychological
differences.

In practice, panelists find the fixed point scale easy to use. They
readily comprehend the concept of graded magnitudes, and have little
or no difficulty using the scale to reflect perceptions. We will discuss
the scale implementation, analysis, and specific issues in the remaining portion of this section.

A Typical Example: Measuring Sweetness of Puddings

Let us consider the study by Moskowitz *et al.* (1974) concerning the
sweetness of pudding with varying sugar levels. These researchers

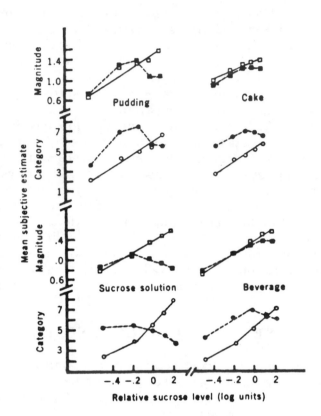

FIG. 5.1 SUCROSE LEVEL VERSUS SENSORY INTENSITY AND LIKING

Relation between sucrose concentration and mean estimate of sweetness or pleasantness, respectively, by the methods of category scaling and magnitude estimation. Symbols: O, sweetness; ●, pleasantness; □, magnitude estimation; and ■, category estimation.

Source: Moskowitz, Kluter, Westerling and Jacobs (1974)

wished to determine how graded levels of sugar in a vanilla pudding, a cake and a beverage transform into perceived sweetness. To do so, they used a 9-point scale. The panelists tested varying sweet stimuli, and chose a scale value to reflect perceived sweetness. Figure 5.1 shows some of the curves which they generated. Each curve represents average ratings.

Various issues arise, with which we deal now.

How Many Categories. Sensory analysts perennially argue about the optimum number of categories to use. Some researchers prefer to use a wide range of categories, whereas others prefer a narrow range of categories. Looking through published reports, one finds citations of as few as three categories, and occasionally as many as 100 categories, a 100 point scale. No fixed number of categories can truly claim optimality, save that the researcher should use as many categories as possible.

Restricting the number of categories to a small range engenders certain counter-productive biases. (1) Panelists shy away from using the end categories. They will often convert the 9 point scale to a 7 point scale by rarely using the 1 and 9 scale points. One should not compensate for this scale contraction by chopping the scale to 7 points for that further aggravates the problem. Panelists then shorten the scale to 5 points by avoiding the two extreme categories. (2) Panelists may distribute their ratings all over the scale to show discrimination, even when most of the stimuli lie in the middle range. A scale comprising a limited number of categories will confound this distribution behavior. The researcher will not know whether the distribution of ratings on a short scale reflects panelist perceptions or a bias to use the entire scale.

Marks (1968) found that biases diminish when fixed point scales have an increasing number of categories. He based these conclusions upon correlations of category scaled perceptions versus known physical stimulus levels. The correlations improve as the number of available categories increase. In light of scale biases, the product tester should increase, rather than decrease, the available number of categories.

Odd Versus Even Number of Categories. Hand-in-hand with the number of categories goes the issue of the parity, or odd-even number of categories. This question predominates in hedonics, or acceptance, where we deal with its implications in greater detail (see Chap. 6). Nonetheless, the issue of odd/even often arises in intensity scaling as well. No compelling reasons exist for selecting either an odd or an even number of categories in intensity ratings.

Numbers or Words or Both. Some product testers prefer to use only numbers on a category scale to reflect gradations of intensity. Others prefer to use words ranging from extremely strong down through barely perceptible to guide panelists. Still other practitioners use a combination of numbers and words. Psychophysicists who use fixed point category scales often avoid word descriptions. Rather, they present the panelists with a numerical scale, basing their choice of scale on the belief that only the numerical scale truly reflects magnitudes.

In some situations, however, the product tester may wish to assist panelists to obtain an idea of the specific meaning of the categories. To do so, the product tester presents words which accompany the numerical scale values. The danger of such an approach lies in the selection of words which, more often than not, fail to show equal interval properties. Table 5.6 shows numerical equivalents to five intensity words as calibrated by the magnitude estimation procedure (see section on magnitude estimation calibration). The intensity words extremely, very much, moderately, slightly and none at all do not generate equal psychological intervals or distances between them. Consequently, the product tester may err by using words jointly with numbers on a fixed point scale. Furthermore, many researchers have run into the problem of trying to find words to accompany 6 point scales, but then having to modify the selection of words for use in a 7, 8 or 9 point scale.

TABLE 5.6
WORD DESCRIPTORS AND RATINGS WHICH ACCOMPANY
CATEGORY SCALES

	Category Descriptor		Rating		Interval	
(1)	Extremely	=	161 }		45	Product = Beverage
	Very Much	=	116 }		37	
	Moderate	=	79 }		36	
	Slight	=	43 }		43	
	None	=	0			
(2)	Extremely Strong	=	183 }		49	Product = Sauce
	Very Much	=	134 }		40	
	Moderately	=	94 }		35	
	Slightly	=	59 }		45	
	Barely	=	14 }		14	
	None	=	0			

Range of Stimuli: Its Effect on the Category Scale. The category scale contains within it the seeds of a paradox. Unless the panelist knows the full range of stimuli ahead of time, he or she will not know where on the scale to assign the first stimulus. If the first stimulus seems strong but the panelist has no idea of the range, then the panelist may assign the first stimulus a high scale value towards the top end of the scale. Suppose, now, that subsequent stimuli seem even stronger. If so, then more than likely the panelist will run out of available numbers on the scale in an effort to match the increased intensity with a higher scale value. The panelist may request permission to change his or her ratings in order to simultaneously exhibit discrimination, as well as to keep the scale ratings within the arbitrarily preset category boundaries.

In order to avoid this difficulty, researchers sometimes present the panelists with the entire range of stimuli at the beginning of the study, and only then allow the panelist to rate the different stimuli. In this way the panelists can adjust the scale use in order not to run out of numbers. The panelist can assign the ratings so that they exhibit discrimination while remaining within the scale confines. Admirable as such a scheme seems at first glance, it also leads to certain difficulties. (1) The panelists may opt to employ the entire range of allowable scale values to match the range of stimuli. Suppose we divide panelists into two groups. One group evaluates a wide range of stimuli which they see beforehand, so that they know the stimulus range; the other group evaluates a narrow range of stimuli which they also see beforehand so that they too know the stimulus range. The panelists in one group do not know that another group will evaluate different ranges of stimuli. In most instances, the two groups of panelists will assign different ratings to the same test stimuli. The group presented with the narrow range of stimuli will expand the range of their ratings to fit the relatively large scale. The group with the larger stimulus range will compress their ratings to fit within the confines of the relatively narrow scale. (2) The pre-presentation of the entire range of stimuli works only when the panelists must evaluate a small number of stimuli. The strategy of showing the entire range ahead of time cannot work when the panelists must use the product over an extended period of time before rating the product. The panelists do not have sufficient time to inspect the entire set of products prior to rating them. In addition, memory factors interfere. By the time the panelist has sampled two or three products without rating the stimuli, the chances diminish of remembering the range and the appropriate location of stimuli in that range.

Analysis of Category Rating Data. Researchers have assumed, often by fiat, that category data conforms to interval scale rules similar to the centigrade scale of temperature. Category scale values possess no true zero point. On a 1-9 scale, the researcher may change the scale values by adding 100 to each scale point, to generate a scale ranging from 101 to 109 without modifying the statistical properties of the scale. Ratios of scale ratings certainly change (a 2:1 differs from a 102:101), but intervals and ratios of intervals do not (a 2-1 equals a 102-101).

Researchers accept assumptions of equal intervals across the entire scale, and average the scale ratings in order to compute a mean rating. A simple arithmetic average suffices. Researchers often compute the variability of the ratings around that average as well, as shown in Table 5.7, and estimate the standard error of the mean, defined as the standard deviation of the mean: (68% of the time the mean should lie between +1 and −1 standard error, when the error of the mean distributes itself normally).

From time to time researchers prefer to look at the distribution of individual ratings, in addition to the average. The distribution of ratings provides additional insight into the data. The distribution shows whether or not the data generate a unimodal distribution of ratings, peaking at the mean, or whether the data generates two distinct distributions, with the mean sufficing to describe neither. Table 5.7 shows both the average and the variability of ratings on a 9 point category scale for three beverage products sweetened with artificial sweeteners. Figure 5.2 illustrates how one product (A) generates a bimodal set of ratings with 2 peak points, whereas the other products generate a unimodal distribution, with 1 distinctive peak point.

A detailed analysis of the distribution of category scale data becomes important in the analysis of hedonic or pleasantness/unpleasantness ratings. By and large, in the evaluation of specific sensory characteristics we expect to see unimodal distributions, where the average truly represents the center of the distribution. In hedonic testing we often see bimodality, as panelists use the scale to rate product likes and dislikes.

Statistical Analysis of Category Data. Let us consider the case of three beverages which generate a series of ratings. We wish to know whether or not the mean bitterness for one stimulus (A) truly exceeds the mean off taste rating for another stimulus (B). For instance, the averages equal 4.55 for saccharin versus 3.35 for cyclamate on a 9 point scale. Can one conclude with confidence that the rating of 4.55 assigned to sample A, saccharin, represents a noticeably stronger off-taste than does the rating assigned to sample B, cyclamate?

We now enter into the realm of *statistical inference*. Heretofore we dealt with the distribution of the ratings, the variability of the ratings and, of course, the average rating. We now wish to infer something about the underlying true mean. If we repeat this study 100 times with panelists retesting the same set of beverage, what chance do we stand of replicating our conclusion that sample A (rated at 4.55) will reverse the next time; so that sample A (saccharin) will receive a lower off-taste score than sample B (cyclamate).

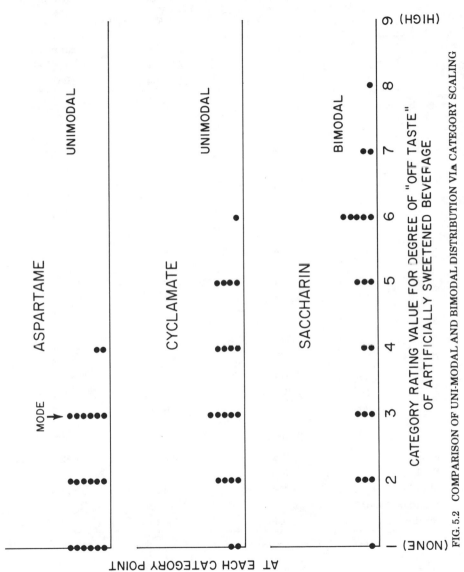

FIG. 5.2 COMPARISON OF UNI-MODAL AND BIMODAL DISTRIBUTION VIa CATEGORY SCALING

TABLE 5.7
MEAN AND VARIABILITY OF CATEGORY SCALE RATINGS OF
OFF-TASTE OF 20 PANELISTS TO 3 VARIATIONS OF
ARTIFICIALLY SWEETENED BEVERAGES

		Sample A (Saccharin) Rating	Sample B (Cyclamate) Rating	Sample C (Aspartame) Rating
Panelist	1	8	3	2
	2	6	5	3
	3	5	2	3
	4	7	4	3
	5	6	5	2
	6	6	5	3
	7	7	2	3
	8	3	3	4
	9	2	4	2
	10	2	2	1
	11	4	3	1
	12	3	5	2
	13	6	1	1
	14	4	1	1
	15	1	2	1
	16	3	3	1
	17	5	4	3
	18	6	4	2
	19	2	3	4
	20	5	6	2
		(Bimodal)	(Unimodal)	(Unimodal)
Mean		4.55	3.35	2.20
Variance		3.94	2.03	1.00
Standard Deviation		1.99	1.42	1.01
Standard Error of the Mean		0.46	0.32	0.23

(Base = 20 panelists each of whom rated 3 beverages)

Statistical inference helps the researcher decide whether or not two samples which appear to differ truly do so, or whether the difference results from accident. In simplest terms, consider saccharin sample A. Statisticians tell us that if we repeat or replicate the study a number of times, our best guess as to its off-taste rating would remain

4.55. However, the average rating from the panel will vary from replication to replication. Sometimes the average rating will exceed 4.55, e.g., become 5.1 or even higher. Sometimes the rating will drop below 4.55. The *standard error of the mean* indicates the variability of the mean. With a high standard error (shown computationally in Table 5.8) we expect the average rating assigned to product A to fluctuate quite a bit over repeated sets of evaluations. With a low standard error of the mean we expect a more constricted variation, still averaging 4.55. A small standard error means tighter, more reliable average ratings from experiment to experiment. A large standard error of the mean suggests large scatter of the means from test to test, but still averaging 4.55.

In this experiment we tested two products, so we got two averages and two standard errors of the means—one for the saccharin beverage, A, and the other for the cyclamate beverage, B. If we repeat this study of beverage off-taste 100 times, the average difference would remain $4.55 - 3.35 = 1.20$. The variation in the difference scores, however, would change. The different scores vary as a function of the standard error of the difference of A and stimulus B. The computational formula appears in Table 5.8. The *standard error of the difference*, defined as the variability of the difference score between A and B, turns out to equal 0.56. This means that 68% of the times we do the experiment, the mean difference of ratings assigned to off-taste of beverage A and off-taste of beverage B lies between $1.20 + 0.56 = 1.76$ and $1.20 - 0.56 = 0.64$.

Furthermore, we can ask whether, in a statistical sense, this difference equals 0, so that our mean difference of 1.20 actually reflected a chance excursion from zero. If it does, then we would conclude that stimuli A and B really do not differ in intensity of off-taste. The *T score*, defined as (mean A − mean B)/(standard error of difference), can help us determine the proportion of times that we would find a difference of 1.20, given the assumptions that: (a) the true difference equals 0, and (b) the variability of that true mean equals the standard error of the difference (0.56). Tables of T show the probability of obtaining a specific T score. In our case, the probability drops below 5%. In fact, we could conclude that with a true mean of 0, the odds become very low, less than 5%, that we would actually observe this difference of 1.20.

Two other interesting facts emerge from this analysis. (1) When we find a small average difference but high variability around the average, we have a much greater chance to find reversals ($B > A$) on repeated trials. (2) The standard error of the mean varies inversely with the square root of the number of panelists. Doubling the number

TABLE 5.8
TEST OF SIGNIFICANCE BETWEEN THE OFF-TASTE RATINGS
OF SACCHARIN- AND CYCLAMATE-SWEETENED BEVERAGES

Saccharin-Sweetened Beverage (Sample A)
Cyclamate-Sweetened Beverage (Sample B)

$$\text{T Value} = \frac{\text{Mean (A)} - \text{Mean (B)}}{(\text{Standard Error of the Difference})}$$

$$\frac{\bar{X}_A - \bar{X}_B}{(S.E.^2 A + S.E.^2 B)^{1/2}} = \frac{4.55 - 3.35}{(0.46^2 + 0.32^2)^{1/2}} = \frac{1.20}{0.56} = 2.14$$

A T value greater than 1.96 means a 95 percent probability that A and B come from different distributions. We would observe a T value of 2.14 less than 5% of the time if A and B came from a single distribution of mean 4.55.

$$\text{Standard error of a single mean} = \left[\frac{\sum_{i=1}^{N} (X_i - \bar{X})^2}{N} \right]^{0.5} = \frac{\text{Standard deviation}}{\sqrt{N-1}}$$

---

of panelists drops the standard error of the mean by a factor of 30%. Doubling the number of panelists reduces the variability to 70% of its size. Hence, to ensure that the differences we observe actually represent the true underlying differences, the product tester may opt to increase the panel size. The increased panel size diminishes the standard error of the mean, increases the T score for the same 1.20 unit difference, and thus increases the chance that we have found a real difference. Product testers often use the T test in order to determine whether or not the difference which they obtain represents a true product or sensory difference. A large difference in ratings between two products may represent an actual difference between the products. On the other hand, quite often the variability associated with the scores becomes so large that we conclude the difference results from chance variability in the mean ratings, rather than resulting from a true, underlying difference.

Fitting an Equation to Category Scale Data. Quite often the product tester may wish to fit a predetermined function to the category rating data. For instance, one may wish to know whether or not a straight line relates ratings of sweetness to the physical concentration levels. Often, psychophysicists relate the category rating data to the logarithm of the concentrations, rather than to the concentration values themselves. In general, the psychophysical function in linear coordinates appears curved, so that a straight line does not adequately represent the relation between stimulus level and the rating. A non-linear transformation, such as converting concentration levels to their logarithmic equivalents, straightens the curve. A logarithm equals the power of 10 which expresses the given number: $\log 100 = 2$, since $10^2 = 100$; $\log 4 = 0.6$ since $10^{0.6} = 4$.

When trying to interrelate the category ratings with the stimulus concentrations, the analyst should consider these specific factors. (1) How well do the stimulus values and ratings correlate? Ideally, in order to ensure that a reasonable equation fits the data, the correlation coefficient should equal 0.9 or more. The correlation coefficient, R, varies from $+1.0$ = a perfectly straight line, through 0 = no relation at all between physical stimulus level and category rating, down to -1.0 = perfect inverse or negative relation. (2) What values of the coefficients of the equation govern the data?

We express the logarithmic equation as follows:

$$\text{Category Rating} = k_0 + k_1 (\text{Log Stimulus Level}) \tag{1}$$

What values do k_0 and k_1 assume? For instance, if $k_1 = 1$, then a 1 logarithmic unit (or 10-fold ratio) increment in stimulus level (e.g., from $2.0 - 20$) produces a 1 unit increase in the category rating, etc. Table 5.9 shows the results for the least-squares estimates of k_0 and k_1 for sweetness ratings, done by category scaling in two ways—(a) assuming that a linear function relates the sensory and ingredient levels:

$$\text{Sweetness Category Rating} = k_0 + k_1 (\text{Sugar Level}); \text{ and}$$

(b) assuming that a logarithmic function relates the sensory and ingredient levels:

$$\text{Sweetness Category Rating} = k_0 + k_1 (\text{Sugar Level}).$$

TABLE 5.9
RESULTS FROM SWEETNESS RATINGS ASSIGNED
TO SWEETENED BEVERAGES

Sugar Level in Beverage (Brix)	Category Rating of Sweetness (10 Point Scale[1])
7	3.4
8	3.9
9	4.7
10	5.5
11	6.3
12	7.1
13	7.3
14	7.6

[1] 0 = No Sweetness

Least Squares Equations

Linear: Sweetness = 0.64 (Concentration) − 1.08
Logarithmic: Sweetness = 15.2 (Log Concentration) − 9.6

Testing Differences Among Many Products

In sensory analysis, quite often the researcher wishes to discover which product(s) from a group of products achieves the highest rating, and if that highest rating has significance, rather than resulting from pure chance alone. Since category ratings or, in fact, subjective ratings in general vary, the question becomes one of comparing the differences or scatter (variability) among means versus the variability around the individual mean.

Statisticians have developed a class of statistical procedures known as *analysis of variance*, in order to assess whether or not several products differ significantly from each other. As we saw in the case of the T test, the product tester must measure the mean and the variability of each product around that mean, either by presenting the same panelist with all products, or by presenting different panelists with one of the products and other panelists with the rest of the products.

Many different variations exist for the analysis of variance procedure. The reader should consult texts on analysis of variance and allied procedures (e.g., Winer 1971). Tables 5.10 and 5.11 show data and the logic involved in testing for differences among four different flavored yogurts to ascertain which flavored yogurt scores significantly higher, and which scores significantly lower in natural flavor.

TABLE 5.10
ANALYSIS OF VARIANCE FOR 4 YOGURTS RATED ON LEVEL
OF NATURAL FLAVOR

Panelist	Ratings of Yogurts			
	Yogurt 1	Yogurt 2	Yogurt 3	Yogurt 4
1	8	8	8	8
2	7	7	9	9
3	2	4	8	8
4	7	5	7	7
5	8	7	8	9
6	7	7	6	8
7	4	6	7	8
8	6	7	6	7
9	6	9	8	9
10	8	8	8	8

EXECUTION OF THE CATEGORY SCALING STUDY

Implementing a category scaling study poses few direct problems, but can ensnare the unsuspecting researcher by its hidden biases. The list below summarizes the sequence of questions which the researcher can pose and follow when implementing the study.

Selection of Stimuli for Testing. Should the same panelist test all stimuli or test only a subset of stimuli? If a subset, then does the number of panelists allow for a reasonable base size of panelists for each product?

Selection of the Appropriate Panel and Panel Size. Ideally, for category scaling one should select a panel of 20 or more, in order to generate a stable base of data with relatively low variability around the mean. Recall that as the base size increases, the variability diminishes proportionally to the square root of the panel size. Doubling the panel size does not double the precision, but increases precision only by a factor of 30%.

TABLE 5.11
LOGIC OF ANALYSIS-OF-VARIANCE (1 Way)

1. Correction Factor $= \dfrac{(\text{Grand Total})^2}{\text{Total Number of Ratings}} = \dfrac{(287)^2}{40} = 2059.2$

2. Sum of Squares, products $= \dfrac{\text{Sum of Square of Total of Each Product}}{\text{Number of Ratings of Each Product}} - \text{CF}$

$$= \dfrac{20779}{10} - 2059.2 = 18.67$$

3. Sum of Squares, Total $= (\text{Sum of Squares of Each Rating}) - \text{CF}$

$$= 2145.0 - 2059.2 = 85.8$$

4. Sum of Squares, Error $= \text{SS(Total)} - \text{SS(Products)} = 85.8 - 18.67 = 67.13$

5. Degrees of Freedom (df)

df (Total) = Total Observations − 1
df (Product) = Number of Products − 1
df (Error) = df (Total) − df (Products)

6. Mean Square = SS/df
   F Value = MS (Product) / MS (Error)

7. Analysis of Variance Table

Source of Variation	df	ss	ms	F Ratio
Products	(4 − 1) = 3	18.67	6.22	3.32
Error	(39 − 3) = 36	67.13	1.87	
Total	(40 − 1) = 39	85.80		

Net Conclusion: The ratio of variabilities (3.32) means that the variability between yogurts exceeds the variability within single products.

Selection of the Attributes to Test. The product tester may instruct the panelists to scale one attribute alone (e.g., sweetness, as did Schutz and Pilgrim (1957) in their psychophysical study of sweeteners). In most product tests the analyst wishes to construct a profile of the product on a variety of different characteristics. Hence, the panelists scale their perceptions on a variety of different attributes.

Selection of the Scale to Use. This selection includes choices regarding the number of points on the scale and the order of the scale (e.g., should the category 1 represent the highest or the lowest value), as well as decisions about whether or not descriptor words will accompany the scale points. Quite often researchers use scales of different sizes for specific characteristics. For instance, the Texture Profile Scale, as propounded by Szczesniak, Brandt and Friedman (1963), uses a 5 point scale for adhesiveness and an 8 point scale for viscosity. Most panelists have trouble working in situations of varying scale length for different sensory attributes, unless the researcher has extensively trained the panelists.

Selection of a Reference Sample and a Reference Category Point. Some investigators prefer to use a standard or a predesignated first stimulus, in order to reduce interpanelist variability. Sometimes the practitioners also require panelists to assign to that reference standard a particular category value, the *modulus*. Fixed standards and moduli will reduce, but not eliminate, interpanelist variability. Other investigators shy away from such a designations, feeling that they bias panelists in the use of the fixed point category scale.

Sequence of Sample Presentation. Most psychophysicists feel strongly that panelists ought to evaluate the samples in randomized order. For small sample sets (e.g., 6 samples), one can systematically rotate the sample order to ensure that each panelist evaluates every sample in a different order. For more than just a few samples, one cannot possibly present samples to panelists in every possible permutation. A set of 8 samples possesses 8! = 40320 different orders, which becomes unwieldy. In such instances the experimenter uses an *irregular order* of samples, with no two samples presented sequentially more often than would occur by sheer chance alone.

Time Between Samples. As with any testing and subsequent scaling, the investigator must ensure panelist sensitivity. The sensory analyst should not present the second sample too quickly after the first, etc. Otherwise, most panelists soon fatigue. Panelists must perform their evaluations slowly to maintain sensitivity. Of course, the actual waiting time between samples in a scaling task varies with the type of sample. Evaluation of sugar-sweetened beverages proceeds fairly rapidly. Beverage flavors for sugar-sweetened products rise quickly in the mouth, maximize, and diminish very rapidly after the panelist has expectorated the beverage and rinsed with water. In such instances, the test can proceed much more rapidly—perhaps 1 sample each 60-90 seconds. In contrast, other sweetening agents, such as saccharin or the neo-naringen dihydrochalcones, deposit intense tasting residuals in the mouth. One must wait 2-5 minutes between samples. Bitter agents and hot foods (e.g., chili products) also deposit a residual taste material in the mouth. To allow the residual taste to diminish requires a substantially longer wait. The product tester should also bear in mind that with increased wait the panelist may forget the previous sample. Thus, while ensuring the maintenance of sensory acuity through long interstimulus times, the product tester may inadvertently promote forgetting of previous stimulus characteristics.

Number of Replicates. The appropriate number of replicates represents one of the thorny issues in product measurement. On the one hand, the researcher obtains the maximum amount of information from the first sample. The second rating determines the average with a weight of $1/2$. The third replicate of the sample has a weight of $1/3$ in determining the average, and so on. Thus, for purely economic reasons, one should simply gather more ratings from more individuals, rather than putting equal effort into securing replicates from one panelist. The issue, however, can become more complicated. On the first replicate, panelists may not react to the stimulus in the same way that they react on the second replicate. Most pronounced for hedonic reasons, this *replicate effect* also occurs in assessment of simple sensory attributes. In an unpublished study conducted as a graduate student at the Harvard University Laboratory of Psychophysics, Richard Young found a strong replicate effect for the evaluation of the brightness of lights. In that study, the experimenter presented panelists with different lights having varying physical brightness values, as assessed instrumentally via a Macbeth illuminometer. The panelists rated perceived brightness on a 9 point scale. The range of brightness scale ratings for the second replicate increased. Perhaps as the panelists became familiar with the range of light stimuli they expanded the scale range, losing the conservatism which pushed the ratings closer to the center of the scale.

When one plans a study using the category scale, one should take into account the precision of the measurement as indexed by the standard error of the mean. Increasing the panel size decreases the error in the data by diminishing the standard error of the mean. Although statistically one often does not care about the source of the error reduction, many panelists or many replicates from a single panelist, in actuality the two strategies lead to quite different results. Replicates from the same panelist present finer tuned data from the same, but limited source. If that source exhibits a quirk in rating stimuli or shows a deficit in perception, the additional replicates will only emphasize that idiosyncracy. In contrast, by enlarging panel size rather than increasing the number of replicates from a panelist, the researcher can more effectively eliminate the idiosyncratic effects of individual panelists. Many R&D sensory analysts forced to work with small panels try to build up the base size of ratings, in order to achieve stable data by increasing the number of replicates. They may achieve stable data, but at the risk of falling prey to individual idiosyncracies which could become even stronger and more firmly entrenched with repeated trials.

A Potpourri of Information on Category Scales

Psychophysicists have extensively explored the advantages and pitfalls of category scaling procedures as a method for assessing sensory intensity. Some of the issues involved concern: the validity of the scale as a true interval scale; response styles of panelists; and the approximation of the scale to a true ratio scale.

Validity as an Interval Scale. Category scales presuppose equal interval properties. However, true interval scales (e.g., temperature) place no restrictions on the upper and lower ends of the scale. For example, with the Centigrade scale of temperature we do not specify the highest temperature level, nor the lowest temperature. One can go down infinitely low although we soon reach a physically meaningful absolute zero level at $-273°$. In contrast, the product tester uses category scales which always have an upper or a lower limit. In actuality, the category scale does not permit true interval scale statistics, even though in practice most researchers use the ratings as if they behaved like true interval-level scale data.

Approximation to a True Ratio Scale. In work on the relation between ratio scales and interval scales, Lawrence Marks (1968) considered what type of function would best fit a category scale if one assumes that the category ratings really possess ratio scale properties. To do so, Marks assumed that the category ratings actually reflect pseudo-magnitude estimates; namely, he treated these ratings as if the ratings came from magnitude estimation scaling (see below). As discussed previously in Chap. 3, magnitude estimates often generate a power function of physical intensity expressed by the equation:

$$M.E. = k \, (\text{Intensity})^n \text{ or Log M.E.} = n \log (\text{Intensity}) + \log k$$

When the product tester uses category ratings in place of magnitude estimates, but goes through the same statistical curve fitting procedure, the power function exponent **n** drops down to approximately 50% of its original value. Marks called these new exponent values of the category scale the *virtual exponents*. Furthermore, Miguelina Guirao (personal communication 1970) found that the values of the virtual exponents increase toward the values obtained by magnitude estimation, when the number of available categories equals or exceeds 15-20.

To all intents and purposes, therefore, a category scale will approximate a ratio scale if the category scale has a sufficiently large number of categories. The scale will still maintain the bias as do all scales with fixed end-points. No fixed point scale can escape that bias.

Response Styles of Panelists. The simplicity of category scales can deceive the user. Just because panelists can use a full scale does not mean that they avail themselves of the full category range. Panelists exhibit different response styles. Some panelists prefer to cluster their ratings in the middle of the range, whereas others prefer to use the upper part of the scales, and still others use the lower parts. Unfortunately, without any other scaling procedure to tie the panelists' ratings together, one will never know whether an individual's use of a narrow portion of the scale reflects a true perception of limited sensory intensities, or whether the narrow range derives from the panelist's response bias, or both. Furthermore, reponse bias increases interpanelist variability above and beyond the variability ordinarily incurred by individual differences.

From time to time, researchers who want to reduce response biases use reference standards to ensure that panelists fully use the scale e.g., in the Texture Profile. Rather than allowing respondents to use any part of the scale that they wish, the researcher maps out the meaning of different scale levels in an attempt to force panelists to use the scale properly. By so doing, one can train the panel members to monitor their progress in scale usage, and quickly detect aberrant response styles.

ALTERNATIVES TO FIXED POINT SCALES

As noted above, fixed point category scales require arbitrary decisions as to the number of category scales to use. Other scaling procedures with supposed interval-level properties remedy some of these problems. In 1946 Baten introduced the concept of a linear scale, which comprised a line of fixed length bounded by endpoint markers. Panelists used this line as a sensory ruler. To scale the sensory intensity of a stimulus, the panelist marked the appropriate region on the line. Recently, Stone *et al.* (1974) used linear scaling to represent sensory intensity, reporting success with it.

Linear scaling possesses advantages, but also disadvantages over traditional fixed point scales. The advantages include: no limitation on the ability of the scale to represent intermediate values; and no recurrent single favorite number, which plagues fixed point scales. The disadvantages include: the necessity of measuring line length with a ruler before data analysis; the fact that biases still remain regarding response position on the scale, narrow range versus wide range, and biased use of the upper portion of the scale versus lower portion of the scale, and the necessary provision of extra room beyond the scale for panelists to rate extremely intense stimuli. Unfortunately, researchers who use category number scaling usually do not use an extra category in the same way as researchers who use linear scaling. The latter researchers allow panelists that extra space beyond end of the line to reflect even stronger stimuli than those previously placed at the line end-points.

MAGNITUDE ESTIMATION SCALING

Magnitude estimation refers to a class of scaling procedures developed over a period of 40 years by S. S. Stevens, his colleagues, students and associates. Magnitude estimation represents the first general approach to the ratio scaling of perceptions. The researcher can develop a numerical scale with the same rigor and usefulness as the scales developed by physicists for length, mass, and temperature, etc.

A Short History of Ratio Scaling

In the late 1930s and 1940s, researchers at the Laboratory of Psychoacoustics at Harvard University, under Stevens' direction, tried to construct ratio scales of perception by various experimental procedures. These researchers dealt primarily with tones and lights, and used this research to develop better measures of visual and auditory perceptions.

The earliest methods for ratio scaling used the methods of *fractionation* and *multiplication*. Let us consider the classic experiment by Beebe-Center (1949) on taste perception for the GUST scale as an example of the procedure. Beebe-Center thoroughly explains the methods, and Guilford's book on psychometric scaling (1954) gives particulars of the scaling procedure. To develop a ratio scale of sweetness, the researcher first prepares a graded concentration series of sugar solutions. Choosing a very low sucrose concentration of 1% arbitrarily equal to GUST, the researcher instructs the panelist to select one of the remaining sugar solutions which tastes two times (or any multiple) as sweet. The panelist samples the remaining stimuli to find the sugar sample tasting twice as sweet. Some sugar solutions will taste sweeter than two times, others will taste less than two times as sweet. Sooner or later the panelist will discover a sugar solution which seems to taste about twice as sweet as the reference sample assigned 1 GUST.

An average concentration obtained from many panelists will show which sugar concentration tastes twice as sweet. This sample has a value of 2 GUSTS. The researcher then repeats the task, this time with the 2 GUST stimulus. That stimulus sample tasting twice as sweet as the 2 GUST sample must equal 4 GUSTS. The process repeats until the researcher has mapped a series of concentrations which lie in the prescribed sensory ratio. Furthermore, one need not work from the reference level of 1 GUST, but could start anywhere, working up (multiplication) or working down (fractionation). Sometimes experimenters find it helpful to do both, and then to average. Figure 5.3 shows the concentration of the GUST scale (Beebe-Center 1949), and Table 5.12 shows a worked example for weight (Stevens and Harper, 1948).

Fractionation and multiplication demand a lot of time. They become tedious and boring procedures. Furthermore, through prolonged tasting one continually runs the risk of exposing the panelist to a desensitizing array of stimuli. For studies of audition (e.g. loudness scaling), fractionation and multiplication represent reasonable methods by which to erect ratio scales. For the chemical senses, multiple extended stimulus presentation to the nose or the mouth can generate too much interference with the scaling task at hand.

Discovery of Magnitude Estimation. Magnitude estimation emerged almost by accident during a study on tonal loudness and visual brightness. During an extensive series of scaling studies at the Laboratory of Psychoacoustics, Stevens and his colleagues investi-

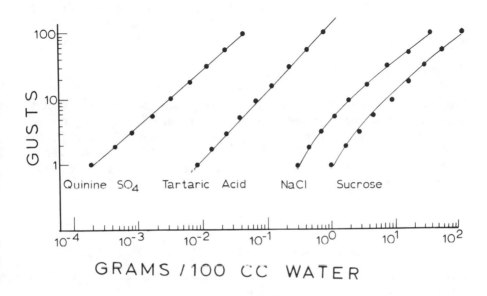

FIG. 5.3 THE RELATION BETWEEN CONCENTRATION OF TASTE MATERIALS AND
THE GUST VALUES
Source: Beebe-Center (1949)

gated the effects of different instructions on the psychophysical function, trying to relate physical stimulus levels to numerically rated
stimulus intensity. On one occasion he inadvertently omitted the
instructions, telling panelists only to match numbers to perceived
intensity. Panelists could select any numbers with which they felt
comfortable, with the exception that 0 represented no intensity at all,
the panelist could not hear the tone or see the light.

Despite the seemingly unstructured task facing the panelists, the
results of this exercise proved encouraging. For one, panelists did not
hesitate to assign numbers of their own choosing. Certainly panelists
differed in the numbers which they selected. Some panelists preferred
to use small numbers (fractions, single digits and low double digit
numbers), whereas others preferred to use higher numbers (10s, 100s).
Panelists tended to use round numbers (1s, 5s, 10s) and did not usually
assign unusual numbers such as 29 or 31, etc.

Panelists can generate numbers ad infinitum. One test of the validity of these numbers uses the correlation between the numbers that
panelists assign and the physical intensity as objectively measured by

instruments. Stevens reported that a straight line in log-log coordinates related the numbers panelists assigned (first called absolute judgments, then later renamed magnitude estimates) to physical intensity:

Log Numbers = n Log I + Log k

The exponent **n** proved a reliable parameter. From experiment to experiment the same exponent appeared for a specific sensory modality, despite panelists' seemingly free-wheeling use of numbers. On the average, the exponent ranged between 0.5 and 0.7 for loudness versus sound pressure, and between 0.3 and 0.4 for brightness versus luminance.

TABLE 5.12

WORKED EXAMPLE OF THE FRACTIONATION METHOD

Standard Weight	Weight Judged Half As Heavy
40	23.3
100	51.6
150	83.3
200	119.9
300	165.0

Relation Between Weight (S) and Weight Half As Heavy (S_n); $Log (S_n) = 1.0105 (Log S) + 0.2699$

Actual Grams Weight	Psychological Weight Scale	100 = 1 = Standard or Reference
17.6	.125	
31.6	.25	
56.4	.5	
100.0	1	
176.3	2	
309.0	4	
583.5	8	
933.1	16	
1607.0	32	
2754.0	64	

Source: Stevens and Harper (1948)

These reliable results encouraged Stevens and his colleagues to further pursue the scaling method. Over the next two decades researchers evaluated the scaling method in a variety of ways which we cover in the next portion of this chapter. Specific questions they answered concerned these issues: the effect of initial stimulus (standard) and prescribed number (modulus); the regression effect—shortening the range of numbers assigned; non-verbal parallels of magnitude estimation scaling; magnitude estimation versus direct ratio estimation; magnitude estimation versus magnitude production; the effect of repeated trials on the rating; age versus ability to assign magnitude estimates; variability of the ratings and the meaning of that variability; proper methods of analyzing the results, including statistical tests; panel size for evaluation; the use of magnitude estimation to scale stimuli without an underlying physical continuum e.g., attitudes; and cross-cultural magnitude estimation with non-English-speaking respondents.

Instructions

We deal first with the proper training of panelists in magnitude estimation scaling. Historical approaches to panelist training follow cycles. The early (1950s) work with magnitude estimation, like research on many other psychometric procedures, used informal training of panelists. The experimenter might simply have instructed panelists to assign numbers to match stimuli. With continued research, however, and with the emphasis on ratio scaling, quite often the instructions became cumbersome. Researchers instructed the panelists to make sure that the ratios of estimates truly reflected ratios of perceptions. Tables 5.13, 5.14 and 5.15 compare the simple, parsimonious instructions and the more complex, rigid and generally less usable, comprehensive instructions.

In many informal studies run by professional psychophysicists, panelists participate in the evaluation without the benefit of any formalized training whatsoever. They may receive instructions simply to match numbers to perceptions, but few other instructions. These studies with simplistic instructions usually generate data which differ little, if any, from studies using more formalized instructions. Based upon these reports from practicing psychophysicists, and the lack of any rigid, formal training appearing in published psychophysics papers, it appears best to provide the simplest and least rigid form of instruction. Panelists should understand the concept of scaling, and the opportunity to use as wide a range as they wish to scale perceptions. Panelists need not demonstrate any superior ability however.

Current Instructions for Intensity Evaluations by Magnitude Estimation

With the increasing use of magnitude estimation scaling as a preferred method for sensory analysis in both academic and industrial circles, researchers have tried to standardize instructions to panelists. The original, simple method for instructing panelists in the university laboratories worked because the experimenter could maintain personal contact with the panelist at all times, monitoring the panelist's comprehension of the scale procedure. In larger scale projects one could no longer ensure that all panelists understand the task of magnitude estimation, because the magnitude estimation scaling approach has developed from a simple, in-laboratory scientific tool to a major method of measurement, used by marketing research as well as by R&D.

TABLE 5.13
TYPICAL MAGNITUDE ESTIMATION INSTRUCTIONS

ASSIGNED MODULUS

In front of you is a series of . . . solutions. Your task is to tell how sweet they taste. Call the first stimulus 10 (reader: you may assign any number here you wish for the modulus, and simply modify instructions accordingly). If the second stimulus tastes nineteen times as sweet as the first, assign it the number 19 times as large. That number equals 10 $\times 19 = 190$. If it tastes one-eleventh as sweet as the first, then assign it a number 1/11 as large. That number equals 10/11 or around 1.0. Use numbers, fractions, and decimals, but make each assignment proportional to the sweetness as you taste it. Remember, 10 equals your reference number, and reflects the sweetness of the first sample.

TABLE 5.14
SUGGESTED INSTRUCTION—WITHOUT EMPHASIS
ON RATIOS (From Stevens, 1975, p. 30)

You will be presented with a series of stimuli in irregular order. Your task is to tell how intense they seem by assigning numbers to them. Call the first stimulus any number that seems appropriate to you. Then assign successive numbers in such a way that they reflect your subjective impression. There is no limit to the range of numbers that you may use. You may use whole numbers, decimals, or fractions. Try to make each number match the intensity as you perceive it.

TABLE 5.15
EXTENDED AND MORE DETAILED INSTRUCTIONS
FOR MAGNITUDE ESTIMATION: CAKES

INTRODUCTION TO MAGNITUDE ESTIMATION

SUPERVISOR: We are going to be using a special method for rating these cakes. In order for you to tell us how you feel about the different characteristics of each cake you will use numbers that you pick yourself. It's really quite simple.

The MORE of a particular characteristic you feel a specific chocolate cake has, the BIGGER the number you should give it. The LESS of a particular characteristic you feel a specific chocolate cake has, the SMALLER the number you should give it. If you feel that the cake doesn't have any amount of a particular characteristic, give it a ZERO.

Now, let's try an example.

(INTERVIEWER: PASS OUT SHAPE SHEETS)

In front of you, you will find a sheet of paper with shapes on them. The shapes have different sizes. Look at the first shape. Find the line of page 2 that has the same letter as the shape you are looking at.

Give numbers to the shapes you look at to show how large or small you think they seem. The number you have selected will be used to compare the size of the next shape you will see. Since you may see shapes after this one which are smaller than this one, we ask that you select a number which is reasonably large for this first shape. However, aside from that restriction, you may select any number you want. Write this number in now. If you have any questions, please raise your hand. (PAUSE)

INTERVIEWER: CHECK TO SEE THAT THE NUMBER IS 0 OR MORE.

SUPERVISOR: Now, look to the next shape in your shape sheet. Find the proper line on page 2. If this shape is bigger than the first shape, give it a bigger number than you gave the first shape. If it's smaller than the first shape, give it a smaller number than you gave the first shape. For example, if you feel that the second shape is half as large as the first shape, you would give it a number half as large as you gave the first one. If you feel that the second shape is five times as big as the first, give it a number five times as large as you gave the first one. If this shape is the same size as the first one, give it the same number as you gave the first one. If you have any questions, raise your hand. (PAUSE)

INTERVIEWER: WITH THE FIRST TWO SHAPES IN FRONT OF YOU, MAKE SURE THE RESPONDENT UNDERSTANDS THE CONCEPT OF RATIOS BY READING THE FOLLOWING:

TABLE 5.15 (Continued)

You gave the first shape letter (FILL IN LETTER), (FILL IN NUMBER), and you gave the second shape, letter (FILL IN LETTER), a (FILL IN NUMBER). This means that you feel the second shape, letter is (FIGURE OUT RELATIVE VALUE — I.E., SHAPE 2 IS TWO TIMES LARGER THAN SHAPE 1) (times larger than/as large as/the same size as) the first shape, letter (FILL IN LETTER). Is that correct? (PAUSE)

IF RESPONDENT SAYS "YES," DATA ARE OK, AND CONTINUE TO NEXT RESPONDENT. IF RESPONDENT SAYS "NO", SAY:

You can change your rating now.

SUPERVISOR: Now, go on to the next shape and continue what you have been doing until you have finished the entire set of shapes. Don't try to remember the size of all the shapes you have looked at. Only remember the size of the last shape you saw. For each shape, we would like you to tell us how big or small it it seems when compared to the one you have just seen. If the shape you are looking at seems larger than the previous one, give it a bigger number than you gave the previous one. If the shape you are looking at seems smaller than the previous shape, assign it a smaller number.

In light of the growing acceptance and proliferation of this technique, researchers have had to develop the standardized instructional format to make the approach portable from market to market. The instructions shown in Table 5.15 present a set of introductory exercises which researchers in sensory analysis have successfully used for four years in marketing research in approximately 38 different locations in the U.S., as well as translations into Quebec French, Parisian French, Japanese, German and Dutch.

The instructions present the magnitude estimation evaluations in a straight-forward manner, instructing panelists to match numbers to perceptions. To introduce the panelists to the task at hand, the panelists first ran through a series of orientation exercises designed to illustrate the wide range of numbers which they can use. Table 5.16 shows typical results from the training exercise, obtained with a panel of 22 individuals.

Once panelists have successfully finished the exercise, they usually can participate in a panel for product evaluation, since they have developed a good idea of how to scale perceptions.

Who Should Participate in M.E. Panels—Age and Abilities

One sometimes hears that magnitude estimation procedures tax the panelist's capacities to evaluate stimuli, since the scale neither imposes arbitrary restrictions on available categories, nor does it impose scale limits. Sometimes such freedom seems disconcerting. Yet, magnitude estimation scaling applies equally well to children ages 7 and above (Moskowitz and Chandler 1979) as to adults. Furthermore, one need not limit the scaling to undergraduate students. Consumers from all walks of life can use the procedure.

TABLE 5.16
RESULTS FROM TRAINING PANELISTS WITH SHAPES TO
SCALE USING THE MAGNITUDE ESTIMATION METHOD

Circles		Triangles		Squares	
Area (cm^2)	Rating	Area	Rating	Area	Rating
7.1	7.8	2.0	4.7	10.1	13.2
19.7	10.0	7.4	10.7	17.9	18.8
43.0	31.1	24.8	22.5	72.4	47.6
91.6	52.2	64.9	49.7	123.0	68.5
145.3	69.5	104.0	65.4	123.0[a]	69.5
216.4	106.9	322.0	92.4	203.0	97.4

[a]Replicate to check scale reliability

Moskowitz (1977) reported that, in the general population, approximately 5% of the panelists will have problems in assigning magnitude estimates to stimuli. These individuals do not seem to understand the matching task. Their difficulties stem more from the task of rating than from inherent difficulties in the magnitude estimation procedure. Other panelists may complain that their ratings do not mean anything. Practitioners often see this among older panelists who have not had formal schooling for a number of years, and who feel uncomfortable with scaling per se.

The important thing to remember, however, remains their actual ratings or performance. Do these panelists scale perceptions so that their ratings correlate with physically measured intensities? If they do, then the product tester can confidently disregard panelist complaints that he or she does not understand the task or has performed the task incorrectly. These complaints result from emotional reactions to the test situation. They arise whenever panelists feel stressed by test demands placed upon them.

Brain damaged panelists have also participated successfully in magnitude estimation panels wherein they rated perceived olfactory intensity, taste intensity, numerousness of grids on a box and area

(Jones *et al.* 1978). Such patients with severe memory defects exhibit good scaling behavior. Their ratings correlate with the physical intensities of the stimuli, in many cases paralleling data obtained for normal panelists.

How Many Stimuli Can One Test with Magnitude Estimation

The appropriate number of stimuli to test depends upon panelist motivation. In traditional laboratory oriented scaling, researchers test between 6 and 12 stimuli in short sessions. Sessions usually last about 20-30 min. each. Panelists soon fatigue, more out of boredom than out of a true sensory loss. One can test many more samples with magnitude estimation (or any other rating method) by keeping the panelists alert. Paying the panelist, or otherwise motivating the panelist acts as an incentive to maintain performance. By doing so, one can achieve long-term evaluations, lasting up to 4 and 5 hours. Moskowitz, Wolfe and Beck (1978) reported success in a beverage evaluation study in which panelists rated 25 colas during a long 4-hr. session. Correctness of performance emerged from a correlational analysis between concentrations of artificial sweetener in the cola and the magnitude estimates. In other studies run at the U.S. Army Natick R&D Command (Massachusetts.), Moskowitz, Dubose and Reuben (1977) reported good results using paid volunteers who evaluated dozens of odor stimuli during the course of a four hour experiment. Again, validity of the ratings emerged from correlations between magnitude estimates of odor intensity for the various odorants, and objectively measured odorant concentrations.

What Do Panelists Do When Evaluating Many Stimuli

During the course of such a long session, panelists sometimes complain that they have forgotten the intensity of first stimulus that they rated. In other studies, with and without reference stimuli, Stevens (1975) reported that despite panelists' complaints about forgetting the first stimulus (the standard), their ratings paralleled ratings made by panelists who always had a standard available to them during the study for reference. Apparently, panelists who scale, either using magnitude estimation or even fixed point scaling, develop their own internal frame of reference. The originally conscious and perhaps labored approach to assigning numbers soon becomes automatic. Panelists feel that a stimulus should receive an estimate of 25 or 50, rather than actually computing the number in their head. Memory for the first stimulus, however faded, integrates into the assignments to the subsequent stimuli. The act of numerical assignment becomes automatic and rapid, rather than forced and considered.

Such a transformation permits the researcher to evaluate several, or even dozens, of alternative formulations in a session, and still remain confident about the accuracy of the results. It also contradicts the more conventional wisdom which dictates (often without justification) that people simply cannot participate in an overly long session, testing many stimuli. That hypothesis or conjecture (for no one has ever proven it) does not hold, as any researcher will quickly discover by doing a study using areas of different shapes and sizes. One need simply instruct panelists to assign numbers to shapes of different areas to match apparent size, and then correlate these ratings with the physical area. Panelists who say that they forgot the first stimulus do as well in their ratings as panelists who do recall the first stimulus, and use it in subsequent evaluations of area.

The First Stimulus and the First Rating

Some psychophysical studies scrupulously use a designated standard as the first stimulus, and designate the first value to go with that standard called the *modulus*. Experimenters studied the effect of standard level upon the resulting magnitude estimation functions (Engen and Levy 1955). A standard selected at the top of the stimulus range will reduce the range of numbers which panelists assign. In order to test this, researchers used the standard psychophysical procedure. They instructed the panelist to rate loudness. The slope of the function in log-log coordinates drops when the standard lies at the top of the range of stimuli, as Fig. 5.4 shows. In other instances, the sensory analyst may place the standard stimulus at the lowest level. In such instances, the psychophysical function steepens as panelists enlarge their range of numbers. By and large, researchers compromise when they use a standard, placing the standard somewhere in the middle range of the stimuli to counterbalance the two effects. When they do so, another phenomenon emerges. Usually the magnitude estimates versus physical intensity conform to a fairly straight line in log-log coordinates (from which we derive the notion of the power function). With the standard in the middle of the range, the ratings in that region become distorted and the psychophysical function shows irregular behavior in the region around the standard. These aberrant results obtained from using standard, or reference, stimuli convinced Stevens and his associates that using no standard at all as a designated, fixed reference would, in fact, generally produce the best data.

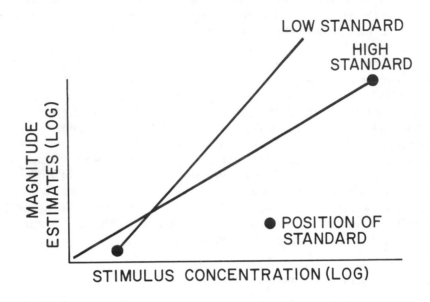

FIG. 5.4 BEHAVIOR OF THE PSYCHOPHYSICAL FUNCTION FOR MAGNITUDE ESTIMA-
TION, SHOWING HOW THE POSITION OF THE STANDARD AFFECTS THE SLOPE OF THE
LINE (OR THE EXPONENT OF THE POWER FUNCTION)
Source: Engen and Levy (1955)

Panelists often feel uncomfortable about a variable first stimulus, and sometimes request a standard against which to reference all of their ratings. The author's observation of panelist behavior during sessions in which panelists receive the standard and then scale the test stimuli show that rarely do the panelists consult the standard after the initial ratings. Thus, if not needed, the standard stimulus, which acts as the reference, serves little or no purpose.

Standards play another role, however, which the experimenter should recognize. They allow the product tester to relate the size of numbers assigned in one study to the size of numbers in another study. Researchers often like to run several small experiments as part of a larger study. Each small study may investigate one condition or test formulation in a larger product set. By using a common stimulus or set of stimuli throughout the entire set of smaller experiments, the researcher can ensure comparability from one study to another. An experiment by Cain on odor intensity scaling for aliphatic alcohols illustrates this point quite nicely (Cain 1969). Panelists scaled different graded series of n-aliphatic (straight chain) alcohols (e.g., butyl alcohol, pentyl alcohol, propyl alcohol, etc.) by magnitude estimation using their own number scales. In order to link together the ratings assigned to different alcohols tested in different sessions, Cain used a common concentration of the chemical acetone, presenting it in every experiment on odors. This stimulus, unbeknown to the panelists, served as an *internal standard*. For the subsequent analysis, Cain indexed the ratings of each panelist by a multiplicative factor, so that the acetone stimulus always obtained a constant rating. He then multiplied the panelists' ratings for the other stimuli by the same indexing factor. Researchers often prefer to use one internal standard or, in some instances, several internal standards, e.g., 5 concentrations of glucose present in sweetness studies (Moskowitz 1971), in order to compare ratings from one study to ratings from another study, while avoiding the biasing effects due to a predesignated reference standard.

The first number which panelists assign sets their scale unit, or modulus. The incorrect choice of a modulus biases the ratings. When the panelist chooses or receives a modulus around 1 or 2, the subsequent magnitude estimates generate high ratios. Panelists do not hesitate to go to 50 or 100. On the other hand, some investigators prefer to force panelists to use a modulus of 100. This high initial scale unit diminishes the range of the magnitude estimates. Panelists feel constrained never to go below 1.0, for fear of running out of numbers. They rarely go above 500, a ratio of 5:1 versus the modulus. Panelists can, of course, assign ratings in the decimals and fractions, but most panelists behave conservatively and avoid that region.

Let us return to the example of tone loudness versus physical energy. When the initial stimulus receives a high modulus, the slope decreases. Panelists constrict the range of the magnitude estimates which they assign to the second and subsequent stimuli. When the first stimulus receives a low modulus, panelists expand the range and ratios of their magnitude estimates to generate a steeper appearing function.

Several rules of thumb emerge from laboratory and commercial uses of magnitude estimation which pertain to the initial stimulus and to the modulus. (1) Vary the first stimulus randomly from the different members of the stimulus set with one exception. The first simulus shoud not lie at the top of the stimulus range or the bottom, but should lie somewhere in the middle. (2) Randomize the sequence of stimuli, in order to minimize any effect of the first stimulus evaluation on subsequent stimulus evaluations. (3) If possible, do not force the panelist to use a specific modulus or first number. Rather, allow the panelist to use any number with which he or she feels comfortable. (4) If one must use a modulus, then allow the panelist a middle modulus value. Some practitioners suggest 10, others suggest 20 or more for this first number. Rarely, however, do practitioners suggest 5 or 1 or 100, since these extremes expand or compress the scale.

Calibrating the Magnitude Estimates in Order to Reduce Variability

By its very nature, magnitude estimation scaling, per se, generates more variability around the average score than does fixed point scaling or linear scaling. Some panelists prefer to use high numbers, whereas others prefer to use low numbers. The mixture of these response styles generates variability in the data independent of the intrinsic variation across products and across consumer preceptions.

Scientists have wrestled with the issue of variability as long as magnitude estimation scaling has existed. In its early days during the 1950s, researchers used magnitude estimation primarily as a method for discovering the psychophysical function relating physical magnitude and sensory magnitude. In so doing, the researcher usually presented the panelist with all of the stimuli in a complete experimental design. If the panelist evaluated one stimulus twice, he or she would evaluate all of the stimuli twice. Each panelist rated the exact same stimuli.

The initial work, focusing as it did on the exponent of the power function, considered variability in the ratings more as a source of annoyance than as a factor to consider in making a statistical decision. The researcher calcuated the geometric mean rating from all of the panelists, and then plotted that mean against physical intensity. From time to time a researcher might publish a measure of stimulus variability, often the interquartile range in logarithmic coordinates. Rarely if ever, however, did the researcher calculate the standard deviation or the standard error of the mean for subsequent use in statistical analysis. In those days, direct psychophysical scaling almost entirely concerned itself with perceptual phenomena and their measurement. It deliberately shied away from the use of anything more exotic, statistically, than the measure of central tendency, whether the geometric mean, the median or the mode. [The *geometric mean* = the nth root of the product of n numbers: e.g., $(X_1 X_2 ... X_n)^{1/n}$.]

Lane, Catania and Stevens (1961) suggested a workable statistical approach to reducing the variability around the mean. They suggested a normalization procedure which they entitled *modulus equalization*. According to Lane *et al.*, the average rating of the stimuli across panelists, e.g., ratings of all the test sugar solutions in a taste test study should remain the same after normalization. However, one could diminish the variability around that grand mean by multiplying all of the ratings of a single panelist by a number, so that the panelist's geometric mean rating equalled the group geometric mean. In order to equate the geometric mean across panelists to the grand geometric mean, the experimenter calculated the necessary multiplier for each panelist separately. The resulting geometric mean of the panelist, after multiplication by the correction factor, would equal the average geometric mean.

For a decade modulus equalization proved a reasonable approach to reducing interpanelist variability. Table 5.17 shows the method. Certainly it did not modify the overall geometric mean, but simply compressed the ratings into a smaller range without destroying the ratios among the ratings assigned by each panelist separately.

TABLE 5.17
EXAMPLE OF MODULUS EQUALIZATION FOR
MAGNITUDE ESTIMATION
(5 Cake Samples Rated On Flavor Strength)

Panelist	Pre-Equalization Sample					
	A	B	C	D	E	$\bar{X}$
1	35	60	120	160	190	(95.8)
2	2	4	17	19	32	(10.6)
3	16	32	48	71	95	(44.0)
4	0.2	0.6	0.8	0.9	1.1	(0.6)

Grand Geometric Mean = 12.56
$\bar{X}$ = Geometric Mean (For panelist 1 = $(35 \times 60 \times 120 \times 160 \times 190)^{1/5}$

Panelist	Post Modulus Equalization				
	A	B	C	D	E
1	4.6	8.0	15.9	21.2	25.2
2	2.6	5.2	22.2	24.8	41.7
3	4.6	9.1	13.7	20.3	27.1
4	4.1	12.2	16.2	18.2	22.3

Grand Geometric Mean = 12.56
Numbers analyzed according to the procedure provided by Lane, Catania and Stevens (1961)

In product testing work, the ability to give each panelist the same, or all of the stimuli represents an unexpected luxury in experimentation which few researchers, sensory analysts, product testers or marketing researchers can afford. In most current studies, the panelists test an incomplete portion of the stimulus set, rather than all of the stimuli, especially when the stimuli comprise food samples which one must first prepare and then consume. To generate a psychophysical function or even to generate profile data on key attributes, in-home use tests could take months or longer when the mode of stimulus delivery becomes lengthy and complex. Panelists might test each sample for a period of 1-2 weeks. Compare this study execution with the traditional psychophysical laboratory approach. Panelists can evaluate 20 auditory or taste stimuli in 1-3 hours to generate the psychophysical data base and the researcher can derive the function from that data.

Moskowitz (1971) suggested another normalization procedure, called *modulus normalization*. This method links together data from panelists or studies which test only part of the stimuli. Panelists receive a set of internal reference stimuli within their set of experimental stimuli. These internal stimuli remain the same from one panelist to another, and from experiment to experiment. The other stimuli vary in random order from panelist to panelist or study to study.

In the initial research, modulus normalization found use in the measurement of sweetness of simple sugars, sugar alcohols, e.g., mannitol, sorbitol, and artificial sweeteners, e.g., saccharin, cyclamate, etc. Since panelists tested each sugar, or a concentration series, with 4-7 levels of stimuli, one panelist could not possibly evaluate all of the different stimuli in one session. In order to link together the ratings obtained in different sessions from different panelists, each panelist evaluated 5 concentrations of the sugar glucose (dextrose), placed randomly in the stimulus set, unknown to the panelists. The stimuli comprised a concentration series by themselves: 2.0M, 1.0M, 0.5M, 0.25M, 0.125M. By modulus normalization, the geometric mean rating assigned to these five common glucose stimuli came to 10.0 for each panelist. The method assigned a multiplier constant to each panelist, so selected that it forced the geometric mean of those 5 stimuli to equal 10 or their product to equal $100{,}000 = 10^5$. That same multiplier, unique for each panelist, then normalized the remaining ratings of stimuli in the set. Thus, modulus normalization permitted comparisons between experiments with different panelists. For example, one could feel more comfortable comparing a 50 for 1.0M sucrose to a 20 for 1.0M dextrose, since by and large these stimuli now lay on the same numerical scale.

This same normalization procedure applies when panelists evaluate an incomplete set of food products. One might, for instance, wish to test various candy flavors in a central location. In a short time period the panelist may only test four flavors, allowing 15 minutes per flavor for a 60 minute session. If one must test 24 flavors, then a single panelist could possibly test only 1/6 of the set. On the other hand, by maintaining a specific two out of the four, or even one out of the four, as the internal reference for all panelists, one can guarantee comparability of ratings across different panelists, even though the panelists did not share any other candy flavors in common but one.

External Calibration

Sensory analysts and marketing researchers often perform product tests in which one panelist evaluates a single product alone, selected from an entire set, rather than rating some or most of the alternative products from the set. In such cases, the traditional category scales, anchored with words, provide the panelist with a reliable frame of reference. Panelists can evaluate even one product alone using the category scale, since the scale generates its own frame of reference. Of course, single or pure monadic evaluations pose difficulties. The practitioner can never guarantee that each panelist uses the scale in the same way. A score of 9 for one panelist may equal a 7 for another panelist using the same scale. Panelists come into test situations with different frames of reference. Those frames interact with the ratings to generate unique scale use by each individual.

The intriguing point of the foregoing discussion concerns the external reference standard provided by the category scale structure. Can the practitioner combine the external reference structure of the fixed point scale with the free number scaling and associated advantages of magnitude estimation?

In a set of early studies in the middle 1970s, Andrew Dravnieks of the Illinois Institute of Technology suggested a method for taking advantage of both types of scales. At the end of the evaluation session where panelists scaled the intensity of odorants of varying concentrations, Dravnieks instructed the panelists to assign a number on their own magnitude estimation scale to represent moderately intense. This number acted as an anchor point. It applied to the set of stimuli which the panelists evaluated, but did not necessarily represent the intensity of any single stimulus. In order to calibrate the responses of panelists, each of whom may have tested different odorants in the study, Dravnieks divided the ratings of each panelist by that panelist's own estimate of moderate (Moskowitz, Dravnieks and Klarman 1976).

Moskowitz (1977) carried this approach further by developing a full scale of word descriptors. The panelists first evaluated a series of stimuli, assigning magnitude estimates to represent varying degrees of intensity. The panelist then scaled normative verbal stimuli, described as extreme, very much, moderate, slight and none at all. Thus, panelists first evaluated several stimuli although they could have evaluated only one stimulus, had the study protocol dictated that design. Then the panelists scaled the words using the same scale, to reflect graded degrees of intensity. The ratings and the calibration or numerical equivalents of the words varied by panelist. Panelists using high numbers to rate stimuli used high numbers to rate verbal equivalents, and vice versa for panelists using low ratings. In order to calibrate the data so as to intercompare the ratings of the panelists the researchers divided each of the panelist's ratings of the stimulus words by the number assigned to moderate. That same divisor calibrated every other word in the panelist's scale, as well as calibrating each rating of intensity.

Points to note about external calibration include the following. (1) The calibration does not depend upon rating of a test stimulus. Rather, the calibration depends upon the panelist's concept of words external to the test stimulus, evaluated after the test stimuli. (2) The calibration allows the panelist to evaluate a single stimulus or many stimuli. No longer must the panelist evaluate all of the test and reference stimuli to assure calibration to a common scale.

The one-point calibration (around moderate) proved effective in the evaluation or products and the coalescing of ratings. The cola study by Moskowitz, Wolfe and Beck (1978) on the sweetness, off-flavor and acceptability of cola flavored beverages showed that one could obtain usable data by averaging together the magnitude estimates from many panelists. In that study, panelists evaluated 44 different formulations over a period of several days. Each day the panelists evaluated a different subset of the formulations. After each day's evaluations, the panelists calibrated their magnitude estimates. The normalization diminished interpanelist variability, and facilitated the discovery of the function of equation relating ingredients to sensory perceptions. Without calibration one probably would not have developed a smooth function due to the variability among products and the additional variability contributed by the divergent scales of panelists.

One can modify the calibration procedure in order to make it more robust by using several different scale points as bases for calibration as Table 5.18 shows. The study proceeds in the following way: Panelists evaluate one or several products; at the end of the evaluation, panelists scale a set of normative words which represent varying degrees of intensity, e.g., extremely, very much, moderately, slightly. By definition, 0 refers to nothing at all or not perceptible.

Rather than using one point, e.g., the top of the scale, extremely, as the basis of the index or normalization, the product tester estimates the average index value by adding up the numerical assignments to extremely, very much, moderately and slightly, and dividing the total by four. This generates an average index number which typifies the panelist's scale. Whereas a panelist's estimate of moderate could vary

TABLE 5.18
CALIBRATION METHOD FOR MAGNITUDE ESTIMATES
(Panelist "X")

Pre-Calibration	Post Calibration
Product Rating	
Product A = 75	47.5
B = 175	110.8
C = 36	22.8
Calibration Words	
Extremely = 260	164.6
Very much = 180	113.9
Moderately = 130	82.3
Slight = 62	39.2
None = 0	0

$$\text{Post Calibration Rating} = \frac{\text{Pre Calibration Rating}}{\text{Index}} \times 100$$

$$\text{Index} = \frac{(\text{Extreme} + \text{Very} + \text{Moderately} + \text{Slightly})}{4}$$

$$\text{Index} = \frac{632}{4} = 158$$

from trial to trial, since it represents estimates of a single point, more than likely the average size of scale will not vary substantially.

Such multi-point calibrations provide these key benefits in analyzing magnitude estimation ratings: a more robust method for indexing panelist's data, independent of any single indexing point which could vary erratically; the ability to correlate magnitude estimates to words which describe intensity; and the ability to ascertain, panelist by panelist, what each magnitude estimate means in terms of a verbal description. Since each panelist assigns the magnitude estimates and calibrates his or her scale, the product tester can obtain an average of the calibrated ratings, and can count the number of panelists whose estimates fall into the region of extreme, very much, moderate, etc.

Experience with this calibration procedure has shown its robustness in many test situations for evaluation of actual products. Furthermore, the procedure generates reliable, sensitive rating data with even as few as 10-15 panelists based upon studies in which one can correlate the average ratings with the known physical intensities. Finally, the sensory analyst and market researcher can use the procedure when panelists scale only one product, rather than having to scale an entire array of products. In a study with beverages tested at home for a two week period, singly and by an entire family, the calibration procedure provided a method to anchor the ratings of families who had no experience with any stimulus other than the beverage which they tested (Moskowitz 1979).

Tables 5.19 and 5.20 show the results of several different studies which illustrate the relative robustness of the calibration scale. Note that even when the data set comprises subgroups of panelists, reducing the base size, the calibration procedure still maintains adequate comparability from one set to another. Furthermore, Table 5.21 shows that the aggregate or average calibration, across a panel of as few as 10 people, generates similar numerical equivalents to verbal descriptors time and time again.

Averaging Magnitude Estimates from Different Panelists

Magnitude estimation saw its first use in evaluating easily perceptible, relatively uncomplicated stimuli, such as lights and tones. Rarely, if ever, during those early days, did Stevens and his associates consider the issues of nonperceptible stimuli, e.g., tones below threshold, or incomplete designs wherein panelists evaluated some but not all stimuli in the set.

The early approach dealt with complete data sets. It did not take into account zero ratings or incomplete data and it used the geometric mean for the average. The geometric mean cannot handle 0's. Once we have a 0 in the data set, the product of a set of numbers with one or more 0's automatically becomes 0. Furthermore, in the traditional approach to calculating geometric means, researchers used logarithmic transformations of the ratings. One cannot compute the logarithmic equivalent to 0. Consequently, laboratory researchers shied away from using stimuli having low intensities which would inevitably generate magnitude estimates of 0 from panelists. Market researchers shied away from the method of magnitude estimation, since panelists often assigned zero ratings which the researcher could not handle.

In product testing and sensory analysis, the constraints imposed by the geometric mean proved impractical for real-world utilization of the

TABLE 5.19
TYPICAL CALIBRATION SCALES FROM DIFFERENT STUDIES
(1)

Scale	M.E. Value	Interval Size	Ratio To Adjacent Value Scale
Extremely Strong	180.4 (3.2)	46.8	1.35
Very Strong	133.7 (1.4)	38.2	1.40
Moderately Strong	95.5 (1.2)	34.9	1.58
Moderately Weak	60.6 (1.6)	30.7	2.02
Very Weak	29.9 (1.5)	29.9	—
Cannot Perceive	0.0 (0.0)		

(2)

Degree of Similarity Scale			
Great Deal	143.5 (1.4)	28.5	1.25
Very Much	115.0 (0.8)	29.5	1.34
Moderately	85.5 (0.8)	29.5	1.53
Slightly	56.1 (1.6)	56.1	—
None At All	0.0 (0.0)		

Exhibit shows mean and standard error of the mean (in parentheses)

magnitude estimation scale. From time to time, researchers have argued that the magnitude estimates conform to a non-normal distribution, called the log-normal distribution (J. C. Stevens 1957), which requires the geometric mean as the appropriate average. Quite often, however, panelists will assign zero ratings, especially when the panelist profiles a product on a variety of characteristics. A sweet beverage may not taste bitter at all. The conscientious panelist will assign to

Table 5.20
PURCHASE INTEREST SCALE
(3)

	Study 1		Study 2		Study 3	
	CLT = Central Location		Intercept = 30-min Test		Pre-recruit = 4-hr Test	
	N = 73		N = 99		N = 219	
	Value	Interval	Value	Interval	Value	Interval
Definitely Would Purchase	173.5 (3.7)	54	198.5 (6.1)	65	162.0 (2.7)	45
Probably Would Purchase	119.3 (1.7)	47	132.7 (3.7)	56	116.6 (1.2)	38
Might Or Might Not Purchase	72.3 (2.1)	37	76.4 (3.4)	37	77.8 (1.2)	34
Probably Not Purchase	34.8 (1.9)	34.8	28.6 (1.90)	28	43.5 (1.3)	43
Definitely Not Purchase	0		0		0	

Numbers in parentheses = standard errors of the mean

that beverage a 0 rating for degree of bitter, no matter what scale he or she uses.

Since 1974, researchers who use magnitude estimation scaling have begun to use arithmetic means of the normalized or calibrated ratings in place of geometric means for these reasons. (1) The data obtained by averaging with the geometric mean leads many to the same conclusions as the results obtained by averaging with the arithmetic mean. (2) The arithmetic mean can account for 0s, whereas the geometric mean cannot. (3) The product tester need not use a complicated logarithmic transformation which removes the investigator from an intimate feel for the data. Rather, most researchers feel comfortable with the actual ratings, and prefer not to transform the ratings into logarithms. (4) With the arithmetic mean, the researcher uses statistical tests which psychophysicists ignored in their original quest for the psychophysical law of sensory magnitude. Whereas psychophysicists feel assured of valid results when the magnitude estimate tracks the physical intensities, sensory analysts and product testers often work with two products which differ from each other in many ways. The

TABLE 5.21
CALIBRATION—INTENSITY
(By Various Breaks in the Population)

	Total	User Group			Age of Respondent		
		A	B	C	18-24	25-34	35-49
Total Respondents:	(113)	(35)	(40)	(38)	(9)	(39)	(65)
Strength of Attribute:							
Extremely Strong	177.8	175.6	181.8	175.8	195.4	176.8	175.9
Very Strong	134.0	130.5	135.9	135.0	131.8	140.3	135.8
Moderately Strong	100.4	103.4	99.6	98.6	98.8	99.9	100.9
Moderately Weak	58.5	58.4	57.4	59.9	56.3	58.6	58.8
Very Weak	26.2	23.0	25.6	29.8	17.8	24.2	28.6
Cannot Perceive	0	0	0	0	0	0	0

TABLE 5.22
COMPARISON OF GEOMETRIC MEAN AND ARITHMETIC MEAN

Panelist	Product			
	A	B	C	D
1	25	70	50	22
2	32	64	38	41
3	61	74	63	61
4	74	32	29	60
5	72	64	31	20
6	10	38	61	59
7	110	130	25	64
8	105	75	27	40
9	105	37	51	60
10	71	62	74	39
Arithmetic Mean	64.1	64.6	44.9	46.2
Geometric Mean	52.9	58.7	41.9	43.3

practitioner wishes to use statistical procedures, e.g., different tests, analysis of variance, to ascertain whether or not two products truly differ in a statistical sense. With arithmetic means and statistical analyses, the entire realm of statistical testing opens up to the magnitude estimation data.

Why Magnitude Estimation Rather Than Category Scaling

In this chapter discussion has covered the method of magnitude estimation scaling, the calibration procedure, and a history of the difficulties and remedies which apply to magnitude estimation. Why use it then when the practitioner can just as simply use fixed point scaling without these detailed operations?

Several benefits accrue from magnitude estimation which makes it a more desirable scaling method in terms of both theory and practice. (1) All fixed point category scales contain arbitrary limits, and magnitude estimation eliminates these biases which reduce scale sensitivity. (2) Magnitude estimation has shown greater sensitivity than fixed point scales, in terms of pointing up differences. In an early study of product acceptability, Moskowitz and Sidel (1971) found that panelists who used magnitude estimates showed as many or more significant differences in their ratings as did panelists using fixed point scales. Only the scaling procedure differed. Furthermore, McDaniel (1974) showed the strong superiority of magnitude estimation over category scales. In neither instance did the panelists have an opportunity to calibrate their ratings, so that the authors used the modulus equalization procedure. (3) When the product tester wishes to correlate sensory responses with measured physical stimulus variation, magnitude estimation recommends itself as a less biased measuring technique to reveal the function relating the two domains. Category scales create a narrow sensory-instrumental function. This constriction inevitably biases the resulting function. The researcher does not know how the sensory perception truly varies with the physical stimulus continuum. (4) Perhaps most importantly, magnitude estimation has captured the attention of many of the psychophysicists who use it as a matter of course in investigating sensory functioning. Their numerous publications in scientific literature have provided a valuable source of information on the technique (Marks 1974; Moskowitz 1977).

A CASE HISTORY WITH MAGNITUDE ESTIMATION SCALING:

The Primavera Sauce Company

Background

The Primavera Sauce Company, PSC, wanted to measure the sensory characteristics of spicy tomato sauces to understand the range of products currently in the marketplace. To develop this snapshot of the current frame of competitors, as well as to measure the sensory charac-teristics of several of their new sauces against competitors, Primavera opted to use magnitude estimation scaling in its panel work.

Let us see how the Primavera Sauce Company performed this cate-gory snapshot of the current competitors and their products. The sequence went as follows: definition of the problem—what aspects of the sauces to scale and why; selection of the scaling instrument—what and why; selection of the panel—who; experimental design—what test products to measure; analysis of the results; and format of the report to management—results and implications.

Definition of the Problem

All manufacturers and scientists concerned with consumer percep-tion and acceptance need and want to know how consumers react to the products currently on the market. These reactions comprise *sen-sory perceptions*, non-evaluative reactions to the sensory impact of taste, smell, and appearance; *performance reactions*, overall liking/disliking, and purchase interest and *image characteristics*, unique-ness of flavor such as Italian flavor, and rich, natural flavor.

The Primavera Sauce Company looked to the method of multiple product evaluation to provide its first insight into the nature of the overall tomato sauce market as it exists today in terms of product sensory characteristics. The goal consisted of measuring products in the market to discover the following: (1) Existence of gaps in the market; do currently marketed products deliver what consumers want? (2) The sensory reaction of consumers to Primavera's test for-mulation versus competitors, and versus the gap between the desired product and existing products. (3) The differences of reactions among consumers; do consumers perceive the products differently as a func-tion of their brand usage, or as a function of their background (demographics).

In setting up the initial study, the sensory analyst and market researchers at Primavera planned to use the data as a focal point in their research program to illustrate to management strategic options. Either the products currently in the market (theirs and competitors) do fulfill consumers' needs, and thus may pre-empt Primavera's entry; or the products currently in market do not fulfill consumers' needs, open-ing up an opportunity for Primavera's entry.

We will deal here only with the issue of the sensory description of test and competitive products by magnitude estimation. In the next chap-ter we consider the measurement of hedonic reactions (acceptance/rejection).

Selection of the Scale

Management at PSC wanted a sensitive measuring procedure to evaluate consumer perceptions of the various sauces. The product tester suggested consideration of three scaling procedures: (1) Magnitude estimation which could reduce the base size and provide clearer diagnostic information because of its ratio properties; (2) fixed point category scales which panelists might find easier to use, but which require larger base or panel sizes due to their lesser sensitivity; and (3) linear scaling on a 6-in. line, with which expert panelists had familiarity through the Quantitative Descriptive Analysis method. The major problem with linear scaling concerned its potential bias because of the restriction of the endpoints of the line. Fixed endpoints on the scale required that one know the full range of stimulus variation before using the scale. Furthermore, unless the sensory analyst could spend many hours transcribing the line lengths into numbers for subsequent analysis, management felt that the linear scaling technique would prove impractical with any panel size larger than a small trained group.

The marketing manager, R&D director, marketing researcher, and the sensory analyst conferred on the pros and cons of the scaling methods. They selected magnitude estimation as particularly suited for the multiple product screening, because of its greater sensitivity. The immediate benefits suggested by the procedure included: an ability to obtain a clear picture of consumer or in-house reactions to the different sauces; a capability to evaluate the effect of market and brand usage differences on product perceptions; and a potential for immediate representation of ratios or differences between the alternative products that PSC had developed for testing, along with the correlation of these ratios of perceptions with the known physical ratios of ingredients.

Panel Selection

PSC's R&D had often used internal panelists for the evaluation of their different test products. In this instance the product tester had to decide whether to use internal consumer panelists (company employees who did not have extensive training), local consumer panelists recruited by a field service (so-called *research guidance panel*, RGP), or a selection of consumer panelists in different markets. Panel composition and panel location become extremely important issues in the evaluation of new products versus the competitive frame of existing, currently in-market products. Product evaluation by one's own employees can often produce misleading results. An internal, or in-house, panel comprising one's own consumer employees may not truly represent the consumer at large. The product tester often has to go outside, to a local or nonlocal field service for a more representative panel. Several factors argued for as well as against the different types of panels.

Local RGP Panels

Pro: (1) More representative of the distribution of consumers across the country even though only 2 or perhaps 3 markets sampled in the study, (2) Less bias as a result of avoiding the incestuous panel development because of greater panel size and geographical diversity.

Con: (1) More expensive, since panels cost money to set up in different locations (viz., running 50 panelists in one location costs far less than running 25 panelists in each of two locations, due to the set-up of the physical facility, shipping, coordinating the different phases in two different sites, rather than in one site), (2) Less experience with the local field service, (3) Possible poorer control of the field execution of the study.

These problems exemplify pragmatic issues which confront the practicing product tester, who must take responsibility for accurate assessment of the company's and competitor's products as part of product maintenance and development. Sometimes the product tester will opt for the simpler, perhaps less representative test. The product tester may restrict the test to one market close to home, or farm out the field work to a testing laboratory which has a reputation for accuracy and reliability. On other occasions, the business implications of accurate representation and valid, reliable data loom large as portents for the commercial success or failure down the road. Thus, the product tester must resort to the more expensive, less wieldy multiple market panel for representative data, and for insurance against misrepresentative data.

After considering the pros and cons, the product tester and the marketing brand manager in charge of sauce products decided to evaluate the products in different markets in a sequential fashion. They decided that the product tester would initially set up the study with the local, external field service (Tru-Data Field, Inc.), analyze the data, and present the findings at an informal progress meeting. If the data revealed the opportunity for better products, and at least some positive performance of one of the Primavera test products by itself and versus the competition, then management would extend the test to two other markets to confirm these initial findings.

The product tester contacted Tru-Data Field, Inc. to implement the study. The panel specifications recommended by the product tester called for specific types of panelists: (1) Current users of the spicy and non-spicy tomato sauces of one or more of at least seven important brands on the market from different large and small manufacturers, with a total panel of 90 consumers; (2) Women heads of households who use a tomato sauce product at least once every two weeks. Quite often in-house sensory analysts in R&D implement internal test panels with consumers who rarely use the product that they evaluate in the test session. These so-called in-house consumer data may pick up sensory perceptions of the product characteristics, but often the consumer panel does not provide the most relevant feedback for modifying the product to improve its acceptability. Since members of the in-house consumer panel do not actually use the product, one should not consider their product wishes as representing the reactions of true product consumers.

Test Design

In product screening studies with many variations, the sensory analyst has available many different options for designing the study.

The consumers can evaluate an entire set of the products in a long session or sessions comprising 3-4 hr per session. One must remunerate the consumers to participate in these extended sessions. Arguments for versus against this strategy appear below:

Pro: The same consumer evaluates many or even all of the variations, reducing interpanelist variability. This reduction enhances the sensitivity of the study.

Con: Unless the product tester properly executes this type of study, the panelists could lose sensitivity to the product by tasting too many samples. One can easily remedy the fatigue problem by requiring panelists to wait at least 5-8 minutes between samples, and lengthening the test session to accommodate the longer waits. One must also pay the panelists to participate in a longer session, thereby increasing the cost of the project.

The consumers can participate for a very short period of time, e.g., 20-30 min, in a central location site area such as a shopping mall. One need not pay the panelists to participate although often panelists receive a small token of appreciation, perhaps a dollar bill or a small gift for their time.

Pro: Less expensive in terms of field work, because the field service intercepts the panelists rather than spending money to pre-recruit them.

Con: No other motivating factor except intrinsic panelist interest in the project, and the coercive ability of the interviewer.

The product tester opted to use the procedure of multiple product evaluation. Panelists participated for a 4-hr test session. This 4-hr testing arrangement ensured accurate product preparation, and provided for rapid acquisition of data needed for a management decision. Owing to the relatively high incidence of sauce users among women heads of households (approximately 50% or more in that location), the Tru-Data field service felt that no additional costs would accrue in trying to find rare, out-of-the-way panel participants. Issues such as the incidence of panelists who qualify become important, and influence the selection of other test methods. Incidence problems arise when panelists must use the products for longer periods of time, when panelist availability becomes low due to the stringent screening requirements e.g., users of specific cigarette brands, or users of a specific product in a category wherein the incidence falls below 5-10% of the general population. Comparisons of costs of the methods appear in Table 5.23.

TABLE 5.23

FIELD COST ($) OF PANELS: PRIMAVERA SAUCE PROJECT[1]

	At a Mall	At Home	Central Location 3 Hr Test Multiple Product Evaluation
Panel Recruiting Cost (1/hr)	2,000	3,000	1,000
Direct Interviewer Cost (25/days)	2,000	3,000	1,200
Rent: 5 Days ($200/day)	1,000	—	400
Panelist's Payment ($)	300	—	2,000
	5,300	6,000	4,600

[1]1981 dollars

Field Set-Up

Product testing, whether sensory analysis or marketing research, often follows a well-orchestrated plan which ensures accurate delivery of key sensory data. The Primavera project represents a choreographed arrangement proceeding in the following manner which also appears in Table 5.24.

TABLE 5.24
SEQUENCE OF ACTIVITIES TO EXECUTE THE
PRIMAVERA SAUCE PROJECT

Pre-Field Set Up

Agree on experimental design
Agree on products and attributes

Prerecruit panelists prior to project implementation
Set up field (1 day before interviewing)

Field Execution (Intensive Screening)	Time (Min) for Implementation During the Interview
Greet panelist	
Orient group of panelists in magnitude estimation	
shapes	
words	20-30
Show panelists how to rate first sample	10
Panelists rate remaining products in random order	
on attributes with rests between samples	100
Panelists profile "ideal" sauce	10
Panelists calibrate ratings	15
Panelists paid	
Total Time	165

Two weeks before the study, PSC notified Tru Data field service to set up the field for the sauce test. Primavera specified the type of panelists it needed, including age, usage history and, importantly, those individuals not to test: employees of other companies involved in the sauce business, market researchers and sensory analysts. All required panelist and screening information appeared on a screener. The screener questionnaire provided the background information on the panelist. The screener solicited information pertaining to age, sex, occupation, income and address. It also requested a partial inventory of purchasing habits regarding the product in question: frequency of purchase and frequency of consumption of specific tomato sauce products.

Prerecruiting the panelists for a test provides several key benefits for the product tester, as we can see in the Primavera sauce project. (1) It permits the product tester to tailor the panel composition to a specific distribution of consumer groups. For example, suppose marketing management wanted the new Primavera sauce to appeal to users of the top two competitors, Sweet and Saucy and Tomato Heaven. By means of the prerecruitment procedure, the product tester could ensure that one-third of the panel would represent loyal users of Sweet and Saucy, another third of the panel would represent users of Tomato Heaven, and remainder would represent loyal users of Primavera products. (2) It prepares panelists to spend at least 2 to 4 hrs evaluating the products, depending upon the specific project. With such advance notification, panelists can arrange their affairs to insure that they have the requisite free time. In contrast, with panels comprising individuals intercepted at a central location such as a shopping center mall, the product tester may find many shoppers taken totally unaware and resistant to the idea of an extended interview. Furthermore, prerecruitment allows a working mother or father to participate on the panel. (3) Prerecruiting permits the product tester to ensure the maximal use of the interviewer's time at the site. Knowing that a group of about 25 panelists will show up at a prearranged time at the testing facility allows optimal scheduling of manpower to meet the short-term work load imposed on the interviewing staff. Contrast this with the random interception of willing panelists at a shopping center mall, who may participate for the half-hour interview. The majority of time in an intercept study passes while the interviewers wait to intercept the panelist rather than the execution of the test interview itself.

Field Arrangement

Prior to actually running the product evaluation, the Tru-Data field service had to locate and set up the test facility to ensure proper stimulus preparation and proper control over the testing sequence. This required a designated set of responsibilities for each member. The preparatory activities included the following.

Provision for Product Storage. Prior to the test use, who would store the product? In this instance, Primavera shipped the tomato sauce products to the test site three days in advance, in numerically coded, marked jars. The competitor products came in the same boxes, with the labels removed and a white label identification number pasted in its place. Although interviewers at Tru Data knew, or could find out, what products corresponded to the blinded commercial brands, in most instances they would not and usually did not. Blinding or disguising the identity of the marketed products in this manner simply provided Primavera with the added feeling of security that panelists in the study would not obtain cues about which products represented the test formulations.

Facilities Layout. To assure correct product preparation, Tru Data field service received precise cooking and serving instructions from R&D at Primavera. For the sauce project, the instructions specified the time needed for heating prior to serving, and specified the serving method. In this study, the panelists tested the products on pasta. The home economist at Primavera recommended a specific brand of pasta. The instructions specified the precise amount (2 tablespoons) of each sauce, and the precise amount of pasta (2/3 of a bowl). The facilities required heating trays to keep the sauce warm, as well as facilities for preparing pasta in large amounts. R&D suggested a maximal holding time, not to exceed 30 min, for either heated sauce or pasta. Additional instructions regarding the facilities included provisions for panelist evaluations.

To ensure adequate privacy and isolation of each panelist, and yet maintain the efficiency of data acquisition during sampling, Tru Data rearranged a large room to serve as the testing site. A kitchen adjoined the test room. There the field service could prepare the product according to specifications. The actual test room contained tables and chairs, with provision for 8 tables and 4 chairs per table, sufficient to seat 32 respondents in a single session although only 25 panelists participated per session. Furthermore, the room contained a sufficient number of windows and fans to provide adequate ventilation.

Implementation of the Study

Tru Data used the following procedure for testing. Panelists reported to the study site at approximately 10:30 AM. An interviewer oriented the group of 25 panelists in magnitude estimation by means of a simple set of exercises requiring the panelists to scale shapes of different sizes and areas according to area (see Tables 5.12-5.15). These introductory exercises allowed the panelists to use a wide range of numbers to scale perceived area. The training procedure required 15 min to implement, but abbreviated instructions can considerably reduce the instruction time. For example, had the product tester wished to compromise on the orientation, he or she could have had the panelists evaluate just a few of the shapes to instill the concept of scaling.

The panelists then received the first, or orientation sauce product. One of the test formulations (different for each panelist) served as the orienting product. The supervising interviewer, or moderator, at the front of the room took the panelists through the evaluation procedure, instructing the panelists to inspect the sauce atop the pasta and then to rate the sample on overall appetizing appearance (liking/disliking). Panelists then smelled the spaghetti sauce aroma, rating it on intensity of aroma, overall liking/disliking of aroma, etc. Next, they tasted the sauce and the pasta, rating the sauce on various taste and texture characteristics. Finally, the panelists rated their overall liking/disliking of the sauce, and their intention to purchase it. We deal here only with intensity characteristics. Chap. 6 will deal with hedonics.

The first stimulus, an orientation stimulus, often generates confusion as to what the interviewer expects from the panelist when rating a sauce. Panelists do not, from their experience, know what the researchers or interviewers expect from them in a taste-testing situation. They do not know how to approach the product evaluation, what characteristics to look for, how to sample the product or how to scale their perceptions. Consequently, the first test product becomes an excellent tool with which to orient the panelists in what they must do, and how they must do it. The product tester may wish to eliminate the ratings assigned to the first product from consideration in subsequent analysis. Thus, to ensure that all subsequent products receive equal weight in the analysis while discarding the first rating, many sensory analysts prefer to have panelists retest the first stimulus somewhere during the product sequence, but with a different identification number.

Subsequently, panelists evaluated the remaining products. In this particular study, panelists evaluated all eight sauce samples comprising four test products and four competitors. In other projects, panelists might not test all products, but just a subset. Each panelist received and tested the sauce formulations in a different, randomized order. Since the first sample (the standard) differed for each panelist, and since the panelists may not have fully understood how to scale the sauces on the first trial, the first sample for each panelist reappeared in the set of products but with a different code number. Hence, panelists evaluated 9 sauces in toto. In order to maintain sensitivity to the product and to minimize the chance of carryover tastes from one evaluation to another, the panelists waited at least 8 minutes between samples. Furthermore, they rinsed their mouths with water, provided specifically for that purpose.

The panelists profiled each sauce product on a common set of attributes, shown in Table 5.25. These scales shown in Table 5.25 require evaluation of the sensory characteristics pertaining to impressions for vision, kinaesthesis (texture), smell, aroma and taste. Together, the attributes provided a sensory signature of each product. The panelists further evaluated each product on image characteristics, including richness of flavor and naturalness of flavor. These image characteristics integrated the panelists' sensory input together with their experience with foods of this type. The image characteristics do not necessarily imply liking/disliking, but rather complex cognitive and intellectual reactions to the product. Finally, the panelists evaluated each product on performance or hedonic characteristics, including overall liking/disliking, liking/disliking of specific characteristics, and purchase interest.

TABLE 5.25
ATTRIBUTES RATED IN THE PRIMAVERA SAUCE STUDY

Sensory	Image	Acceptance
Aroma Strength	Rich Flavor	Liking/Disliking Overall
Taste Intensity	Natural Flavor	Purchase Intent
Sweetness	Italian Flavor	Liking of Appearance
Tomato Flavor	Unique Flavor	Liking of Aroma
Spiciness		Liking of Flavor
Consistency		Liking of Texture
Amount of Aftertaste		Liking of Aftertaste
Tartness		

Order of Attributes

Quite often sensory analysts disagree about the specific order of attributes. Should all of the sensory attributes precede all of the image attributes or should they intermingle? Can the product tester truly mix together sensory characteristics, image characteristics, and hedonic characteristics? How many attibutes can a panelist really handle?

Some product testers prefer to have panelists profile all of the sensory characteristics prior to rating their overall liking of the product. Other practitioners prefer just the opposite order: to first secure an overall, integrated rating of liking or acceptability as the panelist's initial impression, before asking the panelist to provide an exhaustive scaling analysis of the product's sensory characteristics. In this project the product tester chose to secure a liking rating first, following the second approach. In so doing, the liking/disliking rating represented the panelist's immediate impression. On the other hand, little or no data exist to differentiate between hedonic acceptance data obtained alone versus that obtained in the context of sensory data.

In this sauce project, the panelists evaluated the different sauce attributes in order of their appearance. When rating foods, visual impressions usually precede aroma impressions which precede taste and texture impressions. In following this order, the panelists evaluated the attributes in the natural manner of appearance of sensory impressions. However, for specific sensory impressions, e.g., strength of flavor, intensity ratings always preceded hedonic evaluations of the attribute, e.g., liking of the flavor. Thus, panelists evaluated the sensory characteristic and only then evaluated the liking of the specific sensory characteristic.

This study mixes together the attributes so that sensory and hedonic attributes intermingle. Practical experience shows that panelists can make the evaluations with ease. This practitioner does not subscribe to the hypothesis that panelists must rate sensory and hedonic characteristics in totally separate test sessions. Furthermore, the study design secures an entire profile of attribute ratings in one evaluation, rather than running the panelists through a sequence of evaluations, each time securing ratings of all products on one attribute. We can contrast this *multiple attribute evaluation* with the traditional psychophysical approach, espoused by Stevens and his colleagues, for laboratory-based experiments.

Stevens secured ratings for only one characteristic in a laboratory psychophysics study. For example, panelists rating a sugar solution scaled only sweetness. In subsequent studies on taste and hedonics, Moskowitz (1971) followed this approach rather faithfully, instructing panelists in one session to evaluate liking, and in another session to evaluate perceived sweetness. In later studies on sweetness and hedonics (Moskowitz and Klarman, 1975 a,b), panelists scaled sweetness and liking in the same session, one attribute just after the other. This study design required far fewer test sessions to secure the data, since panelists scaled all the different attributes at virtually the same time.

The data on attribute ratings versus sweetener concentration generated the same psychophysical power functions for sweetness as generated when the panelists rated sweetness and hedonics in different sessions. Hence, the evaluation of two or more attributes in a session produced similar results to evaluation of only one attribute in each of two sessions.

The panelists scaled each sauce on the different attributes. In general, panelists seemed able to scale products on at least 10-15 attributes. Requiring panelists to rate a product on more than twenty attributes begins to tire the panelist. The sheer act of scaling reactions on so many attributes begins to bore panelists, so the analyst cannot feel confident about the quality of the data. Unfortunately, no systematic research has appeared concerning either the ability of panelists to scale many attributes in a product testing session, or the point at which the number of attributes becomes burdensome.

After panelists have evaluated the different sauces, they profiled their ideal sauce using the same scales and attributes. By profiling existing products and the ideal product, panelists communicated to the sensory analyst precisely those characteristics which they would like a sauce to possess. How the R&D product developer can generate a product possessing those attributes appears in Chapter 7 on optimization. Panelists generally have little or no problem profiling an ideal product, if they have already profiled one or several existing products which they can taste, smell and otherwise sensorially experience. Panelists do, however, find difficulty in profiling an ideal product if they have no opportunity to base their ratings on prior product experience and if they do not have a physical frame of reference.

Analysis of the Sauce Data

Prior to concluding anything regarding Primavera's potential opportunities in the sauce category, the sensory analyst calibrated the ratings from the various panelists according to the method shown in Table 5.18. The calibration equalized the scale size of different panelists.

The resulting data, first normalized and then aggregated together, appear in Table 5.26 arranged by product and by attributes. Below each product rating in parentheses lies the standard error of the mean, (S.E.) a measure of the dispersion of the ratings after normalization.

Analytical Strategy

Let us follow a typical analytical strategy which the analyst might use to evaluate the results and report the findings and implications to management. Prior to any detailed analysis, the product tester should develop a plan or a strategy which outlines the key questions to answer. The plan points out the specific part(s) of the data which will provide those answers, as well as outlining the necessary statistical tests which one may need to perform on the data. For instance, likely questions to answer include these: how do competitors perform in the evaluation; how do the Primavera test formulations compare to the competitors; do panelists track the known physical changes in the test formulations; what characteristics track acceptability; how well do existing and test products fare versus the desired ideal; and do any ideal attributes show evidence of a bipolar, segmented value, e.g., some panelists may want a stronger spiced sauce whereas others may want a blander sauce?

Comparisons of Sensory Attributes

Panelists evaluating the sauce products noticed the differences between the different commercial and test products as Table 5.26 shows. In many instances, these differences approach or even exceed statistical significance as shown by the T test for significance of difference.

Statistical differences aside, what else do that data show? It indicates that the products differ in terms of taste characteristics far more than they do in terms of texture or aroma characteristics. We see such variations by looking at the range of ratings across representative products in the category. The taste characteristics (sweetness, tartness, spiciness) vary considerably more than do the texture or aroma characteristics. This suggests that the major sensory differences among the products probably occur as a result of the ingredients in the product which produce taste not texture impressions.

The data also tell us that the variability in ratings, as indexed by the standard error of the mean, varies as a direct function of the average ratings. High ratings of tartness show high variability of ratings. The variation in the ratings confirms other results in the evaluation of beverages (Moskowitz, Jacobs and Fitch 1980). With magnitude estimation, variability becomes a relative matter. The Swedish psychophysicist, Gosta Ekman, also found that the variability of magnitude estimates increases with the average rating (see Teghtsoonian 1971). Lest the reader consider this analysis of variability simply as an academic exercise, let us stop for a moment to consider its implication. Suppose that the variability of ratings assigned for an attribute seems overly high compared to the average variabilities on other attributes. This aberrantly high standard error suggests that the panelists may not comprehend the meaning of the attribute. Some panelists rate the product low while others rate it high, because of lack of understanding.

Finally, we learn from the data that the products vary in sensory attributes in a manner correlatable with the physical variations in the products. For instance, test sauce H comprised 15% more thickener than the current sauce A. The rating for the consistency of H exceeds that for A as one might expect. Furthermore, the increment in thickener affects other attributes as well. Variant H, the thicker sauce, produces a lower impression of overall taste intensity, a more intense tomato flavor, etc. A small change in product formulation often exerts its effect on many other attributes.

Comparisons with the Ideal

The panelists evaluated the ideal sauce at the end of the test session, after they had rated the test and marketed formulations. We can compare the ratings desired for the ideal with the achieved product ratings. Specifically products A and H come closest to producing the desired intensity of sweet taste compared to the ideal. Products A, D, G and H come closest to generating the ideal tartness. No product produced either the ideal level of natural, fresh flavor, or the ideal Italian flavor.

A comparison of products versus the ratings for the ideal shows that products can achieve the ideal sensory characteristics, but rarely do products ever satisfy the ideal on the image or hedonic characteristics. Since panelists realize that a sauce can taste too sweet or not sweet enough, they know approximately where to assign their ideal sweetness rating. By tasting products, panelists can report whether or not a product tastes too sweet or not sweet enough. On the other hand, the manufacturer can really never deliver a product having too much natural, fresh flavor. Panelists generally assign the ideal or most desired levels of these characteristics at the top of the scale, or at least very high on the scale. Product ratings for these image characteristics usually lie in the middle range of the scale, and almost never reach the ideal, desired levels of the attributes. Sensory characteristics represent *actionable attributes* which the product developer can achieve by judicious modification of ingredients. On the other hand, image characteristics lack actionability in an R&D sense. Even though panelists may request more natural flavor or more Italian flavor, the sensory analyst usually cannot report that a specific product delivers the desired high amount of natural flavor. No matter how the product developer modifies the formulation, the ideal seems always to lie beyond the reach of any physical product.

TABLE 5.26

AVERAGE MAGNITUDE ESTIMATION RATINGS FOR 8 SAUCE PRODUCTS AND IDEAL

					Products				
		A	B	C	D	E	F	G	H
Attribute	Ideal	Current PSC Product	Competitor 1	Competitor 2	Competitor 3	Current + Spice	Current - Spice	Current - Thickener	Current + Thickener
1. Aroma Strength	110	93.1 (4.9)[a]	94.6 (15.9)	80.8 (5.7)	116.8 (5.5)	94.0 (5.5)	98.4 (6.6)	102.1 (5.4)	96.3 (4.1)
2. Taste Intensity	92	55.5 (4.3)	48.2 (3.8)	53.6 (4.4)	58.3 (4.7)	48.7 (4.2)	48.0 (4.6)	59.4 (4.8)	47.0 (4.2)
3. Sweetness	58	55.7 (7.7)	41.1 (6.4)	41.7 (6.8)	51.4 (7.0)	69.7 (6.3)	62.9 (7.7)	45.0 (6.4)	56.2 (7.8)
4. Tartness	45	46.5 (7.7)	36.1 (6.0)	36.5 (5.3)	48.2 (6.8)	30.2 (4.7)	25.3 (4.9)	47.6 (7.3)	45.0 (5.9)
5. Tomato Flavor	96	54.2 (5.3)	41.8 (4.3)	55.2 (6.5)	49.4 (5.2)	68.8 (5.4)	63.8 (6.0)	52.9 (5.6)	59.8 (5.6)
6. Spiciness	68	67.0 (6.1)	61.8 (4.6)	67.9 (5.8)	78.0 (7.2)	70.2 (5.0)	56.6 (5.7)	67.3 (6.3)	67.9 (5.4)

TABLE 5.26 (Continued)

Attribute	Ideal	Products							
		A Current PSC Product	B Competitor 1	C Competitor 2	D Competitor 3	E Current + Spice	F Current − Spice	G Current − Thickener	H Current + Thickener
7. Consistency	58	49.4 (5.9)	38.3 (4.8)	46.8 (5.8)	54.7 (6.7)	71.1 (6.1)	58.8 (5.3)	49.2 (6.3)	62.2 (5.9)
8. After-taste Intensity	70	65.9 (6.9)	54.5 (5.8)	62.8 (5.3)	71.1 (6.2)	76.4 (5.8)	71.8 (6.8)	76.5 (6.6)	72.1 (6.2)
9. Richness	104	78.5 (6.0)	63.3 (5.8)	74.4 (5.3)	80.8 (6.2)	83.5 (5.8)	82.0 (6.8)	74.2 (6.6)	80.6 (6.2)
10. Unique	60	19.1 (13.2)	13.8 (11.2)	35.6 (8.8)	17.8 (11.2)	63.0 (9.5)	25.2 (11.4)	20.1 (11.7)	35.5 (8.1)
11. Natural	79	30.7 (13.1)	21.9 (10.5)	20.4 (10.3)	52.6 (12.8)	64.8 (9.5)	58.3 (10.4)	48.0 (11.9)	59.7 (10.0)
12. Italian	120	16.2 (12.0)	18.8 (10.3)	24.4 (9.8)	50.9 (11.8)	57.6 (10.2)	54.5 (11.2)	48.9 (11.7)	57.8 (9.7)

[a]Numbers in parentheses = standard errors of the mean

An Overview of the Study

The product tester should report from this study the following: (1) perceptions of the experimental products versus the commercial one, and (2) perceptions of the test products versus changes in ingredients. Do panelists track the changes which the product developer made in the product. If so, how do these make themselves evident? Do they appear as exact sensory correlates, or do they show up as changes in other related characteristics. Changes in sugar level may show up as changes in sweetness, in flavor or in tartness. Also, (3) the product tester should report the performance of products vis-a-vis the ideal product. What gaps exist? Can a specific product variation fill these gaps between products and the ideal?

VARIATIONS ON MAGNITUDE ESTIMATION

During the course of its development, magnitude estimation received attention and often criticism from many quarters. Critics maintained that panelists neither did nor could truly assign numbers on a ratio scale. During the early and mid 1950s, research began on alternative ways of measurement which would validate the magnitude estimation procedure as providing a true ratio scale. S. S. Stevens suggested that magnitude estimation represented just a variation of the general matching operation in measurement. In a magnitude estimation task, panelists adjust numbers to match sensory magnitudes. Following this line of reasoning, Stevens suggested that panelists could adjust other modalities as well, such as line length or the acoustic energy of tones presented through earphones or loud speakers, in order to match intensities of taste or other perceptions.

These speculations on the nature of measurement in general, and on magnitude estimation in particular led to the method of *cross-modality matching*. In cross-modality matching experiments, panelists manipulated the intensity of a continuously adjustable stimulus (e.g., a tone under the control of a sone potentiometer which varied energy). They manually varied the perceived sensory intensity of the adjusted stimulus to match the test stimulus. As the experimenter presented each panelist with stimuli of varying intensity, the panelist scaled perceived intensity by adjusting the matching stimulus, the sound produced by the potentiometer. In different studies, panelists varied the loudness of tones, the pressure on a handgrip dynamometer, and the loudness of noise to match sensory intensity. Figure 5.5 shows cross-modal matches between sound, as the matched stimulus, and other stimuli.

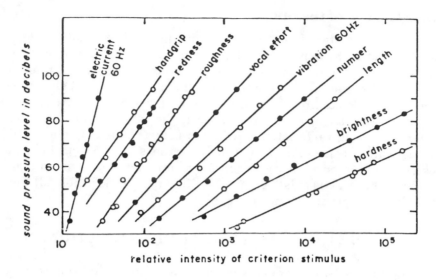

FIG. 5.5 CROSS MODALITY MATCHES BETWEEN THE SENSORY MAGNITUDES OF
DIFFERENT TYPES OF STIMULI AT VARYING LEVELS, AND THE LOUDNESS
OF EQUALLY STRONG SOUNDS

From Perceptual Magnitude and Its Elements, by S. S. Stevens in *Handbook of Perception II*, p. 367

Panelists can perform almost any task demanded of them. Do the matches made with stimuli other than numbers exhibit any predictability or consistency? Stevens and his co-workers suggested the following test to confirm that the matching operation possesses inherent validity. According to Stevens, from experiment to experiment one can develop a power function relating numbers, or magnitude estimates, of a stimulus continuum A to physical intensity. We express this equation by:

Magnitude Estimates $= k$ (Intensity A)^n

where Intensity A = intensity of modality A; for example, percent concentration or molarity of a sugar solution.

Furthermore, the cross-modality matching experiments empirically reveal that the equal intensity match also obeys a power function with a reproducible exponent, **m**:

Intensity B $= k'$(Intensity A)^m

where Intensity B = intensity of modality B adjusted to match A; for example, the measured physical energy of a band of white noise adjusted by the panelist to match the apparent taste sweetness of varying concentrations of sugar solutions.

The panelist has now matched numbers (magnitude estimates, M.E.) to molarities (concentration) of sugar solution A; and has further matched noise levels, B, to molarities of the sugar solution. Combining the two equations should generate a prediction of the matching relation. The experimenter can empirically confirm or disconfirm the prediction when the panelist matches numbers, M.E. directly to noise levels, B.

This roundabout validating procedure predicts the exponent of the direct match between numbers (M.E.) and stimulus intensity B (e.g., noise level), by virtue of the intermediate matching to the third stimulus (e.g., molarity of sugar solutions of varying sweetness). The magnitude estimates of loudness should yield an estimated exponent of n/m, and they do.

If the power function itself possesses validity, and if the magnitude estimates truly lie on a ratio scale, then the exponent from the direct matching function, n/m, should emerge. One empirically confirms this by instructing panelists to assign magnitude estimates directly to the noise levels, intensity B, to discover the exponent. Generally, the direct match substantiates the prediction of the power function exponent hypothesized by cross-modality matches.

Study after study confirmed the validity and reliability of this cross-modality matching procedure. In studying taste perception, Moskowitz (1968 and 1971) instructed panelists to match noises to the taste intensities of simple tastes and pairs of taste mixtures. In that study, the same panelists varied the loudness of bands of white noise to match the perceived taste intensity of the identical stimuli. The two sets of matches generated functions relating magnitude estimates to molarities, and noise matches to molarities. The joint functions predicted the exponent of the power function directly relating magnitude estimates to noise level of white noise. Table 5.27 shows the data for saltiness matches. Note the closeness of such predictions to the actual value of the noise exponent, approximately 0.64, as predicted from previous research on loudness.

Cross-Modality Matching by Children

If the matching operation underlies magnitude estimation, can children who lack training in numbers make these equal intensity matches between stimuli from different modalities? This question focuses on the nature of measurement. If children measure by matching, then they should perform a specific matching operation even without numbers, by adjusting the intensities of stimuli from one modality to match the intensities of those from another modality. Bond and Stevens (1969) explored this issue of measurement by children in an ingenious study. They worked with five-year olds. These children matched tones of varying loudnesses so the tones sounded as loud as the light appeared bright. The equal intensity matches appear in Fig. 5.6. Note how closely the children's matches parallel the matches that the adults made. Apparently, one can measure a child's perception of intensity if he understands the concept of magnitude, even if the child has little or no familiarity with the number scale; and even if the child hasn't the faintest idea of ratios or of the rules of arithmetic.

This simple experiment by Bond and Stevens illustrates the possibility of using one or another form of cross-modality matching with panelists who cannot use number systems, either because of age or because of language problems.

Magnitude Estimation and Cross-Modality Matching With Illiterates

In a recent study on cross cultural taste perferences, Moskowitz *et al.* (1975) tested the taste perception of Indian laborers from the Karnataka region in northern India. These illiterate panelists scaled varying concentrations of sugar (sweet), sodium chloride (salty), citric acid (sour), and quinine sulfate (bitter). Instead of rating perceived taste intensity using numerical magnitude estimation, the panelists scaled taste intensity by drawing an line to match taste intensity. The line length correlated with physical concentrations in the same manner as the numbers from magnitude estimation would correlate with physical concentration.

The success of this field study opens up at least two promising areas for product testing by the different ratio-scaling procedures—magnitude estimation, loudness matching, and line matching. These areas include: use of a device to continuously vary a non-numerical stimulus (e.g., line length or tones), instead of continuously varying numbers; improved measurement with child panelists who need to understand the simpler concept of magnitude which does not depend upon a panelist's concept of the number system for its validity.

BIASES AND REMEDIES IN MAGNITUDE ESTIMATION

Like any other form of measurement, magnitude estimation and its associated measurement procedures fall prey to biases. During the

TABLE 5.27
RESULTS OF EQUAL LOUDNESS — TASTE AND NUMBER
TASTE MATCH
(For Saltiness)
Parameters of the Power Law for Saltiness: $S = kC^a$

Experiment	Magnitude Estimate of of Saltiness	Noise Match to Saltiness	0.64X Noise Match to Saltiness
Pure Salt			
Experiment 1	1.40	1.91	1.22
Experiment 2	1.43		
Experiment 3	1.42	2.07	1.32
Experiment 4	1.00	1.52	0.97
Experiment 5	1.01	1.34	0.86
Experiment 6	1.10	1.64	1.05
Mean	1.22	1.70	1.09
Mixtures of Salt			
With Quinine Sulfate Series 1			
0.002% QSO₄	1.55	2.23	1.43
0.004% QSO₄	1.62	2.13	1.36
0.008% QSO₄	1.65	2.43	1.56
Mean	1.60	2.26	1.45
Series 2			
0.004% QSO₄	1.61	2.12	1.36
0.008% QSO₄	1.60	2.32	1.48
0.015% QSO₄	1.44	2.02	1.29
Mean	1.55	2.15	1.38
Grand Mean—QSO₄	1.57	2.20	1.40
With Sucrose Series 1			
1.0% Sucrose	1.65	2.13	1.36
2.0% Sucrose	1.53	1.98	1.27
4.0% Sucrose	1.51	2.25	1.44
Mean	1.56	2.12	1.36
Series 2			
4.0% Sucrose	1.23	1.78	1.14
8.0% Sucrose	1.44	1.90	1.22
15.0% Sucrose	1.55	1.79	1.15
Mean	1.40	1.82	1.16
Grand Mean	1.48	1.98	1.26
With Acid Series 1			
0.02% Acid	1.61	2.21	1.41
0.04% Acid	1.58	2.16	1.38
0.08% Acid	1.42	2.22	1.42
Mean	1.53	2.19	1.40
Series 2			
0.08% Acid	1.24	1.61	1.03
0.15% Acid	1.60	2.00	1.28
0.30% Acid	1.58	1.81	1.16
Mean	1.45	1.79	1.15
Grand Mean	1.49	1.98	1.27

Estimated exponent relating magnitude estimate to noise level = 0.64
Moskowitz (1968)

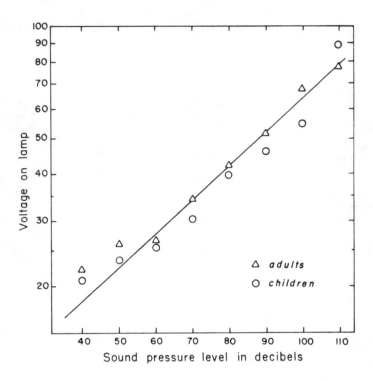

FIG. 5.6 EQUAL LOUDNESS BRIGHTNESS MATCHES: 5 YEAR OLDS VERSUS ADULTS

Median cross-modality matches of brightness to loudness of 5-year-old children and adults. The voltage on a 150-watt lamp varied to produce brightnesses that appeared as intense as the loudness of a 500-hertz tone heard through earphones. (From *Psychophysics* by S. S. Steven, p. 121)

course of its development, magnitude estimation received intense scrutiny by researchers who used it to obtain valid measurements of sensory function, and who, during the course of their studies, have suggested one or another remedy for biases they have discovered.

Round Number Tendency

Panelists prefer to use round numbers more than odd, unusual numbers. Any small study with magnitude estimation soon reveals the tendency of panelists to use 1s, 5s, 10s, 20s, etc. Table 5.28 presents the frequency distribtion of panelists (both adults and children) who assigned numbers to match the taste intensity of beverages containing different sugar and dye concentrations (Moskowitz 1977). Note the preponderance of ratings clustering at round, typical numbers, and the infrequent use of unusual, odd numbers.

TABLE 5.28
PERCENTAGE AND CUMULATIVE PERCENTAGE OF MAGNITUDE
ESTIMATES OF SWEETNESS—ADULTS VERSUS CHILDREN[1]

Magnitude Estimate	Adults		Children	
	Percent Using It	Cumulative Percent	Percent Using It	Cumulative Percent
0	3.80		6.2	
1	.62		3.3	
2	.62		2.3	
3	.41		2.2	
4	.37		2.8	
5	4.10	10	5.5	22
6	.32		2.2	
7	.14		3.0	
8	.46		2.8	
9	.21			
10	4.44	17	7.30	40
11	.02		.35	
12	.21		.05	
15	2.04	21	3.12	46
16	.09		.42	
17	.16		.56	
18	.14		.71	
19	.04		.79	
20	5.40	26	5.30	53
25	5.40	32	3.12	58
30	4.06	36	3.12	63
35	1.64	37	2.04	65
40	4.40	42	3.36	70
45	1.64	44	1.99	73
50	10.37	54	4.46	78
55	.88	55	.84	78
60	4.06	59	1.47	81
65	1.09	60	.64	82
70	3.17	67	1.21	84
75	3.72	72	1.42	85
80	4.57	77	1.18	87
85	1.25	78	5.91	88
90	3.16	81	1.27	89
95	1.09	83	.59	90
100	6.63	87	3.01	93
105	.04	89	.01	94
110	.08	89	.02	94
115	.03	90	0	94

TABLE 5.28 (Continued)

Magnitude Estimate	Adults		Children	
	Percent Using It	Cumulative Percent	Percent Using It	Cumulative Percent
120	.05	90	.03	94
125	1.28	91	.03	95
130	.03	92	.01	95
135	.01	92	0	95
140	.03	93	0	95
145	.002	93	0	95
150	2.25	95	6.2	95

[1] 2700 ratings in total by each group
Moskowitz (1977)
Numbers do not add to 100 because of rounding

This round number tendency plagues magnitude estimation just as it plagues any scale where panelists can use numbers as they wish. Remedies for the round number tendency include the following. (1) Start panelists with different initial stimuli (standards), and let the panelists choose their own moduli. In this way panelists do not overly cluster their ratings on one specific number for each product. Panelists still may prefer to use round numbers (a perennial bias), but at least they will distribute these preferred numbers across different stimuli. (2) Avoid magnitude estimation altogether, and use a continuously variable stimulus as similar as possible to numbers. Line length matching typifies the continuum closest to numbers, since it exhibits a power function exponent of 1.0. If panelists increase or decrease a line to match perceived sensory intensity, they generally do not have favorite line lengths as they have favorite numbers. However, line matching seems considerably less efficient with large panel sizes. Also, high line lengths run up against a physically meaningful upper limit. (3) Index or calibrate the ratings. Since panelists begin with different stimuli and moduli, and since panelists use different scales, the indexing method will convert these round numbers to other values. After normalization, the distribution of ratings around the mean should not appear as lumpy, but rather should become smoother and more continuous.

ABERRANT CONCEPTIONS OF THE NUMBER SCALE

Despite efforts at education, people do not all come equipped with the same conception of the number scale. Most individuals operate within a limited range of familiar numbers, e.g., 1, 2, 5, ... 100 or 200. Rarely do panelists freely use fractions below 1 or numbers above 500. Furthermore, from numerous experiments concerning ranges of stimuli from near threshold to extremely intense and almost painful, the author has observed aberrant conceptions of the number system outside the familiar range.

Specifically, the concept of ratios breaks down below 1.0. Many people fail to realize that fractions exist below 1.0, and that the ratio of 2 to 1 (reduction of 50%) equals the ratio of 1 to 0.5 (also a reduction of 50%). Many panelists seem totally confused with fractions and wish to use negative numbers (an impossibility and directly contrary to the meaning of the scale) for ratings below 1. A number lower than 1 often becomes 1/10 or 1/100, which represent 10-fold and 100-fold decrements. When directly confronted with the fact that 1/10 and 1 lie in the same ratio as 1 and 10, many panelists complain that it just doesn't seem that way. The product tester can do very little to alleviate this misconception of low numbers, except to allow panelists to start evaluations using a moderate size number, e.g., 20 or more, which usually lets them avoid the fractions.

People also become conservative when assigning numbers above 100. The increase from 100 to 200 seems much greater than the increase from 1 to 2, even when panelists feel that they operate on a ratio scale. Apparently one's concepts of ratios break down at the top end of the scale as well as the bottom, perhaps as much due to conservatism in using numbers as to a failure to fully comprehend the true meaning of the ratio scale. The product tester can do little to resolve this problem.

Fortunately, most panelists use numbers between 1 and 100, and rarely need to venture too far beyond 200 or higher. From time to time enterprising researchers suggest that, in light of panelists' aberrant reactions to numbers, the product tester ought to restrict the panelists to 100 point scales. In that range, or so that rationale goes, the panelists actually show consistent understanding of the number scale. Psychophysicists reject this suggestion for the following two reasons. (1) Panelists show different preferred ranges of numbers. By presetting panelists on a 1-100 scale, the experimenter has, in effect, forced the panelists into a fixed point interval scale, albeit a wider scale. (2) A fixed point scale, comprising whatever number of categories, prevents the researcher from calibrating the ratings, because one assumes that all panelists use the fixed point scale in the same way. Yet, an observing practitioner will soon see that panelists show consistent, individual differences, even within a constricted scale such as a 9-point intensity scale. Calibrated magnitude estimates reduce some of the effects of the panelists' idiosyncratic use of the scale. The product tester cannot calibrate an already pre-set scale, however, for fear of tampering with the scale points as they currently exist.

THE REGRESSION EFFECT

People show conservative behavior when assigning ratings to reflect intensity. Individuals tend to constrict the range of the numbers which they assign. Some conservative panelists greatly restrict the number range, often limiting their ratings to a fixed interval as small as 1-5. Other panelists constrict their ratings, but not to such a marked extent. Nonetheless, the *regression effect*, as Stevens and Greenbaum have called it (1966), pervades all measurement and represents a pervasive fact of life with which the product tester must deal.

To the psychophysicist, the regression effect shows up as a diminished exponent when testing sensory intensity versus physical intensity. The reseacher presents stimuli of varied intensities to the panelist. The stimuli may represent graded levels of salt solutions, odorants, or tones, etc. The panelists assign magnitude estimates to these stimuli. The ratings correlate with the physical intensities and fall along straight lines in log-log coordinates suggesting power functions. When a panelist severely restricts the range of his or her magnitude estimates but still accurately scales intensity, the exponent (or slope) of the power function diminishes as Fig. 5.7 shows. The exponent of the power function drops down as the slope of the line flattens in log-log coordinates.

In product testing, the regression effect also occurs. When the product tester desires to develop a psychophysical function relating increases in an ingredient, e.g., mayonnaise level in a tunafish spread, to physical concentration, e.g., amount of mayonnaise, the straight line function which results from the experiment underestimates the true change in perceived mayonnaisiness versus actual level of mayonnaise.

The regression effect can often lead to poorer, less discriminating data. Let us consider what happens when panelists rate three cookies for taste intensity. The cookies vary in the amount of chocolate chips. The panelists systematically underestimate the true psychological ratio of perceived flavor intensity, due to the regression effect and panelist conservatism in scaling. Product A receives a 45, product B a 60 and product C a 90. We would ordinarily conclude that product C tastes twice as strong in flavor as product A. However, in actuality, the ratio of flavor perceptions may lie closer to 2.2 or 2.5, rather than 2.0. Differences in scaling behavior underestimate true differences in per-

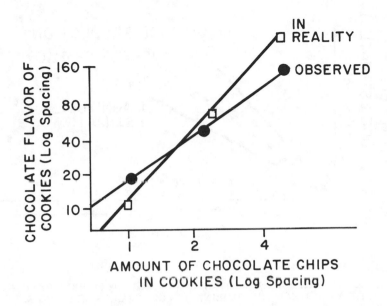

FIG. 5.7 EXAMPLE OF THE REGRESSION EFFECT IN PSYCHOPHYSICAL JUDGMENT

Note that when the researcher asked the panelist to assign magnitude estimates to the perceived amount of chocolate chips, the curve flattens out (filled circles). On the other hand, when the researcher asked the panelist to select the amount of chocolate chips which seems as much as the number (magnitude estimate) seems large, the curve becomes steeper (squares).

ception. Failure to obtain significant differences in scaling, with concomitant actual differences in choice or consumption behavior, may reflect as much panelist conservatism in scaling as it reflects true behavioral discrepancies between what people say versus what they do.

Psychophysicists have suggested a number of remedies to counteract the regression effect. These remedies best apply to laboratory-oriented scaling of intensity of simple stimuli.

Turn the Experiment Around

We have discussed the method of magnitude estimation, in which panelists assign numbers to reflect sensory intensity. Let us turn the instructions around 180°, and instruct panelists to systematically vary the criterion stimulus, e.g., a tone, so that the tone sounds as loud as a number seems large. Experimenters call this the method of *magnitude production*. Numbers become the independent variable. The panelist varies the stimulus, e.g., loudness of the tone, until he or she

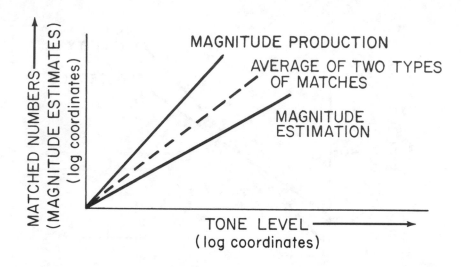

FIG. 5.8 HOW MAGNITUDE ESTIMATION AND MAGNITUDE PRODUCTION FUNCTIONS
APPEAR, AND HOW THE COMBINATION OF STRAIGHT LINES AVERAGE

finds that tone which sounds as loud as the number seems large. Since
panelists show the ubiquitous regression tendency, they will shorten
the range of matched tone levels which they varied, in the same way
that they shortened the range of numbers when they matched
numbers to perceived loudness. When the researcher plots the matching function between numbers on the ordinate and physical intensity
on the abscissa, the magnitude estimation line appears flatter than the
magnitude production function. A geometric average of the two slopes
or exponents produces a better estimate. Figure 5.8 shows the result of
this strategy.

Panelists Match a Third Continuum to Both Stimuli

Let us assume we wish to uncover the function relating perceived
sweetness to sugar concentration. We know that we cannot easily
relate sweetness and concentration by magnitude estimation alone,
and still avoid the regression effect. The researcher can instruct panelists to vary a third continuum, e.g., line length, to match the sweetness
of the sugar solution, and also instruct the panelist to vary the line
length to match the apparent size of numbers. In such an instance we
assume that the magnitude of the regression effect remains
unchanged in both matching operations. Each matching operation
generates its own power function of the form:

Line Length = k (Molarity of Sugar)^n
Line Length = k' (Magnitude Estimate)^m

By combining the equations, the researcher generates the following equation relating molarity of sugar to magnitude estimates:

k" (Molarity of Sugar)$^{n/m}$ = Magnitude Estimate

Moskowitz (1971) first suggested this approach to develop regression free estimates of the power function for sweetness.

EXTREME INDIVIDUAL DIFFERENCES IN NUMBER USAGE—AND SMALL PANEL WORK

Some panelists show very aberrant number usage with little or no conception of scaling. They seem to assign numbers randomly. Other panelists show consistency in assigning numbers, but limit their ratings between 1 and 10 no matter how large the range of physical intensities which they scale.

With a large panel of respondents, these individuals with aberrant number behavior will exert little or no influence on the resulting data. They may introduce a slight amount of extraneous variability, but will probably not influence the average rating to any noticeable degree. The remaining ratings from the panel modify the net effect of these aberrant ratings.

With small size panels in R&D facilities or in universities, aberrant scaling by one or a few individuals causes problems, because the aberrant panelists constitute a sizeable portion of the panel population from which the product tester draws participants. Furthermore, as panelists become increasingly familiar with magnitude estimation or any other scaling, they may settle into a rigid pattern with their number assignment. Any idiosyncracies with which they begin often magnifies. When these overly experienced panelists participate in a test panel, their aberrant, overused rating system produces nonrepresentative results.

Dravnieks (personal communication 1975) suggested that, in order to remedy such a problem, sensory analysts should consider the use of equal-intensity matching as a technique to augment magnitude estimation or other scaling techniques. In the actual research, Dravnieks considered the problems ensuing from repeated evaluations of chemical odors. He had access to a small, repeating panel of participants, who could soon tire of assigning the same numbers time after time.

(1) In the odor evaluation session, panelists had available to them 8 odor streams emanating from an olfactometer. These streams comprised a wide range of concentrations. The olfactometer presented 8 continuous streams of a single odor, in this instance n-butyl alcohol, or butanol. Figure 3.16 shows the schematic of the olfactometer. The continuous air streams comprised a geometric dilution of butanol, from 20% saturation down to $20\%/2^7 = 0.156\%$ saturation. This range of butanol odorants spanned an extremely wide range of concentrations, and, more importantly, generated a wide range of perceived odor intensities.

(2) Panelists sniffed the test stimulus, and then smelled the butanol reference odorants in sequence, until they found a butanol sample (one of the 8) which smelled as strong as the test odorant smelled. From time to time panelists reported that one port or butanol stimulus smelled too strong, but that the next lower port, at half the butanol concentration, smelled too weak. The panel leader recorded a concentration halfway between those two levels, even though no such intermediate value actually existed.

(3) The geometric average of the ports selected by a panel of individuals to reflect the odor intensity of a stimulus acted as a measure of odor intensity.

(4) By means of other, external evaluations, Dravnieks transformed the butanol intensity scale to magnitude estimates. He developed a single reference equation which related butanol concentration in air to magnitude estimates of odor intensity. This calibration equation reflected a consensus function obtained through the cooperative effects of different laboratories, and appears as follows:

$$\text{Magitude Estimate (Odor Intensity)} = 261 \, (\text{Butanol Concentration})^{0.66}$$

By so calibrating the butanol scale to transform it to magnitude estimates, Dravnieks avoided individual differences in scaling behavior which could likely influence the resulting data (Moskowitz, Dravnieks, Cain and Turk 1974).

(5) This calibration method reduces aberrant number behavior, because panelists who scale by equal intensity matching do not have the opportunity to bring into play their own particular idiosyncracies in number use. Panelists do not assign numbers to the stimuli, but rather make the intensity matches within the same modality. On the other hand, the calibration method leaves much to vagaries of the original calibration scale. Once the researcher fixes the scale relating butanol to magnitude estimates, he or she must remain loyal to that calibration scale in order to convert the equal intensity matches to numbers.

DOING THE LABORATORY MAGNITUDE ESTIMATION—
DEMONSTRATION STUDY

Let us follow the sequence of a typical magnitude estimation project for scaling the perception of viscosity. The project typifies experiments which researchers have performed over the past three decades. We will use some specific variations of the general technique and point out other alternatives as we go along.

Study Design

This study concerns how perceived viscosity varies with apparent physical viscosity, and how perceived fluidity varies with apparent physical viscosity. It represents the type of research done by psychophysicists over the past 26 years. The approach reflects a composite of experiments reported by Stevens and Guirao (1964) and by Moskowitz (1972).

The stimuli for this study comprised varying concentrations of sodium carboxymethylcellulose (CMC) dissolved in water, stirred and sheared to produce liquids having perceptually different viscosities. Food scientists use CMC to thicken and stabilize sauces. CMC gum dissolves only with difficulty, so the initial stimulus preparation proceeded slowly, with extensive care taken to ensure that the stimuli fully dissolved. The viscosimeter recorded viscosity in terms of centipoises (1 centipoise = viscosity of water).

Quite often psychophysicists suggest that researchers use graded concentrations representing a wide concentration series. These recommendations apply when the researcher wishes to develop an equation to relate physical stimulus variations to sensory perceptions. In such instances, the function which results generally follows Stevens' power law. Psychophysicists recommend that the researcher arrange stimuli lying in a constant ratio. Such a constant ratio appears as a set of equally spaced points in logarithmic coordinates. Here we used a 5:1 ratio. Along this vein, researchers usually use specific ratios in their studies which they know will yield noticeable changes in perception.

For loudness evaluation, usually, 10 dB changes, corresponding to a 3-fold change in physical pressure, represent standard steps. For taste, the ratio usually equals or exceeds 2:1. Rarely can panelists reliably detect differences less than 1.3:1. For odor perception, the ratio usually equals or exceeds 2, but preferably 4 or more to 1, when testing the odorant samples dissolved in a liquid diluent, e.g., diethyl phthalate; or a ratio of at least 2:1 when the experimenter presents the stimulus in air. For texture, where the exponents vary, the researcher should use the power function exponent as a guide. When sensory texture intensity conforms to a power function with low exponent, e.g., viscosity, the researcher should use large ratios of physical variation. When the power function possesses a high exponent, the researcher can use a smaller ratio of physical variation (Table 5.29).

For convenience, psychophysical researchers prefer to use stimuli which lie in simple ratios. They present these stimuli in random order. The panelist does not know the actual physical relation between the stimuli. The stimuli may represent chemicals at the same physical concentration, but which possess other factors that modify sensory intensity, or they may vary systematically in concentration.

Let us consider food product evaluation using the same design. Perhaps the sensory analyst wishes to evaluate the perceptual responses to gum-thickened salad dressings of various types under various presentation conditions. The test method remains unchanged. The only difference between testing the dressings and our simple psychophysical study resides in the selection of stimuli, and perhaps the method of tasting the stimuli. Psychophysicists work with systematically varied stimuli. In contrast, food scientists and other researchers often work with complex, non-systematically varied stimuli. To the sensory evaluation panelist, both test stimuli remain indistinguishable except for the specific sensory impressions which each stimulus provokes.

Instructions

Recall Tables 5.13-5.16 which present the panelist's instructions. The instructions specify an initial training session in which the panelist rates shapes of different areas. After this initial training, we can feel certain that panelists understand the concept of scaling, and we then can proceed with the product evaluations.

Evaluation of Stimuli

Panelists do not intuitively know how to evaluate stimuli, nor do they know what the experimenter expects of them. Presented with a viscous stimulus, panelists do not know whether to sip the stimulus, shake it, swirl it around a bit, tilt it over its side, or perform any of a dozen other manipulations, and by doing, how to estimate specific characteristics of the stimulus.

Table 5.30 presents the specific instructions regarding the evaluation of the stimuli. Note that the instructions specify a certain set of

TABLE 5.29
SOME RELEVANT EXPONENTS FOR POWER FUNCTIONS—TEXTURE

Attribute	Exponent	Physical Change To Double Perceived Intensity
1. Modulus of Elasticity (Space Cubes)	0.41	5.42
2. Ultimate Strength (Space Cubes)	0.61	3.11
3. Force/Indentation Ratio (Rubber)	0.6 - 0.8	3.17 - 2.18
Force		
1. Dynes/Cm^2 (Handgrip Dynamometer)	1.6	1.58
2. Dynes/Cm^2 (Large muscle group against the floor)	1.6	1.5
Viscosity		
1. Centipoises (Gum Solutions, Suspensions)	0.4 - 0.5	5.65 - 4.0
2. Centipoises (Silicone Oils)	0.4 - 0.5	5.65 - 4.0
Crunchiness		
1. Modulus of Elasticity (Space Cubes)	0.55	3.52
2. Ultimate Strength (Space Cubes)	0.72	2.62
Chunkiness		
1. Size of Grind (Hamburger)	0.55	3.52
Roughness		
1. Grit Size (Sandpaper)	−1.5	1.58 (decrement)

TABLE 5.30
PANELIST INSTRUCTIONS TO ASSESS PERCEIVED VISCOSITY

Please tilt the bottle containing the viscous liquid. Now, look at the bottle, and estimate how viscous the liquid seems inside the bottle. The more viscous (or thick) the liquid appears, the bigger the number you should assign to it. The more liquid or less viscous the liquid appears to you, the lower the rating. Only if the liquid has no viscosity should you assign it a 0.

Calibration

On your scale, rate an extremely viscous or thick liquid, thicker, and more viscous than any liquid you have seen. How high would you rate it. It must score higher than any liquid you rated today.

(1) Extremely viscous liquid

Now how high would you rate:

(2) A very viscous liquid?
(3) A moderately viscous liquid?
(4) A slightly viscous liquid?

0 = No viscosity, by definition

actions on the part of the panelists on which to base their ratings. The panelists and the researcher should follow these specifications as closely as possible. Changes in the physics of the testing situation can easily modify the physical factors which induce the perceptions. Similar effects of presentation mode occur in many other modalities. When evaluating taste stimuli, the panelist can rate his or her initial impression, or integrate the impression over 10 seconds during which time the stimulus remains in the mouth. The two methods of evaluating taste impressions generate different psychophysical functions as Lawless and Skinner (1979) have shown. At the end of the evaluation, the panelists must calibrate their data as described in the final set of instructions (Table 5.30).

Data Analysis

Let us look at the results from six panelists before and after the calibration procedure. Table 5.31 shows the raw data with which we will work. We follow the average point calibration method shown in Table 5.19. This generates calibrated scale values shown in Table 5.31. To compare the effects of the calibration on the data, let us look at the variability of the magnitude estimates. Uncalibrated magnitude estimates will show substantially higher variability. Differences due to stimuli recede in face of the unusually high interpanelist variability which results from the freedom to choose any numbers which he or she wishes.

Averaging

We can compute at least three types of averages: arithmetic means, geometric means, and medians. Since this study on perceptions of gums involved scaling, and since none of the samples had zero levels of perceived viscosity, we do not have to worry about 0 ratings assigned by any of the panelists. If panelists scale taste perceptions, then panelists may or may not assign the weakest stimulus a non-zero rating. With zero ratings, we must confine our analysis to arithmetic means or to medians. Table 5.32 shows the arithmetic mean, the geometric mean and the median.

Function Fitting

Our simple psychophysical experiment on perceived viscosity lets us fit functions to the data. We can choose a variety of different equations to describe the results, including linear, logarithmic, exponential and

TABLE 5.31
DATA BASE FOR RELATING PERCEIVED VISCOSITY OF GUM TO
INSTRUMENTALLY MEASURED VISCOSITY (5 PANELISTS)

Sample	Viscosity (Centipoise)	Ratings By Panelist				
		1	2	3	4	5
1	1	10	.5	5	64	5
2	5	17	.8	12	80	9
3	25	32	1.2	19	150	13
4	125	60	2.0	32	198	19
5	625	88	3.5	46	264	26
6	3125	100	4.7	78	375	31

Calibration Ratings					
	1	2	3	4	5
Extremely	150	8	100	500	70
Very Much	120	6	70	300	40
Moderate	80	4	30	160	20
Slight	40	2	15	40	10
None	0	0	0	0	0
Index =	97.5	5	53.75	250	35

Calibrated Panelist Ratings					
Viscosity	1	2	3	4	5
1	10	10	9	26	14
5	17	16	22	32	25
25	38	24	35	60	37
125	62	40	60	79	54
625	90	70	86	106	74
3125	103	94	147	150	88

$$\text{Calibrated rating} = \left(\frac{\text{Rating}}{\text{Index}}\right) - 100$$

power functions. Each function will exhibit better or worse degrees of
fit to the data. Table 5.33 shows how well each function fits our data
when we use the arithmetic mean.

Note that when we use the power function, the exponent turns out
less than 1.0, similar to previous scientific results published in the

TABLE 5.32
COMPARISON OF GEOMETRIC MEANS, ARITHMETIC MEANS
AND MEDIANS OF MAGNITUDE ESTIMATES ASSIGNED TO THE
PRECEIVED VISCOSITY OF TEST SOLUTIONS

	Viscosity Level					
	1	5	25	125	625	3125
	Pre-Calibration					
Geometric Mean	6.03	10.3	17.0	27.0	39.4	53.2
Median	5	12	19	32	46	78
Arithmetic Mean	16.9	23.8	43.0	62.2	85.5	117.7
Standard Deviation	(26.5)	(32.0)	(60.9)	(78.8)	(104.5)	(148.7)
	Post Calibration					
Geometric Mean	12.9	22.0	37.3	57.5	84.3	113.4
Median	10.3	22.3	37.1	59.5	85.6	102.6
Arithmetic Mean	13.9	22.7	38.9	58.9	85.2	116.3
Standard Deviation	(6.8)	(6.5)	(13.2)	(14.1)	(14.1)	(29.7)

TABLE 5.33
COMPARISON OF LINEAR, LOGARITHMIC, EXPONENTIAL AND
POWER EQUATIONS RELATING VISCOSITY TO PERCEIVED
VISCOSITY USING THE ARITHMETIC MEAN

Linear Function
    Sensory Viscosity = $k_0 + k_1$ (Physical Viscosity) $R = 0.85$
                 = 38.4 + 0.0271 (Physical Viscosity)

Logarithmic Function
    Sensory Viscosity = $k_0 + k_1$ Log (Viscosity) $R = 0.98$
                 = 4.59 + 29.41 (Log Physical Viscosity)

Power Function
    Sensory Viscosity = k_0 (Physical Viscosity)^{k_1} $R = 0.99$
                 = 15.03 (Physical Viscosity)$^{0.27}$

Exponential Function
    Log (Sensory Viscosity) = $k_0 + k_1$ (Physical Viscosity) $R = 0.70$
                       or
    Sensory Viscosity = $10^{(k_0)} \, 10^{(k_1 \text{ Physical Viscosity})}$
                 = $(1.51)(10^{(0.000198 \text{ Physical Viscosity})})$

literature (Stevens and Guirao 1964; Moskowitz 1972). On the other hand, with the linear, logarithmic and exponential functions, we cannot compare the parameters of the specific equations with previous reports in the literature. Thus we do not know whether or not we have replicated previous results.

Other Statistical Analyses

In many magnitude estimation studies, the product tester will evaluate products which bear no relation to each other in terms of underlying ingredients. Rather than searching for an underlying function, the product tester will search for statistically significant differences among products, and try to estimate the ratio of ratings for two stimuli. In our example on the viscosity of gums, we could assume that the two middle stimuli represented two alternative gum compositions. The sensory analyst might then wish to ascertain the ratio of perceived viscosities of the gum, to answer questions regarding which type of gum produces a product which we sense as more viscous.

Furthermore, should one wish to evaluate the significance of the viscosity ratio rather than the significance of difference, then one should convert all of the ratings into logarithms after normalization, and estimate significant difference in logarithms. Significant differences in logarithms equate to significant differences in ratios.

Standardization of Magnitude Estimation

Quite often statisticians prefer to standardize their data, in order to achieve a mean of 0 and a standard deviation of 1.0. When the scale values assigned do not necessitate conclusions about ratios or differences of perception, the statistician and product tester can and often do standardize the ratings of each panelist to put all panelists on the same scale. Panelists who use a wide range of numbers show wide variability (standard deviations) in their ratings. The standardization procedure contracts the range of their ratings. Panelists who use a narrow range of numbers to rate products generate concomitantly small variability in their ratings. The standardization procedure expands their range.

With magnitude estimation scaling, one cannot standardize the ratings and still maintain the ratios intact for the following reasons. (1) Standardization changes the zero point on the scale. Magnitude estimates possess a meaningful zero point, thus changing the zero on the scale changes the ratios among the ratings. (2) Standardization changes the size of the scale unit and also modifies ratios of ratings.

OVERVIEW

This chapter has traced the history and use of different types of intensity scaling. In contrast to descriptive analysis and discrimination measurement, scaling allows the panelist to truly act as a measuring instrument. We can use scales for different purposes: (1) to assign stimuli to different categories for purposes such as classification; (2) to measure the differences between stimuli on attributes which clearly differ; or to relate perceptions to independently varied physical stimulus levels. In all cases, the advent of modern day psychophysical measurement by category scaling and magnitude estimation permits the use of scaling in new and more productive ways. With the appropriate scales of measurement, the product tester can better ascertain how differences in stimuli emerge as differences in the magnitudes of perceived sensory characteristics.

CHAPTER 6

HEDONIC SCALING—LIKES AND DISLIKES

INTRODUCTION

Hedonics represents a substantial component of our response to food and food-stimuli, whether these comprise model systems (e.g., sugar solutions, vanilla odors) or foods we normally consume. Hedonics deals with our likes and dislikes, and encompasses a wide variety of behaviors, such as: choice between two or more products, scales of liking for products, frequency of product consumption, and the behavior which a person will undertake to obtain the product.

CONFUSION OF HEDONICS WITH SENSATIONS

Panelists often confuse hedonic reactions with sensory reactions. All too often, a panelist instructed to evaluate the texture or taste of a product actually rates how much he or she likes the product. Likes and dislikes play such an important role in our responses that when we instruct panelists to scale sensations, frequently they first rate acceptability rather than the quality and strength of sensation. Published reports in the scientific literature abound with these confusions between quality, intensity and liking. For instance, scales for texture often reflect the acceptability of the texture impression (good to poor), rather than the magnitude of a specific textural attribute (e.g., hard to soft).

Researchers in taste and smell have discovered that hedonic reactions emerge in virtually all attribute evaluations. For example, when panelists scale the perceived dissimilarity between taste stimuli, or between pairs of odor stimuli, they do so using perceptions of several different qualities which they integrate together to form an overall judgment of qualitative dissimilarity. Schiffman (1974) in the U.S. and Yoshida (1964) in Japan have reported that panelists use hedonics as the primary or, at least, initial characteristic along which they differentiate taste and smell stimuli. Only with repeated practice and exposure does the impact of hedonics diminish, so that other attributes emerge and play their proper roles.

Distinguishing The Types of Hedonic Reactions

People may prefer one food to another, but consume more of the less preferred food. In study after study, candies rate high in acceptance; yet, in terms of volume, Americans consume far more bread and potatoes than candy. Different measures of hedonics tell us different things. The sensory analyst, the product tester and the marketer should make sure that they correctly use their measurements to predict critical choices or consumption behaviors, rather then measuring an aspect of liking which does not correlate with preference or consumption.

Let us take a look at the scope of hedonics and enumerate the different types of hedonic responses which we can measure, as well as determine how well these measures correlate with behavior.

Basic Hedonic Tone. Since the last century scientists have struggled with hedonic tone as a primary component of perception. John G. Beebe-Center summarized much of what we have learned about hedonics in the last century and the early part of this century in his volume *The Psychology of Pleasantness and Unpleasantness,* published in 1932. According to Beebe-Center, psychologists have long recognized the innateness of hedonics in behavior and in perception. Topics studied by the psychologist include the nature of rapidly shifting hedonic tones (so that at one time a stimulus might seem pleasing, whereas shortly afterwards the same stimulus might seem displeasing), and the time course of hedonics (how rapidly do we react to a stimulus; do likes and dislike precede recognition of stimulus quality, or do they follow it).

Hedonic Functions. In 1879 Wilhelm Wundt suggested that a general law typified how hedonic tone varies as a function of stimulus intensity. According to Wundt, hedonic acceptability rises with physical intensity or with sensory intensity, reaches a maximum level or *bliss point* at some intermediate level, and then diminishes as the intensity further increases. If we measure the intensity of liking, we might find that acceptance begins at neutral, where we cannot perceive the stimulus. As we increase the stimulus intensity, liking increases, albeit at probably a different rate than does sensory intensity. (The relative rates remain a topic for experimental measurement). Eventually, at a region unique and characteristic for each sensory modality, overall liking peaks at the bliss point or optimum level. Any further increase in stimulus or sensory intensity reduces overall liking below the bliss point level (see Figure 6.1).

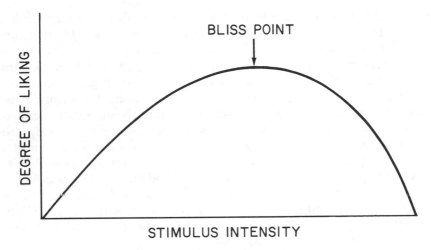

FIG. 6.1 TYPICAL INVERTED U-SHAPED CURVE RELATING "LIKING/DISLIKING" TO EITHER STIMULUS INTENSITY OR PERCEIVED SENSORY INTENSITY. THE EXACT FORM OF THE FUNCTION VARIES ACCORDING TO THE SPECIFIC SENSORY MODALITY

Wundt suggested this curve as a schematic of hedonics magnitude, but could not measure hedonic reactions. Part of this chapter, as well as the chapter on optimization of hedonic reactions, concerns the representation of these hedonic functions and the location of the bliss point levels.

Paired Comparison—The Issue of Choice. During the 1920s, L.L. Thurstone at the psychometric laboratory in North Carolina suggested that researchers could measure hedonics by direct choice behavior. Thurstone suggested a variant of the forced choice procedure, the method of paired comparison. According to Thurstone, people choose stimuli in perference tests as if they operated on the basis of an underlying hedonic level. Thurstone suggested that by measuring choices between different stimuli, and determining the proportion of times a panelist chooses each stimulus over another, the researcher can obtain a reasonable idea of relative separation of the stimuli on the underlying hedonic scale. We will deal with paired comparison designs in this chapter, including the experimental design and the analysis of results. Chapter 3 on psychophysics and sensory perception also illustrates the use of paired comparison procedures.

Direct Scaling of Hedonics. A product tester can ask panelists whether or not they like a stimulus, allowing them to classify their hedonic reactions into liking/disliking. The classification into discrete categories shows the proportion of the population which finds a stimulus pleasing or displeasing. A key example of the categorization comes from the classic study of taste likes/dislikes, reported by Engel in Germany more than half a century ago. Engel (1928) polled the German population to determine what proportion of panelists found different concentrations of sugar, salt, quinine and acid pleasing, displeasing or neutral. As one might expect, with increasing concentrations of sugar (and thus increasing sweetness), an increasing proportion of the population categorized the taste as pleasant, and a decreasing proportion categorized the taste as unpleasant. With sodium chloride a similar, but not as marked curve emerged. As the concentration of acid and bitter stimuli increased, more and more panelists in the population categorized the taste as unpleasant. Figure 6.2 shows Engel's results, which represent the first critical study in taste to measure likes and dislikes.

Direct categorization of likes and dislikes has a distinct advantage over the method of paired comparisons. The method of paired comparisons never directly indicates whether or not the two stimuli both seem acceptable; whether the less preferred stimulus seems neutral and the preferred stimulus acceptable; or, in fact, whether both stimuli seem unacceptable but the preferred one less unacceptable. Paired comparisons rank order hedonics using pairs of stimuli. By themselves, paired comparisons do not allow panelists to scale or categorize their reactions.

Classification of stimuli into discrete categories, as well as ranking by the method of paired comparisons, both lack a metric or unit of acceptability. The paired comparison procedure does not reveal the degree to which the panelist prefers one stimulus over the other. Suppose the panelist always prefers stimulus A (cognac) over stimulus B (salt water). How different in acceptability do these two radically different stimuli appear to the panelist? Without a direct measure of overall degree of liking/disliking, the product tester must rely upon the statistical manipulation of the results, and must use an underlying hypothesis to generate a scale of hedonic magnitude. This underlying scale may or may not already parallel the panelist's own internal degree of liking/disliking. In terms of categorization, if we accept Wundt's schema as describing hedonics, then the strong stimuli beyond the bliss point (e.g., 20% sucrose in water) should show lower liking than the bliss point stimulus lying at maximal acceptance (around 9% sucrose in water). How can the panelist show that gradation for two stimuli when the panelist likes both? The panelist can simply classify each stimulus into one of three categories: like, neutral or dislike; but he or she cannot show degree of feeling. Thus, the

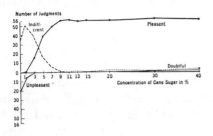

Curve representing the hedonic tone of solutions of cane sugar for 10 observers in 6 sittings.

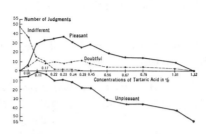

Curve representing the hedonic tone of solutions of tartaric acid for 7 observers in 6 sittings.

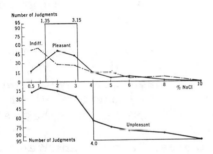

Curve representing the hedonic tone of cooking salt solutions for 7 observers in 7 sittings. Also ideal regions of pleasantness and unpleasantness.

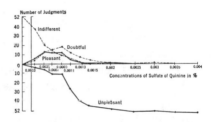

Curve representing the hedonic tone of solutions of sulfate of quinine for 10 observers in 6 sittings.

FIG. 6.2   THE PROPORTION OF INDIVIDUALS IN THE POPULATION WHO CLASSIFY INCREASING LEVELS OF TASTE STIMULI AS PLEASANT, NEUTRAL, OR UNPLEASANT, RESPECTIVELY
Source: Engel (1928)

panelist cannot measure hedonic gradations. The limited number of responses forces the panelist to compromise his or her own responses, and to set arbitrary categories of hedonics. For instance, in a taste test the panelist may classify the extremely sweet taste of 36% sugar as acceptable. While the stimulus does possess some small amount of acceptability, most panelists would feel more comfortable assigning the stimulus a low degree of acceptability, probably near neutrality, rather than classifying the cloying sweet taste of 36% sugar as pleasing. Other panelists in the same study may adopt a more rigid criterion, and classify the taste as neutral. Still others, who avoid the category of neutral entirely, will classify the taste as unpleasant. In these instances, the very lack of a graded measure of liking precludes the panelist from expressing his or her feelings about the stimulus. Rather, the panelist must set an arbitrary criterion for classification.

Direct Scaling of Hedonics—Category and Magnitude Estimation

The sensory analyst and product tester can remedy the biases resulting from restricted response categories by instructing panelists to directly scale their hedonic reactions, using either the fixed point category scale or the magnitude estimation scale. By allowing panelists to freely express their hedonic reactions rather than forcing them to use an all-or-none response, product testers can obtain classification information as to whether the stimulus falls into the category of acceptable or unacceptable, as well as information on the relative degree of acceptability (ranking and either differences or ratios).

Frequency of Choice. Scaling procedures (psychometrics) require panelists to state an opinion. However, in the real world, likes and dislikes emerge along with choice behavior. Faced with many alternatives, including avoiding the stimulus altogether, with what frequency do panelists select the stimulus? Do products with the greatest liking rating emerge as the most frequently selected? At first glance, perhaps. Consider, however, the case of a restaurant. We often consume coffee or bread with our meal. In a direct paired comparison test or through direct scaling, the entree we choose (on a less frequent basis) generally receives a higher hedonic rating than does the bread or beverage. On the other hand, we consume breads and beverages with greater frequency than we consume the entree. In fact, we more quickly tire of the entree than we tire of the bread, beverage and ancillary food items on the menu. To date, product testers seem not to have considered the paradox of hedonic ratings, on the one hand, as indicators of preference or strength of feeling, and the correlation of that rating behavior with other external signs of preference, such as frequency or volume consumed.

Purchase Behavior. Purchase behavior represents a still more complicated variation of hedonic reaction. The consumer expresses interest in a product by spending some amount of money to obtain that product. We may purchase a food product that we dislike because the item costs far less money than its competitor which we like far more. Do we now consider our purchase behavior as the true indication of acceptability, or do we make provisions for variations in acceptability due to external factors, such as price or availability of items? In the

R&D sensory analysis laboratory, the researcher cannot predict whether or not consumers will purchase the product by simple acceptance scales alone, and therefore often evaluates the product in isolation from real world stimulus conditions. The marketing researcher, by contrast, must take these factors into consideration.

ILLUSTRATION OF SCALING METHODS IN HEDONICS—RANK ORDER SCALING

Ranking stimuli in terms of degree of liking/disliking has proved a popular scientific, as well as practical, method for discerning which products consumers like best. Rank order procedures provide the panelist with an unambiguous task—to put the stimuli into a specific order regarding overall liking/disliking. As stated in Chapter 5, the test requirements increase tremendously as the number of stimuli increases, because the panelist must make all of the possible paired comparisons between stimuli.

In the scientific literature on hedonics, ranking emerges as one of the researcher's favorite techniques. A study by Chappell (1953) on the hedonics of sugars showed that panelists have a rank order in their preference for sugars of various types, putting sucrose at the top of the list and maltose at the bottom. The British scientist and writer, R. W. Moncrieff (author of *The Chemical Senses*), reported the results of a large scale study on odor preferences. Panelists ranked all of the different odorants, which represented stimuli ranging from simple chemicals to complex natural mixtures extracted from plants. Table 6.1 shows part of the rank order of preferences which Moncrieff reported.

Rank ordering puts products in a hierarchy, beginning with the most pleasant product (rank = 1) and finishing with the least pleasant (rank = N, where N represents the number of products tested). The differences between the adjacent ranks (between ranks 1 and 2, vs 2 and 3) neither represent equal psychological intervals nor equal ratios of liking. Three fragrances, which seem almost equally pleasant but differ only slightly, may rank 1, 2 and 3. Yet, upon further probing the panelist will indicate that the first three fragrances seem almost equal in pleasantness, or else the three seem widely different from each other.

Let us consider the results of a small study on rank ordering of odor liking/disliking. These results come from a short course on sensory evaluation, given in Switzerland in 1976 (Vaisey-Genser *et al.* 1977). The panelists rank ordered five different levels of maltol (agreeable),

TABLE 6.1
RANK ORDER PREFERENCES OF ODORANTS
(As Reported by R. W. Moncrieff, 1966)

Odor	Average Rank	Odorant Ranked	Quality
Red Rose	5.1	1	Rose
Sweet Orange	24.6	10	Orange
Lavender	30.1	19	Lavender
Citral	37.8	30	Lemony
Almond Flavoring	45.2	40	Almond
Amyl Butyrate	50.6	50	Fruity
Benzyl Acetate	54.7	60	Flowery, Hyacinth
Oil of Citronella	63.9	70	Sweet, Spicy, Floral
Musk	70.3	80	Musky, Nutty
Amyl Cinnamate	75.2	90	Jasmin
Toluene	82.3	100	Benzene but rubbery
Sour Milk	92.6	110	Sour
Castor Oil	104.1	120	Oily, Nauseating
pChlorothiophenol	120.2	130	Pungent, Burnt, Sweetish

(1 = most pleasant)

and five different levels of propionaldehyde (disagreeable). The panelists smelled the odorants from small, wide mouthed bottles. The bottles remained capped until the time of evaluation, thus maintaining a fairly constant odorous sample. The panelists ranked the odorants both in terms of odor strength and overall liking/disliking. Note that with these different samples, in effect the panelist had to make $(5 \times 4)/2 = 10$ paired comparisons to make sure the samples lay in the correct order.

Our first question concerns the overall ranking of the odors in terms of liking versus intensity. Do they track? Table 6.2 shows the different ranks. Note that for propionaldehyde the rank order of liking completely inverts the rank order of intensity. As propionaldehyde increases in odor intensity, it diminishes in pleasantness. In contrast, maltol shows an inverted U-shaped function for liking versus concentration, and thus for liking versus odor intensity. As odor intensity increases, the rank score for liking increases. As the odorant reachers an optimal (bliss) point in the middle of the range, liking maximizes and then diminishes. Unfortunately, we cannot discern the exact nature of this function, nor do we know how much more liked or

TABLE 6.2
RANK ORDER OF INTENSITY AND LIKING FOR MALTOL
AND PROPIONALDEHYDE
(Panel of 25)

Maltol	Concentration	Intensity Ranks						Liking Ranks					
		1	2	3	4	5	Average	1	2	3	4	5	Average
1	187	1	0	3	5	16	4.4	3	3	2	8	9	3.7
2	375	2	1	2	15	5	3.8	4	2	6	7	6	3.4
3	750	4	4	12	3	2	2.8	6	10	6	2	1	2.3
4	1500	1	16	6	1	1	2.4	6	7	5	4	3	2.6
5	3000	17	5	2	1	0	1.5	6	3	6	4	6	3.0
Propionaldehyde													
1	125	0	1	1	2	21	4.7	12	5	3	3	2	2.1
2	250	1	2	3	17	2	3.7	5	8	6	6	0	2.5
3	500	1	4	15	4	1	3.0	5	7	7	3	3	2.7
4	1000	4	14	4	3	0	2.2	1	4	4	10	6	3.6
5	2000	19	4	1	0	1	1.4	2	1	5	3	14	4.0

From: Vaisey-Genser et al (1977)

disliked one stimulus seems versus another. By using the ranking method alone, the product tester has forfeited the opportunity to measure the true psychological magnitude, both of sensory odor intensity and of liking.

MEASUREMENT BY PAIRED COMPARISONS

Paired comparison measurement of product acceptance (really product preference) represents one of the more ubiquitous measuring procedures in the testing armory. Product testers and market researchers use paired comparison procedures to quantify the proportion of times which a panelist selects one product over another. We will consider the typical paired comparison study on the case history of a potato chip product, produced by the Early Bird Potato Company.

Background of the Problem

Early Bird Potato Company (EBC) typifies a solid, small, mature food company, founded around the turn of the century. Its major products use potatoes in one form or another. For the past twenty years, Early Bird Potato Company has marketed Jangles, a natural potato chip which contains a unique flavoring mix that gives Jangles a fresh, non-rancid, clean taste. The Jangles franchise comprises individuals 18-35 years old, who use the product for party dips and snacks.

Recently, competitors of EBC introduced Tangys, a spicy, nacho flavored barbecue potato chip. Tangys garnered a considerable share of the market, due in part to aggressive marketing, but also due greatly to Tangys unusually acceptable flavor. In order to recapture its market share, management at EBC instructed R&D to develop a potato chip product which tasted better than Tangys on a blind basis (unbranded). If R&D could develop such a potato chip, then the marketing group at EBC would advertise this new potato chip as having a more acceptable taste.

As occurs in all such projects, R&D first developed prototypes. From various spice and flavor houses, EBC procured different spice blends to put into its new potato chip formulation, code name Chips. Early product evaluation at the bench suggested that some variations of the Chips formulations tasted too burning, others too bland. Finally, after three months of product development work, bench-top product evaluations and tests with the in-home taste test panel, R&D reported that the new Chips formulation seemed a winner. It differed in quality and spiciness from the current Tangys potato chip, but still tasted acceptable to the panel.

At this point R&D turned the project over to the market researcher for product testing to execute a paired comparison test. The test would show whether, in fact, consumers of potato chips, who had purchased flavored chips in the past several months, would show a definite preference for Chips over Tangys.

Study Design

The marketing objective of the study determined the selection of panelists. Marketing wished to test Chips versus Tangys among three groups of consumers: those consumers who regularly purchased and consumed Tangys or other flavored chips; consumers who regularly used unflavored potato chips; and consumers who had switched from EBC's regular chips, Jangles, to a flavored chip of any type.

The selection criteria for panelists in acceptance testing plays a more critical role than does selection criteria for any other type of sensory test. Panelists differ in what they like and dislike. Panelists who show identical sensory reactions give identical descriptions of products. However those who share similar backgrounds, ages and incomes may differ widely on what they like and dislike. Interpanelist differences dictate the use of larger scale, more representative panels for acceptance testing in general, and of paired comparison measurements for preference in particular.

The marketing group selected three specific groups of consumers for very good reasons. (1) Current Tangys consumers represented those individuals who had already expressed an interest, or a revealed preference, in purchasing flavored potato chips. These current users reflected part of the potential market or franchise towards which the EBC marketing group would target its new Chips entry. A substantial preference for the Chips entry by current Tangys consumers should indicate superiority in terms of unbranded product. (Blind preference may not translate to branded preference overall, when we factor in the package and the promotion strategy). (2) The consumer who regularly purchased unflavored potato chips represented an untapped market of potential customers, and a source of danger as well. These individuals currently expressed preference for, and also purchased unflavored, regular potato chips. If EBC wished to market Chips as an alternative, or line extension to its regular, unflavored potato chip product, then the EBC marketing group should know, ahead of time, the likelihood that users of unflavored potato chips will select Chips, a flavored chip, over EBC's current unflavored potato chip. Marketers call this behavior *cannibalization*. Chips will cannibalize, or take away purchasers of EBC's current unflavored chips. Cannabilization might become economically disadvantageous in the broad scope. By marketing the flavored Chips product, EBC might diminish its own current potato chip business, rather than gain a share of business from the Tangys consumers. (3) The consumers who have switched away from EBC's unflavored potato chips to Tangys or to other competitors' flavored potato chips, or who exhibit dual usage patterns (using both types of chips, flavored and unflavored, albeit on different occasions) represent a group of consumers without strong brand loyalty. These dual users may comprise a substantial portion of the population.

Study Particulars

Quite often R&D product developers implement small scale preference tests locally, at a field site which they can easily supervise. The readings from a local preference test, executed either within one's plant facilities with so-called employee consumers, or extramurally with true consumer panelists, provide data from only one market.

For studies of limited scope and risk (e.g., initial confirmatory evaluations to determine that the product remains on target), the small scale preference test proves more than adequate. With as few as 30-50 panelists, the sensory analyst, product tester or market researcher can quickly obtain a reading as to the chances that consumers do, in fact, prefer Chips over Tangys. For large scale studies where the risk increases (e.g., confirmatory tests about product superiority just prior to the full scale market introduction of Chips), the product tester must augment the sample size, in order to read the reactions from many different regions where marketing will roll out the product, as well as read the responses from many different types of consumers who comprise the franchise (divided into age and sex, location, income, frequency of purchase and item consumption, type of brand selected, etc.).

EBC did extensive homework to develop the acceptable flavored chip. A sequence of tests showed the potential superiority of Chips to Tangys. We now consider the results of a test which assessed preferences for Chips versus Tangys in a variety of markets, representing locations where consumers would face the opportunity of purchasing Chips over Tangys. The product testing took place in three separate markets: one in the northeast (Boston, Mass.); one in the Midwest (Minneapolis, Minnesota); and one in the southwest (Dallas, Texas). These three locations reflect markets in the U.S. with fairly representative populations of potato chip consumers. Furthermore, Dallas, Texas represented a market in which flavored potato chips have captured a high share of the potato chip/savory snack market (a 'developed' market); Minneapolis represented a market where flavored potato chips have just begun to penetrate; and Boston represented a market where flavored snack chips had not yet truly made a successful entry.

These market considerations answer issues beyond product evaluation. The product tester must consider such marketing issues in the analysis of preference data. It does no good to test the potato chip products among a non-representative sample of consumers, in order to obtain a preference measure of Chips versus the competitor Tangys product. The information obtained from a non-representative sample of consumers cannot help the marketer determine whether R&D's new product formulation meets the action specifications for a snack chip— viz., that the new entry beat the competitor in direct preference testing by a significant margin. (We define significant margin later on below, and discuss its implication.)

The field portion of the study required panelists to evaluate the current Tangys snack chip and Chips, EBC's test product, both on a blind basis. In order to do so, the product tester made decisions regarding implementation in terms of panel size and panelist instructions.

Panel Size. The panels comprised 100 individuals per market, divided evenly among men, women and teens (approximately 33/group/market). A base size of 100 represents the typical size of consumer panels used by marketing researchers for evaluating preferences. Furthermore, since preference judgments (prefer A or prefer B) require all-or-none judgments (the panelist cannot prefer A just a little, but must choose one chip of the two), the researcher needs a large base size to counteract small biases and errrors which occur in panelists' data.

From time to time researchers inquire into the appropriate size of panels needed for paired comparison tests. For example, should one use small panels which entail low cost, or larger, more representative panels with higher cost. A good thing to remember concerns the relations between what one wishes to determine, its cost and its importance. For early R&D product testing, the sensory analyst may need to measure preferences among far fewer panelists than at subsequent stages in the cycle, where the majority of work has already led to a fine tuned product. Later preference work usually searches for directionality of feedback.

Appropriate base sizes for panels can range from 20 up to 1000 or more, depending upon the issues at hand. With small base sizes of 20 or so, the error around the mean percent preference becomes so large as to subject the preference ratio to considerable error. With 1000 panelists giving preferences at approximately 50 times the field cost, and perhaps a dozen times the computer analysis cost, the error of prediction around the preference ratio declines quite substantially. One rule of thumb suggests a base of 50 panelists for initial preference tests, and 100+ for later studies.

Panelist Instructions. Simple preference tests do not require particularly much comprehension by the panelists. The panelist tastes a product, rinses his or her mouth, tastes another product, and then indicates which of the two products he or she prefers. Some researchers allow the panelist to state no preference, a third category. Other researchers discourage the no preference response, forcing a preference between the two products. With a no preference category, insecure panelists use that category unduly often, and avoid the definite preference votes. This strategy reduces the effective size of that part of the panel which exhibits definite preference. A drop in panel size invariably increases the variability around the preference ratio, which makes the preference ratio less significant.

In many preference tests the researcher may also seek additional information to further understand the reasons which underlie the judgment. The panelist may judge specific characteristics, such as: which product tastes saltier, and which product does the panelist prefer on flavor, on texture, etc.

When panelists provide these additional pieces of information, the analyst obtains diagnostic information which indicates the reasons underlying the preference.

For our snack chip study the product tester asked these specific questions: which product does the panelist prefer; which product has more flavor; which product does the panelist prefer on flavor; which product tastes spicier; which product does the panelist prefer on spiciness; which product tastes fresher; and which product does the panelist prefer on freshness?

At this point the reader should note several factors which impact on the design of an appropriate paired comparison test; in particular, the positions of the overall preference ratings in the list of questions and the order of the questions on the diagnostic portion of the study.

The Positions of the Overall Preference Ratings in the List of Questions. Should preference ratings come first or come last? Many practitioners prefer to ask the preference questions first, in order to obtain an overall first impression of the panelist's feeling, without requiring the panelist to go into detail regarding specific characteristics. Before panelists state their preferences and ratings on specific characteristics, they state their overall initial impression (prefer A or prefer B). Other practitioners, with just as much vehemence, favor having panelists make their overall preference choice after they have evaluated strengths and preferences on specific attributes. This author feels that both positions have merit. For preference tests and general hedonic evaluations, however, an initial, overall impression, before other evaluations provides a more sensitive, less biased evaluation.

The Order of the Questions on the Diagnostic Portion of the Study. Should all of the intensity ratings of attributes come first, followed by preferences on the characteristics? Should preference questions as a group precede specific paired comparisons of attribute intensities (e.g., should preferences in terms of flavor acceptance, spiciness acceptance and freshness acceptance precede judgments regarding which has more flavor and which has greater spiciness)? Or, should the intensity and preference questions interdigitate, with evaluation first of relative strength, and then relative preference on attributes. This author feels that the latter approach, namely interdigitation or intermixing provides the least biased method for questioning the panelists. Specifically the sequence of ratings in the questionnaire should proceed as follows: (1) overall rating of acceptability (which product do panelists like more); and (2) pairs of attribute questions, with the intensity questions first, followed by the preference questions for specific attributes (which seem stronger on the attribute; which do they prefer for that attribute).

Finally, in order to insure minimal bias in the ratings of preference and intensity evaluations, the product tester should insure that the attributes appear on the questionnaire according to their natural order of appearance: overall rating (liking, purchase interest, etc.); visual intensity and visual preference (appearance); aroma intensity and aroma preference; taste (flavor) intensity and taste (flavor) preference; and texture intensity and texture preference.

The Actual Interview

The product tester developed an interview format lasting 20 minutes, comprising the sections discussed below.

Orientation to the Test. Orientation relaxes the panelist, introduces the panelist to the testing situation, and thus sets the stage for valid data acquisition. A good orientation, dealing with the panelist's concern for his or her performance and lack of experience in product testing, inevitably enhances the quality of the data so obtained. Conversely, a poor orientation, which leaves the panelists confused regarding what to do or the purpose of the study, diminishes the utility of the data. In the orientation the product tester should stress these specific factors: importance of the test; purpose of the test; expectations about what to do; and requirements regarding scale use.

Purpose of the Study. One need not reveal the ultimate purpose of the test. That information could bias the data, since panelists know the underlying rationale for the study. Panelists may unconsciously provide the interviewer with the information he or she wishes to obtain. The panelist need only know that the manufacturer wishes to measure preferences between two types of chips, wants to find out why the panelist exhibits those specific impressions for preference, and wants to determine which of the two samples has more flavor, spice, etc.

What to Do. In any test situation, few if any panelists really know what the experimenter expects of them. Clear instructions help the panelist provide the data needed. What should the panelist do before tasting the product? How much of the product should the panelist taste? Should the panelist give an immediate judgment or first clear the palate? Into what frame of mind should the panelist put herself or himself, e.g., a purchaser of the product or a home use situation? Or should the panelist provide data in the here and now, without regard to what he or she might do outside of the arbitrarily confined test situation? (One would not like to provide data from a test which represents only the test situation itself. Quite often the interviewer can insure the proper attitudinal framework by instructing the panelist to rate the products as if he or she would use the product at home.)

How to Evaluate and What to Look For. Does the interviewer read the questionnaire and record the data? Does the interviewer read the questions, but instruct the panelists to record the data on their own answer sheets? This seems a trivial question, but it actually plays a role. Interviewer bias can enter into the dialog with the panelist when the interviewer reads questions and solicits verbal answers. Eye contact, hints, pursing of the lips and other non-verbal hints convey expectations and information to panelists, even when the interviewer does not mean to.

One Preference Test or Two? We often consider preference testing representing a rigid, fixed test method, wherein we ask the panelist for a single preference rating, presenting to the panelist first stimulus

A and then stimulus B. By varying the order of A and B, so that half the time product B precedes A rather than following A, we assume that we have eliminated any order bias.

Recent work by the author on preference testing suggests, however, that repeated paired preference testing may generate different results on separate pairs. In a set of paired preference tests, following each other closely in the same session, panelists may exhibit varying preferences. Whereas a panelist might prefer A on the first pair, he or she may prefer A or B in the second preference evaluation.

In order to avoid problems of a non-representative first preference test, the EBC product tester chose to run two preference tests back-to-back. In this way the panelist would go through the same evaluations twice. The additional preference evaluation, requiring no more than 8-10 minutes extra, would provide this additional information: data on preferences as a function of order of appearance in the first versus the second pair (how do panelists evaluate the stimuli when A precedes B versus when B precedes A; and do the preferences differ); consistency of preferences over repeated trials (do panelists exhibit consistent preference judgments, or do they vary their preference judgments after having tasted the samples); and increased diagnostic information on intensity and preference of the key attributes.

Results of the Study

The study we have just outlined for the EBC company on snack chips typifies the usual preference study. We present the results in some detail to illustrate specific points. The reader should keep in mind, however, that when running preference tests many of the options purposely selected and explicated in this study may not apply. The product tester can just as easily run a simple, uncomplicated preference test with far fewer panelists in a single location.

The data summarizing this study appears in Table 6.3. However, let us summarize the general results in a simple manner.

Overall Preference. The data from the paired preference tests showed that, in fact, R&D did succeed in producing a snack chip which beat the Tangys on a blind (nonbranded) basis. For example, in general, panelists preferred Chips over Tangys 58 to 42. Table 6.4 shows how to compute the statistical probability that a 58:42 preference would emerge by chance alone, given that the true preference actual equals 50:50. Since the probability of obtaining 58:42 preference drops below 5% by chance alone, assuming a true preference of 50:50 and

TABLE 6.3
SUMMARY OF PAIRED PREFERENCE DATA FOR CHIPS VS. TANGYS

	Overall Preference for Chips	Overall Preference for Tangys	Chips Has More Flavor	Chips Has Better Flavor	Chips Tastes Spicer	Chips Preferred on Spiciness	Chips Tastes Fresher	Chips Preferred on Freshness
1. Total Panel	58	42	68	62	53	54	68	64
a. Regular Tangys User	60	40						
b. Unflavored Jangles User	42	58						
c. Switch or Joint User	72	28						
2. Boston Panel	44	56						
a. Regular Tangys User	57	43						
b. Unflavored Jangles User	38	62		(Data broken down by user segment)				
c. Switch or Joint User	37	63						
3. Minneapolis Panel	60	40						
a. Regular Tangys User	55	45						
b. Unflavored Jangles User	40	60						
c. Switch or Joint User	85	15						
4. Dallas Panel	70	30						
a. Regular Tangys User	68	32						
b. Unflavored Jangles User	48	52						
c. Switch or Joint User	94	6						

Etc.

Number of panelists (expressed as a percent) showing preferences for Chips over Tangys and paired comparison ratings on attributes (total panel only).
No "no preference" responses allowed
Base = 100 panelists/market
Jangles Users = group of consumers who regularly use EBC's "Jangles" (a non-flavored chip)

given this sample size, we accept the hypothesis that R&D has, in fact, created a better product.

Preference by Region. Just because the preference scores seem so much in EBC's favor does not mean that the Chips wins uniformly across markets. We can break out the preference ratings by region, as Table 6.3 shows, in order to determine how consistently Chips wins over Tangys. Does Chips achieve its 58:42 preference equally across different markets, representing different rates and depths of penetration of flavored chips? Or, in fact, do the ratings really show a smashing success in preference in one market, and just a so-so performance in other markets. We see success for Chips in two markets, Dallas, Texas and Minneapolis, Minnesota, representing, importantly, the markets where flavored snack chips have made their most successful showing. Tangys beats Chips in Boston, Mass., where flavored snack chips have not had the opportunity to penetrate too deeply.

TABLE 6.4
STATISTICAL ANALYSIS OF PANEL PREFERENCE DATA

$$\text{``T'' Value} = \frac{\text{Probability of Preferring Chips} - 0.50}{\text{Standard Error of the Proportion}}$$

$$\text{*Standard Error} = \left[\frac{P(1 - P)}{N - 1} \right]^{0.5} \quad \begin{array}{l} N = \quad \text{Base Size} \\ P = \quad \text{Probability of Preference for ``Chips''} \end{array}$$

$$T = \frac{(0.58) - (0.50)}{\sqrt{(0.58)(0.42)/(300 - 1)}} = \frac{0.08}{\text{S.E.}} = \frac{0.080}{0.0285} = 2.803$$

If the probability of Chips winning over Tangys comes from a chance occurrence, we would expect the "T" value to drop below 1.96. It does not. We conclude that with the base size of 300, more than likely the 0.58 proportion of preference for Chips represents a true departure from a 50/50 (or no preference situation).

Preference By User Type. To whom do Tangys and Chips appeal most readily—to current Tangys users or to current unflavored potato chip users? Table 6.3 indicates that the preferences result from an overwhelming acceptance by Tangys users and by joint users; namely, those consumers who already use flavored potato chips, in preference to or along with the regular potato chips. Unflavored chip users show a preference for Tangys, choosing it 58% of the time. This additional information suggests that the market for the flavored chip may comprise different segments. R&D had developed a product which appeals primarily to the flavored snack chip user, rather than appealing to the unflavored chip user. More than likely, Chips will make its major gains among users of flavored snack chips, capturing some of the market held by Tangys. R&D has not made a chip which competes successfully with current unflavored snack chips. The consumers of unflavored chips show a decided preference for Tangys. Furthermore, since we have no information on the preference of Chips versus regular, unflavored potato chips, we do not know whether our new product, possesses any competitive advantage over regular potato chips, either for current Tangys users (those who now use flavored snack chips) or for current, loyal potato chip users.

Requisite Base Size For Preference Data. Our test comprised ratings from 300 panelists, which generated our measure of preference. What would have happened had we run the panel with fewer individuals? How few panelists would we have needed to obtain the same preference score of 58:42, and still feel confident that we have a statistically valid sample? Product testers and market researchers always come up with this query, sometimes before, but seemingly always after having done the experiment. The question really points to the heart of statistical analysis of preference testing, in the following ways.

(1) With increasing panel size, the average preference ratio (e.g., 58:42) should remain the same. Statisticians tell us that the average preference ratio from the data remains the best estimate of the mean or average preference ratio in the population. Hence, we have little or no reason to assume a different preference ratio if we increase the sample or decrease it, so long as the population from which we have chosen demonstrates the same usage and demographic characteristics as the population we originally started with.

(2) With increasing panel size, the variability around the preference ratio diminishes. Small differences or preference ratios have increasing chance of achieving statistical significance with high base sizes of panels. For example, with 100 panelists, a 58:42 ratio just approaches significance. With 1000 panelists, the variability around the mean decreases to $(10)^{0.5} = 1/3.2$ or approximately 29% of its original value. A T test of the difference (58% - 50%) would show an increased T value, since the mean difference (0.08) remains unchanged, but the variability diminishes (see Table 6.4 and Table 6.5). With 10 panelists, the 58:42 ratio lies far away from statistical significance, not because of the ratio, but because the preference ratio brings with it high error.

(3) We can determine the probability of obtaining a preference ratio of 58:42, if we sample from a random distribution (50:50 preference ratio), and obtain data from increasingly larger base sizes. Table 6.5 shows the estimated T value for the preference difference/ratio (58/42), assuming base sizes of 10, 20, 50, 100, 200, 300, 500, 700, 1000, 2000. Note that as we increase the panel size we diminish the variability and increase the resulting T value. We thus increase the probability that the ratio of preference we see (58/42) truly represents a difference, not a parity (viz. 50/50) preference which somehow due to chance and to the distribution of preference ratios, produces this particular value on this test.

What have we learned from our preference study? We have answered our question positively about R&D's success or failure. R&D did successfully produce a better tasting potato chip. We found that the preference test scores show statistical significance. We would not expect a winning ratio, 58:42, given a true parity (50:50) preference situation, and given a base size of 300. We found that preferences differ by market and by usage type. We may have produced a superior product, but not to all panelists and certainly not in all markets.

What have we not learned from the preference study? We have not determined the strength or intensity of an individual's likes. Do people like or dislike each product, and how much? Our test concerned only preference, and not scales for the intensity of preference or acceptance.

TABLE 6.5
"T" VALUES ASSOCIATED WITH A PREFERENCE OF 58 (FOR CHIPS)
VERSUS 42 (FOR TANGYS)

Base Size	"T" Value
10	.49
20	.71
50	1.13
100	1.61
200	2.29
300	2.80
500	3.62
700	4.28
1000	5.12
2000	7.24

$$T = \frac{0.58 - 0.50}{\sqrt{(.58)(.42)/(N-1)}} \qquad N = \text{Base Size}$$

Each product may attract or repel. We have no way to find that out with simple panel preference.

Attributes of the Chips Which Influence Preference

Bear in mind that preference ratings by themselves convey little diagnostic information. Without additional questions pertaining to reasons for preference, the panelist leaves the researcher in the dark concerning specific reasons for preference. Does one product score higher than another because panelists prefer its flavor? Its color? Neither? Both?

Table 6.3 shows the type of diagnostic information obtained from our study for the entire panel. It tells us how many panelists preferred product A to B on the basis of each attribute, and how many felt A to have stronger sensory characteristics. We can use this information in a straightforward manner.

Given the preferences for Chips over Tangys of 58:42, does this overall preference parallel preference for Chips over Tangys on specific characteristics? For example, let us consider some purely hypothetical, but nonetheless, reasonable outcomes of paired comparisons on specific diagnostics. (These possibilities differ from the data in Table 6.3).

1. Outcome A: Tangys preferred to Chips 40:60 (Chips loses) on the flavor attribute. We conclude that on the group level, where we aggregate the panelists together, the preference for Tangys in terms of flavor goes contrary to the overall preference for Chips. Obviously, flavor preference does not predict overall preference. Furthermore, we might expect an even greater win ratio for Chips over Tangys if we improve Chips flavor, keeping everything else constant. Paired preference tests do not tell the marketer how to improve the acceptance of flavor, per se, of Chips. We leave that topic to Chapter 7 on optimization.

2. Outcome B: Chips preferred to Tangys 75:25 on spiciness preference. Here Chips performs overwhelmingly better. If overall preference exactly parallels spiciness preference we might expect a similar preference ratio of 75:25 in favor of Chips in terms of overall acceptability. Usually, spiciness preference would correlate with, or drive, overall preference, but not to such a great extent. Other factors moderate the overwhelming effect of spiciness as a variable to which panelists respond.

The product tester can follow this train of reasoning to determine the sensory and liking factors which determine overall preference. The data permits the product tester to determine the extent to which the strong preferences on attributes impact on overall preference.

Critique of Paired Preference

Paired preference testing occupies the enviable position of a well accepted technique in product testing. At first glance the paired comparison method seems reasonable. After all, what mistake can the analyst possibly make when forcing the panelist to state a preference between products? Let us inquire, however, about the conclusions which practitioners derive or wish to derive from paired preference testing.

Intensity of Preference. Researchers often mistake the preference ratio (e.g., 75:25 in favor of one product) as a measure of the intensity of preference. This conclusion misleads. Preference testing involves head counts, not measures of strength of preference. We have no way of knowing what strength of preference on the part of consumers corresponds to a 75:25 preference for product B over product A.

Reliability of Preference. Preferences change. Preferences may vary from trial to trial, even when panelists evaluate the same pair of products. A repeated paired comparison can produce surprising results. Often panelists shift their criteria for preference from one trial to the next. The simplicity of preference testing deceives. What appears simple on the surface becomes complicated in execution. The psychological processes involved in preference testing integrate many different criteria in ways unknown to the researcher.

Thurstonian Scaling of Preference

We stated in Chapter 3 that discrimination testing can generate a measure of panelist variability which allows the researcher to develop a metric or scale underlying the stimuli. Stimuli close together generate more confusion in discrimination testing than do stimuli far apart on the scale. The same reasoning applies to preferences. Thurstone assumed that when panelists judge preference, choosing stimulus A over B, they do so by appeal to an underlying, or latent, liking function. By means of Thurstonian scaling procedures for paired comparison data, the researcher can generate a matrix showing the percentage of times each stimulus wins against other stimuli by paired comparison testing, and generate the underlying liking scale by statistical analyses. This underlying scale places stimuli at specific points, so that stimuli close together show preference ratios close to 50:50, whereas stimuli far away show wider preference ratios (e.g., 70:30, 80:20, 90:10, etc.) Table 6.6 shows the data base of panel preferences, the logic of Thurstonian analysis for the data base, and the resulting scale.

TABLE 6.6A
WORKED EXAMPLE OF THURSTONIAN SCALE
FOR FOOD PREFERENCES

		Proportion of Time Row Vegetable Preferred to Column Vegetable							
Vegetable	Tur. 1	Cab. 2	Beet 3	Asp. 4	Carrot 5	Spin. 6	St Bean 7	Peas 8	Corn 9
1. Turnip	.500	.818	.770	.811	.878	.892	.899	.892	.926
2. Cabbage	.182	.500	.601	.723	.743	.736	.811	.845	.858
3. Beets	.230	.399	.500	.561	.736	.676	.845	.797	.818
4. Asparagus	.189	.277	.439	.500	.561	.588	.676	.601	.730
5. Carrots	.122	.257	.264	.439	.500	.493	.574	.709	.764
6. Spinach	.108	.264	.324	.412	.507	.500	.628	.682	.628
7. String beans	.101	.189	.155	.324	.426	.372	.500	.527	.642
8. Peas	.108	.155	.203	.399	.291	.318	.473	.500	.628
9. Corn	.074	.142	.182	.270	.236	.372	.358	.372	.500
$\Sigma p_{i > k}$	1.614	3.001	3.438	4.439	4.878	4.947	5.764	5.925	6.494

Food stimuli arranged in order of increasing $\Sigma p_{i > k}$ across the columns.

TABLE 6.6B
SCALED-SEPARATIONS FOR THE NINE VEGETABLES
JUDGED IN TERMS OF PREFERENCES AS FOODS

Vegetable	Scale Value (Thurstonian Scale)
1. Turnip	−0.7
2. Cabbage	1.4
3. Beets	1.9
4. Asparagus	3.3
5. Carrots	3.8
6. Spinach	4.0
7. String Beans	5.0
8. Peas	5.2
9. Corn	5.9

Thurstonian analysis generates scale values for a panel's likes or dislikes, based upon a statistical analysis of paired comparison ratings. Stimuli as different as watches, food flavors and attitudes provide appropriate stimuli for paired comparison scaling and subsequent Thurstonian analysis.

Researchers develop scales from paired comparison or direct preference data, for various reasons. (1) To many researchers, paired comparisons represent the essence of hedonics. People understand choices between two items. Panelists relate well to instructions about choosing the "one you prefer." It seems natural to them. One can straightforwardly translate those preference into scale values, either by Thurstonian analysis using the normal curve as a means for developing scale values, or by other techniques which assume a non-normal statistical distribution underlying the paired comparison data. The researcher need not limit the analysis to an underlying Gaussian or normal distribution as a description of how the percent preferences translate into scale values. (2) With paired comparison methods, the starting data for scale development represents actual choice behavior, not self generated hedonic or rating scales. Marketers often feel more comfortable with actual choice behavior than with scale data. Such face validity attracts. (3) Like any other traditional technique of many years standing, Thurstonian analysis bears the mantle of hoary age. Age and variety of applications automatically make the method credible and respectable in the eyes of the user, unfamiliar with its shortcomings, or with the difficulties of hedonics measurement. (4) Paired comparisons represent a deceptively easy procedure to implement. Panelists do not seem to do anything new and different. Consequently, in the marketer's mind, this simplicity generalizes to the subsequent analysis of the data.

Thurstonian scales lack the following specific benefits which a hedonic scale should have. (1) They have no meaningful zero point. Thurstonian scales typify interval scales. The zero point on the Thurstonian interval scale may shift around without changing the differences between scale values. (2) Thurstonian scales critically depend upon the specific selection of stimuli. Choose a wide variety of stimuli and one will obtain one type of scale. Choose a narrow range of hedonically similar stimuli, and one may distort the scale considerably. (3) They have no meaningful categorization of the stimuli into liking/disliking categories. The paired comparison procedures do not permit the panelist to categorize his or her feelings into the different hedonic classes.

Engen's Experiments With Adults and Children

Trygg Engen (1974) at Brown University reported some elegant experiments in odor hedonics, using paired comparison procedures and Thurstonian analysis. Engen wanted to determine whether or not children's and adults' preferences for flavors differ from each other. He instructed panelists to choose which flavor of a pair they preferred, and subsequently scaled the paired comparison matrix by traditional Thurstonian techniques. The results proved fascinating. Children showed more preference lying around 50:50 or 60:40 for pairs of flavorings, whereas adults showed much stronger preference ratios (see Table 6.2). Recall that large preference ratios translate into large distances between stimuli on the underlying hedonic scale, whereas equal preference ratios closer to 50:50 translate to shorter distances on the underlying scale. The underlying hedonic scale for adults appears wider than the underlying hedonic scale for children, as Figure 6.3 shows.

TABLE 6.7
PAIRED COMPARISON OF ODOR PREFERENCE —
ADULTS VS. CHILDREN
(Engen, 1974)

Proportion of Choices of Odorants[a]

Odorant	Butyric acid	Rapeseed oil	Diethyl phthalate	Neroli oil	Safrole
Butyric acid	—	0.786	0.821	0.786	0.929
Rapeseed oil	0.214	—	0.679	0.750	0.679
Diethyl phthalate	0.179	0.321	—	0.607	0.786
Neroli oil	0.214	0.250	0.393	—	0.536
Safrole	0.071	0.321	0.214	0.464	—

[a]Each entry shows the proportion of six-year-old subjects preferring the odorant in the row to the corresponding odorant in the column on the left

Hedonic Scale Values for Five Odorants from Five Different Age Groups
Based on Paired Comparison

Age group	Butyric acid	Rapeseed oil	Diethyl phthalate	Neroli oil	Safrole	Range
4	−0.55	−0.15	+0.23	0	+0.48	1.03
5	−0.77	0	+0.26	−0.02	+0.53	1.30
6	−1.00	−0.02	+0.08	+0.42	+0.72	1.77
7	−1.05	−0.40	+0.37	+0.34	+0.74	1.79
Adult	−2.00	−0.54	+0.42	+0.81	+1.30	3.30

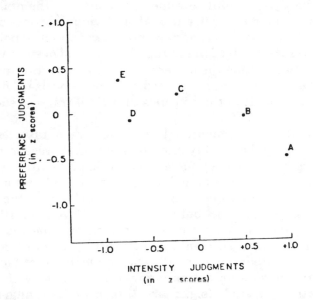

Pleasantness plotted against perceived intensity for the same odorants for seven-year-old children. A = 100% neroli oil, B = 20% neroli oil, C = 10% neroli oil, D = 100% rapeseed oil, and E = 100% ethyl phthalate

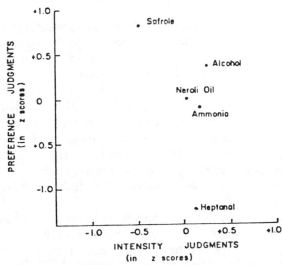

Pleasantness plotted against the perceived intensity for the same odorants by adults

FIG. 6.3   PLOT OF THE HEDONIC SCALE VALUE VERSUS INTENSITY (BOTH IN STANDARDIZED SCORE) FOR CHILDREN VERSUS FOR ADULTS
Source: Engen (1974)

Another important point to remember concerns the ability of the paired comparison method to eliminate individual differences in scaling behavior. The investigator need not worry about panelist understanding of issues involved in scaling. The panelist needs only point to which one of two samples he prefers. The panelist tests stimuli immediately in front of him or her, and need neither memorize a scale, nor fit an individual scale into the confines of an arbitrary, predesignated scale.

In net, paired comparison precedures seem here to stay. Despite their limitations, they will probably remain important to researchers for at least three reasons. (1) They have the mantle of tradition and establishment as the general approach to preference. (2) Computers facilitate the processing of paired comparison data. Witness the extensive work appearing yearly in journals such as Psychometrika on the psychometric analysis of paired comparison or choice data. These articles deal with new, efficient and insightful ways to evaluate and process paired comparison data. (3) They have inherent face validity which always acts as an attractive feature to those who order the implementation of a study (e.g., marketing or R&D managers responsible for initiation of the project).

CATEGORY SCALING

Perhaps no other method has attracted as widespread use in sensory analysis as the category scales of hedonics. As we saw in the previous chapter on scaling, category scales allow the panelist to act as a number generating instrument, to measure intensity of subjective responses. Category scales, whether pertaining to intensity or to liking/disliking, allow the panelist to exhibit graded differences in strength of feeling, by selecting different scale points. In practical applications category scaling and paired comparison procedures often complement each other. Category scaling shows the intensity of sensory and hedonic reactions on different product attributes. Paired comparison methods reveal the overall definitive choice of one product versus another.

With category scales the researcher can transcend some of the limits of the paired comparison method. Specifically (1) he or she can test more samples. Paired comparisons require presentation of many or sometimes all pairs of test stimuli to panelists. This quickly generates an unduly large number of stimuli [$N(N-1)/2$ pairs for N samples]. With category scaling, the researcher need only present each stimulus once to secure the rating. (2) The researcher can measure the strength of liking. Category scales allow for specific gradations of feeling. (3) Category scales facilitate statistical analysis by enabling the researcher to obtain data which one can analyze by statistical means to show significant differences. (4) They also make functional relations possible in order to obtain data to develop a hedonic curve relating strength of feeling to a physical measure, or to the strength of a sensory impression.

A CASE HISTORY—EXAMPLE AND OPTIONS USING CATEGORY SCALING

The Jeveli Meat Company (JMC) had the opportunity to develop and market a line of meat spreads in order to compete with the market leader. JMC could develop a roast beef spread, a ham spread, a chicken spread, or two or three of these. Furthermore, JMC had several options within each product, including selection of the meat source, size of grind, etc.

In order to select the best meat test, the product tester at JMC decided to run a hedonic evaluation test. This test would show whether consumers showed greatest liking for beef, for ham, or for chicken. Marketing management planned to introduce at least one of the three lines by the end of the year. The vice president of marketing instructed the product testing group to obtain information on consumer reactions to the different meats.

The Panelists. As with all hedonic testing, the first issue a practitioner faces concerns the selection of panelists. Should one use extramural, consumer panelists representing the general market, or internal, company employee panelists who represent a group of consumers, albeit probably biased ones. Or, should one use expert panelists, trained in product description by one or another procedure?

The expert, in-house panel represents an extremely biased panel. These individuals, trained in descriptive analysis, often have intimate involvement in the development of the product, often as early as the concept stage, and onwards. With so much experience, these experts hardly represent an unbiased panel. Testing their likes and dislikes will more than likely surface biases developed over their years of product testing experience. Of course, one can always reply that these panelists will show more discrimination, and that through their hedonic reactions they will surely detect any defects in the test products. With so much experience these experts can hardly overlook product faults which the ordinary consumer would miss. This argument represents specious, but widely used, reasons. By using the expert panel to provide hedonic ratings, the product tester has, in actuality, turned the panel into a quality control tool, with the specifications for quality control subtly and secretly instilled from years of training. The hedonic reactions of these expert panelists derive jointly from their individual hedonic reactions and their intellectual understanding of strengths and defects in the product. In-plant testing which uses such expert panelists and hedonic scaling actually uses the hedonic scale as a quality control device to measure defects. The liking/disliking scale measures the distance from a perfect product, in terms of quality assurance specifications.

The extramural consumer panel represents another panel option. The JMC product tester argued that for initial testing, where one wants to rank the products in terms of acceptability, such extramural testing should take place after the internal panel of 100 employees has had a chance to evaluate the product. The product tester further suggested that the evaluations take place during a two stage process. First, the internal consumer panel of non-expert employees would evaluate the meat spreads. If one or more spreads showed promise as reflected by the ratings, then the product tester would move the test outside to several locations, replicating it to obtain more representative data from a large sample of consumers.

The product tester's suggestion appeared reasonable. Both marketing management, responsible for product introduction, and R&D management accepted the suggestion and gave the product tester the go-ahead to implement the test. Furthermore, in a meeting with management, the product tester outlined the logic of the study, and arranged the study implementation in order to meet specific schedules. R&D needed feedback within 3 weeks, in order to ascertain whether it had to change any of the formulations for subsequent retesting. Also, marketing had scheduled a product launch 8 months hence, and needed the final product within 4 months to allow for the storage evaluation, and for scale-up product and plant retooling.

Quite often the product tester schedules tests in order to simultaneously satisfy two groups. Product development/R&D needs lead time for pilot plant scale-up and production. Marketing plans the product launch to begin at a specified time. Marketers must coordinate advertising strategy and development, the purchase of advertising space, promotions and the like. These time constraints can severely impact upon the type and extent of product testing which one can and must do.

Product testers in many companies and universities can call upon in-house panelists of volunteers to participate in acceptance tests. These so-called taste tests usually last anywhere from 15-40 minutes.

They require that the panelists come to a central location facility inside the corporation or university. In that facility, panelists learn what they have to do through orientation, and usually test between 1 and 7 products, rating the products either on overall liking/disliking and/or on specific attributes. The JMC company had developed such a roster of volunteer panelists, by soliciting participation in taste test panels at the start of each employee's tenure. The product tester kept records on product preferences and usage of the panelists through an annual questionnaire. This information allowed the JMC product tester to select those specific individuals who use, or at least, accept canned meat spreads. All too often, acceptance tests with in-house panelists fail to take into account panelist likes and dislikes. Had the product tester simply selected panelists at random from the pool of in-house panelists, we might have obtained non-representative data. If such randomly selected panelists, in fact, rarely or never use canned meat spreads, then one cannot extrapolate their likes and dislikes for canned meat (a product they do not use) to the consumer population at large to which marketing will target the product.

The product tester at JMC selected a panel of 30 individuals to participate. Considerations dictating panel size included the following. (1) The point in the development cycle during which testing occurs. Here, product testing took place in the early part of the development/marketing cycle, with low risk of making an incorrect decision. Thus, the panel size fitted that of a small scale study, rather than a large scale, full-market, nationally projectable study. Had this study formed the basis for the final decision regarding which of the three products to market without any further testing and fine tuning, the product tester would have used a larger panel to insure better representation. Furthermore, more than likely the product tester would have selected extramural consumer panelists from different parts of the U.S., in view of the criticality of that final go/no-go decision. The panel then would have better represented the consumer target population. (2) The nature of the task required a reasonable size panel. The product tester gathered information on like/dislikes, which we know to vary among the population. A small panel comprising 6-9 members cannot provide the necessary representation. A large panel (100+) will cost too much, and management would reject those costs in view of the project stage and criticality. Hence, the tester selected an intermediate number of 30 panelists. At 30, the ratings begin to approach a normal distribution. One could use 28 or 32, etc., but we settle here on a round number. (3) Availability of panel members always influences the selection of panel participants and panel size. The product tester did not pay the panelists. Hence, the success of testing depended, in part, upon panelist good will. Panelists like to participate in product evaluations, as long as the time and the frequency of service do not drain them, or generate undue strain on schedules. Interruptions of work, when too frequent, inevitably lead to the refusal to cooperate. To assure cooperation, the product tester had to recruit a limited number of panel participants, in order to assure future participation of these and other panelists. Too large a panel size demands participation from the majority of available panelists. By running three panels of 30, for three separate test occasions, rather than three panels of 90, the product tester maintains long-term panelist interest by not fatiguing or irritating the panelist with too frequent participation. R&D sensory analysts often overlook the factor of panelist resistance, and settle for those panelists who gladly volunteer their time. However, such accommodating panelists do not necessarily provide better data. In fact, they may provide poorer data, and can provide non-representative answers. The researcher should not depend too much upon the participation of available and agreeable participants to make his or her job easier. Amiability will not generate valid product evaluation over a several year period when the same panelists participate repeatedly.

Questionnaire/Scale Type

In hedonic testing, researchers prefer one or another type of hedonic scale. Scales vary in terms of the following factors: Number of available categories; odd versus even number of categories; bipolar versus unipolar category scales; a scale with verbal descriptors versus one without; and positions of the high and low ends of the scale (should point 1 lie at the top of the scale or at the bottom of the scale?).

Number of Categories. A quick survey of the product testing literature, or an inspection of current, in-use procedures shows a divergence in the number of scale points. Einstein and Hornstein (1970) used 3 points to show liking/disliking. Other researchers prefer a 7 point scale or a 9 point scale, depending upon the individual's own particular preferences. One basic rule to remember concerns the ability to discriminate hedonic differences. Increasing the number of categories available to the panelist helps to increase discrimination. Ease of data analysis counteracts this increase in number of categories. A 9 point scale, 1-9 simplifies statistical analysis. One simply instructs panelists to use a limited number of response categories. This constraint makes them feel at ease, although it may not generate sufficiently sensitive and discriminating data. Furthermore, with a limited number of rating categories, the analyst can estimate both the mean and count the number of ratings in each category. As the number of categories increases, the number of panelists assigning any specific category will diminish.

Product testers and psychophysicists have observed that in the use of category scales of hedonics (and intensity), panelists shy away from using the endpoints of the scale (see Table 6.8 for a distribution of ratings for each point on the scale). Avoidance of extremes on the fixed point scale occurs because panelists show conservative behavior. They often refuse to use the endpoints of the scale unless they come across a stimulus which seems so good or so poor that they feel they must use those endpoints. In intensity evaluation using category scales, the panel director can present a stimulus of such strong or weak intensity to the panelist so as to force the panelists to use the endpoints. Confronted with the extremes, panelists will use the endpoints of the scale, often embarrassed at doing so. With hedonic ratings, which have no necessary underlying physical correlate as immediate as sensory

TABLE 6.8
SAMPLE DISTRIBUTION OF RATINGS FOR LIKING
ON A 9-POINT SCALE

Number Assigned	Product Tuna Spread	Product Hot Chocolate	Product Beer (European Import)
1	0	1	0
2	0	1	0
3	1	0	0
4	1	3	0
5	2	2	0
6	4	6	0
7	12	11	3
8	9	5	9
9	1	1	8
Total in Panel	30	30	20

intensity, the product tester cannot force the panelist to use the endpoints. Hence panelists show much more conservatism. One cannot easily budge the panelists from this conservative center-seeking behavior, the so-called *regression effect* (Stevens and Greenbaum 1966). It should come as no surprise, therefore, to read about experts in the sensory analysis and product testing disciplines arguing for fewer than 9 categories, in light of the tendency of panelists to use fewer categories. On the other hand, when we decrease the nine categories to seven, panelists change their scaling behavior. They avoid the seventh and first categories, the new extremes, thus shortening the effective scale to five points, and so on.

The JMC product tester decided to use the traditional 9 point category scale, proposed by Peryam and Pilgrim (1957), to measure product acceptance. Many researchers use this scale as the measurement tool of choice, for the following reasons. (1) The Hedonic Scale comprises an odd number of scale points, with the middle point reserved for neutrality—neither like nor dislike. Researchers prefer to use such a balanced scale. It provides panelists with an equal number of scale points for liking or disliking. Quite often researchers use scales with an even number of categories. Half the scale pertains to liking, and the other half pertains to disliking. In such instances the scale forces the panelist to decide whether he or she likes each product. Without a neutral point, panelists cannot equivocate. They must categorize their hedonic feelings as like or dislike. Presumably, the ratings that would lie at the neutral point (5 on the 9 point scale) would fall equally often into the liking and disliking portions of the corresponding 8 point scale, which lacks the neutral point. This presumption remains open for definitive experimentation. (2) The Hedonic Scale comprises well defined verbal descriptors which accompany the scale. Many practitioners in product testing insist upon verbal descriptors of hedonics to accompany the scale, as an aid for their panelists.

Table 6.9 shows scales which researchers have used over the years in category scaling of liking/disliking. Some researchers in industry prefer to use unbalanced scales, allowing panelists a total of six categories with four categories reserved for liking and two reserved for disliking. Other practitioners prefer a five point scale, etc. Unfortunately, few studies have investigated the specific idiosyncracies and problems associated with each type of scale.

A continuing source of confusion occurs when choosing descriptor terms representing the 9 point scale. Some practitioners prefer to have category 1 reserved for the best or most acceptable product, and 9 reserved for the poorest or least acceptable product. Other practitioners prefer the opposite, allowing 9 to represent the most acceptable product and 1 to represent the least acceptable product. Still others divide the scale at 5, the neutral point. They show the panelist a V scale containing a 5 at the base of the V, and two different ascending scales which describe increasing degrees of liking versus increasing degrees of disliking.

Another issue in hedonic evaluation concerns the use of unipolar versus bipolar scales. The product tester at JMC could have selected a

TABLE 6.9
VERBAL DESCRIPTORS FOR HEDONIC SCALES

Number of Scale Points	Descriptors
2	Dislike, unfamiliar
2	Acceptable, dislike, not tried
3	Like a lot, dislike, do not know
3	Well liked, indifferent, disliked, seldom if ever used
5	Like very, like moderately, neutral, dislike moderately, dislike very
5	Very good, good, moderate, tolerate, dislike, never tried
5	Very good, good, moderate, dislike, tolerate
5	Very good, good, moderately well, tolerate, dislike
9	Like extremely, like very much, like moderately, neither like nor dislike, dislike slightly, dislike moderately, dislike very much, dislike extremely

Source: Meiselman (1978)

unipolar scale, in which 0 stands for no liking at all. Unipolar scales go in one direction—the lowest number represents the total absence of liking, whereas the highest number reflects the highest level possible of liking. In contrast, the bipolar scale directly recognizes that hedonics represent two continua, meeting at neutrality. Neutral represents the meeting point of two diverging, and perhaps different, psychological scales. Unfortunately, little work has appeared on the relative virtue of using bipolar versus unipolar scales, with one major exception. Moskowitz and Fishken (1979) suggested that in fragrance testing one could obtain greater discrimination between stimuli by using a bipolar scale.

Use of Reference Standards in Category Scaling Evaluation

The JMC product tester, thinking ahead about the implications of product acceptance testing, realized that without external reference standards for comparison (e.g., in-market products) the ratings obtained for the canned meat spreads might become irrelevant. What does a score of 6.7 on a 9 point scale mean? Can one translate that into market share of the product? Can one compare those numbers on the hedonic scale to ratings of competitor products?

In order to answer this question, the product tester selected three meat products in the canned meat category as internal references. For the actual product evaluation, the product tester decided to present six products to the consumer panel on the company premises. Three of the products comprised the three test options which management wanted to test. The remaining three products represented one in-market competitor of each test product. When analyzing the results, the product tester could compare the ratings assigned to the in-market competitor versus the ratings assigned to the test product. By so doing, the analyst could determine whether or not panelists like JMC's product more than the competitor or less than the competitor; as well as whether or not the competitor scores higher then the JMC entry on one or several key sensory attributes of appearance, aroma, flavor and texture, etc.

As a general rule in product testing, one should always test a competitor as a benchmark, unless the test situation rules out that possibility (e.g., in a long term, product storage test). Only by knowing how a competitor performs on one's own scale versus the test product can the product tester, marketing and R&D understand their own product ratings. With a panel which tends to downgrade all products it evaluates (e.g., the meats receive averages of 4.9 versus an expected average of 6.7), the product tester can immediately ascertain that the low rating results from panelist bias, and not from inherent problems in the test product itself. But to understand this bias requires evaluation of external products which one knows to have achieved a reasonable level of product acceptability.

The Test Implementation:

The execution of the hedonic test for product acceptance/rejection proceeded smoothly. Panelists reported to the in-house product testing center during a specified time (9:30-11:30 AM) after the panel recruiter telephoned them during the previous week to set up and confirm their appointments. The evaluation required approximately 45 minutes in toto, and proceeded as follows.

The panelist checked in at the test site. They read the instructions, informing them about the reason for the study (namely, to evaluate different canned meat items), and what to do (to evaluate overall acceptability). Table 6.10 presents the instructions to the panel. As an aside, the sensory analyst or product tester should make every effort to use standardized, pretested instructions in any type of product test, whether for descriptive intensity or for hedonic scaling. Standardized instructions reduce the bias due to different instructions. By their very variation, instructions influence the panelist and generate different responses. Product testers and interviewers often do not realize how

TABLE 6.10

You will test 6 meat spreads. We would like you to rate how much you like each meat spread *overall*.

— First clean your mouth with a water rinse
— Taste the first sample, as shown on your questionnaire.
  (An interviewer will give you the product)
— Rate how much you like the product overall. (Imagine for a minute, as you taste
  the product, that you will have purchased a tin of the product for a meal).
— Use the scale below to rate your feelings:
  9 Like extremely
  8 Like very much
  7 Like moderately
  6 Like slightly
  5 Neither like nor dislike
  4 Dislike slightly
  3 Dislike moderately
  2 Dislike very much
  1 Dislike extremely

Then please rate these attributes as well, using the same scale:

Liking of Appearance
Liking of Aroma
Liking of Flavor
Liking of Texture

---

easily they can influence panelists with subtle cues and hints, conveyed by instructions.

The panelists evaluated the products in a testing booth, where they could neither see the interviewer nor their fellow panelists. Some practitioners prefer this isolation, in carefully controlled conditions because it has the external appearance of good scientific control. No data has appeared which confirms that isolated product testing generates any better data than testing done in a large room with panelists exposed to each other, but working separately. However, traditional product testing procedures in R&D setting dictate the isolation room and sterile testing procedures. The booth eliminated contact between the panelist and the interviewer. The panelist read the instructions regarding how to taste and how to scale using the 9 point Hedonic Scale. The testing booth provided a simple background against which to test the product. A small white booth with overhead lights and interchangeable bulbs, the test site provided isolation between panelists and isolated them from the product server. Neither could see the other. The isolation prevented any transmission of information by unspoken cues, such as facial movements.

The entire product evaluation took approximately 35 minutes. The panelists received their products, and rated each product on five characteristics, all of a hedonic nature. These included overall liking, liking of appearance, liking of aroma, liking of flavor, and liking of texture. The panelists evaluated each of these attributes in the same order with appearance always preceding aroma, which, in turn, always preceeded texture and flavor. Sometimes product testers like to shift the order of attributes for different panelists to avoid biased results from the same repeated order. When the food item stimulates different sensory reactions from many modalities, the rotation of attributes interferes with the natural course of sensory inputs. It may prove infeasible, despite the advised nature of such randomizations.

Most panelists found little or no difficulty with the test. Panelists felt comfortable with the scale, and used it in their own accustomed manner. Little training preceded the actual evaluation. In fact, most product testers do not have to train panelists to use the category scale. As an unwanted consequence, however, panelists use the scale in their own idiosyncratic ways. Some panelists constrict the scale, whereas others expand the scale. The quickness of implementation and the lack of involvement of a trained product tester in the study reduced quality control of the data, since no one monitored the proceedings of the panel until the panelists finished all of the products.

Results

Table 6.11 shows the ratings for the six products, overall, on each of the attributes. Note the following. (1) Panelists varied their ratings with the different products. The ratings show that the beef spread possessed the most acceptable flavor, since the beef spread scored highest in terms of overall acceptance. (2) Panelists exhibited different behaviors when assigning numbers. Some panelists (e.g., panelists 7 and 26) constricted the spread of their ratings to the intermediate range, categories 4-8. Other panelists (e.g., panelists 2 and 24) spread their ratings to the extremes of the scale (see Table 6.12). Does this mean that panelists actually exhibit different likes/dislikes of the products, with some panelists more accepting of some flavors than others? Or, in fact, does this mean that the so-called simple hedonic scale really acts as many different scales, depending upon individual differences in its use. We do not know the answer. In order to decide between these possibilities, we would have to run another study, where we know beforehand through other measures that panelists exhibit the same acceptance level for the products. Then we could distinguish between individual differences in scale use patterns and individual differences in true hedonic reactions to the meats.

The products scored differently. The leading product, ham spread, scores 6.73, with its standard error of the mean equal to 0.30. These scores mean that panelists rating the ham spread felt that the taste fell into the category between like slightly and like moderately. The standard error measures the variability of the mean. In theory, if we repeat this experiment 100 times, we will obtain a distribution of ratings. Our best guess of the average of the distribution remains the average we obtained here, namely 6.73. However, that average would represent a distribution of ratings. Figure 6.4 shows the proportion of times we expect the mean from repeating this study to lie between certain values. The reader will recognize this as a *normal distribution*, with the mean equalling the average mean here of 6.73, and the standard deviation of the distribution equalling the standard error of the mean, here 0.30.

Additionally, it should be noted that the individuals in this study differed from each other in their average ratings of the products. Table 6.12 shows ratings and the average liking ratios for the panelists. The product tester should expect wider individual differences in liking ratings then in intensity ratings, for two reasons. One reason pertains to true individual differences in perception which lead to different scale values. Add to that the well known observation that people differ in what they like/dislike. Even if two panelists perceive products

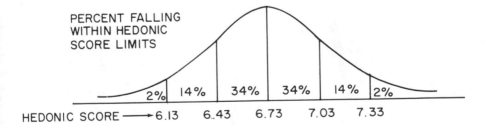

FIG. 6.4 DISTRIBUTION OF AVERAGE RATINGS
OF REPEATED TESTINGS OF CANNED SPREAD
(Mean = 6.73, Standard Error = 0.30)

TABLE 6.11
HEDONIC SCORES AND ATTRIBUTES RATINGS OF
SIX CANNED MEAT SPREADS

	Product					
	Test Ham	Competitor Ham	Test Chicken	Competitor Chicken	Test Roast Beef	Competitor Roast Beef
Overall Liking	6.73 (0.30)	6.46 (0.22)	5.23 (0.29)	3.07 (0.20)	6.43 (0.32)	6.23 (0.30)
Liking of Appearance	6.05 (0.38)	6.31 (0.35)	4.02 (0.48)	4.25 (0.38)	5.70 (0.31)	6.28 (0.49)
Liking of Aroma	6.84 (0.42)	6.71 (0.35)	4.55 (0.48)	5.23 (0.51)	6.34 (0.49)	6.28 (0.33)
Liking of Flavor	7.11 (0.54)	6.92 (0.41)	4.21 (0.43)	4.73 (0.51)	6.42 (0.42)	6.35 (0.38)
Liking of Texture	5.48 (0.54)	6.08 (0.40)	5.21 (0.41)	5.58 (0.49)	6.05 (0.41)	6.93 (0.42)

Numbers in parenthesis = standard error of the mean

TABLE 6.12

RAW DATA FOR HEDONIC SCALE RATINGS OF MEAT SPREADS

| Panelist | Ham | | Chicken | | Roast Beef Panels | | Average |
	Test	Competitor	Test	Competitor	Test	Competitor	
1	7	6	6	2	6	6	5.5
2	9	6	3	1	8	7	5.7
3	7	6	5	4	2	1	4.2
4	8	8	7	4	8	7	7.0
5	8	8	6	4	7	8	6.8
6	6	5	4	3	2	4	4.0
7	7	8	7	4	7	7	6.7
8	7	7	6	3	6	7	6.0
9	7	7	6	3	8	7	6.3
10	7	6	6	4	6	7	6.0
11	5	6	3	5	8	8	5.8
12	6	5	4	3	8	6	5.3
13	6	7	7	4	2	2	4.7
14	6	4	4	2	6	4	4.3
15	5	7	6	3	7	7	5.8
16	5	4	3	2	6	9	4.8
17	7	7	6	4	7	6	6.2
18	6	6	3	3	8	8	5.9
19	6	5	3	2	7	6	4.8
20	8	6	6	3	6	8	6.2
21	7	7	5	3	7	7	6.0
22	8	7	3	2	7	6	5.5
23	9	9	8	1	5	5	6.2
24	8	7	6	1	8	5	5.8
25	8	7	7	4	8	8	7.0
26	8	7	6	5	5	6	6.2
27	6	5	3	2	7	7	5.0
28	7	7	6	4	7	4	5.8
29	7	6	4	3	7	7	5.7
30	6	8	8	4	7	7	6.7
Mean	6.73	6.46	5.23	3.07	6.43	6.23	
S.D.	1.28	1.19	1.61	1.11	1.73	1.79	
S.E.	0.30	0.22	0.29	0.20	0.32	0.30	

identically in terms of sensory characteristics, some panelists will like the product, and others will not.

Statisticians have developed techniques to partial out the variability in the ratings for different products; and to account, on the one hand, for the contributions due to the intrinsic acceptability of each product, and on the other hand for the individual differences. Both sources of information, products which vary and individuals who differ, add error or unexplained variation to the data. We must eliminate the variability due to panelists, so that we can concentrate on variability due to products.

Statistical methods, such as the *analysis of variance* (ANOVA) procedure, partial out that variability. The *two-way analysis of variance* does the following statistical analysis which tells the product tester which of the meats consumers like most. (1) It represents the variability in the rating as a sum of the variabilities contributed by actual differences in product acceptance, and by individual differences. (2) It looks at three sources of variability: products, panelists, and the *unexplained residual* (total variability − explained variability). (3) It looks at the *ratio of variabilities* in the data. The ratio consists of the variability due to products divided by the unexplained or error variability. (4) With a sufficiently high variability ratio, we conclude that the variability of the product looms so large as to have resulted from true differences among products.

Table 6.13 shows a worked example of the analysis of variance, which indicates that panelists like the products to different degrees. Table 6.13 shows the analysis done 1 way (without partialling out panelist variability) and 2 ways (partialling out panelist variability).

If the analysis of variance shows that the variability in ratings due to products substantially exceeds the variability due to unexplained error, then the product tester can conclude the products differ in acceptability. One can then perform subsequent, or post-hoc, tests such as the T test, to find out which products differ from each other.

Interpreting The Differences

We have found that the acceptabilities of the different meat spreads differ from each other significantly. The product tester at JMC tested the meats, and found that the differences in hedonic ratings among the products would not occur except in very rare instances, if, in fact, the six products actually scored equally high in reality. What exactly does this mean? How does the product tester use this information and report it out?

The hedonic scale reflects raters' opinions of the products. The panelists rate the meats according to a combined number/word scale, which we saw in Table 6.10. These numbers or words represent the panelists' own opinions about the products, developed during a very short term exposure to the products. They show that the panelists categorized the manufacturer's three meat spread products as follows: canned ham spread—between like moderately and like slightly;

TABLE 6.13
COMPUTATIONS OF THE ANALYSIS-OF-VARIANCE (ANOVA) FOR LIKING RATINGS OF SIX MEAT SPREADS

Without Factoring Out Panelist Differences (1 Way) (6.13A)
By Factoring Out Panelist Differences (2 Way) (6.13B)

TABLE 6.13 A
ANALYSIS OF VARIANCE (1 WAY) AMONG MEAT SPREADS

Source of Variation	df	SS	MS	F Ratio
Foods	$6 - 1 = \quad 5$	188.73	57.74	23.10
Error	$180 - 6 = 174$	435.07	2.50	
Total	179	723.80		

TABLE 6.13B
ANALYSIS OF VARIANCE TABLE (2 WAY)

Source of Variation	df	SS	MS	F Ratio
Panelists	$30 - 1 = \quad 29$	199.30	6.87	4.22
Foods	$6 - 1 = \quad 5$	288.73	57.75	35.52
Error	$29 \times 5 = 145$	235.77	1.62	
Total	179	723.80		

COMPUTATIONAL TECHNIQUE FOR ANALYSIS OF VARIANCE (2 WAY)

1. Correction Factor (CF) $= \dfrac{(\text{Grand Total})^2}{N} = \dfrac{(1026)^2}{180} = 5848.2$

2. Sum of Squares Panelists (SS panel) $= \displaystyle\sum_{\text{Panelist 1}}^{30} [(\text{Total for panelist})/6]^2 - \text{CF}$

   $\dfrac{36285}{6} = 6047.5 - 5848.2 = 199.3$

3. Sum of Squares Foods (SS$_{Foods}$) $= \displaystyle\sum_{\text{Food 1}}^{6} [(\text{Total}_{Food})/30]^2 - \text{CF}$

   $= 6136.93 - 5848.2 = 288.73$

4. Sum of Squares Total (SS$_{Total}$) $= \Sigma x^2 - \text{CF} = 6572 - 5848.2 = 723.8$

5. Sum of Squares Error $= \text{SS}_{Total} - \text{SS}_{Food} - \text{SS}_{Panelist} = 235.77$

df = degress of freedom
SS = sum of squares
MS = mean square

canned chicken spread—like slightly; and canned roast beef spread—
between like slightly and like moderately.

We do not know how the panelists would feel about the products
outside the test situation. Would they purchase the product? Would
they purchase a product which they rate as disliked slightly, given a
low price of that product which tempts their pocketbooks? Hedonic
testing poses an extremely complicated question regarding an overall
judgment. Like very much may apply to the product in a sterile testing
booth, but like very much for what—extended consumption?

Utilization of the Test Data by Management

Management received a writeup of the JMC analysis of the three
canned meat acceptance values which stressed the points discussed
below.

The ham spread received the highest rating, 6.73. Ham spread
acceptability exceeded the other two test products which rated 5.23 for
chicken spread and 6.24 for roast beef spread, and also exceeded the
acceptance rating of the competitor ham sample (the in-market product rated as 6.46). Based upon these intitial inputs, management
decided to proceed with further development of the ham spread, and to
shelve the other two canned meat spreads. Management reasoned that
the higher acceptance rating of ham spread versus the other meat
types and, most importantly versus the current competitor, promised a
potentially stronger product in the marketplace. The heightened
acceptability suggested points of difference versus the current competition, on which the marketer and the advertising agency could
capitalize.

Product testing also provided key insights into areas for improving
canned ham spread. On the one hand, the flavor acceptance of the
winning test product only slightly beat the acceptance of the leading
competitor, 7.11 to 6.92. Flavor did not pose any problems. Aroma
acceptance also scored at parity, 6.84 to 6.71, which means that both
flavor and aroma acceptability of JMC's canned ham spread equalled
the acceptability scores of the competitor. On the attributes of texture
and appearance acceptability, however, JMC's test product lost to
competition, receiving a substantially lower score of 5.48 to 6.08. Based
upon this input, the sensory analyst recommended to management
that they undertake a product reformulation project in which they
maintain current flavor and aroma, but improve the overall acceptance of the canned ham spread in the key areas of texture and appearance. (Sometimes product testers can recommend even more specific
courses of action, by soliciting verbatims or comments regarding likes

and dislikes. Such freely volunteered comments on texture and appearance could more specifically locate areas which need improvement. The JMC analyst did not solicit that information, however).

What would the panelist do to purchase the product? Would the panelist pay more money to buy the product or go out of his or her way in order to purchase product? Would the panelist select the product in a paired comparison test instead of a product rated lower on the scale?

We bring up these issues to show that management looks to the sensory analysis and product test results searching for marketing and production clues, not just data which stands alone in a nicely bound folder. Sensory·results should mean something beyond the numbers which one has obtained and processed. The practitioner will have a difficult time generalizing consumer behavior from sterile laboratory testing results, unless he or she can tie hedonic ratings to other information or behavior, such as: high hedonic ratings correlated with initial or repeated item purchase; low hedonic ratings indicating eventual consumer rejection of the product and, in some instances, loss of brand loyalty; or high hedonic ratings correlated with selection of one item over another product which scores lower. Sensory analysts and product testers all too often lose sight of the broad ramifications of hedonic tests, concerning themselves strictly with manipulation of the data and reportage of results. Yet, more often than not the marketer relies upon hedonic scale, or paired preference data to help make a key decision in the marketing stream.

Food Acceptance Attitudes and Hedonic Scales

Researchers in the food industry often use hedonic scaling to measure attitudes to foods by paper and pencil surveys alone, without requiring that the panelists evaluate the actual food in a tasting or consumption situation. The category scale allows the researcher to assess overall attitudes to foods. Such a study complements the use of the hedonic scale as a laboratory-based procedure for testing actual foods.

The U.S. Government has played an important role in promoting hedonic scaling of attitudes toward food items in large scale questionnaires. The U.S. Government, first at the Quartermaster Corps in Chicago until 1963, and afterwards the U.S. Army Natick Laboratories in Massachusetts, has sponsored studies on hedonic scaling of attitudes of food items. These studies used the hedonic scale alone, or used it together with a frequency/month scale to measure what soldiers like or do not like. The implementation of the study remained the same—panelists rated the food name on the 9 point scale. A food attitude survey, in contrast to an actual product evaluation, generates ratings for food which depend upon a panelist's generalized memory skills and disposition to the particular items. The ratings also distribute along the scale, showing variation from one panelist to another. Panelists still show the same reluctance to use the extreme points of the scale, and instead cluster their ratings around the middle scale values.

Table 6.14 shows some representative data on food preferences, obtained from the Fort Lewis food preference survey (Meiselman *et al.* 1972). Note that without knowing which stimuli the researcher uses, we could not ascertain whether the ratings in Table 6.14 represent reactions to actual products or reactions to food names.

Extensions of Hedonic Scaling—The FACT Scale

Workers in sensory evaluation have recognized that hedonic scaling captures only one small facet of liking behavior. Schutz (1964) suggested intermixing a liking/disliking scale with a scale that probes what a panelist would do. Table 6.15 shows the FACT scale, which lists certain types of behaviors a panelist would exhibit based upon the attitude to the food, such as eat it as often as I could, etc. To date, little information has appeared on the FACT scale, such as a list of foods and their FACT values.

Time Preference Factors

We may like a food very much, rating it high either in direct taste tests or attitudinally in surveys. Yet, given the opportunity, we may select this highly acceptable food less frequently than we select a less acceptable food. In order to conceptualize these two processes, we turn to the concept of time/preference, as originally elaborated by Joseph Balintfy (Balintfy, Duffy and Sinha 1974). In its simplest form, the theory suggests that likes/dislikes do not remain fixed. Rather, if an individual consumes a food, the acceptability of that food diminishes. Subsequently, if the individual stays away from the food, acceptability rises, as Figure 6.5 shows. Thus, overall liking/disliking ratings coalesce two contributory factors: innate liking/disliking of the product, and change of food acceptability as a function of time since the last serving.

An Overview To Category Scaling of Likes/Dislikes

Category scaling represents an extremely popular way to measure the acceptance of foods. The 9 point hedonic scale predominates as the

TABLE 6.14
FOOD PREFERENCES: DEGREE OF PREFERENCE AND
DESIRED SERVING FREQUENCY[a]

Item		Preference	Frequency/Month
1	Hamburger	6.95	9.25
2	Pizza	6.82	4.64
3	Lobster Newburg	5.44	3.16
4	Ham	6.79	4.05
5	Chicken	7.26	6.40
6	Pot roast	6.79	3.85
7	French fried potatoes	7.28	10.36
8	Mashed potatoes	6.75	8.54
9	Boston baked beans	5.52	3.75
10	Rice	5.46	4.19
11	Fritters	5.25	2.06
12	Sweet potatoes	6.90	7.99
13	Creamed corn	6.13	6.62
14	Carrots	5.40	4.51
15	Brussels sprouts	3.96	1.51
16	Broccoli	4.51	2.22
17	Peas	5.57	3.91
18	Yellow squash	3.88	1.34
19	Banana salad	5.04	2.70
20	Mixed fruit salad	5.70	4.86
21	Waldorf salad	4.08	1.86
22	Cole slaw	5.25	4.89
23	Lettuce tomato salad	6.28	1.74
24	Tossed green salad	6.56	11.14
25	Sugar cookie	5.24	4.75
26	Chocolate pudding	6.25	5.15
27	Devils food cake	6.29	4.14
28	Cherry pie	6.26	5.50
29	Ice Cream	7.32	9.60
30	Strawberry gelatin	5.64	3.46
31	White bread	7.18	16.87
32	Milk	8.03	22.00

Peryam & Pilgrim (1957)

[a]Preference Scale = 9 Point Hedonic Scale (Peryam & Pilgrim, 1957). Scale: 9, like extremely; 8, like very much; 7, like moderately; 6, like slightly; 5, neither like nor dislike; 4, dislike slightly; 3, dislike moderately; 2, dislike very much; 1, dislike extremely

category scale of choice, although other scales also have their place. We should expect to see even wider use of category scaling, as manufacturers become increasingly interested in measuring consumer likes/dislikes. Researchers have answered or generally ignored many

TABLE 6.15
FACT (FOOD ACTION) SCALE

Eat Every Opportunity
Eat Very Often
Frequently Eat
Eat Now and Then
Eat if Available
Don't Like — Eat on Occasion
Hardly Ever Eat
Eat if no Other Choice
Eat if Forced

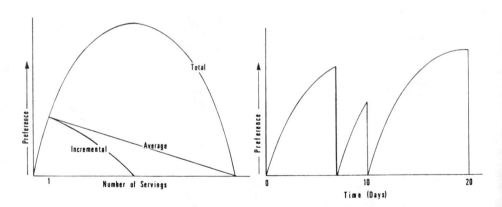

FIG. 6.5 (A) RELATIONSHIP BETWEEN SERVING FREQUENCY, TOTAL PREFERENCE,
AVERAGE PREFERENCE, AND INCREMENTAL PREFERENCE
6.5 (B) PREFERENCE FOR MEAT LOAF SERVED ON DAYS 1, 7, 10, AND 20 OF A
FEEDING SCHEDULE
Source: Balintfy, Sinha, Moskowitz and Rogozenski (1975)

of the scale issues of category measurement. The 1980's may see more investigation of scale properties and validation of the scale. We should also expect the development of models which relate product acceptance data on the scale to predictions of choice behavior in the marketplace.

RATIO SCALING OF LIKES/DISLIKES

One can use magnitude estimation scaling (ratio scaling) to measure likes/dislikes, in the same way that product testers use the hedonic scale or other category scales. Ratio scaling provides another scaling procedure for acceptance measurement. It grew out of psychophysical measurement of hedonics, rather than out of applications in food science. Magnitude estimation provides even more flexibility and utility in hedonic evaluation. It often requires considerably fewer panelists to achieve its goal than do other scaling procedures (Moskowitz 1981). Thus magnitude estimation may have utilitarian benefits as well.

Historical Background—
Sugar Sweetness and Pleasantness

In the early 1970s magnitude estimation scaling began its penetration into the psychophysics of taste and smell. Researchers in the late 1960s had used magnitude estimation and its variants primarily to evaluate sensory intensity. In Stockholm, Ekman and Akesson (1964) demonstrated that panelists could use magnitude estimation scaling to scale both taste intensity and taste acceptability. These early psychophysical studies, like their counterparts in the U.S., sought to uncover the rules governing sensory and hedonic responses. Ekman and Akesson used magnitude estimation to develop and compare functions relating liking versus sweetness versus sugar concentration. Except for the fact that panelists scaled liking as well as sweetness (and saltiness of NaCl), the Ekman/Akesson study paralleled the many scaling studies going on in other psychophysics laboratories.

Ekman and Akesson instructed panelists to assign ratings to match perceived sweetness. In another session they instructed panelists to assign ratings to match degree of liking. Zero, in the second session (liking scaling) meant no liking at all. Psychophysical scaling, at that time new to hedonics, did not use bipolar scale. The Ekman and Akesson study used a unipolar scale of liking.

Figure 6.6 shows the rating of liking versus concentration of sugar or salt. Panelists could and did discriminate between sensory impression and the liking of that sensory impression. Sensory ratings for taste intensity grew according to a power function of physical concentration. As physical concentration increased, perceived taste intensity also increased. Not so for liking. Panelists differed among themselves. Some panelists felt that the sugar stimuli tasted increasingly pleasant at higher concentrations. Other panelists felt that sugar sweetness

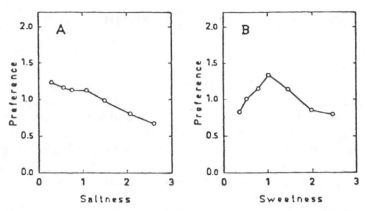

FIG. 6.6 GROUP DATA SUMMARIZING RESULTS CONCERNING PREFERENCE

Diagram A represents the average saltiness preference relation, and Diagram B the average
sweetness preference relation.

Ekman and Akesson (1965)

tasted increasingly unpleasant at higher concentrations; whereas a
third group felt that sugar pleasantness seemed to peak in the mid-
range of concentration.

Moskowitz (1971) repeated the Ekman and Akesson study with
sugar solutions, using unipolar magnitude estimation scaling (0 = no
liking at all). The results from that study confirmed that for overall
liking of sweetness for sugar solutions, liking described an inverted
U-shaped curve with an optimal or bliss point in the middle level at an
approximately fixed sweetness level, corresponding to the sweetness
of 1.0 M glucose (18% w/v).

Why Magnitude Estimation for Hedonics?

If magnitude estimation represents merely another scaling tool in
the product tester's repertoire, then why use it? Does magnitude estimation scaling provide additional information which other scaling
methods cannot provide, and does that information make its use key to
correctly answer certain questions?

At least three reasons address the utility of magnitude estimation
scaling to measure likes and dislikes.

(1) With magnitude estimation, the product tester will more likely
pick up product differences which other measurement techniques
miss. For example, in a study on different types of food products using
unipolar magnitude estimation (0 = no liking or intense disliking),
panelists in several instances showed more discrimination between
products than in a parallel study using the more traditional 9 point

hedonic scale (Moskowitz and Sidel 1971). If one scale picks up more differences than another, we can assume that the more sensitive scale provides a better measuring tool. In her Ph.D. thesis on sensory analysis, Mina McDaniel at the University of Massachusetts showed that magnitude estimation could and did discern more differences among products in the evaluation of mixed alcoholic drinks (McDaniel and Sawyer 1981).

(2) The more sensitive magnitude estimation scale also provides the product tester with enhanced discrimination among product ratings assigned by panelists from different markets, who show different brand usages, etc. Since the product tester or marketing researcher often divides the total panel into subgroups, in order to compare their reactions, the magnitude estimation scale will show more stable data than will a fixed point category scale for the same panel size. Thus, as a first benefit, magnitude estimation of likes and dislikes provides a more sensitive scaling procedure—it finds differences where they exist. However, the small panel size needed for sensitive discrimination does not absolve the product tester from developing a panel which represents the target consumer population.

(3) Magnitude estimation allows the investigator to develop equations which show how liking varies with physical ingredient levels or with sensory levels. Furthermore, with magnitude estimation scaling one can determine exactly at what combination of ingredients acceptability reaches its highest achievable level. Additionally, as the product developer changes ingredient levels in a specific way away from the optimal combination, the magnitude estimation scale allows the analyst to quantify the proportional or ratio loss in product acceptance.

The two benefits, (a) enhanced sensitivity to differences and (b) utilization in developing hedonic curves, make magnitude estimation a very utilitarian tool for the measurement of both perceptions and acceptance.

A Short History of Magnitude Estimation in Hedonics

As noted above, magnitude estimation received its first major use in hedonic testing with the model, laboratory-type solutions of water and either sucrose or sodium chloride. Much of the subsequent work used magnitude estimation to develop functions or curves relating hedonic reactions to graded levels of physical stimuli.

Taste. Moskowitz (1971) studied how hedonics of sweetness change with sugar concentration, and found panelists able to assign magnitude estimates in a reliable fashion to both sweetness and pleasantness. These curves differed from each other. In subsequent studies, the originally unipolar hedonic scale became bipolar, in recognition of the bipolar nature of liking/disliking. In a later study on the sweetness and liking/disliking of sugars and mixtures of artificial sweeteners, Moskowitz and Klarman (1975a, 1975b) used a bipolar magnitude estimation scale. Panelists assigned positive ratings to show degrees of liking, and negative ratings to show degrees of disliking. Zero reflected neutrality—neither like nor dislike. The bipolar magnitude estimates showed the same bliss point, at 1.0 M glucose, which one obtains using a unipolar scale. Thus, we can feel sure that panelists who use a bipolar scale will generate similar data to that obtained with a unipolar scale. Both yield the same conclusion, but with somewhat different numbers to back it up.

In parallel work on sugar sweetness in different foods, Moskowitz, Kluter, Westerling and Jacobs (1974) instructed panelists to rate their liking/disliking of sugar water, cherry flavored KoolAid, vanilla pudding and cake, each sweetened to different degrees with varying amounts of sucrose. Half the panel used magnitude estimation scaling, and the other half used the 9 point hedonic scale. Both scales generate similar appearing functions (inverted U's) relating sugar level in foods to the degree of product acceptance.

Scientists working with magnitude estimation in taste have paid special attention to establishing the validity and reliability of the magnitude estimation method for product testing. The foregoing study of the three foods showed that magnitude estimation scaling could reliably generate the inverted U-shaped function. More importantly, it showed more significant differences among products at adjacent sugar levels then did the category scale ratings (Moskowitz 1981). This sensitivity allows the product tester greater confidence that he or she will uncover existing differences among products, even with reduced panel size.

Smell. Magnitude estimation estimates of odor likes and dislikes go back to the middle 1960s. At Brown University Trygg Engen and Donald McBurney (1964) reported perhaps the first study using the magnitude estimation for odor hedonics. They instructed panelists to rate odor intensity and odor liking on a unipolar scale for a wide variety of odorants. The odorants appeared only at one concentration. Engen and McBurney reported that magnitude estimation of perceived odor intensity varied over a 2:1 range, but that odor liking estimates varied by almost 125:1.

Later studies on odor hedonics (Moskowitz 1977a, 1977b) concerned odor hedonics for a number of odors and flavors. In Sweden, at the University of Stockholm, the Berglunds evaluated the intensity and noxiousness of malodors generated by burning various refuse mixtures. In Sweden this procedure of scaling odor noxiousness by magnitude estimation became an accepted method for the law. It provided the foundation for ordinances regarding air pollution (Berglund 1974).

Finally, in recent work on odors and their mixtures, Moskowitz (1979) evaluated the pleasantness/unpleasantness of simple odors (e.g., the minty smell of pulegone) and their binary mixtures. By regression analysis (curve fitting), one could relate the overall odor liking to odorant concentration by a non-linear function. The function appeared as an inverted U. We will deal with the issues of predicting and optimizing acceptance ratings in Chapter 7 on optimization.

Texture. Researchers in the food industry have used the magnitude estimation procedure to evaluate the acceptability of breads, comprising various amounts of wheat/rye blends and sucrose. These studies (Moskowitz *et al.* 1979a,b) reveal that both experts and consumers can use magnitude estimation scaling equally well to describe perceptions and scale acceptance. Magnitude estimation enhanced the sensitivity of measurement. However, the product tester should bear in mind that magnitude estimation talks only to the issue of scaling method. It does not, nor can it ever, substitute for the specific type of panelist one needs in the study.

Using Magnitude Estimation in Applied Sensory Analysis

In order to use magnitude estimation for product testing, the researcher must apply principles that scientists have found to govern hedonic scale measurement. Specifically, (1) hedonics lie on a bipolar scale. An intermediate neutral point separates the region of liking from the region of disliking. Without a bipolar magnitude estimation scale, the product tester cannot truly achieve the necessary discrimination and hedonic classification. (2) The panelist who uses magnitude estimation uses numbers with which he or she feels most comfortable. At the same time each person's scale differs from that of the others. The high variability generated from panelists' scales combines with the typically high variability resulting from individual differences in hedonics. The researcher must use a normalization procedure to coalesce the ratings from the different panelists, in order to partial out some of the variabilities.

The development of magnitude estimation as a commercial tool for product and concept evaluation began in the middle 1970s. Moskowitz

(1977c) developed a calibration procedure for magnitude estimation which combined the bipolar scale and a normalization method into a single, integrated scaling approach. The technique follows this sequence. (1) The panelist learns how to rate acceptance by scaling word concepts using magnitude estimation scaling. Table 6.16 shows instructions and Table 6.17 shows the words. (2) The panelist evaluates one or several test stimuli using a two phase evaluation. The first phase requires the panelist to categorize the feeling as either liking or disliking, with 0 representing neutral. The second phase requires the panelist to scale the degree of liking/disliking, starting from 0 (neutral) to low numbers (little feeling, e.g., either little liking or little disliking) or high numbers (intense liking or disliking). (3) The panelist calibrates his or her ratings, by assigning numbers to reflect degree of feeling (e.g., like extremely, like very much, etc.). See Table 6.18. (4) The product tester calibrates or indexes the ratings.

A Word About Data Calibration

The calibration method reduces the variability of the ratings by means of a straightforward indexing procedure. One can use other calibration methods as well, such as dividing all of the liking ratings by the value of 'like extremely' on the calibration scale, or dividing all of the liking ratings by the value of 'like moderately.' The first method, division by 'like extremely', compresses the entire range of a panelist's ratings into preset scale limits. After multiplying the ratio (old rating/like extremely) × 100, we will obtain a 0-100 point scale for liking, and a similar scale for disliking. We avoid this calibration procedure because it depends too much on the panelist's own estimate of the top point on his or her scale. However, if the researcher feels that he or she can obtain stable estimates of 'like extremely', then that method of calibration will do just as well. Similarly for dividing liking ratings by 'like moderately', the intermediate point on the scale will be shown. Again, this normalization depends critically upon a stable divisor. In Table 6.18 the reader should note that the calibration derives from an average of 8 scale points, rather than from one scale point. No matter how off scale a panelist goes on a single calibration point, the other remaining 7 points maintain the robustness of the calibration.

We will illustrate this technique with a case history of cookies of different flavors. For now, the reader should bear in mind that anything which one can do with a category scale, and its fixed limits and other biases, one can also accomplish with magnitude estimation.

TABLE 6.16
EXAMPLE OF INSTRUCTION IN MAGNITUDE ESTIMATION
LIKES AND DISLIKES

Name: _____ I.D. # _____ Day: _____ Replicate: _____

TRAINING SECTION

As an exercise, we would like you to express your liking or disliking of different words. A list of words appears below. Using a scale of your own design, show how you feel about each word.

You will use numbers to show how you feel about each word. If you like a word, write an (L) next to it or a (D) next to it if you dislike it. Then indicate just how much you either like or dislike the word by also writing in a number. A large (L) number means you like it a lot, while a large (D) number means you dislike it a lot. A small (L) number means you like it a little, while a small (D) number means you dislike it a little.

Let's begin. Give the first word an L or a D to show if you like it (L) or dislike it (D). If you like it a lot, give it a large L number. If you dislike it a lot, give it a large D number.

EXAMPLE: Say you give the first word an "L10" to show how you felt about it, but you like the second word twice as much. You would then give the second word an "L20". If you dislike the third word, you should give it a D and a number to show how much you dislike it. If you dislike it just a little, you might give it a "D30" but if you dislike it a lot, you might give it a "D150". Match numbers to show how you feel about the words.

Word	L/D	How Much?	Word	L/D	How Much?	Word	L/D	How Much?
Flowers		_____	Cigar		_____	Hate		_____
Mud		_____	Spaghetti		_____	Worm		_____
Perfume		_____	Rattlesnake		_____	Kiss		_____
Murder		_____	Love		_____	Puppy		_____
Sex		_____	Sun		_____	Pollution		_____

TABLE 6.17
MAGNITUDE ESTIMATES ASSIGNED TO WORDS

Word	Value	Word	Value
Sex	138	New York City	0
Love	126	Worm	−5
Kiss	84	Mud	−25
Money	82	Cigar	−31
Sun	73	Rattlesnake	−40
Flavors	58	Pollution	−72
Puppy	47	Hate	−81
Spaghetti	41	Murder	−140
Perfume	37		

TABLE 6.18
EXAMPLE OF CALIBRATION — LIKING/DISLIKING

	Pre-Calibration	After Calibration*
Product A	+60	42.1
Product B	−120	−84.2
Like Extremely =	+280	196.5
Like Very Much =	+180	126.3
Like Moderately =	+90	63.2
Like Slightly =	+40	28.1
Neither Like Nor Dislike =	0	0
Dislike Slightly =	−60	−42.1
Dislike Moderately =	−120	−84.2
Dislike Very Much =	−170	−119.3
Dislike Extremely =	−200	−140.3

$$*\text{Calibration} = \frac{\text{Old Rating}}{\text{Index Number}} \times 100$$

$$\text{Index Number} = \frac{\begin{array}{c}(\text{Like Extremely} + \text{Like Very Much} + \text{Like Moderately} + \text{Like Slightly}) \\ + (\text{Absolute Values of Dislike Slightly} + \text{Dislike Moderately} + \text{Dislike} \\ \text{Very Much and Dislike Extremely})\end{array}}{8}$$

Index Number = 142.5

DOING THE MAGNITUDE ESTIMATION STUDY — A CASE HISTORY

Background

The Jacobs Cookie Company (JCC) has manufactured and marketed cookies for the past 42 years. Beginning with simple chocolate chip cookies, JCC expanded its product line to include many different cookie variations. Furthermore, since 1968 JCC has competed successfully in the food service industry, marketing three types of cookies, chocolate chip, vanilla creme and peanut butter. These three cookies now contribute 71% to the total gross sales of JCC.

During the past six years president Barry Jacobs and the management at JCC have watched the food service industry grow rapidly. Demand for JCC's chocolate chip, vanilla creme and peanut butter cookies expanded 257% over a six year period, with a commensurate increase in profits. However, competition set in. In the past year, two competitors have begun to take away some of JCC's cookie business by selling their cookies at cheaper prices, averaging 17-24% lower. Marketers at JCC decided that they should augment their current line of cookie offerings to expand the market rather than compete on price alone. They have developed five new types of cookies, varying in size, shape, type of flavor, presence/absence of a creme filling, etc.

In a meeting with R&D and sensory analysis, the vice president of marketing for the food service division of JCC suggested that, before going out with new cookie offerings for the trade, JCC should pare down the number of possible alternatives to at most two, and to concentrate on those. The product tester concurred, and proposed a magnitude estimation scaling evaluation of consumer reactions to the 8 different cookies: 3 current and 5 proposed.

Product Selection

For the cookie project, the product tester suggested testing all of the 5 alternatives. As discussed before, the researcher should also have benchmarks against which to evaluate the current performance of the six competitors. Quite often the product tester can purchase existing competitors' products off the shelf and test those. However, in food service systems, one cannot easily purchase the large boxes of cookies manufactured by competitors. In lieu of this competitive testing, JCC decided to test its own 3 current products as typifying the frame of products currently in use. Their acceptance ratings represent target product acceptance values.

Quite often products stale or lose their flavor as they remain in storage. In order to assure herself of the best test possible, with representative, fresh products, the JCC product testers used batch runs of the 8 cookies stored for 2 weeks in a warehouse to simulate real-world use conditions. Although product developers said that they could fabricate the 8 formulations at the bench and bake them in the small ovens, management responded that a better test would entail evaluation of pilot plant runs of the 5 test variations. Bench-top prototypes may allow the product developer the opportunity to experiment with and perfect the product, since the product remains under constant scrutiny and control. On the other hand, pilot plant runs of the test products more closely typify the likely final formulations, with the ensuing lack of control and the resulting inevitable variations in ingredients. What emerges from the pilot plant run in terms of product quality more validly represents what the consumer will purchase and consume in the cafeteria.

Panel Selection

Food service comprises many different types of consumers. One has a difficult time finding the typical user of food service products. Most people fall into the category of food service customer. The JCC product tester did not want to use in-house panelists who had had extensive experience in cookie evaluation, and especially those who had intensive experience with JCC's own offerings, the vanilla creme, chocolate chip and peanut butter.

In order to expedite the study, the product tester contracted with a local field service to recruit 180 respondents for the study. These respondents reflected individuals who satisfied specific criteria:

— High Incidence Group: all panelists ate at least 4 of their meals per week away from home, in a company cafeteria or at school (2/3 of the panel).
— Low Incidence Group: panelists who purchase cookies for home use (for evaluation of other market opportunities) (1/3 of the panel).
— All panelists purchased cookies at least 2 times a week, in order to qualify. The product tester did not want to have panelists participate who do not represent the ultimate consumer.
  Panelists had to volunteer for 1½ hour product testing sessions.

The field service recruited the panelists and arranged six evaluation sessions, two on each of three evenings from 6-7:30 p.m. and from 8-9:30, to accommodate the working panelists.

Study Execution

The panelists reported to the evaluation site at the scheduled time to participate for the 90 minute product testing session. At the test site, a local church basement rented by the field service to do the study, an interviewer greeted each panelist, recorded his or her name, and waited for the full group to assemble.

In order to properly execute a magnitude estimation evaluation, the interviewer or moderator must orient the panelist by means of a short exercise. We saw one version of the orientation pertaining to intensity ratings. In this study, the moderator, or field supervisor, oriented the panelists in the evaluation of the cookies, by means of the short introductory script, similar to the script in Table 6.10, but adapted to magnitude estimation.

The script for the introduction and training followed this specific pattern: introduction to the task; orientation in magnitude estimation; directions for scaling each attribute (here panelists evaluated overall liking/disliking, as well as liking of texture and flavor); and calibration to coalesce the ratings of the panelists by eliminating much of the interpanelist variability.

Test Results

The test proceeded according to schedule. Panelists evaluated the products, and generated the ratings shown in Table 6.19 which gives the mean and the standard error of the mean.

TABLE 6.19

AVERAGE MAGNITUDE ESTIMATES ASSIGNED TO COOKIES
ON THREE ATTRIBUTES
(Overall Liking, Liking of Texture, Liking of Flavor)

Sample	Mean	Liking of Texture	Liking of Flavor
1. Vanilla Creme	74.2 (8.7)	90.6 (9.1)	105.6 (9.6)
2. Chocolate Chip	69.5 (7.6)	81.4 (8.6)	89.9 (7.8)
3. Peanut Butter	43.2 (8.1)	80.6 (7.8)	58.3 (7.4)
*4. Entry A	91.3 (5.9)	56.3 (8.2)	93.6 (9.2)
*5. Entry B	74.7 (6.4)	79.2 (7.9)	82.1 (8.1)
6. Entry C	41.4 (8.9)	61.4 (8.3)	−35.8 (8.8)
7. Entry D	2.2 (9.4)	−20.5 (6.9)	77.9 (7.7)
8. Entry E	−13.9 (7.5)	48.6 (7.3)	−60.2 (6.3)

* = Winning Entries
Second number (in parentheses) = standard error of the mean

Based upon these results, the product tester concluded that two of the new test cookies (entries A and B) performed as well or better than the current vanilla creme, peanut butter and/or chocolate chip cookies. Statistical analysis backed up these conclusions. Entry A (rating = 91.3 on liking) differed significantly from the current three products.

Distribution of Ratings

Quite often the product tester wishes to determine how the ratings distribute along the scale. A moderate or average value with a high standard error could represent a product which some panelists like and some panelists dislike. Or, it might reflect a product which averages around the low area of liking, with a wide distribution of ratings around it. The former situation typifies a bimodal liking distribution, with one mode at liking and another mode at disliking. The latter reflects a unimodal distribution, with a single representative average, but with an unusual scatter of ratings.

In order to plot out the distribution of ratings, let us make use of the calibration scale which we obtained. We can ask the following questions. How many individuals placed their ratings in the top part of the scale, between like extremely and like very much? How many individuals placed their ratings in the second box, between like very much and like moderately? How did panelists distribute their ratings around the rest of the scale?

Market researchers often report out hedonic data in terms of just such a distribution. In category scaling one can easily count the number of panelists assigning ratings in a specific category. For magnitude estimation ratings the product tester does the same thing, only this time using each individual's own calibration scale. By comparing each score to the panelist's own individual calibration data, the product tester can ascertain whether that score belongs in the top box, the second box, etc. By going through this exercise individual by individual, the sensory analyst, market researcher or product tester can plot the distribution of ratings, panelist by panelist and product by product. Table 6.20 shows the distribution for three cookie products. Such a distribution helps management at JCC ascertain whether their cookies run the likelihood of high acceptance by a small faction in the population, but rejection by others. This information does not come from the mean alone. It necessitates information about the underlying distribution of ratings.

Reasons For Preference of One Cookie Over Another

Recall the issue of diagnostic information which we considered with regard to the canned meats. A hedonic evaluation test with magnitude estimation clearly shows the reasons for preference. We array the products in a matrix format, as shown in Table 6.19. To make things easier, the product tester can replace numbers with words to determine whether products score high on overall acceptability and compare these to scores on specific characteristics.

As a first approximation, entries A and B score high versus the current products, because they score well on flavor acceptance. Entry D scores poorly on texture, but well on flavor. That poor texture helps

TABLE 6.20

DISTRIBUTION OF MAGNITUDE ESTIMATION RATINGS OF COOKIES INTO DIFFERENT CATEGORIES
(AS SET UP BY THE HEDONIC SCALE)

	Cookie Entry C			Cookie Entry D			Cookie Entry E		
	Total	Frequent Category Users	Infrequent Category Users	Total	Frequent Category Users	Infrequent Category Users	Total	Frequent Category Users	Infrequent Category Users
Like extremely	5	6	3	3	2	4	2	2	1
Like very much	18	21	12	12	15	8	9	10	6
Like moderately	27	29	25	18	19	16	16	15	16
Like slightly	29	25	35	26	23	32	20	20	22
Neither like nor dislike	4	2	5	4	4	3	3	0	6
Dislike slightly	6	4	7	10	7	15	14	20	12
Dislike moderately	7	8	6	11	12	9	9	8	28
Dislike very much	3	4	3	7	6	9	19	21	5
Dislike extremely	1	1	4	9	12	4	8	4	4
Percent	100	100	100	100	100	100	100	100	100
Magnitude Estimation Mean	41.4	50.3	25.7	2.2	3.8	-0.9	-13.9	-16.5	-8.4
Standard Error	4.9	6.0	7.9	6.0	7.9	8.8	6.0	7.6	9.8

to make entry D a loser. Entries C and E score moderately on texture, and entry C scores poorly on flavor whereas E scores very poorly. Together they represent run of the mill products. Such insights, as provided by the diagnostics, provide an opportunity to uncover the reasons underlying acceptance/rejection. With in-depth comments by panelists about specific characteristics of texture and flavor, the product tester can further discover the reasons underlying rejection or acceptance. Overall scores on texture, flavor and appearance acceptance provide only rough diagnostic information.

Interpretation and Utilization of the Magnitude Estimation Results

Having finished the study, and run the proper analyses on the ratings (including averaging and, when so desired, statistical tests such as analysis-of-variance to evaluate significant differences), the product tester can now use the results to answer product-related questions.

Which Products Seem Like Winners. Based on the average ratings of the eight cookies, we find that the current products score 74.2, 69.5, and 43.2. The marketer uses these numbers as benchmarks for the evaluation of the test cookies. In order to qualify as a potential winner for subsequent introduction, acceptability should equal or exceed the acceptability of the three (or at least 2 of the 3) commercial products. Cookie entries A and B fall into this category of potential winning products. The remaining cookies score too low for consideration.

What Factors Influence Acceptability. Based on our analysis of the ratings, we conclude that acceptability correlates most highly with flavor acceptance, and next with texture acceptance. Among the products which scored well, each possessed an acceptable flavor, as shown by the liking/disliking estimates assigned to flavor in Table 6.19. Texture plays a secondary role. Entry A turned out a winner, but it possessed a less acceptable texture than did the three current cookies.

Can The Marketer Predict Ratios of Choices From Relative Liking Ratings?

Marketers often want to know if the hedonic scores which products receive, on whatever scale, can predict product choice and/or volume consumption. The answer to this query remains a firm no. Other factors besides overall liking influence choice and consumption. These factors include cost of the product, distribution channels and packaging.

In terms of the cost of the product, increases in item cost decrease the likelihood of item selection. Distribution channels have importance as well. Poor distribution in the markets will show poorer consumption, because consumers do not have an opportunity to try the product. Packaging also plays a key role. Consumers often reject products which come poorly packaged. Visual appearance plays a key role in facilitating initial choice and consumption of the products.

Our product tester thus faces the problem of inability to predict purchase behavior from the liking/disliking ratings. This lack of translatability, from ratings to market share, arises because in most product evaluation tests the panelist does not experience the impact of pricing, distribution, packaging, advertising and the other factors which influence choice and repeat purchase.

ACCEPTANCE MEASUREMENT BY MAGNITUDE ESTIMATION
The Primavera Sauce Company (Revisited)

Recall that in Chapter 5 we discussed the product selection and development program of the Primavera Sauce Company. In that project, respondents evaluated both sensory characteristics and acceptance of test sauces and commercial products. We now pick up the thread of that project. Here we will consider the issues of sauce acceptance and sensory factors which correlate with acceptance. Table 6.21 shows the ratings of the attributes and acceptance (liking).

Evaluation of Overall Liking for Tomato Sauce

Table 6.21 shows the different acceptance ratings for the various tomato sauces tested in the blind study. With the magnitude estimation scaling procedure, panelists show widely different ratings for the products, based upon ratings from all 90 panelists. Product E scores a 77.5, and product A scores 16.6 for "overall liking". At the side of Table 6.21 appears a key or legend, which the reader can use to translate magnitude estimates into equivalent verbal categories.

By and large the competitive products, especially Sweet and Saucy (40.6) and Tomato Heaven (25.5) perform reasonably well in terms of acceptance, as one might expect. Test formulation G shows a rating of +38.9, whereas test formulation E shows a high rating of 77.5.

TABLE 6.21
AVERAGE MAGNITUDE ESTIMATION RATINGS FOR EIGHT SAUCE PRODUCTS
(Primavera Project)
Sensory Attributes and Acceptance (Liking)

Attribute	Self-Designed Ideal	A (Current PSC Product)	B Competitor 1 (Store Brand)	C Competitor 2 (Tomato Heaven)	D Competitor 3 (Sweet & Saucy)	E Current + Spice	F Current - Spice	G Current - Viscosity (Thickness)	H Current + Viscosity (Thickness)
1. Aroma Strength	110	93.1 (5.9)	94.6 (5.7)	80.8 (5.5)	116.8 (5.5)	94.0 (6.6)	98.4 (5.4)	102.1 (4.1)	93.6 (5.8)
2. Taste Intensity	92	55.5 (4.3)	48.2 (3.8)	53.6 (4.4)	58.3 (4.7)	48.7 (4.2)	48.0 (4.6)	59.4 (4.8)	47.0 (4.2)
3. Sweetness	58	55.7 (7.7)	41.1 (6.4)	41.7 (6.0)	51.4 (7.0)	69.7 (6.3)	62.9 (7.7)	45.0 (6.4)	56.2 (6.8)
4. Tartness	45	46.5 (7.7)	36.1 (6.0)	36.5 (5.3)	48.2 (6.8)	30.2 (4.7)	25.3 (4.9)	47.6 (7.3)	45.0 (5.9)
5. Tomato Flavor	96	54.2 (5.3)	41.8 (4.3)	55.2 (6.5)	49.4 (5.2)	68.8 (5.4)	63.8 (6.0)	52.9 (5.6)	59.8 (5.6)
6. Spiciness	68	67.0 (6.1)	61.8 (4.6)	67.9 (5.8)	78.0 (7.2)	70.2 (5.0)	56.5 (5.7)	67.3 (6.3)	67.4 (5.4)
7. Consistency	58	49.4 (5.9)	38.3 (4.8)	46.8 (5.8)	54.7 (6.7)	71.1 (6.1)	58.8 (5.3)	49.2 (6.3)	67.2 (5.9)
8. After Taste Intensity	70	65.9 (6.9)	54.5 (5.3)	62.8 (7.0)	71.1 (6.7)	76.4 (5.9)	71.8 (6.1)	76.5 (6.7)	72.1 (6.0)
9. Richness	104	78.5 (6.0)	63.3 (5.8)	74.4 (5.3)	80.8 (6.2)	83.5 (5.8)	82.0 (6.8)	74.2 (6.6)	80.6 (6.2)

Scale | 1
Extreme   164
Very much   123
Moderate   74
Slight   32
None (neutral)   0

TABLE 6.21
AVERAGE MAGNITUDE ESTIMATION RATINGS FOR EIGHT SAUCE PRODUCTS
(Primavera Project)
Sensory Attributes and Acceptance (Liking)

Attribute	Self-Designed Ideal	A (Current PSC Product)	Competitor 1 B (Store Brand)	Competitor 2 C (Tomato Heaven)	Competitor 3 D (Sweet & Saucy)	E Current + Spice	F Current − Spice	G Current − Viscosity (Thickness)	H Current + Viscosity (Thickness)	
10. Unique	60	19.1 (13.2)	13.8 (11.2)	35.6 (8.8)	17.8 (11.2)	63.0 (9.5)	25.2 (11.4)	20.1 (11.7)	35.5 (8.1)	
11. Natural	79	30.7 (13.1)	21.9 (10.5)	20.4 (10.3)	52.6 (12.8)	64.8 (9.5)	58.3 (10.4)	48.0 (11.9)	59.7 (10.0)	
12. Italian	120	16.2 (12.0)	18.8 (10.3)	24.4 (9.8)	50.9 (11.8)	57.6 (10.2)	54.5 (11.2)	48.9 (11.7)	57.8 (9.7)	
13. "Liking"	N.A.	16.6 (14.0)	19.4 (12.2)	25.5 (9.5)	40.6 (13.2)	77.5 (8.1)	47.2 (12.4)	38.9 (12.6)	43.2 (9.9)	Base = 90
Liking/Subgroup										
Primavera users	N.A.	19.0 (18.8)	20.4 (18.5)	21.9 (12.2)	50.6 (18.2)	76.2 (9.8)	41.4 (17.5)	20.3 (21.9)	55.4 (14.5)	Base = 30
Tomato Heaven users	N.A.	14.6 (26.2)	18.3 (15.8)	29.3 (14.7)	30.5 (18.8)	71.0 (13.9)	53.3 (17.3)	57.6 (11.0)	30.9 (12.9)	Base = 30
Sweet & Saucy users	N.A.	−3.6 (26.2)	7.3 (15.0)	1.4 (15.1)	42.2 (11.4)	81.4 (13.7)	25.3 (14.6)	−18.2 (14.9)	43.0 (11.3)	Base = 30

N.A. – Not asked

One can evaluate the differences in the ratings by means of statistical tests, to insure that the ratings truly reflect statistically significant differences. The analysis of variance technique will indicate whether the variation due to product ratings exceeds the variation due to random error, and if so, then by how much. The product tester, if so inclined, could then determine which pairs of sauce products differ significantly from each other by subsequent, or post-hoc, tests of difference (e.g., T Tests). We do not show these tests here, but product testers can, and often do, perform these analyses to further back up the differences. In Table 6.21 note that the products spread apart far more in acceptance ratings, compared to the size of the standard error of the mean. The spread of acceptance ratings shows the panelists find the acceptability of products substantially different from each other.

Evaluation of Purchase Intent Ratings

Purchase interest ratings, another measure of consumer intent to purchase items, often, but not always, parallel acceptability ratings. Those products which score highest on overall acceptability usually score highest on purchase interest ratings. Initially, the concurrence seems to further indicate the validity of the test procedure, which picks up similar trends using two types of scale: liking/disliking, a hedonic attribute, and purchase interest, a performance attribute. In many instances purchase interest ratings correlate so highly with overall liking as to suggest that the two attributes pick up the same overall hedonic response. From time to time, however, liking and purchase interest may correlate only modestly with each other, or even correlate negatively.

Liking/disliking scores fail to correlate highly with purchase intent scores when the product itself has a poor taste intrinsically. However, panelists purchase the product for reasons other than taste or overall acceptability. For instance, breath fresheners often have poor or highly unacceptable tastes (e.g., Listerine), but these tastes signal efficacy. The manufacturer trades off a drop in taste acceptability against the increased perception of efficacy. Purchasers of medicines might reject as ineffective those particular formulations which taste good, because the good taste will not seem efficacious at all.

The purchase interest decision depends upon a complex of sensory and other factors, only some of which stem from the panelist's own personal acceptance. Consider the issue of a beverage, such as a dry-mix, artificially flavored beverage designed for the entire family. A mother evaluating the beverage for her own personal preference might prefer a tarter, more highly flavored product. A child, on the other hand, would prefer a sweeter product. In making her purchase decision, assuming she cannot modify the product to serve two different groups, the mother integrates her own likes/dislikes along with those of her children, to develop a composite estimate. She might show the highest purchase interest rating for a product which tastes neither too tart nor too sweet. This intermediate product provides a hedonic compromise. It neither lies at the top of her hedonic scale, where she would highly accept it but the children might reject it, nor at the bottom of her hedonic scale, where she might hate it but her children might like it very much.

In evaluating the data, the product tester might wish to gain further insights by analyzing the results in subgroups. In this study, Table 6.21 shows the ratings broken out by the different users. The user groups exhibited similar sensory ratings, as one might expect. However, the user groups differed in overall acceptance (For years marketing researchers have recognized that product acceptance/rejection represents the behavior of many divergent segments of consumers who contribute their own personal likes and dislikes. Hence, it should come as no surprise that for these panelists the ratings of hedonic characteristics differ. The researcher should also keep in mind that, had the study involved panelists of different age groups, or panelists in widely different markets, with different competitive frames of reference for tomato sauce products, the data could also reflect the contributions of age, demographic variables, etc. Here, we confine our attention only to the panelists' brand preferences and usage histories.).

Communication of the Results

In the communication of these initial findings, for the heading of the product test report, the researcher might wish to summarize the results in terms of overall ranking of product acceptability (most acceptable to least acceptable); the presence of statistically significant differences in product acceptance (a short, concise statement highlighting the performance of test products versus the competitors, rather than test products versus each other); or the existence of noteworthy group differences in acceptance. [e.g., highlight the higher acceptance ratings, overall, assigned by users of Tomato Heaven (average liking = 38) and Primavera (average = 38) versus Sweet and Saucy user ratings (average = 22)]. Group differences in overall acceptance ratings, as well as in the acceptance ratings of specific attributes and products, can provide valuable marketing insights into reactions of user groups to the category.

Correlates with Liking

A correlation matrix between attributes and overall liking reveals how closely each sensory characteristic or image attribute tracks overall liking/disliking, or purchase interest. Table 6.22 shows the correlation matrix between each of the attributes, and liking ratings assigned by the different groups of consumers.

Specific facts emerging from Table 6.22 include the following. (1) The sensory attributes correlate only moderately with overall liking. Sweetness correlates slightly more with liking (R = 0.75) than does tartness (R = −0.41), and far more than does total taste intensity (R = −0.28). (2) The image attributes, natural flavor, etc., correlate more highly with overall liking (R = 0.85). (3) User groups differ in how their attribute ratings correlate with liking. For instance, perceived spiciness correlates only slightly (R = 0.17) with liking for data from the entire group. On the other hand, it correlates 0.32 for Primavera and 0.31 for Sweet and Saucy users. It correlates virtually to 0 with liking for Tomato Heaven users.

Quite often product testers use the correlations incorrectly. Researchers often fall prey to accepting the attributes which most highly correlate with liking, without realizing that quite often one cannot manipulate these attributes in a reasonable fashion by varying ingredients. The researcher can manipulate sweetness and tartness by changing ingredients, but how does one modify natural tomato flavor with these ingredients? Yet the attribute of natural tomato flavor correlates most highly with overall liking. Chapter 7 will deal with this issue of correlating sensory attributes and liking to engineer a product.

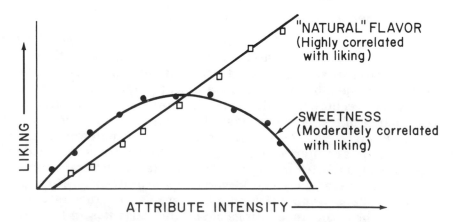

FIG. 6.7   HOW LINEAR CORRELATION FAILS TO REVEAL STRONG, BUT CURVED RELATIONSHIP BETWEEN SENSORY ATTRIBUTES AND LIKING

When using a correlation matrix for keys to product acceptability, the product tester should make sure that the attributes so selected do, in fact, represent actionable characteristics. Image and performance attributes often correlate highly with liking/disliking, because they reflect alternative ways of saying that the panelist likes or dislikes the product (e.g., natural). In contrast, the truly actionable characteristics exhibit optimal levels somewhere in the middle range, (e.g., sweet, in Figure 6.7). Consequently, if the study contains products above and below the optimum, the correlation will turn out lower, as Figure 6.7 shows.

TABLE 6.22
CORRELATION OF SAUCE ATTRIBUTES WITH LIKING RATINGS

		User Group		
	Total	Primavera User	Tomato Heaven User	Sweet and Saucy User
1. Aroma Strength	.19	.17	.10	.21
2. Taste Intensity	−.28	−.41	−.06	−.50
3. Sweetness	.75	.76	.55	.73
4. Tartness	−.41	−.29	−.44	−.37
5. Tomato Flavor	.78	.68	.71	.60
6. Spiciness	.17	.32	−.06	−.31
7. Consistency	.86	.91	.61	.82
8. Aftertaste	.74	.56	.77	.37
9. Richness	.66	.70	.47	.60
10. Uniqueness	.79	.74	.62	.73
11. Natural	.85	.83	.70	.70
12. Italian	.84	.77	.74	.63

AN OVERVIEW

This chapter has illustrated the wide range of approaches and studies used for the evaluation of stimulus and product acceptance. The reader should keep in mind that, in commerical product evaluation, proper product testing probably represents the most important type of test. With accurate measures of product acceptance, the marketer, marketing researcher and R&D product developer can learn about the product. To the marketer, high product acceptance represents one of the keys to increased market share. To the marketing researcher, high product acceptance provides clues to the needs/wants of the consumer. To the R&D product developer, high product acceptance ratings indicate which specific stimulus characteristics generate enhanced acceptance. That information provides the product developer with further direction to modify product formulations.

CHAPTER 7

PRODUCT OPTIMIZATION

INTRODUCTION

Product optimization refers to a class of statistical procedures which maximize a product's overall acceptability, or other criterion variable by one of two distinct methods:

(1) finding that combination of ingredients which generates the highest possible acceptance score, within physically achievable ingredient levels; or
(2) finding that combination of ingredients which, in concert, produces a sensory perception as close as possible to a predesignated sensory profile.

This chapter illustrates these two approaches by case histories in the development of new and improved products for the food industry.

BACKGROUND TO OPTIMIZATION

In order to optimize a product, the sensory analyst or marketing researcher must develop a quantitative, mathematical model to interrelate ingredients, varied by the product developer and sensory perceptions/acceptance ratings, which the consumer panelist scales. The mathematical model summarizes these interrelations. The model shows the expected changes in perceptions and acceptance which result from specific changes in ingredient formulations. The model summarizes the interrelations and allows the marketer to minimize his or her effort when creating new or varied products. In a sense, the mathematical model substitutes for many hundreds or thousands of empirical product formulations. By developing and testing just a small number of formulations, strategically selected by statistical means, the product tester can construct the model to replace much of the trial and error work which ordinarily ensues.

Product optimization traces its roots back to the early 1950s and even before. Statisticians used the statistical procedures of curve fitting to develop equations which summarize how two or more variables interrelate. For example, we dealt previously with the relation between magnitude estimates (scalar ratings) of sweetness and sugar concentration. This relation took the form of a power function: Sweetness = k(Concentration)^n.

The calculations used to estimate the parameters of that equation, intercept k and exponent n, belong to the domain of statistical analysis known as *least-squares regression*.

Statisticians who develop models for product optimization often use simple linear models, of the form:

$$S = k_0 + k_1(X) \tag{1}$$

(S = sensory response; X = physically measured ingredient level; k_1 = coefficient, k_0 = intercept = value assumed by S when $X = 0$). A curve or polynomial model often fits the data better when the panelists evaluate overall product liking/disliking. As we saw before, liking of products increased with physical ingredient level, maximizes at the middle formulation level, and then diminishes with further increases in formula level. We capture this parabolic relation in equation 2:

$$S = k_0 + k_1(X) + k_2(X)^2 \tag{2}$$

Statisticians can estimate the values of parameters k_0, k_1 and k_2 which, in concert, produce a curve that best describes the empirical data obtained from consumer panelists.

These curve fitting techniques not only describe the data, but provide other benefits as well. For example, with the curve fitted to the data, the researcher can calculate the estimated value of S for specific, non-tested values of X. This calculation may require interpolation where the value of X lies between tested X values used to develop the model. Or, the problem may require extrapolation where the value of X lies outside the limits used to develop the model. In either case (but with more trepidation in the case of extrapolation), the product tester can use the quantitative model to estimate the likely value of S for a specified value of X.

Statisticians call this approach of curve fitting the *response-surface method*, RSM. The basis of the response surface method lies in the fact that the analyst can develop an ad hoc or simple descriptive equation which best fits the empirical data points. The equation becomes a de facto model of the interrelations between ingredients and perceptions. The response surface refers to the equation, or to the geometrical surface which the equation describes. Of course, this response surface represents an idealized, smoothed version of the empirical data. Where the empirical data presents jagged points on the surface, the response surface predicts the likely sensory ratings at those points by using the equation. The analyst inserts the value of X, or of several variables (e.g., X,Y,Z), into the proper equations in order to compute the dependent variable, S.

Nature does not always work with one variable at a time. Sometimes in the case of two variables, the consumer response may result from a simple, but differentially weighted, sum of the two variables X and Y:

$$S = k_0 + k_1 X + k_2 Y \tag{3}$$

In equation 3, the panelists ratings for sensory intensity S (e.g., sweetness) behave according to a weighted sum of the two ingredients (X, e.g., sugar) and Y (e.g., acid level). The coefficients k_0, k_1 and k_2 may assume positive or negative values, depending upon how S changes when X or Y changes. For example, if S stands for sweetness ratings, X represents sugar concentration and Y represents acid concentration, then we expect the coefficient k_1 for sugar to assume a positive value. Perceived sweetness should increase with increasing levels of sugar. We know that increasing the acid level diminishes sweetness if we hold sugar constant. Therefore, k_2 should assume a negative value. Statistical curve fitting procedures objectively assign the coefficients and the intercept k_0 in accordance with the best fit to the data. The researcher can, however, predict the likely sign of the coefficient, as well as obtain an idea of the magnitude of the coefficient.

The linear equation typifies the very simplest case. Let us assume, for the time being, that the sensory variable S behaves independently with respect to X, sugar level, and Y, acid level. No interaction occurs among the independent variables, sugar and acid. The sugar level S acts independently of the actual level of acid. Acid levels simply increase or decrease the sweetness rating by a constant amount, independent of the sugar present.

The linear equation (3) represents a very typical equation which describes how sensory perceptions vary with ingredient levels. We saw before that power functions often describe sensory intensity versus physical concentration. By and large, so do linear equations, albeit not quite as well. For the purposes of optimization, we will confine our attention to the simplest linear and non-linear quadratic equations, rather than the power equation, because these simpler equations allow us to handle zeros and negative numbers, whereas the power equation does not.

Interactions Among Variables

For some sensory attributes, and for many hedonic response variables resulting from interactions of two or more ingredients, we obtain curves, not straight lines or planes. If we ask the panelists to rate how much they like the taste of the sugar + acid mixture, we find that as sugar level increases (keeping acid level constant), liking increases but only up to a certain point, the optimum or bliss point. Once we have exceeded that bliss point, liking diminishes with increasing levels of sugar. As the acid level increases (holding sugar constant), liking increases but only up to a certain point, the bliss point. After that, further increases in acid only diminish the liking score. The acid bliss point depends upon the level of sugar, and vice versa. With low acid levels, we tolerate low sugar levels. We will see a low bliss point for sugar in the presence of low acid levels. With high acid levels we find a high level of sugar corresponding to the bliss point. These two ingredients, sugar and acid, interact with each other. Changes in liking vary with changes in the sugar level, the acid level and with a new factor, their interaction.

This example of the interaction of sugar + acid typifies the real world of food products. It occurs for the hedonics of coffee versus sugar level and milk level. To coffee drinkers who prefer regular coffee (milk + sugar), the beverage reaches its bliss point somewhere in the middle concentration range of sugar and milk levels—neither the highest nor the lowest level. Furthermore, the presence of milk affects the bliss point for sugar and vice versa. For a given level of milk in coffee, the bliss point for sugar will differ as compared to the bliss point for sugar alone in black coffee.

In order to represent this relatively complicated state of affairs, statisticians have recommended a simple polynomial, or parabolic, equation, which appears as follows:

$$S = k_0 + k_1X + k_2X^2 + k_3Y + k_4Y^2 + k_5XY \qquad (4)$$

This equation comprises the following portions. (1) It has an intercept, k_0. When $X = 0$ and $Y = 0$, we project the ratings to assume a specific value of k_0. Rarely, if ever, do we test at $X = 0$ and $Y = 0$. Still, we require an additive constant for improved fit of the model to the data by means of the quadratic equation. (2) It has a linear portion, k_1X and k_3Y, which tells us how liking varies with changes in X and Y. (3) It contains a quadratic portion of X and Y, k_2X^2, k_4Y^2, which allows liking to increase with physical level, maximize at some intermediate point, and then drop down again. Without the quadratic portion of the equation, liking would maximize either at the highest or lowest allowable value of X and Y. (4) It has an interaction term, k_5XY, which we use to statistically represent how the consumer panel rating, S, depends upon X and Y, and their interaction together.

Equation 4 seems complicated, but it actually represents the simplest equation which accomplishes these objectives. (1) It represents how the sensory or liking variable, S, varies with X and Y. (2) It allows liking or sensory intensity to maximize at an intermediate level (an especially valuable property to represent overall product acceptability, which we know maximizes at a middle range). (3) It allows for interactions which we know to occur in acceptance of products.

Using the Equation

We can use the nonlinear or linear equation to predict the following: the sensory rating S for a given combination of X and Y values (Merely generalize the equation, as Table 7.1 shows, for a three variable case where the sensory variable S depends upon levels of X, Y and Z.)

TABLE 7.1
GENERALIZED NONLINEAR (QUADRATIC) POLYNOMIAL EQUATION
WHICH RELATES LIKING TO INGREDIENT LEVEL
(3 Ingredients X, Y and Z)

Liking $= K_0 + k_1 X + k_2 Y + k_3 Z$	Linear
$+ k_4 X^2 + k_5 Y^2 + k_6 Z^2$	Quadratic
$+ k_7 XY + k_8 YZ + k_9 XZ$	Cross Terms

A CASE HISTORY USING OPTIMIZATION

The Gonzales Milling Company (GMC) has, for the past sixty years, pioneered in the processing and marketing of bread products in the southwest. Starting from a $3500 investment in 1924, GMC has grown to a 6.8 million dollar company, by the purchase of facilities to process wheat and rye flour.

Recently, Fred Gonzales, the forward looking president of GMC, commissioned an evaluation of the market for rye bread. He found that consumers repeatedly expressed a desire for a richer tasting bread product. In order to satisfy these unfulfilled consumer desires, Gonzales hired a marketing research company in the southwest to do an attitude and usage study on consumers' reactions to rye and whole wheat breads. The results showed that many consumers felt the bread market lacked a rich flavored, highly textured rye bread, which they would willingly purchase.

In preliminary meetings with the R&D and product testing groups, Gonzales suggested that the bakery group at GMC consider producing a number of rye bread formulations to test with consumers. Gonzales could then compare the performance of these test formulations that would represent rather different types of rye bread (see Table 7.2). Formulation I seemed to promise the most acceptable product, in a blind evaluation versus the competition. Formulation I comprised an unusual rye flour which provides an excellent texture and flavor.

TABLE 7.2
RESULTS OF BLIND TASTE EVALUATION OF 6 TEST FORMULATIONS
OF RYE BREAD AND 3 COMMERCIAL PRODUCTS
(Magnitude Estimation)

Commercial	Purchase Intent Scale*	Overall Liking	Flavor Liking	Texture Liking
A	52	24	60	43
B	74	84	71	59
C	39	52	38	64
Test				
E	44	51	61	73
F	32	46	58	34
G	26	29	36	10
H	74	88	81	63
I	86	103	76	123
J	60	70	93	42

*Unipolar scale: 0 = definitely not purchase

Based upon the specific choice of the rye flour in formulation I, marketing management at GMC decided to go ahead and optimize the bread formulation, in order to achieve the highest level of consumer acceptability within predesignated cost constraints.

Initial Testing—Optimization Approach

Based upon the initial work reported out by the product testing group at GMC, marketing and R&D decided to test a trial set of alternative product variations, rather than settling for the evaluation of one proto-type. They would test among a group of panelists, and then reformu-late and optimize that best scoring prototype to correct any problems. Table 7.3 shows the logic of evaluating a variety of alternative formulations all at once in an optimization framework, rather than prolonging the testing time frame.

In order to develop the appropriate set of products, R&D and marketing met together to determine the target population, the type of product, the cost constraints and the time-frame for the project.

TABLE 7.3

RATIONALE FOR TESTING SEVERAL PRODUCTS RATHER THAN ONE PRODUCT

Traditional "Inefficient" Method	Current Multi-Product Approach
1. Develop one prototype which seems viable	1. Develop many prototypes
2. Test vs. one or two major competitors	2. Test all prototypes and most of competitive category
3. Feedback	3. Develop model interrelating ingredients, perceptions, cost acceptance
4. Reformulate	
	4. Optimize
Recycle steps 1-4 Fix one or a few physical characteristics at a time (3-6 cycles) = 9-18 months	5. Plot out optimal formulation *and* cost reductions (1-2 cycles, 3 months)
5. Retest 1 year later for cost reductions (2 cycles)	

Product Recipe Development

Optimization intimately involves the testing of many alternatives to develop a mathematical model. The product developer cannot test just any random set of alternatives and expect to optimize the bread. More than likely, the random set of product variations will not statistically represent the entire population of potential rye breads. Rather, through the technique of experimental design the product developer can formulate a set of alternative formulations which, in fact, do span or cover the range of test products in an efficient manner.

Many different formulations procedures and experimental designs will cover the range of product formulations. These include both full factorial and fractional factorial designs. In full factorial design the researcher tests a full set of combinations which the product developer formulates. For 3 levels of rye and 4 levels of sugar, the full factorial design calls for $3 \times 4 = 12$ products. In fractional factorial design the product tester tests a partial set of the 12 combinations. Fractional factorial designs leave out some of the alternatives, in an effort to economize. They eliminate some, but not the most critical, information about the product, but also save time and money. The product developer and the product tester need not formulate all of the possible combinations in order to develop a representative array of products.

Experimental Designs

The product tester and product developer had various experimental designs from which to choose, shown in Table 7.4. If they wished, for the two factor (two ingredient) rye bread problem, they could avail themselves of the full factorial design or a fractional factorial, response surface (central composite) design. For this particular project, the researchers used the full factorial experimental design. Their informal product development research had shown them the desirability of testing 4 levels of rye bread and 3 levels of sucrose. In this initial optimization, therefore, they decided to use all 12 combinations of sugar and rye as test formulations, in order to insure the best results.

TABLE 7.4
COMPARISON OF TWO EXPERIMENTAL DESIGNS
(Full Factorial versus Central Composite Fractional Factorial)

(A) Full Factorial

		Sugar		
		A	B	C
Rye Flour	A	1	2	3
	B	4	5	6
	C	7	8	9
	D	10	11	12

(B) Central Composite

	Sugar	Rye	
1	High	High	$+\alpha = $ High $+ (2^{n/4})$(High $-$ Medium)
2	High	Low	$=$ High $+ (1.4)$(High $-$ Medium)
3	Low	High	
4	Low	Low	$-\alpha = $ Low $- (2^{n/4})$(Medium $-$ Low)
5	$+\alpha$	Medium	$=$ Low $- 1.4$(Medium $-$ Low)
6	$-\alpha$	Medium	
7	Medium	$+\alpha$	$N = $ Number of Ingredients $= 2$
8	Medium	$-\alpha$	
9	Medium	Medium	

Study Execution

The study aimed to optimize the product among consumers of rye bread. In light of the early staging of this study in the marketing sequence, with many variables open to evaluation, Fred Gonzales suggested spending an additional, relatively small amount of money on a more intensive evaluation of the leading competitor rye breads currently in the market, in order to measure the sensory properties of the competitive frame. [Recall Table 7.2 which shows the sensory profiles and acceptance ratings, for these competitor rye bread products]. The panelists evaluated the bread blind, to eliminate effects due to branding and familiarity with the products, and at a relatively constant state of freshness (2 days at most since baking).

A competitive product profile as the initial portion of a product optimization study provides a valuable framework for the product tester and marketer. It serves no good to find out that the optimal product scores an 87 on the scale, when the competitive products score in the 100-120 range. On the other hand, an average score of 80, with products in the competitive frame scoring around 50-60 represents a substantial breakthrough in terms of product improvement.

Product Optimization Phase. The panel of 35 consumers convened for a 3-hour test session and followed this sequence. (1) They learned magnitude estimation scaling, by means of the orientation procedure outlined in Chapters 5 and 6. This orientation insured quality control of panelist scaling. After having scaled various shapes as to perceived area and words as to degree of liking/disliking, panelists understood the concept of magnitude estimation scaling. (2) A moderator instructed the panelists regarding which specific characteristics to evaluate. These characteristics included simple sensory characteristics pertaining to flavor and texture impressions, as well as acceptance ratings on overall liking/disliking and purchase interest. (3) The panelists rated the products, one at a time (monadically), scaling each product on a different characteristics. (4) Panelists then calibrated their ratings on three separate scales. These comprised intensity of flavor and texture attributes, purchase interest, and overall liking/disliking.

Table 7.5 shows the questionnaire used in the project. Note that the questionnaire comprises two sections, one pertaining to data and the other pertaining to calibration. In magnitude estimation studies, the calibration phase follows the product ratings. Parenthetically, when researchers try to have panelists calibrate their scales prior to evaluating products, they bias the panelists who end up using the calibration values as their limited category scale.

Some Observations on the Test Execution

Panelists sometimes felt uncomfortable when asked to use an open ended scale. Nonetheless, after having evaluated the first bread sample or, at most, the first two bread samples, panelists began to enjoy the test process. By assigning to the products a profile of ratings, the panelists felt that they could communicate to the manufacturer their impressions and their likes and dislikes.

In an analysis of the time required to implement this portion of the study, the field service reported these elapsed times: orientation in scaling—20 minutes; explanation of the attributes—15 minutes; "walking through" the first product—12 minutes. The interviewer reiterated the instructions to the panelists, attribute by attibute, in order to insure panelist comprehension. Although in theory one can do without this phase by having panelists immediately launch into product evaluation on their own, from several years of experience it appears that such step-by-step introductions enhance the quality of the data. Panelists feel free to ask questions pertaining to how to evaluate the bread, to clarify what specific attributes mean, and to obtain assurance that their data means something. Continued evaluation of the remaining 11 products—approximately 4 minutes/product; and calibration—20 minutes.

As panelists obtained increasing experience with the product, and as they developed more confidence in themselves and their rating abilities, a shift occurred in the rhythm of the evaluation. What started out as a group of panelists unable to evaluate the product became, in effect, a data generating system providing data of high quality with low probability of bias, since the interviewer and the panelist did not talk to each other about the panelists' perceptions.

Each panelist evaluated the products in a uniquely different order, starting at a different product and proceeding at his or her own pace. In order to maintain a coherent sequence of evaluations, panelists stopped after completing their ratings of the first 4 products. After all panelists had completed these first 4 evaluations, they waited 5 minutes and proceeded, again at their own pace, to evaluate 4 more samples. They rested again and then rated the remaining 4 bread samples. Afterwards, panelists waited and an interviewer instructed them how to calibrate their ratings. About 3 minutes elapsed between samples.

During the entire time, interviewers in the test facility walked among the panelists, checking the data, to insure that panelists properly carried out the instructions. From time to time an interviewer would ask a panelist to explain an answer (e.g., if a panelist rated bread A as 40 on density, and bread B as 10, the interviewer would ask

TABLE 7.5

BALLOT OR QUESTIONNAIRE FORM USED IN OPTIMIZATION

Ballot—Rye Bread Evaluation

Name: _____

I.D. # _____

Attributes	Products													
	22	19	34	17	16	18	42	79	84	76	25	37	Ideal Bread
I. Surface													
1. Ease of particle removal													
2. Roughness													
II. First Bite													
1. Firmness													
2. Cohesiveness													
3. Denseness													
III. During Chewing													
1. Moistness													
2. Chewiness													
3. Cohesiveness during chewing													
4. Adhesiveness/stickiness													
5. Graininess													

TABLE 7.5 (Continued)

Name: _____

I.D. # _____

Attributes	22	19	34	17	16	18	42	79	84	76	25	37	Ideal Bread
IV. Flavor													
1. Overall flavor strength	—	—	—	—	—	—	—	—	—	—	—	—	—
2. Degree of rye flavor	—	—	—	—	—	—	—	—	—	—	—	—	—
3. Degree of wheat flavor	—	—	—	—	—	—	—	—	—	—	—	—	—
4. Degree of nutty flavor	—	—	—	—	—	—	—	—	—	—	—	—	—
5. Degree of sweetness	—	—	—	—	—	—	—	—	—	—	—	—	—
V. Aroma													
1. Yeasty aroma	L D	L D	L D	L D	L D	L D	L D	L D	L D	L D	L D	L D	L D
2. Toasted aroma	—	—	—	—	—	—	—	—	—	—	—	—	—
VI. Performance													
1. Overall liking—how much	—	—	—	—	—	—	—	—	—	—	—	—	—
2. Purchase intention	—	—	—	—	—	—	—	—	—	—	—	—	—

Products

TABLE 7.5 (Continued)

Calibration page for Magnitude Estimates
(Bread Evaluation)

Name: _____

I.D. # _____

CALIBRATION PAGE

What Product Rating Corresponds to Each Description Word?

Like/Pleasant		Strength/Degree of Rating		Purchase Intention	
Like Extremely	_____	Extreme	_____	Definitely Would Buy	_____
Like Very Much	_____	Very Much	_____	Probably Would Buy	_____
Like Moderately	_____	Moderate	_____	Might or Might Not Buy	_____
Like Slightly	_____	Slight	_____	Probably Would Not Buy	_____
Neither Like Nor Dislike	0	None	0	Definitely Would Not Buy	0
Dislike Slightly	_____				
Dislike Moderately	_____				
Dislike Very Much	_____				
Dislike Extremely	_____				

the panelist whether this meant that bread A seemed 4 times as dense as bread sample B, etc.). Of course, with group testing one cannot do that kind of questioning for more than just a few samples per panelist. Nonetheless, just to have this type of questioning done during the evaluation maintains quality of the data for most of the group.

Results of the Study

Product optimization proceeds according to the straightforward sequence of data base development and display, linear equations for validation, nonlinear models for form. The entries in the form comprise the mean, and occasionally the standard error of the mean. Table 7.6 shows the tabular data display.

The sensory analyst can learn quite a bit from the tabular display of data. If the aim of the study pertains to optimizing overall liking then an inspection of the table can reveal whether or not the overall liking/disliking ratings vary, or if these ratings cluster around a central point, with relatively little excursion from the mean. A small variation around the mean suggests that overall liking remains stable in the face of product modification. This small variation should lower the expectation that the optimization can improve acceptance to any great extent. On the other hand, with high variation two things may occur. Either one can build a model which allows for product optimization, or the data shows so much random variation that no reasonably simple, parsimonious model fits the results.

In addition, if the researcher aligns the products in ascending order of ingredient level, then a quick inspection of the data will reveal whether or not a panelist's rating, either on overall liking/disliking or on specific attributes, roughly correlates with ingredient changes. We will see this analysis of ingredient/sensory correlations in more depth later on.

Table 7.6 shows that panelists feel strongly about some of the bread samples, and reject others. The ratings for purchase intent vary from a low of 18 to high of 49. Furthermore, we can take some solace from Table 7.6 insofar as we can see that the change in ingredients (rye flour and sucrose) did substantially affect several of the flavor and texture characteristics. Like wide changes in acceptability, changes in sensory characteristics due to ingredient modifications promise the possibility of optimizing product acceptability. We would have less confidence in the data if the ingredient modifications left most, or all, of the sensory characteristics unchanged.

Linear Equations. Linear equations provide the analyst with a good first hand idea of the interrelations between ingredients, percep-

TABLE 7.6
DATA BASE OF RATINGS FOR BREAD

	Percent Rye	Percent Sugar	Cost Now	Cost in 6 Months	Surface Ease of Removal	Sensory (Texture) Surface Roughness	Firmness	Cohesive-ness	Denseness
1.	12.0	0	60	96	87	71	33	37	40
2.	12.0	3.0	66	114	78	63	44	64	55
3.	12.0	6.0	720	132	91	61	35	43	36
4.	19.5	0	98	156	78	63	44	64	55
5.	19.5	3.0	103	174	82	66	32	40	39
6.	19.5	6.0	109	192	69	50	47	54	51
7.	27.0	0	134	216	42	49	65	80	82
8.	27.0	3.0	141	234	40	40	51	73	68
9.	27.0	6.0	147	252	45	43	52	69	70
10.	42.0	0	210	336	36	48	83	74	105
11.	42.0	3.0	216	354	37	43	78	80	100
12.	42.0	6.0	222	372	34	39	96	107	119

TABLE 7.6 (Continued)

	Percent Rye	Percent Sugar	Moistness	Chewiness	Chewy	Cohesive Sticky	Adhesive Graininess	L/D*
					Texture			
1.	12.0	0	49	37	34	33	55	21
2.	12.0	3.0	63	34	39	27	5-	13
3.	12.0	6.0	55	33	44	32	5-	30
4.	19.5	0	63	55	70	50	43	14
5.	19.5	3.0	62	48	48	48	41	17
6.	19.5	6.0	64	58	87	46	40	60
7.	27.0	0	50	62	63	53	41	-9
8.	27.0	3.0	58	54	69	45	49	15
9.	27.0	6.0	63	59	67	53	39	37
10.	42.0	0	51	62	60	53	47	50
11.	42.0	3.0	60	69	69	62	49	10
12.	42.0	6.0	80	95	94	83	35	12

*L/D = Like/Dislike

TABLE 7.6 (Continued)

	Percent Rye	Percent Sugar	Flavor Strength	Rye Flavor	Sweetness	Yeasty Aroma	Toasted Aroma	Flavor L/D*	Total L/D*	Purchase Intent
1.	12.0	0	44	27	15	41	13	22	−7	22
2.	12.0	3.0	36	17	19	47	11	−5	16	33
3.	12.0	6.0	41	20	25	42	16	40	23	31
4.	19.5	0	52	34	16	50	17	36	7	49
5.	19.5	3.0	49	28	20	48	14	11	11	26
6.	19.5	6.0	58	26	32	52	16	27	35	49
7.	27.0	0	61	38	11	47	18	11	−11	18
8.	27.0	3.0	55	37	17	45	16	32	7	29
9.	27.0	6.0	62	28	30	47	22	60	30	44
10.	42.0	0	73	53	13	50	17	14	−28	24
11.	42.0	3.0	74	56	14	56	19	−23	−7	32
12.	42.0	6.0	79	54	23	54	21	46	−9	35

*L/D = Like/Dislike

tions and acceptance. For our purposes, we use the simple linear equation, which we express as:

Sensory Characteristic $= k_0 + k_1(\text{Sucrose}) + k_2(\text{Rye})$

This equation generalizes to **n** different predictors, with **n** different ingredient levels, all systematically varied.

Table 7.7 shows the linear equations, including the intercept k_0 and the coefficients for sucrose, k_1 and for rye flour, k_2.

We interpret the parameters of the equation as follows. (1) The intercept k_0 reflects the sensory level we would achieve, hypothetically, when we project the equation down to 0 level of sucrose and 0 level of rye flour. This estimation represents a straightforward projection of our straight line (or plane) equation for the 0 levels of the ingredients. Of course, in real world terms, we do not test in the zero region, so we have no way of knowing what would actually occur for such a blend. Nonetheless, the intercept does represent a best estimate of the rating we would obtain. (2) The value of k_1 represents the slope or the coefficient for rye. It tells the analyst the increment or decrement in magnitude estimation scale units which will occur for specified changes in the physical concentration of rye. For example, suppose the coefficient for rye equals 2.0. This means that increasing the rye level by 1 unit will increase the attribute rating by 2.0 units. The coefficient can assume negative values as well. A coefficient of -0.20 means that a 1 unit increase in rye will generate a loss of 0.20 magnitude estimation units on the specific attribute. The same rules hold for k_2, the coefficient for sucrose.

The coefficients k_1 and k_2 reflect the rate at which the sensory attribute changes with physical concentration. When the sensory attribute behaves virtually independently of sucrose level, k_2 equals 0 or close to 0. With high dependence of a sensory attribute on the levels of sucrose, the value of k_2 increases as well.

High values of the coefficient can mislead. The coefficients depend, in part, upon the size of the units which the researchers use to measure the physical ingredient levels. With everything held constant but unit size of ingredient, changing the percentage sucrose (e.g., 50%) to the fractional amount (e.g., 0.50), but leaving the actual value unaffected, will increase the coefficient by a factor of 100. Similarly, changing the units of measurement from feet to inches will change the coefficient for that measurement by a factor of 12.

Let us look for a second at the numbers shown in Table 7.7. Note that since the units for sucrose and rye both represent percentages, we need not worry about incommensurate coefficients. In fact, we can compare

Product Testing and Sensory Evaluation of Foods

TABLE 7.7
LINEAR EQUATIONS INTERRELATING RYE AND SUCROSE TO PRODUCT PERCEPTIONS

Attribute	Equations $K_0 + K_1(Rye) + K_2(Sucrose)$			Multiple R	Correlations With	
					% Rye	% Sugar
Ease of particle removal	106.47	−1.91	0.99	0.92	−0.91	0.13
Surface roughness	74.21	−0.75	−0.94	0.81	−0.78	−0.19
Firmness	6.52	1.82	0.67	0.95	0.95	0.04
Cohesiveness	23.32	1.55	0.63	0.87	0.86	0.05
Denseness	5.47	2.44	−0.12	0.97	0.97	−0.04
Moistness	46.61	0.31	1.82	0.66	0.39	0.51
Chewiness	20.26	1.29	1.19	0.88	0.86	0.14
Cohesiveness of mass	30.49	0.99	2.61	0.71	0.62	0.34
Adhesive/stickiness	17.74	1.13	0.88	0.88	0.86	0.12
Graininess	529	−0.23	−0.30	0.47	−0.45	−0.12
Flavor strength	27.71	1.13	0.30	0.96	0.96	0.02
Rye flavor	8.06	1.10	−0.30	0.96	0.96	−0.09
Wheat flavor	27.79	−0.02	1.32	0.57	−0.06	0.57
Nutty flavor	6.42	0.33	0.26	0.71	0.70	0.10
Sweetness	18.74	−0.12	1.52	0.61	−0.23	0.58
Aroma/yeasty	40.44	0.26	0.50	0.73	0.68	0.26
Aroma/toasted	11.52	0.20	0.07	0.73	0.73	0.03
Overall liking	21.97	−0.94	2.92	0.71	−0.59	0.41
Purchase intent	25.96	0.02	1.79	0.51	0.00	0.51

the sizes of the coefficients, attribute by attribute, to evaluate the effect that a unit change in percent ingredient level will produce on the sensory perception.

Specifically; a 1 unit increase in percentage of rye produces a 2.44 unit increase in perceived density. Furthermore, the same 1 unit increase, this time in sucrose, produces a 0.12 unit decrease in density, as perceived by the panelist.

Correlations—Multiple and Partial. The multiple linear equation represents the best estimate the analyst can make as to the straight line (or plane) interrelation between sucrose, rye and sensory perception. Some equations fit the data, whereas other equations fail to fit the data. We can try to fit a straight line to a curve. We succeed for some attributes, but fail for other attributes. Figure 7.1 shows how the same equation can fit one data set well, but another data set poorly. Yet, given the restrictions of using only the straight line or the flat plane, the poorly fitting equation still represents the best one can do.

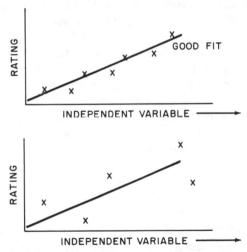

FIG. 7.1 SHOWING HOW A STRAIGHT LINE FIT TO THE DATA MAY OR MAY NOT REALLY DESCRIBE THE DATA

The multiple correlation shows how well the straight line fits the data, or in the case of two or more predictors, how well a plane fits the data. The square of the multiple correlation indicates the relative amount of the variation in the data which the equation explains. $R^2 \times 100$ = pecentage of variability in the data accounted for by the equation. Ideally, a good predictor equation should have a multiple R exceeding 0.9, meaning that the equation accounts for $(0.9)^2 \times 100 =$

81% of the variability in the ratings. Some of the sensory characteristics such as flavor strength, firmness, and denseness show high multiple correlations, meaning that these simple, linear equations adequately describe the data. Other sensory characteristics such as moistness, graininess and nutty flavor show low multiple correlations. Linear equations weighting sucrose and rye do not adequately account for the attribute rating. Perhaps no simple linear equation can fit the data. Either the data exhibits so much curvature as to defy linearity, or the data exhibits too much random error, and no simple equation will fit it at all.

One of the ubiquitous results from virtually all studies on the interrelations between liking/disliking and ingredient levels pertains to the poor fit of linear equations to the data. Our bread data reaffirms that general rule. Rarely, if ever, does liking grow as a straight line relation with formula ingredients. As discussed before in Chapter 6 on hedonics, the German psychologist Wilhelm Wundt speculated that the optimum level or bliss point lies at an intermediate ingredient value. Any well constructed experiment probing a wide variation in ingredient levels to optimize acceptability will test levels which exceed the bliss point, as well as levels which fall below it. The typical linear equation appears in Table 7.7. The multiple correlation for the linear function equals 0.51 for purchase intent and 0.71 for liking. Although the average product rating shows variation with ingredients, the linear equation simply cannot account for these nonlinearities. We deal in greater detail with the nonlinear equation below.

Finally, one should consider how well each ingredient (sugar, rye) tracks or correlates with each sensory attribute. One can assess this partial relation between each component ingredient and perception by means of the partial correlation coefficient, partial R, which Table 7.7 shows. Like the multiple R, the partial R varies between 0 and 1.0. The partial correlation can assume positive values to show an increasing relation, or negative values to show an inverse relation. The partial correlations relate to the multiple correlation by this formula, specific to our case, but generalizable to any number of predictors:

Multiple R^2 = Partial R^2(Sucrose) + Partial R^2(Rye Flour)

Looking at our data, we can see, for instance, that the sensory characteristic of sweetness correlates most with the percent sucrose, since perceived sweetness has a high partial correlation with sucrose. Similarly, with increasing levels of rye flour, the perception of rye flavor also increases. The partial correlation between rye flour and perceived rye flour, 0.96, shows the two linked tightly.

Through visual analyses of these partial correlations, the analyst can ascertain which ingredients correlate with each sensory attribute. Furthermore, these visual checks can confirm the intrinsic validity of the data. If the analyst expects that rye flour level should correlate with perceived rye flavor, then he or she can easily check this hypothesis by considering the partial correlation coefficient. The partial correlation between rye flavor and rye level should attain a high value. In this data, where R&D systematically varied sucrose and rye level, the analyst can immediately assess the validity of the data by looking at the partial correlations between sucrose level and sweetness, and between rye level and perceived rye flavor.

Non-Linear Equations. Linear equations do not often adequately describe how liking covaries with ingredient level. Here, the correlation for a linear equation turns out to equal 0.51 for purchase intent, and 0.71 for liking. We can improve this correlation by using a non-linear equation, which appears in Table 7.8.

The non-linear equation comprises these terms: linear terms (sucrose and rye), quadratic terms (sucrose^2 and rye^2) and pairwise interaction terms (sucrose x rye). The additional terms serve the following purpose. (1) With non-linear, quadratic terms, overall liking can increase with sucrose and/or rye level, peak at the bliss point, and then diminish at levels beyond the bliss point. With a simple linear equation, overall liking must peak either at the highest or the lowest level of ingredients, and cannot peak at an intermediate optimum. Of course, adding non-linear quadratic terms does not insure an optimum in the middle range. Rather, it simply allows the data to show the intermediate peak, if such a peak exists. (2) With multiplicative, cross terms (sucrose x rye), the non-linear equation can represent or model some of the pairwise interactions between ingredients which influence acceptability, above and beyond the ingredients themselves. Sometimes the particular combination of ingredients achieves a level of acceptability which one could not predict from the ingredient levels alone. Other terms to express intreactions exist as well, such a ratio (sucrose/rye), but we use the simplest form (multiplicative) because of mathematical considerations. One can optimize the parabolic equation of the form below most easily:

$$\text{Purchase Intent} = k_0 + k_1(\text{Rye}) + k_2(\text{Rye})^2 + k_3(\text{Sucrose}) \qquad (5)$$
$$+ k_4(\text{Sucrose})^2 + k_5(\text{Sucrose})(\text{Rye})$$

One cannot as easily maximize the equation with a ratio of ingredients as the form of the interaction, even when such an equation fits the data better:

$$\text{Purchase Intent} = k_0 + k_1(\text{Sucrose}) + k_2(\text{Sucrose})^2 + k_3(\text{Rye}) \qquad (6)$$
$$+ k_4(\text{Rye})^2 + k_5(\text{Rye/Sucrose})$$

Goodness of Fit—And the Kitchen Sink

We always improve the fit of the equation to the data by adding extra terms, as we can see in Table 7.8. Mathematicians have shown that one can always improve the fit by increasing the number of predictors, whether these predictors have relevance or not to the actual data. How then, can we measure how well our new predictors behave as additional predictors in describing liking versus ingredients? To answer this question, let us consider how the statistician conceptualizes the problem.

TABLE 7.8
NONLINEAR VS. LINEAR EQUATION RELATING LIKING RATINGS
TO FORMULA VARIATIONS

Purchase Interest	Linear	Nonlinear
Intercept	21.97	31.26
+ k_0(% Rye)	−0.94	+3.54
+ k_1(% Rye)^2	—	−0.081
+ k_2(% Sugar)	+2.92	+3.01
+ k_3(% Sugar)^2	—	+0.14
+ k_4(% Rye)(% Sugar)	—	Not Necessary
Multiple Correlation	0.71	0.83

The first requirement becomes adequate prediction. Does the data follow the curve or equation which we have developed? The second requirement concerns the issue of parsimony. Have we used too many terms, some of which represent accidental or adventitious predictors? Do we need all of the terms in the equation, or can we get away with fewer predictor variables, without using all of the possible permutations (linear, square, cross terms)? When we deal with systems of 3, 4 or more ingredients, the number of possible additional terms increases. In a 3 ingredient system we can appeal to 3 linear terms, 3 quadratic terms and 3 cross terms; or an additional 6 predictor variables. In a 4 ingredient system we appeal to 4 linear terms, 4 quadratic terms, and 6 cross terms, totalling 10 additional terms.

Optimizing the equation with a nonlinear equation which adequately describes the data, the sensory analyst can ascertain those levels of sucrose and rye, which lie within preestablished limits, and which maximize overall liking/disliking.

In order to ascertain the rye and sucrose levels, we use optimization procedures specifically designed for the quadratic equation which always find the optimum, even if the optimum lies at the upper or lower extreme limit of ingredients tested. Of course, in order to make the situation realistic, the analyst should constrain the sucrose and rye levels to lie within technologically feasible limits. The best estimate for such limits comes from the actual limits which we tested in the study itself. Since we have data on rye between 12% and 42%, and since we have data on sucrose between 0% and 6%, we should feel confident to limit our data to within those specific limits.

By doing so we find the optimal levels to lie at 6% sucrose and 21.8% rye flour. This intermediate optimal level for rye flour reveals itself because we have used the non-linear equation (which describes a surface) as the idealized or smoothed counterpart of our data. With such a mathematical equation we can interpolate, using the mathematics to guide us, and estimate the likely reaction to intermediate values.

Estimated Liking. After optimizing and finding out the most acceptable combination of ingredients, we can substitute the optimal levels into our equation in Table 7.8 and calculate the expected liking/disliking value (which solves to approximately 30.5). Since the mathematical equation summarizes the relation between liking and ingredients, and since we have a reasonably good fit of the data to the equation, we can estimate the most likely rating panelists would assign to their liking of that optimized product.

Estimated Sensory Profile. Recall that Table 7.7 showed how to relate sensory attributes to ingredients. Given ingredients, the analyst could estimate the most likely sensory profile corresponding to the optimally acceptable rye and sugar level. Table 7.9 shows the results of this estimation, which one calculates straightforwardly. We use the set of equations in Table 7.7 as surrogates for the actual data. By using the equations, rather than the original data, we can estimate the sensory reactions for levels which we did not even test, but which nonetheless lie within the region of the tested levels.

Constrained Optimization

Consider the issue of cost of goods. We computed our cost of goods for the optimal rye bread as 120.40 units, based upon the equations which tell us how cost of goods varies as a function of sucrose and rye level (see

Tables 7.7 and 7.9). Given constraints on the cost of goods (e.g., cost less than or equal to 95), then what highest level of liking can one obtain? Of course if the cost of goods plays no role, the highest liking will occur at 6% sucrose and 21.8% rye, since the bliss point lies at an intermediate level.

Table 7.9 shows three examples of the constrained optimization, where the analyst has artificially constrained the total cost of goods to lie between 0.0 and 95, 75 and 65, respectively. Notice the drop in liking and the change in sensory characteristics. We should expect these changes. By dropping the cost below the cost of the overall optimum, the analyst has, in effect, forced some or both of the ingredients below their optimal or bliss point levels. One cannot but diminish liking from the overall optimal level obtained before. Of course, with a model one can estimate the percentage drop in acceptability for specific percentage drops in cost, and therefore ingredient levels.

TABLE 7.9
ALTERNATIVE BREAD RECIPES
FOR DIFFERENT COST CONSTRAINTS

	Optimal Product	Current Cost Less Than 95	Current Cost Less Than 75	Current Cost Less Than 65
% Rye	21.8	16.7	12.7	12.0
% Sucrose	6.0	6.0	6.0	1.9
Liking	30.5	28.4	23.8	6.0
Current units costs				
(rye and sucrose only)	120.4	95.0	75.0	65.0
Cost in 6 months	199.8	158.0	125.2	128.2
Ease of particle removal	70.8	77.5	84.6	82.2
Surface roughness	52.1	56.2	59.3	63.6
Firmness	50.1	43.2	36.5	32.2
Cohesiveness	61.0	56.4	50.8	46.8
Denseness	58.0	49.3	40.3	38.6
Moistness	64.1	64.5	63.7	55.9
Chewiness	55.4	48.9	43.7	38.0
Cohesiveness of mass	67.8	62.7	58.7	47.5
Adhesive/stickiness	47.5	41.8	37.3	32.9
Graininess	43.3	46.4	47.3	48.7
Flavor strength	54.1	48.4	43.9	41.8
Rye flavor	30.2	24.6	20.2	20.6
Wheat flavor	35.2	35.3	35.4	30.1
Nutty flavor	15.1	13.4	12.1	10.8
Sweetness	25.2	25.8	26.3	20.2
Aroma/yeasty	49.1	47.8	46.7	44.5
Aroma/toasted	16.3	15.3	14.5	14.0
Purchase intent	37.0	36.9	36.8	29.6

Discussion of the Bread Study—Update

The analyst presented the four solutions, first without cost constraints, and second with three cost constraints. The Gonzales Milling Company accepted the solutions as tentative products. Management suggested testing the products in a subsequent evaluation study, and subjected the optimal formulation as predicted, along with the top two winners, to extended home use tests, using conventional consumer testing procedures. Panelists received a competitor bread, as well as the optimal or cost reduced (but optimal) bread, to try for 1 week. Each panelist received two loaves, one a current competitor (in market), and the other one of the test products (or optimum), both blind wrapped to disguise the brand. The subsequent home tests of the breads revealed that the optimization did, in fact, produce a more acceptable bread, tested without the influence of the wrapper or branding. The overall optimum and the most expensive of the cost reduced bread optima scored well. Thus, by systematically varying the key ingredients of sucrose and rye flour, the Gonzales Milling Company effectively improved the quality of rye bread (see Table 7.10).

TABLE 7.10
RESULTS OF THE FOLLOWUP HOME USE TEST OF BREAD

Group I (Optimum vs. Competitor A)		
67% prefer optimum	26% prefer "A"	7% no preference
Group II (Cost reduced Optimum ($\leq$ 95¢) vs. Competitor A)		
62% prefer Winner "1"	28% prefer "A"	10% no preference
Group III (Cost Reduced Optimum ($\leq$ 75¢) vs. Competitor A)		
53% prefer Winner "2"	25% prefer "A"	12% no preference

Panel = 100 women/group

During a subsequent review of the study, management requested the analyst to evaluate the cost implications of the optimization from the perspective of alternatives which the product tester could have used to arrive at the same result. Specific questions included the following. (1) How long would it have taken the product tester and R&D to develop the same formulation? According to the product tester and R&D's calculations, the only way to have definitely come up with the product would have required testing of all 12 breads versus competition by paired comparisons, using panels of 50 individuals per paired comparison. At the very least, such testing would require 12 paired comparisons evaluations, requiring subtantially longer time. The paired comparison studies would require at least 7 but more likely 10+ weeks, to generate the answer. Furthermore, one could not guarantee that the procedure would finish after the 12 tests. Projects using paired comparisons, more often than not, fail to find significant differences among products. This failure to differentiate many variations prevents development of the integrated data base so important to optimization. (2) Could the research group have provided the same quality data with conventional methods? Probably, but with a few caveats. First, with conventional testing methods and their known insensitivities, the product tester would have had to dramatically increase the panel size to insure equivalent sensitivity. Perhaps doubling or tripling the base size would have equalized sensitivity, as compared to the magnitude estimation method (150 vs 50). Furthermore, with sequential tests the product tester could not certify the comparability of the test conditions, and comparability of respondent populations. Panelists change over time. They become increasingly experienced with the product category, and alter their frame of reference. Over a relatively long term testing regimen, such as that required by conventional test procedures, one could expect drift and random variability in the data, which did not appear in the simultaneous testing done by the Gonzales Milling Company. Thus, in all probability, the product tester could not have acquired data of equivalently high quality, owing to the simple vagaries of panelist experience. Furthermore, statistical complications ensue when only part of the panel sample comprises the same individuals, and part of the panel comprises transient panelists who participate for only one or, at most, a few sessions.

Perhaps the most important benefit of the optimization approach lies in the development of the integrated data base. A data base merges cost of goods, product ingredients, consumer perceptions of sensory attributes, and consumer perceptions of quality or overall purchase interest and/or acceptability. An integrated data base allows the product developer and marketer a better understanding of the product. It permits the product developer to quantitatively evaluate how large and small changes in the levels of the selected ingredients affect perception and acceptance. It affords the product developer, as it did the Gonzales Milling Company, an actionable direction for product improvement. The integrated data base, and the allied methods of optimization, generate testable predictions of consumer perceptions and acceptability, rather than general, non-specific directions such as increase the sucrose level in order to increase flavor. In a sense, the data base represents a tight mathematical model of the product, developed by an engineering approach. It has two aims; solving the problem of interrelations of ingredients and perception, on the one hand, and improving product acceptance on the other.

A SECOND OPTIMIZATION STUDY—BEVERAGES

Let us further evaluate the optimization procedure by a second case history pertaining to a dry mix beverage. The Fraterman Beverage Company (FBC) has, in the past ten years, grown from a small, local company in Massachusetts to a large national company, on the verge of introducing a line of dry mix beverages into an already highly competitive market (estimated 300-400 million dollars/year). FBC's management realized the extremely competitive aspect of the dry mix beverage business, as it saw the category grow from a 128 million dollar business to over 379 million dollars.

Dry mix beverages come in many flavors, with many options. The consumer can purchase the beverage, premixed with sucrose, in cans or in large envelopes; or in small packets and add the sugar to taste. Furthermore, many different flavors abound, including a number of entries in cherry, grape, lemon (virtually a category by itself), etc. Finally, a number of entries allow the purchaser to buy already prepared beverages in the can, in a variety of simple and complex fruit flavors.

Background of the Specific Study

Management at FBC did not know which flavor(s) to market, nor the precise composition of the beverages. Should they introduce a cherry flavor, an orange flavor, or a line of simple fruit flavors backed up by heavy advertising and trade promotion? Or should they concentrate on exotic fruit flavors, hoping by such a strategy to call attention to themselves and develop a unique niche having relatively less competition?

In order to find out the flavor preferences of consumers, FBC commissioned a study to measure what flavors Americans like in beverages. The study would ascertain whether, in fact, FBC could possibly make a viable entry into an already crowded, but eminently profitable market.

In the preliminary, or screening study, FBC's marketing analyst selected various commercially available products, directly from the shelves of supermarkets, as the products to initially test. These competitive products represented dry mix beverages currently in-market. They varied by flavor (e.g., lemon cherry, grape, orange), by type of preparation (premixed, in can, add your own sugar, etc.), and in their appeal to different age groups (some products appealed primarily to adults, others virtually entirely to children, whereas still others appealed to a broad cross section of the consuming public).

In order to determine the flavor preferences, FBC ran a blind taste evaluation of these products. FBC performed the test in the following way. First, the marketing researcher selected the target population. Since marketing management at FBC remained open to the final target population, the marketing researcher suggested testing flavor preferences among a spectrum of panelists, comprising a broad range of ages. They divided the groups into children (7-10), teens (13-17) and adult women (18-49). Forty panelists participated in each group. Next, the testing phase comprised an initial exploration of consumer taste preferences. In order to minimize costs for this initial exploration stage, management requested an evaluation of the products in only one test location. Since the first beverage project aimed simply to guide the management in selecting the general flavor class, the marketing manager accepted the risk of a less than optimal representation of U.S. consumers, in light of the information gained from one location, as well as in light of the lower cost incurred by a one location study. (With a smaller scale test, comprising fewer products and a smaller base size of panelists, quite often the screening study discussed here for the beverage proves feasible to conduct in several locations.). Table 7.11 shows the products.

The panelists participated in a group session. Groups of 20 panelists participated in a 3.5 hour taste evaluation session. During that time, the panelists followed the regimen discussed below, which provided good control over the evaluation.

Panelists volunteered to participate in the test. Through pre-recruiting the week before they set up their appointments. During this pre-recruiting stage, the interviewer obtained background data on age, demographic variables, product usage, etc. Panelists reported to the test site at either 9 a.m. or 1:30 p.m. for adults; and 3:30 p.m. for the children, to insure the test would take place after school. A moderator or head interviewer instructed the panelists in the magnitude estimation method (see Chapters 5 and 6 for details of the instruction). The moderator took the panelists, as a group, through the first product in a step by step fashion. The moderator first instructed the panelists to scale various attributes, including overall liking/disliking of flavor intensity; tartness, liking/disliking of tartness; liking/disliking of flavor quality of flavor type. The panelists evaluated and finished the

TABLE 7.11
SCORES OF PRODUCTS TESTED IN THE FBC
BEVERAGE STUDY—PHASE I: SCREENING OF DIFFERENT FLAVORS
(Liking Ratings by Magnitude Estimation)

Beverage Flavor and Type	Average	Adults	Teens	Children
Cherry A	56.3	43.8	50.9	74.3
B	65.9	49.3	60.1	88.2
C	63.4	51.9	63.3	74.9
Average	(61.9)	(48.3)	(58.1)	(79.1)
Orange A	33.5	30.2	35.4	35.0
B	38.9	40.1	30.2	46.3
Average	(36.2)	(35.2)	(32.8)	(40.7)
Mixed Fruit A	69.6	60.4	70.3	75.1
B	72.8	68.3	61.2	88.9
C	73.1	73.4	64.2	81.8
Average	(71.8)	(67.4)	(65.2)	(81.9)
Lemon A	54.8	89.7	45.3	29.4
B	62.5	73.2	75.1	39.2
Average	(58.6)	(81.5)	(60.2)	(34.3)
Average Standard Error of Rating	4.2	10.8	12.6	13.4

first beverage, randomized among panelists to insure reduction of first-product bias, and then proceeded, at their own pace, to evaluate the subsequent beverages.

After panelists finished each product, they threw away their beverage cups, having tasted at least 1/3 of the cup which they could swallow or expectorate. They waited at least 3 minutes, and then went to the head of the room, where they showed the interviewer their answer booklets. The products in the booklets appeared in random order. The interviewer who dispensed the products determined their next beverage, and dispensed them 1/2 glass of the next beverage. After every four samples (taking about 20 minutes), the panelists took an enforced 10 minute break, to insure the maintenance of sensitivity. (As a parenthetical note, the procedure of forcing panelists to wait between samples, to walk around in the testing room and otherwise distract themselves between separate product evaluations, insures sensitivity and minimizes the boredom factors which so often disrupt sensory analyses.) After the panelists completed evaluating the entire set of products, the moderator at the head of the table instructed them to calibrate their scales (explicated in Chapters 5 and 6).

Results of the Screening Study

We will concentrate on the overall liking/disliking ratings which the panelists provided, and which appear in Table 7.11. These data, broken out by age, show that the greatest opportunity for product acceptance lies in the multi-fruit beverage. These products outscore the competition in terms of overall liking. They also show that adults as well as children like the complex, non-single flavor provided by multi-fruit beverages.

Of course, the screening study that FBC ran provide this information and much more. It told the marketer the strengths and the weaknesses of each competitor product. For instance, by knowing flavor likes and dislikes, and attribute ratings of the products (not shown), the marketer could home in on specific shortcomings of the competitors. Thus, a multi-product screening study, executed before the optimization project, allows the product developer, the sensory analyst, the marketing research analyst and marketer a broad scale perspective regarding what products currently exist. It provides information about satisfaction and dissatisfaction with the existing products. This screening study also revealed the divergence of tastes. It indicated the preponderant acceptance of the red, cherry flavors by children, and the more tart, sharply defined flavors by the adults. Thus, had management wished, it could have simply used this information by itself to guide marketing efforts. By coupling the study with a subsequent product optimization phase, FBC further augmented its opportunities to develop a product with enhanced acceptability.

Product Optimization—Phase I: Selection of Formulations

In subsequent meeting with the marketing and product testing groups, the R&D group, headed by a beverage technologist with over 15 years experience in product formulation, suggested that FBC consider a specific multi-fruit flavored formulation, with pre-specified ingredient levels for the flavor. The beverage technologist suggested that one could improve the product by adding key components to the flavor, at as yet undetermined levels; and by modifying the sugar and acid levels. These variations represent the very standard types of options which one encounters in beverage development.

After numerous discussions and intensive bench-top formulation work with different prototypes, R&D finally presented a beverage formulation for consideration at the biweekly showing of products currently in the FBC testing pipeline. With management concurrence, the product tester and marketing researcher decided to optimize the product in a systematic way, by means of the technology we previously discussed with regard to the Gonzales Milling Company.

Experimental Design. With four formulation ingredients which can vary over a wide range of levels, the statistical design of the study can take on specific complications. For instance, some commonly asked questions, which arose again in the product development meetings, included the following. (1) How many levels of each ingredient should R&D test? Two, three, or more? (2) How many products in total should R&D produce? Each formula variation takes time to develop. The fewer the total number of formula variations, the faster the development time and the lower the cost. On the other hand, as we saw before, the more products one tests the greater the likelihood of developing a representative data base which allows for subsequent product optimization. (3) Should R&D attempt to cover the entire set of permutations and combinations of products? Do experimental designs (layouts of options) exist which can facilitate the evaluation by selecting a key fraction of the possible product variations?

During the meeting, the product tester, well versed in psychophysics, suggested that in order to develop any sort of curve relating ingredients to variations, one would have to use more than 2 levels of the ingredients. At least 3 levels or more should cover the range of product variation. Furthermore, the statistical consultant suggested that all efforts should go into the evaluation of how ingredients and their interactions affect consumer sensory reactions, and hedonic or acceptance ratings. Therefore, one proposed strategy of evaluating ingredients separately, and not in combination of various levels, would not prove feasible. As an aside, a common fallacy in product optimization occurs when we separately evaluate variations in one ingredient (e.g., sugar or acid), keeping the other ingredients fixed. Each ingredient impacts on every other ingredient. Perceptions and acceptance result from the integration of these interactions, not the separate effects of each ingredient alone.

The statistician brought up the possibility of using one of two different designs: fractional factorial design, or the central composite design (Mullen and Ennis 1979; Box and Hunter 1953). These designs appear in Table 7.4. The traditional fractional or full factorial design often appears jointly with analysis of variance, where the researcher wishes to isolate optimal levels of treatments, from those he or she has studied. The central composite design represents a different way of laying out ingredients. Product developers use it quite often to develop equations relating sensory perceptions, or product acceptance versus physical ingredients levels.

After extensive discussion, R&D and the product testing group concurred that they should use the fractional factorial design as suggested by the statistician, for the following three reasons. (1) The design allowed estimation of the non-linear equation which best fits the data. (2) The design allowed the product tester to estimate the linear and the quadratic equations as well as the cross-terms, in a straightforward manner. (3) Relative to the other designs, both the fractional factorial and the central composite designs seemed most appropriate for developing the non-linear equation. Since the study aimed to optimize (requiring an interpolation between tested values of the ingredients), the product developers felt that a design specifically set up for the purpose of developing a non-linear equation would prove the best choice.

The actual sugar, acid and flavoring levels could vary over a wide range. Faced with this wide range of ingredient variation, the R&D sensory analyst brought in the in-house testing panel, which comprised individuals skilled in sensory analysis of beverages. Each panelist had at least 2 years of experience in product evaluation, both in descriptive and in quantitative product analysis. The expert panel pre-screened the formulations. They tasted wide ranges of product formulations, telling the product developer when they thought the product had far too much, or far too little sugar, acid and flavoring. Although the expert panel did not act as surrogates for the consumer, they did act as quality control monitors, indicating those levels where they felt the consumer would absolutely reject the product. Thus, the sensory analyst used the expert panel for screening purposes.

Quite often, management, R&D and sensory analysts feel that with an expert panel they can bypass the product optimization phase entirely. Panelists with years of experience should know their products, or so the rationale goes. This attitude inadvertently eliminates the most critical stage in the development process—fine tuning the formulation by means of actionable consumer feedback. Fortunately, management at FBC took the position that improvement in consumer acceptability provides the necessary key to advertising claims and product loyalty. Thus, management recommended that R&D proceed with their testing plans.

Test Location and Panel

We have previously dealt with the issue of central location test, wherein panelists come to a site and test the product for long or short periods of time. For the current project, management suggested that the panelists should test the products at home, under the more normal, ecologically valid test situations of common, everyday usage. Home-use tests provide the marketer and the product tester with both benefits and problems: The benefits include: a realistic testing environment; long term product exposure, not just a short taste test; the ability to modify the product formulation at home, in a normal environment to suit one's own tastes as consumers usually do; and exposure to and evaluation by the whole family, not just one individual. Problems, on the other hand, include: loss of stimulus control—panelists can prepare the product in different ways, even though one provides explicit instructions; loss of control over the evaluation—panelists test the product how and when they want; and loss of opportunity to spot errors and problems in testing as they occur, because of lack of contact between panelists and the product tester, except (possibly) after the test has actually finished.

In view of the benefits and the problems, the product tester suggested packing the product in pre-weighed packages, with explicit directions. These instruction regarded: the amount of water to add to the mix (sucrose already comprised part of the dry mix), and how to make it; how long to hold the mixture; the temperature of refrigeration; evaluation instructions involving panelist orientation to magnitude estimation; advice on the scaling of specific characteristics; calibration instructions; and a method for self-checking the ratings.

Table 7.12 shows the experimental array of products agreed upon by the tester (with the job of implementing the study), and the sensory panel of in-house experts (who had pre-tested the ingredient limits of the formulation in order to provide directionality for an otherwise extremely large range of alternative ingredient levels).

Study Implementation

Once the product developers reached a consensus with management and product testing regarding the number of products, the volume necessary for each product, and the method of product packaging and developing, they proceeded to produce the alternative formulations. They also purchased and repackaged for test purposes three of the leading product competitors, which they had already tested in the screening phase. Product development takes time. In the brand manager's schedule, the development time occupied a full 3 weeks of manpower, with 1 bench scientist designated as product development leader, and 2 laboratory assistants designated as aides in the formulation and packaging.

Since this test comprised home-use evaluations, R&D packaged

TABLE 7.12
EXPERIMENTAL DESIGN OF BEVERAGE PROJECT
INGREDIENT LEVELS

Product	Acid	Sweetener	Flavor A	Flavor B
1	50	120	22	25
2	50	110	22	50
3	50	100	22	0
4	55	110	22	0
5	55	110	22	25
6	55	100	22	50
7	60	120	22	50
8	60	110	22	0
9	60	100	22	25
10	50	120	11	50
11	50	110	11	0
12	55	110	11	50
13	55	120	11	25
14	55	100	11	0
15	60	120	11	0
16	60	110	11	25
17	60	100	11	50
18	50	120	0	0
19	50	110	0	25
20	50	100	0	50
21	55	120	0	50
22	55	110	0	25
23	55	110	0	0
24	60	120	0	25
25	60	100	0	50
26	60	100	0	0
27	50	100	11	25

separate products for each test variation. Initial suggestions about the base size or number of panelists centered around 30 panelists/product. With 27 different test formulations and 3 commercially available products, this came to 450, each of whom tested 2 products. Each family received 2 of the 30 products for a base of 30/products. This number compares with 500-600 panelists, often used for paired product testing. Here, FBC used the 450 panelists to provide information about a wider range of products, albeit with fewer panelists/product.

The product tester and marketing researcher contracted with a testing service which had mail-out facilities. They selected families with specified usage patterns of dry beverages. Among the criteria, the families had to consume a variety of different fruit flavored beverages, with low brand loyalty to any particular brand; and had to consume at least 2 packages/week. This specification (for late spring product usage) insured sampling an adequate number of potential consumers who showed low brand loyalty, and who used the product regularly. The mail-out service kept records of product usage on its roster of families in the United States. It could easily select from its files those families, their composition and address, which satisfied these screening or eligibility criteria.

The panel testing service received the coded packages, with the product disguised regarding ingredient formulation, and packaged in simple cardboard containers with the name of the panel testing service printed along with the product identification code. The service mailed out the questionnaire which contained the following sections: (1) orientation to the study (an introduction which the panelist reads); (2) instructions on scaling by magnitude estimation (self administered); (3) instructions on product preparation; (4) instructions on testing; and (5) instructions on calibrating. Furthermore, all of the family members participated in the study. The panel testing facility mailed out separate questionnaires, one for each member of the family, in order to obtain responses from the different individuals.

As in any long-term test, panelists participating in home-use tests do not always complete the evaluations. For this reason, many researchers and product testers prefer to use central location facilities where they can insure test completion. In the FBC beverage study, an average of 70% of the panelists returned the questionnaire. This return rate generated a base of 21 responses per product. The questionnaires came back, slowly, then in a rush, followed by the lagging final questionnaires. Seven weeks after the questionnaire mailing, the panel testing service closed out the study, and ignored the remaining forms which late-comers mailed in.

Data Analysis

For the first time we now deal with relatively simple, albeit sequential, monadic evaluations. Panelists in this beverage study did not possess a standard or a modulus against which to compare previous results. They tested only 2 of the 30 products. They did, however, possess a calibration scale. By normalizing the data, the product tester could bring into line the ratings of the panelists, even though no panelist tasted more than two products. The data analysis first required calibration of both the intensity and the hedonic ratings.

Table 7.13 shows the results. Note the following. (1) The rating of acceptability comprises total ratings (all panelists combined), as well as those by adults, children and teens, respectively. (2) The ratings for sensory characteristics by adults, children and teens agree with each other in most instances, suggesting that these different panelists could and did evaluate the products similarly. We show only average sensory ratings for adults, children and teens combined. (3) The ratings for liking vary by age group. Teens showed a smaller range of liking than did adults. (4) The ratings for the different groups on overall product liking/disliking show group differences. Individuals showed different taste/flavor/product preferences.

Linear Regression. As we did previously, let us do the initial data analysis using the method of regression analysis. The linear equation allows the analyst to ascertain how sensory perceptions and overall liking/disliking vary as a function of the ingredient levels. Did panelists pick up differences in the ingredient levels of the juices, even though they tested only two products, and did not have an opportunity to test a wide variety of products? The regression analysis, showing the coefficients and the partial and multiple correlations, appears, in Table 7.14.

The regression analysis shows that panelists can track changes in acid and less so, in sugar, even in the unusual situation of testing only a limited part of the product set. We have a reasonably high multiple correlation relating ingredients and tartness (sourness) level, with acid playing a major role. As acid increases, tartness increases as well. Thus, we conclude from the initial analysis that panelists can and do react singly to products, even without comparing many products. In their minds panelists maintain a scale of absolute intensities. Their performance in this test, with evaluation of a limited subset of products, showed slightly lower correlations of attributes to ingredients compared to what one usually finds when panelists evaluate all of the stimuli in one session. This stands to reason. In the home-use test panelists had no general frame of reference which they could use in assigning their ratings.

As a general rule, the analyst can expect to find these variations in the test results when doing the study by different methods. (1) When panelists evaluate all of the products in a single session and ingredients systematically vary, panelists perform best in terms of tracking the physical concentration. Their sensory attribute ratings parallel concentration changes. In fact, in such a central location study one can often reproduce the classical psychophysical experiment in which panelists scale varying levels of a stimulus in random order. The fact that we deal now with foods, flavors and other consumer items, rather than with pure, simple model systems, makes virtually no difference at all to the results. (2) When panelists evaluate a subset of the total number of product variations, and when each panelist tests a different subset of products, we find panelists still able to track the physical variations, but less well. Whereas the multiple correlations between ingredients and perceptions above might range around 0.90+, the multiple correlation for the same attribute in this balanced incomplete design might range around 0.70-0.80. (3) When panelists evaluate only one product of the total set, we find that panelists still track the physical ingredient levels. However, correlations between their sensory attribute levels and physical levels falls to around 0.5-0.7, much lower than the foregoing.

By inspecting Table 7.14 even before going on to optimization, the sensory analyst, marketer and general manager can feel assured that the data makes sense. Panelists do discriminate the different levels of ingredients. Of course, this discrimination might show up in different attributes. Flavoring changes may show up equally as changes in the perceived levels of flavor, as well as in perceived levels of sweetness. The analyst should realize that sweetener level affects other attributes, such as flavor and tartness (inversely). Sweetener level exerts an effect beyond influencing and correlating with perceived sweetness.

OPTIMIZATION

Table 7.15 shows separate non-linear equations which relate overall liking of the product by total sample by adults and children, respectively, to ingredients. Note that the equations differ from each other. We should expect that. These different groups of consumers exhibit different likes and dislikes. Furthermore, the unconstrained optima, lying within ingredient limits, show different formulations. Each individual group of consumers shows its own preference for the products. Finally, the sensory characteristics for the different products also differ. Adults prefer the less sweet product; children prefer the sweeter product.

SOME OTHER CONSIDERATIONS FROM A MARKETING/SENSORY ANALYSIS PERSPECTIVE

The non-linear models of liking allow us to predict how each group will react to the product which the other group finds most acceptable.

TABLE 7.13
DATA BASE—AVERAGE RATINGS ASSIGNED TO 27 BEVERAGE PRODUCTS
(Multi-Flavored Beverage)

	Total L/D	Adult L/D	Child L/D	Teen L/D	Purchase Intent	Flavor Strength	Natural Juice Flavor	Sweetness	Tartness	L/D Flavor	L/D Color	L/D Thickness	Freshness	Similar To Juice	L/D Appearance
1	18	12	32	19	−6	67	46	63	43	10	45	28	54	43	46
2	24	16	47	31	1	71	46	65	47	7	47	25	57	44	40
3	34	8	53	89	1	73	51	69	45	22	50	35	64	53	48
4	35	14	72	64	11	73	52	69	46	29	56	31	58	50	48
5	43	30	63	61	9	76	59	66	60	41	51	34	67	53	49
6	18	13	54	−3	−1	71	51	66	57	14	52	30	58	46	50
7	25	27	29	13	16	77	76	57	56	17	49	27	63	55	48
8	12	−4	49	18	−24	73	72	50	62	6	51	29	58	47	55
9	11	4	59	−21	−2	74	51	59	63	3	49	27	58	47	50
10	23	18	58	−1	6	70	50	62	49	15	48	27	58	45	41
11	26	9	60	48	−10	65	48	62	42	13	44	23	56	45	51
12	15	13	31	7	−9	71	49	65	54	13	40	15	61	50	38
13	26	28	51	−5	10	69	54	58	55	26	53	28	61	48	50
14	18	5	18	64	−4	70	45	62	58	6	50	21	56	43	53
15	16	12	38	8	−15	67	54	60	51	19	47	29	57	46	47

TABLE 7.13 (Continued)

	Total L/D	Adult L/D	Child L/D	Teen L/D	Purchase Intent	Flavor Strength	Natural Juice Flavor	Sweet-ness	Tart-ness	L/D Flavor	L/D Color	L/D Thick-ness	Fresh-ness	Similar To Juice	L/D Appear-ance
16	18	23	15	4	0	75	49	65	62	12	54	22	61	44	48
17	3	16	12	-42	-3	75	50	59	70	-2	49	28	56	47	39
18	4	-13	46	5	-16	59	43	56	48	3	43	18	52	43	40
19	-15	-26	35	-39	-34	59	38	54	49	-25	45	5	45	32	28
20	-19	-32	37	-46	-36	63	46	54	45	-19	44	5	50	39	33
21	0	-6	-8	25	-23	63	45	51	5	-6	55	23	56	41	38
22	11	11	58	-35	-5	66	42	55	55	3	44	22	51	44	42
23	16	20	1	15	6	68	51	63	49	9	52	25	60	47	49
24	15	5	29	30	-13	67	49	59	58	12	52	25	60	50	44
25	13	9	30	8	-12	70	46	56	59	10	44	23	58	47	45
26	-16	-21	16	-33	-23	65	38	57	51	-24	42	10	47	39	35
27	14	7	77	-35	-6	73	56	69	43	7	46	23	64	53	39

Adult Only

L/D = Like/Dislike

For purchase intent, 0 = might/might not buy, − = not buy, + = buy

TABLE 7.14
LINEAR EQUATIONS RELATING RATINGS TO BEVERAGE INGREDIENTS

Attribute	Multiple R	k_0 +	k_1(Acid) +	k_2(Sweetener) +	k_3(Flavoring A) +	k_4(Flavoring B)
1. Total Liking	0.75	−70.47	0.60	0.40	1.15	−0.18
2. Women's Liking	0.66	−144.21	1.71	0.43	0.96	−0.16
3. Child's Liking	0.59	156.90	−1.66	−0.28	0.97	−0.25
4. Teen Liking	0.67	−99.73	−0.07	0.97	2.02	−0.62
5. Purchase Intent	0.62	−94.63	0.95	0.25	0.87	−0.07
6. Flavor Strength	0.97	27.94	0.87	−1.10	0.45	−0.01
7. Natural Juice Like	0.82	−49.34	1.27	0.22	0.65	−0.04
8. Sweetness	0.58	82.37	−0.26	−0.09	0.29	−0.06
9. Tartness	0.95	−31.30	1.76	−0.15	0.23	0.06
10. Liking of Flavor	0.73	−113.46	0.97	0.54	1.04	−0.15
11. Liking of Color	0.59	6.01	0.17	0.08	0.17	0.02
12. Liking of Thickness	0.83	−45.93	0.84	0.16	0.66	−0.08
13. Freshness	0.62	20.68	0.47	0.07	0.32	−0.02
14. Similar to Juice	0.66	8.03	0.56	0.04	0.34	−0.03
15. Liking of Appearance	0.89	−12.09	0.88	0.04	0.57	−0.12

R = multiple correlation

TABLE 7.15
NONLINEAR EQUATIONS RELATING LIKING TO INGREDIENTS

	Group		
	Adults	Children	Total
Intercept	−1547.40	1491.50	−1115.60
(Acid) = A	41.62	−11.81	30.79
(Acid)^2 = A^2	−0.39	0.05	−0.33
(Sweetener) = B	6.86	−20.10	4.60
(Sweetener)^2 = B^2	−0.04	0.08	−0.03
(Flavor A) = C	6.89	−3.43	8.49
(Flavor A)^2 = C^2	−0.09	−0.02	−0.04
Flavor B = D	−2.43	5.46	−2.56
(Flavor B)^2 = D	−0.01	−0.02	0.00
AB	0.03	0.04	0.05
AC	−0.12	0.06	−0.12
AD	0.05	−0.20	0.05
BC	0.02	0.01	0.00
BD	−0.00	−0.03	0.00
CD	0.015	−0.01	0.00
Multiple R	0.89	0.77	0.89
Optimum Formula			
Acid	56.81	50.00	51.38
Sweetener	117.92	160.06	114.54
Flavor A	16.99	22.00	22.00
Flavor B	45.13	29.93	0.00
Optimum Liking =	33	73	40

SENSORY ATTRIBUTES OF THE OPTIMUM FORMULAS

		Group		
		Adults	Children	Total
1.	Flavor Strength	72.4	70.8	70.9
2.	Natural/Juicy	57.4	48.8	54.9
3.	Sweetness	59.7	65.3	65.5
4.	Tartness	57.4	48.3	46.9
5.	Freshness	60.3	57.3	59.9
6.	Similar to Juice	48.8	46.4	48.5
7.	Cost*	236.85	201.9	188.9

*From cost formula

By substituting the optimum ingredient levels in each liking equation, the marketer can ascertain the expected liking generated by each group. What adults find highly acceptable children may find less acceptable, and vice versa (Table 7.16).

The problem of satisfying several groups simultaneously commonly occurs when we deal with segmented markets in which consumers have different taste preferences. In order to overcome this problem and to select a product which has a reasonable chance of success, the product tester, market researcher and marketer must settle for a less than optimal product which satisfies the key consumer segments to at least a minimal degree.

TABLE 7.16
COMPARISON OF RESPONSES OF DIFFERENT SUBGROUPS
TO OPTIMAL BEVERAGE

Formulation						Expected Liking Rating		
			Flavor					
	Acid	Sweetener	A	B	Total	Adults	Children
Optimal Beverage for								
Total	51.38	114.54	22.00	0.0	40		
Adult	56.81	117.92	16.97	45.13		33	
Child	50.00	160.00	22.00	29.93			73

Systematic Cost Reductions

The optimization method allows the analyst to change the constraints on the cost of the product and then evaluate the effect on acceptance. Let us consider the issue of optimizing the beverage by selecting different cost constraints. Recall that Table 7.13 provides ratings of sensory and hedonic characteristics. We also can estimate the total cost of goods. We estimate the unit cost of each item in the beverage formula and the inflation factors, both as they currently exist and as they affect the prices of ingredients.

Optimization requires that we select the highest point on the parabolic, or inverted U-shaped curve. This represents the highest estimated acceptance level. Add to this the requirement that a linear combination of ingredients must achieve a value equal to or lower than a pre-set value. Mathematicians have developed optimization procedures for parabolic curves which allow them to maximize the curve (find the highest point), such that the curve remains (a) subject to point or ingredient constraints (no ingredient shall exceed an upper or lower limit pre-specified by the analyst) and (b) subject to linear combination constraints. Cost of goods represents a linear combination of ingredients, which we can represent by means of a linear equation.

Table 7.17 shows the schedule of cost reductions which one can achieve by systematically lowering the cost of goods of the beverage. Note that as the permitted cost diminishes, the ingredient levels diminish, but not equally. The sensory perceptions change due to the changing ingredient levels. Furthermore, at first the change diminishes acceptance only marginally, but when we come to large cost reductions, acceptability will begin to drop down rapidly. This exercise parallels the cost reduction exercise we did for bread (Table 7.9).

With systematic cost reductions optimized by means of the non-linear model, the marketer, sensory analyst and marketing researcher can insure the most acceptable products at the lowest cost, or at least at pre-determined low costs. Consequently, the procedure allows the product developer an opportunity to map out the sequence of cost reductions at the inception of the project, after having developed the alternative prototypes and subjected them to consumer testing. This systematic procedure contrasts sharply with less systematic, trial-and-error methods whereby the marketer reacts to changing cost-of-goods by requesting rapid reformulations of current products. Given a model which interrelates ingredients, perceptions, acceptance and cost, the marketer can estimate at the outset the likely change in consumer perceptions and acceptance level incurred by specific cost reductions.

Formula Modifications and Line Extensions

From time to time, marketers in the food industry want to develop line extensions of current products, or modify current products to change one or another sensory characteristic. Perhaps, for a bread, the rye flavor tastes too strong. A beverage may taste two sweet or too tart, or the marketer may want a less tart beverage to appeal to children. In the usual course of events, the marketer requests that R&D develop a variety of alternative modifications which embody the flavor or other sensory change. These modified formulations, representing possible line extensions, go out for consumer testing. The product developer reformulates the products in order to improve their taste/flavor, or

TABLE 7.17
SEQUENCE OF ALTERNATIVE OPTIMA—BEVERAGE

	Adults				Total		
	Overall Optimum	Cost ≤ 210	Cost ≤ 185	Cost ≤ 160	Overall Optimum	Sweetness ≤ 60	Tartness ≤ 45
Acid =	56.81	55.39	54.10	53.20	51.38	55.12	50.00
Sweetener =	117.92	14.76	113.20	100.00	114.54	120.00	113.46
Flavor A =	16.99	15.04	12.97	6.80	22.00	10.44	22.00
Flavor B =	45.13	24.80	4.70	0.00	0.00	13.62	0.00
Liking =	33.4	30.2	23.3	7.4	40.0	27.5	39.1
Flavor Strength =	72.4	70.9	69.3	67.1	70.9	68.2	69.8
Natural Juices =	57.4	54.5	52.0	44.2	54.9	52.8	52.9
Sweetness =	59.7	61.0	62.1	62.0	65.5	60.0	66.0
Tartness =	57.4	53.7	50.0	48.7	46.9	50.8	44.6
Freshness =	60.3	59.1	58.0	54.8	59.9	58.0	59.1
Similarity to Juice =	48.8	47.7	46.8	43.8	48.5	46.5	47.7
Cost Now =	237	210	185	160	188	199	185

otherwise correct any deficits which the product may possess.

With a model interrelating sensory characteristics, acceptance, cost and ingredients, the marketer can short-cut this tedious process. We illustrate the development of a less sweet or less tart beverage in Table 7.17. Here, the marketer decided to explore the acceptance change which would occur if the consumers assessed a less intense tasting beverage. Since the model interrelates the various ingredients, it becomes a straightforward matter to determine the necessary ingredients which maximize the acceptance of the product; but at the same time require that the ingredients stay within limits pre-specified by R&D, and that the sensory characteristics stay within limits, as specified by the marketer. By treating sensory characteristics as constraints, just as we treated ingredients as constraints and cost of ingredients as a linear constraint, the marketer can now evaluate the effect on acceptance and attribute perceptions.

An Update on The Results and Their Implementation

These results provided direct formulations which the marketers and market researchers could test, and then introduce. In any new product development effort, the product tester who optimizes a product must subsequently test the optimum formulation to confirm its acceptability, preferably in an extended (home) use test. The extended use test provides the final product test regarding acceptability.

The FBC market research group submitted the product formulation to subsequent testing, and found that, in fact, the optimum product performed quite acceptably. Afterwards, the product entered into other testing phases, including tests of the concept underlying the beverage as well as the test market simulation. The product then appeared in the market in limited roll out. The marketing group launched it in three locations, where it performed acceptably in terms of initial consumer satisfaction and repeat purchase.

SENSORY CHARACTERISTICS AS ATTRIBUTES— OPTIMIZATION IMPLICATIONS FOR PRODUCTS

In many studies the manufacturer may wish to optimize acceptance, but has no systematically varied products. Rather, the manufacturer may possess ratings on marketed products without systematic variations in ingredients. The product tester may have available different types of beverages of the same flavor, varying in sweetness, tartness, flavor impact, flavor quality, etc. These products, purchased from the competitors and augmented by test variants fabricated with alternative ingredients, represent a variety of different formulations. No two products from the set will differ by only the ingredient type alone.

The product tester can still use the ratings of products on attributes to gain an idea of the optimally acceptable product, and synthesize the optimally acceptable sensory profile. The logic follows this sequence. (1) The sensory characteristics (e.g., flavor, taste and color) comprise surrogate ingredients. They behave as perceptual ingredients. (2) By varying the types of physical formulations, the product developers have generated products comprising an array of different perceptual levels of sensory characteristics. (3) By relating overall liking to the sensory attributes, and to their non-linear interactions and square terms, the analyst can discover the *sensory profile* which produces the maximum level of acceptability. The panelist may not have tested any product which possesses the specific characteristics. On the other hand, we synthesize the optimal profile of sensory attributes just as we optimized the profile or recipe of actual ingredients. (4) The results provide a sensory profile, or a sensory recipe, which gives direction for future product development. The method does not provide the actual physical recipe, because the researcher cannot integrate the ingredients into this model.

Let us consider our bread and our beverage data in light of this sensory optimization. The first criterion concerns the selection of the relevant sensory attributes to serve as our surrogate ingredients. We eliminate actual ingredients from consideration at this point, and imagine instead that the products typify a wide variety of alternative compositions. We must choose attributes which behave as surrogate ingredients, representing non-evaluative sensory judgments. Attributes such as rye flavor and firmness suggest themselves for the bread, whereas perceived sweetness, tartness and flavor intensity suggest themselves for the beverage. The considerations listed below represent some criteria for the selection of the surrogate attributes.

(1) Each attribute should not correlate with the other attributes. The modest or low correlation means that the attributes selected as ingredients behave independently of each other, just as the ingredients behave independently of each other. (2) The attributes should show relatively low interpanelist variability. Panelists ought to agree with each other as to what these attributes mean. (3) The attributes make sense as descriptors of sensory experience. They reflect sensory perceptions, not image perceptions, or restatements of liking. A bread can have too much rye flavor as well as too little. A beverage can taste too sweet as well as not sweet enough. We must choose those attributes in preference to attributes such as "natural" which behave like an image attribute.

Model Development

Let us follow the same analytical approach that we used previously when optimizing liking versus ingredients. First, let us substitute the sensory attributes in place of ingredients, and represent liking as a weighted linear combination of two bread attributes, or beverage acceptance as a weighted combination of the three attributes. This approach shows a modestly good fit of the data (see Tables 7.18 and 7.19).

Recall the principle of optimization. Each sensory attribute, as well as each ingredient, may (but need not) show an intermediate bliss point. We could never ascertain the intermediate bliss point without the non-linear terms which allow curvature. Thus, we must again introduce both square terms and the cross product terms into the equation to describe liking. For bread acceptability, we need but 3 additional terms (the two square terms and the one cross term). These additional terms improve the fit. For beverage acceptability we have at most 6 additional terms (3 square terms and 3 cross terms). We can reduce the 6 terms to a fewer number, since all terms do not contribute that much to the data.

TABLE 7.18

SENSORY ATTRIBUTES OF BREAD AS SURROGATE INGREDIENTS*

Linear
  Liking $= 32.66 - 0.01$ (Firmness) $- 0.74$ (Rye Flavor)
    $R = 0.58$

Nonlinear
  Liking $= 41.22 - 0.02$ (**Firmness**) $- 0.05$ (Firmness)$^2 - 0.89$ (Rye Flavor) $- 0.13$ (Rye Flavor)^2
                $+ 0.16$ (Firmness) (Rye Flavor)
    $R = 0.62$

---

*Note: no intermediate optimum of either perceived firmness or rye flavor

Tables 7.18 and 7.19 show the equations which we can develop by this approach. As we might expect, the non-linear equation improves prediction of overall liking versus sensory characteristics. As a side issue, this simple exercise reveals that in order to relate sensory characteristics to overall liking/disliking (which may exhibit intermediate bliss points), the product tester should consider using the quadratic or parabolic equation.

TABLE 7.19
SENSORY ATTRIBUTES OF BEVERAGES AS
SURROGATE INGREDIENTS

Linear
  Liking (Total) = $-$ 120.091 + 1.89 (Sweetness) + 0.38 (Tartness)
    R = 0.68

Nonlinear
  Liking (Total) = $-$ 917.99 + 14.17 (Sweetness) $-$ 0.40 $(Sweetness)^2$
                  + 16.45 (Tartness) $-$ 0.07 $(Tartness)^2$
                  $-$ 0.14 (Sweetness) (Tartness)
    R = 0.75

Attribute Limits	Lower	Upper	Optimal By Linear Equation	Optimal By Quadratic Equation
Sweetness	50	70	70	70.0
Tartness	40	70	70	47.5

Note: intermediate optimum of perceived tartness

By using the straightforward methods of optimization, one can ascertain that set of sensory levels for perceived flavor or taste characteristics which, in concert, generate the highest liking. Of course, we must stay within the boundaries of achievable levels of sensory values. We cannot project the optimum level out to sensory values about which we have little or no data. It should come as no surprise that when we try to maximize the equation, one or several sensory attributes will show their optimum at the upper or lower level that we tested. We cannot avoid this problem and force an intermediate sensory level. We cannot a priori engineer products simply by fabricating very high or very low sensory attribute levels. Only by modifying ingredient levels can one develop products representing very high or low sensory characteristics.

AN OVERVIEW TO OPTIMIZATION
BY NON—LINEAR METHODS

The two foregoing exercises in product optimization show that the product tester can provide extremely powerful feedback to marketing and R&D through well designed and executed studies. The basic requirements for providing this feedback necessitate two considerations. (1) It requires recognition that one needs responses to a pattern or array of products, rather than response to a single formulation and the ensuing directional information. Only the pattern of varying ingredient (or sensory) levels versus acceptability provides sufficient information to construct a roadmap which can guide product reformulation with adequate precision. (2) It requires recognition that the product tester needs to use a sensitive scaling device to measure differences among the products. The researcher cannot use insensitive scaling methods, which provide little or no discrimination. If one used insensitive scales, then the ratings of products would cluster near each other, and hinder the discovery of relations between acceptance and either ingredients or sensory characteristics.

This model summarizes the relations between ingredients, perceptions and liking. Products must vary in terms of sensory characteristics in order to evidence these interrelations. Because of its sensitivity, magnitude estimation may well provide the most sensitive measurement procedure, appropriate with either large or with small numbers of panelists (experts or consumers) testing each variation. Hedonic scales (e.g., fixed point category scales) show less sensitivity to differences. Hence, they require more panelists per product to achieve stable data. The use of fixed point scales would place an unduly large strain on the field costs to actually implement the optimization project (Moskowitz 1980).

Finally, through optimization, the product tester, product developer, marketer and management can develop an action oriented description of the product. The model tells them in quantitative terms the likely effects of changes in ingredients. Furthermore, the model provides the manufacturer with an unambiguous insight into the relations between cost of goods, product acceptance and sensory perceptions.

PROFILE FITTING—AN ALTERNATIVE APPROACH

Recently, Moskowitz, Stanley and Chandler (1977) suggested that in some instances the marketer may wish to copy an existing product, using one's own ingredients. As the cost of ingredients increases in an inflationary economy, manufacturers continually seek to reduce the cost of goods by substituting ingredients which cost less, and yet maintain an identical or at least highly similar profile of sensory attributes. With established brands, marketers must carefully assess the effect of such substitutions on consumer reactions. The sensory profile of the cost modified product could differ so much from the currently marketed product that consumers would reject it. New suppliers of food ingredients often provide similar, but not identical, ingredients which differ in graded degrees from the current ingredients. Even when the manufacturer changes from one ingredient supplier to another who sells almost identical ingredients, the manufacturer always runs the risk of accidentally modifying the sensory profile of the product, and changing it to a less acceptable one.

The logic of the profile fitting system appears as follows. (1) Linear equations relate sensory attribute perceptions to ingredients. (2) Given the linear equations (e.g., those appearing in Table 7.7 for rye and Table 7.14 for beverage), the analyst can estimate the likely sensory profile of a combination of ingredients by using the equations. In order to do so, the analyst inserts the relevant ingredient concentrations or input levels into the equations, and calculates the expected sensory attribute level. Since a separate equation governs each attribute, the analyst must substitute the same set of ingredient levels into each equation, and calculate the expected level. We saw this for the evaluation of the sensory characteristics of the optimally acceptable product. Once we discovered the actual levels which maximized acceptance, we could estimate what the product would taste like or feel like by using the equations. (3) Let us turn the problem around 180°. We now specify a desired profile of perceptions. These perceptions can represent an existing product which the manufacturer wishes to copy; the profile may represent an ideal product developed by the panelist's own estimation; or it may even represent the sensory characteristics of a product as connoted by an advertisement. (4) By reversing the regression procedure using the method of *goal programming* or *multiple objective programming* (a reverse regression method), the analyst can discover that combination of ingredients which produces the desired or goal sensory profile. Furthermore, these ingredients must lie within specified, pre-designated limits. It does no good to determine that the ingredients for the designated profile assume 0 or negative values, in order to best solve the reverse regression problem. The ingredients must lie within pre-designated limits, specified a priori by the sensory analyst and the product developer.

Examples With Bread and With Beverage

Given this approach which appears schematically in Fig. 7.2, we can reanalyze the bread and beverage ratings. Having already developed the linear equations for the attributes, we proceed immediately to the analysis. The analyst should bear in mind that the profile fitting optimization proceeds most smoothly and validly when the attributes represent sensory attributes, not image attributes. Generally, these

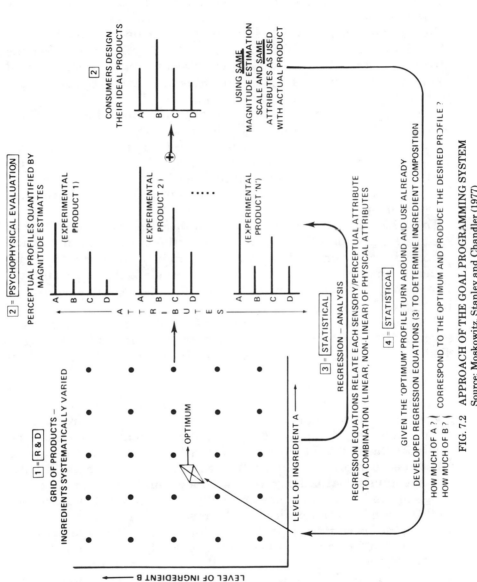

FIG. 7.2   APPROACH OF THE GOAL PROGRAMMING SYSTEM
Source: Moskowitz, Stanley and Chandler (1977)

sensory attributes generate acceptable linear functions relating ingredients and sensory perceptions (in terms of the multiple correlation and goodness of fit). The analyst should not use hedonic attributes (e.g., overall liking/disliking or liking/disliking of specific sensory characteristics) or image attributes as the goal or target levels to achieve. The ideal levels of these attributes often lie far out of the range of achievable levels. Furthermore, more often than not these hedonic attributes behave in a non-linear way versus concentration. Overall liking and disliking of specific attributes peak at intermediate bliss point levels, and do not fall on a straight line.

With respect to the rye bread project of the Gonzales Milling Company, recall that the panelists evaluated 12 breads on a variety of attributes (Tables 7.6). At the end of the evaluation, the panelists scaled their ideal product using the same attributes and the same scale. This comparability of existing and designed products plays a key role in the achievement of successful profile fitting, since we must have commensurate attributes and scales.

Table 7.20 shows the results of the profile fitting procedure. Having specified a goal profile, the multiple objective programming method searched for a combination of sucrose and rye flour which would generate an attribute profile as close as possible to the desired profile. The ingredients had to stay within the designated 0-6% sucrose and 12-42% rye flour ranges.

With several different alternative profiles, we would of course obtain several different formulations. Furthermore, with only two ingredients varying we have few degrees of freedom to move around, in order to satisfy all of the different constraints placed upon the system. Each sensory characteristic acts, in turn, as a constraint. With a limited number of sensory characteristics, the statistical method can juggle the sucrose and rye flour levels to generate the desired values. As the number of sensory characteristics increases, and as some desired values conflict with each other, the optimization technique must make compromises and satisfy some more than others. Finally, in some unusual situations the desired level may lie so far out of the range of the levels which one can achieve by reasonable ingredient modification, that this desired level forces the ingredients to lie at the upper or the lower ingredient limits. If, for example, ideal rye flavor lay at a rating of 200, and the rye breads could only achieve a maximum level of 90, then the rye bread within the range of variation would not achieve a rating of 200. Yet, by forcing the ideal level to this unreasonably high value, the analyst would push the actual concentration of rye to its limit, which in this study remained at 42%.

Table 7.20 shows two of the alternative solutions for different

TABLE 7.20
PROFILE FITTING—BREAD
(Gonzales Milling Company)

Attribute	Profile A		Profile B	
	Desired Level	Obtainable Level	Desired Level	Obtainable Level
Firmness	100	100.0	70	70.0
Denseness	100	127.2	60	87.6
Moistness	100	71.1	80	64.8
Chewiness	100	92.5	80	68.5
Flavor Strength	100	88.7	100	67.7
Rye Flavor	100	60.5	60	42.9
Formula				
Rye	37.85		26.1	
Sucrose	6.0		6.0	

sensory characteristics, and for some reasonable versus unreasonable desired levels placed on the ideal profiles which one would like to achieve in the formulation.

A second set of optimizations, this time with our fruit flavored beverage comprising three ingredients, appears in Table 7.21, again with

TABLE 7.21
PROFILE FITTING—BEVERAGE PROJECT
(FBC Company)

Attribute	Profile A		Profile B	
	Desired Level	Obtainable Level	Desired Level	Obtainable Level
Flavor Strength	89	79.9	50	62.7
Natural/Juicy	96	62.7	50	44.2
Sweetness	82	64.6	50	54.9
Tartness	66	64.2	50	50.0
Formula				
Acid	60		54.9	
Sweetener	100		120.0	
Flavor "A"	22		6.0	
Flavor "B"	0		50.0	

two alternative solutions showing the flexibility of the profile-fitting approach. With beverages, the technologist faces the continuing problem of providing the consumer panelist with an acceptable beverage that tastes natural. If when we use the attribute of naturalness at its highest level possible, which lies far outside the range of achievable levels versus ingredient modification, we would force the formulation to generate extreme stimulus levels, which might not taste quite acceptable.

INTERLINKING OUR THREE OPTIMIZATIONS

The three optimizations (ingredients versus liking, sensory attributes versus liking, and ingredients versus sensory attributes) share some common aspects. If ratings for the sensory attributes predict liking very well, behave independently of each other, and correlate highly with ingredient levels, we may expect the non-linear optimization by means of sensory attributes (versus liking) to generate a highly acceptable product. The sensory profile which generates the highest empirical liking allows us, via the final profile-fitting optimization, to determine that combination of ingredients which provides the most acceptable product. In turn, this provides the highest empirical liking score.

Each problem of optimization deserves special and separate consideration. On some occasions the analyst will find that the three optimizations link together perfectly, whereas on other occasions they do not. In such instances, this author recommends that, wherever possible, the analyst choose an experimental design of ingredients which systematically vary. The analyst should then develop the non-linear model relating ingredient levels and overall liking/disliking ratings. This form of optimization most directly relates ingredients to an overall acceptance rating. The method provides the most direct, fool-proof way to generate highly acceptable products.

DO PANELISTS' IDEAL PROFILES REFLECT
THE MOST ACCEPTABLE PRODUCT?

Product testers, market researchers and marketers traditionally have asked panelists to profile their ideal product. They have related this profile to existing products, in order to obtain direction for product modifications. Do these self-designed ideal products lead the road to the most acceptable formulations?

We can test this hypothesis by appealing to rating data. We possess good non-linear equations relating ingredients to perceptions in terms of predicting overall liking/disliking ratings. We further know the consumer panelist's self-designed ideal profile for the product. We could substitute the formulation for the consumer's self-designed ideal product profile into the equation for overall liking/disliking. The liking score for the self-designed ideal often scores less than optimal. In many cases, the self-designed ideal points towards the optimum, but really lies some distance away from the optimum. What the consumer designs himself or herself does not necessarily produce the most acceptable product. Traditional research, using only one or a few products in descriptive analysis, could not have tested this hypothesis and revealed the estimated acceptance of a self-designed optimum for a product. Only with a model relating ingredients and perceptions can the analyst confirm or disprove the validity of the self designed ideal profile as an optimally acceptable product.

If self designed profiles, in fact, do not maximize acceptability, then which method should the product tester adopt? Of what value does the profile-fitting become, if it cannot maximize acceptance? To reiterate the foregoing points, it seems most appropriate to use the experimental design of ingredients and base the optimization on the liking scores. This exercise directly develops an equation relating liking to ingredients, independent of a consumer's scaled perceptual attributes. The product tester, market researcher and marketer can feel more certain that the optimized product emerging from the non-linear liking model will, in fact, score highest on overall liking.

Profile fitting, in turn, does best for copying existing products whose sensory profiles possess desirable characteristics. The manufacturer wishing to imitate those characteristics should use the profile procedure to do so, but should not concern himself or herself with maximization of overall acceptability.

AN OVERVIEW TO CONTINUOUS-VARIABLE OPTIMIZATION

We have seen three different methods of optimizing the product: (1) igredients versus liking (non-linear), (2) sensory attributes versus liking (non-linear), and (3) ingredients versus sensory attributes (linear). These optimization procedures require the panelist to scale the product(s) on a variety of sensory or performance characteristics, using a scale which sufficiently differentiates among the various products. The scale must provide different rating levels for different products;

otherwise, no matter how the products vary physically, they will all generate the same attribute profile. As a consequence, the researcher will find it impossible to fit a model or equation to the data. As stated previously, the magnitude estimation scaling procedure may provide the best method to generate these numbers on which to base the equations. That should come as no surprise to the reader. Magnitude estimation scaling has, for the past thirty years, provided the numerical basis for scientific equations relating perceived sensory intensity to physical stimulus levels.

The optimization methods further require that the analyst scale perceptions for a variety of products, not just one variation. The product developer must produce these systematic and continuous ingredient-level variations. Traditional product measurement often tried to secure directional feedback for optimization from the evaluation of a limited number of alternative products (sometimes as few as just one); but in these less efficient methods panelists would indicate where the sensory attributes lay on the scale, as well as where they wanted the attributes to lie. These procedures generated the desired sensory changes. However, one ran the risk that the self designated ideal profile would, in fact, not score high on acceptability.

Researchers, product testers, marketers and manufacturers who use single stimuli, or several stimuli (but too few for model development), may miss the opportunity to obtain actionable, validating data on directions for product reformulation. The economics of producing and testing just a few prototypes, attractive as they seem, more than likely would lead to a quagmire and dead end when the time comes to evaluate the results and suggest alternatives. This author would not follow that dead end path when other methods of a more actionable nature present themselves.

OPTIMIZING DISCRETE PRODUCT CHARACTERISTICS

Product developers and manufacturers often face an entirely different problem which demands optimization. During the development of a product prototype, the manufacturer can vary the type of flavor, the type of color, and the shape. Each one of these characteristics or variables, flavor, color and shape, can assume one of several different alternatives. If, in the development of a candy bar, the manufacturer can choose from among 4 flavors, 5 shapes and 3 colors of the coating, then the number of combinations comes to 60 ($4 \times 5 \times 3$). Increasing the number of variables or the number of options within a variable further increases the total number of alternative prototypes which the manufacturer can produce.

How to select the optimal combination of discrete alternatives constitutes the remainder of this chapter on optimization. We now face a different problem. The problem becomes how to select a combination of discrete alternatives to go together, in order to maximize an overall criterion (e.g., rated purchase interest), subject perhaps to other criteria remaining within bounds (e.g., cost, perceived youth orientation or perceived adult orientation of the product).

THE CEREAL PROBLEM

The Fitch Cereal Manufacturer (FCM), a small manufacturer of cereals located in the Midwest, has for the past five years considered introducing a new cereal, compatible with its extruding machinery. FCM markets four cereals, three targeted for children and one targeted for adults. In the light of the growing opportunities for nutritionally fortified adult and children's cereals, FCM commissioned a strategy study on the opportunities for introducing a cereal into the market.

This strategy study revealed the following factors, which dictated the type of cereal that would pay out most effectively for FCM. (1) Consumers (primarily mothers of young children) stated that they wanted non-gimmicky children's cereal. (2) The increasing emphasis on taste and flavor, coupled with the interest in health, suggested that the cereal should offer a health benefit. Consumers evidenced high interest in vitamins and other fortifications. They also showed interest and credibility in adding bran for its laxative, bulk properties. At the time of the project, bran-enriched products began to appear regularly on the shelf in food stores. The facing or space devoted to bran cereals and bran breads had grown at the rate of 18%-25% yearly, reflecting the increased consumer interest and demand. (3) Consumers said that they wanted a tasty cereal, not just another me-too formulation with little or no appeal other than fancy packaging. (4) A study of candidate names for the cereal suggested that a name connected with health would add considerably to consumers' initial interest in the cereal, and would favor initial product purchase. On the other hand, in the category of adult cereal, the taste/flavor/texture factors would determine the level of re-purchase. (5) Consumers behaved in a fickle manner in their selection of cereals. Many consumers felt that dry cereals had such short life cycles that consumers had little time to build up awareness and brand loyalty to any particular cereal before the manufacturer withdrew it, and introduced another entry.

Armed with this information, the group marketing manager, with responsibility for new cereals, commmissioned his R&D product development staff to develop alternative prototype formulas. These prototypes embodied different flavors, shapes and colors, in an effort to find that combination of factors which (1) signalled health benefit, (2) tasted good to adults, and (3) tasted good to children.

Prototype Development

The FCM product developers had the opportunity to fabricate a variety of alternative cereal prototypes. They suggested certain prototypes, given their bench top capabilities, and the pilot plant feasibility in terms of time available for development of the product prototypes. This array of cereal options provided the product developers with a potential set of $2 \times 3 \times 3 = 18$ variations.

The variations in Table 7.22 emerge from the method of experimental design. By means of the proper selection of alternative formula options, the product developer can test key variations or a subset from among the options which he or she can produce. Of course, with few alternatives the product developer can test all options or all combinations. On the other hand, the judicious use of experimental design and the development of a model permits prediction of consumer reactions to the combinations not directly tested. This ability to test a limited set of alternatives, not the entire set, becomes critical in test situations involving possibly hundreds or thousands of alternative combinations.

In this situation, FCM chose discrete options in terms of physical product variations. The preceding approaches, which built a model based upon continuous variations of ingredient levels, no longer applies. Here we must choose which options or type to manufacture—not which level. We select from among available options rather than interpolating.

Marketing researchers and marketers have introduced the concept of tradeoff analysis, which we will use here. Tradeoff analysis permits the researcher to represent the combination of product options in a product as the arithmetic sum of *component utilities*. Each flavor, each color, and each texture carries with it an intrinsic utility, as yet undetermined. Any product comprising one of the flavors, colors and textures represents the sum of three component utilities. In order to maximize overall acceptability, therefore, the analyst must select the proper flavor, color and texture so that the sum of their utilities will generate the highest score.

When the marketer has an opportunity to have consumers evaluate all of the combinations, he or she can select that product which scores highest in actual ratings. Even better, the marketer might seek to represent the full data as a model, and look at the model to see which combination of options generates the highest utility or acceptability. When we work with incomplete product sets, representing the fractional design, we cannot limit our selection to the products empirically tested. Rather, we use those tested products to represent the entire set of alternatives. We base the parameters of the model on the products we test, but generalize the model to the full set of options.

Theory of Tradeoffs and Discrete Option Optimization

Let us consider, in mathematical terms, what we just described above in verbal terms. Overall liking (or, in fact, any other characteristic judged by consumers) correlates with the presence or absence of each option or each cereal variable (flavor type, color type and texture type) by means of a simple additive equation:

$$\text{Liking} - k_0 + k_1(\text{Honey}) + k_2(\text{Cinnamon}) \mid k_3(\text{Maple}) \mid k_4(\text{Red}) + k_5(\text{Brown}) + k_6(\text{Tan}) + k_7(\text{Smooth}) + k_8(\text{Rough}).$$

This additive equation implies these things. (1) Overall liking equals a linear sum of the component utilities, or part-wise liking values of the components. As yet we do not know those utilities. We compute them through simple statistical methods using our data base on product ratings. (2) The coefficient k_1 represents the partwise utility, or partwise liking for honey flavor. The coefficient k_2 represents the partwise utility, or partwise liking for cinnamon flavor, etc. (3) Each option possesses its own unique coefficient, which indicates the partwise utility or partwise liking contributed by the presence of that specific attribute. (4) In order to estimate the overall liking which we can expect for a given combination of cereal characteristics, we use the equation for computation purposes. For a product which has a honey flavor, and thus does not have a cinnamon flavor or a maple flavor, we put a 1 in the spot reserved for honey, and a 0 in the place of cinnamon and maple. In that way, the product of the partwise utility and the code for presence (present $= 1$; absent $= 0$) will correctly emerge as a non-zero number for honey, and a 0 for cinnamon and maple. No matter what their partwise utilities equal, the absence of these two remaining flavors means that their contributions effectively equal 0. (5) The coefficients k_i can assume 0 values if the presence of the flavor or shape, etc. contributes absolutely nothing. A coefficient can assume a positive value if the presence of the particular flavor or shape, etc. adds some partwise liking, or can assume a negative value if the presence of the

TABLE 7.22
EXPERIMENTAL DESIGN OF 18 DIFFERENT CEREALS VARYING
IN TEXTURE, COLOR AND FLAVOR

Product	Type of Texture	Type of Color	Type of Flavor
1.	A	A	A
2.	A	A	B
3.	A	A	C
4.	A	B	A
5.	A	B	B
6.	A	B	C
7.	A	C	A
8.	A	C	B
9.	A	C	C
10.	B	A	A
11.	B	A	B
12.	B	A	C
13.	B	B	A
14.	B	B	B
15.	B	B	C
16.	B	C	A
17.	B	C	B
18.	B	C	C
A	Low (Smooth)	Tan	Honey
B	High (Rough)	Brown	Cinnamon
C		Red	Maple

particular characteristic diminishes liking.

By representing the data as an additive function of contributions from components, the researcher and marketer can immediately evaluate the expected overall liking of various combinations of alternatives, by simply adding together their partwise utilities. Furthermore, if the marketer generates an additive equation for other sensory characteristics as well as overall liking, it becomes a straightforward matter to compute the estimated sensory properties of the optimal product, even though the sensory analyst or product tester has not directly tested that specific formulation.

Specifics About the Cereal Study

In order to properly implement the evaluation of options, the marketer and the product tester had to answer these specific questions pertaining to research particulars. (1) What constitutes the optimum number of products to evaluate? Through the method of experimental design, this problem resolved itself into a full set of 18 alternatives, representing 100% of the full set of 18. Other experimental designs could equally apply in this instance. Recall that we tested 27 variations out of 81 for the beverage product. (2) What constitutes the best method of testing—long-term home-use test, short term exposure in a mall-test situation, or central location pre-recruit test with 3 hour evaluations? Based upon the discussions with inputs from R&D and the product tester, the company decided to test the products in a short term, central location intercept evaluation. (3) Who should make up the panel? Panelists would comprise cereal users, half adults (generally women ages 18-49) and half teens (ages 13-17).

Study Implementation

The final approval for the study came from management. The product tester and field service executed the study. In order to properly implement the study and to insure adequate data collection, the product tester followed these steps. (1) He developed written instructions for the field service, specifying the type of panelists to select, including age, etc. (2) He specified criteria for rejecting any panelist. (3) He specified the amount of product served to each panelist. In the actual field evaluation, each panelist evaluated a total of 6 of the 18 products, with a half bowl of cereal and milk. (4) He specified questions to ask the panelists in the form of a script, which comprised an orientation (to the test and to the magnitude estimation procedure), the actual product evaluation, and the calibration method.

The study took place in two cities, allowing the product tester the opportunity to look at city differences (We will not consider the issue of regional differences here, but will take up the issue in the chapter on Marketing Research and Sensory Analysis).

In order to achieve a reasonable base size for the study, allowing for 40 panelists/product (20 adults and 20 teens/children = 40), the product tester used these computations to arrive at the final base size:

18 products $\times$ 40/Ratings/Product = 720 Total

Each panelist tasted 6 of the products in random order (720 Total Tastings)/6(Tastings/Panelist) = 120 Panelists (60 Adults, 60 Teens). Since this study occurred in two markets, and since the aim included an analysis by market, a total of 240 panelists participated.

Field studies with consumers take longer to set up than do in-house studies with company panelists who work at the company site or at the university. However, once the product tester has contracted out the field portion of the study, the field service can manage the data collection, putting to work several interviewers to intercept the panelists at the mall, interview them, etc. In this study, the field service estimated total time to complete the data acquisition around 2 weeks. In fact, the study took 10 field days, with 5 interviewers working each day.

Results of the Study

Let us first look at the method for representing the full set of 18 product formulations in terms of discrete options. Table 7.22 shows the original specifications. Note that the design codes each option of flavor, color and texture as 0, 1, or 2 (or A, B, C), respectively. We use those letters or numbers simply as discrete numerical codes to represent the fact that these products represent different qualitative nuances. In this usage context, the numbers possess simple categorization properties, not higher level quantitative properties.

In order to better use the mathematics of discrete optimization, we must transform these data into a *binary code*. With 3 levels of cereal flavor, corresponding to honey, cinnamon and maple, we actually test three variables. Each variable assumes the value 1 if the attribute appears in the product, or 0 if the attribute does not appear (see Table 7.23). Table 7.24 shows the average ratings from the panelists who tested the cereals. It also provides the cost of goods. Since all panelists tested only a subsample of the actual set of formulations, but calibrated their ratings, we can compare the ratings of all panelists even though they did not all sample the same cereals. The calibration step in magnitude estimation provides us with that capability (see Chapters 5 and 6).

Development of Equations

By transforming data into a binary code, we set the stage for developing the additive equation which provides us with estimates of our partwise utilities, or partwise liking ratings. Table 7.25 shows the equations for the various different attributes. Note that in Table 7.25 the ingredient levels, or independent variables, take on only binary values (1 = present; 0 = absent). Each sensory or hedonic attribute which the panelist judges possesses its own unique equation, which relates the presence or absence of the 8 options in the cereal to the consumer reactions. Table 7.25 presents the full set of trade-off equations.

Some of the linear equations fit the data better than other equations.

TABLE 7.23
CEREAL VARIATIONS, CODED INTO BINARY CODE*

Product	Texture Type		Color Type			Flavor Type		
	Smooth (1)	Rough (2)	Brown	Red	Tan	Honey	Cinnamon	Maple
1.	1	0	1	0	0	1	0	0
2.	1	0	1	0	0	0	1	0
3.	1	0	1	0	0	0	0	1
4.	1	0	0	1	0	1	0	0
5.	1	0	0	1	0	0	1	0
6.	1	0	0	1	0	0	0	1
7.	1	0	0	0	1	1	0	0
8.	1	0	0	0	1	0	1	0
9.	1	0	0	0	1	0	0	1
10.	0	1	1	0	0	1	0	0
11.	0	1	1	0	0	0	1	0
12.	0	1	1	0	0	0	0	1
13.	0	1	0	1	0	1	0	0
14.	0	1	0	1	0	0	1	0
15.	0	1	0	1	0	0	0	1
16.	0	1	0	0	1	1	0	0
17.	0	1	0	0	1	0	1	0
18.	0	1	0	0	1	0	0	1

*1 = Present; 0 = Absent

TABLE 7.24
AVERAGE RATING OF 18 CEREALS ON ATTRIBUTES

	L/D Texture	Texture Rough-ness	Color Dark-ness	Crisp-ness In Milk	L/D Taste	Crunchi-ness	Sweet-ness	Natural Flavor	Graham Flavor	Total L/D	Liking Bran User	Liking Non User	Liking Adult	Liking Teen	Cost of Goods
1.	58	78	98	127	50	124	71	54	82	48	53	43	55	32	10
2.	73	79	89	129	61	121	86	72	94	46	43	49	47	44	16
3.	51	75	87	132	39	117	87	68	95	34	47	19	44	13	44
4.	72	95	89	141	52	129	75	55	88	41	39	43	43	35	19
5.	69	88	83	145	63	137	90	61	88	50	87	12	63	9	32
6.	61	92	85	145	61	130	94	76	85	64	75	53	72	44	64
7.	78	80	65	145	63	128	86	69	69	46	42	50	53	25	35
8.	66	78	64	149	63	129	86	69	76	62	73	50	68	42	47
9.	60	83	75	150	67	139	105	86	85	60	74	44	64	50	79
10.	56	85	92	159	61	142	87	64	89	55	61	49	65	23	4
11.	84	77	80	145	72	126	83	54	85	68	74	62	79	20	15
12.	64	77	84	135	70	124	101	79	90	58	83	35	73	23	48
13.	72	89	84	153	54	145	82	53	75	52	67	36	59	30	19
14.	60	84	79	142	60	137	83	57	84	51	52*	50	69	8	30
15.	62	71	63	137	53	122	96	75	75	44	63	26	57	9	63
16.	65	83	59	144	43	131	72	47	62	30	24	35	35	1	33
17.	66	95	67	149	59	149	103	82	83	50	50	50	55	41	45
18.	68	84	66	147	71	134	92	80	79	75	100	51	83	53	78

L/D = Liking/Disliking
Manufacturers Variable Cost

We should expect this. Just as the equations for some sensory characteristics fit the empirical ratings better than others, so here, in the
discrete option case, some attributes which consumers rate seem more
tractable to description by means of a simple additive equation. This
results from two factors. (1) The additive equations in Table 7.25
represent a very simple model of how the consumer combines partwise
contributions of the different cereal options. The sensory variables
generate better equations than do the hedonic variables. (2) The additive equation allows no interaction among components. The special
synergistic behavior of certain specific combinations of color and
shape, unique to that color and shape, never show up in the additive
equation. The linear equation makes no provision for such synergism,
whereas the non-linear liking equation, with continuously varying
factors, has that provision. By working with discrete, non-continuous
options in a selection study, the product tester and the product developer relinquish the opportunity to work with interactions, and with
non-linear functions.

SIMPLE OPTIMIZATION

Let us take the example of overall liking/disliking of the cereal.
Consulting Table 7.25 (equation 10), we see that for our three flavor
options, one option (maple) always obtains a utility or partwise
hedonic value of 0; whereas cinnamon flavor obtains a value of -1.33
and honey obtains a value of -10.50. In binary coding of this type,
mathematicians have shown that one variable of the three (choosen
arbitrarily) must obtain a utility or partwise contribution of 0. All of
the other variables in that set of flavors will obtain utility values
relative to that 0. The differences in utility values remain constant. For
example, had we chosen cinnamon to obtain a utility value of 0, maple
would have assumed a value of $+1.33$ and honey a value of -9.17. The
same rationale applies to the options of color and texture.

Given the array of partwise utilities or contributions to liking, how
do we select the combinations which maximize overall liking? Recalling the meaning of the utilities, we simply select that combination of
cereal options which provides the highest arithmetic sum of overall
liking. We select maple for flavor (utility = 0), tan for color (utility = 0)
and rough for texture (utility = 0). Our additive model allows us to
estimate the overall liking which a panelist would assign to this combination (which, recall, we did not test): $0 + 0 + 0 + 59.56 = 59.56$ (59.56
= additive constant).

Suppose, now, the product tester suggests, for one or another reason,

TABLE 7.25
TRADE OFF EQUATIONS RELATING PRESENCE/ABSENCE OF CEREAL CHARACTERISTICS TO PERCEPTIONS AND ACCEPTANCE

Attribute	Multiple R	K_0	Texture		Color		Flavoring			
			Smooth $+k_1$	Rough $+k_2$	Brown $+k_3$	Reddish $+k_4$	Tan $+k_5$	Honey $+k_6$	Cinnamon $+k_7$	Maple $+k_8$
1. Texture L/D	0.49	62.9	−1.00	0	−28.30	−1.61	0	5.83	8.66	0
2. Roughness	0.58	81.00	0.33	0	−5.33	2.68	0	4.67	3.16	0
3. Darkness	0.89	60.98	6.79	0	22.35	14.52	0	4.51	0.36	0
4. Crispness (In Milk)	0.61	148.01	−5.33	0	−9.50	−3.50	0	3.83	2.16	0
5. Taste Liking	0.49	63.50	−2.68	0	−2.17	−3.84	0	−6.33	2.83	0
6. Crunchiness	0.67	134.45	−6.22	0	−9.33	−1.66	0	5.49	5.48	0
7. Sweetness	0.78	99.84	−2.11	0	−4.85	−4.02	0	−16.99	−7.32	0
8. Natural Flavor	0.82	81.74	2.11	0	−7.02	−9.34	0	−20.33	−11.49	0
9. Artificial Flavor	0.83	75.82	4.44	0	13.51	6.83	0	−7.32	0.19	0
10. Total Liking	0.47	59.56	−3.55	0	−2.33	−3.52	0	−10.50	−1.33	0
11. Bran User Liking	0.59	74.95	−4.56	0	−0.34	3.30	0	−25.98	−10.48	0
12. Non User Liking	0.44	44.34	−3.44	0	−3.83	−10.02	0	4.65	7.49	0
13. Adult Liking	0.51	68.61	−7.33	0	0.83	0.82	0	−13.82	−1.99	0
14. Teen Liking	0.51	34.68	9.56	0	−9.52	−12.85	0	−7.67	−4.67	0
15. Cost of Goods	—	77.09	1.22	0	−130.06	−115.07	0	−142.65	−131.87	0

Only Linear Equations Used

TABLE 7.26
ALTERNATIVE CEREAL OPTIONS

	"Liking" Additive Units	"Cost" Additive Units	"Teen" Liking
(1) OPTIMUM			
Rough Texture	0	0	0
Tan Color	0	0	0
Maple Flavor	0	0	0
Additive Constant	59.56	77.09	34.68
Total:	59.56	77.09	34.68
(2) NEXT BEST PRODUCT In Terms of Cost (Cost Reduction: Maintain Liking)			
Rough Texture	0	0	0
Tan Color	0	0	0
Cinnamon	−1.33	−31.87	−4.67
Additive Constant	59.56	77.09	34.68
Total:	58.23	45.22	30.01
(3) NEXT BEST PRODUCT In Terms of Teen Liking			
Smooth Texture	−3.55	1.22	9.56
Tan Color	0	0	0
Maple Flavor	0	0	0
Additive Constant	59.56	77.09	34.68
Total:	56.01	78.31	44.24

that the manufacturer should seriously consider another combination of color, flavor and texture. In fact, based upon knowledge of federal regulations on color, the product tester and the head of regulatory affairs suggest that the color option which came out with the highest utility, tan, may soon come under Food and Drug Agency (FDA) scrutiny as a potential carcinogen. What amount of liking do we lose by selecting a separate color, e.g., red. In order to answer that question, the analyst need only appeal to the additive equation to determine the likely overall rating of liking for that specific combination of options.

By exchanging tan (utility = 0) for red (utility = - 3.52), we expect the net liking to drop down to 56.04.

The set of equations also provides a handy method to compute the sensory profile for the product, based upon the other sensory characteristics. Since each specific characteristic itself possesses a unique additive equation, it becomes a straightforward matter to compute the likely flavor intensity, rating of appropriateness for adult, etc.

Table 7.26 presents some alternative product formulations which emerge from this analysis, based upon the optimal product and its sensory profile, as well as upon less than optimal products (based upon alternative strategies, which suggest other alternatives for use). Furthermore, note that Table 7.26 presents an estimate of the cost of the specific products. In continuous variable optimization, we can use cost as a dependent variable, which we predict from a linear combination of ingredient factors. Here we also have a perfect equation relating cost of adding different flavors, textures, colors, etc.

AN OVERVIEW TO OPTIMIZATION IN GENERAL

The optimization methods presented here show a range of techniques which a product tester, sensory analyst and marketer can use in the search for optimal products. Traditionally, such a search often required long time frames, with considerable back and forth testing and reformulation based upon consumer feedback and subsequent confirmatory testing. These procedures took months, and sometimes years to accomplish, as the manufacturer tried to select that combination of ingredients which provided the best consumer response at the lowest cost.

Optimization reduces that trial and error. It requires development of a sufficiently large number of alternative product variants, which generate a data base from which one can predict reactions to similar product formulations not tested. The optimization procedure thus departs from the traditional methods. Those traditional methods relied upon one or two easily fabricated alternatives, simple and straightforward testing, and then a qualitative evaluation of the results to suggest the next steps. Although at each stage the process seems simple enough, back and forth trial-and-error procedures take longer and cost quite a bit more money. They often lead to blind alleys. The bits and pieces of research, time for prototype development, and other associated costs often add up to greater expenditures than do the time and cost involved in extensive prototype development.

The optimization method provides a unique insurance policy for the manufacturer, the product developer and the sensory analyst in several respects. (1) It generates the best scoring product, in actuality, from a wide set (always good to know—with 15 or more different formulations tested, some should by chance alone prove out as viable opportunities for further work). (2) It provides clearer understanding of how ingredients impact on perceptions, cost and acceptance. (3) It offers a quantitative feedback system for pinpointing changes which the manufacturer must make in order to improve acceptability, as well as the sensory and cost implications of changes which achieve optimality. (4) It provides quantitative feedback regarding sub-optimal formulations which satisfy other important business and marketing constraints that may reflect cost considerations or sensory restrictions. The product may have to possess specific sensory characteristics to set it apart from the competition .

In net, therefore, the optimization method promises a bright future for product testing. The approach dictates the type of experimental design, generates the data, and develops the model for use by product developers and managers. In effect, optimization methods provide the manufacturer with a high-technology method to discover products having improved acceptance, developed at lower research and manufacturing costs, and in a vastly shorter time frame.

CHAPTER 8

PRODUCT MEASUREMENT AND MARKETING RESEARCH

INTRODUCTION

In their traditional role, R&D sensory analysts have shied away from dealing with the consumer in the marketplace, preferring to concentrate on simple, well established laboratory procedures which bear the hallowed imprimatur of science. In contrast, the marketing researcher tests responses to products in a relatively disorganized, non-sterile world. Whereas, R&D sensory analysts often work in laboratories, marketing researchers work with consumers at home, or in crowded shopping malls, or by telephone. Marketing researchers also assess the consumer's attitudes towards entire product categories, specific products, and advertising, as well as the consumer's general awareness of products in the marketplace.

R&D sensory analysts and market researchers share many of the same research and testing needs, however. Each can profit from the other. This chapter deals with consumer marketing research, both from the vantage point of problems which researchers tackle and from the point of view of methods for testing.

A CASE HISTORY—YOGURT

We will concentrate on the approach of marketing research, and its interface with sensory evaluation, by means of a case history on fruit yogurt. As preface, the Simon Yogurt Company (SYC) has, for the past forty years, manufactured natural yogurt having little or no added flavoring. During the past five years, several companies in the Chicago area have introduced fruit flavored yogurt, and have gained considerable strength among the consumers. Yogurts with new flavors (e.g., fancy fruit), and with simple flavors have, since 1974, increased their market share by 19%, representing profits of several million dollars in this particular market. At the same time the Simon Yogurt Company, based in Chicago, has seen its share of the market for its franchise (Midwest) erode by 11%.

Management at SYC met with a marketing consulting group to discuss the problems of their declining share of market. After several meetings, the principals of SYC and the marketing consultants decided to explore the yogurt market, hoping to enter it with a flavored yogurt or line of flavored yogurts. These flavored yogurts could carry the Simon name, but did not have to, if the consumers felt that the Simon name would add little additional leverage. Management at SYC stood ready to develop a new brand with a completely new identity, to support the introduction of the flavored yogurt.

Normally, marketing researchers enter here with information about how consumers perceive the current market of yogurts, as well as the volume of yogurt consumption. Sometimes the marketing researcher commissions a study to determine how consumers think about different brands of yogurts in order to further understand the dynamics of the marketplace. What, perceptually, in the mind of the consumer, leads to similar perceptions of brands as sharing common aspects, and what differentiates brands from each other? Furthermore, market researchers study the market structure in order to discover whether or not there exist any segments of the market which have unfulfilled needs. For instance, if some consumers wish to have a yogurt with a unique flavor, e.g. to use as a dip, this might represent a possible need which a product could satisfy. If no yogurt exists specifically designed for dips, and if consumers wish to use yogurts for dips, then this gap may represent a real opportunity in the marketplace. Product measurement enters at a later stage, after the marketing researcher has discovered opportunities in the marketplace, and after the product developer has fabricated one or several prototypes.

Competitive Frame Analysis

We saw an example of competitive frame analysis in the previous chapters concerning the introduction of a new snack potato chip, and a beverage. A market researcher interested in the product opportunity might approach the problem with a different point of view. Market researchers test the alternative competitors in order to see which competitor products score highest among several groups of consumers in the population. The researcher might also evaluate other products, such as sour cream, which compete with yogurt as dips.

The market researcher at SYC performed a competitive frame analysis on the leading 6 yogurts marketed in the Chicago area. Since the study concerned reactions to the actual products among a wide variety of users, the marketing researcher commissioned a study on consumer perceptions of yogurts, blind and branded, as well as image. Consumers in the Chicago area tested the yogurts in a short, 40 minute test in a mall in the metropolitan Chicago area (in a location some 12 miles north of Chicago itself). A total of 160 panelists participated, comprising these groups:

1. Half males, half females.
2. Half users of yogurts with flavoring, half users of regular yogurts.
3. A cell of 60 regular users of the SYC yogurts.
4. A cell of 100 panelists who do not use the SYC yogurts.

Each panelist evaluated 3 of the 6 yogurts "blind" (viz., not identified as to brand), then evaluated the other 3 yogurts branded (viz., identified as to brand). Finally each respondent rated the sensory, acceptance and image characteristics of 3 of the products based upon the package alone.

In total, 160 consumer panelists participated. Since each panelist scaled 3 of the 6 products blind, a separate set branded, and still a separate set in terms of image (product name, no product) all on the same attributes, and with the same scale, the product tester and market researcher had the opportunity to assess the following aspects, for each group of panelists:

1. Reactions to the branded versus the blind product—what does branding the product do to ratings? When panelists evaluate a product knowing the brand, do they always like the product more, or do they sometimes like the product less because of the brand?
2. Expectations set up by the pictorial display of the product. What do the pictures suggest about the product's sensory characteristics?

Table 8.1 presents a partial display of the results of the competitive frame analysis. The marketing researcher examining Table 8.1 found that:

1. Regular users of flavored yogurt like the set of products more than do users of unflavored yogurt.
2. SYC users show the least satisfaction with flavored yogurt as a category. This suggests that SYC users may represent that particular segment of the population currently dissatisfied with the array of flavored products on the market.
3. Males like the products, on the average, more than did females (not shown).
4. The variability of liking ratings for flavored yogurts exceeded the variability of liking for unflavored yogurts (not shown). This suggests that in the category of flavored yogurt panelists show quite a good deal of inter-individual variability among themselves in likes and dislikes.

TABLE 8.1
PARTIAL RESULTS OF THE RATINGS OF 6 YOGURTS
(Blind, Branded, Package-Image)

Liking Ratings

Yogurt		Total	Unflavored Yogurt Users	Flavored Yogurt Users	SYC Users
A	Blind	52	30	74	35
	Branded	57	35	78	50
	Package	58	31	85	56
B	Blind	54	47	61	42
	Branded	50	42	58	70
	Package	47	34	60	88
C	Blind	65	53	78	50
	Branded	59	47	70	41
	Package	62	58	65	45
D	Blind	46	61	32	22
	Branded	54	67	30	16
	Package	57	72	42	24
E	Blind	50	54	47	46
	Branded	55	59	51	42
	Package	57	58	55	38
F	Blind	59	71	46	51
	Branded	59	70	48	45
	Package	55	50	60	47

	Average Rating		
	Blind	Branded	Package
Total	54	56	56
Unflavored User	45	56	62
SYC User	41	44	50
Flavored User	53	53	51

A, B, C, F — Fruit flavored yogurt
D — Unflavored yogurt
E & F — Fruit and spice flavored yogurt

5. Branding the products sometimes increases liking, but also can decrease liking. Branding products produces different effects, depending upon the specific product.

6. Men show greater susceptibility to branding than do women. The change in their ratings due to branding exceeds the change of ratings assigned by the women respondents.
7. The expectation of product acceptability set up by showing consumers the picture of the product differs from the rated acceptability obtained when panelists evaluate the products in actuality, both blind and branded. Apparently, some pictures of products (or, in effect, the package) set up positive expectations, whereas others set up negative expectation. The sensory analyst and market researcher do not know for sure the underlying reason for the difference between liking ratings for the package (pure image) and liking ratings for the actual physical products.
8. One can assess the effects of package (or image) and of brand by age (not shown here), by brand usage (shown in terms of regular users of SYC versus non-users), by male versus female, etc.
9. The products differ from each other in terms of their sensory and hedonic characteristics (Table 8.2).
10. These differences between products change when they appear in branded form for the test, as well as when they appear in pictures. To the sensory analyst differences in the product characteristics which result from the presentation mode of products (blind, branded, picture) suggest that sensory perceptions interact with the panelist's expectations. Panelists do not, and probably cannot judge a product solely on the basis of its sensory characteristics. Rather, panelists react to the brand, their expectations of the product, and to their memories of the products. This should indicate that consumers do not judge products in a vacuum, but judge even the so-called "objective" sensory characteristics against the context of expectations. We often lose sight of the powerful effects of cognition, which plays a key role in determining product perceptions.

Consumers in the yogurt study also profiled their ideal product using the same characteristics and the same magnitude estimation scale that they had used to profile the blind, branded and pictures of test products. The profile of the ideal (Table 8.2) revealed that:

1. Some products showed the right levels of sensory characteristics.
2. Other attributes, such as "fruit flavored" showed so much discrepancy between the ideal and any of the products that it suggested the attribute reflected a non-achievable goal. The R&D product developer could not possibly deliver on the desired level of real fruit flavor, despite consumer's requests to the contrary.

TABLE 8.2
ATTRIBUTE PROFILES OF THE SIX EXISTING YOGURT PRODUCTS
AND THE SELF DESIGNED IDEALS

Yogurt	Sweetness	Strength of Real Fruit Flavor	Spice Flavor	Consistency	(Blind Test) Liking
A	64	90	22	80	52
B	78	84	16	74	54
C	60	102	34	96	65
D	29	5	8	74	46
E	60	42	54	103	50
F	47	61	50	84	59
Ideal	64	76	—	80	—
Ideal: Unflavored User	94	20	12	78	
Ideal Flavored User	34	132	86	82	

A competitive frame test, such as the one we just saw from SYC (Table 8.2) provides a powerful method with which we can diagnose consumer reactions to existing products in the marketplace. The competitive frame test provides the researcher with a spectrum of the sensory profiles of existing products. To the marketing researcher the relative liking ratings provide a numerical index of how products compare to each other in terms of the key attribute of overall acceptability. The sensory characteristics themselves provide further information, or "diagnostics". These attributes allow the product tester or marketing research analyst to understand why some fruit yogurt products score high and why some score low. Do the differences in acceptability arise because:

1. One yogurt fares poorly in the acceptability of texture or flavor?
2. Yogurt possesses too much or too little flavor relative to the ideal.
3. The yogurts taste equally good "blind", (yogurts A and B) but the brand of one (A) acts as a positive factor, enhancing acceptance, whereas the brand of the other (B) acts as a negative factor, diminishing acceptance.
4. The yogurts differ on one or a few key sensory characteristics which dramatically affect overall liking.

The study of the yogurt market reported here shows some other important factors, to which a marketing sensory analyst attends when evaluating the results.

Consumer acceptability (liking) of the different products varied by user group. This suggests to the sensory analyst that if the consumer truly perceives the product's sensory characteristics in similar ways (i.e., they rate the texture, the flavor, appearance, etc. similarly in terms of non-evaluative sensory characteristics), then the differences in acceptability arise because of differences in consumer desires for product characteristics. Some user groups may prefer a stronger flavored product, whereas others may prefer a weaker flavored product.

The market for yogurts does not represent a homogeneous category. Individuals in the market show widely divergent likes and dislikes. Variations in taste allow manufacturers to market many brands to the different segments of the consumer population.

Furthermore, within subcategories, such as the strongly flavored spiced yogurts, the higher inter-respondent-variability suggests an even wider fractionation of panelists into different likers and dislikers. Presumably, for the yogurts having added flavor and spice, consumer panelists will differ considerably as to whether or not they accept that added flavor, or whether they reject it.

Product/Concept Test

A later stage in the sensory analysis done by a market researcher concerns the product/concept test. Either after or before the marketing researcher has evaluated the existing products in the market, the creative group at the advertising agency or the marketing group in the company itself, may develop a strategy to market a new product. Prior to the test of any specific product, the marketing group may evaluate the variability of dozens or even hundreds of different product concepts which stress alternative benefits and positionings of the product. They may test dozens of possible ideas for products, narrowing and focusing down the set of possible ideas to just a few.

SYC management decided that, in the light of the varied acceptance of flavored yogurts, and in view of the fact that SYC did not market a spicy fruit yogurt an opportunity existed to increase their market share by adding a spicy flavored yogurt or set of yogurts to their line.

Parallel research by marketing researchers on consumer attitudes (in contrast to actual product perceptions) showed little or no interest in long-term purchase and repurchase of "wildly" flavored yogurts. The research did turn up extensive consumer interest in a lemon-spice yogurt, with a mild spicy flavor. When marketers looked at the competition from current, in-market flavored yogurts they realized that this idea for the lemon-spice yogurt represented another yogurt product in a competitive, crowded citrus flavored yogurt market. The second best idea concerned a sweet curry-flavored yogurt, which one could use as a dip, as well as eat at a meal or as a snack.

After extensive discussions at SYC, management and marketers decided that the fruit and curry yogurt might serve as a good extension of their current yogurt line, for the following reasons:

1. SYC would probably not have to develop an entirely new brand image for this fruit and curry product. Developing a new brand image for a product often costs more money than building a new brand based upon an existing product which consumers have learned to accept, and to which they have shown some loyalty.

2. Initial tests of the different consumer attitudes towards alternatives to unflavored yogurt showed that in terms of attitudes alone (without products in the evaluation), consumers evidenced a positive attitude towards a curry/fruit yogurt. Table 8.3 shows the array of favorable versus unfavorable responses to alternative concepts, which generated the possiblity of developing a curry and fruit yogurt. Note that in such concept tests, which precede development of prototypes, consumers may not evaluate actual products, but rather they rate how good they think the idea seems to them. Whether or not the execution of the idea, in terms of an actual product prototype, lives up to the consumer's expectations, remains for the next step.

TABLE 8.3
RESULTS OF CONCEPT TEST ON DIFFERENT
TYPES OF FLAVORED YOGURTS

Percent of Panelists Who Responded	Concept Statements				
	Fruit Flavors			Spice & Fruit	
	Raspberry	Lemon	Banana	Allspice	Curry
1. Would buy at least once in next 2 purchases	25	34	10	15	18
2. Unique	20	15	25	40	40
3. Other similar products on market to choose from	40	80	42	18	12
4. Would tire of this quickly	22	18	30	60	30

Based upon the data in Table 8.3 (which confirmed interest in a curry product) the market researcher, together with marketing and with the product tester, discussed the type of flavored yogurt which consumers might wish to purchase. Product developers formulated a number of alternative yogurts at their facility, testing the products first informally, and then through research guidance panels in the local area.

After the product developers finished their initial testing, and bench top reformulation from consumer feedback, they presented four different prototypes to marketing for decision regarding which product(s) to carry to further testing. Marketing selected two of the four products, one representing a strongly fruit flavored curry yogurt, and the other representing a yogurt with weaker fruit flavor, and a slightly different qualitative note of curry. Note that in order to develop these prototypes, the product developers spent about 2 months, screening alternative options in terms of flavor, consistency, etc. Only after extensive internal, and small scale external tests did the product developer recommend testing these two prototypes.

The marketing researcher suggested that management do a product/concept test. In the product concept test, the interviewer first exposes the consumer to a concept. This concept may comprise simply a card which states the product benefits. The concept may present a rough graphical layout of the product as a prototype advertisement (which includes pictorial designs, figures, etc., in the rough sketch). The concept may comprise a finished print advertisement or a finished commercial for television.

The concept sets the stage for consumer expectations of the product. The concept represents products' taste, appearance, usage, etc., sometimes subtly without mentioning sensory characteristics, but on other occasions bluntly and forcefully.

In some product/concept tests, the panelists rate the product, after tasting it. Panelists evaluate the product against the background of expectations which the concept generates. Let us look at how the two products scored. In this case, the panelists comprised individuals from 3 cities representing different markets for SYC products. A total of 100 panelists participated from each city, providing a base of 300 individuals. Usually market researchers work with a large sample of consumers, rather than with a small sample. Large sample size insures that the data represent the responses of the population, rather than the responses of the limited, isolated group of individuals. This requirement for projectibility of the data to the population of consumers at large requires larger-scale sampling, in contrast to the more technically-based research of laboratory sensory analysis.

In the actual study, panelists performed the following tasks.

Looked at a print advertisement which provided a pictorial representation of the yogurt container, as well as read a statement about the product (viz., that the product tasted delicious, could be used on many occasions, etc.). For better or worse, this advertisement reflected the best which SYC could develop, for the product, at the time.

Panelists studied the concept board (viz., print ad) for a minute. (Sometimes, a researcher might ask some questions about the concept board itself, such as its persuasiveness, believability, communication of attributes, etc. Here, the advertising simply set the stage for subsequent product evaluation.)

The panelist tasted the yogurt from the container, eating as much as he/she wished.

Panelists rated their impressions of the product, viz-à-vis the print ad on directional scales, which asked the panelists questions such as "relative to the expectations set up by the concept, did the product taste too spicy, just right, or not spicy enough? These directional scales instruct the panelists to indicate which direction the products lie vis-à-vis the concept or the print advertisement. Usually the scales do not measure the actual spiciness of the product itself.

In this study panelists used three point directional scales to rate a variety of characteristics, as Table 8.4 shows, for each product, for two groups of consumers.

TABLE 8.4
PRODUCT CONCEPT TEST—PERCENT OF RESPONDENTS STATING
"TOO MUCH," "ABOUT RIGHT" OR "TOO LITTLE"
CURRY-FRUIT YOGURT

Attribute	Total	SYC User	Other User
Spiciness			
Too Strong	40	52	28
Just Right	35	28	42
Too Weak	25	20	30
Fruit Flavor			
Too Strong	25	22	28
Just Right	60	50	70
Too Weak	15	28	2
Aftertaste			
Too Strong	45	41	43
Just Right	20	40	11
Too Weak	35	19	46

In other studies, the researcher may opt to use a broader scale for directionality, such as five points in place of three points. A five point directional scale permits finer distinctions in the magnitude of directional change.

Through data shown in Table 8.4 the product developer can ascertain areas of satisfaction versus dissatisfaction. Perhaps the consumer feels that the product tastes too spicy, or not spicy enough, relative to the concept. Through directional scales the panelist can communicate this impression to the product developer. Of course, when the panelist reads the concept statement or the advertisement and assigns his or her ratings, the research will reveal a compromise between what the concept or advertisement communicates and what the panelist perceives as the ideal product, towards which the product developer should strive. If the panelist desires a weak flavored yogurt, and if the advertisement connotes an extremely strongly flavored yogurt, then the panelist may have problems indicating the direction of change needed.

Another Approach To Product/Concept Testing

Alternatives exist to the traditional concept/product test which allow the marketer to test many different concepts and many different products in the same session. These methods have utility for evaluation of beverages and foods.

One approach proceeds as follows:

The interviewer informs the panelist that the panelist will assess several products and advertising/or/concepts in a single category (e.g., flavored yogurts). This introduction sets up the general framework of expectations, but does not convey specifics to the panelist which could bias the results. The introduction aims for a bias-free interview, in which the panelist evaluates all stimuli separately.

Panelists evaluate one or perhaps several products, using magnitude estimation scaling, to provide a "snapshot" of the products on attributes. Table 8.5 provides this data for the test yogurt product, as well as for 3 other and similar yogurt products currently on the market. Table 8.5 shows data similar to the data we have previously seen for product evaluation on a variety of sensory, performance/acceptance and image characteristics (See Table 8.2).

After panelists have evaluated the array of products, they then evaluate one of the print advertisements (or concept boards) They scale each advertisement on precisely the same characteristics, and use the same scale as they had used for evaluation of the products. In effect, the panelists react to the advertisement or concept as yet another product.

Having finished the first concept or advertisement (one of the several chosen to test in random order), the panelist waits for a few minutes, and then scales the second advertisement again exactly as if the panelist would rate a yogurt product, using the same scales and the same attributes.

This sequence can continue, with panelists rating an entire array of test products, commercial products (in random order), and finishing the set of ratings with evaluations of one to several different advertisements, concepts, and the like.

After having finished ratings for products, and then ads or concepts, the panelist profiles the "ideal" product on the same scales, using the same attributes.

This experimental design and research strategy possesses advantages over and above the standard product/concept test.

TABLE 8.5
ALTERNATIVE PRODUCT CONCEPT TEST
SINGLE RATINGS OF SEVERAL PRODUCTS AND SEVERAL CONCEPTS
(Ratings of "Total" Group Only)

Product	Spiciness	Fruit Flavor	Natural Flavor	Aftertaste	Purchase Intent
A*	84	92	62	52	84
B	63	89	71	64	88
C	89	108	50	80	62
Concept					
D	108	120	85	60	104
E	95	134	102	57	96
F	72	116	120	58	117
G	103	94	94	64	81
Ideal	74	128	140	31	143

*Current Test Product = A
Current Competitors = B & C

— It can assess many products and concepts (or ads), faster, and with less inter-panelist variability.
— It sets up a general, not a specific framework for overall evaluation.
— It obtains measures of products and concepts as perceived by the consumer.

— In order to develop "directional" scales, for modification, the analyst or marketing researcher need only look at the gap between what products deliver, versus what advertisements promise.

— One can easily distinguish between actionable attributes on which one can deliver, and attributes on which one cannot deliver no matter how the product developer modifies the formulation.

Let us take a look at the implementation of this modified approach with our spicy fruit yogurt. To keep things as parallel as possible with the first study, we will consider the results of a test with 300 individuals, each of whom evaluated the three yogurts, and then scaled four test concepts in random order.

Table 8.5 shows the summary results, on the products, and on the advertisements. Note that in Table 8.5 the marketing researcher has immediately available the consumer's profile reactions to the three products and four concepts or ads. One can report those out to management, in terms of what each concept connotes, versus what the test product delivers and compare it to competition. In addition, the marketing researcher obtains a measure of satisfaction for each yogurt product, and for each concept without confounding one stimulus with another. In some instances the products may score very high in acceptance, but consumers may dislike the concept. On other occasions the reverse occurs. The creative group at the manufacturer's company, or at the advertising agency may have developed a stunningly successful concept for advertising the yogurt, but R&D may not have developed a product which tastes quite that good.

Table 8.5 also presents the differences between the product(s) and the advertising, which represents the analog to the directional information which we saw before. Notice another thing, however. By directly scaling products and concepts separately but in the same session, and on the same scale, the marketing researcher and product tester can distinguish between two types of attributes. On the one hand, consumers rate attributes such as fruit flavor intensity, spiciness, etc. The advertisement promises levels of these sensory attributes. By and large the products come reasonably close (within 15%) to delivering the attribute levels. These sensory attributes typify actionable attributes. By modifying the physical product the product developer can modify the perception of these attributes, increasing perceived flavor intensity, etc., or decreasing it. Sooner or later product modifications will come close to the levels suggested by the advertisement. On the other hand, concepts often deal with such characteristics as "natural flavor". The concept or ad connotes a much higher level of "natural flavor" than any product can deliver. Perhaps the product developer can modify the ingredients in such a way as to deliver more "natural flavor." Probably not, however. The attribute "natural flavor", like other "buzzword" or "image" attributes typify inherently inactionable characteristics. More than likely, the product developer can never sufficiently modify the product so that the product will live up to expectations generated by this inactionable characteristic. We see this clearly in the large gap between the ratings of products and the ratings of the advertisement or concept. The very large gap serves as a warning signal to us that more than likely, the attribute represents one which may find a place in advertisements, but does not provide useful directionality for product modification Similar distinctions between actionable and inactionable attributes occur in the evaluation of an individual's self-defined ideal product. The ideal levels of some characteristics lie close to levels achieved by product formulations. The ideal levels of the inactionable characteristics often lie far away from the levels achieved by any of the potentially many different formulations (Moskowitz, Jacobs & Fitch, 1980).

An Update on the Results

Based upon the results of the concept/product test, the marketing researcher and the product tester concurred that product A showed best promise for a spicy fruit yogurt. As a result of the test, therefore, the marketing researcher suggested proceeding with formulation A. As further support for this position, the marketing researcher pointed to the higher acceptability of A, in terms of characteristics, by various subgroups in the population, segmented by brand usage, sex, age, etc.

MARKET SEGMENTATION AND PRODUCT TESTING

Marketers deal with segmented markets, comprising consumers with different need and wants. Some of these characteristics pertain to demographic differences, such as age, income, residence, type of job, etc. Other characteristics come from attitudes towards specific products or entire product categories. Brand usage, degree of brand switching, etc., represent yet another, more complicated segmentation. Some consumers remain loyal to a brand of cereal. Other consumers switch fom cereal to cereal, choosing new cereals either on the basis of price, on the basis of promotion, or more often than marketers like to admit, on the basis of the premiums inside the box. Finally, marketers deal with an entirely different set of segments, derived from structuring the consumer market into "lifestyle" segments. Some individuals fall into the "young marrieds and freespending, devil-may-care" group. Others belong to the more conservative, savings-oriented, non-curious, consumer group. Studies on segmentation in the population have concerned these different types of consumers.

R&D sensory analysts usually do not confront nor deal with the problem of wide individual differences in the evaluation of items. Individual differences in sensory analysis often has come to mean differences in ability to sensorically discriminate differences in food, rather than meaning response differences due to varying attitudes and lifestyles. Laboratory-oriented sensory analysis often coalesces the responses of many consumers, differentiating some by age, sensory acuity, and other biologically related factors. The marketer and marketing researcher use more marketing-oriented methods of clustering segments in the population.

A CASE STUDY WITH MARKETING SEGMENTS

The manufacturers of Crunchy, a new granola and coconut based candy, did extensive research prior to introducing the Crunchy product line into the Southwest. Using the Fritz product development group (FPDG) the marketers and R&D group developed a variety of alternative formulations. In their marketing surveys, prior to any product testing, the cereal manufacturer found that different segments of the population stated different reasons for accepting a coconut-granola candy. Specifically:

1. One group of consumers, (specifically teens) find this type of candy highly acceptable in taste, without the connotation of a "children's candy". These consumers would purchase "Crunchy", and products similar to it because of taste factors, and because of the unique positioning of the product. Capitalizing on consumer acceptance of granola as a youth-oriented product, the manufacturer felt that it could attract teens and other candy lovers with a sweet candy which contained granola, and had good taste properties.

2. Another group of consumers exhibited high interest in things having to do with "natural" and " healthful". These primarily health oriented consumers comprised roughly 18% of the population. They clearly preferred natural foods. They consumed a lot of granola and other sweetened natural products in cereals, and represented a likely target for the marketer.

3. Other segments of the population uncovered in the study included the businessman who might use the product as a quick-pick-me-up.

The business person's lifestyle places so many demands on his or her time that a nutritious candy might prove extremely attractive, as a substitute for a heavy snack or a meal.

4. A final segment uncovered in the population comprised dieters, who wanted to lose weight. These calorie-conscious individuals spanned a wide range of consumer ages, incomes, etc., representing individuals primarily interested in health, but from a fitness point of view and from an appearance point of view. These consumer segments would probably accept the "crunchy" product as an aid to dieting, and as a meal substitute.

Testing Acceptance/Perceptions With Segments

Uncovering segments in the population has turned into straight-forward statistical procedure. The reader should bear in mind that segmentation theory, and the mechanisms for analysis of data and extracting viable segments in the market now comprise a well developed discipline in marketing and marketing research (Wells, 1975). We deal here with the product evaluation section of the project. We will look at the issue of segments from the point of view of the marketing researcher and product tester interested in two things:

1. Consumer acceptance/rejection of the product, through product testing.

2. Those specific sensory characteristics of products which trigger acceptance/rejection, and the possibly different sensory cues which operate for the various segments. (For instance, the teens may like the candy because of the sweet taste, whereas older consumers may like Crunchy because the box says "dietetic" or "natural").

In the actual product-study, marketing suggested a test of the following array of products:

1. Current Crunchy (not yet launched), representing marketing and R&D's best guess as to the most acceptable formulation.

2. Four other test formulations of variants of "Crunchy" varying in the type of coconut, the level of sugar in the product, etc.

3. Two competitors in the marketplace, Coco-Gran, and Gran-Crisp, which represent products currently in-market but less than a year old. (Marketing evaluations suggested that throughout the U.S. only about 6 brands in total, in addition to Coco-Bran and Gran-Crisp possessed any significant share of the market.)

After discussions with the marketing researcher and product tester, marketing accepted the recommendation for testing in a central location facility, in which panelists would participate for a 90 minute test session. Realizing that they needed to test 7 different product variants, the product tester and market researcher agreed that for the sake of statistically better data they should insure that each panelist or consumer respondent evaluate all of the 7 product formulations. Only in this way could they insure "clean" bias-free data in which they could evaluate the relative performance of the test formulations versus the competitive frame of products. Furthermore, only with 7 or more products could the marketing analyst draw out a meaningful correlation between the sensory characteristics of the formulations and overall acceptability, for the total group of consumers and for the specific subgroups.

From time to time problems arise in trying to do such market evaluation studies correctly. Often marketers, marketing researchers or sensory analysts complain that due to logistical factors and problems they cannot afford to do the test, although they can afford to do a simple paired comparison between two products, e.g., current Crunchy versus Gran-Crisp. Yet, as the records of many companies show, these same practitioners often have to implement such simple studies over and over with small modification in the product, with each modification made from previous feedback. The product tester and marketer can substantially increase cost and time efficiency in marketing research studies by evaluating the range of competitor products in one integrated project, rather than evaluating the products over a long, drawn out sequence.

Results

The data from the multi-product evaluation appear in Table 8.6 which provides the following information:

1. Acceptability of the candy products, for the total samples of panelists, and for the specific subgroups of interest. In order to identify the different subgroups or segments the marketing researcher administered a questionnaire based upon previous research. This questionnaire contained questions, which when answered and scored according to a key set up by the previous research, classified consumers into one or several different segments, on the basis of the consumer's attitudes. (Of course, the product tester would have less problem classifying the consumers on the basis of their age, brand usage, etc. One accomplishes this classification by straightforward questions.)

2. Sensory characteristics of specific products, evaluated by the total sample. In this study, as in numerous other studies, consumer

panelists agree with each other in their ratings of sensory characteristics. These characteristics do not carry with them evaluative connotations.

The ideal product on all of the attributes, presented in terms of total sample, and subgroup. The panelists profiled their ideal product after having had the opportunity to evaluate each of the 7 test products. In this way one can anchor ratings of the ideal against the framework of ratings assigned to actual products. The product tester and the market researcher can compare the consumer's ideal profile with the actual ratings of products, in order to determine the gap between desired attribute levels, and levels which actual products obtain.

3. Differences in the rated acceptability of the products. As one might expect, different subgroups in the population of consumers find different products acceptable. Marketers have known about this for years. Such differences in acceptance in the population enables more than one brand to compete successfully for consumer attention, as each brand or product garners its share of consumers.

4. A wide range of different sensory characteristics which the product generates. Consumers can and do distinguish between products on the basis of the product's taste, texture, appearance, flavor, etc. Obvious as this point seems, marketers and management often overlook the key fact that engineering an acceptable sensory impression often goes a long way to insure consumer satisfaction with the product.

5. Quite different ideal sensory profiles emerge depending upon the particular segment. Some consumer segments desire a hard texture, with less sweetness. Other groups in the population feel they would like to have a product with a softer texture, and a greater amount of sweetness. We often do not know the reason underlying such differences in ideal products, although we know that children consistently design a sweeter product than do adults.

6. Gaps between the ideal and actual delivered levels on specific attributes, e.g., "natural tasting". Natural tasting, refreshing and a host of other attributes reflect characteristics more relevant for image and advertising than for R&D product development. Few, if any product developers, know exactly how to improve a product's natural taste. Certainly one may not necessarily improve the natural taste by adding more natural ingredients to it. In studies with beverages conducted by the author, the addition of natural fruit juice to a beverage did not raise the perception of "naturalness" at all. Instead, the natural fruit juice merely incresed the amount of cloud in the beverage, making the beverage appear darker. At a sufficiently high concentration this natural ingredient interacted with the rest of the beverage ingredients to yield a heightened bitter taste.

TABLE 8.6

(A)
LIKING RATING OF PRODUCT—BY USER GROUP

Acceptability	Total	By Age			Psychographic Profile	
		Children	Teens	Adults	Businessmen	Diet-Conscious
Crunchy	74	46	88	80	58	79
Test A	61	54	65	54	64	58
Test B	70	68	79	63	73	78
Test C	54	58	43	61	53	44
Test D	63	52	65	72	68	55
Coco-Gran	59	47	46	64	65	46
Gran-Crisp	68	69	75	60	73	54
Ideal	145	152	163	120	149	140

(B)
PROFILES OF THE IDEAL PRODUCT—BY USER GROUP

	Total	Children	Teens	Adults	Businessmen	Diet-Conscious
Sweetness	74	92	74	56	69	54
Flavor Strength	65	54	73	68	70	83
Hardness	80	76	82	82	75	73
Coconut Flavor	54	58	64	40	47	69
Denseness	88	83	80	101	94	85
Natural Flavor	122	108	140	118	93	145

TABLE 8.6 (Continued)
(C)
ATTRIBUTE PROFILES

Acceptability	Sweetness	Flavor Strength	Hardness	Coconut Flavor	Denseness	Natural Flavor
Crunchy	59	80	88	58	85	72
Test A	71	59	74	74	83	89
Test B	60	64	80	60	75	77
Test C	43	72	74	48	93	36
Test D	39	68	63	71	68	29
Coco-Gran	79	58	57	64	74	94
Gran-Crisp	79	72	68	79	67	90
Ideal "Total"	74	65	80	54	88	79

An Overview of Segmentation Research in the Crunchy Study

Our Crunchy project reveals that individuals in the population differ in what they like and dislike, in the candy category. Marketers know that these differences pervade reactions to many consumer items. Individuals segment into different demographic groups, attitudinal groups, and lifestyle groups. Groups show different preferences and acceptances of products. Furthermore, characteristics which attract one group to a product (e.g., super sweet taste and flavor) may repel another group, even though both groups share the identical set of sensory perceptions of the specific products.

R&D sensory analysis has not, until recently, recognized the importance of the segmentation method for the assessment of foods. Rather, R&D sensory analysts have concentrated on the more biologically related factors of hunger, age, satiety, etc. as determinants of acceptance, or sensory characteristics of foods. As the marketing researcher becomes increasingly aware of the science of sensory analysis, and as sensory analysts bring their methods more in line with consumer research rather than relying upon expert or non-representative panelists, we may expect an increasing cross fertilization between the market researcher and the sensory analyst. Certainly, the realization that different consumer segments exist in the market represents a fact of life with which the sensory analyst must deal in the evaluation of foods.

TESTING CONSUMER PERCEPTION:
BLIND VERSUS BRANDED PRODUCTS

Branding a product, by testing it within the context of its marketed package, influences product acceptability, oftentimes dramatically, as well as influencing some of the ensuing sensory perceptions. We saw this in our first case history-The Simon Yogurt Company. This fascinating topic of blind versus branded testing represents a unique challenge to product testing and to the psychology of perception. How can the presence of non-tasted stimulus influence one's sensory perception of taste, flavor, aroma, etc., so that it influences one's acceptance of the product.

We saw in an earlier chapter (3) that coloring a food can modify its taste. Miscolored foods simply taste less acceptable. Thus, the sensory input for a product, in terms of taste, aroma, texture seems linked with an additional overlaid impression of "quality", or "type of product". The latter impressions do not represent sensory impression per se, but rather cognitive impressions, which act as organizers or modifiers of the sensory input. Give an individual a white mass of fairly tasteless material, with a spongy rubber texture, and the individual will not know what to do with the stimulus as he or she tastes it. Tell the individual that the spongy rubbery mass represents the raw materials for Chinese bean curd and suddenly the individual reacts in an entirely different way. The sensory inputs remain unchanged, but a new organization of these inputs into a coherent whole has emerged, based upon non-sensory information about the product. The panelist may report nuances which he or she did not detect before. The product may even "taste different" than it did because of this additional information.

Similar changes in perception become obvious when the marketing researcher tests a product blind (without identification) versus branded (with identification). The branded product may consist simply of the product plus its name. On the other hand, more elaborate studies can use the product package as a method of branding.

In some instances the research may call for the point of purchase visual displays which appear in the store, as a further reinforcement of the brand.

Branding can exert a substantial effect on perceptions of products, but the directions of the effect (increase or decrease in rating levels) vary, depending upon the product, the brand, and the consumer and the attribute. We will consider in detail one case history, chocolate bars, and inspect the effects of branding on two other categories (potato chips, yogurt).

A Case History of Blind vs Branded Evaluation-Chocolate

The study reported below took place in Paris in 1977. The study concerned the reactions of female French consumers to different chocolates, tested both blind and branded.

The business issue which generated the research derived from concerns by a manufacturer of a French chocolate, Brand 'Q'. During the two years before the research, beginning in late 1974, Brand Q lost share, in a consistent downturn of sales. Furthermore, consumers seemed not to care about Brand Q, at least as reported from storekeeper interviews. The research project aimed to determine whether the change in share resulted from

Possibility 1: Poorer product, versus competition.
Possibility 2: Poorer image, versus competition.

Marketing researchers suggested that a panel of 50 females, who regularly purchase chocolate candies, would suffice for a small scale

study of chocolate product perceptions. The marketing researcher contracted with a field service in Paris to pre-recruit the 50 female consumers to participate in the study. These women participated in one of
two sessions, lasting about 1.5 hours each. In each session 25 women
participated.

The actual product evaluations followed a specific sequence:

Respondents oriented in magnitude estimation scaling, by means of
an orientation procedure, (adapted from Chapters 5, 6, translated into
French). In other market research projects, the approach has worked
when the researchers have translated instructions into German, Dutch,
Italian, and Japanese for the specific groups of panelists in those
countries. Thus, the instructions and the scaling technique works
validly just as well in other languages and alphabets besides English.

Respondents scaled the four chocolates singly, in random order,
presented "blind". (Nestle's, Beaumont, Poulain, Brand Q). These four
chocolates represented different qualities of chocolates available to
the French consumer, but did not represent "high-class" chocolates.
The respondents waited 5 minutes between samples.

Respondents then waited about 15 minutes. They then evaluated the
same four chocolates, this time by taking the chocolates out of the
wrapper in which the chocolates came as marketed. The wrappers
showed the price, and clearly identified the product. The wrapper itself
constituted part of a consumer's overall impression of the chocolate
product.

Respondents used the same scale and same attributes for "blind"
and "branded" products.

After having finished the evaluations of the eight chocolates, the
respondents profiles their 'ideal' chocolate bar product.

At the end of the evaluation the respondents calibrated their magnitude estimates by the procedures discussed in Chapters 5 and 6.

The average ratings appear in Table 8.7. The magnitude estimation
scale clearly shows the effect of branding upon the perception of overall acceptability, as well as upon the perception of some of the attributes. For example as a result of branding, Nestle's acceptance rating
goes up from a 31.6 to a 55.6 whereas another product, Beaumont,
drops down from a 70.1 to a 50.3. With respect to the size of the scale
and the size of the standard error of the mean these changes reflect
quite dramatic changes in a panelist's acceptance rating.

Table 8.7 shows clearly that the resulting loss of share for Brand Q
probably comes from an intrinsically inferior product, rather than
from poor image. In fact, the rating of overall liking for Brand Q,

51.3 branded versus 27.8 blind, shows that Brand Q's image or brand helps an otherwise poor tasting product to achieve a higher acceptance level. We also see that consumers respond to Brand Q, when branded, as primarily a children's product (rating = 75.7, appropriate for children). The other, more successful chocolate products, rate equally high for children and adults, suggesting a less focused image, and greater appropriateness to a wider target audience.

Sensory characteristics and image characteristics also show susceptibility to branding, as Table 8.7 shows. Even though we conceive of our senses as accurate registrators of outside stimuli, a brand (or other type of label) placed onto the product can modify our impressions and ratings of sweetness, etc. The susceptibility of sensory impressions (in contrast to image characteristics, such as milk chocolate) should come as a surprise to many of the psychophysical researchers, who assume that perceptions reflect the stimuli veridically. They do not.

Marketing researchers and product testers who obtain this type of information about products from consumers can provide a very valuable service to both marketing and to R&D.

Marketing discerns the strengths and weaknesses of the particular products which the consumers have evaluated. One can discover and measure the gap between the competitive products in order to see whether one chocolate possesses more chocolate flavor than does another chocolate. This type of information regarding particular sensory or image characteristics, as well as ratings of overall liking/disliking signal the marketer whether there exists an opportunity in the marketplace because the sensory quality of the competitors provide less of a chocolate flavor than one's own product provides. This piece of intelligence provides a clear opportunity for the marketer to advertise that fact in a creative, enticing and convincing way. The marketer further learns about the impact which the package and brand exerts on consumer perceptions of the product. From the size of the gap between ratings of blind products and branded products the marketer can learn whether improvements in the product arise from the change in the product, or arise from changes in the type of packaging. For example, the data in Table 8.7 tells the marketer that through proper positioning of the product and proper marketing/packaging, the product can signal increased chocolate flavor, even though by itself the product has not changed at all. The sheer presence of the label wrapper enhances consumer's impressions of specific attributes.

R&D uses the information in a different way. R&D seeks to improve product quality by modifying the ingredients. R&D's reaction to the data in Table 8.7 consists of an evaluation of the attributes of the product vis-à-vis each other blind, branded, and versus the ideal. If the

TABLE 8.7

CATEGORY SNAPSHOT OF CHOCOLATE BARS

(Blind versus Branded Ratings)

Product	Liking	Attributes						
		Hardness Texture	Taste	Sweet-ness	Milk Choco-late Taste	Appropriate For		
						Adult	Children	
Nestle (blind)	31.6	46.1	23.5	65.3	54.5	44.6	48.4	
Nestle (branded)	55.6	64.8	56.4	76.6	68.5	57.0	57.9	
Poulain (blind)	26.0	32.9	14.3	61.8	53.5	40.5	41.7	
Poulain (branded)	27.1	45.5	5.9	54.8	48.9	43.5	45.6	
Beaumont (blind)	70.1	63.6	56.4	79.7	66.0	65.1	70.1	
Beaumont (branded)	50.3	57.4	47.5	65.9	69.2	55.1	54.7	
Brand Q (blind)	27.8	60.4	24.3	64.3	38.4	29.3	40.3	
Brand Q (branded)	51.3	63.6	37.9	69.2	59.9	34.7	75.7	
Ideal	141.6	109.5	130.2	86.6	82.8	114.3	100.9	
Average Standard Error of the mean	9.4	5.7	6.2	7.3	7.1	5.3	5.7	

ideal level lies within the range of product ratings (i.e., if the product variations encompass the ideal, or bracket it), then the product developer has learned that he or she can vary ingredients, in order to bring the product closer to the ideal. For example, if sweetness represents an actionable attribute (so that the ideal level of sweetness lies close to some level achieved by one or another product), then the product developer knows that formulation changes can solve product problems involving sweetness of ingredient. The product developer can narrow the gap between a product's sweetness level and the ideal or target sweetness level. On the other hand, if the consumer desires a chocolate flavor so far beyond the score of any product tested, this information acts as a clear warning signal to the product developer. The attribute of "chocolate flavor" behaves as an image attribute, and not only as a sensory one. By trying to narrow the gap between existing products and the extremely high or (extremely low) rated ideal levels, directly scaled by the consumers, the product developer may undertake an impossible task. One cannot close the gap, because such closure requires an extraordinary change in ingredients, which could reduce the acceptability of the product dramatically.

Table 8.8 and 8.9 present other data, pertaining to yogurt and potato chips. These studies revealed the base effect which branding plays upon the perception of products. Branding perhaps more than any other factor (including panelist age, sex, brand use history etc.) influences how a consumer reacts to a product.

Effect of Age and Sex on Branding

Marketing researchers often classify their consumer panelist population into subgroups, or cells. (R&D sensory analysts usually do not.) This section concerns the results of a small study on the susceptibility of consumers to branding with these consumers falling into different age groups. Benzaquen of Yeshiva University conducted the study, in the New York City area, with interesting results. The base results appear in Table 8.10. Here we look at the data in greater detail.

The study comprised 50 consumer panelists, who regularly consume chocolate candy. These individuals participated singly in an hour-long session study, run on two consecutive days. On day 1 panelists evaluated four bars of candy with wrappers removed to prevent identification. On day 2, the same panelists evaluated the same four bars of candy, this time branded, so that they knew the candies. As in the standard magnitude estimation scaling, the interviewer oriented the respondents in magnitude estimation scaling. After orientation, the interviewer had panelists evaluate the four products. Panelists gener-

TABLE 8.8
YOGURTS
(Blind versus Branded Product Ratings)*

| Product | Liking | Sweet-ness | Con-sistency | After-taste | Appropriate for | |
					Children	Adults
Yoplait (blind)	43.3	30.7	46.0	27.5	50.8	54.7
Yoplait (branded)	50.0	32.5	43.3	25.9	51.9	53.3
Dannon (blind)	50.0	28.1	41.5	27.6	55.7	58.6
Dannon (branded)	64.7	33.2	56.8	23.3	65.6	64.1
Laroche (blind)	26.3	38.1	32.8	40.3	50.7	57.3
Laroche (branded)	44.2	32.6	40.5	27.8	50.8	50.2
Nova (blind)	64.5	44.9	67.7	24.9	61.9	62.5
Nova (branded)	60.0	34.4	66.4	15.5	61.0	62.9
Ideal	133.5	40.4	92.3	15.5	115.2	113.5

*Base of 50 housewives, Paris

TABLE 8.9
POTATO CHIPS
(Blind versus Branded Product Ratings)*

Product	Liking	Purchase Intent	Crisp-ness	Greasi-ness	Fresh-ness	Potato Flavor	Appro-priate With Dips
Lays (blind)	21.8	54.1	68.2	75.7	59.4	51.9	46.2
Lays (branded)	46.4	74.5	88.7	80.5	88.5	87.8	82.7
Pringles (blind)	4.9	32.5	80.1	60.8	69.9	24.0	47.5
Pringles (branded)	−30.7	36.7	85.7	35.7	79.9	39.2	64.4
Ruffles (blind)	27.5	61.1	88.6	59.7	67.6	51.3	75.4
Ruffles (branded)	75.5	83.9	78.1	50.6	79.8	69.8	87.2
Wise (blind)	21.5	43.4	79.9	117.4	70.4	39.0	54.1
Wise (branded)	75.3	93.5	76.5	97.8	88.5	89.7	77.8
Ideal	138.0	157.6	122.0	20.5	133.3	112.6	119.8

*Base of 50 panelists, N.Y. market (local high school)

ated profile ratings for each candy, on a variety of characteristics. On day 2 panelists repeated the same exercise with the branded products. On day 2 the panelists also scaled their ideal profile of the ideal chocolate product (a fudge filled center product), and then calibrated their ratings.

The products comprised three basic children's candies and a fourth adult candy (Forever Yours) with the adult candy possessing a more bitter-chocolate note than the children's candies. The panelists comprised five different age groups, half male and half female. The arrangement provides the marketer, marketing researcher and the sensory analyst with an opportunity to study the influence of age, sex and branding upon panelist's perceptions of the products.

Based upon the data in Tables 8.10A and 8.10B the marketing researcher and marketer learns that:

1. Branding a candy bar affects consumer acceptance of the candy bar. The liking ratings differ, depending upon blind versus branded presentation, although not to the same degree. Some candy bars (Forever Yours, Milky Way) show greater susceptibility to branding, whereas other candy bars show less susceptibility.

2. Younger children show more robust, less brand-sensitive ratings than do some of the older panelists in the study (See Table 8.10A).

3. Candy tastes segment. Forever Yours, an adult oriented candy with a bitter-sweet chocolate taste, appealed more to adults than it did to children.

Sensory analysts, and sometimes marketers, forget about the effects of branding on product perceptions and product acceptance. Tests of products without identification may contradict actual results obtained later on when the marketer evaluates, or even test markets the same candy or product under a label. This data on candy, broken out by ages, shows the effect, and how it differs age-by-age. The previously exhibited sets of ratings on yogurt, candy, and potato chips confirm the critical role which branding or other identification methods play on consumer perceptions.

EFFECT OF ANOTHER FACTOR—PRICE

We will illustrate the powerful effect of another variable, stated item price, on consumer's ratings. Marketing researchers and marketers realize that a consumer's hedonic rating of a product does not completely correlate with the success of the product in the marketplace. If the manufacturer distributes the product poorly, so it appears in only a few outlets, or if the manufacturer prices the product too high (or too low), then consumers may not purchase the product, or purchase lesser amounts than expected. We illustrate this price-purchase relation through a study of lotion, rather than foods.

TABLE 8.10A
HOW AGE AFFECTS LIKING OF CANDIES

| | Average | Age | | | | | Sex | |
		7-15	16-25	26-35	36-45	46+	Male	Female
Snickers								
Blind	62.9	95.6	46.6	64.1	48.4	61.4	77.3	47.9
Branded	77.7	95.0	92.6	76.9	63.9	64.4	85.4	70.0
Forever Yours								
Blind	46.8	49.5	37.6	66.9	30.7	54.2	52.1	41.5
Branded	50.1	26.5	47.9	51.1	54.0	70.1	53.0	46.8
3 Musketeers								
Blind	55.6	88.0	52.2	44.0	46.2	43.7	64.6	46.6
Branded	74.5	83.4	45.0	77.3	73.6	93.5	79.3	69.6
Milky Way								
Blind	60.7	66.1	38.0	61.1	58.1	80.5	67.9	53.2
Branded	93.4	107.2	97.0	69.7	90.0	104.6	87.4	99.4
Average								
Blind	56.5	74.8	43.6	59.0	45.8	59.9	65.4	47.3
Branded	74.1	78.0	70.6	68.7	70.3	82.9	76.2	71.4
% Change due to branding	31%	4%	62%	16%	53%	39%	16%	51%
Ideal	161.8	175.3	168.6	169.0	156.1	140.8	162.7	160.9
Children's Candies (without Forever Yours)								
Blind	59.7	83.2	45.6	56.4	50.9	61.8	69.9	49.2
Branded	81.8	95.2	78.2	74.6	75.8	87.5	84.0	79.6
% Change due to branding	37%	14%	71%	32%	49%	42%	21%	62%

TABLE 8.10B
HOW BRANDING AFFECTS ATTRIBUTE RATINGS OF CANDIES

Product	Liking	Inside Chewiness	Chocolate Flavor	Overall Quality	Sweetness
Snickers (blind)	62.90	60.21	36.85	65.84	53.00
Snickers (branded)	78.00	63.25	53.17	84.16	62.20
% Change (branding)	+124%	4%	44%	27%	18%
Forever Yours (blind)	46.85	65.30	43.38	59.89	68.3
Forever Yours (branded)	50.05	52.64	56.11	61.74	66.90
% Change (branding)	7%	19%	28%	17%	−2%
3 Musketeers (blind)	55.62	60.10	44.79	60.36	64.90
3 Musketeers (branded)	74.57	55.25	61.44	82.37	76.10
% Change (branding)	+34%	−9%	39%	36%	18%
Milky Way (blind)	60.68	59.68	50.59	88.20	74.80
Milky Way (branded)	93.39	67.26	64.03	104.96	76.10
% Change (branding)	+54%	+13%	27%	19%	2%
Average (blind)	56.52	61.32	43.90	66.82	65.25
Average (branded)	74.10	59.37	58.68	83.30	70.30
% Change (branding)	31%	−3%	34%	25%	8%

The lotion product typified a health-oriented lotion, with a unique set of ingredients designed to heal and otherwise improve the quality of skin. After several years of research on consumer needs and wants, and after four years of intermittent laboratory formulation work, the lotion manufacturer developed a prototype lotion they called Health. Health comprised a number of unique ingredients designed to sooth and heal hands chapped by exposure to dishwater or cold weather.

In an attempt to optimize the formulation of "Health" the manufacturer suggested evaluating different formulations of Health, comprising:

Color variations
Fragrance/perfume variations
Emollient (thickener) variations

Each of these cosmetic variations performed identically in clinical tests, but the aesthetic appearance, fragrance and tactile properties influenced consumer perceptions.

In the actual evaluation of the 18 alternative formulations of Health and 3 competitors (A, B, C) the marketing researcher realized that consumers would have to test each lotion for at least four days. With a large array of alternative lotions, the consumer researcher and sensory analyst came up with an experimental design in which the panelists would test an incomplete portion of the actual formulations. In this manner, each consumer respondent could test 5 of the lotions over a five week (35 day) period, using the lotion for four days, and then waiting two days, before using the next lotion. Studies of this type come up frequently in consumer research where the manufacturer wishes to test a wide array of products, under actual use situations, but must limit each respondent to a subset or incomplete block, of alternative formulations.

The study proceeded, with each of the panelists evaluating 5 of the 22 lotions. Altogether, more than 140 respondents participated, with each product evaluated by approximately 36-41 different individuals at home.

As part of the study, the marketing researcher suggested that the respondents rate samples on two characteristics pertaining to overall acceptability: liking and purchase interest. Liking refers to one's own acceptance of the product, whereas purchase interest calls into play a host of other factors which include stated item price, the consumer's own frequency of use and current need for the product, etc. As a test of the impact of price, the marketing researcher instructed the respondent to rate overall liking (using magnitude estimation), based upon sensory impressions and performance impressions of the product. Furthermore, the respondents scaled purchase interest in the lotion, assuming the lotion price varied between $1.00/jar and $2.00/jar. In this way, one could evaluate the change in purchase interest due to price changes, given a fixed lotion acceptability rating. Only the ancillary factor of price varied.

Table 8.11 shows the ratings, averaged across the panelists. As expected, with increasing price of the jar of lotion, purchase interest declines. It declines at different rates, depending upon the intrinsic lotion acceptance.

Perhaps the most interesting factor to emerge from this type of study consists of the equation which relates change in purchase interest to the change in acceptability, and the change in price. We expect that purchase interest will increase as consumers find the lotion more acceptable, but that purchase interest will decrease as the price of the lotion increases. Which factor exerts more power—acceptability based upon sensory characteristics, or stated price/jar of lotion?

In order to answer this question, let us construct an equation to relate overall purchase interest (PI) to two factors, acceptability (L/D) and Price (P). We chose an equation which eliminates the size of units

TABLE 8.11
OVERALL LIKING AND PURCHASE INTENT RATINGS[a]
AT FIVE PRICE LEVELS FOR SKIN LOTIONS AND "IDEAL PRODUCT"

Products Tested	Overall Liking	Purchase Intent at Five Price Levels				
		$1.00	$1.25	$1.50	$1.75	$2.00
Ideal Product[b]	151	160	138	105	82	63
A[c]	60	99	74	54	33	22
B[c]	72	96	73	51	34	24
C[c]	71	92	73	56	38	23
D	70	91	83	59	38	25
E	62	90	73	55	32	23
F	57	86	64	47	29	22
G	60	84	68	45	27	13
H	40	83	63	39	25	12
I	36	82	69	53	35	26
J	54	81	63	45	25	15
K	53	80	59	35	18	13
L	47	79	57	37	21	10
M	46	79	50	29	15	7
N	44	78	64	41	22	15
O	43	76	54	31	22	13
P	42	74	55	39	20	16
Q	42	74	61	39	15	10
R	41	71	59	43	25	19
S	41	71	51	26	14	9
T	39	70	55	35	24	19
U	38	67	58	40	25	20

[a]Normalized mean ratings using magnitude estimation scaling
[b]In the actual test, two digit identification numbers used to identify each product
[c]Commercial products "blind tested"

as a key factor which could influence the answer. (Since acceptability appears in terms of magnitude estimates, and since price of the lotion appears in terms of dollars/jar, we do not want to obtain a measure of relative importance which depends upon the choice of units, and which would change when we change the cost of goods to cents/jar.)

The power equation has the form:

$$PI = k(L/D^m)(P)^m \tag{1}$$

provides us with the appropriate, simplest equation. The exponent for liking (m) tells us how rapidly purchase increases as a function of increases in liking rating. (If m exceeds 1.0 then, recalling Chapter 3, purchase interest will grow more rapidly than we expect on the basis of increasing liking. Doubling liking will more than double purchase intent. On the other hand, when m drops below 1.0, then doubling the product liking rating will less than double purchase interest. For instance, for $m = 2.0$, doubling liking increases purchase interest by $2^2 = 4$ times. For $m = 0.5$, doubling liking increases purchase interest by $2^{0.5} = 1.41 = 41\%$ not 100%.)

The actual equation appears as:

$$PI = 645 \, (\text{Price})^{-2.37} \, (\text{Liking})^{0.45} \tag{2}$$

These data and the equation (which summarizes the data) tell the marketing researcher and the sensory analyst that:

Purchase interest varies with both liking and stated item price.

Increases in liking or product acceptability generate a relatively slowly increasing purchase intent. Changes in the formulation to increase purchase interest by increasing liking will show less of an effect than will pricing changes.

Increases in price, decrease purchase interest more than an increase in liking increases purchase intent. Small changes in price exert a greater proportional effect on changes in purchase interest than does the same proportional change in liking. Keeping liking constant, doubling the price decreases purchase interest by 81%, from a fixed level (e.g., from 100 down to 19). Halving the price, increases purchase interest by 517%, from a fixed level of say 10, up to 51.7.

IMPORTANCE OF ATTRIBUTES TO CONSUMERS

Marketing researchers often evaluate the importance of different attributes to consumers as keys to enhance product acceptability. If the marketing researcher can ascertain what characteristics "drive" or enhance consumer acceptance of products, then these charactertistics provide insights regarding the direction to modify products.

Marketing researchers have used at least two different methods to distinguish between important and unimportant attributes:

Direct ratings of importance.

Multiple linear (or non-linear) regression relating liking to attribute level.

Direct Ratings of Importance

Respondents in product evaluations often have an idea (whether clear or fuzzy) as to how important different product characteristics seem to them. For example, in the evaluation of cereal, the marketing researcher may ask the panelist to scale the relative importance of texture, flavor, appearance, health benefits, etc. Respondents usually comply, and provide answers which agree fairly well from individual to individual, except when we probe a benefit or characteristic (e.g., nutrition) in which some, but not all individuals, feel overrides all other attributes.

Linear Correlations Versus Non-Linear Correlations and Equations

Quite often marketing researchers use another, more statistical approach. They hypothesize that overall liking relates to the sensory characteristics (and other characteristics) by means of a specific equation, called the general linear equation. We express that equation as:

$$\text{Overall Liking} = k_o + k_1 (\text{Attribute 1}) + k_2 (\text{Attribute 2}) \text{ etc.} \qquad (3)$$

(k_o = additive constant, k_1 = multiplicative coefficient, attribute 1 = a specific sensory or image attribute.)

Sometimes (but not all that often) the marketing researcher or the R&D sensory analyst has tested sufficiently large variation either in the number of products or the number of panelists. By coalescing all of this data and using a linear equation, the analyst can estimate the coefficients $k_1 \ldots k_n$ for the different attributes. Those attributes showing a high value for the coefficient (viz., unit increases in the consumer's rating on the attribute generate high increases or decreases in liking or purchase interest ratings) represent attributes which we define as "important". On the other hand, low values for a coefficient represent less important attributes, since changes in the attribute level do not generate large changes in liking.

One can furthr generalize this approach by considering the observation made by Moskowitz (1981) with regard to ingredients, but apply it to sensory characteristics. A better representation of overall liking versus consumer rated characteristics comes from the parabolic equation for two sensory attributes, written below

$$\text{Liking} = k_o + k_1 (\text{Attribute 1}) + k_2 (\text{Attribute 1})^2 + k_3 (\text{Attribute 2})$$
$$+ k_4 (\text{Attribute 2})^2 + k_5 (\text{Attribute 1}) (\text{Attribute 2})$$

(one can easily generalize this approach to 3 or more sensory attributes.) According to this approach, each attribute, just as each ingredient, reaches a bliss point or peak level in the middle of the range. The researcher or analyst should use the parabolic equation to find that optimum, and to represent the fact that attributes interact with each other.

A consequence of this non-linear equation becomes the recognition that importance, as represented by the single coefficient k, no longer remains a single number. Importance equals the momentary rate of change of liking or purchase intent versus an attribute. For a linear equation, the momentary rate of change of liking versus attribute equals the coefficient, and it remains fixed. For a non-linear equation (e.g., a parabolic or curvilinear equation) the momentary rate of change varies rather than remaining fixed. The importance of the characteristic or attribute thus changes, depending upon the attribute level. Moskowitz (1981) has suggested that when marketing researchers and sensory analysts use this more complex parabolic equation, relative importances for attributes at the optimum point of acceptability all become equal. Only as we go away from the optimum or bliss point do attributes assume varying, non zero importance values. As one moves further away from the optimum, bliss region, some attributes assume greater importance than others, in affecting overall acceptability. Those attributes where the liking rating shows a flat terrain (little change in liking with changes in that attribute) exert less importance than attributes where liking markedly changes with attribute level.

A Case Hisory Comparing Methods
To Assess Attribute Importance

The Phipps Company, manufacturers of liquors developed 20 variations of a new liqueur comprising unique flavors, with varying ingredient combinations. Commissioning an outside marketing research firm to do its ratings, the Phipps Company suggested that the research measure the relative importance of different liqueur characteristics to the consumer.

The marketing research company executed the study, using a panel of 120 consumers, each of whom rated 5 of the 20 formulations in a 4 hour session. Thus, about 30 consumers rated each product. Of course, to insure no order or product selection bias, each consumer in the panel rated a unique set of 5 liqueurs. The data base appears in Table 8.12. At the end of the evaluations, the consumers scaled the relative importance of the characteristics, as influencing acceptability, using the

TABLE 8.12
DATA BASE OF RATING LIQUEURS

Product	Purchase Intent	Liking	Liking of Flavor	Liking of Texture	Flavor Strength	Sharpness of Taste	Sweetness	Aromatic	Aftertaste	Smoothness
1	21	-25	-43	-28	77	58	55	38	71	36
2	49	19	2	37	88	67	69	55	82	56
3	60	42	34	61	93	78	65	56	74	70
4	63	30	20	45	91	79	68	45	77	54
5	62	29	22	34	92	90	71	77	83	80
6	69	45	26	48	73	58	54	47	61	55
7	81	67	61	64	80	70	55	50	60	64
8	55	29	11	33	84	68	64	55	75	51
9	87	45	42	66	91	81	65	53	68	85
10	52	6	3	29	76	65	58	45	63	46
11	68	38	22	51	75	72	60	50	73	63
12	66	41	31	55	78	66	65	40	85	61
13	78	51	37	59	85	73	64	52	76	81
14	17	-41	-47	-10	68	44	39	30	56	36
15	76	24	31	13	100	101	73	75	95	73
16	61	-2	10	12	99	105	70	73	86	60
17	67	57	43	47	71	59	49	43	57	54
18	33	-10	-7	15	74	63	58	42	77	46
19	82	70	56	76	93	80	65	78	76	71
20	38	5	-3	-27	101	97	81	82	88	46

same magnitude estimation scale as they had used to evaluate the actual set of formulations. In this way the marketing researcher obtained a measure of relative attribute importance directly from a consumer, who has had previous experience with the product.

Let us look at different ways of evaluating importance. Table 8.13 shows the relative importance of the characteristics, as consumers directly evaluated them. Note that the truly sensory characteristics achieve lower importance value on the scale than do image characteristics and score lower on the scale than hedonic ratings of different sensory characteristics. To the marketing researcher this presents a paradox. Although hedonic and image characteristics of products play a key role in determining importance and acceptance, nonetheless the only way the marketing researcher and the product developer can modify acceptance comes from modifying the product's sensory characteristics. Yet, at first glance panelists assign these characteristics relatively less importance.

TABLE 8.13
DIFFERENT MEASURES OF IMPORTANCE

Attribute	Direct Rating of Importance	Correlation With Liking	Correlation With Purchase Intent
1. Liking of Flavor	130	0.96	0.90
2. Liking of Texture	107	0.88	0.90
3. Flavor Strength	114	0.15	0.30
4. Sharpness of Taste	113	0.16	0.39
5. Sweetness	102	0.18	0.29
6. Aromatic	88	0.24	0.35
7. Aftertaste	99	−0.07	0.08
8. Smoothness	141	0.70	0.90

By accepting consumer's direct rating regarding the importance of characteristics, the marketing researcher and the marketer often incorrectly focus in on the non-actionable hedonic or image characteristics as the key characteristics to modify. Many of these characteristics correlate so highly with overall liking that they represent restatements of like and dislike.

A further problem arises in the evaluation of a consumer's own prima facie rating of what constitutes an "important" versus a nonimportant characteristic. Do consumers know? On the basis of one or several stimulus evaluations we know that consumers, can adequately evaluate the sensory properties of food products. At the same time, however, can these same consumers quantify the relative importance of each attribute? Although consumer panelists as well as expert panelists rate relative importance, how validly do they make those ratings.

Let us now look at the behavioral correlations between overall liking and each attribute (also shown in Table 8.13). In contrast to the self-estimated importance value, the correlation emerges from actual behavior which the panelists exhibit. By computing a simple correlation between each attribute and overall liking, the marketing researcher and the sensory analyst can discern which attributes correlate highly with liking, versus which sensory characteristics correlate only modestly. At first glance, this again suggests the relatively lower importance of the actionable sensory characteristics as determinants of overall liking, since behaviorally these sensory characteristics exhibit low correlation coefficients.

A similar result occurs when the marketing researcher or sensory analyst puts the ratings into the form of a multiple linear regression to find the relative weights or importance values assigned to each characteristic of our liqueur. A multiple linear correlation shows the hedonic attributes as relatively critical determinants of liking, with the sensory characteristics as less important.

The use of correlations, linear regression or self-estimated importance values characterizes much of what marketing researchers do in their analysis of rating data, and how they discover those particular factors critical to increased acceptance. Again and again, from study to study the factors emerging as most important comprise those image and hedonic attributes over which the product developer and manufacturer have no control.

Let us take a closer look at an alternative way of evaluating relative importance of attributes using the parabolic equation discussed previously. The method follows these steps:

1. For our liqueur data, classify the attributes into the sensory, image and hedonic attributes.

2. Select only the sensory attributes as appropriate for the evaluation. The remaining attributes reflect derivative perceptions from advertising, expectations and the like, over which the product developer has no control.

3. Develop both a linear and a non-linear (parabolic) equation relating liking to separate sensory characteristics.

4. If the linear equation fits the data, we assume that the sensory characteristic maintains a fixed importance value over its entire range of magnitude. Relative importance then equals the relative size of the coefficients in the equation. The order of relative importance parallels

the order of the simple correlation between each sensory attribute and overall liking.

5. If the non-linear equation fits the data, but the linear equation does not, then we conclude that the relative importance of the sensory attribute continuously varies over the range of sensory magnitude. The relative importance will vary according to the attribute level, in a more complex way.

Table 8.14 shows the approach in a schematic form.

TABLE 8.14
DEMONSTRATION OF HOW TO COMPUTE RELATIVE IMPORTANCE*

1. Prototypical Equation (1 Sensory Variable) versus Liking

(A) Linear: Liking = $k_0 + k_1$(Attribute)

Rate of change of liking with respect to attribute = k_1 = constant, no matter what value attribute assumes.

(B) Nonlinear: Liking = $k_0 + k_1$(Attribute) + k_2(Attribute)^2
Rate of change of liking with respect to attribute equals

$k_1 + 2k_2$(Attribute)   (We call this the 1st partial derivative of liking with respect to attribute)

2. Prototypical Equation (2 sensory variables) versus liking

(A) Linear: Liking = $k_0 + k_1$(Attribute 1) + k_2(Attribute 2)
Rate of change of liking with respect to attribute 1 = k_1
Rate of change of liking with respect to attribute 2 = k_2

(B) Nonlinear: Liking = $k_0 + k_1$(Attribute 1) + k_2(Attribute 2) + k_3(Attribute 1)^2 + k_4(Attribute 2)^2 + k_5(Attribute 1)(Attribute 2)

Rate of change of liking with respect to attribute 2 = $k_2 + 2k_4$(Attribute 2) + k_5(Attribute 1)

Rate of change of liking with respect to attribute 1 = $k_1 + 2k_3$(Attribute 1) + k_5(Attribute 2)

*Based upon non-linear equations: importance = rate of change of liking

COMPARISON OF MARKETING RESEARCH & R&D SENSORY ANALYSIS

Traditionally, R&D sensory analysis concerns itself primarily with in-laboratory formulations of products. The major focus of R&D sensory analysis concerns the product itself, and how that product performs vis-à-vis competitors (for reformulation), or vis-à-vis specific standards for quality assurance. Until recently, many sensory analysts worked almost exclusively with in-house expert panels, or with in-house, but non representative consumer panels.

In recent years the R&D sensory analyst has discovered the consumer and has changed or at least augmented its focus from strictly in-house, small scale panel work to external panel work. In most instances this augmentation has allowed the R&D analyst an opportunity to better tailor the panels of consumers to answer questions regarding the perceptions and acceptance of products. Nonetheless, R&D sensory analysis still bases decisions on relatively small size panels for testing formula variations. The interest of the analyst focuses upon the perception of the product, and the correlation of that perception of the product with antecedent ingredient or storage/quality changes.

Marketing researchers deal directly with consumers in terms of their perceptions of products, brands, attitudes, etc. The product tester or marketing researcher uses sensory analysis as a tool in "product testing". Such product testing considers products in their totality. The product tester may instruct consumers to rate the sensory and acceptance characteristics, the fit of a product to a marketing concept, or evaluate the product against different competitors, under different types of labels, etc.

Marketing researchers use different terms and different analyses than do R&D sensory analysts. R&D analysts often focus on how ratings of products correlate with physical variations. These R&D analysts sometimes use technical terms to describe product nuances. In contrast, the marketing researcher uses the consumer's vocabulary. By interspersing words which connote sensory characteristics together with "buzz" words from advertising (e.g., natural, refreshing), the consumer researcher obtains a snapshot of the product in terms of consumer ratings. Furthermore, marketing researchers work with consumers who have had little or no experience in descriptive sensory analysis, and who evaluate the samples under non-laboratory test conditions (in a mall, at home, etc.).

It should come as no surprise that the R&D sensory analysts and marketing researchers rarely talk to each other. They share the goal of measuring human reactions but for different reasons. The laboratory R&D sensory analyst, testing under relatively sterile, non-real world conditions presents a stark, almost unreal figure to the marketing researcher. In an attempt to isolate factors which relate to physical changes, the R&D sensory analyst often eliminates the particular variables to which consumers respond (such as packaging), and on the basis of which consumers make purchase decisions. In contrast, the marketing researcher seems undisciplined to R&D. The marketing researcher deals with product evaluations, couched in consumer language, in a relatively uncontrolled world. The marketing researcher cannot understand how one can possibly achieve good, valid data from a non-representative panel of 10-20 individuals in a laboratory. Marketing research practice has stressed representation of the target population by large base sizes, of 100+ individuals. To the laboratory based researcher, a panel size of 100+ in one's own facility would strain resources.

The two types of practitioners look at data differently as well. The marketing researcher attends to the major effects of product differences and why these product differences occur. Can we trace the differences to specific physical characteristics of the product? Or do the differences emerge because some respondents in the population evaluate products based upon different histories of brand usage. Age, sex, or brand usage play a role. What about frequency of brand usage—do infrequent users show different ratings than frequent (viz. heavy) users. The marketing researcher deals with as few as 1 or 2 products, in a study, and rarely tests more than 5. Thus, the marketing research analyst must look for patterns in the variation among panelists. Differences in adults versus children, in regionality (east versus midwest versus west), in user pattern (loyal users of one brand A, versus loyal users of the other brand B) all provide grist for the marketing research data mill. Rarely, however, does the marketing research analyst correlate changes in product ratings with systematic variation in the formulation or in the ingredient levels. More often than not the marketing research analyst studies reactions to two products which differ qualitatively, rather than quantitatively, on ingredient dimensions.

The R&D or laboratory based sensory analyst usually works with a smaller base of panelists. The panel members usually show greater homogeneity of age, brand usage, etc. The use of in-house consumer panels severely limits the R&D sensory analyst's ability to evaluate differences as a function of market, age, etc. When one uses 20-30 panelists, and segments the data into different cells based upon panelist's age, one usually ends up with an exceptionally fragile data base of ratings comprising 3-5 panelists/cell.

These differences between the two types of researchers inevitably lead to communication problems. On the one hand, the R&D sensory analyst must issue reports to the marketing group regarding the in-house consumer and expert panels' perception of product quality. Marketers look for representativeness in the panel to assure themselves that these data truly represent the reactions of the target population. The R&D sensory analyst, with his or her ability to assess many alternative formulations, cannot provide this representation of the target population in the data. Consequently, the marketer often puts the R&D report aside as not germane to the final marketing objectives. Yet the R&D sensory analyst can extrapolate responses to new, untried ingredient formulations. The marketing researcher, in contrast, usually cannot discern the patterns in the data and make predictions as to reactions of consumers to a new untried formulation. The marketing researcher always deals with one or two products which he or she tests. From this limited array of products even the most creative and dedicated marketing research analyst would find it difficult to generate a pattern of different consumer responses to a systematically varied set of formulations. The data and the array of stimuli militate against prediction of such responses, by severely limiting the type and range of products which the marketing researcher tests. Creativity comes from analysis, with a limited stimulus array. Perhaps more would come from a wider stimulus array as well.

In the last eight years the author has had success in developing testing systems with marketing research and R&D jointly. Through numerous tests, some of which have appeared in the technical and marketing literature (Moskowitz, Jacobs & Firtle, 1980: Rabino & Moskowitz, 1980), marketing research and R&D have cooperated to develop and test variations in a variety of products (e.g., bread, beverages, sauces, lotions, etc.). Quite often the tests require evaluations of the existing competitive frame of formulations on the market, as well as evaluation of different test products which vary in physical formulation. The results of those tests, presented in Chapter 7 show that a marriage of large scale testing by marketing research methods, with the R&D approach of evaluating a wide variety of alternative formulations, provides the manufacturer with these benefits:

1. Discernment of patterns of responses due to product variations (ingredient levels, etc.)
2. Discernment of patterns of responses due to region, age and brand usage variations among consumers.
3. Ability to optimize a product formulation so that the product

gains the maximum acceptance from one or several selected segments of the consumer market, and simultaneously appears different from competitors or costs less than competitors.

Only continued research, however, with joint efforts between R&D and marketing can bring together the different talents of each into a more coherent testing and product assessment system which will improve profitability in both short and long runs.

AN OVERVIEW

With the increasing costs of developing and marketing new products and fine tuning current ones, product testing has emerged as a vital facet of the marketing researcher's armory of technical tools. The marketing researcher approaches product evaluation from a more global point of view than does the R&D sensory analyst. Factors such as type of panel, brand usage, and regional variations become important. Descriptive analysis and other fine-tuned tools for laboratory analysis and early tests recede into the background.

To a great degree the market researcher has ignored much of the scientific contributions and methods of the R&D sensory analyst, preferring to concentrate on test techniques which have received approval from marketers. Only in the past five years or so has a dialogue emerged between the two branches of sensory analysis. To this day, however, no parallel to R&D sensory analysis exists in marketing research. Marketing researchers execute product tests, but do not specialize, as food scientists do, in the science of product (or sensory) measurement. To the market researcher and marketer, product testing represents another facet of the premarket stream of testing just as thirty or forty years ago sensory analysis comprised a small part of food science. As interest grows in the consumer evaluation of foods, and as marketers begin to see how optimization methods can aid product penetration and add to profits, we can expect to see far greater interest and advances in product testing by marketing researchers.

CHAPTER 9

LABORATORY LAW—AND LORE

INTRODUCTION

Perhaps no other area in product measurement causes as much confusion, consternation, and ultimately frustration as the procedure for product testing, and the physical testing laboratory or field site. Test methods and physical arrangements reflect the biases of their users. How many times does the visitor see a corporate laboratory facility with exquisite facilities for product testing. And just as often, how many times does the visitor see poorly equipped product evaluation laboratories, from otherwise rich and prosperous companies. Yet, beneath the exterior trappings both companies may do equally good (or poor) work.

This chapter concerns the nuts and bolts of product measurement, from the point of view of execution. We divide the chapter into several sections, including the following: (1) Panelists—who, how to get them, and how to keep them. (2) Facilities—what should they look like, what accoutrements does the product tester absolutely need to run a product evaluation properly, and what accoutrements represent frills. (3) Products—how to present them.

PANELISTS—TO GET THEM AND KEEP THEM

Without panelists the product testing laboratory cannot function. Panelists represent the sensory analyst's instruments, by which one measures the products. All too often companies spend thousands of dollars or even more money on expensive instruments to assess the physical and chemical properties of foods, and yet they neglect to spend a small fraction of that large amount on the human consumer.

Laboratory based sensory analysts often make do with in-house panelists, selected from company employees. Sometimes, the sensory analyst will further select panelists to develop an expert panel, of highly interested, dedicated individuals. In other situations, such individuals simply do not exist. The sensory analyst must select panelists who may have less than an enthusiastic outlook regarding the product evaluation procedure.

In-house panelists present opportunities and problems. Since these individuals work at the plant, the sensory analyst can call on them without much ado, often with only a 10-20 minute warning ahead of time. In this respect, in-house panelists provide one ideal source of panelists, close at hand. Furthermore, corporate management can insure the continued participation of such individuals by making panel participation a precondition of employment (as several food companies do). Given a sufficiently large number of individuals working in a plant or a laboratory, the sensory analyst can often call upon a wide range of individuals, no more than one or two buildings away. This arrangement seems perfect. The cost of the panel declines to effectively '0' dollars, in terms of out-of-pocket expenses. Panelists close at hand allow the sensory analyst to perform the work without having to worry about arranging matters with an outside panel recruiting service, although one must develop an in-house panel recruiting service to insure the steady flow of panelists.

Problems arise with internal panels, however, sometimes severe, sometimes mild.

Motivation

How does the sensory analyst motivate a panelist, other than appealing to the individual's own altruistic nature? Perhaps a few minutes to a half hour off provides sufficient incentive for those individuals with repetitive, dull jobs in the company. What about those highly paid, motivated panelists who must interrupt their work in order to participate for the half hour testing session. Such interruption annoys and interferes with work. The interruption could possibly reduce the quality of data obtained by the sensory analyst. No research has appeared on the quality of data obtained by interruption of an interesting versus a boring task. One might guess, however, that the quality of data could differ, if not on sensory characteristics, then perhaps on evaluation of hedonic characteristics.

Panelist Resistance

Resistance to testing arises when the same panelist over-participates in testing. Panelists like to donate their time, when this time does not interfere with other things that they must do. On the other hand, in small companies, the same panelists participate, day after day, several times per week. Such a regimen becomes tedious, and generates psychological resentment. Certainly the participation reflects laudable company or laboratory behavior, but people still resent the repeated interruptions. Panelists soon begin to refuse to participate, making up excuses. The hostility can break out into the open, evidencing itself in snide remarks about the sensory evaluation function in the corporation, which defeats the entire purpose. Small companies, with few employees who can serve on the panel, especially fall prey to panelist resistance. Larger companies may not, if the sensory analyst can space out the participation of the panelists over longer periods of time, in order to avoid calling upon any single individual too often.

The Professional Consumer

Some participants in company panelling like the panel work so much that they volunteer for it on a continuing basis. The sensory analyst, happy to get a warm body to participate, comes to depend upon these repeaters as the mainstay of the panel, even though their data may soon become expertised. The vicious cycle of panelist availability and panel composition forces the sensory analyst to depend upon these motivated individuals as members of the panel in order to build up the base of ratings. The selection of such convenient participants in place of otherwise randomly selected panels of participants biases the data. Such professional panelists in companies may provide distorted, non-representative ratings.

The Overly High True Cost of Internal Panels

On casual inspection internal panels of consumers (or experts) appear to cost very little. After all, runs the argument, these individuals constituting the panel already work for the company, have come to the laboratory or the test site for other purposes, and spend only a short period of time in the test laboratory. Sensory analysts and R&D directors across the country and the world use this argument repeatedly to develop and maintain in-house sensory analysis facilities, with non-paid participants, representing a selection of the employees. Let's look, for a minute, at the true costs of running such an internal panel. Assuming a $40.00/hr overhead these expenses arise: (1) Laboratory costs, in terms of rent. (2) Cost of the personnel involved in the test set-up (usually a sensory professional and a technician), which takes approximately 4 man-hours. (3) Cost of recruiting the panelists (4 man-hours). (4) Cost of the people participating in the test (2/3 of an hour, including time to get to the site, participate, and return). (5) Opportunity cost, incurred by interrupting an individual's job, and perhaps changing one's attributes about the job at hand for the next few hours. One cannot estimate this cost, but certainly these opportunity costs arise in some, if not all cases. The total man-hours involved comes to 30 man hours $\times$ $40/man hour = $1,200. Note that this price of $1,200 reflects the following: (1) Test of 1-2 products on a limited set of attributes. (2) Test with a limited number, of non-representative consumer panelists. One probably incurs a substantially higher cost, after considering the cost of product preparation, analysis of the data, reporting, etc. The costs cited above reflect only the field costs.

The Case For Extramural Product Testing Panels

Alternatives exist to internal panels which provide the sensory analyst with an opportunity to substantially improve the quality of the panelists and to obtain data in far greater quantity and quality than hitherto. Field services exist outside of companies. Market researchers use these services as primary sources of panelists. These field services charge for recruiting panelists, provide interviewing staff if the sensory analyst wants to contract out the field work, and provide facilities set up and clean up as well. Various benefits accrue from using the field service, and/or extramural panelists: (1) Lower testing cost, because one can test without incurring major overhead expenses. The field testing represents a direct business cost, deducted from the operating expenses, rather than a cost buried in the overhead section. (2) Ability to tailor the panel to select users, who have not participated before, and who show specific product usage patterns, or who belong to specified demographic groups. If the sensory analyst wishes to test a children or teen's cereal, he or she can do so using a panel of children or teens, rather than testing the product on in-house adults who act as surrogates for children or teens. (3) Ability to keep panelists for up to 4 hours by paying them. The author has had success in product evaluation projects wherein panelists participated for several hours, evaluating up to 20 or more beverages, a dozen cakes, a dozen candies, respectively in the test session. By interspersing breaks in a long test session, the sensory analyst avoids sensory fatigue, or a true loss in the panelist's ability to discriminate product differences. By paying panelists a reasonable amount of money (e.g., $30.00 for 4 hours) the sensory analyst can secure relatively enormous amounts of information hitherto unobtainable, except with greater costs. The monetary payment, and the fact that panelists volunteer for the study, setting aside time to participate, eliminates the boredom factor so prevalent in other long interviews. It thus insures higher quality of data.

Extramural panelists can provide a valuable source of data for the sensory analyst, and represent the target group of consumers. Furthermore, since the sensory analyst remunerates these individuals for repeated participation, one can develop a selected group of these individuals into an expert panel, who participate over an extended period of time.

How To Keep In-House Panelists Happy

Sensory analysts from time immemorial have tried different methods for rewarding in-house panelists to continue participating in product evaluation sessions. Some of the rewards include: (1) Participation in a "select" club comprising members of the panel. (2) A certificate, given after the individual has completed a prespecified number of panel evaluations (3) Cookies, or other food rewards (or perhaps even product rewards) at the end of the test session. (4) One new way to keep panelists happy calls for developing a reporting framework which tells panelists how they themselves performed versus the group, in rating product acceptance, and rating the specific sensory characteristics of products. People like to know how they stand vis-à-vis other individuals. Do they share the same tastes with other people, or do their tastes differ? A customized report to each individual (or perhaps a computerized version of such a report), showing the individual's acceptance and perception ratings versus those of the other panel members provides an ongoing incentive to the panelist to continue participating. One need only listen to panelist discussions at the end of the evaluation session, when they talk about the products they liked or they disliked. These panelists show interest in the task, once they immerse themselves in the task, and just after they have finished. They lose interest when away from the testing situation. The report keeps up this flagging interest, and bridges the psychological time gap between one test occasion and the other.

A Note On Panel Size

Novice sensory analysts often worry about the correct size of the panel. When one has no constraints on costs, and can spend as much as desired, panel size becomes no problem at all. One can use large panels, or small panels, depending upon the nature of the problem.

Most R&D sensory analysts operate within constraints on the number of people that they call upon, and time constraints which limit the amount of testing that they can do.

As a consequence of these constraints, the sensory analyst often resorts to a few rules of thumb: (1) Expert panels necessitate fewer individuals than do consumer panels. (2) 3-6 individuals comprise a valid expert panel. (3) 30+ individuals comprise a consumer panel (e.g., for acceptance testing). Marketing researchers, on the other hand, usually work with much larger panels, using base sizes of 100+ to represent the target consumer population.

In actuality, no hard nor fast rules exist about the appropriate size of panels to use. We do not know if 3-6 individuals suffice for an adequate expert panel. No data exist on the appropriate base size for such expert panel ratings. Do we estimate panel size on the basis of the number of individuals needed to discriminate between products? If so, then laboratories find that 3-6 ratings provide too few ratings on which to base a statistical judgment. With 6 expert panelists, one often must load the number of ratings, by rerunning the evalation over extended periods of time, so that each expert panelist provides 4-5 such judgments of the same product, bringing the number of ratings up to 20-30.

In terms of consumers, one often hears the magic number 30, because of the central limit theorem in statistics. According to this theorem, numbers drawn from any population of data, whatsoever, soon generate their own normal distribution. Even if the original population did not show a normal distribution nonetheless the samples drawn at random from this original non-normal distribution will distribute themselves normally. Furthermore, the number 30 also assumes importance, because around 30 the small sample distribution (viz., the so-called 'T' distribution) becomes virtually identical to the large sample Z distribution. With a sample size of 30, one can begin to use statistics appropriate for large samples.

These concepts reflect statistical consideration, but they do not take into account issues continually confronting the sensory analyst and the market researcher.

In sensory tests of perception, with little or no individual differences other than sensory differences and sensitivity (or scale usage), base sizes of 4-6 experts and 30+ consumers (for effective or hedonic testing) may underrepresent the actual distribution of sensitivities in the population. Furthermore, we know that individuals differ in what they like and dislike. Can a panel size of 30 represent the entire population? If the population comprises discrete groups of consumers, some of whom like the product and others who dislike the product, one may obtain an average acceptance rating around neutrality, without faithfully representing any group in the population. Given a small base size of 30 consumers who rate liking/disliking, the sensory analyst will not know whether large variations in the ratings come from variations around a middle group of liking (unimodal distribution of liking) or whether, in fact, the variation represents a bimodal distribution of likes/dislikes. A panel size of 30 presents simply too few individuals to discover the existence of a bimodal distribution. On the other hand, when the sensory analyst knows for certain that he or she has sampled from a homogeneous population of consumers, then the base size of 30 may constitute quite an adequate sample.

Base sizes also, vary, depending upon the sensitivity of the particular scaling device. Some procedures, such as paired comparisons, or categorization, allow the panelist only gross response categories. These all or none responses (same, different, prefer A, prefer B) require many more panelists to counteract errors than other scaling procedures which allow the panelist more freedom in choosing response categories. For example, to achieve the same difference in paired comparison (or preference) scaling requires more panelists than when the sensory analyst uses category or fixed point scaling. A stable distribution of preferences arises when the number of panelists approaches or exceeds 40 or more. The distribution becomes exceedingly stable with base sizes of 100 or more. On the other hand, when the panelist can use a set of categories to show degree of liking, the sensory analyst can achieve a stable (albeit not necessarily representative) data base with fewer panelists. Furthermore, when panelists can use magnitude estimation (a continuous scale, with infinite range), along with a mechanism for calibrating data to reduce interpanelist variability, the number of panelists needed diminishes even more.

Each test situation differs from every other test situation. No hard nor fast rules exist as the requisite number of panelists which one should use. However, the sensory analyst can keep in mind these specific considerations: (1) The more panelists, the greater the sensitivity of the test to differences. (2) With increasing number of panelists, the standard error decreases in proportion to the square root of the panel size. This means that increasing the panel size by a factor of 4 (at $4 \times$ the cost) will diminish the standard error of the mean by a factor of 2. This increases sensitivity to differences. The average ratings will remain unchanged (in theory) but the variability around those ratings should diminish. Differences previously found will replicate themselves, but this time the differences will possess enhanced statistical significance. (3) Sometimes the sensory analyst or marketing researcher can overkill the test, by testing too many panelists. With increasing panel size, small differences can become statistically significant. Yet, these so-called differences actually reflect a statistical artifact, obtained by inflating the sample size. A narrow line of judgment divides significance due to real differences among samples (or among individuals) versus significance due to the inflated panel size.

Selecting the Proper Panel

How can the sensory analyst insure that the panelists represent the appropriate population for the study? Can one simply grab anyone off the street, or out of the laboratory to participate in a sensory analysis session, or must one make special efforts to develop and tailor a specific population? Obviously, one can choose the former approach—select panelists at random from the population, indoctrinate them as much or as little as one wants, and then have the panelists participate in the evaluation. This approach works in the following cases: (1) The panelists perform a conceptually simple task (e.g., detection thresholds for tastes). (2) Sensory evaluation requiring free descriptions of perceptions. (3) Simple ratings of liking/disliking (overall hedonic) without need to explain to panelists the criteria on which they must judge, or indoctrinate the panelists extensively as to what they should attend.

The "quick and dirty" approach does not work in cases such as: (1) Evaluation of specific sensory characteristics, needing explication and indoctrination. (2) Evaluation of consumer acceptance by specific groups in the population exhibiting the proper usage pattern of products (acceptors, rejectors), or the proper age (quota samples for ages, in accordance with research specifications), etc.

Many sensory analysts maintain files on the likes/dislikes of the testers in their laboratories. Such files can contribute significantly to better consumer data, where interest focuses on the acceptability of foods. The sensory analyst or marketing research analyst should test the foods with those individuals who regularly consume the foods, rather than testing with a randomly selected sample of available panelists. A file on likes/dislikes, consumption habits, and the like provide the sensory analyst with a ready reference on the panel specification. Sometimes one can computerize this information, and retrieve it with a sort program to insure that one has produced the proper panel composition.

THE TEST LABORATORY OR FACILITY

With the recent expansion of interest in scientific sensory analysis it should come as no surprise that researchers and practitioners have focused considerable attention on the physical facilities of the test laboratory. As companies and universities have come to recognize the importance of sensory analysis as a discipline vital to insuring product quality, those in command of funds have allocated increasing amounts of monies to develop adequate test facilities.

Sensory analysis facilities come in all shapes and sizes. A fancy, elegant and modern equipped laboratory does not, however, guarantee accurate data. Nor does a seemingly less controlled laboratory preclude the collection of good data. Rather, adequate facilities comprise certain key elements, cosmetized or not, which when properly used, assure adequate data. The next section concerns the setup of such a laboratory.

Panelist Facilities

A well equipped test laboratory should have provision for testing the panelist in both social (face to face) conditions as well as in relatively isolated conditions. In many sensory analysis laboratories the interviewer isolates panelists from each other by means of booths, in which the panelist sits. The rectangular booths have an open back. The panelist sits in the booth, with his or her face turned to a wall, on which a shelf protrudes. The walls of the booth on either side of the panelist effectively isolate that individual from other panelists who simultaneously participate in the evaluation.

In less well equipped laboratories, wherein one cannot so easily construct such a booth, the sensory analyst can still isolate the panelists from each other by constructing a partition which fits on top of the test table. In this way, two or even more panelists can sit at the same table, with the movable partition placed in such a way as to effectively isolate one individual from another.

In other test situations, such as marketing research studies, the interviewer must make do with relatively unsophisticated laboratory facilities, without dividers or partitions. In a test with one interviewer and one panelist (one-on-one), the sensory analyst need not worry about the interference from other panelists. When the test requires a classroom setting, with several panelists sitting at the same table, the optimum strategy to isolate the panelists consists of seating panelists at separate ends of the table, or at entirely separate, but small card tables.

Relatively little, if any, information exists on the effect of isolated testing versus non-isolated testing on the data which the sensory analyst collects. Does isolation, and the exceptional care to make private testing facilities for each panelist pay out in terms of increased sensitivity of the results? The following benefits obtained by isolating panelists seem immediately apparent: (1) Prevention of cheating. (2) Prevention of discussion of results. (3) Prevention of disturbances by one panelist of others.

These benefits generate distraction-free testing. In effect, the partitions, or other such devices eliminate outside interference. By themselves, they do not guarantee better data. In fact, the adept sensory analyst or field supervisor probably can obtain just as sensitive data in less controlled surroundings by setting up the test situation properly, to reduce or eliminate all external influences on the panelists. Like other cosmetic niceties of testing, the partitioning booths display the care and expected validity of the data which hopefully the sensory analyst has built into the experimental design, and test controls. Isolation of one panelist from all others to insure uncontaminated ratings should remain a goal of all testing, with or without the partitions and dividers.

Isolation of Panelists from the Interviewer

Interviewers can communicate expectations to panelists through many means, some of which may escape detection. Non-verbal as well as verbal communication continually occurs between interviewer and panelist, in the form of shrugs, raised eyebrows, pupil dilation, muscular movement of the lips, the body, etc. When done at critical times during the course of the interview, these nonverbal communications reinforce or punish the panelists for their responses. This interaction effectively modifies behavior.

In the sensory analysis laboratory, one should make every effort to isolate the panelist from the interviewer. In the already difficult world of product development this isolation can become hard to achieve. The product developer often attends the evaluation sessions, as an onlooker. The developer's ego-involvement in the project interferes with the objectivity of the evaluation, and can bias the results, if the interviewer allows communication to pass in a 3-way mode between the panelist, the product developer and the interviewer. And, as stated above, nonverbal communication occurs so frequently and subtly that its absence in such an open test situation reflects the rare exception rather than the rule.

R&D sensory analysts can prevent this communication by isolating the panelist from the interviewer, in the following ways:

(1) Use interviewers who do not know very much about the aims of the project or about the product constituents. The interviewer should simply execute the study, without any preconceived ideas as to the correctness or incorrectness of the answers. In a small test laboratory one has a difficult time finding such willing, effectively unbiased interviewers.

(2) Erect a partition between the interviewer (or the food dispenser) and the panelist. The panelist sits at one side of the partition (e.g., in

the testing booth), and the interviewer or food server works on the other side. All communication occurs by non-verbal means (e.g., pressing a button which lights a light) and the interviewer passes instructions to the panelist. These instructions appear on a self-explanatory card. In order to avoid signals, the instructions must appear on a card or a sheet, rather than come from an interviewer through the spoken word. Speech carries with it intonations. Intonations themselves act as hints, cues, and the like. If one absolutely requires oral communication of instructions, one can standardize the presentation by tape or video cassette, or some other standard manner, which prevents the communication of nuances.

(3) Have the panelist evaluate the products at home, with a questionnaire containing all of the training instructions, questionnaire, etc. Mail panels and home use testing provide relatively poor control over the testing situation, but truly isolate the panelists from the interviewer.

(4) Have the panelist report to the test site, pick up the questionnaire with the product, and go to a table in the test room, away from the interviewer. In central location evaluations the interviewer can control communication by orienting the panelists verbally, through talking, show them how to evaluate the first product, and then let the panelists evaluate the remaining products at their own pace, in an uninterrupted manner.

Marketing researchers have the same problem with interviewers, and perhaps even more so. Many sensory tests conducted by market researchers occur in one-to-one interviews, in a central mall. The interviewer (or recruiter) intercepts the panelist, and administers the test in a secluded spot, designated for the test purpose. In such situations the interviewer can inadvertently correct answers. Perhaps the interviewer wants to obtain the proper quota of panelists of a certain user group, and has trouble finding those panelists. Sometimes through nonverbal communication the interviewer can induce the panelist to respond that the panelist falls into a user group of specific products. During the interview the panelist may have expressed negative reactions to the product, but may not want to go on record as having done so. Or, the panelist may give the same response for all questions. We all crave variety and become suspicious when the same response occurs time after time. Interviewers can communicate their anxiety to panelists in many subtle ways, influencing the panelist to change the negative rating to a neutral or to a positive one. Even the interviewer may not know exactly how he or she has communicated this information.

Personal, one-to-one interviewing suffers from inconsistencies in individual performance. No individual who interviews can perform identically, time after time, interview after interview. During the course of the interview, the intonation, interviewer attitude and length of interview will differ. The bright, chipper attitude which an interviewer has in the morning may give way to tension, boredom, or concern in the afternoon. How these affect the results remains unknown. Yet, they may affect the hedonic reactions of panelists to products, or perhaps the distribution of ratings. They most certainly affect the depth to which an interviewer will probe nonquantitative reactions, in open ended questions. The early bird, so interested in probing more deeply into likes and dislikes turns into the weary interviewer, who wants to complete the interview as quickly as possible to fulfill the quota.

Interviewers actively involved in the project show the highest motivation. This generates a paradox. The interviewer who knows too much about the product and who becomes too motivated communicates wants and expectations. The energy and enthusiasm works to maintain interest, but can bias the results. The objective interviewer loses motivation more quickly, but may provide less biased data.

We do not have any hard and fast rules about involvement of interviewers with panelists. R&D sensory analysis has solved the problem by physical isolation. That works when panelists understand the routine task of evaluation. Isolation effectively eliminates interpersonal cues. In the harder, more personal tasks involving direction from the panel leader, or complex responses beyond marking a paper, one has a more difficult, if not impossible time, isolating the panelist from the interviewer.

PHYSICAL FACILITIES FOR STIMULUS PRESENTATION AND ENVIRONMENTAL CONTROL

One should design the test environment in view of what the panelists have to do. In a laboratory concentrating primarily on flavor research, and which evaluates foods with noticeable aromas or odors, the sensory analyst must quickly eliminate those odors from the test environment. One can install a vacuum system above the panelist booths, with a continually present operating vacuum to serve as a low pressure center. A gentle sweep of air continually passes over the testing area, gathering up in its path the accumulated volatiles, and ending up in the vacuum system. Failing that, one might open a window in the test site, place two fans near that window (one in back of the other), with both fans blowing outwards, towards the open window. This creates a wind tunnel, which replaces the vacuum but not as nicely. The sensory analyst must also put fans in different areas of the test location, making sure that the fans do not interfere with the running of the test by blowing directly on the panelist or the product. The fans rapidly sweep away any volatiles which aggregate. The fans should not make too much noise, but they can produce a pleasing white noise which serves as a background noise carpet.

Lighting. Lighting affects our perception of foods. Each type of light bulb generates a different spectrum of wavelengths. Sunlight differs from the yellow-tinged incandescent lights, and both differ from the blue-finged flourescent lights. Products look different under different lighting situations. Some lights enhance the color of the products and others suppress or modify the color. We know that appearance comprises a critical characteristic of the product, and substantially affects overall acceptance. Thus, the product tester should pay careful attention to lighting, selecting that light which comes closest to daylight. Ideally, one should run the test in an environment illuminated by daylight itself so that one need not depend upon the artificial light. Daylight varies, however, depending upon the time of day and the ambient weather conditions. Morning light comprises a different spectrum of wavelengths than does evening or afternoon light. The same product will look darker and richer in the morning light, and appear more washed out at noon.

Sometimes sensory analysts want to eliminate the effect of light altogether. They can blind-fold the panelists, to insure that no visual impressions get through. This blindfold presents a problem since one must then interview the panelists one-to-one, because the panelist can neither feed himself or herself, nor record the responses. Other strategies include changing the multichromatic white light to a single light (e.g., red, blue) or pure chroma. The single color diminishes the color differences among samples, allowing the panelist to concentrate more fully upon the other characteristics of the product. Furthermore, the light allows the panelist to test the product with at least some visual assistance. The individual can serve himself or herself, and record the answers without the help of an additional interviewer. The monochromatic red or blue light will not eliminate many nuances due to surface appearance, however. If the panelists evaluate a product with a stippled surface versus a product with a clear surface, these differences may show up in the colored light, perhaps less clearly.

Expectoration. Many sensory analysis laboratories have equipment for expectoration of samples, using a dentist's arrangement. The panelist can expectorate the sample into a dentist's bowl, which continually removes the material. A stream of water continually washes the bowl, insuring the removal of the material. Other facilities make no such attempts to provide a method to remove unwanted material. Panelists in the former test situation, having a disposal method for their use may feel freer to ingest or at least test larger quantities of product. They may fill their mouth with more of the test product, knowing that they can, in the privacy of the test booth, eliminate most of that material or the liquid. The whole mouth exposure, with larger samples can influence the panelist's impression. These impressions can differ from the impression obtained by the panelist who gingerly tastes a small sample, knowing that he or she will have to swallow whatever sample he or she selected. We know that whole mouth stimulation by liquids generates a different taste impression of stimuli compared to the impression with small samples (e.g., 10-20 cc).

In marketing research studies one cannot provide the same type of control over the ingestion and expectoration. Fortunately, one can make do with large cups into which a panelist can expectorate liquids. On the other hand, for cakes and other solid food no simple way exists for evaluating taste impressions, without simultaneously forcing the panelist to ingest the product. The best solution may involve lengthening of the market research interview, so that in the evaluation of several products the interviewee does not rapidly consume a relatively large amount of food in a short period of time.

PRODUCTS—HOW TO SERVE THEM

We now move on to the issue of products. How many products should one test. Should the sensory analyst show all of the products to the panelist first? These questions, and many others pertaining to actual product preparation constitute this section, and represent issues which arise daily in virtually every testing laboratory and marketing research facility.

Number of Products That a Panelist Can Test

Controversies rage in the product evaluation literature, less supported by hard fact than by the heat of emotion. Some practitioners maintain, rather vociferously, that individuals cannot possibly assess more than two or three products in a sensory analysis or market research test. Without adequate evidence, these pontificators about test policy claim that panelists lose their sensitivity to differences after the first two samples. They point to the fact that experienced perfumers and flavorists claim that they need to take long breaks between samples in order to rest their noses and palates. Yet, if we go a little more deeply into these allegations of lack of sensitivity we find them relatively unconvincing. No good evidence or data has shown that panelists lose their abilities to detect differences with repeated exposures. Perfumers and flavorists who complain about 'fatigue' do so because they expose themselves during the course of their work to high odor or flavor levels over long periods of time. This evaluation regimen predisposes one to sensory adaptation, as scientific investigators have shown. With less intensive and shorter exposures, such adaptation should not occur, or if it does occur, it should not play an important role.

Panelists can test many different products, in a testing sesson. The number of testable products depends upon several factors: (1) Panelist expectations. (2) Panelist motivation. (3) Distracting influences. (4) Type of Product.

Panelists who expect to test many products, and who take out time to test these products can do so. Complaints that one cannot test many products more often arise from the desire by that individual to return to work or shopping, rather than from true sensory fatigue. Tell a motivated panelist that the taste evaluation session will last three hours, and the panelist will make arrangements to participate for 3 hours. Tell the panelist that the session will last 10 minutes, and exceed that by 3 minutes, and panelist will consult his watch and report that he can no longer taste the samples. He has become fatigued, more from expectation than from actuality.

One can motivate the panelists in different ways to test these products. Money motivates, or rewards, but in any event, motivated panelists can test many more products than can unmotivated panelists. Distractions such as people passing in and out of the testing area, creating a noise or other scene, will distract the panel, and reduce the number of products that panelists can evaluate.

Finally, and most importantly, the type of product influences panelist's ability to test. If one wishes to test spicy products, then one must realize that these products stimulate a variety of sensations, and can leave residual tastes in the mouth. During a short test the panelist can evaluate at most two or three of these products during the evaluation. Eventually a noticeable after-taste builds up in the mouth, interfering with subsequent evaluations. On the other hand, with a longer test session (several hours) the sensory analyst can wait a longer time between product evaluations, allowing the residual effects to dissipate, and allowing sensitivity to reestablish itself. In contrast to spicy products, one can test many more beverages in a shorter session. Beverages, especially both sweetened carbonated and noncarbonated beverages do not leave a noticeable residual in the mouth. Consequently the sensory analyst can effectively test up to 7 per half hour, allowing at least 2-3 minutes for residual tastes to dissipate.

The list in Table 9.1 indicates the approximate number of products that one can test in a 3-4 hour test session based upon the author's experience.

In general, three factors determine the number of testable products: (1) The type of stimulus (food, liquid, spicy, non-spicy, etc.). (2) The type of evaluation (paired comparison, monadic evaluation), which determines the inter-trial interval. (3) The depth of exposure to the stimulus (brief exposures, such as evaluations of acceptability, require less intense exposure to the stimulus than do exposures in an intense product profiling exercise). The longer the time of exposure to a single stimulus the more likely the panelist will experience build up of residual stimulus on the tongue, and the less likely will the panelist have an opportunity to rid himself or herself of the residual. Brief exposures allow testing of more stimuli than do extensive exposures.

TABLE 9.1
NUMBER OF PRODUCTS TESTABLE IN A FOUR HOUR
EVALUATION SESSION

Beverages
15-20 Beverages, separating each sample by a 5 minute wait.

Sauces
12-15 Sauces, if the sauces have low to moderate spice levels, and if a 10 minute wait elapes between sauces. Watch out for residual material in the mouth. The panelist should carefully rinse between samples.

Candies
12 samples, with careful rinsing.

Cakes
12 samples. Take care to prevent panelists from eating too much of the cake at the start of the session.

Syrups
12 samples. Take care not to have the panelist eat the carrier pancakes so that they fill up at the start of the session.

Ice Cream
10 samples.

Spicy Foods
8-10 samples. Take care not to allow panelists to go too quickly through the set. One must allow at least 10 minutes between samples.

Testing The Products—What Does The Panelist Do

It may surprise many researchers to learn that panelists often do not know what to do when evaluating stimuli. Present the panelist with a food, and some panelists will look at the food, mash it (or otherwise test its texture), smell it and then taste it. Other panelists will chew the food slowly to savor its flavor, and then swallow it. Other panelists will immediately chew and swallow the food. Left to themselves, these three panelists will describe the products in different ways. The first panelist may talk about texture and appearance; the second will talk about the flavor and taste, and the third may talk primarily about liking or disliking, and fail to discuss sensory characteristics whatsoever.

The foregoing example typifies the tremendous individual differences in the motor activities and focus of attention involved in evaluating foods. We often lose sight of the fact that individuals differ in the way they interact with foods. Left to themselves each panelist does something different to the food, and experiences a unique, idiosyncratic, different pattern of forces for texture evaluation, or pattern of chemosensory stimuli for taste and smell evaluations.

Part of profile training concerns how the panelist should go about experiencing the food, by manipulating it physically. Instructions for texture profile analysis comprise specific activities which the panelist must perform in order to experience and rate characteristics such as hardness, brittleness, viscosity, chewiness, etc. Only by specification of motor behavior involved in evaluation can one insure that each panelist senses comparable patterns of forces.

Aroma Evaluation

In order evaluation, one tests aroma in several ways. For the simplest evaluation panelists can simply sniff the food, as one would normally present the food (viz., in an open tray, etc.). This mode of evaluation presents an array of odor notes in the manner which a panelist would ordinarily experience them, at the correct concentration in air. The sensory analyst does not control the precise concentration of the aroma stimulus. Fortunately, however, psychophysicists tell us that the perceived odor intensity grows according to a power function of concentration with very low slope or exponent (around 0.5, or even less). This implies that a 10-fold change in ambient aroma level concentration should produce only a 3-fold change in perceived aroma level. Quite often we see variations of 2:1 in a single aroma stimulus, due to changes in volatiles. Thus we should not feel surprised to find high variability in aroma ratings assigned by panelists, since we begin with two large sources of variability—the panelist and the stimulus.

Evaluating concentrated headspace in products represent another method for aroma evaluation. Here, the sensory analyst can better control the stimulus, and can instruct the panelist specifically how to evaluate the odor, with the opportunity to further standardize the evaluation. Finally, for flavor-in-the-mouth (which usually comprises odor perception as its major constituent), the panelist's own individual method for chewing the stimulus and manipulating the bolus in the mouth will determine the release of the aroma-stimulating chemicals. One can take care to specify a certain pattern of chewing, in hopes of further controlling what the panelist does to the food.

Texture

The mechanics of texture evaluations also present problems. Some individuals like to chew their foods thoroughly, whereas others like to chew their foods only partially, before swallowing. The sensory analyst often specifies the number of chews which the panelist makes before swallowing or making the evaluation. To at least some extent these specifications standardize the array of forces to which the panelist attends in making the evaluations.

In consumer product testing similar considerations apply regarding the test procedures. Consumers, like R&D panelists, do not know what to do when evaluating a product. The interviewer can help by giving the panelist specific instructions regarding what the consumer must do when evaluating the food. Of course, one cannot standardize marketing research panels, in different cities, to the same degree as one can control in-house R&D laboratory panelists. Consequently, the marketing researcher does not put as much trust in what the consumer does when evaluating the product as does the R&D sensory analyst.

Order of Products and Number of Products
Simultaneously Available

Some practitioners prefer to show the panelist all of the samples at the start of the testing, in order to familiarize the panelist with the range of product variation. Product testers who use fixed points (e.g., category scales) or limited line lengths (e.g., the 6" line used in Quantitative Descriptive Analysis and similar procedures) often must resort to showing the range ahead of time. The panel leader shows the panelist the entire range of stimuli, in order to insure that the panelist does not run out of available categories to use, or run out of usable line lengths. When the interviewer has at his or her disposal the entire range of product variations, and when the evaluation of the upper and lower limits of these products causes no problem, then such preshowing and familiarization may not bias the ratings.

On the other hand, nature rarely provides the product tester with the convenient opportunity to show panelists the upper or lower limits, or the set of products ahead of time. For example: (1) The panel may have to test so many variations that it proves impractical to show the panelist extremes on each dimension. (2) The product developer may not know the extremes of each dimension. In sequential testing the product developer may vary the product formulations, taking into account previous consumer or panelist data in the reformulation. (3) In cases with large numbers of alternative products, each panelist may receive an incomplete set of product alternatives, according to a balanced incomplete block design. Various designs allow the product tester to partition the full set of products among panelists in such a way that each product appears equally often, and panelists never see the same product twice. In such partial or "incomplete block" designs, one cannot show the panelist an entirely different set of products, representing the extremes.

Scaling procedures such as magnitude estimation do not require the panelists to see the extremes of the dimensions. Magnitude estimation does not limit the panelist's range of numbers to an arbitrarily preset scale. The sensory analyst can use an incomplete design with only one or a few of the many product variations shown to panelists.

Order of Products. Sensory analysis carries with it inherent biases resulting from a variety of physiological factors. For example: (1) Sensory fatigue. By presenting a strong stimulus and then a weak stimulus within a too-short a period of time, the sensory analyst runs the risk that the panelist will not detect product nuances in the weaker stimulus. (2) Contrast effect. Following a highly acceptable product with a neutral product may tend to modify the rating assigned to the neutral product, with the neutral product subsequently assigned a lower number than expected. (3) Convergence effect. The first stimulus may influence the rating assigned to the second stimulus, so that the second stimulus rating lies closer to that of the first than expected, had these two stimuli not appeared in direct succession. (4) Tried first bias. In the hedonic evaluation of foods, many panelists uprate the product tried first, or prefer that product over the product tried second. The tried first bias pervades product testing.

In order to eliminate many of these order biases, product testers often use prespecified designs, in which each product appears in every order position an equal number of times. Designs and procedures exist whereby the statisticians can analyze the responses assigned to each product, and discern and factor out effect due to order position. When one has many different products to test, and relatively few individuals on which to test them, other methods of eliminating order biases become more suitable. The sensory analyst can permute or randomize the order of appearance of each product, so that each panelist receives a totally unique order. When one must test 10 products, such a permutation becomes a necessity, for even with a large number of different panelists who will test 10 products, one cannot test all 10! (10 factorial) permutations an equal number of times (10! = 3628800).

Sometimes it proves beneficial to place some constraints on the order in which panelists test items, especially when the sensory analyst or the market researcher knows that one stimulus tastes so strong as to overpower the perceptions of a subsequently very weak stimulus. This problem requires case-by-case consideration. For instance, one may decide not to test those specific combinations, wherein the strongest stimulus in the set immediately precedes the weakest stimulus, but test all other combinations. One may further decide not to begin the test with the two strongest, nor the two weakest stimuli, in order not to constrain the panelists' responses to an unusually high or unusually low first rating, respectively.

How Many Products at One Time

Some sensory analysts favor having the full set of products always available to the panelist. The panelist can refer to the products he or she previously tested. In this way, the panelist can assess each new product within the physical framework of products already evaluated, thus (presumably) increasing the accuracy of the data. As a panelist tests each new product, he or she can, if desired, retest the previous product ad libitum in order to refresh his or her memory.

Other practitioners prefer a single assessment of each product, and then onto the next product, without giving the panelists the opportunity to go back and retaste or resmell the products already tried. These practitioners feel that little or no additional information will emerge from retesting the product, because the panelist has already made a decision. Furthermore, an opportunity to retest the product will diminish the panelist's sensitivity. As the panelist has more products in front of him, the temptation becomes great to resample and to dawdle over previous decisions, as well as to worry about the correctness of the previous rating. A rating procedure, or a paired comparison procedure turns into a trial and error and often exasperating session.

These two approaches typify two opposite ends of the spectrum.

Psychophysicists have tackled the same problem, in a slightly different way. They have investigated the use of a standard, always present in a session, versus presented only on the first trial. Panelists presented with the standard stimulus for comparison prior to every new stimulus rated intensity similarly to panelists who saw the standard only as the initial stimulus. This means that the opportunity to try at least one of the previous stimuli did not influence the panelist's ratings. In fact, panelists soon ignored the standard, going on to the evaluation of the stimulus as if the standard had not appeared at all. These stimuli differ from those one would encounter in sensory analysis of food. The same principle would apply, however.

In reevaluation of previous stimuli one runs another risk. What should the sensory analyst do if the panelist wishes to return to a previously rated stimulus in order to change the rating? Should one permit that change? If so, then all of the previous ratings may require change. Should the panelist change all of those ratings? This would entail a retasting of the entire set of intervening samples.

Finally, consider what happens in reevaluation of previous stimuli, from the points of view of (a) actual behavior in the test situation (stimulus control) and (b) time to complete the study. When the panelist can retaste the stimuli previously evaluated, quite often he or she will break the routine of cleaning the mouth between samples. This inter-sample routine maintains sensitivity. In the effort to show correct ratings, the panelist sacrifices the choreographed behaviors specified by the product tester for the sake of valid data. After ignoring the first interstimulus waiting period, the panelist may lose the continuity of the task, and cease evaluating the products in the routine, and efficient manner. The behavior becomes irregular, the panelist tries other samples, becomes confused, and the original time estimated to complete the evaluation can in some instances dramatically increase. The compulsive panelist may reevaluate every sample, turning an evaluation session into a herculean effort to rank order the products on the spot.

In net, this author suggests that panelists not retest samples, unless the evidence to do so seems overwhelming. If the panelists must retest the samples they should do so only once, with the interviewer interjecting the retested sample as a new sample, right then and there in the sequence. Under no circumstances can or should the panelist break the sequence of evaluations whenever he or she wishes to do so in order to make sure that the answers seem correct. The damage caused by the loss of control over the sequence of evaluations far outweighs the damage caused by errors in one or two products or from one or two of the panelists.

The Standard Stimulus

Should one use a standard stimulus, starting each panelist on the same reference stimulus (to presumably equate their initial experiences) or should one randomize the initial stimulus, so that each panelist begins with different stimulus? Some practitioners prefer the former, for they can check the panelists' reactions to a known initial stimulus, and thereby quickly diagnose the presence of a problem in comprehension. On the other hand, other practitioners just as strongly prefer the latter, where each panelist receives a uniquely different stimulus as the first stimulus. Only by so doing can one remove the bias which occurs in the rating of the initial samples (such as that sample receiving the highest liking).

Sometimes sensory analysts compromise, by selecting a first sample common to all panelists, but use that first sample simply as a training sample. The panelist repeats the first sample somewhere in the remaining set of products. With N products, this generates N + 1 total evaluations (e.g., with 6 products, the panelist will actually test 7 products in total).

Psychophysical practice currently dictates randomization of the first stimulus, simply as a precautionary measure to avoid sequence effects. We still do not know the residual effect upon hedonic and sensory ratings incurred presenting a constant first stimulus versus varying that first stimulus. To insure no sequence effects, or no tried-first biases, which could influence the remaining samples, psychophysicists often randomize the initial stimulus and discard the rating anyway.

Retasting the standard, like retasting any stimulus, also remains a matter of contention. Some product testers and psychophysicists allow the panelist to retest the standard, in order to refamiliarize themselves with the standard, even though these same researchers do not permit panelists to retest any of the other stimuli in the sequence. Other practitioners do not permit panelists to retest the first stimulus, treating that standard as just another stimulus which the panelist must evaluate.

Reference Standards for Specific Attributes

Quite often sensory analysts interested in specific characteristics use a variety of reference standards to illustrate in straightforward ways specific sensory nuances that a panelist might forget. In texture, one might show the panelist a sample representing a high degree of cohesiveness, since panelists often do not know what cohesiveness means until they chew the reference. In aroma evaluation, multiple reference standards often concretize specific qualities or aroma notes, which otherwise would elude the panelists. In quality evaluation of stored carrots, for example, panelists often report the aroma of violets. In the actual evaluation of stored carrots, one might wish to have available a reference standard of the chemical of ionone at low concentrations, which smells like violets. Of course one can overdo this, by having too many reference standards present. Many references will confuse all but the most experienced panelists who represent the individuals least needing the standards in the first place.

THE ACTUAL EVALUATION

The test session comprises two main sections: (1) Orientation of panelists. (2) Evaluation of the products (and calibration, in the case of magnitude estimation).

Sometimes novice sensory analysts feel that once they have set up the study properly, with the correct written instructions and with the correct order of samples (randomized for each panelist, respectively), a study simply flows. In reality this rarely occurs. Sensory analysis sessions, whether conducted in-house with one's own R&D panel, or conducted by marketing research with an external panel of consumers, vary in the quality of evaluations, depending upon the choreography of the session. Choreography of orientation and evaluation define what the interviewer expects from the participant. It puts the participant at ease, and insures higher quality data than data obtained by panelists who go through the session, without such orientation and direction. Furthermore, a well choreographed session insures that panelists receive sufficient feedback about their performance at the appropriate time(viz., those points during the course of the evaluation where feedback will insure better data, without biasing the responses).

Orientation

One can orient panelists in many ways, depending upon the specific goals of the study. Orientation can occur in a short mall test. The interviewer intercepts the panelist, brings the panelist through a short evaluation, asks the panelist to taste two products, and then to indicate a preference. The orientation requires one or two sentences to convey the test requirements.

On the other hand, orientation may call for an extensive explanation of what the panelist must do in evaluation, what attributes to look for, and how to scale perceptions. This orientation may last 30 minutes, but the study itself will provide richer information than would simple paired comparison. One must orient the panelists in order to insure adequate quality control of panelist comprehension.

Orientation in Scaling

Let us first consider how to introduce panelists to the concept of scaling. Panelists have little or no problem in ranking stimuli, other than knowing the basis on which to rank the stimuli. One requires little orientation time to introduce panelists to the concept of ranking. Paired comparisons behave similarly. Panelists know how to express a preference between two products. Instructing the panelists in paired comparison becomes a straightforward task, demanding little effort. Panelists may ask about neutral or indifferent categories in paired comparison, for they legitimately do not know what to do when they come across samples which seem equally acceptable (or equally sweet, etc.). The interviewer answers this according to the convention chosen (viz., forced choice or use of a nonpreference category).

When orienting panelists in the use of category scales, the interviewer should explain the arrangement of the scale, including the limits. Panelists cannot exceed the limits and the interviewer should emphasize that the differences in scale points represent equal psychological differences. Sometimes the interviewer will show the panelist the entire scale, in numerical form. Other times the interviewer will show panelists only the word equivalents of the scale (whether describing sensory intensities or degrees of liking). As discussed in the chapter on category scaling (Chapter 5), panelists usually do not know exactly what to do when using a category scale. They may resort to conservative rating behavior. The panelists confine their ratings to the middle of the scale. If panelists evaluate only one or two products this conservatism produces a cluster of responses around the middle category. On the other hand, when panelists repeatedly use the scale and become familiar with the limits of the scale and the product range they sometimes may break out of this conservative scale usage. More often than not the sensory analyst and marketing researcher will find panelists who participate infrequently, and will act conservatively in scaling when they do participate. Rarely does the researcher obtain good data from a small number of panelists, using category scale procedure unless the interviewer has previously indoctrinated the panelists more thoroughly into the scaling procedures so as to reduce this conservatism.

Magnitude estimation, as discussed previously, requires slightly more orientation. Laboratory researchers in years gone by simply instructed panelists or unpracticed students to match numbers to the perceived intensity of stimuli. The interviewer or sensory analyst need not emphasize the concept of ratios in orientation but merely should emphasize the concept of matching magnitudes of numbers to magnitudes of perceptions.

Although many novice researchers feel that extensive indoctrinated orientation provides better data, little work has appeared on the relation between the amount or depth of orientation and the quality of the ensuing data. Simply stated, extensive and compulsive orientation does not necessarily guarantee good results. The appearance of care in the development of the study helps but does not insure usable data. Surprising as this may seem, it stands to reason that the study design, the intrinsic difficulty of the task, and the nature of the evaluation have as much to do with the results as does the indoctrination of panelists regarding what they must do in the test. A painfully implemented, thorough orientation does not guarantee success of an otherwise weak study design. One will not obtain good results if the products themselves show no difference from each other, or if the products show no consistency (viz., that different samples of the same test stimulus differ adventitiously in ways that could markedly influence the results by reducing reliability).

Product Evaluation

We have already dealt with the mechanical behavior that the panelist must use in the evaluation of products. We suggest that panelists need to know exactly what they must do when evaluating the products. We deal here with ancillary issues, including the time between samples, and time allocated to a sample, the method for clearing the mouth, and specific instructions to panelists concerning how to avoid adaptation.

Time Allocated To Evaluating A Sample

Panelists and consumers differ in their response styles. Some individuals prefer to give products a quick going-over, evaluating the product rapidly on a series of attributes after a short inspection and a quick taste. Other panelists show more care and seriousness (but not necessarily better data). These panelists behave in a relatively compulsive manner. Give one of these panelists an opportunity to rate 8 separate attributes of the product and this panelist will retaste or resmell each product once for each attribute in an effort to insure the 'correctness' of the ratings. The latter group of panelists fear that their data will somehow become invalid if they do not take such precautions.

Panelists who spend a lot of time inspecting each sample always run the risk of adapting to the product and losing their sensitivity. More insidiously, however, such intensive inspection fatigues the panelist, leading to discouragement, or boredom during the course of the product test. On the other hand, panelists who evaluate the product quickly may distort their ratings. They may not attend to each of the attributes, giving each its full attention, but rather these panelists 'skim' through the samples, providing surface impressions.

Which group provides better data? Does the rapid, relatively disinterested response style (characterizing much consumer data) generate poorer data than the intense concentration preferred by panelists who want to get every answer right. We have no idea as to which group, if either, provides better data. In at least one study, consumer data with less motivated individuals and expert panel data with more interested panelists show equivalent goodness-of-fits of ratings to underlying physical stimuli (Moskowitz, et al., 1979). Apparently, individuals showing superficial interest in the task, and less willingness to spend time evaluating the product intensively do not necessarily generate any poorer (or any better) data than do the more detail oriented panelists.

As panelists evaluate a series of products (e.g., beverages, chips, etc.) the time taken to complete each evaluation decreases. Panelists become familiar with the stimuli, and the questionnaire. They develop their own efficient method for evaluating the products. Motor learning occurs, so that the acts of evaluating a product, tasting it, and recording the answer on an answer sheet becomes more efficient. Panelists do not necessarily pay less attention to any one product. Rather, they have learned how to extract the information from their evaluation more quickly and efficiently. Estimates of the time taken to complete an evaluation of a dozen beverages, for example, should take into account the rapid reduction in evaluation time needed once the panelist has rated the first two or three beverages. Panelists become exceedingly efficient during the course of their product evaluations, seemingly avoiding adaptation during their tasting and doing evaluations quickly and smoothly.

Panelists may also spend a lot of time evaluating a product when they do not understand the instructions on scale usage. They may have difficulty following the scaling instructions when they evaluate the product. Quite often these panelists dawdle. They appear as though they try hard to actually evaluate the product correctly. A simple question by the interviewer regarding the task will reveal that the panelists have not grasped how to scale their perceptions. Simple as many ballots appear, panelists surprise the interviewer by failing to comprehend a simple category scale (or more often, the magnitude estimation scale). In the test protocol and design, the sensory analyst and market researcher should insert a control section, which insures that the interviewer can discover whether or not the panelists have comprehended the instructions.

Inter-Sample Time

One cannot rush a panelist through the evaluation task and expect to obtain valid results. Panelists and consumer respondents need time to reestablish their sensitivity to the next product, after evaluating the last product, and in general to relax while evaluating. By making the pace of the evaluation more rapid, the interviewer runs the risk that panelists will walk out, or even worse, give an invalid answer, by simply filling in the appropriate questionnaire blanks with random answers. Unmotivated panelists, especially, feel social pressure to conform to the external behavior and decorum requirements. Often they provide invalid data without informing anyone that they cannot keep up with the pace.

At least 45 seconds to 1 minute should elapse between samples. In the beginning of a test session in which panelists will rate many products, the rest between samples should exceed 1 minute, perhaps lasting 2-3 minutes, since the panelists have no doubt concentrated time and effort on the evaluation of the initial sample. Concentration to that degree produces fatigue. Subsequently, however, the panelists who become adept in the evaluation may wish to finish the testing, and subtly apply pressure to the interviewer to quicken the pace of the evaluations, in order to finish the task. Ideally, at this point, the panelist has developed sufficient proficiency to properly evaluate the samples without spending too much or too little time. Quite often, panelists like to speed up after they have attained this proficiency. The interviewer must slow the panelists down, lest the panelists rush too quickly through the evaluations.

Various methods will slow the evaluation pace: (1) Force the panelist to take a break between samples, and instruct panelists in a group testing situation (central location test site) that they can receive their products only after a specified time has elapsed. (2) Require panelists to walk to a central dispensing area for the product. The walk takes time. One cannot rush through the evaluations if one has first to dispose of the previous product in one area of the test room, go back to one's sitting area to obtain the test booklet (with the product code written in), and then proceed with that test booklet to the product dispensing area. (3) Force the panelists to stop at every fourth or fifth product, so that all panelists keep in tandem at specific checkpoints along the way. (These methods work when panelists evaluate a large number of products in a modified group setting, wherein 20+ panelists evaluate the products, in a unique randomized order each, but do not communicate with each other).

In one-on-one interviews, the interviewer controls the inter-sample time. The reviewer must realize that it does no good to quicken the interview to finish the study. Interviewers may become bored with their task, but the sensory analyst or market researcher must stress the importance of proper rest periods between samples.

During this inter-sample period, the panelist can clear out his or her mouth. Some practitioners prefer that the panelist chew on something, such as an unsalted bread stick. Other practitioners prefer that the panelist rinse out his or her mouth with warm water, and still others do nothing, but wait, hoping that the saliva will wash away the residual detritus in the mouth. This author feels that a water rinse does the best job. Bread sticks, or other so-called neutral carriers can become caloric when the panelist evaluates more than just a couple of products in a session. Furthermore, we do not know the effect on taste perception or acceptability of continued ingestion of the bread sticks. At least for water we know that several mouthwashes of water will eliminate most of the residual material in the mouth. The panelist can expectorate the water into a large cup, or funnel, provided specifically for that purpose. Often, however, the panelist does not even expectorate the water, but swallows it entirely. During the course of an evaluation session panelists learn to measure how much stimulus and water to take in order to maintain their sensitivity, but not become overloaded.

Amount of Sample To Serve

How much sample should one show to and serve the panelist? In many home use tests, the panelist sees the entire sample package, and can form an impression of the product in literally its entirety. For instance, in the evaluation of a cake product, the panelist can see the entire cake, untouched in any way, and uncut. The panelist forms an impression of the overall appearance of that cake during eating. In contrast, in central location testing, the panelists may receive only a wedge of that cake served by the interviewer and cannot evaluate the appearance of the entire cake. The rating of overall cake acceptability, as well as ratings of the sensory characteristics may vary according to the size of the cake served, and the position of the cake slice relative to the entire cake itself. Edge pieces may make a more favorable impression than smaller, inside pieces, and thus receive higher ratings.

Similar problems pervade other product categories as well. The evaluation of tomato sauce introduces the variables of appearance and flavor. Large amounts of tomato sauce on pasta provide a good indication of appearance of color and richness. Furthermore, large amounts of sauce allow the full flavor to emerge. The panelist can fill his or her mouth with the product, allowing all of the taste buds exposure to the stimuli, and allowing the nasal receptors in the mucosa direct stimulation (by smelling the full portion) and indirect stimulation (through retrograde stimulation, coming from the back of the mouth, upwards into the nasal cavity). The impression of such a rich stimulus differs quite substantially from that of a small and weak stimulus, with scarcely enough material to provide a decent impression.

Finally, similar problems pervade beverage testing as well. One obtains quite a different impression of the beverage when testing a large amount rather than testing a small amount. One also obtains a different impression by swallowing the beverage than by sipping, swirling it around in the mouth, and then expectorating. We have taste receptors at the back of the tongue which swallowing stimulates. Furthermore, the act of swallowing allows the retrograde stimulation of the nasal mucosa, further enriching the sensory experience. The stimulus more naturally coats the mouth, swirling around, and stimulating in the pattern most appropriate to ingestion. Product tests with small samples cannot provide this natural pattern of stimulation.

In order to efficiently test products, and to insure that the testing approach provides representative data, the recommendation below provides the sensory analyst and the marketing researcher with some ideas:

(1) Provide the panelists with more sample than the panelist can possibly ingest in a single bite.

(2) Insure sufficient uniformity of appearance, even when this requires the production of more samples, (e.g., for cakes).

(3) Instruct the panelists that they must swallow some of the product in order to obtain a better idea of the product characteristics. Discourage, if possible, a simple tasting and expectoration, with the panelist not really exposed to the totality of the product. Such cursory exposure can create the wrong impression. A highly spiced product may taste absolutely delicious if one tastes just a small piece, e.g., a highly spiced snack chip or an ethnic spicy Indian dish. Let one sample a whole mouthful of the product, and the ratings will change, often quite dramatically. The sensory analyst and market researcher need, of

course to know both, but the true ratings reflect experience with the full mouthful of product.

(4) If necessary, decrease the number of samples which one tests, in order to have the panelists test more of each sample. Alternatively, lengthen the period of the testing (often considerably). Panelists can test many more products during a long, leisurely evaluation than they can test in a hurried one-to-one, central interview.

(5) Critically lay out the scheme for evaluation, requiring visual inspection, and then eating of a specified amount of the sample, predetermined by the interviewer. Often, standardizing the amount of sample consumed will help standardize the sensory impressions gained by the different panelists.

The sensory analyst and marketing researcher should always keep in mind that individuals use different and idiosyncratic methods for sampling products. Some individuals naturally evaluate products by taking a lot into their mouths. Others approach the task more gingerly, evaluating just a little bit, in a timid, almost frightened, and certainly very conservative manner. These evaluations generate rather different sensory impressions, and consequently they lead to different ratings. Such interpanelist variability may add to the already-existent variability due to differences in usage of scales.

Serving Utensils

How does one properly serve the sample? Should one use clear plates, white plates, paper plates, glass plates? For beverages should the panelists see through the beverage, or should they evaluate the beverage in opaque glasses? If so, what color? And so forth.

The mode of presentation affects appearance, which in turn can affect product sensory characteristics, and ultimately acceptance ratings. A beverage served in opaque cups assumes the color of the cup, when the beverage has no clear color of its own. A colored beverage with cloud, which makes the beverage appear opaque or translucent may look different in the white cup than it will look in a clear glass.

Similarly for food items. Presenting the food on a colored plate will induce color contrast, or eliminate the contrast, depending upon the colors of the food and of the plate, respectively. A clear plate will diminish the food's visual impact, whereas a white dish can enhance the impact of a dark food, but lower the impact of a similarly colored white or light food. These visual changes can substantially affect perceptions, and thus change acceptability ratings.

Finally, large items on small plates, and small items on large plates can detract from the aesthetics of the testing situation, and change ratings, at times substantially.

No hard nor fast answers exist to the proper serving utensils for products. Perhaps one should settle for neutral colors for plates, clear glasses for beverages usually consumed in glasses, and white cups or bowls for soups consumed in bowls. In terms of ambient lighting, the interaction between the lighting in the test location, the reflectance from the food and the reflectance spectrum from the utensil certainly can modify one's reaction to the product. One should not, however, abandon hope and resort to the ubiquitous red light to mask all differences. More than likely that drastic decision will certainly modify the panelists' reactions to food, driving the acceptance ratings downwards. People like to see what they evaluate. The panel leader must ascertain the best possible lighting conditions for the task.

One can improve acceptance of poor food by serving it with silver, elegant napkins and table cloths. To avoid biasing the ratings upwards or downwards, the panel leader should serve the food in a neutral environment, with the utensils most appropriate for the product, as one might serve it at home or where one normally consumes it.

Serving Temperature

Serving temperature makes a difference in how panelists respond to foods. Too hot or too cold provokes negative reactions. Foods ordinarily served cold (e.g., beverages) lose their acceptability when served several degrees above the typical serving temperature.

Each food product shows its own range of acceptable serving temperatures. These temperatures refer to the temperature at which the panelist tastes the product, not to the temperature of the refrigerator or kettle. Food temperature equilibrates towards ambient room temperature as the food stays out of the refrigerator or the kettle. The temperature measured in the refrigerator may show a temperature several degrees colder than the product at the time of testing.

Figure 9.1 shows the results from both a laboratory evaluation and a paper and pencil survey by D. Waterman, at the U.S. Army Natick Laboratories, concerning how people feel about foods served at different temperatures. Note the wide spread in acceptability which ensues when people rate product acceptance at a temperature different from the temperature suitable for it. Some foods exhibit moderate sensitivity to temperature shifts (e.g., pecan pie), whereas other foods exhibit greater temperature sensitivity (e.g., fried eggs). In order to maintain temperature at the optimum level the product tester should perform a trial and error run through the evaluation to determine that temperature at which the panelists taste the product. One should also determine

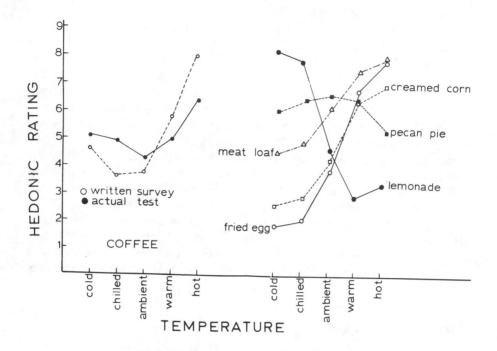

FIG. 9.1　RELATION BETWEEN TEMPERATURE AND PRODUCT LIKING
Source: D. Waterman

the requisite source temperature of the kettle, of the refrigerator, etc., at which to maintain the product in order to assure the desired temperature during serving. Keep in mind, however, that foods show time-temperature relations. An overly hot kettle can damage food flavor, so that one should take precautions to insure the quality of food as well as optimum temperature at the time of serving.

PANELIST SELECTION AND TRAINING

For decades practitioners in product testing have argued the merits and deficits of various procedures to select panelists for various end uses. Some individuals in sensory analysis favor the selection of so-called sensitive or discriminating individuals to participate in product testing, whereas other practitioners, with just the same degree of conviction, equally prefer to use unpracticed individuals. Traditional sensory evaluation run in R&D laboratories often opts for experts; psychophysics and allied behavioral science research, as well as marketing research opt for the unpracticed or so-called 'naive' panelist as the participant.

We can specify the types of selection procedures which practitioners have used, and caution the sensory analyst and marketing researcher to use his or her judgment in selecting the type of panel (whether comprising practiced consumers, experts, or first-timers).

Selection on the Basis of Sensitivity

Many researchers feel that the best panelists come from those individuals with demonstrated sensory acuity. In order to test such acuity, the sensory analyst must subject the panelist to an acuity test. Some tests for acuity stress the panelist's ability to detect taste or smell stimuli at specific concentrations. In these acuity tests the sensory analyst presents the panelist with stimuli of varying concentration, near the threshold region. Those panelists who can detect the stimulus at the low levels comprise the "sensitive" group of panelists from which the sensory analyst selects the panel participants. In contrast, the less sensitive panelists do not fall into the acceptable group, and the sensory analyst eliminates these less sensitive individuals from the final panel.

Sensory acuity tests vary according to the tasks they involve; detection threshold (ability to recognize the presence/absence of stimulus), recognition threshold (ability to recognize the quality of the stimulus in the threshold region), or differential threshold (Just noticeable differences; and, the ability to discriminate between two similar concentrations of a material).

When developing or using a sensitivity test for panel selection, the practitioner should take these factors into account:

(1) Do the stimuli which the sensory analyst uses in the screening evaluation represent the type of stimuli which the panelist will evaluate in the actual study? Sometimes the ambitious product tester develops a screening program, using as probes a wide variety of different taste/smell/texture stimuli, at low concentrations. These stimuli may represent the four taste qualities (sweet, salty, sour, bitter), a variety of pleasant and unpleasant smells (e.g., minty smell of methyl salicylate; sweaty smell of isovaleric acid), or texture stimuli. Yet, in the actual evaluation of stimuli whether model systems or actual foods the panelist will come into contact with only a limited range of alternatives. The panelist may participate in a panel on the detection of the wet-dog smell of meat, after exposure to radiation. Yet, one might read about the screening program for this project which utilizes sensory acuity in such unrelated areas as ability to detect and properly recognize the

minty smell of methyl salicylate, (oil of wintergreen). Only when the panelists come from a pool of individuals who participate in many different sensory tests can the sensory analyst rely upon such broad scale screening of different stimuli as a valid procedure to identify sensitive panelists. When the panelist participates in focused evaluations on a single type of stimulus, ideally the sensory analyst should tailor the acuity test to reflect the particular stimulus range under consideration.

(2) Does acuity guarantee good panel data? Can the experimenter predict the accuracy of the data (and by what means), based upon adequate or superior performance on the screening test? Researchers all too often believe that the panelist who shows superior sensory acuity in threshold work will provide commensurately improved performance on intensity scaling at above threshold levels, or commensurate sensitivity on other threshold stimuli, different from those in the initial screening phase. No good data exists on the translatability of this type of general screening to dissimilar tasks, or dissimilar stimuli.

(3) What, in fact, does the superior performances on threshold or discrimination reflect? Does such superior performance reflect greater-than-normal sensitivity to stimuli. Or, perhaps, does such sensitivity reflect a different strategy for attending to the stimuli as presented. Sometimes, changing the strategy or criteria in terms of attending to new 'cues' of a stimulus can improve panelist performance in screening, and place that panelist into the 'superior' or 'more sensitive' category.

John Amoore has pioneered methods for categorizing individuals in terms of their sensitivity to various smell stimuli, using well defined sniff techniques, with standardized presentation methods, and standardized stimulus concentrations (Amoore, Venstrom & Davis, 1968). Using such an approach, Amoore has effectively categorized populations of individuals in terms of their ability to detect the putrid odor of isovaleric acid, and has used this scientific screening method to isolate individuals in the population who suffer from a smell deficit. Such 'anosmics' also show diminished ability to detect the odor of isobutyric acid (which to normals, possesses a sweaty, nauseating odor). Amoore recognized the importance of a screening procedure which one can use to classify an individual into a particular class, and limited the classification of individuals to average, and below average sensitivity both to isovaleric acid and to a limited range of similar-smelling compounds. Figure 9.2 shows the threshold value for isovaleric acid, which Amoore has published, along with a categorization of panelists into two classes (normal, anosmic to isovaleric acid). Additionally, Figure 9.2 shows how the same panelists perform in detecting other similar and

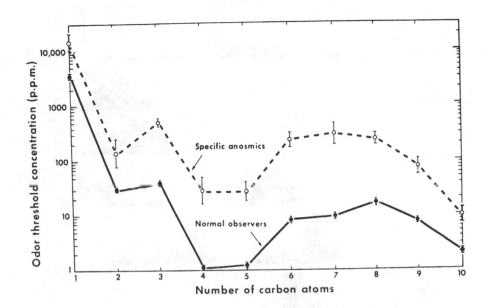

FIG. 9.2 DISTRIBUTION OF ANOSMIA IN THE POPULATION
Odor thresholds for normal fatty acids. The thresholds of the specific anosmics have higher values
then those of the normal observers towards all these fatty acids, but the sensitivities of the two groups
tend to converge at the extremes of chain length. From: Amoore, Venstrom and Davis (1968).

dissimilar odors. It reveals that the classification of panelists into
normal and anosmic for one test stimulus predicts their performance
on only a limited set of other odorants. In net, Amoore's approach
reflects the ideal—use of a screening procedure specifically designed to
categorize individuals into one of two classes, and the validation of the
procedure by testing a limited number of similar, but not identical
compounds.

In the scientific literature other practitioners have also selected
panelists on the basis of sensory acuity. Much of the work involving
anthropological evaluation of the sensory acuities of populations utilizes the chemical phenylthiocarbamide (PTC). Such panel work, with
a variety of populations scattered throughout the world has shown
that individuals fall into two groups, PTC sensitive and PTC insensitive. Those who comprise the PTC-sensitive class can taste the fishy,
bitter, and rather unpleasant taste of this sulfur containing chemical.
In contrast, the individuals categorized as PTC-insensitive show
higher-than-average thresholds (See Figure 9.3). Although traditionally used as a simple population classification device (along with blood

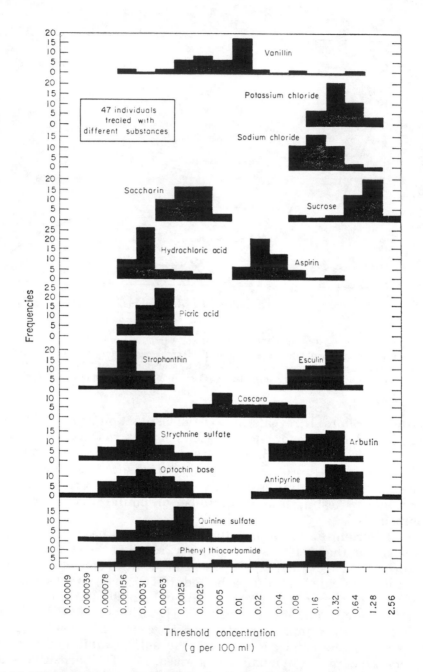

FIG. 9.3 DISTRIBUTION OF SENSITIVITY TO CHEMICALS IN TERMS OF THRESHOLDS
(Blakeslee and Salmon, 1935)

type, and other biological parameters of human physiology), recent work by L. Bartoshuk (1978) and her colleagues at the John B. Pierce Foundation (associated with Yale University) reveals that sensitivity to PTC correlates with sensitivity to the bitter taste of saccharin. Individuals showing PTC sensitivity also show sensitivity to the bitter off-taste of saccharin previously reported and documented extensively (Bartoshuk 1978; Rader, Tihany & Zienty, 1966). Thus, the selection of a panel of individuals with enhanced PTC or saccharin-bitter sensitivity would generate different data for the taste profile and acceptance of diet carbonated beverages comprising saccharin as the primary sweetener. In such a case, the scientific selection of panelists by taste acuity to a compound in a simple state (unmixed with anything else) has implications for panel ratings of supra-threshold stimuli of the same chemical, in a more complex mixture (viz., carbonated beverages).

Selection on the Basis of Discriminating Power

Sometimes marketing researchers look for discriminating panelists in the population, defining discriminating panelists in an operational way, rather than defining it by standardized acuity tests with model systems. Using the triangle test procedure, a marketing researcher may present the panelist with two identical and one different stimuli, with the odd sample differing only slightly. Panelists who correctly select the odd stimulus in the triangle fall into the category of discriminating panelists. The marketing researcher selects these individuals as the 'discriminators' in the population.

Panelist selection on the basis of discrimination tests, rather than threshold tests with the actual products, provides better information about panelist performance, for these reasons: (1) The sensory analyst or marketing researcher measures discriminating power on the actual product which the panelists will evaluate, rather than having to extrapolate panelist acuity from model systems to the actual product. Such a strategy allows conservatism in selecting panelists. The sensory analyst and the marketing researcher can rest assured that the ad hoc selection of panelists to participate in the 'discriminator group' reflects actual performance on the product under scrutiny. (2) The discrimination test calls into play all of the panelist's acuities, and integrative powers, and blends the sensory inputs into an overall impression. Consequently, one has set the stage for evaluation of 'differences' in much the same way that people exposed to the product outside may make their judgment of difference. Through such triangle discrimination testing (or similar methods) the sensory analyst has developed a general measure of discrimination, not just discrimination on the key sensory characteristic.

Prior to adopting discrimination testing as the method for panelist selection, one should consider what marketing researchers have to say about the issue. In a set of publications, Day (1965) suggested that discrimination reflects a probabilistic process, not a fixed process. One cannot classify a panelist as a discriminator, except in terms of the specific product, and the specific characteristics. Moskowitz, Jacobs and Firtle (1980), confirmed Day's hypothesis in a study of fruit flavored carbonated beverages. Panelists who showed ability to discriminate on the basis of sweetness differences did not necessarily show the same ability to discriminate on the basis of flavor differences.

Selection on the Basis of Ability to Scale or Rank Order Stimulus

A very sensitive method for testing discrimination ability and sorting panelists into groups involves the use of a scaling or ranking method. Suppose the sensory analyst or marketing researcher wishes to determine who among the panelists represents a potential candidate, on the basis of sensory capabilities. By providing the panelist with a graded series of stimuli, or different concentrations, which taste or smell noticeably different the sensory analyst or market researcher can quickly determine which individuals in the population can scale the different intensities or rank order them correctly. Moskowitz, Jacobs & Firtle (1980) categorized panelists in this way for discriminating ability in carbonated beverages. In a laboratory demonstration procedure for panelist selection and training, Vaisey-Genser et al. (1977) showed how to select panelists based upon a ranking of bitter quinine. Panelists fell into different groups on the basis of their performance in ranking these bitter materials.

Selecting on the Basis of Articulateness

Quite often sensory analysts and marketing researchers deal with situations where they cannot perform quantitative tests on products. Rather, these researchers deal with panelists as sources of ideas, or reactions to products or to concepts, as in the focus-group. Selection of panelists to participate in these idea-generating sessions represents one emerging area for product measurement. How does one select the best panelist for a focus group session, or a panelist to participate in a creative session? One has no guidelines for creativity, nor any standardized statistical methods by which to test an individual's performance in this type of task.

In contrast to the previous straightforward and relatively objective quantitative methods, moderators or group session leaders interested in qualitative performance of panelists try to select individuals who feel they can articulate their thoughts. These individuals should present themselves with confidence, and demonstrate the ability to present their ideas and reactions clearly in the group. They should not overpower the other group members, nor demand overly much of a moderator's time. Those demands and behaviors diminish the quality of information.

From time to time the researcher may have need for special groups with articulateness in specific areas. Perfumers, flavorists, food scientists, home economists and the like represent sources of panelists who qualify on the basis of their background, on the basis of their shared language, and their ability to pay attention to salient characteristics to which the normal consumer may not attend. In such instances the researchers select on the basis of experience, not on the basis of performance in a standardized test. We often confuse participation by such panelists (e.g., perfumers, home economists) with participation by individuals selected on the basis of unusual sensory acuity. In fact, perfumers, flavorists and home economists possess the same acuity as do normal individuals. Acuity reflects a biological process and variable, not a psychological variable. These special panelists differ from the ordinary consumer by virtue of their ability to recognize subtle cues, and their ability to communicate those cues to the panel leader.

Selection on the Basis of Demographic Variables

Marketing researchers often select their respondent panelists on the basis of market or region. Usually, these individuals test consumer reactions to products, and know that consumers in different locations have had different exposures to the products that they will evaluate. Some consumer panelists may not have had any exposure whatsoever to the finished test product; others may come from markets where the test product has fared well, and where consumers have purchased and used the products for weeks, months or sometimes years .

Sensory analysts who work at the R&D level usually do not concern themselves with adequate representation of panelists from different markets. Rather, these researchers limit their interest and focus to reactions of panelists from a single location, since they work primarily in R&D at the early stage of product development. Only when the product development project has moved sufficiently far along does the

R&D sensory analyst evaluate products using panelists from different markets. In fact, in many companies which house both an R&D sensory analysis facility and a marketing research group, the R&D testing facility limits itself deliberately to local testing, and allows the marketing researcher to execute the consumer tests all over the country.

Generally, selection on the basis of demographic variables precludes selection on the basis of biological variables, such as specific sensitivity. In most consumer testing involving different markets, spread around the country, one cannot control the sensitivity of panelists, nor pretest these panelists sufficiently well to assure selection of sensitive individuals. From time to time the marketing researcher may include a triangle or double triangle test as part of the product evaluation interview, in order to select these individuals from the panel who fall into the group of discriminating panelists. On the other hand, the nature of the research process in a nation-wide study precludes the selection of such sensitive individuals as a special panel, unless one takes special care to do so, prior to the actual evaluation.

Selection on the Basis of Product-Related Behavior

The type of product which a panelist uses, from a specific category, will affect that panelist's ratings generally in terms of liking or purchase interest, but also in terms of specific sensory and image characteristics. Marketing researchers who concern themselves with attitudinal reactions to products, as well as with the panelist's specific sensory reactions to product prototypes attempt to balance the composition of a panel in terms of product usage. When testing lemonade products, for example, the marketing researcher may select panelists on the basis of the type of lemonade which the panelist regularly uses, and perhaps on the loyalty or lack of loyalty of that panelist to specific brands of lemonade. When testing snack chips, the marketing researcher may select a panel comprising half heavy chip users and half light or occasional chip users (viz., 3 times weekly or more often for heavy user, less than 3 times weekly for light or moderate user).

Such panelist specifications reflect the marketing researcher's and marketer's interest in the response to the food as a gestalt, or an entirety. This focus of attention on the totality of product related behavior differs from the focus of the R&D sensory analyst, who generally tests products to determine necessary reformulations or to assess the degree of stability in the product's sensory character. Consequently, in reports by marketing research the reader often notices detailed evaluation of a few products evaluated by a wide cross section of different panelists. The analysis takes into account primarily the reactions of different types of consumers to the same, or to a limited selection of products. In contrast, the R&D sensory analyst usually does not evaluate the product using a wide cross section of panelists, and rarely specifies the panel composition in terms of such detailed user-group specifications.

BLIND VERSUS BRANDED VERSUS ADVERTISING/CONCEPT EVALUATION

In previous sections in this book we have discussed extensively the issue of types of questions to ask in an interview, and types of products to evaluate. One can evaluate product prototypes, finished products, blinded products (without advertising or labelling), branded products (with advertising or labelling), and concepts and advertisements as if they represented actual products.

In order to insure the optimal collection of valid data, this author suggests the following sequence of evaluations in the interview: (1) Blind products first, without any identification at all. (2) Branded products afterwards, evaluated after the panelists have completed all of the blind product evaluations. (3) Concept evaluation (using one or several different concepts or concept boards). (4) Advertising evaluation (using one or several finished or partly finished advertising copy or commercials). (5) Ideal product evaluation (where appropriate).

The foregoing sequence provides the sensory analyst and the marketing researcher with an opportunity to measure the consumer panelist perceptions of the products, and yet test these products and concepts in a sequence which generates the least amount of bias.

In all instances, when the sensory analyst and marketing researcher test different variations of blinded, branded products or concepts/ads, one should make sure that panelists have evaluated all blinded products in a randomized order, before going on to branded products (all tested in a randomized order), and then having done that proceed to test advertisements and concepts. Randomization will reduce the order bias, and lead to better data.

SETTING UP CONSUMER EXPECTATIONS

Questions in product testing often arise pertaining to how much the consumer or expert panelist should know about the test when participating. If the sensory analyst wishes to evaluate a new flavored beverage, with an unusual flavor, what should the interviewer tell the panelist ahead of time, at the start of the session? Should the interviewer provide the panelist with only a rough idea; viz., that the panelist will test a flavored carbonated beverage, having a new taste? Should the interviewer tell the panelist a little more, such as the type of flavor to expect? If not, then when the panelist tests the flavored beverage and does not recognize the flavor, the panelist may downrate acceptability, because the panelist expected something entirely different from what he or she tasted. On the other hand, had the interviewer presented the panelist with a description of the beverage flavor, the panelist may have uprated the flavor, because of expectations.

From time to time researchers engender even greater expectations on the part of the panelist, by presenting the panelist with the point of purchase package and promotional materials, as part of the introduction to the evaluation. Promotional and advertising material often generate strong panelist expectations.

The practitioner must consider the aims of the study, and then select the optimum method by which to introduce the panelists to the task, and to convey to them the information. Too much information can bias the ratings upwards or downwards. With too little information and unformed expectation the panelist may evaluate the products in an incorrect manner based upon the paucity of information which leads to an incorrect frame of reference.

In one study that this author ran, panelists evaluated a flavored snack chip, under two conditions. In one condition the sensory analyst told the panelist what the snack chip should taste like—viz., strongly spiced. Thus, the sensory analyst set the stage for the panelist's frame of reference, viz., to evaluate strongly flavored snack chips. The results of that study differed from results of another cell of the same test in which the sensory analyst did not tell the panelist anything at all. The panelist knew that the test required an evaluation of snack chip, but did not know whether he or she would evaluate low-flavored snack chips or highly flavored chips. The major differences occurred in the initial ratings of the product (viz., those tried first), for the two conditions. Setting up the frame of reference changed the average acceptance rating, and diminished panelist variability in acceptance ratings.

AN OVERVIEW

When developing the protocol for a sensory test, and when implementing that protocol with consumers or expert panelists, the sensory analyst and marketing researcher makes decisions pertaining to panelist selection, training/orientation, conduct of the experiment, etc. Quite often the small changes in a research design, or the change in the project execution at the field level can dramatically alter the data (in terms of directionality and quality), and thus alter the final R&D or marketing decision.

This chapter has presented some of the 'Law and Lore' of product testing, from the marketing and R&D points of view. It stresses that one cannot adopt a single procedure, a single scale, or a single method for implementing the study. Rather, the researcher must keep in mind the ultimate test goals, the type of information required, and the types of consumers and products. Only that information provides the requisite information to develop the proper field execution, including sample size, number of products per panelist, types of orientation for the panelist, and proper procedures for evaluating the food.

CHAPTER 10

CORRELATING SENSORY RATINGS WITH OBJECTIVE MEASURES OF FOOD

INTRODUCTION

Correlating sensory ratings with instrumental measures represents a growing area of research in food science in general, and product testing in particular. Through analyses the food scientists can more adequately discern what specific physical/chemical factors in foods correlate with human sensory perceptions. The correlations lead to better, more scientific understanding. They also open up the possibility that given sufficient information the food scientist can some day engineer the physical properties of foods to generate predesignated sensory characteristics. We saw the potential of that engineering approach in Chapter 7 on optimization.

A history of R&D sensory analysis reveals that attempts to correlate sensory with more objective instrumental measures go back to the beginning of the century. Researchers have always wanted to relate what a person perceives to the physical variables which one can measure by so-called objective means. For example, researchers have tried to correlate the sour taste with the number of hydrogen or H+ ions. They often had little success when they varied acids. They had greater success when they varied the concentration of a specific acid and measured perceived sourness.

Interest in instrumental texture measurement led to substantial refinements in texture measurement. A history of texture measurement reads like a catalog of machines. One reads of evaluation of gel stiffness, by means of the Bloom Gelometer, the Volodkevitch texture tester and other machines to test firmness. During those early days, research focused on the plumbing and configuration of such machines. Rarely, if ever, did the researcher venture out to collect good, hard, scientific data on human sensory perception. Apparently, during the formative years of food science and technology, practitioners and scientists seemed more interested in the perfection of their instrumental measures than in the relation of these measures to valid measures of sensory perception. A glance through the food literature of the past fifty years, scattered in all sorts of journals quickly reveals the relative ignorance of sensory measurement, and the weight of attention that researchers paid to their instruments. (see Voisey, 1976 for a history of texture testing machines).

CORRELATION ANALYSIS VERSUS
FUNCTIONAL RELATIONS

Early studies, and in fact many current studies today, proceed in the following simplistic fashion. The scientist develops a texture-measuring device capable of shearing the product, or otherwise deforming it, by applying pressure, straining the stimulus, puncturing the stimulus, or applying other specific external stimuli of known physical value. The machine may comprise a blade, weighted down with a specific weight necessary to shear the meat (or in more scientific terms, the force, generated by the blade, which shears the meat).

In the R&D sensory analysis laboratory the researcher obtains panel ratings of perceived toughness for this meat sample (or a parallel sample). Perhaps the sensory analyst has taken alternate sections from the meat muscle so that the Warner Bratzler shear cuts some pieces while the panelist bites into adjacent, virtually parallel pieces from the same animal, and scales toughness (or tenderness) on a prescribed scale.

Such an experimental design and approach typifies the initial data gathering phase. In order to measure the relation between the rating of perceived toughness and the Warner-Bratzler value, the sensory analyst may correlate the instrumental ratings with the subjective ratings. This will develop a measure of association between the two sets of observations. The correlation indicates the degree of relation. A correlation +1 indicates a perfect (linear) relation, a correlation of 0 indicates no relation at all and a −1 indicates a perfect inverse, or negative relation between rated tenderness and shear values.

Correlation quantifies the degree of linear relation between two variables. Generally, in texture and flavor research some underlying instrumental variant may correlate highly (0.7 or more) with a single textural attribute or a flavor attribute, whereas some other objective measures correlate far lower (0.2 or so). Rarely, however, will the experimenter find correlations of 0.8 or more, when one evaluates a wide cross section of different types of related stimuli, trying to correlate a sensory characteristic to the physical measurement. High correlations (0.9+) usually result from systematic variation of a single underlying physical parameter, and the measurement of a known correlate of that parameter, (e.g., increasing the concentration of a flavor oil, and then measuring flavor intensity).

Functional relations differ from correlations. Functional relations, or equations show how changes in the underlying physical continuum relate to changes in perception, and what sensory ratings to expect for specific physical measures. In order to construct the functional relation, the researcher uses the statistical method of regression analysis. With regression analysis, the researcher lines up the different objective measures of the physical variable alongside the subjective intensities as scaled by panelists, and tries to fit a line (or a curve). For instance, going back to the example of meat toughness, vs the Warner Bratzler shear value, the panelists may have evaluated six samples of meat, varying in perceived toughness. Each sample has associated with it a measure of instrumental toughness from the Warner Bratzler shear. The combination generates a function of the form:

$$\text{Toughness (Sensory)} = k_0 + k_1 \text{ (Warner Bratzler Measure)} \quad (1)$$

Equation 1 shows a linear equation. Regression analysis tells the researcher the value of k_0 (the intercept; value of toughness expected for a 0 value of Warner Bratzler Shear), and k_1 (slope; unit change expected in toughness rating for a unit change in the Warner Bratzler measurement).

We now consider several case histories of sensory instrumental measures; a full study for texture of bread, and a synopsis of other studies on flavor of ginger oil and the aroma of canned beef. The studies have appeared in the scientific literature. We will consider a detailed exposition of the approach which the experimenters used, the logic of analysis, the types of relations which the researchers used, and a critique of the findings. From it, the reader should obtain a fairly good insight into how one goes about conceptualizing and developing usable subjective instrumental correlations.

CASE HISTORY—BREAD TEXTURE

Background

We continue now with further exposition on the Gonzales project on rye bread.

Researchers at the U.S. Army Natick R&D Command (Massachusetts) wished to determine how ingredients in bread produce rheological or physical properties, instrumentally measured, and how these objective or controllable properties generate sensory perceptions. Led by Dr. John Kapsalis of the Food Sciences Laboratory at the Natick R&D Command, the research team picked bread as the most likely first medium with which to investigate the correlations between ingredients, objectively measured rheological or instrumental-texture properties, and consumer/expert panel perceptions. They repeated the project on bread originally commissioned by the Gonzales Milling Company (see Chapter 7) but used instrumental measures as well.

We now consider some of the work on rye bread done at the U.S. Army Natick R&D Command, in parallel with the project on optimizing the rye bread.

The Physical Stimuli

The research team selected rye bread for the study. In order to assure a wide variety of alternative formulations, the group systematically varied the amount of rye flour and sugar in the rye bread, to produce 12 variations. The rye flour varied at four levels (12%, 19.5%, 27%, 42%), and the sugar added, at three levels (0%, 3%, 6%). Table 10.1 presents the actual composition of the twelve formulations. Note that when the rye flour decreased the wheat flour increased, to maintain a constant total weight of flour + sugar.

TABLE 10.1
COMPOSITION OF RYE BREADS*

	Rye Flour	Wheat Flour	Sugar
1.	19.5	67.5	0
2.	19.5	64.5	3
3.	19.5	61.5	6
4.	27.0	60.0	0
5.	27.0	57.0	3
6.	27.0	54.0	6
7.	12.0	75.0	0
8.	12.0	72.0	3
9.	12.0	69.0	6
10.	42.0	45.0	0
11.	42.0	42.0	3
12.	42.0	39.0	6

*All numbers in percent

The Food Engineering Laboratory prepared breads, and kept them frozen until use, when they removed the breads. Half the breads they apportioned to the texture measurement group, and the remaining breads they apportioned to the sensory analysis laboratory for testing by expert panelists. In many similar studies the researcher takes care to insure that the products which panelists test and the products which instruments evaluate remain identical to insure parallelness. For bread one need not worry about naturally occurring variation from one bread to another. One can bake several loaves and feel fairly confident about maintaining parallel samples for instrumental and sensory assessment. Not so in meat, or other biologically varying stimuli. Meat muscles vary from animal to animal, within animals and within a single muscle. In order to feel confident that the machines and the panelists measure the same things, researchers who study meat and other such intrinsically variable products cut adjacent slices, assigning one slice to the panelist for evaluation, and the neighboring slice to the machine. In other tests, where the machine does not destroy the sample (called nondestructive tests) both the machine and the panelist can evaluate the same sample. However, most flavor and texture testing belong to the category of destructive tests, because the measuring instrument grinds, tears, shreds, bends, evaporates, burns, or otherwise changes the physical constitution of the food during the course of measurement.

In many other evaluations of sensory-instrumental (textural) relations scientists do not have the opportunity to systematically fabricate the stimuli in a nice, experimental design, such as the factorial design for bread discussed above. All too often the researcher must make do with the variations which nature provides, in different muscles, in different fruits, etc. Our experimental design represents a unique case. More normally the researchers face cross-sectional (and seasonal) variation in products, not longitudinal or systematic variation in one ingredient. With cross-section variation the researcher seeks correlations of sensory responses with one or a few underlying mechanical or texture measurements. In reality, the products differ from each other in flavor, appearance, as well as in texture. Furthermore, as a consequence of these gross qualitative variations, the researcher does not know how one product truly differs from the other, having confined the measurements primarily to differences in one or a few mechanical properties. As a consequence, the correlations between sensory and instrumental measures diminish. Quite often panelists rate a product on the basis of many attributes for which the researcher has not accounted. The complexity of the stimulus vs the ratings assigned by the panelist do not show up in the single or in the limited set of objective instrumental measurements, selected as the predictor variable(s).

The Instrumental Measures

The texture researcher who works with food such as bread has available many different instruments by which to measure the instrumental aspects of food texture. One can measure the physical properties using well defined chemical/physical measures (e.g., density, pH., etc.). More often the texture researcher uses one or several different machines, specifically constructed to measure texture on an instrumental basis.

The machines fall into two classes; integrative and analytic.

Integrative Machines: Machines such as the Kramer Shear Press and the General Foods Texturometer, as well as the Warner Bratzler Shear and the Armour Tenderometer, integrate many forces into a single number or set of numbers, reflecting one or several texture characteristics. These machines do not measure a single mechanical property of foods. Rather these machines squeeze or slice the food (or apply any of a hundred different, complex, operations to the food), and measure the force needed to achieve a certain change in the food, or measure the new physical configuration which the food assumes, after the machine has applied the forces. Table 10.2 presents a list of some of these instruments. We call these machines integrative because they integrate a variety of simpler forces into a set of more complex forces, depending upon the physical configuration of the test cell in which the experimenter places the food, and depending upon the physical configuration of the device which ruptures or otherwise deforms the food.

Analytic Instruments: These machines such as the Instron Universal Testing Machine, manufactured by the Instron Corporation in Canton, Mass., apply well defined forces to the product, and measure strains or deformations over time resulting from the application of those simple stimuli. Unlike the integrative machines, in which a complex of forces join in ways difficult to determine, the applied forces from the Instron reflect fairly simple, straightforward physical variables which engineers can easily understand, and which the engineers can model by using basic physics.

The reader should note that in a sense all machines behave as integrative instruments. Only when the test cell of a machine applies a single, pure, well defined force to the food and records a simple response (e.g., deformation) do we say that the machine behaves as an analytic machine. Much of the difference comes from the configuration of the test cell in which the researcher tests the food.

The research group could have tested the 12 bread samples with either type of machine. Quite often researchers measure the textural correlates of foods using a combination of integrative and analytical machines, in an effort to obtain a textural instrumental profile of the product. The General Foods Texturometer, (Friedman, Whitney & Szczesniak, 1963) exemplifies an integrative machine which these researchers could have used to obtain a profile of a number of different

TABLE 10.2
MACHINES FOR TEXTURE MEASUREMENT

NAME	GENERAL TYPE
Adams Consistometer*	radial flow
Armour Consistometer	rotating tube viscometer
Armour Tenderometer	penetration
Asco Firmness Meter	squeezing
ASTM Grease Penetrometer*	penetration
Baker Compressimeter*	compression
Ball Compressor*	compression
Bloom Consistometer	torque
Bloom Gelometer	compression
Babb Compressimeter	compression
Bostwick Consistometer*	linear flow
Boucher Jelly Tester	compression
Brinell Hardness Tester*	compression
Butter Extruder*	extrusion
Butter Consistometer	spreading and cutting
Carbide Penetrometer	biting
Child-Satorius Shear	shearing
Christel Texturemeter*	multiple-probe puncture
Chopin Alveograph*	bubble pressure
Chopin Teleplastometer	kneading
Crusell Consistometer	extrusion
Curd Firmness Tester	cutting
Dassow's Shear-Jaw Device	shear
Dexometer	biting
Dough Extensimeter	extension
Fiberometer	cutting
Firm-O-Meter	squeezing
Gel Characterization Apparatus	compression
General Foods Texturometer*	biting
Geneva Texturometer	puncture
Grunewald Tenderometer	biting
Hamden Deformation Tester	compression
Hoeppler Consistometer	compression, penetration
Hutchinson Cone Penetrometer	penetrometer
Karlsruhe Device	twist
Kramer Shear Press*	compression/shear (presently, multiple cells)
"KT" Biting Device	biting
Lundstedt Curd Tester	penetration
MacMichael Viscometer	rotational shear
Magness-Taylor Pressure Tester*	puncture
Martin Consistometer	rotational shear
Martin Tenderometer	shear
Maturometer	puncture
McCollum Firmness Meter	puncture

TABLE 10.2 (Continued)
MACHINES FOR TEXTURE MEASUREMENT

NAME	GENERAL TYPE
Minnesota Shear Stress Apparatus	shear
MIT Denture Tenderometer	biting
Monsanto Resonance Elastometer	oscillation
New Jersey Pressure Tester (forerunner of the Magness-Taylor Pressure Tester)	puncture
Panimeter	compression
Pea Tenderometer*	shear
Penn State Testing Machine	compression
Plastometer	in-line tube viscometer
Platt Compressimeter (forerunner of the Baker Compressimeter)	compression
Plumit	penetration
Recording Dynamometer	compression
Ridgelimiter*	sag
Ridgelimeter	displacement
Rigorometer	extensibility
Rotating Knife Tenderometer	cutting
Sectilometer	like curd firmness tester
Shortometer	compression
Slice Tenderness Evaluator (STE)	puncture
Smith Tensiometer	tensile strength
Succulometer*	expulsion of fluid
Swift's Tenderness Testing Device	compression
Tarr-Baker Delaware Jelly Tester	compression
Torsiometer	torsion
Variable Pressure Viscometer	extrusion
Volodkevich Bite Tenderometer	biting
Warner-Bratzler Shear*	shearing
Winkler Device	biting
Wolodkewitsch Apparatus	different cells

*denotes commercially available devices
From Szczesniak (1972)

texture measures for the bread.

After consideration of the various machines available, the research group selected the simplest one, the Instron Universal Testing Machine, in order to obtain relatively simplistic measures of the forces needed to characterize the texture of the bread (as objectively measured, rather than as subjectively measured).

The research group secured a variety of measurements using the Instron, and supplemented these measurements with some simpler, non-instrumental (but still objective) measurements of density, thickness, etc. In all this exercise provided a reasonable data base of different characteristics with which one could correlate the sensory texture measures. Figure 10.1 shows a typical, annotated tracing of the curve which the Instron generates as it compresses the food in a test cell.

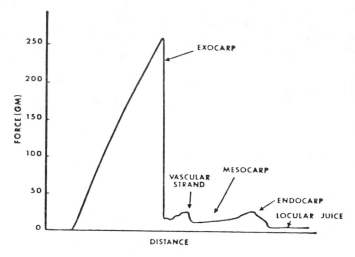

Instron force-distance curve for a ripe tomato

FIG. 10.1 TYPICAL FORCE-DEFORMATION CURVE WHICH THE INSTRON PRODUCES
As the instrument applies more strain to the food, the shape of the food changes. It deforms. The nature of the strain deformation curve gives the texture researcher a clue to the food's textural properties.

Before proceeding, let us again distinguish between two types of instrumental measures: destructive and non-destructive measures. Destructive Measures: These measures change product characteristics as they quantify. When the researcher applies a pressure to the product, this pressure modifies the cellular structure of that product. Quite often these modifications remain permanently and thus in testing the textural characteristic the researcher has, in effect, modified the product, and destroyed that which he or she had measured. Most textural measures require destructive testing of one sort or another. Non-Destructive Measures: These measures leave the product intact after the measurement. The experimenter may weigh the product; calculate its density or thickness, or even subject the product to examination by means of sound waves (Finney, 1970). These measurements do not modify the product's cellular characteristics. Consequently,

TABLE 10.3

SUMMARY OF THE PHYSICAL MEASUREMENT OF BREAD TEXTURE
FOR THE TWELVE RYE SAMPLES

Bread Product	% Rye	% Sugar	Stress at[1] E = 0.6	Modulus of Elasticity	Strain Loading Energy	Hysteresis Loss	Density (gm/cm^2)
1	19.5	0	1.54	3.86	0.370	0.899	0.2945
2	19.5	3	1.19	2.59	0.287	0.880	0.3052
3	19.5	6	0.93	2.17	0.239	0.887	0.2695
4	27	0	3.09	8.29	0.742	0.860	0.4200
5	27	3	1.73	5.05	0.441	0.874	0.3474
6	27	6	1.96	5.60	0.498	0.889	0.3627
7	12	0	1.15	3.35	0.306	0.889	0.2558
8	12	3	0.93	2.42	0.242	0.883	0.2762
9	12	6	0.75	2.30	0.194	0.884	0.2202
10	42	0	10.40	19.40	2.17	0.924	0.6133
11	42	3	4.43	10.60	1.04	0.913	0.4971
12	42	6	6.01	12.70	1.29	0.918	0.5289

[1]Definition of stress

panelists can eat the same products which the experimenter has measured, rather than having to test parallel products, which in reality differ (if ever so slightly) from the products instrumentally measured.

Data Base: Bread Project

The data base of measurements appears in Table 10.3. Note that with such a data base the experimenter has, in effect, generated a texture profile (instrumentally, of course) for the product.

INITIAL ANALYSIS—REDUNDANCY OF PHYSICAL MEASURES

Physical texture measures, like sensory attributes of texture (or flavor) correlate with each other. Rarely do we find totally uncorrelated, independent physical measures. In order to obtain a reasonably good idea of which attributes highly correlate with each other (and thus which may represent redundant textural characteristics) the research group used a correlational analysis of the set of physical measures, which appears in Table 10.4.

TABLE 10.4
INTERCORRELATION AMONG THE INSTRUMENTAL
TEXTURE MEASURE

	1	2	3	4	5
1. Modulus of Elasticity	1.00				
2. Hysteresis Loss	.69	1.00			
3. Stress at E = 0.6	.99	.73	1.00		
4. Strain	.99	.72	.99	1.00	
5. Density	.97	.65	.94	.87	1.00

Recall that the correlation analysis computes a Pearson Correlation coefficient between every pair of characteristics, measured instrumentally. Since the Pearson correlation varies between +1, 0 and −1 (with a continuum of numbers in-between) the correlation coefficient gives the researcher an idea of which pairs of textural characteristics behave similarly, and which vary independently. It makes no sense to work with correlated attributes as predictors or sensory responses, when one texture characteristic in effect expresses the same thing as another.

For bread we find many textural characteristics highly correlated with each other. Having had the opportunity to systematically modify the physical composition of the bread by altering its ingredients, we find that we have measured the same property by several (but not all) of our instrumental texture measures. We can narrow down the set of these measures to a fewer number, such as the modulus of elasticity and the hysteresis loss of the product.

In many instances we do not find such highly intercorrelated characteristics. In fact, our bread project reflects an unusually simplistic case. The ability to change the sugar and rye levels overwhelmingly influenced the instrumental characteristics in the same way. For naturally varying stimuli, however, such high intercorrelations of these factors may not occur as sharply as Table 10.5 shows.

TABLE 10.5
CORRELATION COEFFICIENTS BETWEEN OBJECTIVE
MEASUREMENTS FOR 7 VARIETIES OF SPAGHETTI

		Tensile		Multiblade	
		Stress	Force	Energy	Force
Tensile	Stress	1			
Tensile	Force	0.57	1		
Multiblade	Energy	0.49	0.46	1	
Multiblade	Force	0.38	0.91	0.52	1

Source: Voisey and Larmond (1973)

One should keep in mind that just because two or several textural measures (either subjectively or instrumentally assessed) highly intercorrelate for one food, they may not intercorrelate highly for another food. In other words, high correlation between measures in one product category does not suffice to label the two attributes or two physical measures as redundant to each other. One can state, however, that for the particular foods the two specific attributes do parallel each other.

For our bread study, we selected two characteristics to act as the instrumental measures, against which we correlate the different sensory perceptions. We selected the modulus of elasticity as the first and the hysteresis loss as the second variable. These two variables correlate moderately. Ideally, they should correlate "0", but it becomes difficult to find such uncorrelated variables for bread.

TABLE 10.6
DATA BASE OF RATINGS OF RYE BREAD TEXTURE BY A PANEL OF 7 EXPERTS, TRAINED IN THE TEXTURE PROFILE METHOD

Bread Sample	Firmness	Ease of Surface Removed	Cohesiveness	Denseness	Moistness	Chewiness	Adhesive-Stickiness	Cohesive-Chewiness	Graininess	Surface Roughness
1	45.4	81.9	52.7	51.8	50.4	64.6	60.5	54.5	28.0	88.8
2	28.7	95.7	30.9	23.8	56.5	57.2	51.7	48.7	47.7	99.5
3	29.5	81.1	33.5	30.1	46.8	37.5	55.7	54.1	37.8	71.8
4	71.8	15.3	83.7	83.6	53.1	67.0	70.5	62.4	28.2	28.5
5	68.6	13.1	77.0	80.2	62.9	63.9	55.1	67.1	35.9	28.0
6	53.9	31.7	73.5	73.7	55.0	60.7	69.0	70.6	29.6	31.9
7	48.4	66.4	35.2	34.1	40.5	55.2	28.0	39.3	33.0	85.6
8	37.2	85.0	46.9	23.0	41.2	44.4	31.5	41.0	33.0	81.3
9	32.4	86.2	39.8	25.2	43.9	38.8	28.2	41.3	40.8	75.4
10	92.8	1.8	29.7	94.6	31.7	52.9	69.1	38.0	51.8	20.3
11	71.7	9.4	63.7	92.7	63.7	77.5	68.8	67.6	40.4	21.2
12	92.1	2.5	82.7	108.3	89.6	82.3	82.5	61.0	21.2	9.6

CORRELATES OF TEXTURE MEASUREMENTS

Having decided upon the appropriate objective or instrumental measures to describe texture, we next correlate each sensory characteristic with the objective measure of texture. In most scientific studies the researcher first correlates single objective measures with single subjective ones, rather than developing a multiple relation between several texture measures and a single sensory characteristic. The simplistic approach helps the scientist and sensory analyst understand exactly how a specific texture measurement relates to a specific sensory characteristic.

Table 10.6 presents the data base of ratings from the 7 member expert panel at the U.S. Army Natick R&D Command. These ratings parallel the ratings for bread texture obtained by the Gonzales Milling Company in their product optimization work. However, the previous data derived from consumers who regularly purchase rye bread, whereas the ratings we now consider come from expert panelists who may or may not purchase the bread.

Table 10.7 presents the sets of correlations between the modulus of elasticity and the hysteresis loss, respectively, and each of the sensory characteristics of texture, as evaluated by the expert panel trained in the Texture Profile Method (as described by Szczesniak *et al.* 1963).

The expert panel used magnitude estimation scaling to rate different texture characteristics, and the external calibration procedure to calibrate their scale (See Chapter 5).

TABLE 10.7
SIMPLE CORRELATIONS BETWEEN THE TWO INSTRUMENTAL
MEASURES OF TEXTURE (MODULUS OF ELASTICITY,
HYSTERESIS LOSS) AND SENSORY TEXTURE RATINGS

	Modulus of Elasticity	Hysteresis Loss
1. Surface Ease of Removal	−.81	−.35
2. Surface Roughness	−.77	−.35
3. Firmness	.91	.50
4. Cohesiveness	.19	−.16
5. Denseness	.83	.44
6. Moistness	.09	.07
7. Chewiness	.48	.29
8. Cohesive Chewiness	.07	−.14
9. Adhesive/Stickiness	.67	.36
10. Graininess	.18	.14

Table 10.7 shows that each objective texture measure correlates to different degrees with sensory texture attributes. The differences in the size of the correlation coefficient indicate that modulus of elasticity better correlates with most of the sensory textural characteristics.

In seeking instrumental correlates of sensory aspects of texture, researchers have realized that many sensory characteristics interact to generate the overall impressions of texture. We react to a medley and pattern of physical forces when we evaluate texture. The sensory analyst and food scientist cannot coalesce all of these instrumental measures into one overall instrumental measure of texture, nor can one coalesce all of the textural characteristics, as perceived by human observers, into a single measure of subjective texture. Furthermore Table 10.8 shows that a particular sensory texture attribute may or may not correlate with other sensory texture attributes.

Having completed the correlation exercise the researcher now knows that some instrumental measures (or analogs) of texture characteristics better relate to specific sensory aspects of texture than do others. On the other hand, the researcher does not know the relation. Do small changes in the instrumental measure of modulus of elasticity generate large changes in the perception of bread firmness? Or small changes? Correlation analysis only reveals the existence of linear relations between sensory and instrumental measure, but does not reveal the nature of those relations. It assumes a simple linear relation, but does not reveal the size of the coefficient (multiplier) nor of the intercept in the relation [which we express as: Sensory Characteristic $= k_0 + k_1$ (Instrumental Measure)].

TABLE 10.8

INTERCORRELATIONS AMONG TEXTURE ATTRIBUTES OF BREAD

	1	2	3	4	5	6	7	8	9	10
1. Surface Ease of Removal	1.00									
2. Surface Roughness	.97	1.00								
3. Firmness	−.94	−.89	1.00							
4. Cohesiveness	−.64	−.68	.53	1.00						
5. Density	−.97	−.94	.95	.68	1.00					
6. Moistness	−.41	−.45	.34	.73	.51	1.00				
7. Chewiness	−.68	−.60	.69	.72	.78	.77	1.00			
8. Cohesive Chewiness	−.51	−.57	.30	.82	.57	.74	.64	1.00		
9. Adhesive Stickiness	−.73	−.75	.70	.58	.84	.57	.71	.66	1.00	
10. Graininess	.14	.17	−.14	−.70	−.22	−.51	−.44	−.46	−.22	1.00

Function Fitting—The Simplest Case

To obtain a deeper understanding of how one sensory characteristic and one instrumental measure of texture relate to each other, we must use a statistical method to fit a curve to the data. The curve summarizes the relation between the sensory characteristic and the instrumental measure. With such a relation, the researcher can accomplish the following goals, hitherto impossible with just the data itself, or even with the correlation between the two measures: (1) Learn the nature of the relation—what happens when the objective instrumental measure of texture changes by a fixed amount or a specific percentage? How does the sensory texture perception change? (2) Ascertain what instrumental measurement will generate a predesignated sensory texture perception. (3) Fit different types of equations to the data, with each equation generated from one or another hypothesis about the true, underlying relation between texture perception and the physical measurement. One can fit linear equations, power equations, logarithmic equations and exponential equations, to see which equation best describes the data, as well as to see what each equation implies about the sensory—instrumental relation. (We will see an example of this approach below).

Let us subject the attribute of firmness to a function fitting exercise. In order to do so, we use the method of regression analysis, to fit a prespecified curve. In the simplest of cases, we can assume a linear relation between perceived bread firmness and measured modulus of elasticity:

Sensory Firmness $= k_0 + k_1$ (Modulus of Elasticity)

Regression analysis estimates that value of k_0 (the intercept) and k_1 (the coefficient) which in concert generate predictions of firmness which lie statistically as close as possible to the empirical, or actual measures of firmness. In other words, regression analysis determines those parameters, intercept k_0 and coefficient k_1, which generate a prediction of firmness, for each value of the modulus of elasticity. Furthermore, these predictions represent the best that one can do. The predictions reflect those which differ in the smallest degree from the actual empirical values observed in the experiment.

The equations appear in Table 10.9.

The equation tells the researcher the following additional information:

(1) At a theoretical 0 level of modulus of elasticity, we expect a firmness value of 30.68. Obviously, no bread can have a 0 modulus of elasticity. One can project the straight line downwards, and estimate

TABLE 10.9
SAMPLES OF LINEAR RELATIONS BETWEEN MODULUS OF
ELASTICITY AND SENSORY ATTRIBUTE OF TEXTURE

Firmness = 3.898 (Modulus of Elasticity) + 30.68

R = 0.91

F Ratio (1,10) = 45.97; viz., probability $\leq$5% that the equation results from chance or no true relation between the two variables

---

the likely value obtained at "0" level of the independent variable.

(2) For a unit increase in the modulus of elasticity, we expect a 3.9 unit increase in perceived firmness of bread,

(3) With a correlation of 0.91 for the equation, we conclude that a linear equation accounts for 82% of the variability in the ratings of firmness. Other physical factors besides the modulus of elasticity determine the perceived firmness of bread, but these factors would play a lesser role.

In order to estimate the percentage variability accounted for by the equation, the analyst computes the correlation between the stimulus level and the response of firmness, squares that correlation (called multiple R^2), and then multiplies the square by 100%. The remaining variation unexplained by the modulus of elasticity probably comes from other factors which affect firmness.

(4) Given a desired firmness rating of 50, a modulus of elasticity rating of 4.97 will probably come closer to generating that desired firmness rating than any other value could.

We can follow the same exercise, this time for hysteresis loss versus firmness. We would generate a different equation, as well as generating a different goodness-of-fit statistic. The difference tells us that we will have a more difficult time relating perceived firmnesss to the hysteresis loss than we had relating perceived firmness to the modulus of elasticity. The correlation (R = 0.52) means that for this particular equation, changes in hysteresis loss account for only 27% of the variability in ratings of firmness (See Table 10.10).

Other Equations and Models

Linear equations specify that additive increments in the independent variable generate additive increments or decrements in the response or dependent variable. The size of the coefficient tells the researcher the magnitude of the change in perception which accompany a unit of increment in the instrumental measure.

Sometimes other types of equations better describe the data, as we saw for power functions versus sensory perceptions. Psychophysicists have suggested that the sensory system transforms ratios of physical measures into sensory ratios. In order to determine the nature of this transformation, the researcher must calculate a different type of equation; the power function, expressed as:

Sensory Intensity $= k_0(\text{Physical Intensity})^{k_1}$

When k_1 exceeds 1.0, our sensory system expands physical ratios to larger sensory ratios. When k_1 falls below 1.0, the sensory system contracts physical ratios to smaller sensory ratios. When $k_1 = 1$, the sensory ratios equal the physical ratios.

Let us investigate how hysteresis loss and modulus of elasticity relate to perceived firmness, given these new ways of conceptualizing the relation. Does our perceptual system contract ratios of the modulus of elasticity to generate smaller ratios of perceived bread firmness? Or does it expand these ratios of the modulus of elasticity to large ranges of bread firmness? Or do ratios of modulus of elasticity generate identical sensory ratios of firmness.

To answer this question, the researcher first must put the equation into a form that appears as a straight line. A power function of the form: $S = k_0 I^k$ becomes a straight line after a logarithmic transformation of both the independent texture measure (I), and the sensory texture rating (S).

Log S $= \log k_0 + k_1[\text{Log (I)}]$

In fact, by transforming the equation to logarithms on both sides, and computing the intercept log k_0, and the exponent k_1 (as the coefficient), the researcher quickly can answer the foregoing question.

The power equations appear in Table 10.10, for both modulus of elasticity and for hysteresis loss versus the sensory measurement of firmness.

From this exercise we learn the following: (1) If we conceptualize the problem in terms of how the sensory system transforms ratios of instrumental measures into sensory ratios, we find that the sensory system compresses the physical ratio of modulus of elasticity variable into a smaller ratio of perceived firmness. (2) The power equation produces a slightly better fit of the predictions to the data. We know this by calculating the correlation coefficient, for firmness versus modulus of elasticity and for firmness versus hysteresis loss. (See Table 10.10). Again, the coefficients k_1 differ for the same sensory

TABLE 10.10

HOW MODULUS OF ELASTICITY AND HYSTERSIS LOSS RELATE TO
PERCEIVED FIRMNESS OF BREAD BY DIFFERENT EQUATIONS

Modulus of Elasticity (M.E.) versus Firmness (F)
1. Linear: $F = 3.91(M.E.) + 30.7$ $R = 0.91$ F Ratio = 45.26
2. Logarithmic: $F = 69.16(\text{Log M.E.}) + 7.68$ $R = 0.96$ F Ratio = 133.72
3. Exponential: $\text{Log } F = 0.029(M.E.) + 1.52$ $R = 0.85$ F Ratio = 26.37
4. Power: $\text{Log } F = 0.54(\text{Log M.E.}) + 1.33$ $R = 0.95$ F Ratio = 84.8

Hysteresis Loss versus Firmness (H.L. = Hysteresis Loss)
1. Linear: $F = 606.73(H.L.) - 484.5$ $R = 0.50$ F Ratio = 3.25
2. Logarithmic: $F = (\text{Log H.L.}) + 116.99$ $R = 0.48$ F Ratio = 3.04
3. Exponential: $\text{Log } F = 4.29(H.L.) - 2.11$ $R = 0.44$ F Ratio = 2.38
4. Power: $\text{Log } F = 8.50(\text{Log H.L.}) + 2.14$ $R = 0.42$ F Ratio = 2.18

attribute of firmness, regressed against each of the two different physical parameters.

Choosing the Correct Function From the Simple Set

Too many cooks spoil the broth. Too many alternative equations spoil the simplicity of subjective-instrumental relations. Given an opportunity to relate one or several instrumental measures to one or several sensory texture attributes by means of one to several types of simple equations, the researcher can quickly lose sight of the more parsimonious paths to relate sensory and instrumental measures.

Should the researcher limit his or her investigation simply to power functions, or linear equations? Or, perhaps should the investigator use any equation which describes the data and provides a good fit to the results. Psychophysicists use power functions as the primary equation which relates sensory ratings to underlying instrumental measures, basing their selection upon theory. The theory states that ratios of sensory intensities derive from ratios of physical intensities. In order to determine how the sensory system constructs sensory ratios from physical stimulus ratios, the researcher must use a power function. No other type of equation provides this insight into the mechanism of conversion. In fact, the mathematical psychologist R. D. Luce has proven that when the sensory analyst wants to develop a psychophysical law of perceptual ratios, and relate that to physical ratios, only a power equation can properly relate the two types of variable (Luce, 1959).

When working with sensory intervals or differences, such as those specified by category scales, Luce showed that the sensory information lies on an interval scale, whereas the objective, instrumental measures lie on a true ratio scale. What mathematical relation transforms physical ratios to sensory intervals? According to Luce, a logarithmic function provides the appropriate equation to relate the ratios of instrumental measures to the difference in subjective measures.

No such compelling reasons suggest themselves for the adoption of the eminently attractive linear function or the exponential function. However, the linear function provides a very simple equation to relate sensory and instrumental measures. Psychophysically the linear function lacks a theoretical justification. One rarely sees the exponential function used at all, for it lacks a theoretical justification. The researcher has a difficult time using it in least-squares fits.

The foregoing justifications represent theory-based approaches regarding how one ought to interrelate sensory and instrumental measures. The arguments suggest that the researcher should choose the function according to theory. Even if the function selected does not provide the optimum fit of the equation to the data, the researcher should use that function, for the following reasons:

(1) The researcher can build up a base of comparable parameters, such as the size of the power function exponent. (2) The researcher can understand the nature of the sensory transformation of physical measures, within the framework of theory rather than against statistical and data reduction frameworks. By using the power function, the researcher conceptualizes the way the sensory system transforms physical ratios to sensory ratios. Simple, ad hoc, linear equations can never provide this insight.

So much for theory.

Let us consider matters from the other side. It does little or no good to continue to fit data with a function which provides a poor fit. For example, if power functions just do not fit the data (e.g., they cannot account for "0" ratings of a sensory variable) then the researcher has reached an impasse. In many instances food science deals with complex systems in which the empirical data simply do not describe or generate a power equation. For instance, for the evaluation of the texture of rubber foam samples (Moskowitz and Kapsalis, 1976) or rubber samples (Harper and Stevens, 1964) the magnitude of perceived sensory characteristics departed from power functions in the middle of the function and at the top and bottom of the function, respectively.

Power functions did not describe the data. Using theory to select the equation for description obscures, not clarifies. The investigator can lose insight by forcing a predesignated equation onto the data.

AD HOC FUNCTION
FITTING: ARGUMENTS PRO AND CON

In some cases, the researcher may wish to use more ad hoc methods for fitting equations—viz., selecting that set of equations which best describe the data in an empirical way. No longer does the investigator aim to understand the relation in terms of hypothesized, underlying mechanisms operating in the sensory system. Instead, the selection of the equation reflects the researcher's desire to describe the relation for predictive purposes, rather than for understanding the mechanism.

When the researcher has several instrumental measures which he or she wishes to relate to one sensory characteristic, the problem does not pose many difficulties. Problems arise when one can relate one or several instrumental measures to that single sensory characteristic. The researcher then faces the following problems: (1) How many independent physical measures can or should one use when developing the equation. (2) How should one transform the physical measures (e.g., linear, exponential, logarithmic, power transform), if one wishes to transform them so that the data becomes linear. (3) How should one combine the separate instrumental measures to develop the predictor equation (add, multiply, exponentiate one by the other).

Number of Measures

Statisticians tell us that as the researcher uses more predictors to predict a single dependent variable (e.g., hardness) some measures of overall goodness-of-fit increase as well [e.g., the multiple R^2 (which accounts for the percent of the variation in the data accounted for by the equation)].

For the study of bread texture, we could substantially improve the goodness of fit by adding into the equation a second predictor, and further improve that goodness of fit measure even more by adding in yet a third predictor variable.

Surprisingly, the added variables do not have to represent particularly good predictors of the dependent texture characteristic, in order to marginally increase the predictability of the equation. They merely need to enter into the predictor equation in order to improve the goodness of fit, overall. Their presence does not add anything theoretically, and in fact may distort the relationship which really underlies the rating. Nonetheless, statistically, the presence of these other predictors, does improve the predictability. Of course, with such accidental or irrelevant predictors, which really add just marginal predictability the researcher should not expect to obtain reliable coefficients for other, similar data sets. Replicating the experiment and utilizing adventitious predictors simply to increase predictability does little or nothing to increase the reliability of the parameters of the equations. The fact that the researcher uses such irrelevant predictors means that, in fact, coefficients assigned to these predictors and to the other, key predictors, will differ, as one replicates the bread texture experiment and develops equations. The accidental nature of the prediction almost guarantees that these adventitious predictors will fit the random variability in the data, accounting for variability unaccounted for by the more basic and critical measures, such as modulus of elasticity.

Parsimony versus Predictability

Researchers often lose sight of the tradeoff between parsimony and predictability. A parsimonious equation represents an equation containing relatively few independent predictors. The lean, sparse, predictor equation has little or no room for predictors which add little in the way of accounting for substantial variation in the data. Parsimonious equations allow the researcher to build up a data base on the parameters (e.g., exponents of the power function). The equation does not possess complicating terms which by their very presence change the other key parameters on which the scientist builds up a data base. For instance, add an additional independent variable to the simple power function and one can radically change the exponent. The exponent varies according to the basic trends in the data. Adding another predictor variable to generate a two-variable power function (from $S = kI_1^N$ to $S = k^1 I_1^N \times I_2^M$) will change the exponent N to N', and in doing so will obscure the true value of N.

**Fitting Data By Theory versus
Fitting By Ad Hoc Combinations**

Recently, Cussler and collegues (Cussler *et al.* 1979) suggested that the researcher should use theory to combine specific instrumental measures together as predictors of sensory response to taste and texture. According to Cussler, the appropriate method of combining physical or instrumental texture measures derives from underlying theory about the true combination of forces which produce the texture percept. These true combinations of forces may differ from the simple forces that the researcher finds easy to measure. Accordingly, the researcher should develop a mathematical model of how physical forces combine to generate the effective texture forces which act jointly upon the receptor system. These instrumental measures do not combine in a simple additive, nor multiplicative way. Rather, underlying theory of what really occurs often dictates very unusual, unexpected methods of combination. In combining the physical measures based upon the theory, Cussler accurately predicted the perception of roughness/smoothness and of viscosity, as Figures 10.2 and 10.3 show. For most studies involving instrumental-sensory correlations, we have little or no theory which dictates how we combine the instrumental measures. For example, we do not know the ideal conditions under which we should evaluate the forces and the combination of forces underlying the perception of bread firmness. Lacking a theory regarding the type and interaction forces impinging upon the mouth, when we chew, we do not know those physical forces to which we must attend and how to combine them.

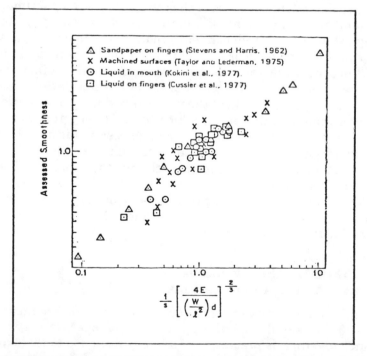

FIG. 10.2. PREDICTION OF PERCEIVED ROUGHNESS/SMOOTHNESS VERSUS EMPIRICAL
ESTIMATE OF ROUGHNESS AND SMOOTHNESS
(Cussler *et al.*, 1979)
Each set of data comes from the different panels. The points marked with an x equal the reciprocals of
assessment of roughness which varies inversely with smoothness

Multiple Linear Correlation and Combinations of Predictors

Faced with the problem of developing sensory-instrumental relations, and with many predictors from which to choose, many researchers avail themselves of the simple statistical procedure known as multiple linear regression. With multiple linear regression (readily available on most computer systems), the researcher hypothesizes the following simplistic relation between a single texture characteristic and one or several independent physical measures of texture (A, B . . . N):

$$\text{Sensory Characteristic} = k_0 + k_1(A) + k_2(B) \ldots k_n(N)$$

This equation states, in an ad hoc manner, that the sensory characteristic equals a linear, weighted combination of the physical measures, A,B,C . . . N.

Geometrically, the multiple linear regression appears as a plane. The coefficients $k_1 \ldots k_n$ tell us how much change in the sensory characteristic (e.g., firmness) to expect for a unit change in independent variable A (e.g., modulus of elasticity), or variable B (e.g., hysteresis loss). Large coefficients mean that we should expect a relatively large change in the sensory characteristic for a unit change in the independent variable; small coefficients mean that we should expect a relatively small change in the sensory characteristics. The size of the coefficients k_1, k_2, etc., primarily depend upon two factors: (1) The true relation between changes in the physical measure, A, and sensory changes. (2) The size of the unit of measurement for A (changing the unit of measurement, e.g., from grams to kilograms dramatically reduces the size of the coefficient as well, even though we have produced only a simple multiplicative linear change).

Researchers find the multiple linear regression an attractive method by which to relate perceptions of sensory characteristics to weighted combinations of physical measures.

One can use the statistical procedure virtually at any location which possesses a computer facility. Virtually every computer center or computer package of statistical routines contains a progam to compute multiple linear regression.

The conceptualization of the relation between sensory attributes as an instrumental measure as a plane becomes straightforward. In fact, multiple linear regression really reflects the generalization of the straight line relation ($S = k_0 + k_1(A)$) to two or more independent variables (A,B).

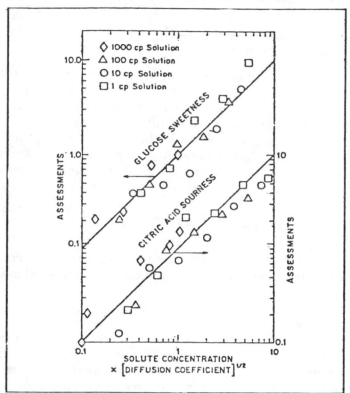

FIG. 10.3. PREDICTION OF TASTE INTENSITY VERSUS CONCENTRATION OF TASTE
MATERIAL, ACCORDING TO THE SIMPLISTIC APPROACH (LEFT PANEL: MOSKOWITZ
AND ARABIE, 1970) AND AFTER REANALYSIS BY THEORY (CUSSLER *ET AL.*, 1979)
Relation between assessed sweetness and sourness and transport to the surface of the tongue, based
on data from psychophysical ratings.
Source: Cussler *et al.* (1979)

Researchers usually can gain an intuitive idea of the meaning of the
coefficients as indicators of the direction and magnitude of the change
which one expects for unit changes in the physical variables.

With multiple linear regression the researcher also has an opportunity to construct the best possible predictor equation, using a limited set
of independent variables as predictors. The method of step-wise linear
regression often used in such model building proceeds according to
these steps:

(1) The computer arrays all predictor variables on one side of the
equation. (2) The computer arrays the dependent variable on the other
side. (3) The computer computes the correlation betwen each predictor
variable separately, and the dependent variable. (4) In the first step,
the computer selects that independent predictor variable which correlates most highly with the dependent variable. viz., the instrumental

measure which provides the best fit or prediction of that sensory attribute. This generates the first equation: $S = k_0 + k_1(A)$, (5) The computer calculates the residuals. The predictor, or independent instrumental measure (A), when used in the first equation, explains only a part of the variability in the data or sensory attribute ratings. Some of the residual, unexplained variability remains. We now must find another predictor to explain that residual. (6) The computer then searches among the remaining independent predictor variables for another predictor variable (e.g., B,) which explains the maximum amount of the residual variability. This generates the next equation. $S = k_0' + k_1'(A) + k_2(B)$. The coefficient k_1, which we saw above, usually changes, when we introduce the new predictor, B, into the equation. In fact, unless each predictor acts totally independently of every other predictor, the addition of a new predictor in the equation changes the magnitude of the coefficients previously calculated, and may even change their sign; e.g., k_0' may change from $+$ to $-$, or from $-$ to $+$. (7) The computer calculates the residual (Predicted-Observed) given these two predictors, in order to find the remaining residual unaccounted for by the weighted linear combination of A and B. (8) The computer then searches among the remaining independent predictor variables for that specific predictor which explains the maximum amount of the residual variation. This generates the third step in the regression:

$$S + k_0'' + k_1''(A) + k_2'(B) + k_3(C)$$

The process repeats itself until several things have occurred. Either (1) The researcher has run out of available predictors, having literally thrown everything into the predictor equation that he or she could muster. (2) The researcher has prespecified a goodness-of-fit measure, in order to insure that only significant predictor variables enter into the equation. One may not wish to add spurious predictors, and so specifies that the addition of any new predictor should occur only when the predictor variable can truly explain a resonable amount of variation in the data. Otherwise, if the predictor explains only a small amount of the residual variation, the process stops. The researcher then uses the limited number of good predictors, rather then using all of the predictors.

Kramer (1976) and other researchers have made extensive use of the multiple linear regression method to develop texture predictions on the basis of independent measures.

In the case of our bread data, we could begin to add additional predictor factors, beyond modulus of elasticity and hysteresis loss, as predictors. Table 10.11 shows what happens when we continue to add other measures as predictors to the data: (1) We increase the predictability (as indexed by the multiple correlation). (2) We may lower the true measure of goodness-of-fit, as indexed by the F ratio, which relates explained variability and unexplained variability, taking into account the number of predictors that we use. As the number of predictors increases, we explain an increasing amount of variability in the sensory rating, but at a decreasing rate. As we accrue more predictors the F ratio first increases, but then peaks, and finally begins to decrease.

The multiple linear regression system provides a nontheoretical method for relating our textural sensory ratings to the independent, instrumental measures. Multiple linear regression does not specify what occurs in terms of how the physical variables combine to generate the sensory responses. It tells us that if we assume that the variables combine in a noninteractive, linear fashion, then we can discover the relative weighting factors for the variables (viz., the coefficients in the equation).

Nonlinearities and Interactions

If we pursue the concept of many instrumental measures interacting to generate a single sensory perception, then we will probably find that these independent instrumental measures do not behave in a simple manner. Generally, they do not add linearly, according to the scheme dictated by multiple linear regression. It seems too simplistic to imagine that the sensory system partials out the forces assessed by the instrumental measures, weights some of them by constant weighting factors, and then adds the weighted values together. That linear system may describe the data in a statistical sense, but the equation may not lead to a deeper understanding of how sensory characteristics indeed relate to the underlying physical variables. Complex nonlinearities and interactions occur. The sensory-instrumental equation should generate a prediction as a function of the underlying physical measures, as well as a function of the particular synergistic interaction of the physical variables.

When people assess the perceived thickness or viscosity of liquids in the mouth, they do so in a predictable way. Shama and Sherman (1973) have shown that panelists do so by responding to viscosity, and then changing their motor movements to generate different rates at which they swirl the liquid in the mouth. People do not assess the textural world around them in a fixed motor manner, as an instrument would do. Through complex sensory feedback, people adjust the motoric actions and forces that they bring to bear upon a food. Depending upon the type of food that they eat, people exert a stronger force or a weaker

TABLE 10.11
EXAMPLES OF WHAT OCCURS IN THE PREDICTION OF BREAD
FIRMNESS AS WE ADD INCREASING NUMBERS OF
INDEPENDENT MEASURES

1. Firmness = 30.68 + 3.898 (Modulus of Elasticity)   R = 0.906
                                                          F = 45.97 (df = 1,10)

2. Firmness = 244.62 + 4.493 (Modulus of Elasticity)   R = 0.918
   −244.3 (Hysteresis Loss)   F = 24.0 (df = 2,9)

3. Firmness = 52.359 + 12.556 (Modulus of Elasticity)   R = 0.96
   −35.20 (Hysteresis Loss) − 16.11 (Stress)   F = 30.4 (df = 3,8)

4. Firmness 27.1 + 23.35 (Modulus of Elasticity)
   −0.27 (Hysteresis Loss) + 26.44 (Stress)   R = 0.97
   −305.18 (Strain)   F = 28.7 (df = 4,7)

5. Firmness = 25.50 + 22.72 (Modulus of Elasticity)
   −4.49 (Hysteresis Loss) + 30.47 (Stress)   R = 0.97
   −325.47 (Strain) + 32.03 (Density)   F = 20.3 (df = 5,6)

force when making their judgments.

Let us add to this picture the complexity of the forces which already exist in the mouth. More than likely, the kinaesthetic sensory system will pick up a pattern of forces, and respond to that pattern by integrating the information into a single perception. The researcher chooses to model or to describe the complex pattern of interacting physical forces by means of a simplistic, tractable, but not necessarily intrinsically valid equation for these reasons: (1) We do not know the physics at the receptor site. Therefore we do not know the precise forces which impinge upon the actual surface of the receptor area. (2) We do not know the pattern of forces. Therefore, we cannot plot the effective or true stimulus in terms of forces and time.

If the researcher wishes to predict the likely sensory response, he may have a half dozen to several dozen instrumental variables from which to choose. If nonlinearities and interactions exist, then a half dozen instrumental variables generate an additional 6 square terms, and 15 (viz., (6)(5)/2) pairwise cross terms. The original set of 6 predictor variables now increase to 27. With three way interaction terms (product of three variables) the ternary interaction terms increase to an additional 20 [(6 × 5 × 4)/(1 × 2 × 3)].

Further complexities arise when we consider ratios of variables, square roots of the products of variables, etc, as predictors of responses. The simplistic method of multiple linear regression provides a straightforward but nontheoretic answer to this mèlange of predictors. It does not increase complexity in the prediction system. It does provide a method for prediction of the likely sensory preception, in a quantitative way.

Relating Instrumental Measures
To Acceptability

Let us close this section on texture measurements with the important question on the relation between acceptability (or quality) and the underlying instrumental measures. In actuality, many of the studies which appear in the scientific literature strive to develop and validate instrumental test methods which will predict the textural quality of foods. Although the researchers recognize that people first react to the sensory characteristics of foods as precursors of judgments of quality (good-bad, or another hedonic dimension), much research tries to correlate instrumental measures with hedonic reactions.

Many researchers treat hedonics (like/dislike, product quality) as a sensory characteristic, and use the multiple linear regression method (or simple correlation analysis) to relate hedonics to the physical measurements. All well and good, until we recall that according to the scientific literature, acceptability describes an inverted U shaped curve versus the physical concentration of an ingredient or versus the sensory characteristic (see Chapter 6). In other words, the equation relating quality or hedonics and instrumental measures must allow acceptability or quality to first increase with increasing physical level, peak (at the "bliss" point), and then diminish as the physical intensity increases beyond the bliss point level.

In the case of our bread project the nonlinearity implies that in actuality the simple linear regression relating sensory characteristics to the modulus of elasticity and to the hysteresis loss cannot apply when we wish to relate acceptability of the bread to those two characteristics. The multiple linear regression equation may describe some, or perhaps a substantial amount of the variability in the acceptance ratings, but it cannot truly represent how liking (or another quality parameter) varies with the underlying instrumental measures. Furthermore, if the R&D sensory analyst or the texture scientist models quality using a simple additive, linear regression equation, then the bliss point or predicted optimal combination of instrumental measures will always lie at the upper or lower extreme level of the variables. The optimum level can never lie in the middle (See Fig. 10.4).

The same problems in modelling quality or acceptability versus instrumental measures arise when modelling acceptability versus ingredients. We dealt with that issue in the chapters on hedonics

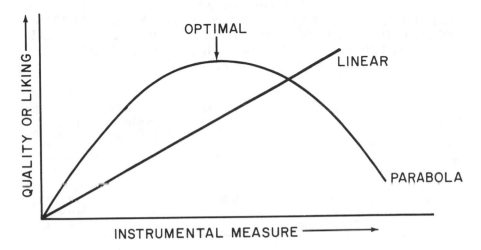

FIG. 10.4. PROTOTYPICAL RELATION BETWEEN HEDONICS (LIKING) OR PRODUCT
QUALITY VERSUS INSTRUMENTAL MEASURES

(Chapter 6) and optimization (Chapter 7). Similar problems and solutions arise here as well. Specifically: (1) One may choose an equation which accounts for nonlinearities, and interactions, in order to represent possible optimal quality levels at the middle levels of the instrumental measures. The pairwise (or higher order) interactions allow for the variables to interact together, and provide a mechanistic way to portray those interactions. (2) By expressing the sensory-instrumental equation in terms of a second order (quadratic) equation, the researcher can represent the complex relation in manner similar to the way one represents the relation with multiple linear regression. (The mathematics for computing the coefficients remains the same).

Table 10.12 shows how acceptability ratings, by the panel, relate to the modulus of elasticity and hysteresis loss. Note that the nonlinear equation provides a better fit than does the linear equation for predicting overall liking and that the optimal level lies in the middle range for modulus of elasticity rather than lying at the extreme level.

Such complex analyses, using nonlinear equations become critical if the researcher wishes to truly represent how product quality varies with the underlying physical variables chosen as instrumental predictors. By sweeping all of the variables under the rug (in a figurative sense), using the mechanistic, and straightforward method of purely linear multiple regression, the investigator cannot determine how quality truly varies, and where peak conditions exist for product acceptance.

TABLE 10.12
COMPARISON OF LINEAR AND NONLINEAR EQUATIONS RELATING
TWO INSTRUMENTAL MEASURES (MODULUS OF ELASTICITY AND
HYSTERESIS LOSS) TO LIKING RATINGS OF BREAD
ASSIGNED BY EXPERTS

Type of Equation	Equation	Overall Multiple Correlation Coefficient	Optimial Levels
Linear	Liking = 6.9 − 5.24(ME) + 12.7 (HL)	0.88	ME = 19.4 HL = 0.887 Liking ≃ 45
Non-Linear	Liking = −3.8(10⁴) + 5.52 (ME) + 8.7(10⁴)(HL) − 0.24(ME)² − 4.9(10⁴)(HL)²	0.94	ME = 11.53 HL = 0.882 Liking = 18

Proxy Variables, True Variables and Sensory Perceptions

When the researcher selects a variable or set of variables to measure instrumentally and to correlate with the sensory percepts or with acceptability, the selection represents a guess as to what variables affect the sensory responses to the food. We should recognize that many potential predictors of sensory characteristics need not, themselves, reflect actual forces to which the person would react in the eating situation. The forces chosen as independent texture predictors should predict, but may not represent physical reality. These predictor forces may act as proxy forces. Time after time, measurements of these proxy forces allows the investigator to predict the likely consumer reaction.

Let us take an example from commodity grading to illustrate this point. Consumers judge the quality of many fruits by color, rejecting mottled fruits as having already spoiled. When eating the fruits, and classifying fruits into fresh, green, or spoiled, the panelist may not even look at the surface, but rather judges from the volatiles and from the fruit texture. Yet, by knowing that surface appearance correlates highly with fruit quality, we can use surface appearance as a surrogate predictor of quality. The color and appearance correlate with the internal characteristics of the fruit. Quality graders find grading the color easier than actually opening the fruit and determining degree of freshness by measuring the volatile aroma constituents, or measuring the hardness of the fruit.

Approaching this quality grading situation naively, the critic might say that color has little or nothing to do with the appreciation of the fruit in the mouth. Furthermore, in order to truly measure the quality of the product, its hardness, and the key types and levels of the flavor producing volatiles, the scientist may demand the requisite physical measurements. On the other hand, pragmatically, the color of the fruit surface could just as easily predict the likely quality or grading (or acceptance) rating as do the other, more complex physical measures.

The researcher faces the same problem in correlating texture measures and product quality. One can use proxy measures of instrumental texture to substitute for other texture characteristics, harder to measure, without necessarily losing any power of predictability. The researcher does not know the true, or underlying physical forces generating the perception of texture quality or acceptability. One can only discover that basic information by knowing the actual mechanical forces and structures involved at the receptor site. However, through the use of convenient proxy predictors the researcher can go a long way towards explicating relations between an objectively measured textural property (e.g., modulus of elasticity, hysteresis loss, or others), and rated quality/acceptability.

An Overview To Texture Research

Texture researchers, perhaps more than any other researchers in food science, have available to them a wide variety of different measuring systems. Engineers, such as Peter Voisey in the Canadian Department of Agriculture, have devised numerous instruments which apply different types of forces to products. Other researchers, such as Essex Finney in the U.S. Department of Agriculture, have developed innovative procedures such as nondestructive testing by means of sound stimuli directed towards the foods. Bakers have their farinographs and amylographs, meat scientists have the different types of shear presses, and the Instron Universal Testing machine, whereas those interested in gels have the Bloom Gelometer, and its modern descendents for texture testing.

Given the abundance of these instruments there arises the real possibility of too-many, rather than too few independent instrumental measures which can serve as predictors of sensory perceptions. With the emphasis upon replacing human panels by instrumental measures it should come as no surprise that researchers continue to seek that single instrument which best predicts human texture responses.

The product tester should keep in mind that the information gained from human scaling of texture perceptions allows for only the most rudimentary modelling by analog or instrumental means. To date, it appears that no single set of machine parameters can predict responses to all or even most items within a single food category. Rules generated for modelling the sensory-instrumental relations for one type of fruit will probably not apply, or apply only modestly to another type of fruit. Rules generated to predict the texture of meats will apply to some meats, but not to others. Since we usually remain ignorant of the precise physics and mechanics of the testing situation at the receptor site, we really do not know the appropriate physical factors which represent the best measures. Even the so-called engineering oriented instruments, such as the Instron Universal Testing Machine, which provide simple, rheologically well defined measurements, do not tell the researcher what forces exists at the sensory texture receptors. Perhaps the Instron provides better control over the component variables which it measures. However, the Instron does not provide the texture researcher or the product tester with the rules which combine these fundamental physical measures into a sensory texture perception. In a sense, research has a far way to go before approaches aimed at correlating sensory and instrumental measures can truly become a predictive science, with fundamental rules to guide correlations, and with predictions emerging according to scientific "first principles." Research has entered in the pragmatic, data-gathering stage, skipping over the theoretical stage, and rushing into an era of increased instrumental sophistication. Our knowledge and wisdom have not advanced commensurately.

SENSORY-INSTRUMENTAL RELATIONS—FLAVOR

The second half of this chapter concerns correlations between chemical constitution and the sensory characteristics of flavor. Simple psychophysical and sensory analysis tells us that in many instances we can correlate the specific odor characteristics of a product to a chemical or combination of chemicals. In the most simple of cases, one odorant chemical causes, or correlates with the sensory characteristics. These so-called character-impact compounds play a key role in flavor of some, but certainly not all foods.

Prior to the early 1960's, many flavor researchers had to remain content with these character-impact compounds. Although complex substances such as coffee possessed dozens (and with increasing sophistication of measurement finally hundreds) of compounds, researchers could not study the relation between the single chemical constituents of coffee, and coffee flavor. Researchers lacked an adequate instrument to fractionate the components of coffee or other flavors into components. They thought however, that the answer lay in more sensitive measurement of the component chemical. Better resolution of the underlying chemical mixture would surely elucidate the relation between perception and chemical constitution, or so the went the consensus.

During the late 1950's and early 1960's chemists developed the separatory gas chromatograph, an instrument which selectively and differentially retards the passage of chemicals through a column of adsorbing substance. The chemist injects a slug of atmosphere (or headspace) over a food into the gas chromatograph. The air slug injected into the inlet port at the start of the column emerges as a series of different slugs of vapor at the end of the column. By means of adsorption, the column separates the complex mixture into its components, based upon selective affinity of the column component (so-called liquid phase) with the chemicals in the injected slug.

The gas chromatograph allows the chemist to fractionate a complex flavor chemical into its components, and thereby to discover which common chemicals the similar flavors share. Researchers can use statistical procedures such as regression analysis and cluster analysis, in order to relate chemical composition to flavor quality. With regression analysis, the researcher obtains different samples of a flavored material, perhaps from different sources of that flavor. The product tester measures sensory ratings of the stimulus. The chemist develops an instrumental profile of the components of the flavor. The regression procedure relates concentration of flavor components to sensory quality. With cluster analysis and related procedures, the researcher classifies the flavor stimuli into common or similar-quality categories, and looks for a common set of chemicals, which when combined in the proper way, reproduce that classification as closely as possible.

Generally, flavor researchers have had success in identifying the different flavor compounds in foods. The number of reports grows continually, as researchers use new and improved analytic separatory techniques to discover compounds present in foods at increasingly lower concentrations. The thermal conductivity detector of the early gas chromatographs, a relatively insensitive detecting device, has given way to the more sensitive flame ionization detector, which has a 1,000 times more sensitivity to flavor chemical substances. The flame ionization detector, in turn, has given way in some instances to an even more sensitive electron detectors and to the plasma chromatograph, which has a sensitivity 1,000+ times greater.

Unfortunately, researchers have had substantially less success in relating the chemical constituents of flavors to the sensory characteristics of complex foods. We still lack a comprehensive theory which relates chemical constituents to underlying odor perception. We do not even possess general approaches which relate combinations of chemicals to the emergence of specific flavors. Flavorists and perfumers possess a wealth of knowledge, obtained from experience, and from trial and error research in the fabrication of odorous substances. Even they, however, have not developed a general theory which predicts the likely odor sensation which one will perceive, given a specific set of components.

With this limitation, let us look more closely at some studies in sensory-instrumental correlations, in which the experimenters have used gas chromatographic separation and measurement. We will deal with two critical studies in regression analysis, and one critical study in discriminant analysis (a form of clustering).

The Odor of Ginger—Its Relation to Chemicals

Our first study comes from research reported by Bednarcyzk and Kramer (1975). These authors collected various substances which possess a strong ginger flavor. They subjected the compounds to separatory gas chromatography, using a device with moderate sensitivity. The researchers measured the relative concentrations of the components via the thermal conductivity detector. The peaks appear as in Figure 10.5, which shows a typical tracing of a gas chromatographic 'run'. Each peak represents a chemical, or a combination of chemicals which the instrument could not resolve into further subcomponents (either due to the rate at which the slug passed through the column, or because the column and the sensitive liquid phase could not distinguish between the two compounds). Other methods, such as nuclear magnetic resonance, allowed Bednarcyzk and Kramer to identify the chemicals corresponding to each peak.

Each compound possesses a unique flavor. Not all compounds in the chromatogram tracing in Figure 10.5 seem "gingery." In fact, relatively few do. Having isolated the components, the researchers then procured pure chemicals of the same type, and instructed panelists to evaluate these chemicals alone and in mixtures. The panelists tested all chemicals in applesauce as the carrier. The panelists scaled each sample, rating overall flavor strength, ginger flavor, and other characteristics. As these authors reported, different chemicals added to the applesauce base changed the character of the flavor. Some chemicals found in the separation phase added a more lemony taste. Another compound emphasized a more woody, soapy, and harsh taste.

In order to quantify the relations between relative ginger flavor and

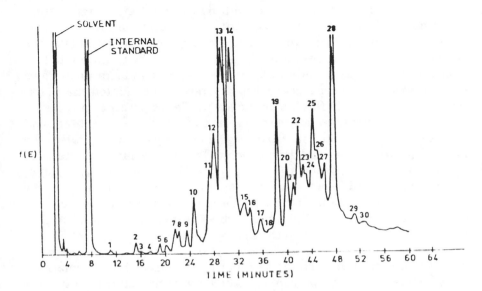

FIG. 10.5   TYPICAL GAS LIQUID CHROMATOGRAPHIC SEPARATION

Typical gas-liquid chromatogram for steam distilled ginger essential oil. Each peak represents
a chemical or combination of chemicals.
Source: Bednarcyzk and Kramer (1975)

the compounds, Bednarcyzk and Kramer selected four different chemicals, from the compounds which they had isolated in the initial, gas chromatographic separation:

Peak 14 (nerolidol)—woody, soapy green smelling
                                  compound reminiscent of ginger.
Peaks 11, 4, 19—all contain other compounds in the mixture, and
                                  generate a ginger flavor.

Finally, using the different peaks as independent variables they related the rating of ginger flavor to the concentration of the peak chemicals, by means of the simple linear regression equation:

Intensity = 13.96 + 0.52(A) + 1.25(B) + 0.993(C) + 0.971(D)

Although Bednarcyzk and Kramer did not explicate how the specific chemicals or mixtures develop the ginger flavor when mixed together, they used the gas chromatographic separation to obtain chemical precursors of ginger flavor. Their testing method specifically selected those chemicals which already possessed a ginger flavor.

The research of Bednarcyzk and Kramer differs from texture research. In the subjective-instrumental correlation of flavor characteristics, the researcher can taste or smell the components, and preselect those which possess the requisite quality. They cannot do this easily for texture. Thus, this study by Bednarczyk and Kramer follows in the tradition of those researchers who have investigated character-impact compounds in flavors as the key to flavor perception.

The next illustrative study comes from the Swedish Institute of Food Preservation Research, in Goteborg. The project investigated the aroma of canned beef, and developed models to correlate instrumental and sensory data (Persson and Von Sydow, 1972). Canned beef aroma, in particular, and beef aroma in general, presents a challenge for relating sensory responses to objective measurements of flavor chemicals. No single chemical stimulus truly characterizes the aroma of beef. Beef aroma arises from the interaction of many different chemical compounds. Furthermore, the quality of beef aroma varies with the processing conditions. The researcher cannot treat beef aroma as a single, fixed sensory percept, produced by one character-impact compound.

The beef aroma study represents the more difficult but also more realistic evaluation of sensory-instrumental relations. It considers the nebulous impression of beef aroma which contains no specific character-impact compound. This contrasts with the relatively straightforward project on ginger flavor, reported by Bednarcyzk and Kramer (1975).

In the actual experiment, the investigators stored meats at varying temperatures, ranging from $-20°$ C to $+8°$ C, for varying lengths of time, and under different headspace (or processing) conditions. In some instances the investigators stored the beef in packages containing large headspaces or empty areas in the storage bag. In those headspaces gases could collect. Oxygen played a role in modifying the gaseous composition. For other samples, the experimenters packed the beef tightly, with less than 0.5 ml of headspace, thus effectively eliminating any headspace. This eliminated the oxygen as a potential flavor modifying agent.

In order to determine the objective measures of chemical composition underlying meat flavor, Persson et al. sampled the headspace, or space above the storage packet of meat, using a simple, widely used sampling procedure. They extracted samples of the gas with a syringe. Furthermore, in order to measure both the compounds present in the meat itself, as well as the compounds present in the vapor phase above the meat, the reseachers homogenized the samples, held the samples in a water bath and then collected samples of the gases above the meat. The gases would presumably contain many, if not all of the volatiles which give rise to the flavor.

Equations

The 17 samples each generated a unique gas chromatographic spectrum of tracing. The spectra or tracings differ from each other, as do the flavor profiles of these samples. The researcher aims to relate the instrumental spectrum to the flavor characteristics, sensorically measured, realizing that for the complex perception of meat flavor, no single peak will characterize the meat. (This complication contrasts sharply with the relatively simple problem solved by Bednarczyk and Kramer, in the evaluation of ginger).

Persson *et al.* developed a wide variety of different mathematical models, to relate sensory perceptions and flavor scores from the gas chromatographic separating phase. The researchers isolated 44 peaks, comprising at least 44 different compounds. They then studied a number of different relations between sensory attributes and peak height, for single peak heights, and pairs of peak heights. (Using three peak heights in combination would have unduly multiplied the number of possible relations). Table 10.13 shows three different types of univariate functions relating sensory characteristic (R) to peak height (X). These univariate functions comprise the linear, the logarithmic and the power equation. Furthermore, Table 10.13 shows the combination rules selected from many possible combination rules for pairs of peak heights. (These include simple additive models, square root models, ratio models, etc.).

TABLE 10.13
RULES RELATING SENSORY RESPONSES (R) TO PEAK HEIGHT (X)

Models for Relating Response Data (R) to Stimulus Data (S)

$$R = A \cdot S + B$$
$$\log R = A \cdot \log S + B \text{ (Stevens' law)}$$
$$R = A \cdot \log S + B \text{ (Fechner's law)}$$

$S = X_i$	$S = X_i / X_j$
$S = X_i + X_j$	$S = \sqrt{X_i \, X_j}$
$S = X_i - X_j$	$S = \sqrt{(X_i^2) + (X_j^2)}$

Given a set of different peaks and combination rules from which to choose, the authors reported that a possible 44,000 (approximate) equations could fit the results. The reseachers thus had to select from among the possible 44,000 those specific equations which provided reasonably good correlations between the rating of flavor and the peak heights (weighted according to the model). Of the 44,000 equations, approximately 500 equations showed correlation coefficients exceeding 0.85 (which value the authors selected as their cutoff point). The authors rejected any equation which showed less than a multiple correlate 0.85 (or 72% of the variability accounted for). Table 10.14 shows some of the models which the authors discovered.

The Persson-Von Sydow study represents a refining step in the complicated process of relating sensory and instrumental measures. As in the case of texture measures, the authors state that "When using this technique in quality control work, it is not necessary to know the chemical identity of the peaks included in the calculations as long as one is certain that the peaks originate from the food and are not artifacts. However, in process and product development work the identity of the peaks may be important to know, e.g., when trying to make corrections in formulation or process in a direction giving improved flavor quality."

Like texture, the researcher need not specify the underlying reality of the system. Rather, the researcher needs to model the empirical relation between sensory and instrumental measures, in an ad hoc way, making sure that the variables chosen as the independent predictors in fact predict the dependent variable, flavor intensity, fairly well. The chemicals may not necessarily cause the meat flavor. Their presence, and the correct equation, however, suffice to predict the intensity of the meat flavor.

The final illustrative study comes from the continuing work of John Powers at the University of Georgia, in Athens, Georgia. The study concerns the assessment of those instrumental correlates of a flavor (e.g., gas chromatographic peaks) which predict the classification of a flavor into one of several predetermined groups. The focus shifts here, from a prediction of the magnitude of an intensity response for a single sensory characteristic to the rules by which the researcher can assign flavor stimuli to different predesignated flavor categories. The experimenter (or the panelist) develops the classification rules, and classifies the stimuli into the predesignated categories. Statistical methods can elucidate which objective or instrumental measures predict the classification. When the researcher has 44 peaks from which to choose (or often, even more peaks), and has the opportunity to classify the aroma stimuli into two classes (e.g., fresh-stale, good-bad, Type A-

TABLE 10.14

EXAMPLES OF ACTUAL MODELS RELATING OFF FLAVOR SCORES OF CANNED MEAT (R) TO INSTRUMENTALLY MEASURED PEAK HEIGHTS (X_i)

Equation No.	Model	Correlation Coefficients		A		B	
		Exp. 1	Exp. 2 and 3	Exp. 1	Exp. 2 and 3	Exp. 1	Exp. 2 and 3
2	$\log R_{cal} = A \cdot \log X_{20} + B$	-0.885	-0.879	0.307	0.315	-0.405	-0.399
5	$\log R_{cal} = A \cdot \log X_{23}/X_{39} + B$	-0.882	-0.883	0.266	0.275	-0.087	-0.057
28	$\log R_{cal} = A \cdot \log (X_{15} + X_{20}) + B$	-0.889	-0.877	0.316	0.321	-0.434	-0.418
29	$\log R_{cal} = A \cdot \log (X_{18} + X_{20}) + B.$	-0.889	-0.880	0.313	0.319	-0.434	-0.418
34	$\log R_{cal} = A \cdot \log \sqrt{X_8^2 + X_{20}^2} + B$	-0.887	-.887	0.317	0.320	-0.408	-0.416
41	$R_{cal} = A \cdot (X_{19} - X_{27}) + B$	0.924	0.552	0.0373	0.0236	1.75	2.48

X_1 = Peak Height of Peak i R_{cal} = Estimated Rating   Exp = Experiment Number

From: Persson & Von Sydow (1972)

Type B), the researcher must develop a classification rule which: (1) Selects the proper peaks in the gas chromatogram (obviously, fewer than 44). (2) Measures their heights (or areas). (3) Weights the peak values, according to a specific rule. (4) Calculates the weighted value (Sum of Peak$_i$ × Weight$_i$). (5) Sorts the flavor stimulus into one of the two groups, depending upon the results of the weighting.

This method of multivariate analysis, known as discriminant function analysis, searches for the optimum weighting formula, by which one can sort the different flavor samples into the correct, prescribed categories. In a sense, researchers use discriminant analysis to parallel human sorting behavior, (see Powers, 1976).

One can generalize this pairwise approach, to multiple discriminant analysis, wherein the experimenter or panelist has specified several different categories, into which one can sort the stimuli. For N categories, one must develop N-1 equations, to properly sort the sets of samples into the N categories.

In the actual experiment, panelists evaluated different potato chip samples generating ratings of sensory quality. In the same study, the experimenter isolated the headspace, or volatiles, comprising the flavor sensitive ingredients in gas vapor, and subjected the mixture of gases to a gas chromatograph, for separation. The resulting trace led to the separation of many different components. Table 10.15 shows how one can combine some (but obviously not all) of the peak heights into a single weighting scheme, to predict the pairwise classification of the products into the classes of fresh versus stale.

Of course, the experimenter must preselect the instrumental measures to use, in order to select those particular peaks which properly classify the products into different groups. As with any other multivariate procedure, increasing the number of predictors (either in multiple linear regression or in discriminant analysis) allows the experimenter to more accurately relate the instrumental measures to sensory responses (whether intensity ratings or classifications). On the other hand, the researcher always runs the risk of including too many predictors in the equation, which would automatically generate a 100% correct classification (even if the additional predictors do nothing but fit random variability).

An Overview to the Science of
Sensory-Instrumental Correlations

This chapter discussed methods by which experimenters can relate objectively or instrumentally measured variables to sensory or to hedonic responses. The results of most empirical research today on

TABLE 10.15
RESULTS OF MULTIPLE DISCRIMINANT ANALYSIS OF
POTATO CHIP ODOR INTO QUALITY CLASSES

Table A—First "step" of a stepwise discriminant classification of blends of fresh and stale potato chips (ground), nine specimens of each blend

Blends		Blends					
Fresh	Stale	100% fresh	80:20%	60:40%	40:60%	20:80%	100% Stale
100%	—	(1)	3	2	1	2	0
80%	20%	0	(8)	0	1	0	0
60%	40%	3	3	(0)	2	1	0
40%	60%	0	2	2	(5)	0	0
20%	80%	0	2	1	5	(1)	0
—	100%	0	1	0	0	0	(8)

Variable	F-Value
Peak 2/Peak 1	34.59

Table B—Classification at Step 5

Blends		Blends					
Fresh	Stale	100% fresh	80:20%	60:40%	40:60%	20:80%	100% Stale
100%	—	(7)	0	2	0	0	0
80%	20%	3	(5)	1	0	0	0
60%	40%	1	1	(4)	0	3	0
40%	60%	1	1	1	(3)	3	0
20%	80%	1	0	2	0	(6)	0
—	100%	0	0	0	0	0	(9)

Variable	F-Value
Peak 4/Peak 1	4.48
Peak 3/Peak 2	1.21
Peak 1/Peak 3	1.73
Peak 4/Peak 2	1.15
Peak 4/Peak 3	0.60

Table C—Weights and correlations of discriminant function

	Peak Areas									
	PK05	PK07	PK09	PK10	PK18	PK19	PK22	PK23	PK26	PK31
Weight	0.459	0.715	−9.83	−17.7	−18.4	4.96	−0.868	18.7	24.9	−35.5
Correlations	0.42	−0.12	−0.12	−0.08	−0.21	0.24	−0.07	0.15	0.38	−0.28

() = number correctly placed into appropriate category (6 categories in all)   Source: Powers (1976)

complex foodstuffs reveals that experimenters have had to content themselves with empirical models, to describe the relations in an ad hoc way. Food scientists, rheologists, chemists, physiologists and psychologists have only just begun to tackle the problem of what really occurs at the receptor site when the panelist evaluates a stimulus. Without that information, researchers must settle for non-theoretical equations or other statistical techniques, which describe those empirical relations which exist. These equations do not give a general model of why, in theory, the relations do exist.

Faced with this constraint, the product tester should keep these things in mind: (1) Sensory-instrumental correlations find their greatest use in quality control and product development, where the researcher attempts to ascertain what has gone awry to reduce product quality, or what to do to improve product quality (or at least to maintain it). (2) The domain of stimuli which the experimenter studies varies biologically by the very nature of food itself. Although psychophysicists, rheologists and other analysts deal with well controlled stimuli in the laboratory in order to discover the laws of perception, precise stimulus control becomes well nigh impossible in foods which people purchase and consume. As a consequence, one should expect to see poorer predictability in data generated from real foods than from simpler model systems. One cannot even conclude that the simpler model systems provide information which will generalize to the real food. Perhaps the methods for evaluating psychophysical relations apply equally to model systems and to real foods, but the type of data one obtains, and the nature of the human response differ dramatically, when the consumer panelist rates a simple mixture chemicals versus evaluating a real, consumable food.

With ongoing developments in chromatography, in rheology and in the measurement of physical variables, and with growing maturity of research in food science and other disciplines, the researcher of the next decade should see important breakthroughs in the following areas: (1) Conceptualizations or models of what really occurs at the receptor site (à la Cussler and colleagues, in psychorheology). (2) Better measurement and definition of consumer responses, the keystone of interrelating domains of instruments and people. (3) Development of both pragmatic and theory-based models of how the receptors transform physical and chemical stimuli into sense perceptions.

CHAPTER 11

QUALITY CONTROL FROM THE SENSORY POINT OF VIEW

INTRODUCTION

Many manufacturers receive their first introduction to product testing through problems with product quality. Perhaps during the course of a production run something goes wrong in one of the processes, causing a change in the product characteristics. Consumers sense these changes, and either reject the product outright, never purchasing it again, or complain to the manufacturer, or both. Quality control seeks to maintain or upgrade product integrity in the face of numerous ingredient and processing changes which modify the sensory characteristics of the product, and alienate the consumer franchise.

Fifty years ago, researchers practiced a relatively crude form of quality control. Workers with gel foods could avail themselves of the Bloom Gelometer. Workers in meat science often used the Warner Bratzler Shear Press as an objective measure of food texture quality. In fact, many of the earliest texture measuring devices grew out of the desire of food workers to develop "objective" grading instruments for food quality.

With the gradual emergence of food science into the stream of modern technology, (in the 1920's—1940's), one reads of increased interest in product quality control. As the production lines geared up for an expanding population and expanding national and international markets, food processors expanded beyond the 'mom and pop' shop, to produce food items for a waiting, yet critical audience of customers having increasingly high expectations. World War II presented unique problems in product quality control. Foods manufactured in the U.S. ended up in storage, for days, weeks or perhaps months at a time in hostile environments (both politically and climatically). A processed meat might remain on the shelves in a steamy jungle for three months after arriving from a shipping convoy. Military concern with soldier morale recognized the responses of soldiers to their foods. Scientific committees studied the nature and improvement of food stability in an effort to insure food quality.

As discussed in the introduction to this volume, the history of sensory analysis sometimes parallels the developing interest in quality control. Many of the techniques we use today, such as the discrimination and affective tests, as well as the descriptive test, trace their origin to attempts to obtain a measure of quality. Questions needing answering included: (1) Has the product changed in any way from a reference standard? (2) What does the modified product taste like? (3) Do consumers like the stored product more than the control, test product? (4) How long can one store a product, before it begins to develop an off-taste? What type of off-taste does the product develop? Does that off-taste/flavor impact on the product's acceptability?

A CASE HISTORY—CANNED MEAT

Let us consider a case history from the meat industry. The Allen Meat Company, famous for its processed meats (processed ham, processed salami, bologna, etc.) has, during the past four years, embarked on an ambitious marketing program, geared to increasing its distribution out of the local Pennsylvania area, where it has its base operations. In order to develop this program, management took these steps: (1) Stored the processed meats for a longer time, under refrigeration. (2) Changed some of the spice mixes, to accommodate the taste of the Ohio and Illinois customers. However, due to processing costs, the Allen Meat Company continued to process all meats in the same plant, with the same personnel. (3) Stored the meats in larger warehouses, prior to shipment. (4) Procured the services of a contract shipping line, to take care of all of its shipping. Previously, it had used it own fleet of trucks. (5) Changed the meat procurement system, to a low bid system, with bids solicited from at least three suppliers.

In light of these changes in production, storage, procurement, etc. it should come as no surprise that without an adequate quality control program, the quality of the Allen processed meats could soon deteriorate. Some problems in quality control which could develop include the following: Suppliers of meat could provide lower quality materials, in order to increase margins. Without quality control, the consumer would know that the quality has diminished, but management would probably not know where in the production sequence the problem had arisen.

With increased distances in shipping, the Allen Meat Company runs the risk of loss of quality in transit. The carrier van may overheat, subjecting the meat products to higher than normal temperatures, which favor the growth of bacteria and mold. Perhaps, from time to time the refrigerated carrier develops a leak, emitting noxious (albeit not necessarily dangerous) gases into the cargo storage area.

The plastic film in which the Allen Company packages its products (either for the final point of purchase for consumers, or as copacking for other manufacturers) could absorb the noxious odorant. Such odorants can and often do migrate through the package to impart an off-odor to the product. Consumers perceive this off-odor as a loss in quality, again not knowing necessarily from whence the off-aroma originated.

The spices which Allen uses to season the meat themselves may not pass quality control standards. Perhaps the company which supplies these spices decided to increase its profit margin by cutting costs, and adulterating some of the more expensive spices with cheaper spices. The cheaper spices may seem identical in flavor to the more expensive spices. With aging, however, and the inevitable modifications of flavor which occur within the products, the cheaper spices may not season the meat adequately, or may not blend with the other flavors. This failure would modify the originally tailored meat flavor which customers have come to expect.

With these possibilities in mind, let us construct a company-wide quality control system, using product testing procedures as the prime guide. The system we design will reflect the premier approach in sensory quality control. Some companies may prefer to select only those parts of the quality control system, which they feel most applicable to their current problem.

"FINGERPRINTING" THE PRODUCT

Quality control systems seek to maintain quality, and to register deviations from a pre-set standard. In order to insure that quality remains constant, the quality control engineer and the product tester must establish a benchmark or control sensory profile (or sensory fingerprint) against which to compare test samples.

Certain technical requirements apply here: (1) Common Language: One should profile the standard or reference product sample in terms of well defined sensory characteristics. (2) Standard Scale: One should adopt a common scale to insure comparable measures of the test sample and the quality control standard. (3) Standard Test Conditions: One should profile the product under standard conditions, in order to insure reproducible test conditions and reproducible ratings from one test to the other.

By fingerprinting a product, we refer to the process of profiling its sensory characteristics by quantitative scaling: (1) Using a limited series of attributes, (2) With shared meaning of each attribute among members of the panel. (3) Using a specific scale.

The sensory profile of the standard becomes, de facto, a numerical description of the target or reference. Products which differ sensorically from the standard profile represent products where quality control has failed. Consumers (or expert panelists) can differentiate between the test product and the reference standard.

The sensory profile of the reference product allows the manufacturer to specify the product's sensory characteristics in a form one can store for future reference. If the new batches of product differ from the standard batch produced in any way, one can often obtain good diagnostic information by comparing the test product profile to the reference profile. Sometimes, one can spot the underlying cause for the disparity. On other occasions the reference and the current product may differ on characteristics, but the reason for the difference eludes the manufacturer. Nonetheless, the profile allows the manufacturer to determine that changes have occurred.

The Allen Product: Some Specifics Using the Profiling Method to Develop a Standard

The product tester and quality control engineer had the opportunity to develop different profiles, by selecting among many different types of attributes to characterize the product and many different types of scales to measure perceptions. The sensory analyst and the quality control engineer both realized that the product with which they deal would exhibit high intrinsic variability from batch to batch. They would have to face these considerations in developing the profile scaling system: (1) They would have to develop a profile system which allowed for certain swings in product sensory characteristics, without setting off an "alarm". They would also have to develop a profile system which could detect and measure the critical swings in characteristics which alter acceptability. (2) They would have to develop a sensitive system for scaling, but also employ a system that panelists could easily use, without those panelists having to invest a great deal of time in evaluation.

Attribute Selection For the Quality Control Profile

Both quality control engineer and product tester recognized that packaged meat (and especially the spicy bologna, which now occupies our attention) comprises a variety of attributes. In order to generate the attributes, they brought together eight employees from the plant, who had expressed interest in participating in a sensory quality control panel. Together with these panelists, the product tester and the plant quality control supervisor formed a 10-person group.

The group discussed their perceptions of the sensory attributes of spicy bologna. Attributes which emerged includes amount and type of spice, appearance (smooth, mottled), presence versus absence of discoloring spots, flavor intensity, fat and mouthfeel properties, etc. These characteristics appear in Table 11.1.

TABLE 11.1
LISTS OF ATTRIBUTES TO CHARACTERIZE
SPICY BOLOGNA PRODUCTS

Appearance	Aroma	Taste	Texture
Darkness	Fatty*	Saltiness	Mouth Coating*
Spotty*	Tallow	Sharpness	Fatty
Glistening*	Spicy	Spiciness*	Tallowy
Shiny	Italian	Flavor Intensity*	Smooth
"Textured"	Hearty		Greasy
	Herb-like*		Dry
			Juicy
			Succulent
			Soft
			Hard*
			Bendable
			Mushy
			Firm

*Final set of 8 attributes

During the course of the four descriptive sessions, run on four separate days, the group refined the vocabulary, and developed a common language to describe the perception of spicy bologna on the one hand, but also generated descriptors for some of the other meat products as well. With Allen's assortment of 6 spicy meat products, the additional attribute lists would come in handy for subsequent quality control meetings.

The group finally reduced the vocabulary to 8 attributes to describe the key perceptions of the spicy bologna. The attributes covered appearance, flavor, aroma, and oral texture. They excluded some characteristics which possessed idiosyncratic meaning to one or another panel member, and excluded other attributes as irrelevant to spicy bologna. Finally, the panel members agreed upon the 8 attributes.

The panelists then set about developing a set of reference standards from packaged meats already on the market, seeking wherever possible to show the ranges of the attributes with a wide selection of packaged meats. In some instances, the product development group at Allen manufactured some samples containing unusually high and low spice levels to illustrate the attribute range. For attributes such as 'mouth coating' (for fat), the panelists tested marketed products which possessed a high degree of mouth coating.

As painstaking as it seems, the quality control supervisor had to pay attention to the key attributes, and had to make every effort to instill into the panel participants a common meaning for each of these characteristics. Unlike consumers, these quality control panelists eventually must learn each attribute in detail, without a reference standard present during the day-to-day grading. Thus, the product tester and quality control engineer had to indoctrinate the panelist to recognize and memorize the quality profile of the standard product, and then to contrast the reference sample to products having overly high or overly low levels of each key characteristic. On some occasions, and with products simpler than spicy bologna, panelists do not need extensive training in descriptive analysis in order to select the vocabulary or select the range of attributes to taste and smell. For simple quality control issues, e.g. for candy bars (e.g., milk chocolate candy bars) defects will reveal themselves more readily, either from visual inspection or from taste inspection. On other occasions, e.g., when training a plant individual in sorting products into quality groups, the quality control specialist may have to expend even more time explicating the nuances which determine the grade into which a product falls. Product categories differ from each other. Meats represent one of the most difficult categories for which to develop a quality control system.

Selecting A Scale

The quality control specialist suggested the following ground rules to follow in selecting a scale: (1) Panelists should understand the scale and feel comfortable using it. (2) The scale must allow a rapid statistical analysis of ratings without extensive intermediate computations. (3) The scale must allow reference standards as nodal points on it in order to refresh the memories of the quality control panel, and to aid their evaluations.

A survey of the techniques currently in progress by the quality control supervisor uncovered these procedures: (1) Four companies used 6 point scales (0-5). (2) Three companies used verbal descriptors of amount. (3) Six companies used verbal descriptors of good to bad on the different characteristics. (4) Two companies used a 100 point grading scale. (5) Three companies used the QDA (Quantitative Descriptive Analysis Method), with a 6 inch line as the scale.

The survey also revealed the following: (1) The 6 point scales seemed insensitive to many differences. Panelists usually clustered their rating around the scale points 3 and 4, or 1 or 2 for the attributes which ordinarily take on low values. The quality control specialist admitted rarely finding differences with that type of scale, but stated that the company had used the scale for 20 years, and had developed sufficient background information to contraindicate using any new scale, despite the known lack of scale sensitivity. (2) Companies using the verbal descriptors of amount also restricted the quality grading system to a limited number of categories. In most instances these verbal scales showed a demonstrable lack of sensitivity, except in the most obvious instances, (viz., with exceptionally poor products). (3) The companies using the 100 point scale seemed 'on target' in terms of their quality control program. They had selected a scale with a large range in order to enhance sensitivity, but recognized that on a day to day basis panelists would feel most comfortable with a closed end, fixed point scale. The panelists did not need the full range of scale points (as they would have with the magnitude estimation scale), since the scale aimed for better (but not perfect) detection of problems on specific attributes. (4) The companies using the 6 inch line scale, or a variant thereof also reported success, but mentioned two drawbacks; Need to evaluate pairs of products (owing to a failure to home in on the proper point on the line from memory alone), and an intermediate time-consuming step of securing the final product rating by measuring the line length assigned, and converting the line scale 'rating' to a number. These steps limited the utility of the line-scaling method to situations wherein one could afford the additional time to transform the data into numerical values.

Based upon this initial survey of the extant procedures, the Allen quality control supervisor decided to adopt a 100 point scale, in light of these specific benefits: (1) Panelists felt comfortable with the closed end scale because they felt anchored, and because they had to deal with a limited product variation which did not require magnitude estimation. They knew the upper and lower limits. (2) The 100 point scale provided sufficient room to show differences from the standard product. (3) With the fixed point scale, one could specify the scale value appropriate for the reference standards. (4) The panelist could record the information on either sheets, or on mark sense cards, for immediate optical-scaling which converts the rating sheet into a punched card format. In planning for the future, the quality control specialist suggested a system that could take the ratings, on a daily basis, feed it into the computer for comparison to references, and also maintain a data bank.

Training With the Scale and the Reference Products

Training lasted about 4 hours. The 8 panel participants, the quality control specialist and the R&D sensory analyst met in the afternoons. They used the 100 point scale to evaluate products on 8 attributes, testing a variety of product variations showing difference in attribute levels.

The results of this training generated a target profile for the "standard" as shown in Table 11.2. Despite experience with the scale and with the product, panelist ratings vary, from person to person, and from one test occasion to another. Thus, in the development of acceptable or tolerance limits for products, the quality control supervisor must allow a range of ratings around the expected value. Unlike measurements in physics and chemistry, the selection of a target value for sensory perceptions must also permit a range of acceptable product variation.

TABLE 11.2
TARGET OR REFERENCE PROFILE—ALLEN "SPICY BOLOGNA"
(Using an 100 Point Intensity Scale, 0 = None, 100 = Extreme,
0 = Dislike Extremely, 100 = Like Extremely)

	Target Scale Value
Appearance	
Spotty	38.2
Glistening	10.6
Aroma	
Fatty	41.3
Herb-like	35.4
Taste	
Flavor Intensity	40.6
Spiciness	39.5
Texture	
Mouth-Coating	21.6
Hard	27.3
Consumer Liking	68.6

In order to develop the quality control limits, the panel used the scale to evaluate 14 batch runs over a three week period. The panelists profiled each batch run on the 8 sensory characteristics. At the same time, the R&D sensory analyst ran a parallel consumer-acceptance panel in the R&D facility, using untrained panelists. They evaluated the overall acceptability of each of the plant runs, and acceptability of each attribute, again with a 100 point scale (to maintain commensurateness of scales). The consumers evaluated liking of the product overall and liking of taste and texture as well.

At the end of the run, the sensory analyst and quality control specialist had generated the following information: (1) Data on 14 product variations of the spicy bologna, (2) For each variation, attribute ratings from the 8 quality control panelists. (3) Acceptance ratings (overall and on attributes) from consumer panelists.

An analysis of the ratings showed relations between changes in each attribute (intensity), and overall ratings of product acceptability. (See Table 11.3).

The next job required specification of quality control limits. One can specify these limits in several different ways: (1) For each of the 8 sensory attributes considered singly, relate *overall acceptability* (by consumers) to variations in the sensory attribute level. Then, select the attribute level which generates what one might consider to represent a significant loss of acceptability, and use that attribute level as a quality control, cutoff limit. (2) For each attribute of the 8, relate its level (rated by the panelist in the quality control group) to *liking of that attribute*, rated by the consumer panel. Then, select the attribute level which generates what one would consider a significant loss of acceptability on that attribute. Use a region around that attribute level (viz., those attribute levels; upper and lower) as the quality control, cutoff limits.

The R&D sensory analyst chose the first option—to relate attribute level to overall acceptability, recognizing that one needed to first specify the consumer's overall reaction, and then ascertain how each sensory attribute (rated by experts) relates to the consumer's overall acceptance.

In order to develop the appropriate quality control limits, and determine what change in acceptability constituted a significant change, consider the data in Table 11.3, which presents the results of the evaluations. Using the rating assigned to each product as a single observation, the quality control specialist calculated the equations relating consumer liking to each sensory characteristic rated by the experts.

The quality control specialist suggested that they reject a batch which fell below a cutoff point. They could choose upper and lower target levels, (i.e., a point on the sensory attribute scale) corresponding to a significant change in acceptability versus the current product.

TABLE 11.3
EXAMPLE OF RATINGS OF SPICED BOLOGNA PRODUCT ATTRIBUTES
BY EXPERT QUALITY CONTROL PANEL AND CONSUMER RATED
"LIKING" FOR 14 TEST BATCHES

	Expert Panel Rating				Consumer Liking		
	(1)	(2)	(3)	(4) Mouth	(1)	(2)	(3)
Batch	Spotty	Fatty	Flavor	Coating	Total	Taste	Texture
1	36.3	32.0	39.1	21.6	31.0	32.0	49.1
2	41.2	38.5	47.2	21.4	20.0	20.1	69.8
3	34.5	44.2	30.3	28.4	18.6	10.3	10.5
4	38.9	29.6	43.6	16.2	52.0	47.3	72.1
5	28.4	42.3	38.5	19.5	47.4	46.9	61.7
6	42.3	33.1	43.2	29.3	48.6	45.8	45.2
7	40.6	31.7	43.1	22.4	57.5	57.3	52.8
8	33.1	31.3	42.0	31.3	63.1	65.1	80.6
9	38.2	41.3	40.6	21.6	66.4	65.8	60.9
10	34.1	35.6	34.7	12.8	27.8	25.3	43.5
11	36.5	33.8	41.8	18.4	60.9	54.1	73.3
12	37.5	37.2	39.7	18.6	31.2	28.9	56.8
13	32.6	38.4	39.3	12.3	45.6	35.2	48.3
14	30.2	40.1	45.4	23.7	26.0	30.1	59.6
Average Standard Error	6	6	6	8	10	12	12

100 point scale

Table 11.4 presents quality control limits as deviations from a target profile.

TABLE 11.4
QUALITY CONTROL CHART
Limits on Attributes to Remain Within Limits of Acceptance:
Target Profile Approach

Attribute	Current (Control)	1.25 × Standard[1] Error (S.E.)	Current ± 1.25 S.E. Low	High
1. Spotty	38.2	1.25 × 6 = 7.5	30.7	45.7
2. Fatty	41.3	1.25 × 6 = 7.5	33.8	48.8
3. Flavor	40.6	1.25 × 6 = 7.5	33.1	48.1
4. Mouth Coating	21.6	1.25 × 8 = 10	11.6	31.6

[1] 90% significance

An Overview of This Phase in Quality Control

The Allen Meat Company had to develop its own standards for grading quality. It had to develop its quality grading and control procedures in several steps, insuring that each step would generate practical information. The steps included: (1) Attribute selection. (2) Scale selection. (3) Development of Quality-Control limits. (4) Setting up a procedure which showed when a product exceeded limits using the internal, quality control panel. When a company can avail itself of a single standard of identity, the quality control specialist may not need to go through the full exercise of developing a descriptive language. One can compare the products to the gold standard in order to find out whether or not the two differ from one another, and if so how, and then use that information, along with measures of changes in consumer acceptance.

On the other hand, without having constructed the attribute scales, and correlated attribute levels with consumer acceptance the Allen Meat Company would not have known how changes of each sensory attribute correlate with changes in consumer acceptance. Sensory changes, such as darkness of meat, for example, may or may not generate dramatic changes in acceptability. How can the quality control panel priorize the sensory characteristics, without first correlating them with actual consumer ratings of acceptability? The quality control panel may arbitrarily select certain attributes as important, but they must subject these results to the acid test of consumer acceptance, in order to rank sensory characteristics from most critical to least important.

A Follow-up—Using the Method to Evaluate Quality Losses

Recall that the Allen Meat Company underwent a period of expansion in their marketing. Having developed the method for evaluating one particular product (spicy bologna), let us follow the panel through these steps: (1) Evaluating the product as it comes out of the factory. (2) Profiling the product as it ages, during storage. (3) Profiling the product after transportation and storage on the warehouse shelves. (4) Profiling the product after storage in the manufacturer's shelves.

Table 11.5 presents 6 different profiles of Allen's spicy bologna, taken from different plant runs, and other profiles for storage, etc. Although the product emerges with reasonable quality control (viz., the product's characteristics remain within quality control limits, as determined by panel), we can see that the distribution and storage process, either at wholesale or at retail does affect some of the product's sensory characteristics. It does throw up some warning signs indicating possible loss of consumer rated acceptability. Note specifically that the transportation and storage modify acceptability modestly, by changing sensory and acceptance characteristics. On the other hand, storage on the store shelves can deteriorate the product, often severely.

STORAGE STABILITY EVALUATIONS

Let us consider another case, this time in the candy industry. The Moss Candy Company has manufactured a wafer-thin chocolate candy for the past 35 years. During this time, it has changed warehousers, distributors, etc. Recently, consumer complaints indicated that from time to time the wafer candy possessed an off taste. The Moss Candy Company had developed a rigorous internal quality control program for screening batch lots as they came out of production, and as they went into storage. However, it seemed that in various store

TABLE 11.5
PROFILE OF THE SPICY BOLOGNA
ON THE 100 POINT QUALITY SCALE

	After Initial Run	After 2 Weeks Storage	After Shipment to Ware-house 1	After Shipment to Ware-house 2	2 Months on the Shelf 1	3 Months in the Store
1. Spotty	33.2	39.2	47.4	38.6	50.1	56.3
2. Glistening	42.7	19.8	18.8	27.6	32.4	39.3
3. Fatty	39.3	35.1	33.3	39.8	40.1	45.2
4. Herblike	32.6	30.1	28.2	34.3	26.1	22.6
5. Flavor Intensity	47.4	50.5	56.3	54.1	58.9	61.4
6. Spiciness	41.3	49.3	51.2	48.7	50.9	46.4
7. Mouth Coating	23.7	36.6	41.4	46.5	50.1	56.3
8. Hardness	20.6	28.3	26.1	30.5	38.6	41.5

locations quality control had slipped. The product appeared to remain on the shelves too long.

The problem of declining storage stability plagues most foods. As a food ages, the chemicals and constituents interact with each other, and with the oxygen in the package and atmosphere. This modifies appearance, texture and flavor, even though the product remains hidden on the shelf. Perhaps the product never undergoes dramatic changes in temperature, or storage conditions. Nonetheless, continued exposure to oxygen resulting in chemical interaction develops new chemicals inside the package which generate modified flavor, and change acceptance.

In order to measure how product quality changes with storage time, the Moss Candy Company decided to run a test with products of different ages, recognizing that these products represent different batches from product lines, ages from 1 week to 6 months.

The marketing manager and quality control specialist at the Moss Candy Company authorized field representatives in various parts of the country to purchase products from the shelves, making sure to purchase an equal number of products from the front (or the facing), closest to the consumer, from the middle and from the back. With this sampling procedure, they could feel sure of having selected a variety of products. From the code dating on the products the manufacturer knew which plant had produced the product, and the age of the candies.

In order to develop a measure of 'quality' the quality control manager for the Moss Candy Company suggested an evaluation of consumer's overall acceptability, using the internal panel of consumers at the company. At the insistence of the sensory analyst, the test comprised ratings both of acceptability and of specific sensory characteristics of each candy, including flavor, appearance and texture characteristics. The product tester reasoned (quite correctly), that the storage period would modify the sensory characteristics of the candy. Some panelists might feel that the change would not impact on product acceptability, whereas others, perhaps from the outside consumer population, might feel that in fact the storage period and the change in product characteristics would severely impact overall acceptance. In order to insure that the data would reveal changes in product quality, the product tester suggested that panelists rate each sample on a complete profile of attributes.

Table 11.6 shows the results of the project. It reveals that as the product ages, a number of perceptual characteristics change, at first slightly, but then more noticeably as the product remains on the shelf for more than 3 months (12 weeks). Furthermore, some but not all of these sensory changes parallel the changes in product acceptability.

The product tester obtained this information by the following, reasonably simple, and straightforward method: (1) Recruitment of an internal consumer panel, inexperienced in product evaluation. (2) Orientation in magnitude estimation scaling (although the panelists could have used category scaling as well). (3) Evaluation of the candy

TABLE 11.6
RESULTS FROM TESTING THE MOSS CANDY WAFER AFTER
DIFFERENT STORAGE PERIODS

	1 Day	1 Week	2 Weeks	4 Weeks	8 Weeks	12 Weeks	16 Weeks
Liking	87.3	84.1	86.1	75.2	69.1	56.4	51.3
Texture							
Liking	89.6	80.4	73.2	65.9	62.6	48.4	47.9
Hardness	60.3	64.1	66.7	75.4	81.6	80.7	83.7
Crispness	43.3	46.8	45.5	50.9	46.2	40.8	39.7
Flavor							
Liking	88.1	84.3	85.4	77.9	73.4	69.1	65.2
Sweetness	91.3	88.6	96.4	84.6	75.3	79.4	81.5
Chocolate	75.6	70.3	68.9	69.5	65.2	68.3	63.8
Appearance							
Brownness	47.3	49.2	46.4	40.1	37.2	38.5	36.3
Off Color	11.9	12.5	11.8	18.4	21.3	31.9	32.4
Liking	85.2	81.3	78.2	70.4	61.3	64.2	60.7

products, at different storage times, but during the same session.

In this particular study, the Moss Candy Company fortunately had at its disposal the field services to pick up products from around the U.S., to insure that it could test different plant batches, prepared on different dates. The research design permitted a clear understanding of how storage period influences acceptance. Using this data, the quality control specialists developed a formula or equation which related changes in overall acceptability to time in storage, and used that equation to predict the particular storage time when overall acceptability diminished to specified levels or criterion cutoff points. Furthermore, by following the same logic, this time using sensory characteristics as the dependent variable the quality control specialist related to sensory intensity versus time in storage.

ANOTHER CANDY PROBLEM

Let us now turn to another problem with the Moss Candy Company, this time involving quality control but with a slight variation. A year later, the Moss Candy Company wished to do a similar project, to measure storage stability for a new product, Granola Twist, which they had just launched in August. In this instance, however, the field service could not easily collect samples manufactured at different times, since the Moss Candy Company had just begun manufacturing the product two months previously. Now (October), the quality control manager decided to institute the testing program for the new, Granola Twist candies.

In order to develop the proper quality control system when the panelists do not have all of the products in front of them, the product tester and the quality control manager decided that panelists should evaluate the products singly or "monadically". As each batch aged, the panelist would select a sample from the aging batch, taste it, and rate it on characteristics and on overall acceptability.

The immediate problem becomes one of developing a panel which could rate the products singly (or monadically)., In order to do so, the panelists had to: (1) Possess a constant frame of reference over time to equate ratings assigned on different testing periods. (2) Use a common scale on each testing occasion.

To develop such a panel for single product evaluations using consumers, rather than experts, requires sampling the reactions from many different consumers at each aging period. One can accomplish this quality control task readily if one uses 30 or so panelists on each testing occasion, with different panelists on each testing occasion, in order to fully randomize the experiment. One must insure that each batch of panelists has the identical instructions, to make their frames of reference comparable.

Table 11.7 shows the results. Note that the attribute and acceptance ratings seem more 'jagged' and less smooth (versus time) than the previous study on the chocolate candy. When panelists do not have the full range of products in front of them, they have a sparser reference frame against which to rate the test products. Trained panelists with ingrained good and reproducible frames of reference products tend to generate less variable data. The trained panelists, possessing as they do continuity from one evaluation to another, can more readily rate the products against their frame of reference. On the other hand, these trained panelists, do not represent the ultimate consumer. Their reaction about product quality and storage stability could mislead management at the Moss Candy Company. Products which the expert quality control panel rejects as different and unstable in storage might taste perfectly acceptable to the consumer of Granola Twist.

Product testers and quality control specialists often face the problem of shifting product quality over time. All too often they cannot

TABLE 11.7

RESULTS FROM MONADIC STUDY OF AGING VERSUS
PRODUCT CHARACTERISTICS OF GRANOLA TWIST

	Time After Production					
	1 Week	2 Weeks	4 Weeks	8 Weeks	12 Weeks	16 Weeks
Liking	92.4	87.4	79.6	85.7	80.3	65.4
Hardness	53.4	59.7	65.6	58.4	69.4	74.4
Sweetness	63.8	64.3	60.6	59.7	61.5	66.3
Flavor Strength	80.2	83.3	79.1	65.4	60.9	64.2

develop a single array of products representing the full spectrum of aging. Once they make the product they must let it age, and sample from that aging batch in a systematic manner, at certain intervals. They cannot set up different products to age at different starting points, in order to cull a set of products which panelists can evaluate in one session. Thus, panelists must rely upon memory and instruction to maintain a specific, constant frame of reference. Such test situations demand a trained expert panel or an indoctrinated consumer panel for efficient evaluation services for those working within a limited monetary budget. However, the marketer and R&D manager must insure that the ongoing expert panel continues to represent consumer reactions, or at the very least that there exists a way of predicting consumer responses from expert panel responses.

SAME-DIFFERENT PANELS AND QUALITY CONTROL

Perhaps the simplest panel to run quality control studies, the difference panel comprises a group of individuals with the job of comparing two products which may differ in some respects. If these so-called sensitized individuals do not pick up the differences, the manufacturer assumes the consumer will not perceive the differences either. Difference panels provide a deceptively simple way to evaluate quality. Most manufacturers strive to develop a product which seems perceptually unchanged as it ages. Consequently, the difference panel which says different (as an "all-or-none" response) has performed its task perfectly. The panel simply registers the existence of a difference, or the lack of a difference. The panelist does not scale perceptions. The manufacturer does not know whether the difference impacts at all on sensory characteristics, or if it does impact, then in what sensory characteristic, and by how much. The manufacturer simply knows that a statistically significant number of the panelists stated that two products seemed different. Chapter 4 provides methods for evaluating differences which a quality control specialist can use in evaluating products.

RISKS AND BENEFITS IN SENSORY QUALITY CONTROL

Using panelists to perform quality control functions exemplifies a rational way to control product quality. One need not worry about using instrumental measures to assess the physical characteristics of products, and then worry whether or not consumers would react in the same way. It could well turn out that specific characteristics which physically seem only slightly different, actually correlate with a major shift in the sensory characteristics of the product. Other, larger shifts in the physical constitution of the product might, in fact, generate subjectively smaller shifts, or no noticeable shift at all.

The discrimination test puts quality control into an all-or-none mode. One may discard an expensive batch of products or ingredients simply because the panelist correctly discriminates that product from a control sample. Yet, the product difference may not impact on acceptance, or may even enhance acceptance. Using discrimination testing alone without scaling as the quality control procedure generates the risk that such all-or-none responses could lead to costly, unnecessary product destruction.

With product profiling as an adjunct to discrimination testing the quality control specialist and the product tester can quantify the changes which occur over time, or changes due to different suppliers of materials. The method of profiling allows for consumer reactions of liking in tandem with consumers ratings of attributes. By such an approach, the manufacturer will learn: (1) Whether panelists perceive two products as same or different. (2) What sensory characteristics cause the difference. (3) How these changes relate to storage time. (4) How these changes impact on product acceptability.

AN OVERVIEW TO QUALITY CONTROL

Sensory quality control represents a growing area in product testing. Through the proper use of product measurement, the marketer can determine the effects of storage on consumers acceptability, and perhaps find out the most efficient point to pull products off the shelves. Sometimes, good quality control information can illustrate the reason for either a sudden or a gradually developing consumer rejection. The R&D product developer can use quality control procedures to assess the impact of different supplier ingredients and different formulations over time. Finally, the business manager and marketer can ascertain how changes in ingredient supplier, transportation, storage and instore placements modify product quality, and thus change acceptance.

REFERENCES

American Society for Testing and Materials. Manual of Sensory Testing Methods, ASTM Special Technical Publication, No. 434, Philadelphia, 1968.

American Society for Testing and Materials. Correlations of Subjective-Objective Methods in the Study of Odor and Taste. ASTM Special Technical Publication No. 451, Philadelphia, 1968.

American Society for Testing and Materials. DS48. Compilation of Odor and Taste Thresholds, Philadelphia, 1973.

AMERINE, M. A., PANGBORN, R. M. and ROESSLER, E. B. Principles of Sensory Evaluation of Food, Academic Press, New York, 1965.

AMOORE, J. The Stereochemical Specification of Human Olfactory Receptors. Perfumery and Essential Oil Review, 1952, 43, 321-323, 330.

AMOORE, J. A Plan to Identify Most of the Primary Odors. In: Olfaction and Taste III, (C. Pfaffmann ed.) New York, Rockefeller University Press, 1969, 158-169.

AMOORE, J. E., VENSTROM, D. and DAVIS, A. R. Measurement of Specific Anosmia. Perceptual and Motor Skills, 1968, Monograph Supplement, 2-V26.

ARABIE, P. and MOSKOWITZ, H. R., The Effects of Viscosity Upon Perceived Sweetness. Perception and Psychophysics, 1971, 9, 410-412.

BALINTFY, J. L., DUFFY, W. J. and SINHA, P. Modeling Food Preferences Over Time. Operations Research, 1974, 22, 711-727.

BALINTFY, J. L., SINHA, P., MOSKOWITZ, H. R. and ROGOZENSKI, J. G., Jr. The Time Dependence of Food Preferences. Food Product Development. November, 1975.

BARTOSHUK, L.M. Taste of Saccharin: Related to the Genetic Ability to Taste the Bitter Substance Propylthiouracil (Prop). Science, 1979, 205, 934-935.

BARTOSHUK, L.M. Taste Mixtures: Is Mixture Suppression Related to Compression? Physiology and Behavior, 1975, 14, 310-325.

BARTOSHUK, L. M., DATEO, G. P., VANDENBELT, D. J., BUTTRICK, R. L. and LONG, L. Effect of *Gymnema Sylvestre* and *Synsepsalum Dulcificum* on Taste in Man. In: Olfaction and Taste *III*. (C. Pfaffmann, ed.) Rockefeller University Press, New York, 1969, 436-444.

BARTOSHUK, L. M., GENTILE, R., MOSKOWITZ, H. R. and MEISELMAN, H. L. Sweet Taste Induced by Miracle Fruit. Physiology and Behavior, 1974, 12, 449-456.

BASKER, D., Polygonal and Polyhedral Taste Testing, Journal of Food Quality, 1980, 3, 1-10.

BATEN, W. D. Organoleptic Tests Pertaining to Apples and Pears. Food Research, 1946, 11, 84-85.

BEDNARCYZK, A. A. and KRAMER, A. Identification and Evaluation of the Flavor Significant Components of Ginger Essential Oil. Chemical Senses and Flavor, 1975, 1, 377-386.

BEEBE-CENTER, J. G. Standards for Use of the Gust Scale. Journal of Psychology, 1949, 28, 411-419.

BEEBE-CENTER, J. G. The Psychology of Pleasantness and Unpleasantness, Van Nostrand Reinhold, New York, 1932.

BEEBE-CENTER, J. G., ROGERS, M. S. and ATKINSON, W. Intensive Equivalences for Sucrose and NaCl Solutions. Journal of Psychology, 1955, 39, 371-372.

BEEBE-CENTER, J. G., ROGERS, M. S., ATKINSON, W. H. and O'CONNELL, D. N. Sweetness and Saltiness of Compound Solutions of Sucrose and NaCl as a Function of the Concentration of Solutes. Journal of Experimental Psychology, 1959, 57, 231-234.

BERG, H., FILIPELLO, F., HINREINER, E. and WEBB, A. D. Evaluation of Thresholds and Minimum Difference Concentrations for Various Constituents of Wines. I. Water Solutions, Food Technology, 1955, 9, 23-26. II. Sweetness: The Effect of Ethyl Alcohol, Organic Acids and Tannin. Food Technology, 1955, 9, 138-140.

BERGLUND, U. Dynamic Properties of the Olfactory System. Annals of the New York Academy of Sciences, 1974, 237, 17-27.

BERGLUND, B., BERGLUND, U. and LINDVALL, T. On the Principle of Odor Interaction. Acta Psychologica, 1973, 35, 255-268.

BERGLUND, B., BERGLUND, U., EKMAN, G. and ENGEN, T. Individual Psychophysical Functions for 28 Odorants. Perception and Psychophysics, 1971, 9, 379-384.

BERGLUND, B., BERGLUND, U., ENGEN, T. and EKMAN, G. Multidimensional Analysis of Twenty-One Odors. Scandinavian Journal of Psychology, 1973, 14, 131-137.

BLAKESLEE, A. F. and SALMON, T. N. Genetics of Sensory Thresholds: Individual Taste Reactions for Different Substances. Proceedings of the National Academy of Sciences, 1935, 21, 84-90.

BOND, B. and STEVENS, S. S. Cross Modality Matches of Brightness to Loudness by 5 Year Olds. Perception and Psychophysics, 1969, 6, 337-339.

BORING, E. S., LANGFELD, H. S. and WELD, H. P. Psychology: A Factual Textbook. John Wiley & Sons, New York, 1935.

BOX, G. E. P. and HUNTER, J. S. Multi Factor Experimental Designs for Exploring Response Surfaces. Annals of Mathematical Statistics, 1957, 28, 195-241.

CAIN, W. S. Odor Intensity: Differences in the Exponent of the Psychophysical Function. Perception and Psychophysics, 1969, 6, 349-354.

CAIN, W. S. Odor Intensity: Mixtures and Masking. Chemical Senses and Flavor, 1975, 3, 339-352.

CAIN, W. S. Olfaction and the Common Chemical Sense: Similarities, Differences and Interactions. In: Odor Quality and Chemical Structure. (H. R. Moskowitz and C. Warren, eds.). American Chemical Society, 1981, 109-122, Washington, D.C.

CAIN, W. S. and DREXLER, M. Scope and Evaluation of Odor Counteraction and Masking. Annals of the New York Academy of Sciences, 1974, 237, 427-439.

CAIRNCROSS, S. E. and SJOSTROM, L. B. Flavor Profiles—A New Approach to Flavor Problems. Food Technology, 1950, 4, 308-311.

CAMERON, A. T. The Taste Sense and the Relative Sweetness of Sugars and Other Sweet Substances. Report 9, Sugar Research Foundation, NY 1947.

CAUL, J. F. The Profile Method of Flavor Analysis. Advances in Food Research, 1957, 1-40.

CHAMBERLAIN, A. F. Primitive Taste Words. American Journal of Psychology, 1903, 14, 146-153.

CHAPPELL, G. M. Flavour Assessment of Sugar Solutions. Journal of the Science of Food and Agriculture, 1953, 4, 346-350.

COHN, G. Die Organischen Geschmackstoffe. Berlin, Siemroth, 1914.

COLLINGS, V. B. Human Taste Responses as a Function of Locus on the Tongue and the Soft Palate. Perception and Psychophysics, 1976, 19, 69-71.

CORIN, J. Action des Acides sur le Gout. Bulletin de l' Academie Royale de Belgique: Classe de Sciences. 1887, 14, 616-637.

CROCKER, E. C. and HENDERSON, L. F. Analysis and Classification of Odors. American Perfumer and Essential Oil Review, 1927, 22, 3-11.

CUSSLER, E., KOKINI, J. L., WEINHEIMER, R. L. and MOSKOWITZ, H. R. Food Texture in the Mouth. Food Technology, 1979 (October) 33 (10), 89-92.

DAVSON, H. (ed). The Eye. Academic Press, New York 1966.

DAY, R. S. Measuring Preferences. In: Handbook of Marketing Research (R. Ferber, ed.). McGraw Hill, New York, 1974, (3-101)-(3-106).

DE MAN, J., VOISEY, P. W., RASPAR, V. F. and STANLEY, D. W. (eds.). Rheology and Food Texture. AVI., Westport, 1976.

DESOR, J. and BEAUCHAMP, G. The Human Capacity to Transmit Olfactory Information. Perception and Psychophysics, 1974, 16, 551-556.

DRAKE, B. Food Crushing Sounds, An Introductory Study. Journal of Food Science, 1963, 28, 233-241.

DRAKE, B. and JOHANNSEN, B. Sensory Evaluation of Food. 1969, 2 volumes. Swedish Institute of Food Preservation Research, Gothenburg, Sweden.

DRAVNIEKS, Personal Communication, 1974.

DUBOSE, C. N., MEISELMAN, H. L., HUNT, D. A. and WATERMAN, D. Incomplete Taste Adaptation to Different Concentration of Salt and Sugar Solution. Perception and Psychophysics, 1977, 21, 183-186.

EINSTEIN, M. A. and HORNSTEIN, I. Food Preferences of College Students. Nutritional Implication. Journal of Food Science, 1970, 35, 429-437.

EKMAN, G. and AKESSON. Saltiness, Sweetness and Preference. A Study of Quantitative Relations in Individual Subjects. Report 177, Psychology Laboratories, University of Stockholm, 1964.

ENGEL, R. Experimentelle Untersuchungen Uber die Abhangigheit der Lust und Unlust Von der Reizstarke beim Geschmacksinn. Pfluegers Archiv fur die Gesamte Physiologie. 1928, 64, 1-36.

ENGEN, T. Psychophysical Scaling of Odor Intensity and Quality. Annals of the New York Academy of Sciences, 1964, 116, 504-516.

ENGEN, T., Effect of Practice and Instruction on Olfactory Thresholds Perceptual and Motor Skills, 1960, 10,195.

ENGEN, T. Method and Theory in the Study of Odor Preference. In: Human Responses to Environmental Odors (A. Turk, J. W. Johnston, Jr., D. G. Moulton, eds.). N.Y., Academic Press, 1974, 122-142.

ENGEN, T., KUISMA, J. E. and EIMAS, P. D. Short Term Memory of Odors. Journal of Experimental Psychology, 1973, 99, 222-225.

ENGEN, T. and LEVY, N. The Influence of Standards in Constant Sum Methods. Perceptual and Motor Skills, 1955, 5, 193-197.

ENGEN, T. and McBURNEY, D. H. Magnitude and Category Scales of the Pleasantness of Odors. Journal of Experimental Psychology, 1964, 68, 435-440.

ERICKSON, R. P., DOETSCH, G. S., and MARSHALL, D. A. The Gustatory Neural Response Functions. Journal of General Physiology, 1965, 49, 247-253.

FECHNER, G. T. Elemente der Psychophysik. Leipzig, Breitkopf und Hartel, 1860.

FICK, A. Anatomie des Geschmacksorganes. In: Lehrbuch der Anatomie und Physiologie der Sinnesorgane. M. Schaunberg and Co., Lahr. 1864.

FINNEY, E. E. Mechanical Resonance Within Red Delicious Apples, and its Relation to Fruit Texture. Transactions of the American Society of Agricultural Engineers, 1970, 13, 177-180.

Food and Container Institute. Symposium on Monosodium Glutamate. Chicago, Illinois 1948.

FRANK, M. The Classification of Mammalian Taste Fibers. Chemical Senses and Flavor, 1974, 1, 53-62.

FRIEDMAN, H. H., WHITNEY, J. E. and SZCZESNIAK, A. S. The Texturometer—A New Instrument for Objective Texture Measurement. Journal of Food Science, 1963, 28, 390-396.

FRIJTERS, J. E. R. The Paradox of Discriminatory Nondiscriminators Resolved, Chemical Senses and Flavor 1979, 4, 355-358.

GESCHEIDER, G. A. Psychophysics: Method and Theory. Lawrence Erlbaum Associates, New Jersey 1976.

GRAHAM, C. (ed.) Vision and Visual Perception, N.Y., John Wiley, 1965.

GRIDGEMAN, N. T. Sensory Item Sorting. Biometrics, 1959, 15, 298-306.

GUGGENHEIM B. (ed.) Health and Sugar Substitutes. S. Karger, Basel, 1979.

GUILFORD, J. P. Psychometric Methods. McGraw-Hill, N.Y., 1954.

HAHN, D. Die Adaptation des Geschmackssinnes. Zeitschrift für Sinnesphysiologie, 1934, 65, 104-145.

HALPERN, B. P., and MEISELMAN, H. L. A New Model for Taste Psychophysics: The Role of Pulsatile Stimulation. Proceedings of the Sixth International Congress on Olfaction and Taste, Information Retrieval Ltd., London, 1977, 483.

HANIG, D. P. Zür Psychophysik des Geschmackssinnes. Philosophische Studien (Wundt) 1901, 17, 576-623.

HARMAN, H. H. Modern Factor Analysis. University of Chicago Press, Chicago, Illinois 1966.

HARPER, R., BATE-SMITH, E. C., and LAND, D. G. Odour Description and Odour Classification. American Elsevier, New York 1968.

HARPER, R., LAND, D. G., BATE-SMITH, E. C., and GRIFFITHS, N. M. Odour Qualities: A Glossary of Usage. British Journal of Psychology 1968, 59, 231-252.

HARPER, R., and STEVENS, S. S. Subjective Hardness of Compliant Materials. Quarterly Journal of Experimental Psychology, 1964, 16, 204-215.

HOROWITZ, R. M. and GENTILI, B. Dihydrochalcone Sweeteners. In: Symposium: Sweeteners, (G. Inglett, ed.). Avi Publishing Company, Westport, Conn., 1974, 182-193.

HSÜ, E. H. A Factorial Analysis of Olfaction. Psychometrika, 1946, 22, 31-42.

HUTCHINGS, J. B. The Importance of Visual Appearance of Foods to the Food Processor and the Consumer. In: Sensory Properties of Foods (G. G. Birch, J. G. Brennan and K. J. Parker, eds.) Applied Science Publishers. London, 1977, 45-56.

IKEDA, K. On the Taste of the Salt of Glutamic Acid. 8th International Congress of Applied Chemistry, 1912, 18, 147.

INDOW, T. and STEVENS, S. S. Scaling of Saturation and Hue. Perception and Psychophysics, 1966, 1, 253-272.

JONES, B. P., BUTTERS, N., MOSKOWITZ, H. R. and MONTGOMERY, K. Olfactory and Gustatory Capacities of Alcoholic and Korsakoff Patients. Neuropsychologia, 1978, 16, 323-337.

JONES, F. N. Scales of Subjective Intensity for Odors of Diverse Chemical Nature. American Journal of Psychology. 1958, 71, 305-310, 423-425.

JONES, F. N. Information Content of Olfactory Quality. In:Theories of Odor and Odor Measurement, (N. Tanyolac, ed.). Robert College, Istanbul, 1968, 133-146.

KANIG, J. L. Mental Impact of Colors in Foods Studied. Food Field Reporter, 1955, 23, 57.

KARE, M. R. and HALPERN, B. R. (eds.). Physiological and Behavioral Aspects of Taste. University of Chicago Press, Chicago, Illinois 1961.

KARE, M. R. and MALLER, O. (eds.) The Chemical Senses and Nutrition. Baltimore, The Johns Hopkins Press, 1967.

KARE, M. R. and MALLER, O. (eds.) The Chemical Senses and Nutrition. New York, Academic Press, 1977.

KATZ, D. The World of Colour, London, Kegan Paul, 1935.

KATZ, H. S. and TALBOT, E. J. Intensities of Odors and Irritating Effects of Warning Agents for Inflammable and Poisonous Gases. Technical Paper 480, Bureau of Mines, U.S. Dept. of Commerce, 1930.

KELLY, A. T. The Psychology of Personal Constructs. New York, W. W. Norton, 1955.

KENNEDY, L. M. and HALPERN, B. P. A Biphasic Model for the Action of the Gymnemic Acids and Ziziphins on Taste Receptor Cell Membranes. Chemical Senses, 1980, 5, 149-158.

KRAMER, A. General Guidelines for Selecting Objective Tests and Multiple Regression Application. In: Correlating Sensory and Objective Measures. (J. Powers and H. Moskowitz, eds.). American Society for Testing and Materials, 1976, STP 594, Philadelphia, Pennsylvania, 48-55.

LAFFORT, P. Data on the Physiochemical Determinants of the Relative Effectiveness of Odorants. In: Theory of Odor and Odor Measurements (N. Tanyolac, ed.) Robert College, Istanbul, 1968, 247-270.

LANE, H., CATANIA, A. C. and STEVENS, S. S. Voice Level: Autophonic Scale, Perceived Loudness and Effects of Side Tone. Journal of the Acoustical Society of America, 1961, 33, 160-167.

LARSON-POWERS, N. and PANGBORN, R. M. Paired Comparison and Time Intensity Measurements of the Sensory Properties of Beverages and Gelatins Containing Sucrose and Synthetic Sweeteners. Journal of Food Science, 1978, 43, 47-51.

LAWLESS, H. and CAIN, W. S. Recognition Memory for Odors. Chemical Senses and Flavor, 1975, 1, 331-337.

LAWLESS, H. and SKINNER, E. Z. The Duration and Perceived Intensity of Sucrose Taste. Perception and Psychophysics, 1979, 25, 180-184.

LEMBERGER, F. Psychophysiche Untersuchungen uber den Geschmack Von Zucker und Saccharin. Pflueger's Archive für die Gesamte Physiologie, 1908, 123, 293-311.

LITTLE, A. D. Flavour Research and Food Acceptance. Reinhold Publishing Corporation, New York, 1958.

LOCKHART, E. and GAINER, J. M. Effect of Monosodium Glutamate on the Taste of Pure Sucrose and Sodium Chloride. Food Research, 1950, 15, 459-464.

LUCE, R. D. On the Possible Psychophysical Laws. Psychological Review, 1959, 66, 81-95.

MACKEY, A. O. Discernment of Taste Substances as Affected by Solvent Medium. Food Research, 1958, 23, 580-583.

MACKEY, A. O. and VALASSI, K. The Discernment of Primary Tastes in the Presence of Different Food Textures. Food Technology, 1956, 10, 238-240.

MAGIDSON, D. J. and GORABACHOW, S. W. Zür Frage der Sussigkeit des Saccharins: Das O-Benzoylsulfimid und seine Elektrolytische Dissoziation. Chemische Berichte, 1923, 26B, 1810-1817.

MARKS, L. E. Stimulus Range, Number of Categories, and the Form of the Category Scale. American Journal of Psychology, 1968, 81, 467-479.

MARKS, L. E. Sensory Processes: The New Psychophysics. Academic Press, New York, 1974.

McAULIFFE, W. K. and MEISELMAN, H. L. The Roles of Practice and Correction in the Categorization of Sour and Bitter Taste Qualities. Perception and Psychophysics, 1974, 16, 242-244.

McBURNEY, D. H. and LUCAS, J. A. Gustatory Cross Adaptation Between Salts. Psychonomic Science. 1966, 4, 301-302.

McBURNEY, D. H. A. Psychophysical Study of Gustatory Adaptation. Dissertation Abstracts, 1965, 48, 1145-1146.

McCREDY, J. M., SONNEMANN, J. C. and LEHMANN, S. J. Sensory Profiling of Beer by a Modified QDA Method. Food Technology, 1974, 28, 36-46.

McDANIEL, M. R. Ph.D. Dissertation. The University of Massachusetts, Amherst, 1974.

McDANIEL, M. R., SAWYER, F. M. Preference Testing of Whiskey Sour Formulations: Magnitude Estimation versus the 9-point Hedonic. Journal of Food Science, 1981, 46, 182-186.

McGILL, W. J. The Slope of the Loudness Function: A Puzzle. In: Psychological Scaling: Theory and Application, (H. Gulliksen and S. Messick, eds.). New York, John Wiley & Sons, 1960, 67-81.

McNULTY, P. B. and MOSKOWITZ, H. R. Intensity-Time Curves for Flavored O/W Emulsions. Journal of Food Science, 1974, 39, 55-57.

MEISELMAN, H. L. Effect of Presentation Procedures on Taste Intensity Functions. Perception and Psychophysics, 1971, 10, 15-18.

MEISELMAN, H. L. Scales for Measuring Food Preference. In: Encyclopedia of Food Science (M. S. Petersen and A. H. Johnson, eds.). Avi, Westport, CT., 1978, 675-678.

MEISELMAN, H. L. and HALPERN, B. P. Enhancement of Taste Intensity Through Pulsatile Stimulation. Physiology and Behavior, 1973, 11, 713-716.

MEISELMAN, H. L., VAN HORNE, W., HASENZAHL, B. and WEHRLY, T. The 1971 Fort Lewis Food Preference Survey. U.S. Army Natick Laboratories, Technical Report, TR-93-PR.

MOIR, H. C. Some Observations on the Appreciation of Flavour in Foodstuffs. Chemistry and Industry, 1936, 55, 145-148.

MONCRIEFF, R. W. The Chemical Senses, 2nd Ed., Leonard Hill, London, 1966.

MONCRIEFF, R. W. Odour Preferences, Leonard Hill, London, 1966.

MOSKOWITZ, H. R. Scales of Intensity for Single and Compound Tastes. Ph.D. Dissertation, Harvard University, Cambridge, Massachusetts, 1968.

MOSKOWITZ, H. R., Sweetness and Intensity of Artificial Sweeteners. Perception and Psychophysics, 1970, 8, 40-42.

MOSKOWITZ, H. R. Intensity Scales for Pure Tastes and Taste Mixtures. Perception and Psychophysics, 1971, 9, 51-56.

MOSKOWITZ, H. R. The Sweetness and Pleasantness of Sugars. American Journal of Psychology, 1971, 84, 387-405.

MOSKOWITZ, H. R. Scales of Viscosity and Fluidity of Gum Solutions. Journal of Texture Studies, 1972, 3, 89-100.

MOSKOWITZ, H. R. Perceptual Changes in Taste Mixtures. Perception and Psychophysics, 1972, 11, 257-262.

MOSKOWITZ, H. R., Perceptual Attributes of the Taste of Sugars. Journal of Food Science, 1972, 37, 624-626.

MOSKOWITZ, H. R. Models of Sweetness Additivity. Journal of Experimental Psychology, 1973, 99, 89-98.

MOSKOWITZ, H. R. Models of Additivity for Sugar Sweetness. In: Sensation and Measurement—Papers in Honor of S. S. Stevens (H. R. Moskowitz, B. Scharf and J. C. Stevens, eds.), Reidel, Dordrecht, Holland, 1974, 195-228.

MOSKOWITZ, H. R. Magnitude Estimation: Notes on What, How, When and Why to Use It. Journal of Food Quality, 1977, 1, 195-228.

MOSKOWITZ, H. R. Sensory Measurement: The Rational Assessment of Private Sensory Experience. Master Brewer's Association of America, Technical Journal, 1977, 14, 111-119.

MOSKOWITZ, H. R. Sensory and Hedonic Functions for Chemosensory Stimuli. In: Chemical Senses and Nutrition (M. R. Kare and O. Maller, eds.). New York, Academic Press, 1977, 71-99.

MOSKOWITZ, H. R. Respondent and Response Types in Magnitude Estimation Scaling. Food Product Development, 1977, (May), 95-97.

MOSKOWITZ, H. R. Odor Psychophysics and Sensory Engineering. Chemical Senses and Flavor. 1979, 4, 163-184.

MOSKOWITZ, H. R. Mind, Body and Pleasure. An Analysis of Factors which Influence Sensory Hedonics. In: Preference Behavior and Chemoreception. (J. Kroeze, ed.). Information Retrieval Ltd., London, 1979, 131-148.

MOSKOWITZ, H. R. Changing the Carbohydrate Sweetness Sensation. Lebensmittel Wissenschaft und Technologie, 1981, 14, 47-51 (A).

MOSKOWITZ, H. R. Utilitarian Benefits of Magnitude Estimation Scaling for Testing Product Acceptability. Paper presented to ASTM Oct. 1980.

MOSKOWITZ, H. R. Relative Importance of Perceptual Factors to Consumer Acceptance: Linear versus Quadratic Analysis. Journal of Food Science, 1981, 46, 244-248 (C).

MOSKOWITZ, H. R. and ARABIE, P. Taste Intensity as a Function of Stimulus Concentration and Solvent Viscosity. Journal of Texture Studies, 1970, 1, 502-510.

MOSKOWITZ, H. R. and CHANDLER, J. W. Magnitude Estimation for Child Respondents, A Psychological Approach. Viewpoints, 1979, 29-35.

MOSKOWITZ, H. R., DRAVNIEKS, A., CAIN, W. and TURK, A. Standardized Procedure for Expressing Odor Intensity. Chemical Senses and Flavor, 1974, 1, 235-237.

MOSKOWITZ, H. R., DRAVNIEKS, A. and GERBERS, C. Odor Intensity and Pleasantness of Butanol. Journal of Experimental Psychology, 1974, 103, 216-223.

MOSKOWITZ, H. R., DRAVNIEKS, A. L. and KLARMAN, L. Odor Intensity and Pleasantness for a Diverse Set of Odorants. Perception and Psychophysics, 1976, 19, 122-128.

MOSKOWITZ, H. R., DUBOSE, C. N. and REUBEN, M. J. Flavor Chemical Mixtures: A Psychophysical Analysis, In: Flavor Quality, Objective Measurements (R. Scalan, ed.). American Chemical Society, Washington, D.C. 1977, 29-44.

MOSKOWITZ, H. R. and FISHKEN, D. What Effects Do Repeated Evaluations Play in Fragrance Perceptions. Perfumer and Flavorist, 1979 (May). 45-52.

MOSKOWITZ, H. R. and GERBERS, C. Dimensional Salience of Odors. Annals of the New York Academy of Sciences, 1974, 237, 3-16.

MOSKOWITZ, H. R., JACOBS, B. and FIRTLE, N. Discrimination Testing and Product Decisions. Journal of Marketing Research, 1980, 17, 84-90.

MOSKOWITZ, H. R., JACOBS, B. and FITCH, D. Distinguishing Actionable from Inactionable Attributes. Journal of Food Quality, 1980, 3, 47-60.

MOSKOWITZ, H. R. and KAPSALIS, J. G. Towards a General Theory of the Psychophysics of Food Texture, Proceedings of the Fourth International Congress of Food Science and Technology, Madrid, Spain, 1974.

MOSKOWITZ, H. R. and KAPSALIS, J. G. Psychophysical Relations in Texture. In: Rheology and Texture in Food Quality. (J. DeMan, P. W. Voisey, V. Rasper and D. W. Stanley, eds.) Avi Publishing, Westport, CT., 1976, 554-582.

MOSKOWITZ, H. R., KAPSALIS, J. G., CARDELLO, A., FISHKEN, D., MALLER, G. and SEGARS, R. Determining Relationships Among Objective, Expert and Consumer Measures of Texture. Food Technology, 1979, 84-88.

MOSKOWITZ, H. R. and KLARMAN, L. The Tastes of Artificial Sweeteners and Their Mixtures. Chemical Senses and Flavor, 1975(a), 1, 411-422.

MOSKOWITZ, H. R. and KLARMAN, L. The Hedonic Tones of Artificial Sweeteners and Their Mixtures. Chemical Senses and Flavor, 1975(b), 1, 423-429.

MOSKOWITZ, H. R., KLUTER, R. A., WESTERLING, J. and JACOBS, H. L. Sugar Sweetness and Pleasantness: Evidence for Different Psychological Laws. Science, 1974, 184, 583-585.

MOSKOWITZ, H. R., SHARMA, K. N., KUMARIAH, V., JACOBS, H. L. and SHARMA, S. D. Cross Cultural Differences in Simple Taste Preferences. Science, 1975, 190, 1217-1218.

MOSKOWITZ, H. R. and SIDEL, J. L. Magnitude and Hedonic Scales of Food Acceptability. Journal of Food Science, 1971, 36, 677-680.

MOSKOWITZ, H. R., STANLEY, D. W. and CHANDLER, J. W. The Eclipse Method: Optimizing Product Formulations Through a Consumer Generated Ideal Sensory Profile. Canadian Journal of Food Science and Technology, 1977, 3, 161-168.

MOSKOWITZ, H. R., WOLFE, K. and BECK, C. Sweetness and Acceptance Optimization in Cola-Flavored Beverages Using Combinations of Artificial Sweeteners. Journal of Food Quality, 1978, 2, 17-26.

MOULTON, D. The Interrelations of the Chemical Senses. In: The Chemical Senses and Nutrition (M. R. Kare and O. Maller, eds.), Baltimore, Johns Hopkins, 1967, 249-262.

MULLEN, K. and ENNIS, D. Rotatable Designs in Product Development. Food Technology, 1979, 33, 74.

MYERS, C. S. The Taste Names of Primitive Peoples. British Journal of Psychology, 1904, 64, 601-606.

New York Academy of Sciences, Recent Advances in Odor: Theory, Measurement and Control, New York, 1964, 116.

New York Academy of Sciences. Odor Evaluation, Utilization and Control, New York, 1974, 237.

O'MAHONY, M. Salt Taste Sensitivity: A Signal Detection Approach. Perception, 1972, 1, 459-464.

O'MAHONY, M. and ALBA, M. D. C. Taste Descriptions in Spanish and English. Chemical Senses and Flavor, 1980, 5, 47-62.

O'MAHONY, M. and THOMPSON, J. The Harvey's Bibliography of Taste, Bristol, 1975.

OSGOOD, C. E., SUCI, G. J. and TANNENBAUM, J. The Measurement of Meaning. University of Illinois Press, Urbana, 1957.

PANGBORN, R. M. Taste Interrelationships. Food Research, 1960, 25, 245-252.

PANGBORN, R. M. Taste Interrelationships II. Suprathreshold Solutions of Sucrose and Citric Acid. Journal of Food Science, 1961, 26, 648-655.

PANGBORN, R. M. Taste Interrelationships III. Suprathreshold Solutions of Sucrose and Sodium Chloride. Journal of Food Science, 1962, 27, 495-500.

PANGBORN, R. M., BERG, H. W. and HANSEN, B. The Influence of Color on Discrimination of Sweetness in Dry Table Wine. American Journal of Psychology, 1963, 76, 492-495.

PANGBORN, R. M. and SIMONE, M. Body Weight and Sweetness Preference. Journal of the American Dietetic Association, 1958, 34, 924-928.

PANGBORN, R. M. and TRABUE, I. Bibliography of the Sense of Taste. In: The Chemical Senses and Nutrition (M. R. Kare and O. Maller, eds.) Baltimore, The Johns Hopkins Press, 1967.

PAUL, T. Beziehung Zwischen Saurem Geschmack und Wasserstofionen Konzentration. Berichte der Deutsche Chemische Geselleschaft, 1916, 49, 2124-2137.

PERSSON, T. and VON SYDOW, E. A Quality Comparison of Frozen and Refrigerated Cooked Sliced Beef. Journal of Food Science, 1972, 37, 234-239.

PERYAM, D. R. and PILGRIM, F. J. Hedonic Scale Method of Measuring Food Preferences. Food Technology, 1957, 11, 9-14.

PFAFFMANN, C. M. The Sense of Taste. In: Handbook of Physiology Vol. 1 American Physiological Society, Washington, D.C. 1959, 507-534.

PFAFFMANN, C. M. Specificity of the Sweet Receptors of the Squirrel Monkey. Chemical Senses and Flavor, 1974, 1, 61-67.

POWERS, J. J. Experiences with Subjective/Objective Correlations. In: Correlating Sensory and Objective Measurements—New Methods for Answering Old Problems. (J. Powers and H. Moskowitz, eds.) American Society for Testing and Materials, STP 594, 1976, Philadelphia, 111-122.

RABINO, S. and MOSKOWITZ, H. R. Optimizing the Product Development Process: Strategical Implications for New Entrants. Sloan Management Review, 1980 (Spring), 45-51.

RADER, C. P. TIHANYI, A. S. and ZIENTY, F. B. A Study of the True Taste of Saccharin. Journal of Food Science, 1967, 32, 357-360.

RIFKEN, B. Unpublished Observations, 1979.

SCHIFFMANN, S. S. Contributions to the Physicochemical Dimensions of Odor: A Psychophysical Approach. Annals of the New York Academy of Sciences, 1974, 137, 164-183.

SCHLEPPNIK, A. A. Structure Recognization as a Peripheral Process in Odor Quality Coding. Symposium of Odor Quality and Chemical Structure, (H. R. Moskowitz and C. Warren, eds.). American Chemical Society, Washington, D.C. 1981, 161-175.

SCHUTZ, H. G. A Matching Standards Method for Characterizing Odor Quality. Annals of the New York Academy of Sciences, 1964, 116, 517-526.

SCHUTZ, H. G. A Food Action Rating Scale for Measuring Food Acceptance. Journal of Food Science, 1965, 30, 365-374.

SCHUTZ, H. G., and PILGRIM, F. J. Sweetness of Various Compounds and its Measurement. Food Research, 1957, 22, 206-213.

SHAMA, F. and SHERMAN, P. Identification of Stimuli Controlling the Sensory Evaluation of Viscosity: Oral Methods. Journal of Texture Studies, 1973, 4, 111-118.

SHAW, J. and ROUSSOS, G. (eds.). Sweeteners and Dental Caries. Information Retrieval Ltd., Washington and London, 1978.

SHEPARD, R. N. The Analysis of Proximities: Multidimensional Scaling with an Unknown Distance Function. Psychometrika, 1962, 27, 219-246.

SMITH, D. V. Taste Intensity as a Function of Area and Concentration: Differentiation Between Compounds. Journal of Experimental Psychology, 1971, 87, 163-171.

STEVENS, J. C. A Comparison of Ratio Scales for the Loudness of White Noise and the Brightness of White Lights. Ph.D. Dissertation. Harvard University, Cambridge, 1957.

STEVENS, S. S. On the Theory of Scales of Measurement. Science, 1946, 103, 677-680.

STEVENS, S. S. On the Brightness of Lights and the Loudness of Sounds. Science, 1953, 118, 576.

STEVENS, S. S. Matching Functions Between Loudness and Ten Other Continua. Perception and Psychophysics, 1966, 1, 5-8.

STEVENS, S. S. Sensory Scales of Taste Intensity. Perception and Psychophysics, 1969, 302-308.

STEVENS, S. S. Psychophysics: An Introduction to its Perceptual, Neural and Social Prospects. New York, John Wiley & Sons, 1975.

STEVENS, S. S. and GREENBAUM, H. Regression Effect in Psychophysical Judgment. Perception and Psychophysics, 1966, 1, 439-446.

STEVENS, S. S. and GUIRAO, M. The Scaling of Apparent Viscosity. Science, 1964, 145, 1157-1158.

STEVENS, S. S., MORGAN, C. T. and VOLKMANN, J. Theory of the Neural Quantum in the Discrimination of Loudness and Pitch. American Journal of Psychology, 1941, 54, 315-335.

STONE, H. and OLIVER, S. M. Effects of Viscosity on the Detection of Relative Sweetness Intensity in Sucrose Solutions. Journal of Food Science, 1966, 31, 129-134.

STONE, H., SIDEL, J. L., OLIVER, S., WOOLSEY, A. and SINGLETON, R. Sensory Evaluation by Quantitative Descriptive Analysis. Food Technology, 1974, 28, 24-34.

STUIVER, M. Biophysics of the Sense of Smell. Rijksuniversiteit, Groningen, The Netherlands, 1958.

SZCZESNIAK, A. S. Instrumental Methods of Texture Measurement. In: Texture Measurements of Foods (A. Kramer and A. S. Szczesniak, eds.), Reidel, Dordrecht, Holland. 1973, 71-108.

SZCZESNIAK, A. S., BRANDT, M. A. and FRIEDMAN, H. H. Development of Standard Rating Scales for Mechanical Parameters of Texture and Correlations Between the Objective and Sensory Methods of Texture Evaluation. Journal of Food Science, 1963, 28, 397-403.

SZCZESNIAK, A. S., LOEW, B. J. and SKINNER, E. Z. Consumer Texture Profile Technique. Journal of Food Science, 1975, 40, 1253-1256.

TAUFEL, K. and KLEMM, B. Untersuchungen über naturliche und kunstliche Susstoffe. Untersuchungen Nahrungs Genusmittel, 1925, 50, 264-273.

TEGHTSOONIAN, M. The Judgment of Size. American Journal of Psychology, 1965, 78, 392-402.

TEGHTSOONIAN, R. On the Exponents in Stevens' Law and the Constant in Ekman's Law. Psychological Review, 1971, 78, 71-80.

THURSTONE, L. L. A Law of Comparative Judgment. Psychological Review, 1927, 34, 273-286.

VAISEY-GENSER, M., MOSKOWITZ, H. R., SOLMS, J. and ROTHE, H. Sensory Response to Food: A Sensory Workshop, Forster Verlag, Zurich, Switzerland, 1977.

VOISEY, P. Instrumental Measures of Food Texture. In Rheology and Texture in Food Quality (J. DeMan, P. W. Voisey, V. F. Raspar and D. W. Stanley, eds.). Avi Publishing, Westport, CT., 1976, 79-141.

VOISEY, P. W. and LARMOND, E. Exploratory Evaluation of Instrumental Techniques for Measuring Some Textural Characteristics of Cooked Spaghetti. Cereal Science Today, 1973, 18, 126-133, 142-143.

VON SKRAMLIK, E. Mischungsgleichungen im Gebiete des Geschmacksinnes. Zeitschrift für Sinnesphysiologie, 1921, 5-3B, 36-78, 219.

VON SYDOW, E., MOSKOWITZ, H. R., JACOBS, H. L. and MEISELMAN, H. L. Odor-Taste Interaction in Fruit Juices. Lebensmittel, Wissenschaft und Technologie. 1974, 7, 18-24.

WATERMAN, D. Personal Communication, 1974.

WEBER, E. H. DePulsu Resorptime, Auditor, et Tache: Annotations Anatomical et Physiological. Leipzig, Koehler, 1834.

WEBER, E. H. Cited in Boring, B. G. Sensation and Perception in the History of Experimental Psychology, New York, Appleton-Century Crofts, 1942.

WELLS, W. D. Psychographics: A Critical Review. Journal of Marketing Research, 1975, 12, 196-213.

WHORF, B. L. Language, Thought and Reality. (J. B. Carroll, ed.). Cambridge, Mass. M.I.T. Press, 1956.

WINER, B. J. Statistical Principles in Experimental Design, 2nd Ed., New York, McGraw-Hill, 1971.

WOODROW, H. and KARPMAN, B. A New Olfactometric Technique and Some Results. Journal of Experimental Psychology, 1919, 2, 431-447.

WOSKOW, M. Multidimensional Scaling of Odors. Ph.D. Dissertation. University of California, Davis, 1964.

WOSKOW, M. Multidimensional Scaling of Odors. In: Theories of Odors and Odor Measurement. (N. Tanyolac, ed.). Istanbul, 1968, 147-148.

YAMAGUCHI, S., YOSHIKAWA, T., IKEDA, S. and NINOMIYA, J. Studies on the Taste of Some Sweet Substances. Agricultural and Biological Chemistry, 1970, 34, 181-197.

YOSHIDA, M. Studies in the Psychometric Classification of Odor. Japanese Psychological Research 1964, 6, 111, 124-155.

YOSHIDA, M. Dimension of Tactual Impression (1) (2). Japanese Psychological Research, 1968, 10, 123-137, 157-173.

YOSHIDA, M., KINASE, R., KYROKAWA, J. and YASHIRO, S. Multidimensional Scaling of Emotion. Japanese Psychological Research, 1970, 12, 34-61.

YOSHIKAWA, S., NISHIMARU, S., TASHIRO, T. and YOSHIDA, M. Collection and Classification of Words for Description of Food Texture. I, II, III. Journal of Texture Studies, 1970, 1, 437-442, 443-451, 452-463.

ZWAARDEMAKER, H. Die Physiologie des Geruchs. Engelmann, Leipzig, 1895.

INDEX